# THE CULTURAL HERITAGE OF INDIA

VOLUME III

## THE PHILOSOPHIES

# THE CULTURAL HERITAGE OF INDIA

VOLUME III

THE PHILOSOPHIES

EDITOR
HARIDAS BHATTACHARYYA, M.A., B.L., P.R.S., DARŚANASĀGARA
*Formerly Head of the Department of Philosophy, Dacca University, and Honorary University Professor of Indian Philosophy and Religion, Banaras Hindu University*

CALCUTTA
THE RAMAKRISHNA MISSION
INSTITUTE OF CULTURE

PUBLISHED BY
SWAMI NITYASWARUPANANDA, SECRETARY
THE RAMAKRISHNA MISSION INSTITUTE OF CULTURE
CALCUTTA

*First Published in 1937*
*Second Edition: Revised and Enlarged 1953*



PRINTED IN INDIA
BY P. C. RAY, SRI GOURANGA PRESS LTD.
CALCUTTA

## PUBLISHER'S NOTE

THE Ramakrishna Mission established this Institute of Culture in 1938 in fulfilment of one of the projects to commemorate the Birth Centenary of Sri Ramakrishna (1936). At the same time the Institute was vested with the entire rights of *The Cultural Heritage of India.* This publication is thus one of the major responsibilities of the Institute; it also serves to fulfil a primary aim of the Institute, which is to promote the study, interpretation, and dissemination of the cultural heritage of India.

The first edition of *The Cultural Heritage of India*, in three volumes and about 2,000 pages in all, the work of one hundred distinguished Indian scholars, was published in 1937 by the Sri Ramakrishna Birth Centenary Publication Committee as a Birth Centenary memorial. This work presented for the first time a panorama of the cultural history of India, and it was immediately acclaimed as a remarkable contribution to the cultural literature of the world. This edition was sold out within a few years and the work has long been out of print. When considering the question of a second edition it was felt that instead of reprinting the work in its original form, advantage should be taken of the opportunity to enlarge the scope of the work, making it more comprehensive, more authoritative, and adequately representative of different aspects of Indian thought, and, at the same time, thoroughly to revise the old articles to bring them up to date.

According to a new scheme drawn up on this basis, the number of volumes will be increased. The plan of arrangement has been improved by grouping the topics in such a way that each volume may be fairly complete and fulfil the requirements of those interested in any particular branch of learning. Each volume will be self-contained, with separate pagination, bibliography, and index, and will be introduced by an outstanding authority. Since due regard will be paid to historicity and critical treatment, it is hoped that this work will provide a useful guide to the study of the complex pattern of India's cultural history.

In keeping with the ancient Indian tradition of imparting instruction to students without remuneration, the distinguished band of scholars, who have co-operated so ably in this task, have done their work as a labour of love in a spirit of service to scholarship and world understanding. Equally essential to the success of the undertaking was the assistance of the Government of India who made a generous grant towards the cost of publication. Without this dual co-operation it would have been impossible to set out on a venture of this magnitude ; and to the contributors as well as to the Government of India we therefore express our deepest gratitude.

In presenting this third volume of the second edition of *The Cultural Heritage of India,* it is perhaps necessary to explain how it happened that the third volume was the first to be published. In the first edition of this work there were a fairly large number of representative articles on philosophy and religion, the two subjects which, under the new scheme, have been assigned to Volumes III and IV. Thus these two volumes acquired an advantage over the others, which required a much greater proportion of fresh material, and it was therefore thought expedient to publish them first. Volume III will thus be followed by Volume IV.

Professor Haridas Bhattacharyya, M.A., B.L., P.R.S., Darśanasāgara, who was formerly Head of the Department of Philosophy at the Dacca University, and latterly Honorary University Professor of Indian Philosophy and Religion at the College of Indology, Banaras Hindu University, is a well-known figure in the world of philosophy. In entrusting him with the editing of this volume, the Institute knew that it was being placed in capable hands. We feel deeply indebted to him for the way in which he has given unsparingly of his time and energy in tackling the many difficulties inherent in a work of this nature.

India's greatest treasure is her ancient spiritual wisdom. The time has come when that treasure should be fully discovered and offered not only to the people of India, but also to those of other countries so that a foundation may be laid upon which to build the peace, the unity, and the concord to which all nations aspire. This volume on philosophy will, it is trusted, play some part in this noble mission.

August 1953

# CONTENTS



PART I

## THE PHILOSOPHICAL SYSTEMS

## PART II

## THE VEDĀNTA

PART III

THE RELIGIOUS PHILOSOPHIES

PART IV

THE PROBLEMS OF PHILOSOPHY

# ILLUSTRATIONS

## ABBREVIATIONS

| | |
|---|---|
| *A. V.* | *Atharva-Veda* |
| *Ai. U.* | *Aitareya Upaniṣad* |
| *B. G.* | *Bhagavad-Gītā* |
| *B. S.* | *Brahma-Sūtra* |
| *Bhā.* | *Bhāgavata* |
| *Bṛ. U.* | *Bṛhadāraṇyaka Upaniṣad* |
| *Chā. U.* | *Chāndogya Upaniṣad* |
| *Ī. U.* | *Īśa Upaniṣad* |
| *Ka. U.* | *Kaṭha Upaniṣad* |
| *Ke. U.* | *Kena Upaniṣad* |
| *Mā. U.* | *Māṇḍūkya Upaniṣad* |
| *Mbh.* | *Mahābhārata* |
| Mm. | Mahāmahopādhyāya |
| *Mu. U.* | *Muṇḍaka Upaniṣad* |
| *Pra. U.* | *Praśna Upaniṣad* |
| *Rām.* | *Rāmāyaṇa* |
| *Ṛ. V.* | *Ṛg-Veda* |
| *S. V.* | *Sāma-Veda* |
| *Tai. U.* | *Taittirīya Upaniṣad* |
| *U.* | *Upaniṣad* |
| *Y. V.* | *Yajur-Veda* |

# PREFACE

THE preparation of the second edition of *The Cultural Heritage of India* was taken in hand in June, 1947, after the first edition had long been out of print. According to the new scheme of publication, the different volumes were not only to be revised, but also to be improved by the addition of new articles to make them more comprehensive. It was also decided to attempt a presentation of the contents in a logical order, and to arrange the articles in such a manner that they might form a homogeneous group from some angle of vision and at the same time not make the volumes unwieldy in size. The third volume devoted to the philosophies of India was the first to be completed and is being released for publication first.

Of the thirty-nine articles contained in the present volume thirteen are old. Most of these have been revised by the authors themselves for the present edition; the one on 'Pūrva-Mīmāṁsā' has been revised and enlarged by Mm. Chinnaswami Sastri; and a few only are reproduced without any noticeable change. A welcome innovation is the inclusion of the contributions of two distinguished scholars, Mm. Anantakrishna Sastri and Mm. Yogendranath Bagchi, whose original articles in Sanskrit and Bengali respectively are appearing in translation.

According to the plan of arrangement of subjects in different volumes, Buddhist and Jaina cultures, including their philosophies, have been assigned to Volume I. In Volume II will be presented the ethical and philosophical speculations to be found in the epics (including the *Bhagavad-Gītā*), the Purāṇas, and the legal literature. The present volume has thus been practically confined to the Brāhmaṇical systems of Indian philosophy, including the Lokāyata or Cārvāka philosophy, which is a rather anti-Vedic mode of thought.

The need to orient philosophical thinking to spiritual requirements has been constantly kept in view. It is hoped that the multiplicity of approaches by different authors to the Vedāntic thought will serve to bring out the personal character of philosophical appreciation in India. And this conviction will be strengthened by a perusal of the succeeding articles that show how the same basic Vedāntic text was used to elaborate philosophical views in consonance with the sectarian attitude towards the ultimate principle and the origin, nature, function, and destiny of the world of dependent beings. The importance of the Vedānta as the highest achievement of the Indian mind has been recognized by devoting one-third of the total number of the articles to its different aspects and interpretations. As basic to the theistic interpretations of the Vedānta, the article on the 'Philosophy of the Bhāgavata' will be found a useful addition.

As compared with the Vedānta, the Sāṁkhya-Yoga and the Nyāya-Vaiśeṣika groups have two comprehensive articles devoted to each. The second has a third article devoted to the special problem of religion as treated in it, while the first has received supplementary treatment by an article on 'The Path of Yoga in the Gītā'—the only article on that book to be included in the present volume, as also by an article on 'The Philosophy of Śaivism' which, like the Yoga system, combines Sāṁkhya and theistic elements in a novel manner. Similarly, the article on the 'Philosophy of the Yogavāsiṣṭha' serves to exemplify a unique synthesis of Sāṁkhya-Yoga, Upaniṣadic, and Buddhistic modes of thought. The other systems, viz. Pūrva-Mīmāṁsā, Cārvāka, and Tantra, are each represented by a single article ; but an elaborate treatment of the last is reserved for the fourth volume. Two articles of general philosophical interest without linkage to any definite school are 'The Philosophy of Mysticism' and 'Philosophy in Popular Literature'. The key to the understanding of the mutual relations of the different systems (including Buddhism and Jainism) in their historical development is furnished by the opening article on the 'Rise of the Philosophical Schools'. Roughly speaking, two-thirds of the entire volume are devoted to an exposition of the different philosophies mentioned above.

A significant departure from the usual method of presenting Indian philosophy has been the discussion of major philosophical topics irrespective of their affiliation to definite systems of thought. The nature of the physical world, the soul, and the mind has been discussed in three different articles, while the almost unanimous Indian belief in the possibility of transcending the narrow range of empirical thought by means of proper mental discipline has found expression in an article on 'Extra-sensory and Superconscious Experiences'. The problem of psychological types, now so widely discussed in the West, had its prototype and counterpart in different branches of Sanskrit literature and has been delineated in the article on 'Types of Human Nature'. The different philosophical sciences have been synoptically treated in four articles, viz. 'Indian Epistemology', 'Indian Psychology', 'Indian Ethics', and 'Indian Theism'. This additional innovation will, it is hoped, serve the purpose of giving a bird's-eye view of the fundamentals of Indian philosophical thinking in its different aspects. A further interesting addition has been the inclusion of an article on 'The Art of Philosophical Disputation', which will give an idea of how the

Indian philosophers carried on debates, and how different objectives in view affected the modes of their attack and defence in arguments. Finally, the peculiarity of Indian philosophy as a spiritual discipline has been sought to be brought out in the last article of the present volume, namely, 'Philosophy of Values', where the different ends of life—religio-ethical, hedonistic, and spiritual—have been delineated, interrelated, and graded.

But while the interest of the scholar and the student has not been forgotten, it has been kept constantly in mind that by far the larger number of readers of *The Cultural Heritage of India* would be men and women, who are seekers after spiritual truth wherever found, without the highly technical equipment of a philosopher. The present volume has been so designed that almost all the articles would be found interesting and intelligible by the cultured lay public on account of their diversified contents and easy mode of presentation. A philosophical work cannot, however, read wholly like a novel ; its subject-matter being recondite, it naturally requires a certain amount of preliminary training in philosophical concepts. Again, where thought is wound up with life and life is linked up with socio-religious conviction or convention, a certain amount of imaginative penetration into national attitudes and age-long beliefs becomes indispensable for understanding the particular mode of handling philosophical problems. Belief in *karma* and rebirth, for instance, started in India certain types of speculation which are rare, if present at all, in other countries where a single life is supposed to be vouchsafed to man to make or mar his destiny. Similarly, the emphasis upon the rôle of the individual in the attainment of spiritual advancement, as compared with divine aid and prophetic intercession, is unmistakable in Indian thought ; and so the technique of expanding the self and increasing the dimensions of personality received an elaborate treatment in the Indian systems not to be found in other countries. Much harsh criticism can be avoided by taking into account these basic assumptions of the Indian philosophers almost as a class. When philosophy ceases to be an adventure of merely speculative ideas and becomes a propaedeutic to the art of spiritual life, an acknowledgement of the native propensities and particular constitutions of different types of minds ushers in a diversity of prescriptions for meeting the needs of individual lives and leads to the recognition of multiple paths of spiritual approach.

It is not to be thought, however, that philosophies in India grew up in water-tight compartments and no attempt was made to arrive at a universal philosophy on the basis of rigid logical thinking. Philosophical controversies, in which hard hits were given and taken in fixing the number of the sources of knowledge and defining the nature of the real, would have been unmeaning without the belief that the laws of rational thinking were identical for all. In fact, each system claimed that it was the most coherent and the most comprehensive from the intellectual point of view. One might begin the speculative life in any tradition and end it in any realization, but in between the two lay the realm of *manana,* logical thinking, without which faith becomes a superstition and realization a make-believe. The controversial literature in Indian philosophy is a vast one, testifying at once to the virility of thought and the keenness of feeling that what cannot be rationally justified has no right to intellectual allegiance. Diversity of social practices and even mutual interdiction of social contact did not prevent the crossing of academic swords. Religious conversion not infrequently followed defeat in philosophical debate; the honest vanquished did not sneak back into his old credal fold after being worsted in an intellectual combat. And this is true not only of the adherents of different faiths like Brāhmaṇism, Buddhism, and Jainism, but also of the champions of different sects and philosophical standpoints within the same religious persuasion.

It is a happy sign of the times that the facile and complacent statement that outside Greece no philosophy proper grew and thrived is much less repeated now with the passing of years. Those who read Indian philosophy only through the translation of the Upaniṣads could dub it as poetry, symbolism, religion, etc. because of their mystical and unsystematic character. But as more and more classical philosophical texts are becoming available in intelligible and authoritative translations, the attitude of sneering is being gradually replaced by feelings of wonder and appreciation. The boldness of speculation and the candour to accept logically inevitable, though emotionally unpalatable, conclusions displayed by some Indian thinkers, have amazed many in the West, while their skilful dialectic and incisive rapier thrusts have caused delectation to the souls of those who can appreciate subtleties in debate and niceties in argument. Linguistic precision of a high order was necessitated by the exigencies of controversy, and though the mnemonic parsimony in words was responsible for an aphoristic style in the basic texts, the commentators wrote elaborately and in precise terms when defending the position of their own schools and attacking rival and opposing views. A watchful opponent would immediately pounce upon the weak link in an argument and deliver a smashing clincher (*nigrahasthāna*). Philosophical disputation may sometimes have been carried on in a highly technical language, far removed from the medium of normal conversation and exposition, and may even have degenerated into logomachy, and this is specially noticeable in the neological schools of Navadvīpa and Mithilā; but the distinctive feature of every considerable commentary is the statement of all *prima facie* objections (*pūrvapakṣa*) together with its own reply thereto in quite intelligible language. The criticisms disclose wide knowledge of the opposing systems of thought; and as the controversy was handed down in the schools, this knowledge had to be kept up to date by later participants in the wordy duel. An intelligent understanding of any fact of a controversial character presupposes a knowledge of more than one system of thought. An indirect gain has been that in many cases we are able to fix the relative dates of philosophers from this literature of controversy even when we are unable to determine absolutely the exact time when they flourished.

This leads us to consider a matter of peculiar interest to students of Indian philosophy. The philosophers kept themselves so much in the background that not only did they not in most cases date their compositions, but even the names of some of them are not ascertainable now, although their works are very well known, and also the different names probably assumed by a philosopher at different times are not recognizable as belonging to one and the same person. It is seldom that a philosopher was actuated by the motive of making a name for himself: he was most interested in advancing the cause of his own particular school either by rebutting criticisms or by adducing new arguments in support. This will also explain why, instead of propounding new philosophies in their own names as mostly done in Western countries, the great thinkers of India preferred to advance their own views under the garb of an interpretation of some famous text, and they even quoted predecessors in their own line of interpretation. Those who followed either put a new interpretation on the same text or supported the commentary by their sub-commentaries and glosses, and in this way rival schools of interpretation grew up on the basis of a single text. This is particularly true of the Vedāntic system. Some like Vācaspati have commented on the basic texts of different schools without betraying their own predilections, while some others have not hidden their pronounced leanings in favour of a particular school of thought, as, for example, Vijñāna Bhikṣu for theistic Vedānta.

The fundamental distinctions of the systems are so great that eclecticism has seldom been attempted. But certain notable associations took place pretty early. The Sāṁkhya and the Yoga were coupled together, because Yoga took over the metaphysical tenets of Sāṁkhya and foisted on them its practical discipline and theism of a kind. Similarly, the Nyāya and the Vaiśeṣika could easily combine, the one supplying its logic and the other contributing its physics, though they did not give up altogether their distinctive tenets. Even the earliest commentators seem to have combined the two in their expositions, which shows that the syncretism of the Mithilā and Navadvīpa (Nadia) schools of the twelfth century was not an accidental event. Still, it would be candid to admit that though the two reciprocally influenced each other owing to a commonness of attitude towards ultimate principles, the association was not so close as between Sāṁkhya and Yoga. Far less knit together than the above pairs are the Mīmāṁsās, though one is called Pūrva and the other Uttara as if they form one continuous doctrinal scheme. The Pūrva-Mīmāṁsā with its emphasis upon the life of sacrificial action harks back to the Vedas, the Brāhmaṇas, and the Āraṇyakas, while the Uttara-Mīmāṁsā has primarily in view the absolutistic metaphysics of the Upaniṣads.

Though the theistically inclined Vedāntins have freely quoted from the Purāṇas as authorities, the Upaniṣads, the *Bhagavad-Gītā,* and the *Brahma-Sūtra* of Bādarāyaṇa form the common triple source of all schools of Vedānta (*prasthāna-traya*) to match the above three bases of the Pūrva-Mīmāṁsā. But as Jaimini and Bādarāyaṇa mutually refer to each other, some sort of relation between their systems was probably sought to be established, especially as the deprecation of the sacrifices was not unequivocal in the Upaniṣads, and those who upheld the necessity of joining rituals with gnosis (*jñānakarma-samuccaya*) could point to many Upaniṣadic passages in support of their position.

Beyond the pale of the three groups stood the heterodox systems which protested against this or that aspect of the orthodox position. The minor dissenters rose and fell, as they had no well-conceived theory either of reality or of knowledge. Probably many of them were antinomian also and so were given short shrift even by the major dissenters, Buddhism and Jainism. Only one had a lasting influence—the Cārvāka or Lokāyata—and had to be reckoned with by all subsequent thought. But its texts were suppressed; and it had to live only as a tradition, though it had all the elements of a systematic philosophy—epistemology, ontology, ethics, attitude towards religion, etc. Both Jainism and Buddhism, however, developed full-fledged systems of thought and became religious institutions in addition, and with them Brāhmaṇism had to wage wars of offence and defence to maintain its integrity and influence. Jainism launched considerable attacks but was less heeded as it chose to fight from its own citadel of primitive concepts mixed with high philosophy and refused to come down to the even ground of common terminology. Buddhism won greater prestige and patronage as a religion, at least in North India, and, though it too had a small armoury of special words, it had greater linguistic affinity with Brāhmaṇism. Perhaps it also contained a larger admixture of Brāhmaṇa converts who knew the weak points of their earlier faith and philosophy. Buddhism also developed greater diversity of speculative systems owing to the greater exercise of free thinking inside the church than was done by Jainism. So with Buddhism the battle of wits was longer and keener, and important changes of front had to be made to withstand the Buddhistic onslaught. Brāhmaṇical, Buddhistic, and Jaina philosophies contended most on the epistemological issue with fruitful results all around. How they influenced one another's religious beliefs, practices, and artistic representations is a different story with which we are not concerned in this volume.

When philosophies develop as schools of thought and vigorous champions are not wanting in any camp, it may be taken for granted that attempts would be made to grade the systems in a scale of excellence. Taking as their motto that men look outward before they look inward and that they look inward before they look upward, some professed to arrange the Nyāya-Vaiśeṣika, Sāṁkhya-Yoga, and Mīmāṁsā-Vedānta in an ascending series. The first is concerned with an elaborate discussion about the properties of physical things, and there the soul has no privileged position in reality, possessing in fact consciousness as a contingent property on the empirical plane in association with mind and object. The second professed to evolve the world out of Prakṛti but gave to Puruṣa the dominant rôle in starting the world process and endowed the soul with essential intelligence in addition to, and apart from, the empirical consciousness generated by association with Prakṛti. But it chose to think of spirit in terms of finitude and multiplicity, and though in the Yoga God was introduced, His rôle was not very vital in the system. The last pair went beyond the second in acknowledging the necessity of the divine principle, whether in its plural form for ritualistic purposes, namely, to invoke with *mantras* the deities even though they are not boon-givers, or in its unitary form as a personal God of grace or as an impersonal Brahman of which the finites are only illusory forms. The Advaita reached the startling conclusion that finitude had no reality in an ultimate reference, and personality could not be ascribed to a being in which all finite personalities merged without retaining a vestige of their distinctive experiences. The One without a second is non-dual in all its aspects and possesses consciousness as essence but not as an attribute. Here the climax of philosophical thinking is reached. The theistically inclined West has not hidden its dislike for this culmination of Indian thought and has professed to find it ethically unsatisfactory because of its tendency to transcend moral distinctions. Even Bradley who comes nearest to Śaṅkara did not hesitate to admit that human experiences are not altogether lost but are retained in the Absolute, though distributed, transmuted, and rearranged there.

It must not be supposed, however, that this Vedāntic claim of finality for its own position has been accepted by other systems. Each claims to be the genuine *mokṣa-śāstra* as teaching the only right way to liberation, howsoever interpreted. Insensibility, isolation, dissolution, eternal life in God, and merger in the Absolute are the alternatives advocated by the different systems. The principal gain from philosophical knowledge is escape from the ills of the present life and the stoppage of the wheel of rebirth, and not necessarily the attainment of a blissful state. All agreed, however, that there was no possibility of obtaining salvation without getting rid of the ignorance which leads one to mistake the non-soul for the soul, the impure for the pure, the painful for the blissful, and the evanescent for the eternal. In this view the orthodox systems were joined by the heterodox ones of Buddhism and Jainism. *Avidyā, ajñāna, aviveka,* and such cognate terms were used to indicate that the root-cause of involvement in *saṁsāra* was intellectual deficiency or lack of wisdom which must be first got rid of to liquidate the distressed condition of the embodied soul. True, the theists suggested divine grace and its counterpart, human devotion, as causative factors for bringing about liberation, but even they looked upon right knowledge as basic to true *bhakti.* Right rapture, self-realization, God-vision, etc., all proceed from true *bodhi,* and therefore philosophy must inform moral praxis and spiritual exercise.

In the following pages has been unfolded by Indian scholars the story of the attempts made by India down the ages to grapple with the fundamental problems of life and thought. As elsewhere, the modes of approach have been many in keeping with the needs of diverse types of minds and in consonance with different philosophical traditions. Many of the writers are themselves adherents of the philosophic creeds they expound, and this lends additional weight to their utterances, which are not merely summaries of book-learning, but are also confessions of personal faith. They have very generously laid aside controversial issues as inappropriate in this work which is dedicated to the great saint of modern India, Sri Ramakrishna, who was toleration incarnate in theory and practice.

In between the two editions the Indian world of scholarship has suffered extraordinarily heavy losses by the death of some who, through their translations of original texts and their scholarly interpretations, made Indian philosophy better known and respected abroad. Mm. Dr. Pramathanath Tarkabhushan, Mm. Dr. Ganganath Jha, Dr. Surendranath Dasgupta, S. S. Suryanarayana Sastri, Professor M. Hiriyanna, and Professor K. C. Bhattacharyya, whose contributions we are proud to include in the present volume, have all left us, as has Dr. B. M. Barua who died before he could write the article assigned to him. We also mourn the death of

V. Subrahmanya Iyer, K. A. Krishnaswami Iyer, and Swami Tyagisananda,—esteemed contributors who did not live to see the publication of this volume. We pay our tribute of respect to their memory, and would put on record our special appreciation of the readiness with which the late Dr. Surendranath Dasgupta agreed to write the introduction to this volume when he was severely handicapped by protracted illness and also by preoccupation with the concluding fifth volume of his monumental work, *A History of Indian Philosophy,* which unfortunately he could not leave completed.

My task as Editor, though enjoyable, has not been an easy one, and would have been more difficult but for the spirit of accommodation readily shown by the contributors. I wish to record my gratitude to the monastic workers of the Institute of Culture who have so greatly helped me in preparing the manuscript and seeing the work through the press. I am also indebted to Mr. Arthur Hughes, I.C.S. (Retd.), who generously volunteered his services to the Institute. He not only proved a great help in toning up the literary aspect of the manuscript, but also made valuable suggestions in course of his scrutiny. My thanks are due to Sri P. Seshadri Aiyar, B.A., M.L., for translating the article on 'Brahma-Mīmāṁsā' from the original Sanskrit. My thanks are also due to Professor Jnanendra Chandra Datta, M.A., for translating from the original Bengali the article on 'The Art of Philosophical Disputation' as well as for preparing the Index, which, it is hoped, will facilitate the search for relevant information. The Bibliography is by no means exhaustive: it is limited to English translations and expositions and is intended to lead inquisitive readers to the original works and specialized treatises on the subjects concerned.

It is hoped that this new edition will worthily maintain the reputation of its predecessor and serve not only to unfold the spiritual aspirations of an ancient nation, but also to forge a powerful link in the chain of human fellowship and universal concord.

HARIDAS BHATTACHARYYA

Calcutta
August 1953

# INTRODUCTION

**KAPILA**

# 1

## INTRODUCTION

AT least three different races seem to have contributed to the traditional heritage of India in civilization, culture, philosophy, religion, and art. These were, firstly, the Indus valley people; secondly, the different hordes of Aryans that in all probability came from the West; and thirdly, the Dravidians who from very early times had settled in the South. The relation between the Dravidians and the Indus valley people has not yet been definitely ascertained, though many surmises about it have been made. The Indus valley people, who were in all probability somehow related to the Sumerians, have left in the buried debris remarkable marks of their great civilization. It has been suggested that a statuette found in Mohenjo-daro probably represents an ascetic in the yogic posture. Phallic symbols in stone are found in abundance. There is also a statuette of Paśupati in association with various animals. Images which have been regarded as being those of Mother Earth also go to show that the cult of Śiva or Paśupati and of Śakti as the Mother may have been current at the time. I noticed in Harappa a site which was very probably a hall of sacrificial fire. These people knew the art of writing, as is quite manifest from the innumerable seals found there, which are similar to the Susa seals. It is unfortunate that up till now there seems to be no progress in deciphering the writings on these seals, which would have thrown much light on the various aspects of the cultural life of these people. In the museum of Harappa I noticed a pottery painting which seemed to portray the belief in the post-mortem existence of the soul and its future destiny.

These people lived in brick-built cities, built in a closely compact fashion, which gave them protection from outside enemies and also afforded many amenities of civilized life. In the Vedic literature we find many references to the quarrel between the *devas* and the *asuras* and to Indra's exploits in the land of the Śiśnadevas (phallus-worshippers) and to the cities of the *asuras* being destroyed by Śiva. Patañjali in his *Bhāṣya* on Pāṇini's grammar thinks that the *asuras* had begun to imitate the performance of Vedic sacrifices but mispronounced the Sanskrit words and the accents, and this was the reason why they were defeated in their struggle with the *devas*. It is needless here to give copious examples of the contact of the Aryans or the *devas* with another race, called the *asuras*, who were probably in some way related to the old Assyrians. But anyhow nothing exists now of the Indus valley people and their civilization.

Some of these people may possibly be traced to the Brahuis of Baluchistan; others must have merged with the Indian people in general, and their religious culture must have also influenced the development of the Aryan religious culture. It is curious to note that in the *Atharva-Veda* we have quite a long section devoted to the praise of the worshippers of Rudra, though they are called the Vrātyas, i.e. people outside the orthodox pale.

## THE VEDAS

The Vedic literature that has come down to us by oral tradition forms the earliest compositions of the Aryan people. We do not know how much of these compositions forms a part of the heritage of the Aryans before they came to this country and how much of these was composed here in India. We have no evidence to show that the Vedic people had any knowledge of writing or of building cities as the Indus valley people had. The date of any part of the Vedic literature is also very uncertain. Conjectures that have been made regarding it from the affinity of the Vedic language with the Avestan language, as found in the inscription of Darius of known date, are as uncertain as other conjectures made by Tilak and Jacobi. The average Hindu regards the Vedas as *anādi* or beginningless. This is true only in the sense that the beginnings of the Vedas are not ascertainable.

The Vedas reveal different strata of religious and philosophic culture. There are passages which indicate that the Vedic people worshipped the nature gods in their diversity; there are also passages which show that there was a tendency to exaggerate the power and influence of one or other of the gods over others. This has been styled as henotheism by Max Müller. There is another stratum which seems to encourage the performance of sacrifices, during which the Vedic verses could be torn from their context and made to form parts of the liturgy of different rites in the sacrifices. These sacrifices gradually attained such importance that the reality of the gods practically vanished. The verses or *mantras* were themselves practically the gods, and the effect of the sacrifices was not produced as a gift of charity from the gods, but it followed automatically from the scrupulously punctilious performance of the different parts of the sacrifice and the proper pronunciation and accenting of the *mantras*. From this followed the well-known theory of the Mīmāṁsā interpreters that all Vedic passages are to be explained and interpreted as commands (*vidhis*) or prohibitions (*niṣedhas*) irrespective of their verbal tense, and that all stories found in the Vedic literature are to be regarded as emphasizing Vedic commands. These stories, called *arthavādas,* need not necessarily have any factual validity. We find, parallel to these, many charms and incantations in the *Atharva-Veda,* as also sacrifices for injuring other people for one's own interests, e.g. the *Śyena-yāga.*

In another stratum we find the performance of sacrifice being replaced by different kinds of meditation. We also find many passages which display doubt or scepticism about our knowledge of the origin of the world, and also some which contain descriptions of a monotheistic character.

The Mīmāṁsā philosophy deals mainly with the ways and methods of sacrifices in accordance with the Brāhmaṇas, the Śrauta-Sūtras, and the Kalpa-Sūtras. But it lays great emphasis on the theory of Vedic commandments. The earliest writer now available to us is Jaimini, whose *Mīmāṁsā-Sūtra* was interpreted by Śabara some time about the second or third century B.C. This commentary was further commented upon by two Mīmāṁsā leaders of thought, Kumārila and Prabhākara, who lived probably round about the seventh century A.D. While Prabhākara tries to show that the Vedic commands are performed by us out of an inherent impulsion of oughtness in us, Kumārila tries to explain it on hedonistic grounds, namely, that we perform the Vedic commands because such performance is beneficial to us in the end. The Mīmāṁsā philosophy does not admit either God or creation. It admits the uncreated character of the Vedas and regards them as eternal. It also believes in the self-validity of knowledge and regards all errors as being due to non-discrimination between cognition and memory. In most other details the Mīmāṁsā philosophy, as developed by its later exponents, follows the lines of the Vaiśeṣika thought.

## THE VEDĀNTIC SCHOOLS

We now turn to the philosophical inspiration of the Upaniṣads. The earlier Upaniṣads are generally regarded as limited to eleven. But in later times many other works trying to follow the style of the Upaniṣads have been called by that name, though their spurious nature can hardly be denied. The earlier Upaniṣads form the concluding part of the Vedic literature and are known as Vedānta. These are to be distinguished from the other forms of the Vedic literature known as the Saṁhitās, the Brāhmaṇas, and the Āraṇyakas. Some Upaniṣads are composed in verse, some in prose, and others in both. They are the outburst of the joy and emotion of intuitive experience. In our modern approach to the study of the Upaniṣads we are disposed to think that the different passages of the Upaniṣads are often in conflict with one another, and it does not seem probable that they are the compositions of the same author. There is a long history among the series of the Upaniṣads of a quest for the ultimate truth. There are many passages in which attempts have been made to express the nature of this ultimate truth, but their expression is emotional and intuitive and very seldom argumentative. The doctrine of the absolute validity of the Vedas had already gained a very strong hold on the minds of the people. Moral, civil, and criminal laws, as well as all customary laws among the higher castes, were regarded as but reflections of the social system of the Vedic people. The validity of the Smṛtis was wholly dependent upon their Vedic texts or upon Vedic customs as practised by virtuous Vedic people. Some of the Upaniṣads were manifestly anti-sacrificial. But their validity with regard to the ultimate truth could never be challenged. Consequently, the apparent differences of opinion among the various passages of the Upaniṣads had to be brushed aside, and a definite unity and uniformity of purport of all passages in the Upaniṣads had to be demonstrated.

The two earliest attempts in this direction are to be found in the *Brahma-Sūtra* of Bādarāyaṇa and the *Bhagavad-Gītā*. But in spite of this the difficulty remained more or less the same. The important question was whether reality was one, or both one and many; whether it was a concrete universal or explicitly many. Other forms of ideas, slightly different from the above well-defined positions, may also be found among some of the later exponents of the Vedānta.

The earliest expositions of the Upaniṣads, the *Brahma-Sūtra,* and the *Gītā,* that are now extant, were made by a South Indian monk, Śaṅkarācārya, though we know from quotations and references that other interpretations on semi-dualistic lines had been made by other exponents anterior to him. In this connection it will be well to remember that the Vedic culture and other forms of ideas that had grown in the North penetrated into the South and were absorbed by the Dravidian people as forming part and parcel of their own culture. The Vedic Smṛtis similarly spread in the South though partly modified in some respects. No very definite information is available regarding the earliest Tamil writings. But we know that the cult of *bhakti* or devotion had become very prominent in the South in the writings of the Āḷvārs in the middle of the first millennium of the Christian era. Śaṅkarācārya was not only the greatest expositor of the Upaniṣads on monistic lines, but was also a great preacher. Like Buddha he established a monastic order, which is carrying on its work even to the present day. It will be wrong to say that he routed the Buddhists by his philosophical arguments. Rather the philosophical enunciation of his views sometimes seems to show that he was himself influenced by some of the Buddhist arguments. His representation of the world as unreal reminds us of the Buddhist view of

Nāgārjuna as explained by Candrakīrti. But while some Buddhists regarded the illusory nature of the world as being without any firm basis of truth and reality, Śaṅkarācārya tried to explain the ultimate reality as being the Self or Brahman, and contrasted this absolute vision with a relative perspective in which the illusory world appeared as real until it was contradicted. While Śaṅkarācārya called the two perspectives *pāramārthika* and *vyāvahārika,* the Buddhists called them *pāramārthika* and *sāṁvṛtika.* The view-point of Śaṅkarācārya is anticipated by Asaṅga and Vasubandhu (fourth or fifth century), particularly in the latter's work *Vijñaptimātratā-siddhi.* The philosophical difference between the two view-points is almost negligible. This explains why many of the opponents of Śaṅkarācārya called him a crypto-Buddhist.

Śaṅkarācārya, in the course of his discussions in the commentary on the *Brahma-Sūtra,* criticized the views of most of the contemporary systems of philosophy, such as the Sāṁkhya, the Nyāya, and the Buddhist schools. In Buddhism he tried to refute the idealism of Diṅnāga but not the view of Vasubandhu. The enunciation of his own views regarding the Vedānta is not convincingly clear. This gave rise to various schools of thought which claimed to be the proper interpretation of the monistic ideas of Śaṅkara, but which differed from one another sometimes in a very remarkable manner. Some of the leaders of these schools of Vedāntic thought were Vācaspati Miśra, Sureśvara, Padmapāda, Prakāśātman, and Prakāśānanda. The interpretation of the Vedānta by these leaders of thought developed in the hands of many successive followers through many centuries. The Vedāntic school of thought has produced many great dialecticians, of whom Śrīharṣa in the eleventh or twelfth century and Madhusūdana in the sixteenth seem to be the most notable. The vast development of the Śaṅkara school of the Vedānta seems to have taken place in the region north of the Vindhya hills. But though the intensive development of the monistic Vedānta of Śaṅkara took place in the Āryāvarta, it always had innumerable devoted followers in the South.

We have already seen that even before Śaṅkarācārya wrote his commentaries, there had been semi-dualistic interpretations of the Upaniṣads and the *Brahma-Sūtra.* One of these is called the Bhedābheda or the concurrence of dualism and monism without assuming either of them as illusory. Bhāskara, in his commentary on the *Brahma-Sūtra,* tried to establish this view on the analogy of the unity of the sea and the diversity of waves, foam, and billows—the forms in which that unity appears. The application of the modern critical apparatus raises considerable doubt whether the monistic interpretation of the *Brahma-Sūtra* by Śaṅkarācārya is always loyal and faithful to the views preached in the text itself.

Rāmānuja, a Tamil Brāhmaṇa of the eleventh century and disciple of Mahāpūrṇa and Yāmuna, wrote a commentary on the *Brahma-Sūtra* on the lines of an earlier work called the *Bodhāyana-vṛtti,* in which he tried to establish a philosophy called the Viśiṣṭādvaita. This assumed the reality of the world and the individual souls, both of which were merged in God and were dependent on Him in His transcendental aspect. In the formulation of his views Rāmānuja was greatly influenced by Nāthamuni and the writings of the Āḷvārs. The doctrine of *bhakti* preached in the *Pañcarātra* and in the writings of the Āḷvārs and of Yāmuna found its philosophical expression in the writings of Rāmānuja. Some of the most prominent names of great philosophical and devotional reputation of this school are Veṅkaṭa, Meghanādāri, and Lokācārya. The doctrine of devotion as *prapatti,* either involving complete dependence on God or that associated with personal endeavour, was emphasized respectively in the Teṅgalai and the Vaḍagalai schools of the Rāmānujists. In this connection we may also mention the name of Nimbārka, a well-known commentator of the *Brahma-Sūtra.* His views were very much like those of Rāmānuja.

It was round about the eleventh century that the great work *Bhāgavata* was written. In the thirteenth century, we find another great writer of the Vedānta in the South called Madhvācārya or Ānanda Tīrtha. He was a violent opponent of Śaṅkara and his monistic doctrine, and he preached a doctrine of absolute pluralism in his various works. Among his followers two great scholars of outstanding eminence, Jaya Tīrtha and Vyāsa Tīrtha, shine forth as two of the greatest philosophers and dialecticians of India. Though most of the great followers of Śaṅkarācārya belonged to North India, yet there were some great names in the monistic schools in the South as well, such as Dharmarājādhvarīndra, Nṛsiṁhāśrama, and Appaya Dīkṣita. The disciples of Madhva had therefore ample field for philosophical disputations with these monists, though by the twelfth or thirteenth century Buddhism had practically died out of India. Vyāsa Tīrtha wrote his great work *Nyāyāmṛta* to refute the various forms of monism, and particularly the Vivaraṇa school of interpretation as started by Padmapāda and Prakāśātman and continued or developed by many later writers. He also challenged in his *Tarka-tāṇḍava* the logical definitions that were introduced by the great Gaṅgeśa, the founder of the new school of Nyāya, which developed further in Bengal in the hands of Raghunātha, Gadādhara, and Jagadīśa. Madhusūdana Sarasvatī, a Vedāntin of Bengal, in his *Advaitasiddhi* refuted the views of Vyāsa Tīrtha against monism, and these refutations had their refutations and counter-refutations in the writings of Vyāsa Tīrtha's followers and the followers of Madhusūdana.

Another great writer, Vallabha, of the fifteenth and sixteenth centuries wrote a commentary on the *Brahma-Sūtra* following a peculiar line of modified monism. All these teachers and exponents of the Vedānta had a successive series of disciples who kept alive the traditional views as explained by their teachers and often enlivened them by their own contributions. The influence of Madhva is very definitely demonstrable in the commentary of Baladeva Vidyābhūṣaṇa, a native of Orissa. Caitanya, the great saint of Bengal, also derived much inspiration for his cult of *bhakti* during his pilgrimage to the South. Jīva Gosvāmin, a follower of Caitanya, also wrote an important work on the cult of *bhakti,* and in this he was wholly inspired by the *Bhāgavata.*

Apart from the rise of the monistic, dualistic, and semi-dualistic theories of religion and philosophy based on the teachings of the Upaniṣads and also the vernacular development of Śaivism and the cult of *bhakti*, it is curious to note, on the evidence of such an outstanding personality as Bhartṛhari, that when the *Mahābhāṣya* of Patañjali, the grammarian, was practically lost in the North, it survived in the South, and many eminent grammarians like Candrācārya and Vasurāta developed it there. On the basis of that a philosophy of grammar was written by Bhartṛhari, whose teachings are now preserved in the great work called *Vākyapadīya* (the only philosophy of grammar now extant). We also remember that the great commentary on the Vedas by Sāyaṇa was written in Vijayanagara somewhere in the fourteenth century.

## BUDDHISM AND JAINISM

It is important to note that excepting the schools of Cārvāka and the Lokāyatas all orthodox schools of Indian thought believed in certain fundamental postulates or dogmas, e.g. (1) the existence of the soul; (2) the possibility of ultimate liberation from sorrow or bondage; (3) belief in the doctrine of Karma and rebirth; and (4) the acceptance of the ultimate validity of the Vedas. The Buddhists and the Jains were regarded as heretical, as they did not believe in the validity of the Vedas. The Buddhists did not also believe in the reality of souls as permanent entities. Leaving the Upaniṣads aside, we can think of the Buddhists and the Jains as having made attempts to enunciate philosophical doctrines as early as the sixth century B.C. The Buddhist and the Jain doctrines and their philosophies gradually expanded through internal criticism by rival sects within the faiths and through external criticism by rival faiths. Buddha, who lived in the sixth century B.C., engaged himself in solving the problems of suffering and death by trying to discover their causes through meditation and *yoga.* His teachings were collected within a hundred years of his death by his disciples; and these works, which were all written in Pāli, were grouped under three collections called the Piṭakas, viz. the *Sutta Piṭaka,* the *Abhidhamma Piṭaka,* and the *Vinaya Piṭaka.* Though solitary ascetics probably existed long before Buddha's time, yet Buddha was the first person who established a monastic order and laid down the rules of monastic living in the works contained in the *Vinaya Piṭaka.* The central doctrine of Buddhism is based upon the causal theory involving the formula 'this happening, that happens', which proceeds in a cyclic order in a sort of 'chain-reaction', such that from a group or conglomeration of a momentary nature other conglomerations proceed *ad infinitum.* The start is made from the idea of ignorance (*avidyā*) which consists in the imputation of reality and permanence to unreal and momentary entities. From this proceed greed, action, birth and rebirth, and so on until the ultimate ignorance and greed are destroyed by knowledge (*bodhi*). Since all things are impermanent, there cannot be any permanent soul or God. All experiences are pure suffering, and our object is to seek the cause and trace the origination of this suffering and to determine the method of its final destruction. For this, Buddha advised a right course of conduct, meditation, and philosophy; and he also gave a formal shape to *yoga* for the first time. The teachings of Buddha were all collected in Pāli; but his philosophy, known as the Abhidhamma, was compiled in Sanskrit in a book of eight chapters called *Abhidharma-kośa* written by Vasubandhu, sometimes described as a friend of Samudragupta (A.D. 320-80). A French translation of the Chinese translation of the work by Hiuen Tsang is now available, and a Sanskrit commentary on it by Yaśomitra has been published by Wogihara from Japan. The Pāli Buddhism, called also the Hīnayāna, developed in North India till at least the fifth century and is now found in Ceylon, Burma, and Siam, and much of it has been published in the Pāli Text Series.

Some time about the second century B.C. many learned Brāhmaṇas, well versed in the Upaniṣads, had become Buddhists. They therefore interpreted Buddhism from a somewhat different angle which had more affinity with the Upaniṣads. They generally wrote in Sanskrit or Gāthā (a form of corrupt Sanskrit). There were three councils of Buddhist monks, and Buddhism became split up into at least as many as eighteen sects. Of these, four schools of thought played their rôle as philosophical systems in constant conflict with the Hindu systems of thought till the tenth century. These were the Vaibhāṣika, Sautrāntika, Yogācāra, and Mādhyamika. The Vaibhāṣika school is well explained in Vasubandhu's *Abhidharma-kośa.* A few texts of the Sautrāntika school are available in Sanskrit, the leading figures of this school being Diṅnāga, Kamalaśīla, Śāntarakṣita, Dharmakīrti,

Dharmottara, and others. The important works on the Yogācāra system were written by Aśvaghoṣa, Maitreya, Asaṅga, and Vasubandhu (*Vijñapti-mātratā-siddhi*). An elaborate work on the subject, called the *Yogācāra-bhūmi-śāstra,* was published in Japan some years ago. The basis of the Mādhyamika system is to be found in the *Prajñāpāramitā-Sūtra* which is an Āgama. The most efficient treatment of the philosophy of this Āgama was made by the acutest of the early dialecticians, Nāgārjuna, for whom the latest date would be the second or more probably the third century A.D. He was followed by Āryadeva, who wrote his *Catuḥśataka* about the fourth century. Candrakīrti wrote an important commentary on Nāgārjuna's *Mādhyamika-Sūtra* and also an important independent work called *Mādhyamakāvatāra.* The theory of Nāgārjuna consists in interpreting Buddhism as a philosophy which denied substance or reality to everything and regarded all appearances as being purely phenomenal, illusory, and contradictory. By his dialectics he attempted to refute any and every thesis that could be put forward. Yet in a phenomenal sense he admitted rebirth, the laws of morality, and causation as dependent origination. The Yogācāra school or the Vijñānavādins believed only in the reality of thought-waves and denied the objective existence of all sensible things as such. The ultimate reality was thought. The Sautrāntikas also went a great way with the Vijñānavādins, but they held that the reality of objective entities could be arrived at, though only in an inferential manner, from our mental experiences. In the course of time the distinction between the Sautrāntikas and the Vijñānavādins gradually tended to vanish. The Vaibhāṣikas admitted both the mental and the extra-mental entities conditioned by each other and working out the scheme of the universe according to the cyclic law of *dharma-cakra,* based on the causal doctrine of dependent origination, *pratītya-samutpāda.* Everything is regarded by Buddhism as momentary and therefore sorrowful.

The Mahāyāna Buddhism expatiates on the cultivation of the great virtues called the *paramitas,* the supreme virtue being the highest wisdom, called *prajñā. Prajñā* and the means to it (*upāya*) appear under various analogical forms as deities. They turn up also in connection with the methods of Buddhist *yoga* in later times in the Buddhist Tantras as found in Tibet and India. Tibet probably had had some form of demonology and sorcery; and when Buddhism was introduced in Tibet about the seventh or eighth century, the pure Buddhism as taught by Buddha became largely modified by various forms of local beliefs and faiths. This also exerted a back-pressure on popular Hinduism. Thus we find the introduction into the popular Hindu religion of many kinds of image-worship and the muttering of mystical syllables and unmeaning *mantras* (called *dhāraṇī* in Buddhism), associated with various typical geometrical forms representing the field of force of the different forms of the newly introduced divinities. These geometrical forms are called *cakras*. *Cakra* is also the name of the six principal nerve-plexuses by concentration on which a *yogin* could control all his passions and ultimately attain liberation. Some processes of the control of nerves and involuntary muscles as well as the washing of internal vacuities in the body seem to have been developing from the time of the *Maitrāyaṇī Upaniṣad*. This was gradually called in later times Haṭha-yoga, Tantra-yoga or Ṣaṭ-cakra-sādhana.

We know that some form of phallic worship was current among the Indus valley people as early as 3000 B.C. Though there are occasional references to the Mother cult or the Śakti cult in the Vedic literature, it did not seem to have taken deep root there. On the other hand, both the Śaiva and the Śakti cults were prevalent in the South from the early times. Some sort of Śakti cult seems to have been mixed up with the aberrant forms of Buddhism giving rise to various forms of Tantras in the middle ages, particularly in Bengal and Kashmir. The ideas of *prajñā* and *upāya* became symbols of Śakti and Śiva; and this evolved a form of worship which seems to reflect sometimes the idea of Prakṛti and Puruṣa and sometimes that of Māyā and Brahman.

The Mahāyāna Buddhism spread northwards to Gāndhāra, Tibet, China, Japan, Turfan, and the whole tract of Turkistan. Early and mediaeval Buddhist paintings and sculptures are preserved in many places in India, such as Sanchi and the caves of Ajanta; and many Buddhist paintings have also been discovered in Tibet and Turfan. A great collection of Buddhist works, of which the Sanskrit originals have been lost, are available in their Chinese translations in China. Buddhism not only spread over China, but it also influenced the thoughts of many Chinese philosophers. The philosophical teachings of Lao-tze are very similar to those of the Upaniṣads, though no contact between China and India is traceable at that early period.

Jainism as originating from Mahāvīra seems to be somewhat earlier than Buddhism. The Jaina Āgamas, which form the trusted religious documents of the Śvetāmbara school, are not generally admitted as authentic by the Digambara school of Jainism, which has a large philosophical literature written in Sanskrit. The difference between the two schools of Jainism is inessential. The Jains believe that the whole world is populated with minute monads in different grades of evolution. These monads, including human souls, are awakened to knowledge and feeling from within by the internal action of *karma*. Human souls are, in essence, possessed of omniscience and omnipotence, but such powers are obstructed by the accumulated coverings on them on account of their inherited *karmas.* The Jains lay great stress on morality in general and on non-injury in particular. In philosophy and logic they have developed a relativistic view that affirmations or denials of any kinds of facts can only be made from seven different kinds of alternative perspectives. Thus from different points of view something may be either affirmed or denied of a thing, or it may be indescribable. This may lead in a permutative manner to seven kinds of affirmation or denial. The Jains believe in a realistic and pluralistic world, and they do not believe in any kind of transcendental illusion or Māyā. They also do not believe in the existence of any supreme God as the creator of the world. Man creates his own destiny by his own efforts or actions. When a man becomes absolutely free from all passions, he is called a Jina ; and he shines in his full powers of omniscience and omnipotence. From very early times the Jains have developed a system of logic ; and we have a history of their dialectical skill in arguing with their opponents, the Hindus and the Buddhists.

## SAṀKHYA AND YOGA

The beginnings of the Sāṁkhya system of thought may be discovered in some of the early Upaniṣads. If we try to link up the various strands of thought that we find in the *Mahābhārata,* the *Gītā,* the Purāṇas, and the *Caraka Saṁhitā* (IV. 1), otherwise known as the *Ātreya Tantra,* and also in other relevant Buddhist and Pāñcarātra texts, we are led to the conclusion that the Sāṁkhya system of thought must have passed through various stages of development, which shaped and reshaped it at various times both theistically and atheistically. We know that some time before the third century there was a theistic Sāṁkhya work known as *Ṣaṣṭitantra-śāstra,* containing sixty chapters, some description of which is found in the *Pañcarātra* and the *Ahirbudhnya Saṁhitā.* The *Sāṁkhya-kārikā* of Īśvarakṛṣṇa, probably written about the beginning of the third century, is regarded as a representative work of the classical school of Sāṁkhya ; and it is referred to in discussions by Vasubandhu in his *Abhidharma-kośa.* Īśvarakṛṣṇa's *Sāṁkhya-kārikā,* which is said to have been based on the *Ṣaṣṭitantra-śāstra,* had no place for God in it, though we are almost certain that the *Ṣaṣṭitantra-śāstra* must have been a theistic Sāṁkhya work somewhat resembling the theistic Sāṁkhya view of the *Bhāgavata Purāṇa.* A later Sāṁkhya work called the *Sāṁkhyapravacana-Sūtra,* commented on by Aniruddha and Vijñāna Bhikṣu, was on atheistic lines. Vijñāna Bhikṣu, however, wrote a commentary on the *Brahma-Sūtra* called the *Vijñānāmṛta-bhāṣya,* towards the middle of the second millennium A.D., in which he tried to interpret the *Brahma-Sūtra* as if it were a work of theistic Sāṁkhya. He also wrote a commentary (still unpublished) on the *Īśvara-Gītā* of the *Kūrma Purāṇa,* in which he explained the Sāṁkhya in a similar manner. In this connection we must bear in mind that another school of Sāṁkhya, known as the Pātañjala school of Sāṁkhya or the system of Yoga, appears in the *Sūtra* form somewhere about the second century B.C. We know that some forms of *yoga* practice were probably prevalent in India as early as 3000 B.C. A definite form of *yoga* practices and some of the stages of *yoga* meditation were given probably for the first time by Buddha. This Yoga doctrine seems to be quite unrelated to the Sāṁkhya doctrine. The attempt of Patañjali, and later of Vyāsa, seems to have based the *yoga* practices on the Sāṁkhya metaphysics, revising and reviewing the *yoga* methods in accordance with the Sāṁkhya doctrines. The Pātañjala school of the Sāṁkhya or the Yoga is theistic, but it has no connection with the *Ṣaṣṭitantra-śāstra.* The commentary of Vyāsa on the *Yoga-Sūtra* of Patañjali was further commented upon first by Vācaspati Miśra and then by Vijñāna Bhikṣu. Bhoja in the tenth century also wrote a commentary on the *Yoga-Sūtra.*

The metaphysical theory underlying the classical Sāṁkhya, attributed to Kapila, Āsuri, and Pañcaśikha and as appearing in Īśvarakṛṣṇa's *Kārikā* as well as forming the metaphysical basis of the Yoga, may briefly be stated as follows. The origin of all forms of subtle and gross matter is to be found in the three classes of reals, *sattva* representing lightness and illumination, *rajas* representing energy, and *tamas* representing inertness and mass. When these reals or *guṇas* are in a state of equilibrium there is no movement or evolution. But besides this primitive matter or Prakṛti as equilibrium of the *guṇas,* there is also an infinite number of souls, Puruṣas, which are of the nature of pure intelligence and absolutely inactive. The concept of pure intelligence should not be confused with any kind of concrete thought but should be regarded as being like contentless sparks in association with which thought may become illuminating and living. The Prakṛti has within it a sort of inherent teleology that the combination of *guṇas* should serve the Puruṣas in providing them with experience, and ultimately detach them from the bondage of Prakṛti itself through the dissolution of individual minds or *buddhis,* leaving them supremely alone in their nature as pure intelligence.

Roused by this inherent teleology, the equilibrium of Prakṛti is disturbed, and various combinations take place among the *guṇas* with varying degrees of predominance of the different *guṇas.* In the first stage there is a predominance of *sattva,* which leads to the evolution of *buddhi* or the cosmic mind which is a sum total of the individual minds that become associated with the different Puruṣas in order to make their experiences possible, for there cannot be an experience without a mind. From this cosmic mind or *buddhi* we have a successive series of evolutions on the subjective side, such as the ego (*ahaṅkāra*) and the eleven senses, cognitive and conative, forming the entire psychic apparatus of the individual mind. From the ego we have another series of evolutions on the physical side through the gradual predominance of *tamas* or mass, forming the five *tanmātras* (subtler states of matter) and the five gross elements, the *bhūtas.* There is a great divergence of opinion among the various schools of the Sāṁkhya regarding the order and manner of the evolution of these categories. Prakṛti is, however, the original matter-stuff from which we get the mental world on the one hand and the material world on the other as a result of the various combinations of the five elements. There is no real association between the individual *buddhis* and the individual Puruṣas. But there is such a beginningless transcendental illusion in the *buddhis* that the distinction between the Puruṣas and the *buddhis* is not realized and the experiences of the *buddhis,* which are of the nature of a subtle material form, are intelligized by their respective Puruṣas and are interpreted as belonging to them. This is explained by the theory of transcendental reflection of the Puruṣa on the *buddhi* or that of mutual reflection of the one on the other. This illusion is regarded as the bondage of the Puruṣa. The classical Sāṁkhya thinks that this illusion is of the nature of the non-apprehension of the difference between the Puruṣa and the Prakṛti, and this is the cause of all our sorrow. When the difference between the Puruṣa and the Prakṛti is ultimately realized, the illusory association between them is cut asunder and the Puruṣa becomes ultimately free in its nature as pure intelligence ; and this is the state of *mokṣa,* the destruction of all sorrow.

The Pātañjala school of Sāṁkhya agrees essentially with the doctrines of the classical school of Sāṁkhya. But it regards the nature of the transcendental illusion as a misapprehension of one thing as another (*anyathā-bhāva*). It does not think that philosophical knowledge alone is sufficient for explaining the dissociation of *buddhi* from the Puruṣa. It lays great emphasis on the psychological nature of our passions, and on the sorrow that proceeds from them. It lays down rules of morality and spiritual life which are called *yamas* and *niyamas* and introduces a system of breath-control and meditation (*dhyāna*) and contemplation (*samādhi*). It is enjoined that the object of *samādhi* should be in an ascending scale of subtler and subtler states and, in the ultimate stage, the object should be pure contentless vacuity. The practice of the control of mental states, including the different stages of *samādhi,* is said to produce miraculous powers (*vibhūti*) as well as different types of wisdom and intuition called *prajñā*.

According to both the Yoga and the Sāṁkhya, objects in the outer world come in contact with the individual *buddhis,* which take diverse forms in accordance with that contact and are intelligized by the illusorily associated Puruṣas. The Yoga writers introduce the concepts of the subconscious and the unconscious mind as determining instinctive tendencies, and also as showing how, by the processes of *yoga,* the efforts of the conscious mind can dominate over the subconscious and the unconscious, and may ultimately succeed in disjoining the different psychical strands that constitute the unity of the mind, and thus effect the ultimate disintegration of the mind. The Yoga writers further think that the variety of material forms and life is due to the specific combinations of the *guṇas.* They believe in the existence of God as a Puruṣa who had never been associated with any passions, *karma,* or its fruits. God has a permanent will limiting the flow of energy in and through the manifestations of Prakṛti, which explains the order of psychic and objective evolutions for the fulfilment of the purpose of Puruṣa in accordance with the moral order of *karma.* If the limitations in the direction of the flow of energy could be removed, then anything could be transformed into any other thing. When a mind is absolutely disintegrated, it returns unto the Prakṛti, and the Puruṣa becomes free and shines alone in its state of pure intelligence.

The Sāṁkhya-Yoga and the Vedānta have practically influenced not only the various forms of Hindu religious literature, such as the Purāṇas, the Tantras, the *Mahābhārata,* the *Gītā,* and the Pāñcarātra and other sectarian literatures related to them, but also many of the Buddhist Tantras. The idea of the conjoined Prakṛti and Puruṣa has also influenced various forms of worship, art, and iconography. The Sāṁkhya had also its influence on the science of medicine.

### VAIŚEṢIKA AND NYĀYA

The *Vaiśeṣika-Sūtra,* supposed to have been written by Kaṇāda, constituted in all probability a system of thought akin in some respects to the Mīmāṁsā, but devoted itself to the interpretation of man and the world, assuming six fundamental categories, namely, *dravya* (substance), *guṇa* (quality), *karma* (action), *sāmānya* (universality), *viśeṣa* (specific property), and *samavāya* (relation of inherence). The *Sūtra* was probably written somewhere about the sixth or the seventh century B.C., though the earliest commentary available to us is probably as late as the tenth century A.D. We have, however, an earlier compendium which states the general view of the Vaiśeṣika but is not a commentary on it, though it goes by the name of *Praśastapāda-bhāṣya.* On this was written, about the ninth or the tenth century, a commentary called *Nyāya-kandalī* by Śrīdhara. It is curious that the Vaiśeṣika as a system of philosophy was not taken up seriously in early times. Most of its doctrines, however, were incorporated in the *Nyāya-Sūtra* by Akṣapāda probably in the third century. The Nyāya system accepts the Vaiśeṣika categories as its basic metaphysical doctrine but lays great emphasis on the development of logic (*ānvīkṣikī*) which had taken its start in the medical discussions as found in the *Caraka Saṁhitā* (III. 8), written some time about the first century. Later on when logical disputes arose between the Hindus, Buddhists, and Jains, the *Nyāya-Sūtra* began to be commented upon by Vātsyāyana, Uddyotakara, Vācaspati, and others, and in these works as well as in some Buddhist logical tracts we can trace the development of the logical controversy between the Naiyāyikas and the Buddhists. The subject of *pramāṇas,* and particularly *anumāna* (inference), received the special attention of Gaṅgeśa and his followers from about the twelfth to the seventeenth century. Mithilā and Bengal deserve special credit for initiating this new school of Nyāya, the technique of which was almost unanimously accepted by most writers on philosophical controversies all over India. Clarity and precision of expression of all definitions have been the chief objects of this new school of Nyāya studies.

The Nyāya philosophy, which became syncretized with the Vaiśeṣika, accepted the doctrine of the plurality of souls which were permanent and unconscious. Under certain conditions these souls happen to possess certain intellectual, volitional, or emotional qualities as a result of their coming in contact with bodies, sense-organs, etc. The Nyāya believes in the existence of God, by whose will atomic action takes place for the formation of molecules and other grosser bodies. It further holds that it is only through philosophical knowledge and dissolution of doubt and ignorance that the souls can be finally liberated and freed from the bonds of *karma* and rebirth. In the state of liberation the souls remain merely as entities devoid of all consciousness, volition, or feeling. Like the writers on other systems of Indian philosophy, the writers of the Nyāya school also enter into long discussions against the Buddhist doctrines of momentariness, soullessness, etc. throughout the long centuries of their virile intellectual contests.

As we have already said, the Sāṁkhya-Yoga and the Vedānta had the greatest influence on Indian literature, particularly religious literature on sectarian lines. Thus, for example, the Kashmir Śaiva literature that flourished principally in Kashmir for some centuries, beginning from the seventh or the eighth century, is in reality an eclectic combination of the

Sāṁkhya-Yoga and the monistic Vedānta. There are a large number of texts on Kashmir Śaivism which await further study.

The philosophies of the Sāṁkhya-Yoga and the Vedānta seem to have coalesced in many respects. In the later Vedāntic writings we come across both *yoga* and the three *guṇas* of *sattva, rajas,* and *tamas*. Of course, *yoga* is used here more in the general sense of concentration and meditation, and does not follow the theory of scalar ascension through subtler and subtler states to ultimate vacuity as recommended by Patañjali's *yoga*. The *prāṇāyāma* or breath-control of the Yoga was almost universally accepted in the systems.

## LATER APPLICATIONS

The application of the Sāṁkhya-Vedānta ideas forms the material basis of the philosophy of literature (*alaṅkāra*). The main inquiry of this science is to establish the fact that literary communication depending on suggestiveness differs from the ordinary modes of communication of meaning as referring to things either directly (*abhidhā*) or indirectly in a secondary manner (*lakṣaṇā*). This suggestiveness (*vyañjanā*), which is the chief function of poetry or drama, manifests to the reader or the audience either certain truths of literary implication or rouses disinterested literary emotions. Long discussions about the nature of disinterested emotions often reveal the view that in such literary experiences either the soul is enjoyed as pure bliss, or that by the over-abundance of the *sattva* qualities there is a reflection of the pure self as blissful. It is for this reason that whatever may be the nature of the emotions, painful, pleasurable, heroic, or the like, they are all ultimately lived through as pure enjoyment. Whatever may be the obstacles to the realization of this enjoyment (*rasa*), whether they be of the nature of wrong grammatical construction or defects of style or contrariness to usage or traditional beliefs or incompatibility of any sort, they are regarded as defects (*doṣas*) of literature. The main object of style is also the adaptability of language for the true suggestion of *rasa*. All descriptions that contribute to the literary art should have for their object the communication of literary enjoyment. The ultimate object of literature is creation of beauty. This beauty is manifested in and through the properly adapted structure of language, the choice of words and images by utilizing their penumbral shades, leading to the ultimate suggestion or revelation of disinterested joy. Great emphasis is laid on the fact that the joy of literature is not the satisfaction of any practical desire or need but the spontaneous overflow of transcendental joy devoid of the bonds of time, place, and necessity. It is at once personal and impersonal.

If we had had any opportunity here to discuss the theory of plastic art and painting, we would have seen that art-creation, whether of persons or situations or ideas, was made in reality in the contemplation (*dhyāna*) of an object associated with exhilaration or joy. This was translated later on into lines and colours or materials of stone or clay. Religious ideas also inspired the architecture of temples. The ideas represented in the various images of gods are always summed up in the *mantras* for contemplation (*dhyāna*) relating to their worship.

Similar application of philosophical principles may also be traced in the case of some of the practical sciences. Thus, turning our attention to the science or art of medicine, we find that it originally started from some form of sorcery or charm, as well as from the knowledge of the healing properties of various plants. As such, *Āyurveda* is regarded as an *upāṅga* of the *Atharva-Veda* in which we find references both to charms and to medicinal plants. We find therein diseases classified as wet, dry, and moving. These in later times came to be regarded as *kapha* (phlegm), *pitta* (bile), and *vāyu* (bio-motor force). In the work of Vṛddha Vāgbhaṭa these three are identified with *tamas*, *sattva*, and *rajas*. We find in the *Bhela Saṁhita* that one of the functions of the *pitta* as existing in the head is to arrange for the nervous adaptations involved in the acquirement of knowledge. Caraka employed some of the Vaiśeṣika concepts in a somewhat different meaning in the interpretation of his medical system. In the fourth book of the *Caraka Saṁhitā* we find a whole chapter devoted to the Sāṁkhya principles, which are somewhat different from those of the classical Sāṁkhya. The origin of the deductive and inductive methods as well as experimental methods can be traced to the *Caraka Saṁhitā*. Logical forms of debate and the definition of logical categories are to be found in the *Caraka Saṁhitā* for the first time. Caraka also introduced concepts of heredity which are very much the same as our modern ideas on the subject. He thought also that all developments in the biological world in man, animal, and plants proceeded more or less on the same plan. He seems to distinguish a so-called biological self (*bhūtātman*), on which life and life-functions depend, from a superior Self which is above all biological conditions. The biological self is destroyed with the body, but the superior Self is unaffected. Caraka distinguishes mental diseases from the physical. The mental diseases are those which manifest themselves in the body and the mind, and are due to passions and wrong emotions of the mind. They have to be slowly rooted out by patient efforts. The object of life is the attainment of physical and mental well-being and pleasure, and Caraka has a complete code of ethics as supplementary to the medical treatment. The *Caraka Saṁhitā* is not only a work of medicine, comprising medical theories, recipes of medicine, and diagnostic methods which were known at the time, but is also an epitome of Hindu culture from a realistic perspective. It was written probably some time about A.D. 100, though certain additions to it were made somewhere about the fifth century. The older Suśruta or the Vṛddha Suśruta of the Dhanvantari school is not available now. But the *Suśruta Saṁhitā* that is now available is plainly based upon the metaphysical theory of the classical Sāṁkhya.

## THE SCEPTICS AND ATHEISTS

Besides what has been said above, there were many other strands of thought whose development cannot now be traced, as the corresponding literature is now practically lost. We can find only allusions to them from different parts of other philosophical literature. There is at least one very prominent passage in the *Ṛg-Veda Saṁhitā* in which doubt is expressed about the origin of this world, and it is further said that even if there were any Lord of the universe in the highest heaven, He also might or might not have known anything about the origin of the universe. There were also different forms of atheistic beliefs called the Cārvāka or the Lokāyata which did not accept the existence of souls, God, rebirth, or the efficacy of any kind of religious rites. Some of them (the Suśikṣita Cārvāka) admitted the existence of souls, more or less permanent during the present life, while others denied it. They also did not admit any *pramāṇa* other than perception. We find references in Buddhist works to other heretical schools which did not believe in any kind of morality. Thus there is a passage in which one Pūraṇa Kassapa is supposed to say that if one killed as many men as there were sands on the beach of the Gaṅgā, there was no sin, and that if one did as much good to so many people, there was no virtue in that. But these ideas and views regarding the disbelief in post-mortem existence of souls were very unpopular ; and I do not know how far they were developed, as no literature on the subject is available.

Jainism is a fairly well-developed system, and it is highly moralistic and lays great emphasis on non-injury to living beings. But in spite of its great antiquity and its consistent development throughout the centuries in the hands of its adherents, we cannot affiliate it to the Vedic schools of thought, nor can we find any statement of the reasons which led to the foundation of the school. In the case of most of the Vedic schools of thought also it is difficult to find out how the original exponents or the founders of the systems came to formulate them ; yet their affinity with the Upaniṣadic ideas is in most cases traceable. If we read the Piṭakas it is not difficult to discover the extent to which Buddha was indebted to the Upaniṣads and wherein he differed from them and why he did so. In its later development Buddhism seems to have come nearer the Upaniṣadic thought. The *Vaiśeṣika-Sūtra* offers another great difficulty. Though it is accepted as one of the orthodox Vedic systems, yet its theory of categories, its absolutely pluralistic views, and its denial of consciousness to self separate it from the Upaniṣadic thought. Its subsequent syncretization with the Nyāya did not improve its position from this point of view. Though the Nyāya admits a plurality of souls, it does not think that these are of the nature of consciousness. They are only substantive entities which may be associated with intellectual, volitional, or emotional qualities as a result of proper collocation of causes and conditions. God, in the Nyāya system, is not the creator of the world but the original prime mover by whose will the atoms are set in motion for the formation of molecules and grosser bodies, and thereby for the formation of a world in which the moral order and the law of Karma may be fulfilled. It has already been pointed out that the Mīmāṁsā philosophy is primarily engaged in explaining the various ways in which the Vedic commandments are to be fulfilled. Its views regarding the world, soul, etc. appear gradually at a later date, and for this it is largely indebted to the Vaiśeṣika. It differs from the Nyāya on the doctrine of self-validity of knowledge, which is denied by the Naiyāyika.

It has been said above that some of the elements of the Sāṁkhya can be traced to the Upaniṣads. But there seems to be little doubt that the Sāṁkhya was not worked upon as a system of philosophy at the time of the Upaniṣads. A study of the later literature is bound to convince one that different systems of the Sāṁkhya were formed under different influences at different times. The classical Sāṁkhya and the Pātañjala Sāṁkhya (the Yoga) are but two well-known examples. The Yoga was probably current as a system of practical exercises and was taken up by Buddha and formulated by him in his own manner. The Pātañjala Sāṁkhya took up the *yoga* practices and supplemented them with the Sāṁkhya metaphysics with some consequential changes, e.g. the admission of God, the psychological theories of *vāsanā,* etc. The word *yoga* had probably caused considerable perplexity in the minds of the early writers. Thus, for example, the *Gītā* does not seem to take *yoga* in Patañjali's sense as the cessation of mental states (*citta-vṛtti-nirodha*). Yet in the colophon of every chapter, the *Gītā* is designated as the Yoga-śāstra. Later on we find that some elements of the Yoga had been accepted by most systems of Indian thought including the Vedānta, though the Sāṁkhya elements were mostly disregarded. The Sāṁkhya literature, as it is available to us, is but meagre ; and we have no record of the manner in which the Sāṁkhya system was thought out. There is also great divergence of views even with regard to the significance of the three *guṇas—sattva, rajas,* and *tamas.* We are not even certain whether the three *guṇas* existed as such as the original entities or if one was produced out of any other. The formation of the *tanmātras* (the subtle entities) and the *bhūtas* (the gross entities) also offers the same difficulties.

The unsystematic ideas of the Upaniṣads, containing germs of dualistic and monistic thoughts, were systematized in the *Brahma-Sūtra* or *Vedānta-Sūtra,* and this passes as the Vedānta school of thought. It has been pointed out before how in the hands of different interpreters at different ages the significance of the Vedānta philosophy changed from pure monism to pure pluralism almost beyond recognition.

### SOCIAL AND MORAL CODES

It has also been mentioned before that some postulates or dogmas were held fast as the bed-rock of most systems of Indian thought, with some variation in the case of Buddhism and Jainism. As a necessary adjunct of these postulates, the highest moral conduct and the most elevated and pure spiritual life were demanded of those who wanted to attain the highest wisdom, which was the *summum bonum,* as it led to the highest good defined as pure bliss or pure consciousness. In Buddhism also the final state of going out of empirical existence, called *nirvāṇa,* is somehow regarded as the highest bliss. Of course, bliss or consciousness in the highest state is only a transcendental reality, as in the absence of a personal ego it cannot be experienced as a psychological state. In the case of the Vaiṣṇavas or the Śaivas, emphasis has been laid on devotion by which the saint enters into communion with God. Throughout the middle ages in the vernacular writings in Hindi, Marathi, Gurumukhi, and Bengali, the idea of the Vedāntic monism as well as the doctrine of devotion (*bhakti*) has been very effectively preached among the masses ; and this has led very greatly to the uplifting of the moral temperament of all Hindus in general.

Apart from the course of the philosopher or the saint we have the course of the householder. The way of conduct of the Vedic people is supposed to have been collected in the Smṛtis, and these Smṛtis seem to codify the social conduct of every Hindu of every community or caste in all essential details. It cannot be denied, however, that owing to the historical change of circumstances the mandates of the Smṛtis became more rigorous and narrow with the advance of time, and the later Smṛtis and Nibandhas sometimes differed widely from the older ones ; and sometimes royal intervention also changed the nature of specific laws on various subjects.

A study of the *Mahābhārata* convincingly proves that during the period of its writing people became critical as regards the concept of the well-established moral and social laws. We find in the *Mahābhārata* on the one hand the uncritical adherence to the concepts of well-known virtues (e.g. not to break one's promise, etc.), and on the other hand we find grave and upsetting discussions on the nature of truth or the status of a Brāhmaṇa, and on the inviolability of certain social practices enjoined on the Brāhmaṇas or the Kṣatriyas.

We cannot also forget in this connection that the stories and instructions contained in our various Nīti-śāstras always keep us wakeful about the correct behaviour in society of normal persons in various situations. The ideal of conduct advocated in the Nīti-śāstras is wise in the sense that it is often utilitarian and hedonistic.

## PHILOSOPHIC METHOD AND OUTLOOK

Philosophical speculations in India can be traced to the intuitive experiences of the Upaniṣads and some of the Vedic hymns. All the Hindu systems of thought either directly or indirectly accept the validity of the Vedic writings. The difference was with regard to their specific import. Consequently we find that the systems of the Nyāya-Vaiśeṣika, Sāṁkhya-Yoga, Mīmāṁsā, and the schools and sub-schools of the different systems of the Vedānta, in fact, almost all the schools of thought, were kept alive through a series of commentaries and sub commentaries as well as independent compendiums or manuals written through the ages by the successive adherents of these schools. This led to the rise of great controversies and dialectical writings by the opposing schools of thought among the Hindu, Buddhist, and Jain writers. Philosophy and logic therefore developed mainly from the fourth or the fifth century to the sixteenth or the seventeenth century. The entry of Islam into India does not seem to have affected the growth of Indian philosophical thought. It is in and through the controversial literature of the commentaries of the above period that we can discover the attempts at a solution of the philosophical problems which we often share in common with Greek and modern European philosophy, though it is not always easy to recognize them as being essentially the same on account of the Indian perspectives through which they appear.

But apart from the discussion of the problems of metaphysics, epistemology, or logic, Indian philosophy as a whole had an outlook entirely different from that of Western philosophy. Philosophy in India began with a quest after the highest truth—truth not as mere objective certitude but as one which was closely linked up with the development of our personality for the attainment of the highest freedom, bliss, and wisdom. It therefore demanded not only a philosophical discipline of reasoning, but also the discipline of our conduct and the control of our emotions and passions in various ways. The object of philosophy is not merely to be able to argue with wisdom, but to transform ourselves into perfectly wise beings, enjoying absolute freedom from all bondage and the bliss that follows from it. Indian philosophy believes that the world about us is a moral world and that by following a moral life both objectively and subjectively we are bound to attain perfection at some time or other. It is for this reason that most systems of Indian philosophy are associated with some form of monastic life which the highest spiritual aspirants may adopt for a fuller realization of their goal. Philosophy does not mean puzzling out intellectual thoughts and problems; it is a light with which we should illuminate all the dark corners of our being and realize in this life the ideals that are set up before us by our thought and wisdom.

PART I

# THE PHILOSOPHICAL SYSTEMS

# 2

# RISE OF THE PHILOSOPHICAL SCHOOLS

## THE PRINCIPAL TRADITIONS IN INDIAN PHILOSOPHY

THE schools of Indian philosophy have sprung from two or rather three original sources or traditions. The Brāhmaṇical systems based on the Ātman doctrine of the Upaniṣads and the Buddhist schools on the Nairātmya doctrine of Buddha conceive reality on two distinct and exclusive patterns. The Upaniṣads and the systems drawing their inspiration from them conceive reality on the pattern of an inner core or soul (Ātman), immutable and identical amidst an outer region of impermanence and change to which it is unrelated or but loosely related. This may be termed the substance view of reality (Ātmavāda). In its radical form, as in the Advaita Vedānta, it denies the reality of the apparent, the impermanent, and the many, and equates them with the false. The Sāṁkhya does not go so far ; still it inclines more towards the substantial, the permanent, and the universal. The Nyāya with its empirical and pluralistic bias accords equal status to both substance and modes. Not only do these systems accept the Ātman, but what is more, they conceive all other things too on the substance pattern. The Ātman is the very pivot of their metaphysics, epistemology, and ethics. In epistemology, substance makes for unity and integration of experience ; it explains perception, memory, and personal identity better than other assumptions. Bondage is ignorance of the self or the wrong identification of the self with the non-self (*ātmanyanātmādhyāsa*). Freedom is the discrimination between the two.

The other tradition is represented by the Buddhist denial of substance (Ātman) and all that it implies. There is no inner and immutable core in things ; everything is in flux. Existence for the Buddhist is momentary (*kṣaṇika*), unique (*svalakṣaṇa*), and unitary (*dharmamātra*). It is discontinuous, discrete, and devoid of complexity. Substance (the universal and identical) is rejected as illusory ; it is but a thought-construction made under the influence of wrong belief (*avidyā*). This may be taken as the modal view of reality. The Buddhists have brought their epistemology and ethics into full accord with their Nairātmya metaphysics. Their peculiar conception of perception and inference and the complementary doctrine of mental construction (*vikalpa*) are necessary consequences of their denial of substance. Heroic attempts have been made to fit in this theory with the doctrine of Karma and rebirth. *Avidyā,* which is the root cause of pain, is the wrong belief in the Ātman (*satkāya-dṛṣṭi-*

*prabhavāḥ sarve kleśāḥ*) ; and *prajñā* (wisdom) is the eradication of this belief and its attendant evils.

The terminology employed above is after the best Jaina epistemological treatises. Philosophical views, they say, are principally two—the Dravyārthika-naya (substance view) and Paryāyārthika-naya (modal view).[1] Each view, carried to the extreme, denies the reality of the other. One emphasizes the universal and the continuous to the exclusion of the changing and the different, and the other holds the opposite view. The Vedānta is cited as the exponent of the extreme form of the substance view ;[2] and Buddhism (Tathāgatamata) represents the exclusive modal view.[3]

The Jaina system ostensibly reconciles these two opposed views by according equal reality to substance and its modes. There is no substance without modes, nor are there modes without substance.[4] Reality is manifold (*anekāntātmaka*) ; it is not of one nature ; it is unity and difference, universal and particular, and permanent and changing. The Jaina philosophy shaped its epistemology on this pattern and formulated the logic of the disjunction of the real (Syādvāda). This view may be said to constitute the third stream of Indian philosophy, lying midway between the two extremes of the Ātmavāda and the Anātmavāda. Seemingly partaking of the nature of both, it was essentially un-Brāhmaṇical and un-Buddhistic. It was un-Brāhmaṇical in that it accepted a *changing* Ātman and even ascribed different sizes to it ; no Brāhmaṇical system could ever accept that. It was un-Buddhistic in that it accepted a permanent entity, Ātman, besides change. As a result, the Jaina found favour with neither. The synthesis of two views is a third view, and is no substitute for either. The Jaina system had comparatively little influence on the course of Indian philosophy, and was little affected by other systems. Jainism has remained practically stationary down the ages.

Indian philosophy must therefore be interpreted as the flow of two vital streams—one having its source in the Ātman doctrine of the Upaniṣads and the other in the Anātmavāda of Buddha. Each branched off into several sub-streams. There were lively sallies and skirmishes, but no commingling of the two streams. Throughout the course of their development they have remained true to their original inspirations. The Brāhmaṇical systems are wedded to Being, Buddhism to Becoming ; the

[1] '*Samāsatastu dvibhedo dravyārthikaḥ paryāyārthikaśca.*' *Pramāṇa-naya-tattvāloka*, VII. 5. See also *Sammati-tarka, Gāthā*, 3.

[2] *Pramāṇa-naya-tattvāloka*, VII. 17-18.

[3] *Ibid.*, VII. 28, 30-31.

[4] '*Dravyaṁ paryāyaviyuktaṁ paryāyā dravyavarjitāḥ ; kva kadā kena kiṁrūpā dṛṣṭā mānena kena vā.*' *Sammati-tarka, Gāthā*, 1. Cf. also the Jaina dictum, *dravyaparyāyātmakaṁ vastu prameyam.*

former espouse the existential and static view of reality, the latter the sequential and dynamic; for the one space, for the other time is the archetype. The Brāhmaṇical systems are relatively more categorical and positive in their attitude (*vidhimukhena*), while the Buddhists are more negative (*niṣedhamukhena*). Again, the former are more dogmatic and speculative, the latter empirical and critical. Subjectively minded, Buddhism is little interested in cosmological speculations and constructive explanations of the universe. The Brāhmaṇical systems are bound to an original tradition; they all accept the authoritarian character of the Vedas. Buddhism derives its inspiration from a criticism of experience itself. The tempo of development is quicker and intenser in Buddhism than in the Upaniṣadic tradition.

An opposite view has been advocated by a not inconsiderable section of the schools of Indian thought. They interpret Indian philosophy as having developed out of one tradition, the Upaniṣadic. Buddhism and Jainism are treated as deviations, rather than radical departures, from the Ātmavāda of the Upaniṣads. This, however, ignores the sharp differences and exclusive attitudes inherent in these systems. Similarly it overlooks the internal differences within the fold of Buddhism, and considers it one unitary system instead of a matrix of many systems. Nairātmyavāda is the genus of which the different Buddhist systems—the Vaibhāṣika, the Sautrāntika, the Mādhyamika, and the Yogācāra—are the species; they are the various attempts to express the same denial of substance.

The entire course of the development of Indian philosophy is proof of our contention. No Buddhist system did ever accept the reality of the Ātman, the permanent and the unchanging. No non-Buddhist system except the Cārvāka, on the contrary, could ever reject it as unreal.

It may be said that this state of affairs is true of the later scholastic phase of Buddhism, and not of the original teachings of its Master. Reliance may be placed on certain texts affirming the Ātman. But we have to consider, as against this, more numerous passages which deny the self in unmistakable terms. It will not do therefore to select those texts that favour a preconceived interpretation and to ignore the others. A systematic exegesis of the texts and a synthesis of the doctrines can alone prove fruitful. Such syntheses have been made by the Buddhist systems from time to time, notably by the Ābhidharmika, the Mādhyamika, and the Vijñānavāda systems. The modern exponent has to take these into account, as *prima facie* they claim to embody and express the original teachings. In the case of Buddhism too, we must accept the law of evolution that the later phases are potentially contained in the earlier. The theory of a primitive soul-affirming Buddhism followed by a soul-denying scholasticism does not solve any problem; it adds one more. 'In the attempt of bridging the difference between the Upaniṣads and Buddha we would have immeasurably increased the distance between Buddha and Buddhism. Nor can we find any adequate reason for such a gross misunderstanding of Buddha by his followers.'

It may be said that the denial of the self is beset with such insuperable difficulties that it could not have been seriously maintained by any philosopher. The answer is that the doctrine of an entity, immutable and impervious to change (Ātmavāda), is also beset with equally insuperable difficulties, though of an opposite kind. The Buddhist schools have made very consistent and commendable efforts to explain phenomena on their own hypothesis, as the Brāhmaṇical systems have on theirs, though in the opposite direction. The deep opposition between these radical standpoints stimulated the systems on either side; they gained in depth and maturity. It also helped the emergence of the dialectical consciousness, which we find in a systematic form in the Mādhyamika philosophy. Dialectic is the consciousness of the total and interminable conflict of the ideas of reason, of philosophical views. It presses towards their resolution in the Absolute which is the negation of the opposites (*advaita, advaya*). The Advaitic turn in the Buddhistic and Brāhmaṇical systems is a necessary outcome of this.

## THE CLASSIFICATION OF THE SCHOOLS

It is customary to speak of the six orthodox and six heretical systems.[5] The Sāṁkhya, the Yoga, the Nyāya, the Vaiśeṣika, the Pūrva Mīmāṁsā, and the Vedānta (also called the Uttara Mīmāṁsā) constitute the former; the four classical schools of Buddhism (the Vaibhāṣika, the Sautrāntika, the Vijñānavāda, and the Mādhyamika), Jainism, and the Cārvāka make up the latter. This traditional enumeration errs by being at once too narrow and too wide; too narrow, as it does not include many other schools—the non-Advaitic schools of the Vedānta, the various Śaiva systems, the philosophy of language, etc. which are not mentioned at all. If the intention is to include the basic systems only, then it is too wide. For there are only three basic systems (the Sāṁkhya, the Nyāya-Vaiśeṣika, and the Advaita Vedānta) on the Brāhmaṇical side, and three (the Ābhidharmika, the Mādhyamika,

[5] Haribhadra's *Ṣaḍdarśana-samuccaya* deals with the Buddhist, Nyāya, Sāṁkhya, Jaina, Vaiśeṣika, and the Jaiminīya systems; it adds, however, that where Nyāya and Vaiśeṣika are treated as one system, Lokāyata is to be regarded as the sixth. *Sarva-darśana-saṅgraha* is a much fuller compendium. Besides the above, it expounds the Cārvāka, Rāmānuja, Mādhva, Nakulīśa-Pāśupata, Śaiva, Pratyabhijñā, Raseśvara, Pāṇinīya, and Pātañjala systems and ends with the statement that the author had already treated of Śaṅkara's system elsewhere. The *Sarva-darśana-kaumudī* and the *Sarva-siddhānta-sāra-saṅgraha* (ascribed to Śaṅkarācārya) are other short compendia.

and the Yogācāra) belonging to Buddhism. The Jaina may be taken as different from both these groups.

The Nyāya-Vaiśeṣika is rigorous realism and pluralism. It advocates a mechanistic theory of causation, and is committed to the logic of difference rather than of identity between substance and attribute, whole and parts, and so on. The Sāṁkhya-Yoga is dualism, as it recognizes the ultimacy and exclusiveness of two realities—spirit and matter. Emphasizing identity and continuity of cause and effect, it does not, however, rule out all difference and emergence. It may be said to advocate the logic of identity-in-difference or the organic conception of things. Though realistic, the Sāṁkhya is not rank realism comparable to the Nyāya. The Advaita Vedānta denies duality: spirit is the sole reality, and matter (*jaḍa*) is unreal. The Advaita conception of the transcendence of substance (Ātman) is really the logic of pure identity; difference and change are illusory.

The Mīmāṁsā, as a school of realism, agrees with the Nyāya in its ontology; it has, however, some important differences in its epistemology. The Śaiva and the Vaiṣṇava schools very largely adopt the Sāṁkhya and, in some cases, the Vaiśeṣika categories within a theistic framework; they are a blend of religion and philosophy.

Though all Buddhist schools rejected the reality of substance (*pudgala-nairātmya*) and were thus subjective and critically minded, in the earliest realistic phase this was interpreted in such a way as to retain the reality of the separate elements (*dharmas*). The Theravāda and the Sarvāstivāda (the Vaibhāṣika) are the chief exponents of this dogmatic pluralistic phase. The Sautrāntika is a critical edition of this realism. The Madhyamika philosophy (*c.* second century A.D.) represents the central and second phase of Buddhism. It denied the reality of the separate elements too (*dharma-nairātmya*), and established a critical absolutism through the dialectic. The Yogācāra is absolutist idealism; criticizing the Mādhyamika, it identifies the Absolute with Consciousness (*vijñāna*) and rejects the reality of the object.

This division of Buddhist thought into the realistic, the absolutistic, and the idealistic schools and phases is in full accord not only with its logical and chronological development, but also with the testimony of the historians[6] of Buddhism.

As an eclecticism or synthesis of all view-points, the Jaina system may not be treated as a basic philosophy. But a combination of views introduces a new pattern and implies a different view which is distinct from the components taken singly. Reality for the Jaina is not merely many,

[6] Buston's *History of Buddhism* (trans. by Obermiller), II. pp. 52-54.

but manifold (*anekānta*) ; the formulation of it in thought is therefore manifold (Syādvāda, *sapta-bhaṅgi-naya*). The Jaina cannot therefore subscribe to the logic of either pure identity or difference, but accepts a disjunction of all modes.

## STAGES IN THE FORMATION OF THE SCHOOLS

Every system of Indian philosophy has passed through three or four well-defined stages of development. A seer or a great man of insight gives utterance to his intimate vision of Reality. This is the *mūla mantra,* the original inspiration, which initiates a new path and is the basis of a new philosophy. The second stage consists in defining and systematizing the suggestions in aphoristic (*sūtra* or *kārikā*) form ; a philosophical system is thus formulated. Then there is further elaboration—drawing implications, application of experience to details, removing discrepancies, etc. A further stage is reached when the systems indulge in the criticism and refutation of other systems to strengthen their own position. Doctrinally, the stages are suggestive, systematic, and scholastic ; from the literary point of view, they are canonical, *sūtra* (*śāstra*), and *ṭīkā* stages.

Centuries of gestation and fermentation must have preceded the systematization of the doctrines of a school in the *sūta* form. The very ease with which the doctrines are formulated leads to this conclusion. We have direct evidence of a succession of teachers in the case of the Vedānta, the Mīmāṁsā, and the Sāṁkhya. The classical schools of Buddhism attained their present form as a result of the age-long disputation and discussion among the numerous Buddhist sects and schools.

The *sūtras* are mnemonic aids, and could never have been meant to be taken by themselves ; some sort of oral exegesis must always have accompanied them. This points to the propagation of the doctrines among specific circles and also to a continuity of tradition. The *sūtrakāras* are in most cases the final redactors rather than the authors of the systems.

Two aspects of the exegesis (*bhāṣya*) may be discerned ; discussion on points of issue (*vārttika*) and explanation or elaboration (*bhāṣya* proper). Some of the *bhāṣyas* (e.g. the *Nyāya-bhāṣya*) still retain traces of this. The commentaries on each *sūtra* which have come down to us must be taken as the crystallization, in their final form, of these age-long discussions and elaborations so essential to make up a complete and coherent system. The *ṭīkās* (sub-commentary or gloss) pay attention to minute details and revel in subtlety. Theoretically, there is no conceivable end to this process, and *ṭīkās* on the various *bhāṣyas* still continue to be written.

Polemic (*parapakṣanirākaraṇa*) is also an integral part of each system. It is an evidence of the maturity not merely of one system, but of several contemporary ones from which it is differentiated. In spite of the heroic language used, polemic does not mean that rival systems are refuted out of existence; they are only differentiated from each other. Confusion of standpoints is warded off, and clarity results. Very often, criticism is employed against sub-schools and undesirable trends within a system in order to stabilize a standard view. All these aspects are exemplified in each system. Philosophical schools have attained their fullness because of criticism and opposition.

## THE AGE OF THE DARŚANAS

The dates of the systems are still very largely conjectural. The problem is complicated by the fact that the *sūtras,* which form the basis of a system of philosophy, are not unitary works. With regard to many of them,[7] e.g. the *Brahma-Sūtra,* the *Nyāya-Sūtra,* and the *Yoga-Sūtra,* it has been shown with some plausibility that they are of multiple authorship and therefore belong to different periods of time. No one date can therefore be assigned to the origin of a system. Regarding the reputed originators of the systems, the traditional account is scanty and legendary. Kapila, the founder of the Sāṁkhya, is quite a mythical figure; Patañjali's identification with the author of the *Mahābhāṣya* is not generally accepted; Kaṇāda and Akṣapāda are nicknames; Gautama and Bādarāyaṇa are family appellations; and we know next to nothing of Jaimini. With regard to the Buddhist systems we are by no means in a better position. Max Walleser observes about Nāgārjuna thus: 'It has to be agreed that even today, an exact fixing of Nāgārjuna's lifetime must remain entirely doubtful having regard to the contradictory sources of the tradition, always supposing that a writer of this name existed at all.'[8] The historicity of Maitreyanātha,[9] the founder of the Yogācāra school, is just beginning to be accepted.

This is hardly the place to discuss the particular problems regarding the date and life of the founders of the schools. What can be attempted with regard to the rise of the philosophical schools in general is mainly this. It is possible to fix with a reasonable measure of certainty the higher and the lower time-limit of the age of the *darśanas* and to determine an order of priority among them.

The *terminus a quo* is supplied by the references to what might be

[7] See Belvalkar, 'The Multiple Authorship of the *Vedānta-Sūtras*', *The Indian Philosophical Review*, II. 2. pp. 141-154; see also his *Sreegopal Basu Mullick Fellowship Lectures,* Lecture IV. Vidyabhushan, *History of Indian Logic,* pp. 49-50. Dasgupta, *A History of Indian Philosophy*, I. p. 230.

[8] *Life of Nāgārjuna,* p. 6.

[9] See G. Tucci, *On Some Aspects of the Doctrines of Maitreya*[*nātha*] *and Asaṅga,* pp. 2ff.

construed as the beginnings of the classical schools in some of the older dialogues of Buddha (sixth-fifth century B.C.) and the Jaina canons (especially the *Sūtrakṛtāṅga* and *Bhagavatī-Sūtra*). In the *Brahmajāla-Sutta, Sāmaññaphala-Sutta,* and elsewhere we find again and again short and stereotyped sketches of the six *tithiyas* (heretics). We find in them the beginnings[10] of the Cārvāka (Ajita Keśakambala), the Sāṁkhya (Pūraṇa Kassapa), the Vaiśeṣika (Pakudha Kaccāyana), the Jaina (Nigantha Nātaputta), the Ājīvaka (Makkhali Gosāla), and dialectical scepticism (Sañjaya Belaṭṭhiputta). As in both the Buddhist and the Jaina canons the interest is in moral consciousness, they characterize the other systems as species of Akriyāvāda (inaction). We have meagre information about their metaphysical tenets. It is, however, certain that the Brāhmaṇical systems, including the Sāṁkhya, were just beginning to get into shape.

The *terminus ad quem* is provided by the pointed references to well-known Buddhist doctrines and schools in the *Brahma-Sūtra,* the *Nyāya-Sūtra,* etc. Allowing about two or three centuries for the evolution of thought, we cannot be grossly wrong if we put the emergence of the systems, in almost their present form, in the second century B.C.; the process must be deemed to have been complete by the end of the third century A.D., if not a little earlier.

Jacobi, who has made a special study of the subject, says: 'The results of our researches into the age of the philosophical *Sūtras* may be summarized as follows: *Nyāya-Darśana* and *Brahma-Sūtra* were composed between A.D. 200 and 450. During that period lived the old commentators: Vātsyāyana, Upavarṣa, the Vārttikakāra (Bodhāyana), and probably Śabara Svāmin. The *Vaiśeṣika-Darśana* and the *Mīmāṁsā-Sūtra* are about as old, or rather somewhat older than the *Nyāya-Darśana* and the *Brahma-Sūtra.* The *Yoga-Sūtra* is later than A.D. 450, and the *Sāṁkhya-Sūtra* is a modern composition.'[11] Jacobi bases his argument on the contention that the references to Buddhist doctrines in the *Nyāya-Sūtra* and the *Brahma-Sūtra* are to the Śūnyavāda and not to the Vijñānavāda. Hence, they are posterior to Nāgārjuna (A.D. 150), but prior to Asaṅga (A.D. 350). The argument is not very conclusive, because Nāgārjuna's date[12] itself is not fixed with absolute certainty. The Śūnyavāda is much older than Nāgārjuna, and hence reference to it does not necessarily mean posteriority

[10] For a very suggestive and full exposition of these philosophers see Dr. Barua's *Pre-Buddhistic Indian Philosophy.*

[11] *Journal of the American Oriental Society,* XXXI. p. 29, 'The Dates of the Philosophical *Sūtras* of the Brāhmaṇs'.

[12] 'It is a good working hypothesis, though nothing more, that he lived in the latter half of the second century A.D.' Winternitz, *History of Indian Literature,* II. p. 342.

to him. In his *Vigrahavyāvartanī*, Nāgārjuna makes distinct references to the Nyāya objections.[13]

It must never be forgotten with regard to the Indian systems that they have all along been developing side by side, and cross references are quite natural. The argument is also inconclusive, because of the possibility of multiple authorship and stratification in the case of the basic *sūtras*.

The consensus of opinion among scholars now is in favour of accepting a somewhat earlier date for the *darśanas*. We may assign them to the period covering a century and a half before and roughly two centuries after the Christian era. It is not possible, in the present state of our knowledge, to assign a more exact date.

The above discussion should also help us to fix the relative priority of the systems. The Sāṁkhya is admitted on all hands to be the oldest system; it is even pre-Buddhistic in its origin, if not in its final form. This is the dominant philosophy of the epic period. That all other systems, including the Buddhistic schools, have arisen as a criticism of the Sāṁkhya, and that the Sāṁkhya itself does not show the influence of other systems, is sufficient proof of its early formulation. The *Vaiśeṣika-Sūtra* is next to the Sāṁkhya only. Buddhist doctrines are not directly referred to in this. Its theory of knowledge, especially the doctrine of *anumāna* (inference), is less developed than that of the Nyāya; its language and terminology also clearly point to an older period. All these considerations apply to the *Mīmāṁsā-Sūtra* also. Next in order come the *Nyāya-Darśana* and the *Brahma-Sūtra*, and last of all the *Yoga-Sūtra*.

### THE DEVELOPMENT OF THE SYSTEMS

The ideological development of the philosophical systems is of greater interest than their chronological sequence. A general outline of this development may be indicated.

The Sāṁkhya grew as the first synthesis, on a rationalistic basis, of the Upaniṣads. There are two chief tenets of the Upaniṣads: the immutability and purity of the self (Ātman), and the creation of the world from the self which was taken as the sole reality. To the Sāṁkhya, it appeared axiomatic that what changes cannot be conscious, and what is conscious cannot change. It therefore tried to remove the apparent contradiction in the Upaniṣads by sacrificing the sole reality of Ātman, and by bifurcating

[13] *Vigrahavyāvartanī*, I. 1-6 and 20. The Yogācāra view is attacked in the *Brahma-Sūtra*, II. 2. 27-29 (Rāmānuja) or II. 2. 28-31 (Śaṅkara) and the Mādhyamika in II. 2. 30 (Rāmānuja) or II. 2. 31 (Śaṅkara).

the real into two—the real as changing (*pariṇāmi-nitya*) and the real as unchanging (*kūṭastha-nitya*). Nothing is common to both of them ; they thoroughly exclude each other. In calling them both real we are, however, using a common measure. Causation for the Sāṁkhya is self-becoming and is a continuous movement. And though it emphasizes the identity aspect of things, it does not rule out difference. In a rigorous formulation of the real, this has to be eschewed. The real cannot be heterogeneous or composite.

Prakṛti is independently real, as real as Puruṣa, and in that sense, it can be called a 'self' existing by itself. Prakṛti exists and acts *by* itself but is not *for* itself ; the value of its existence is for another (*saṅghāta-parārthatvāt*). The Sāṁkhya would not go to the extent of asserting that Prakṛti would exist even if there were no Puruṣa. The *raison d'être* of Prakṛti's existence and activity is the satisfaction of the needs of Puruṣa. Not only is the real bifurcated into two, but even in Prakṛti's nature there is the bifurcation of existence and value.

The Sāṁkhya position is inherently unstable. In it there are elements which are mutually conflicting. This arises because of the adoption of two patterns of the real (Puruṣa and Prakṛti). And this in turn necessitates the sundering of existence and value and the admission of identity and difference as equally real. Criticism, as the drive towards rigour and consistency, can take either of the two directions. If change and impermanence are the sole pattern of reality, then Puruṣa (self) must be replaced by the states of the *buddhi* (mind), and change itself must be construed as the momentary flashing of things into existence and their subsidence. For, the acceptance of an *abiding* entity (Prakṛti) which *changes,* introduces heterogeneity into the structure of the real ; it partakes of the substance and modal views at once. If change is to be accepted as real, the permanent element must be discarded as unreal. This is exactly what Buddhism does when it explains all things on one single pattern of impermanence and non-substantiality.

The other direction in which the Sāṁkhya could be given consistency is to deny change and impermanence ; it is to take Puruṣa (spirit) as the norm of the real. This would tend to monism, and in its rigorous form, to the absolutism of the Vedānta, by the rejection of difference and change as illusory. An intermediate standpoint is that of the Vaiśeṣika which accepts the changing and the permanent, and not the changing permanent, as real. The Sāṁkhya holds that the permanent (Prakṛti) itself changes ; for the Vaiśeṣika, the permanent, viz. the atoms (the ultimate parts of things) and the other substances like Ātman, *kāla, diś,* and *ākāśa,* do not change at all, but a new thing is produced *in* them when they are brought together. The same mechanical conception underlies the Vaiśeṣika notions of substance and attribute, whole and parts, etc.

In the Sāṁkhya there are idealistic and realistic trends in a unified state. Prakṛti exists only for the Puruṣa, though it does not owe its existence and activity to the latter. It rightly holds that empirical existence is conditioned by the wrong identification of spirit and object; but it has not much justification for holding that Prakṛti will not be affected if this wrong identification ceases on the attainment of knowledge. Consistency would demand that one or the other should be made exclusively real: either spirit is all and the object is an appearance, or everything is object, the spirit itself being conceived as an object (*jaḍa*). The first is the position of the Advaita Vedānta, and the second is that of the Nyāya-Vaiśeṣika realism, which objectifies everything (*viṣaya*) and converts the Sāṁkhya dualism into pluralism.

There were several stages in the attainment of the final form in the Vedānta. From the Sāṁkhya dualism we have first the establishment of the monism of the older Vedānta and then of the Advaitism of Śaṅkara. The older Vedānta of the *sūtrakāra* Bādarāyaṇa and his pre-Śaṅkara commentators criticized the dualism of the Sāṁkhya, but generally accepted the modification (*pariṇāma*)[14] of Brahman. They did not perceive any contradiction in conceiving Brahman as both unity and difference.

It was left to Gauḍapāda and his illustrious successor Śaṅkara to revolutionize the Vedānta by introducing the theory of *vivarta* (appearance), by a searching criticism of the earlier Brahmapariṇāmavāda and asserting Advaitism as the true teaching of the Upaniṣads. This development, which was a turning point in the history of Indian philosophy, was brought about by two sets of influences: one, the drive towards self-consistency which was at work in the older Vedānta too, and the other, the adoption of the technique (dialectical method) already perfected by the Mādhyamika and also used by the Vijñānavāda. We have definite evidence of this influence in Gauḍapada, though in Śaṅkara the traces are almost obliterated. There was, however, an adoption of the technique of the Mādhyamika dialectic, and not the borrowing of its tenets. Influence is not necessarily acceptance or borrowing of doctrines. That too is influence which stimulates the systems to modify, revise, or even reaffirm their doctrines. Influence may be expressed through opposition as well as by acceptance. In this sense alone have the Brāhmaṇical systems, the Vedānta and the Nyāya, been influenced by Buddhism.

[14] The fact that the *Brahma-Sūtra* finds it necessary to controvert, at several places, the Sāṁkhya interpretation of the Upaniṣadic doctrines means that it was a rival in the field of the Upaniṣadic exegesis.

The Nyāya-Vaiśeṣika system, as it emerged at the end of its long-sustained duel with the Buddhist systems, very rigorously established the objectivity of relation (*samavāya*), of the whole (*avayavin*), of the universal (*sāmānya*), and even of non-existence (*abhāva*). It minimized and even denied the work of thought. It objectified and externalized all thought-forms, and put them up as categories of the object. In order to realize the truth of this, one has to look into the polemic found in the works of Vātsyāyana, Uddyotakara, Vācaspati Miśra, Jayanta, Udayana, Śrīdhara, and a host of others. The Nyāya brought its ontology and epistemology into full accord with its basic principle or assumption by resisting the subjectivistic and critical attitude of the Buddhist schools all along the line.

An almost analogous and parallel development obtained within the Anātma tradition (Buddhism). Like the Sāṁkhya on the Upaniṣadic side, the first attempt to synthesize the teachings of Buddha was the Ābhidharmika system. We may comprise under this the Theravāda as well as the Sarvāstivāda. Internal evidence within the Mahāyāna systems and historical evidence unmistakably point to the Sarvāstivāda as the matrix from which the Buddhist systems developed as departures and deviations. The Ābhidharmika system is analogous to the Sāṁkhya in a more vital sense. We may consider its *dharmas* (the Skandhavāda) as the Buddhistic version of the Sāṁkhya conception of Prakṛti and Puruṣa. The inadequacy and inconsistency of the Ābhidharma system—the theory of elements—led to the Mādhyamika dialectic.

The tempo of development was intenser and quicker in the Anātma tradition. Schools and sub-schools multiplied rapidly, and in the welter of ideas Mahāyāna was born. It was a revolution in Buddhism, but was in a sense the reaffirming of the oldest and central teaching of Buddha. Here too two influences may be seen at work. The one is the passion for consistency ; the very dynamism of the Nairātmyavāda must have made the realist phase (the theory of the elements) seem just a step. Then there was the Sāṁkhya and probably the other systems which conceived reality from a totally different standpoint. The difficulties in each standpoint with regard to philosophical problems were there as ever. This must have led an acute and sensitive mind to reflect that the fault lay not in this or that system ; there was something fundamentally wrong about the constitution of reason itself. Kant was led, in similar circumstances, when faced with the impasse created by rationalism and empiricism, to examine the claims of reason in his *Critique of Pure Reason*. We have reason to think that the opposition in philosophy created by the Sāṁkhya and the Vedānta on the one hand and the Ābhidharmika philosophy on the other was much more total and basic than that between rationalism and empiricism. Reflective criticism was inevitable. The Mādhyamika dialectic is the expression of this.

'The basic ideas of the Mādhyamika system—the Absolute as devoid of empirical determinations, the falsity of appearance, and the distinction between the ultimate and phenomena—were accepted. There was, however, a reaction against what appeared to some as its extreme and unqualified rejection of phenomena. The idealism of the Yogācāra (Vijñānavāda) school is to be understood as a significant modification of the Mādhyamika negativism (Śūnyavāda). It contends that the sole reality of consciousness cannot be denied, while the duality of subject and object with which it is apparently infected must be considered non-existent (*śūnya*) ; the duality is unreal ; but that, where the negation of duality (*dvaya-śūnyatā*) obtains, *does exist* ; it is not nothing (*śūnya*).'

'The critical philosophy of Kant led to the idealistic systems of Fichte, Schelling, and Hegel in the West ; here, too, the Yogācāra idealism follows as a direct outcome of the Mādhyamika. This is the third great phase of Buddhism.'

'Tāntricism (Vajrayāna, Mantrayāna, etc.) supervened on the Vijñānavāda. Tāntricism is a unique combination of *mantra,* ritual, and worship on an absolutistic basis ; it is both religion and philosophy. It was especially this phase of Buddhism that was propagated in Tibet when it disappeared from India.'[15]

There was a corresponding Tāntric phase on the Brahmanic side too. The necessary ingredients of the Tantra—*mantra,* ritual, and worship—are already present in the *Ṛk-* and the *Atharva-Saṁhitās* and the Brāhmaṇas. What it needed was a philosophic basis. And when absolutism and the theory of emanation (Śaktivāda) were developed, Tāntricism was established. It is found either by itself or as a complementary part of the absolutist and non-absolutist systems, especially of the Śaiva schools. There is, however, no doubt that this phase was the outcome of the Buddhist influence.[16]

A word may be said about the religio-philosophical schools which were systematized in the post-Śaṅkara period. These fall under two main groups ; the Śaiva (including the Śākta) and the Vaiṣṇava schools. We have definite evidence regarding their great antiquity and wide-spread character ; though systematized later than the classical schools of philosophy, they have been cultivated as cults and groups for centuries. They derive their inspiration from the religious strain found not only in the *Ṛg-Veda,*

[15] Quoted from the writer's article on the 'Schools of Buddhism' in *Philosophy—Eastern and Western.*

[16] See Dr. B. Bhattacharya's *Esoteric Buddhism,* p. 163: 'It is thus amply proved that the Buddhist Tantras greatly influenced the Hindu Tāntric Literature.'

the Upaniṣads, and the *Bhagavad-Gītā,* but also from the canonical sources, variously called the Āgamas (Śaiva) and the Saṁhitās (Vaiṣṇava). The lives and inspired utterances of the saints (Śaiva Nāyanārs and Vaiṣṇava Āḷvārs) have impressed these systems with a religious stamp. They emphasize devotion and self-surrender to God as necessary means to salvation ; they are thus, implicitly or otherwise, opposed to the doctrine of knowledge as the sole means to liberation (*mukti*). All of them formulate their systems as a vehement protest against absolutism—the impersonolity of the Highest ; they all affirm the reality and individuality of the finite selves (Jīvas). Though these systems incorporate philosophical elements, their main interest is religious. As such, they may rightly be regarded as schools of theology rather than of philosophy.

# 3

## THE SĀṀKHYA

THE origin of this system and the logical consistency of its teaching have, for a long time, been matters of controversy; but its importance in the history of Indian thought has never been questioned. Its characteristic ideas and the terminology in which it gives expression to them are met with in the religious and philosophical literature of India almost as commonly as those of the Upaniṣads. They especially pervade the Purāṇas, including a large part of the great epic of the *Mahābhārata.* We shall not concern ourselves here with the logical or chronological controversies touching the doctrine, but shall merely give a brief sketch of it, selecting in particular such features as will help us in understanding its significance to practical life.

The Sāṁkhya is frankly dualistic. It recognizes two ultimate entities —nature and spirit—neither of which can be derived from the other. The former is termed Prakṛti and the latter Puruṣa. Since these two conceptions are of fundamental importance to the doctrine, we shall begin our sketch with an explanation of them.

*Prakṛti:* There are two commonly known ways of explaining the origin of the physical world. It may be traced to a manifold of ultimate reals which are supposed to be simple and atomic; or it may be derived from a single substance which is assumed to be complex and all-pervasive. The former is described as the theory of creation (Ārambhavāda), for in it the things of the world are explained as generated by the putting together of two or more atoms; and the latter, as the theory of evolution (Pariṇāmavāda), for in it the same are looked upon as the result of transformations within the primal substance. The Sāṁkhya adopts the second mode of explanation, and Prakṛti is the name which it gives to the principle or entity out of which is evolved the objective universe in its infinite diversity. This primal entity is not directly perceived and its existence, like that of the atoms in the other view, has only to be inferred. Here, as elsewhere generally, the Sāṁkhya prefers a rationalistic explanation and does not, like some other systems, invoke the aid of revelation in support of its conclusions. The very name of the doctrine, derived from *saṁkhyā* which means *buddhi,* indicates that it is based on reflection rather than on authority. Prakṛti, or Mūla-prakṛti as it is sometimes designated to indicate that it is the first cause of the physical universe, is thus one and complex; and its complexity is the result of its being constituted of three factors, each of which is described as a *guṇa*. By the word *guṇa* here we should not understand what it is commonly taken to mean, viz. 'a quality', for the Sāṁkhya refuses to recognize the distinction between substance and attribute. There is indeed no harm in speaking, for the sake of convenience, of either apart from the other; but to think of the two as really separate from, or external to, each other is, according to the present doctrine, to indulge in an illegitimate abstraction. The so-called quality and substance together form a single whole, and it is the concrete unity of both that any material thing represents. The term *guṇa* means here rather 'a component factor' or 'a constituent' of Prakṛti. These three constituents, though essentially distinct in their nature, are conceived as interdependent so that they can never be separated from one another. It means that they are not mechanically placed together, but reciprocally involve one another and form a unity in trinity. That is, they not only coexist but also cohere. The three *guṇas* are named *sattva, rajas,* and *tamas.* Each of them stands for a distinct aspect of physical reality: roughly, *sattva* signifies whatever is pure and fine; *rajas,* whatever is active; and *tamas,* what is stolid and offers resistance. From the standpoint of the experiencing mind, they are also described as being of the nature respectively of pleasure (*sukha*), pain (*duḥkha*), and bewilderment (*moha*), for they give rise to, or condition, those feelings. The above description shows that the *guṇas* are not merely distinct, but are also, in some measure, antagonistic in their nature. The antagonism, however, is not such as to preclude their acting together; and their harmonious action is illustrated by the example of a lamp-flame—the result of co-operation between the wick, oil, and fire which, in their separate nature, appear to be hardly fitted so to co-operate. In other words, the physical universe is an orderly whole which has its own laws to obey and there is no ultimate contradiction in it, though it may consist of opposing elements.

It is not only Prakṛti that consists of these *guṇas*. Everything that emerges from it is also similarly constituted, for the doctrine maintains that effects are essentially identical with their material cause. In fact it is by a proper synthesis of the common and enduring features of the things of experience that the conception of Prakṛti has been reached, as the idea of gold, for instance, is reached by a comparison of golden things like bracelets and rings. These cosmic constituents are in a state of equilibrium in Prakṛti until it begins to differentiate itself; and the diversity of the things that then spring into being from it is due to the diversity in the proportion in which the *guṇas* enter into their make-up in the complex process of Prakṛti's evolution. 'It is just as in a game of dice: they are ever the same dice, but as they fall in various ways, they mean to us different things.' Though only three in number, the *guṇas* thus really stand for a manifold of distinctions. In later Sāṁkhya, it is expressly stated that their number is infinite and that they are only arranged in three groups on the basis of their likenesses and differences.[1] Prakṛti is not only complex and all-pervasive, it is also undergoing change perpetually. Naturally, the things that develop out of it are also conceived as sharing in its fluid character. Thus the paper on which these lines are printed may appear to be static; but it is really changing every instant, though at the same time it maintains its identity as long as it lasts. An important difference between the two is that while Prakṛti, which is by hypothesis omnipresent, can have no change of place but only change of form, the things derived from it on account of their finiteness can have both. A plant, for example, may grow or wither where it is; and it may also be shifted from one place to another. It is change of form that is meant by *pariṇāma* or evolution. The evolutionary process, in the case of Prakṛti, is supposed to be periodical. That is to say, every period of evolution or *sṛṣṭi* is followed by a period of dissolution or *pralaya* when the whole diversity of the universe becomes latent or 'goes to sleep', as it is stated, in Prakṛti. But even in *pralaya*, we must remember, Prakṛti does not cease to be dynamic; only its component parts, the *guṇas*, constantly reproduce themselves[2] (*sadṛśa-pariṇāma*) then, instead of acting on one another and giving rise to a heterogeneous transformation.

As regards the things that emerge from Prakṛti, it will suffice to call attention to only one point which it is necessary to know for understanding the Sāṁkhya explanation of experience. It is the distinction between the things in which *sattva* predominates and those in which *tamas* does. Most of the things of the material world as well as our physical frame belong to the latter class. They are objective. The former in which *sattva* preponderates indeed are not subjective, because they also are derived from Prakṛti and are therefore physical; but on account of their finer structure, they are well adapted to assist in the revelation of external objects to spirit, which, as we shall presently see, is unable by itself to apprehend anything. To state the same in another way, the activity of these *sāttvika* developments is a necessary condition of mental life, although they do not by themselves explain it. Of this group, the most important member is what is described as the *antaḥkaraṇa* or the 'internal organ'. It is really threefold, consisting of *manas, ahaṅkāra*, and *buddhi*, but it is not necessary to give a detailed description of them

[1] *Sāṁkhya-pravacana-bhāṣya*, I. 61, 127-128.
[2] *Sāṁkhya-tattva-kaumudī*, 15-16.

here. Its chief function is to receive impressions from outside and to suitably respond to them; and it is assisted in the proper discharge of this function by the various senses that belong to the same group. This whole apparatus, consisting of the internal organ and its several accessaries, may be taken as roughly corresponding to what modern psychology calls the brain and the nervous mechanism associated with its functioning. It is specific to each individual and, together with certain other factors, accompanies him throughout his worldly existence or *saṁsāra*. This relatively permanent 'accompaniment' is known as the *liṅga-śarīra* or 'subtle body'. It does not part from one even at death, and is cast off only when freedom is fully achieved.

To sum up the conception of Prakṛti: The whole of the physical universe emanates from it; and since Prakṛti is conceived as ultimate and independent, the explanation so far may be characterized as naturalistic.

*Puruṣa:* What prevents the doctrine from being a philosophy of nature, pure and simple, is its recognition of Puruṣa by the side of Prakṛti, which does not exhaust the content of the universe, but leaves out the very element by virtue of which we become aware of the existence of the physical world. And it is that element of awareness or sentience which Puruṣa represents. While the doctrine thus differs from naturalism, it does not identify itself with absolutistic systems like the Advaita, for it preserves till the last the dualism of Prakṛti and Puruṣa. No truly satisfactory explanation of experience is possible, according to the Sāṁkhya, if we do not admit the equal and independent reality of both the material and the spiritual elements. The existence of Puruṣa, like that of Prakṛti, may therefore be said to have been reached through reason. If the latter is postulated on the principle that effects presuppose a cause that is immanent in them, the former is postulated on the principle that objects point to the subject, or more strictly, that the non-sentient implies the sentient. Another argument in support of the same conclusion is based upon the design found in the physical world. The bodily organism, for example, with its many well-adapted parts suggests that it is meant to serve a definite end; and there are numerous other instances in nature with a similar teleology implicit in them. The entity, whose ends such adaptations and contrivances serve, is Puruṣa. In other words, spirit is the principle *for the sake of which* nature evolves.

Both Prakṛti and Puruṣa alike are thus deduced from an investigation of the nature of common things; the only difference is that while the one is the result of arguing from those things to their source or *first* cause, the other is the result of arguing from them to their aim or *final* cause. The world is derived from a principle which is like it in its nature, but subserves the ends of another which is quite unlike. Puruṣa is manifold in contrast to Prakṛti ; and the doctrine may for that reason be described as pluralism. The conception is, in other respects also, the very opposite of Prakṛti. Puruṣa is not complex but simple ; it is not dynamic but static, knowing neither change of place nor change of form. It is passive while Prakṛti is ever active, which means that it is to be identified more with feeling or the affective side of the mind than with the intellect or the will. It cannot consequently either *know* or *will* anything in the ordinary sense, unless it is assisted by the internal organ and its various adjuncts. In itself, it is a mere witness or looker-on (*sākṣin*), as it is described. Like Prakṛti, however, it is supposed to be omnipresent, though its manifestation during the transmigrating state or *saṁsāra* is confined to the limits of its physical accessaries like the body and the internal organ.

The exact manner in which these two disparate entities are, or seem to be, brought together is a difficult point and remains one of the perplexities in the system. But our present purpose does not require any discussion of it. Whatever the ultimate explanation may be, Prakṛti and Puruṣa virtually act as one ; and we shall therefore take it for granted that they co-operate. It is, indeed, a matter of experience that there is no spirit without a living organism or a living organism without spirit. This complex of nature and spirit is only the empirical self and is to be distinguished, according to the Sāṁkhya, from the true or transcendental self, viz. Puruṣa ; but, from the practical standpoint, the distinction is of no importance. The Prakṛti element that most intimately enters into this union is the internal organ. There are other elements also, like the sensory organs, but they are all, in one sense or another, entirely subordinate to it. The coming together of these is the necessary presupposition of all experience, for spirit without nature is inactive and nature without spirit is blind. In the resulting union, each finds its complement and the defects of both are made good. And we may point out, by the way, that experience is not explained here, as in naturalism, to be a product of unconscious matter ; it is, on the other hand, taken to emerge from a certain association of spirit with it—an association through which the two behave as if they were one. Matter is merely the medium for spirit to manifest itself, not its source. This association of the two is found not only ordinarily, but also in what is known as *jīvanmukti* or 'freedom while still alive' when a persan has become fully enlightened and has transcended all the weaknesses of human flesh. Such a man, when he departs this life, will, no doubt, continue to *be,* Puruṣa being considered immortal. Spirit then remains in itself, wholly emancipated from nature. That condition is described as *kaivalya*—'isolation' or 'aloofness'—to distinguish it from *jīvanmukti* in which Puruṣa continues to be associated with the body, senses, and so forth, though no longer in bondage to them.

The empirical self is not a detached entity like the Puruṣa, but exhibits the result of innumerable forces that have acted upon it in the course of its beginningless history. It is consequently not passive and does not remain a mere spectator of whatever happens to be before it, but is active and meddles with the external object as it apprehends it. It does not, however, through such meddling import any new features into the object presented; it only selects certain aspects of it and omits the rest. According to this theory of selective apprehension, all the characteristics that can ever be known of an object actually belong to it; and if any of them are not apprehended by a particular person or at a particular time, it is entirely due to subjective limitations. Hence the sensory organs and the *antaḥkaraṇa,* though they help perception in one sense, may be said to hinder it in another. The nature of the selection made in the case of any object depends upon the past life or character of the person in question; and this is the reason why a thing that attracts one may completely repel another. The aspect under which an individual perceives the world is thus intimately personal to him; yet the doctrine does not maintain, as one school of Buddhism does, that there is no external reality at all. The different world-views are, no doubt, relative to the subject; but they, at the same time, point to an objective world which is common to all and is real in its own right. The chief argument in support of this realistic position is that, although there are differences among men in their views of things, there are as certainly points of agreement also among them. If there are occasions when each can speak only for himself, there are others when one can speak for all. Here is an important feature of the system, for it neither sides with the view that things are precisely as they are apprehended, nor with the other which holds that the mind makes its own things. It avoids either extreme and allots equal importance to the subjective and objective factors in explaining the phenomenon of experience. It is *we* who know, just as truly as it is the *world* that is known. Men obtrude their personalities into their judgements, and subjective prejudices undoubtedly affect their knowledge of things; yet they never create the things they perceive. But our knowledge, though pointing to an external universe, is one-sided. This is a fundamental defect of human experience; and to it we should add another, arising from the fact that the *whole* of the world is presented to no man at one and the same time. All knowledge, as it is familiar to us, is therefore personal and fragmentary. It may not indeed amount to an error of commission (*viparīta-khyāti*); but it is partial and, so far as it is not recognized to be partial, it becomes an error, though only an error of omission (*akhyāti*). This incomplete knowledge, with the resulting over-emphasis on a part of what is given, explains the conflicts and inconsistencies of life whether they be found in the same person at different times or between different persons at the same time.

Such a view of knowledge is not without its lesson for us. The lesson is twofold: It behoves us to feel less positive than we ordinarily do about the correctness of our own views, and be more regardful of the views of others. In other words, it teaches us the need for humility and charity in our intercourse with fellow-men, and impresses upon us the need for doing our utmost to see things not only as they appear to us, but also as they may appear to others. The differences between one man and another may at first sight appear unbridgeable; but it may be that they can be easily adjusted, if only each tries to learn and appreciate the others' point of view. In one word, it bespeaks toleration, which, as a matter of fact, is a striking feature of all Indian thought.

If all knowledge be thus imperfect in its very nature, what is truth? The Sāṁkhya holds that it is comprehensive knowledge in which one part supplements and corrects another. It is knowledge which knows no exclusions or preferences and lays appropriate emphasis on all aspects of the object known. It may be asked whether such knowledge is at all possible so long as its means continues to be the internal organ which, as a product of Prakṛti, is of a triple nature and consists not merely of *sattva*, but also of *rajas* and *tamas*. In answering this question, it is necessary to remember that it is not the internal organ *as such* that limits our view of the world in the manner described above; for, in its intrinsic nature, it is essentially *sāttvika* and is therefore well fitted to be the means of revealing all that is. In point of fact, however, *rajas* or *tamas* predominates in it as a result of the past history of the person to whom it belongs; and it is the relative predominance of either that accounts for whatever limitations it may possess as an organ of knowledge. By subduing these elements through proper self-discipline and restoring the internal organ to its original purity, man may completely transform his outlook upon life and the world. *Rajas* and *tamas* cannot, of course, be entirely eliminated; but when the internal organ is purified or 'the heart is cleansed', as it is said, their presence will be harmless for all practical purposes. But it should not be imagined that this complete knowledge is merely an aggregate of all possible views of the physical world. It is rather an experience in which they have all been integrated and, according to the account given of it[3], is best described as intuitive. It overcomes the idiosyncrasies of individual views; but it does so by a synthesis, not by a mere summation of them.

In this synthetic view, which represents the climax of philosophic thought, all things are seen as they actually are. So soon as this whole and disinterested truth about the world dawns upon one's mind, one sees through Prakṛti and realizes its absolute distinctness from Puruṣa. And it is a knowledge of this distinctness (*viveka-jñāna*) rather than that of the world as it is, that is stated here to be the means of release. Such knowledge is attainable in the present life; and it is the attainment of it that is the final aim of life according to the Sāṁkhya. The whole realm of nature is conceived in the system as leading up to this consummation. It is designed for this end and exists solely for it. Only the approach to the ideal is through worldly life, the character and duration of which depend upon the moral and intellectual equipment of particular individuals. But all alike have to pass through the trials and troubles of common life (*bhoga*) before their minds are turned towards the final goal (*apavarga*). It means that the true ideal does not suggest itself to any one that has not seen for himself the imperfections of *saṁsāra*. The Sāṁkhya ideal of life may appear to be one that can never be actually reached; but what is important to note is the possibility of a progressive approximation to it. In the case of all ideals, we may say, it is a continual advance in the right direction that matters more than even their actual realization.

Such a view of the goal of life means a long course of discipline to reach it, and we have now briefly to consider the nature of this discipline. But before proceeding to its consideration, we may draw attention to what is a common feature of all the Indian systems. They are motived by the purpose of not merely discovering truth, but also realizing it in life. It is such realization that marks the attainment of truth, in the proper sense of the term, and not merely arriving at a speculative notion of it. To give our intellectual assent to a doctrine, however vital that may be, is therefore not all; we must see that it inaugurates a new life. This is the significance of the personal discipline prescribed in all the systems as the necessary accompaniment of philosophic study. The discipline in the present case is only briefly referred to in the Sāṁkhya works, but it is fully described in the sister system of Yoga. If Kapila has enlarged upon the theory, Patañjali has done the same in regard to the practical side of the teaching. The discipline comprises what are described

[3] *Yoga-Sūtra,* I. 49.

as the eight *aṅgas* of *yoga*. They are *yama* or self-restraint, *niyama* or observance, *āsana* or posture, *prāṇāyāma* or regulation of breath, *pratyāhāra* or withdrawal of the senses, *dhāraṇā* or steadying the mind, *dhyāna* or contemplation, and *samādhi* or meditative trance. The aim of this discipline is to assist man in the ascent from the narrow view congenital to him to the larger vision which brings freedom with it. A characteristic feature of it is the gradation in the training which it prescribes. It recognizes different levels of fitness in the disciples and regulates the training accordingly. It does not aim at extirpating evil propensities all at once. Another noteworthy feature of the same is that it is based upon the psychologically sound principle that vice is not overcome by attempting to repress it directly, but by sedulously practising the contrary virtue which will eventually supplant it. This eightfold discipline may be divided into two stages.

(1) The first is concerned with the right direction of the will, and represents the attainment of the good as distinguished from the true. We have already mentioned the need for charity and humility in our dealings with others. The discipline in the present stage is devised to develop this unselfish side in man's character. More particularly, it relates to the acquirement of virtues comprised in the first two *aṅgas* of yogic discipline, namely, *yama* and *niyama*. The former is mostly negative and consists of non-injury (*ahiṁsā*), truth-speaking (*satya*), abstention from stealing or misappropriation of others' property (*asteya*), celibacy (*brahmacarya*), and disowning of possessions (*aparigraha*). The latter is mostly positive and includes purity (*śauca*), contentment (*santoṣa*), right aspiration (*tapas*), study (*svādhyāya*), and devotion to God (*Iśvara-praṇidhāna*). These together may be described as the 'ten commandments' of the Sāṁkhya-Yoga. It is on this pre-eminently moral foundation, and not on the mere cultivation of the intellect, that any spiritual training should rest, if it is to be fruitful. Without such a foundation, there is no possibility of salvation; and he who lays that foundation firmly, even though he may stop short at that, may be taken to have achieved much. The key-word to this discipline is impersonality. Man must overcome the egoistic impulses in him, which are the source of so much evil in the world. The discipline is consequently ascetic, but it is not so in the negative sense of the term, as is shown by the nature of the virtues enjoined under the second head of *niyama*. The impersonal attitude thereby attained is known as *vairāgya*, and its cultivation is recommended in order to awaken the spiritual will. Any dabbling in *yoga*, without this preliminary purification of natural impulses, is fraught with danger; and it is such hasty recourse to yogic practice that is

responsible for much of the odium that has come to be attached in the popular mind to that discipline.

(2) The next stage of the discipline, consisting of the remaining six *aṅgas,* is for the specific cultivation of the power of mental concentration. Its details being somewhat technical, we shall refer here only to its general features. Of the six *aṅgas,* the first three are devised to secure control of the physical frame with a view to facilitating the control of the mind. They refer, as already noted, to right bodily posture, regulation of breath, and the withdrawal of the senses from their respective objects. Of the succeeding three, two assist in getting a direct but gradual mastery over the ever-fitful mind. The objects chosen for meditation may be any in this stage. The last consists essentially in direct meditation on the Sāṁkhya truth. When success in this final stage is achieved, all operations of the internal organ are suspended and spirit returns to itself, so to speak. The disciple then becomes a *jīvanmukta.* He may thereafter continue to live upon the earth, but he is virtually divorced from Prakṛti and therefore remains 'far from passion, pain, and guilt'.

There is one point in the above account which requires a word of explanation. We have mentioned God in describing *niyama* ; but we have not, so far, referred to his place in the doctrine at all. Of the two systems to which we have alluded, the Sāṁkhya, in its classical form, is definitely atheistic. It believes in the permanence and supremacy of spirit, but knows nothing of God. Here it shows its rationalistic bias, for no syllogistic proof, as is well known, can be given of his existence. The Sāṁkhya, no doubt, like the other Indian systems, is essentially a philosophy of values. But according to its teachers, all that is presupposed by the reality of the higher values is the reality of the human spirit. This is clearly indicated by the manner in which the 'design argument', already referred to, is utilized here. It is regarded not as pointing to a designer, but to one that constitutes the end or final aim of the design. The Sāṁkhya concludes from the presence in nature of means adapted to the accomplishment of particular ends, not God as their author, but the self for whom it supposes them to exist. Patañjali holds a different view and postulates the existence of God or Īśvara over and above that of Puruṣas. The allusion to God appears in our account of *niyama* because the course of discipline, as we remarked before, is entirely taken over from his system. Devotion to God would consequently have no place in the discipline which is strictly in conformity with the Sāṁkhya teaching. Here is an important difference between the two doctrines which agree in so many respects. But the Yoga conception of Īśvara is vastly different from the familiar one of the Vedānta. Īśvara of the former is one of the Puruṣas, so that, though omnipresent, he is not all-comprehensive. There are other Puruṣas as well as Prakṛti to limit his being. Secondly, he is not responsible, in the ordinary sense of the term, for the creation of the world which, as we know, is the spontaneous work of Prakṛti. But he is a perfect Puruṣa and has always been so. He is therefore unique, and even the liberated Puruṣas do not stand on the same footing. Still, on account of his perfection, he serves as a pattern to man as to what he might become. In this respect, he resembles a *guru* who should likewise be an embodiment of the ideal. Apart from serving as an ideal, he, out of his abundant mercy, sympathizes with suffering men and helps them to attain spiritual freedom, if they only trust in him and meditate upon him. Accordingly, Patañjali recognizes not only the *yoga* discipline as detailed above for securing freedom, but also an alternative one of *bhakti* or devotion to Īśvara and communion with him which, without all the elaborate preparation of *yoga*, qualifies one for *samādhi*—the immediate means of release.[4]

We have so far referred to the attainment of the good and the vision of the true ; and the Sāṁkhya, like the generality of Indian doctrines, subordinates the one to the other. There remains another value of life, viz. the aesthetic, and we shall refer to a few important features of it before we conclude. An impersonal view of man and nature, but devoid of enlightenment in the above sense, is, according to the Sāṁkhya, the characteristic feature of aesthetic experience. The narrow view common to human life is not overcome here by the acquisition of complete knowledge ; but the conditions of ordinary personal life are, all the same, transcended, though only temporarily, as in the case of a *jīvanmukta*. The aesthetic attitude is therefore disinterested like the insight that brings freedom with it. The detachment characteristic of the attitude is the result chiefly of the *ideal* status of the objects portrayed in art, which divests them of all personal references and thereby renders them similar to the actual things as contemplated by the perfected *yogin*. Art, indeed, may be defined as the layman's *yoga,* for it also affords an escape from the realm of the *guṇas*. Great artists attain such detachment directly through the impulse they receive from nature—from 'woods and rills, the silence that is in the starry sky, the sleep that is among the lonely hills'. But that is not so, to any conspicuous extent, as regards ordinary men; yet even they can rise to that level with the help of the artistic creations of a genius. In either case, we must note, the stimulus comes from outside, although response to it is impossible without

[4] This is according to Bhoja. See his gloss on *Yoga-Sūtra,* I. 23.

a certain aptitude in the individual. In other words, the act of will, as compared with the acquisition of right knowledge, plays here quite a secondary part. The impersonal attitude comes of itself; it is not sought deliberately and found. Speaking of this distinction between the artist's success and the saint's, a thinker,[5] who is known to have developed a theory of art on the basis of the Sāṁkhya philosophy but with particular reference to poetry, states—somewhat exultingly—that the bliss of peace, which the *yogin* strains himself to win, is no match for that with which the poetic muse spontaneously requites her votaries. But he is really reversing the truth here, because the artistic attitude is temporary and will be followed sooner or later by what, in spite of the culture it may involve, must be regarded as a lapse into the routine of ordinary life. The saint also, who has achieved true freedom, may revert to common life from his state of trance; but it can, in no sense, be taken as a lapse, for the knowledge and wisdom he has gained remain with him ever after, inspiring all his thoughts, words, and deeds.

[5] Bhaṭṭa Nāyaka. See commentary on the *Dhvanyāloka,* p. 29.

PATAÑJALI

# 4

# YOGA PSYCHOLOGY

## THE PHILOSOPHICAL PRESUPPOSITIONS OF YOGA

THE Yoga system of Patañjali is not primarily a psychological system and its treatment of psychological problems is only incidental to its main metaphysical and ethical purposes. But it differs from other systems of Indian thought, excepting Buddhism, in being more systematic in its handling of psychological problems. The Yoga system was forced to this course almost inevitably by its presuppositions, and so without a knowledge of those presuppositions it is not easy to understand its main lines of speculation. The Sāṁkhya-Yoga twins started with a dualism of matter (Prakṛti) and spirit (Puruṣa), and although neither could explain when exactly spirit became involved in matter, both assumed, as did the other Indian systems, that it was possible to put an end to the undesirable entanglement of spirit in matter. Both assumed that spatio-temporal existence was somehow painful in its ultimate nature,[1] though to ordinary minds the world presented many pleasurable aspects; and both concerned themselves with the task of eradicating pain without caring to state precisely whether the dissociation of spirit from matter would lead to some kind of happy existence.[2] Both, again, assumed that spirits were infinite in number and that each spiritual being must earn its release from the grip of matter by individual effort.[3] They agreed also that the final state of a released soul was one of splendid isolation (*kaivalya*)—complete freedom from material contact and no communion of any kind with any other released soul.[4] In this state of salvation the soul was supposed to recover its innate purity, self-illumination, and freedom through the falling off of the drapery which served to produce a sense of identity with material existence. Although orthodox speculation had a tendency to think that Nature, of herself, moved away from the proximity of an enlightened soul, so that both entanglement and release of spirit were really her doing[5] (the soul, inactive by nature, being incapable of effecting either the bondage or

[1] *Yoga-Sūtra* (*Y. S.*), II. 15; *Sāṁkhya-kārikā*, 1.

[2] *Y. S.*, II. 14; III. 51; IV. 30; *Sāṁ.-kār.*, 1.

[3] *Y. S.*, II. 22; *Sāṁ.-kār.*, 18, 56. So also in Buddhism an *arhat* is advised to be a lamp unto himself; similar is the Jaina belief.

[4] *Y. S.*, III. 50, 55; IV. 26, 34; *Sāṁ.-kār.*, 17, 19, 21, 64, 68. The term was used in this technical sense both in Jainism and in Buddhism.

[5] *Sāṁ.-kār.*, 62; also 56 f.; *Y. S.*, II. 18. Bhoja ascribes the association and dissociation of nature and spirit to the will of God (Īśvara). See *Bhojavṛtti* on *Y. S.*, I. 24.

the salvation), the general philosophical attitude was that the soul must desire, strive for, and deserve its freedom from the shackles of material existence. The tentacles of Nature were supposed to be multiform: beginning with gross material objects and passing through finer stuff, Nature might assume almost the form of the spirit itself to prevent the soul from realizing its true essence. This increases the risk of spiritual degradation, for under the impression that spiritual safety has been obtained the soul may rest in a false sense of security and thus ultimately fail to achieve its proper object. Nature, in the course of evolution, makes herself almost indispensable to spirit, for she evolves successively into the intelligence-stuff (*buddhi* or *mahat*), the ego-principle (*ahaṅkāra*), and the eleven organs (the five organs of sense, the five organs of action, and mind) to make spirit fit for apprehending the external and internal worlds, and she evolves at the same time the objective world of subtle essences (*tanmātras*) and gross elements (*mahābhūtas*) to complete the subjugation of spirit. Nature in this way takes vengeance on spirit for disturbing her original placidity and the equilibrium of the three *guṇas* or elementary principles of which she is composed. She now begins to spin out of herself the gossamers that, though in reality of the flimsiest strength so far as spirit is concerned, begin to bind the soul which, through its ignorance and false identification with these evolutes of Nature, loses its spiritual orientation and gets more and more involved in the meshes of material existence. The Yoga system professes to free the soul from this material bondage by laying down a progressive scheme of self-realization based upon discriminatory knowledge (*tattvajñāna, vivekakhyāti*). The main objective of Yoga psychology is to lay bare the process of thinking in its ethical aspect of progress towards or away from that self-illumination which is identical with salvation; incidentally it has to discuss the difficulties and dangers that beset the path of the aspirant for liberation at different stages of progress. The means it suggests to achieve this *summum bonum* of the spirit is to turn the material impediments themselves into weapons of attack so that Nature becomes ultimately hoist with her own petard and retires from the field of battle.[6]

Now, spirit is enclosed within a triple barricade of matter and until all the barriers fall off the soul would remain in bondage to matter. The physical body supplies the gross vestment of spirit, and material comforts often pass for spiritual blessings. This was the basis of the Cārvāka philosophy where the soul and the body were identified and the existence

[6] By concentration on Nature's objects they are subdued and seen through. See, for instance, *Y. S.*, I. 17; II. 10, 11; also *Vibhūtipāda* of *Y. S.*

of a disembodied soul (or even a purely spiritual soul) was denied.[7] Then there is the belt of the external sense-organs. As contrasted with the organic sensations mediated by the gross body, these bring reports of external objects and fascinate the soul by the beauties of diversified Nature. The reaction to sensory knowledge is effected by means of the organs of action, and this brings in more knowledge of the external world and more material pleasures. Then there is the group of internal principles (*antaḥkaraṇa*)—mind (*manas*), ego (*ahaṅkāra*), and intelligence (*buddhi*)—which forms the last and the most insidious chain of bondage forged round the soul. Thus the Yoga philosophy reiterates the main Upaniṣadic conclusion that the soul must not be identified either with the body or with the senses or with the mind or even with the ego and the intelligence-principle, and that one must penetrate into the inner spiritual core after ripping open the 'sheaths' (*kośas*) of materiality.[8]

## THE NATURE OF SELF-KNOWLEDGE

But how are we to think of the soul apart from these? If the soul is the principle of consciousness and matter the unconscious stuff of reality, what would remain of consciousness if the necessary paraphernalia of cognition were removed? How would a soul function without a body, a group of sense-organs, and a group of internal principles? If the stream of consciousness dries up for want of materials and means, how are we to know that the soul has not evaporated at the same time? The Yoga philosophy cuts the Gordian knot by denying that the process of awareness in time, which involves the duality of subject and object, belongs to the soul as such ;[9] and thus, by introducing the distinction between relational thinking and self-illumination, it throws to the side of unreality the whole process of empirical thought and reserves for the soul's insight the entire field of spiritual reality. But the language employed was not always happy, for it was often asserted that self-illumination was identical with the knowledge of the ultimate distinction between soul and matter (*vivekakhyāti*)—a position which would involve the persistence of the knowledge of the non-spiritual at least as the opposite of the spiritual reality—as something, however diaphanous, from which the self distinguished itself. Possibly what was intended was that the rise of pure spiritual insight was identical with a cessation of the awareness of the non-spiritual, the psychological duality of compresent subject and object being transcended in a logical duality of which both terms could not simultaneously exist. In other

[7] *Sarva-darśana-saṅgraha* (Abhyankara's Ed.), pp. 2, 13; *Ṣaḍdarśana-samuccaya* (with Guṇaratna's *Tarka-rahasya-dīpikā*), p. 306.
[8] *Tai. U.*, II. 2-5; see *B. G.*, III. 42.
[9] *Y. S.*, I. 2, 3; IV. 25, 34.

words, we are to understand by the rise of spiritual insight (*prajñā*) a positive realization of the true nature of the self and not a mere consciousness of distinction between Nature and spirit.[10] But this introduced a second danger. As the knowledge of the self could not be characterized by the categories of objective contemplation, it was not easy to say what kind of knowledge dawned on the cessation of objective knowledge. Although the Sāṁkhya had talked of the redeemed soul as eternal, pure, illumined, and free,[11] and the Yoga presumably followed suit, it was evident that both took insight not as the attribute but as the essence of the soul, just as the Vedānta did in the case of Brahman.[12] The refusal to regard insight as the essence would have landed the Sāṁkhya-Yoga in the same predicament as the Nyāya-Vaiśeṣika where the dissociation of spirit from mind was supposed to reduce the former to the condition of an insensate stone (*śilā-śakala*)[13]—a contingency which the Sāṁkhya-Yoga could not face in view of its theory that the soul in its true essence is insight (*bodha-svarūpa*). But omniscience, such as is acquired by the highest sages, was not what the released soul recovered on attaining its proper nature after the disappearance of the material vestments; for while omniscience is an *attribute* of the advanced spirit, insight is the *essence* of the soul released. Unlike Jainism, which ascribed to the delivered souls a sort of ubiquity and both omniscience and bliss,[14] the Yoga denied all but knowledge as essence to these; its main line of enquiry therefore was directed towards emptying the thought-process of all phenomenality in order to arrive at the noumenal consciousness of the self. The process consisted in attenuating the phenomenal series with the ultimate object of erasing it altogether from the surface of the soul[15]—no mere improvement of the thought-process could lead to self-realization, for the two were entirely different in kind. In order to get insight one could not jump off the one into the other but must win every inch of ground through the painfully slow and slippery process of self-discipline.

### PHENOMENAL CONSCIOUSNESS: ITS NATURE, CONDITIONS, AND TYPES

The starting point of the enquiry is constituted by an investigation into the nature of phenomenal consciousness, which is an unceasing flow

[10] *Y. S.*, I. 51; III. 50.

[11] *Nitya-śuddha-buddha-mukta-svabhāva;* see *Y. S.*, IV. 18.

[12] The word used is *citiśakti* in *Y. S.*, IV. 34.

[13] Radhakrishnan, *Indian Philosophy,* II (1st Ed.), p. 225; *Ṣaḍdarśana-samuccaya* (with Guṇaratna's commentary), p. 188.

[14] The general belief is that the Siddhas have no body and the occupation of boundless space by them is not to be physically understood. See Sinclair Stevenson, *The Heart of Jainism,* p. 169; *Sarva-darśana-saṅgraha* (Abhyankara's Ed.), p. 88.

[15] *Y. S.*, I. 2, 3, 4, 51; II. 6, 20; III. 50; IV. 34.

of cognitive states, using the word 'cognition' in its most extended sense to include all types of awareness, impulse, and affection. This is called *cittavṛtti,* mental modifications or fluctuations of the mind-stuff, the word *citta* being a comprehensive designation of the collocation of the five vital airs, the eleven organs (including the mind proper), and the other conditions of knowledge like egoism (*ahaṅkāra*) and intelligence (*buddhi*).[16] It roughly corresponds to the Western conception of consciousness as a stream in which there are both apprehension of objects and appropriation by the self of the states of awareness as its own.[17] This aspect of *citta* is called *kārya-citta,* which is conditioned in the nature and extent of its operations by the nature of its organic basis.[18] It must be remembered that all types of beings are not capable of the same type of experience nor do two individuals of the same species agree about their mental contents. The reason for this is to be sought in the law of Karma which determines what type of embodiment and experience is to be expected of any particular embodied soul, when unaided by yogic proficiency.[19] The contracted field of knowledge and activity is at once an effect of ignorance and demerit ; for the *kāraṇa-citta* or the potential mind-stuff is essentially ubiquitous (*vibhu*) and yogic practices can recover this potential ubiquity in any individual case (the Sāṁkhya denying, however, the absolute ubiquity of the *kāraṇa-citta* and admitting only its relative expansiveness in different types of bodies).[20]

This then is the first handicap which the potential *yogin* has to meet. The *citta* is not a perfectly uniform pliable stuff it differs from individual to individual, making the task of one easier than that of another. Past *karma* has set limits to its capacities, so much so that certain types of embodiment are only expiatory in character without the right and the capacity to improve one's lot by personal endeavour, just as probably other embodiments are only meant for enjoying the fruits of past *karmas* and are equally devoid of the capacity of improvement (the gods, for instance, being regarded by some as incapable of acquiring saving knowledge except when re-embodied as men).[21] All individuals do not have to begin at the same point on the onward path and the same disciplines are not necessary for all to bring about spiritual insight. The *citta,*

[16] Dasgupta, *The Study of Patañjali,* p. 96; *Yoga Philosophy,* p. 261; *Yoga as Philosophy and Religion,* p. 94; Radhakrishnan, *Indian Philosophy,* II. p. 345.

[17] See James, *Principles of Psychology,* I. p. 225.

[18] Dasgupta, *St. of Pat.,* pp. 95-6; Radhakrishnan, *Ind. Phil.,* II. p. 345; see also Dasgupta, *Yoga Ph.,* p. 262; *Yoga as Ph. & Rel.,* pp. 92-4.

[19] *Y. S.,* II. 13; IV. 4.

[20] Dasgupta, *St. of Pat.,* p. 95; *Yoga as Ph. & Rel.,* pp. 93-4; *Yoga Ph.,* p. 262.

[21] See the writer's article on 'The Vicissitudes of the Karma Doctrine' in *Malaviya Commemoration Volume,* p. 515.

again, is differently equipped with instinctive cravings in different kinds of beings in accordance with the types of their embodiment. As beings have been coming and going during the whole period of their eternal life, they must have assumed many shapes in the course of transmigration and a deposit of impressions of those different lives is left in the *citta* as *vāsanās.* These *vāsanās* become active according to embodiment, so that a human body is never prompted by bovine instincts nor a cow by human impulses.[22] These *vāsanās* are eternal in the sense that they are not habits, memories, and dispositions acquired during the lifetime of the individual, nor do they disappear like these with the cessation of the body. The *yogin* has to fight not only against visible enemies but also against invisible foes ; for, in addition to the conscious contents of his mind, there are also native tendencies like natural introversion and extroversion, innate propensities peculiar to the species carried over from past lives, and also latent deposits (*saṁskāra*) of past activities of this life. It is not enough therefore to stop the flow of conscious states alone, for latent tendencies of different kinds sprout up into overt thoughts and activities so long as they are not totally burnt up by the fire of discriminating knowledge (*viveka*).[23] When therefore *yoga* is defined as *cittavṛtti-nirodha* (suppression of the modifications of the mind-stuff), it must be understood not only as the stoppage of the flow of presentations but also as the eradication of those potencies or latent tendencies that generate new streams of thought and new lines of action.[24] Much of yogic direction is therefore aimed at the uprooting of potencies that make for fresh bondage through lapse in inhibition. Hence the *yogin* (in Brāhmaṇism, Buddhism, and Jainism) is enjoined to consolidate conquests as well as to attack new outposts if he wishes to attain the condition of a *kevalin* or an *arhat ;* the different *samādhis, bhūmis,* or *guṇasthāna*(*ka*)*s* mark the line of advance in spirituality,[25] and woe unto him who forgets that positions attained with arduousness can be retained only by vigilance and effort, and that to make no effort to advance is the surest way to court retreat.

Now this *citta,* whose modifications must be suppressed in order to obtain insight, is not homogeneous in character. There are distracted

[22] *Y. S.,* IV. 9; Dasgupta, *St. of Pat.,* p. 111.

[23] Dasgupta, *Yoga as Ph. & Rel.,* pp. 96-7; *Yoga Ph.,* p. 280, 285-6; *Y. S.,* I. 51; II. 26; III. 50; IV. 26-34.

[24] *Y. S.,* I. 2, 50-1.

[25] *Y. S.,* I. 17, 18; II. 27; IV. 29. See also Warren, *Buddhism in Translations,* pp. 288-89, 374; also p. 109; C. A. F. Rhys Davids, *Buddhist Psychology,* pp. 110-19; Suzuki, *Outlines of Mahāyāna Buddhism,* Ch. XII; also *Essays in Zen Buddhism* (First series), pp. 70-2; S. Stevenson. *The Heart of Jainism,* p. 185 f.; Nahar and Ghosh, *An Epitome of Jainism,* Ch. XXXVI; J. Jaini, *Outlines of Jainism,* p. 48 f. See in this connection Suzuki, *Essays in Zen Buddhism* (First Series), pp. 81-2. Also Law, *Human Types* (Puggala-Paññatti), p. 82; Mrs. Rhys Davids, *A Buddhist Manual of Psychological Ethics* (Dhamma-Saṅgaṇi), pp. 43-75.

natures (*kṣipta*), unsteady minds (*vikṣipta*), passionate and stupid egos (*mūḍha*), attentive dispositions (*ekāgra*), and intuitive tempers (*niruddha*).[26] The perpetually restless, the occasionally steady, the infatuated, the mono-ideistic, and the restricted exhaust the different types of minds, and they are faced with difficulties of different degrees and kinds in realizing their true selves. We need not refer to the difference in the grades of beings in which, according to Buddhism, trance conditions of different orders are natural.[27] Men are themselves obstructed by different elements in their nature ; the impulsive, the vacillating, the scatter-brained, the obstinate, and even the speculative are all infected with a latent danger to a greater or less extent. So insidious are the ways of mentation that alike in truthful thought (*pramāṇa*), false knowledge (*viparyaya*), verbal knowledge or objectless and inarticulate thinking (*vikalpa*), sleep and dream condition (*nidrā*), and memory (*smṛti*)[28] we are really carrying on some process of thinking or other that draws the soul away from its proper vocation. All avenues of empirical or phenomenal knowledge must be closed before transcendental cognition can arise.

### OBSCURATION AND EMERGENCE OF PURE EXPERIENCE

The reason why phenomenal knowledge must be abolished is that it owes its origin and continuance to the operation of non-spiritual factors. According to the Sāṁkhya-Yoga, phenomenal cognition arises when the intelligent but inactive Puruṣa comes into proximity with non-intelligent but potentially active Prakṛti and sets up the evolutionary process in the latter. Intelligence-stuff (*buddhi*), egoity (*ahaṅkāra*), and mind (*manas*), though bearing psychical titles, do not really belong to spirit—they are all successive stages in the evolution of blind Prakṛti and represent that aspect of Nature in which the approximation to the psychic character of Puruṣa assumes greater and greater prominence. The reflection of the Puruṣa on this constellation produces an illusory spiritual double and Nature seems to have become conscious through this reflected intelligization. According to a different view, there is a double reflection—that of Puruṣa on *buddhi* and that of *buddhi* on Puruṣa—with the effect that while Nature assumes a psychical aspect Puruṣa begins to identify itself with the intelligized phenomena of *buddhi*.[29] The effect of this reflection of Puruṣa

[26] *Vyāsabhāṣya* on *Y. S.*, I. 1; Dasgupta, *Yoga as Ph. & Rel.*, p. 95 f.; *St. of Pat.*, p. 97 f. Vijñāna Bhikṣu points out that *nirodha* is not a negative but a positive condition of the *citta* and its highest form is of two kinds—*samprajñāta* and *asamprajñāta*. See *Yogasārasaṅgraha*, I. For the relation of these natures to the stages of yogic progress, see *Bhojavṛtti* on *Y. S.*, I. 18.

[27] See Warren, *Bud. in Trans.*, p. 289.

[28] *Y. S.*, I. 5, 6.

[29] See Dasgupta, *Yoga as Ph. & Rel.*, pp. 15-23; *Tattvakaumudī* on *Sāṁ.-kār.*, 27. See Sinha, *Indian Psychology*: *Perception*, p. 124, for the distinction between Vācaspati Miśra and Vijñāna Bhikṣu; see Dasgupta, *St. of Pat.*, pp. 15-24, in this connection.

on *buddhi* is similar to that of a motionless person on a rippling surface of water: the water bodies forth a man and at the same time distorts his real form, stature, and posture. If the man on the shore were to look at his own figure in the water, he would be under the impression that his whole frame is dancing in the ripples, although as a matter of fact he is standing motionless. The apparent process or change is due to the medium of reflection and does not indicate the real nature of the man. So also Puruṣa, which is inactive and has no essential relation to Nature, begins to consider itself as an active agent and a cognizer of worldly happenings as soon as it forgets that its phenomenal double is really a creation of Prakṛti.[30] We need not discuss seriously the palliating theory that Nature evolves in order ultimately to redeem the soul; for it is doubtful if without effort the soul would ever get rid of Prakṛti, and even the cessation of effort in Puruṣa requires some kind of active participation in the plan of salvation by Puruṣa itself. The whole yogic scheme would be unmeaning if no personal effort is needed to put a stop to the ceaseless flow of mental states; what the Yoga probably intended to convey is that the *sense* of effort and appropriation is phenomenal, though the transcendental operation of the soul must be presumed to sustain the spiritual effort and progress. We may, in fact, see here something analogous to the distinction between the logical ego and the psychological ego of Kant—there is no empirical knowledge of the existence and operation of the former either in the Yoga or in Kant. Consciousness is a function of the confluence of the logical ego and the thing-in-itself in Kant; so also in the Yoga the noumenal Puruṣa and the undifferentiated Prakṛti must co-operate before any phenomenal knowledge can arise and a sense of agentship can invade the soul. Without knowledge on the part of the phenomenal ego, the thing-in-itself of Kant and the Prakṛti of the Sāṁkhya-Yoga lapse back into an uncharacterizable condition; similarly, without objective cognition, the ego ceases to be known and lapses back into a transcendental or logical condition both in Kant and in the Sāṁkhya-Yoga. There is, however, this distinction between Kant and the Yoga system that while the former denies that the logical ego can know itself, the latter postulates a spiritual illumination of the transcendental ego in its released condition—an illumination so different in kind from empirical knowledge that consciousness ceases to be an attribute and becomes an essence. Students of philosophy are familiar with the concept of Brahman as *caitanyasvarūpa* in Indian speculation and of the ultimate Reality as absolute experience in Western thought; the Sāṁkhya-Yoga

[30] *Sāṁ.-kār.*, 19, 20; *B. G.*, III. 27.

rejects the personal soul of the theistic systems, the illusory soul of the Vedāntist and the Buddhist, the unconscious soul of the Nyāya-Vaiśeṣika, and the embodied soul of the Jaina, and is thus left with soul as experience much in the manner of Śaṅkara's Absolute. When insight becomes wholly immanent and ceases to be transeunt, it ceases to be a form of activity; hence knowledge has very seldom been regarded as a *karma* by Indian thinkers. The Yoga does not deny that phenomenal thinking is a form of activity, but it agrees that the rise of pure experience is not a mode of activity at all. In fact we are told that concentration (*dhyāna*) becomes perfect when self-reference is lost and the self becomes almost emptied of all contents and only the object to be contemplated shines forth;[31] this indicates that, prior to the final leap, the spirit loses the activity that differentiates and reacts upon the object, and, being divested of all relativity, it loses the flow of awareness which is responsible for the sense of activity. Like the central point of a revolving wheel the soul remains unmoved in the midst of changes— it is the unmoved mover of the phenomenal series which, being gradually contracted, leaves the unmoved mover alone behind.[32] As one-pointedness (*ekāgratā*) comes nearest to this ideal of psychical immobility, the *yogin* is enjoined to cultivate it as a means of total suppression of psychical states.[33]

## THE EFFECTS OF IGNORANCE

The relation to their conduciveness to the realization of the nature of the self divides mental states (*vṛttis*) into *kliṣṭa* (afflicted or hindered) and *akliṣṭa* (unafflicted or unhindered).[34] The former can all be reduced to one category, namely, states of ignorance (*avidyā*), while the latter can all be called states of knowledge (*prajñā*). Now, ignorance takes the forms of mistaking the not-self for the self (*asmitā*), the impure for the pure (*rāga*), the really painful for the pleasurable (*dveṣa*, inasmuch as in anger and hatred there is a peculiar pleasure attached, though the experience is really painful),[35] and the evanescent for the eternal (*abhiniveśa*).[36] The combined effect of all these forms of ignorance is that men

[31] *Y. S.*, III. 3. See also *Y. S.*, I. 43. This is Laya-yoga. From this Vedāntic leanings of Yoga may possibly be inferred, but Yoga does not teach union with the object of contemplation.

[32] The distinction between Buddhism and Brāhmaṇism on this point is that while Buddhism thinks that the evaporation of the phenomenal series does not leave any permanent substance behind, Brāhmaṇism believes that an abiding entity called soul (Ātman) is left behind.

[33] *Y. S.*, III. 11, 12.

[34] *Y. S.*, I. 5.

[35] *Y. S.*, II. 2-9.

[36] The terms may also be taken in *Y. S.*, II. 5 without reference to II. 3. In that case the *yogin* would be expected to get beyond ignorance about the nature of the self, all attachments towards pleasurable things, all hostile tendencies towards harmful things and all tenacity of mundane existence. Ultimately they could be all reduced to interest in the physical and

look upon the pleasures of the body as the delights of the soul, the impure bodies of friends and relatives (including women) as pure and desirable, the really beneficent sufferings of the body as objects of aversion, and the changing scenes of the mental and physical worlds as constant and abiding. The *yogin* must cultivate a habit of thinking in which things would appear in their true perspectives—the attractions of the physical world, the pleasures of the senses, the delights of the body, and the pride of possession would all disappear; even the distinction between virtue (*puṇya*) and vice (*pāpa*) would vanish, for this is true only of the phenomenal ego, and not of the transcendental self.[37] It is not enough to kill the manifestations of the afflicted states; for in addition to the condition of active manifestation (*udāra*) these states are sometimes intercepted by other states (*vicchinna*), sometimes they operate with reduced intensity (*tanu*) through the practice of certain forms of meditation and activity like study, austerities, etc., and sometimes they even sink below the level of consciousness and lie dormant (*prasupta*) in the form of *vāsanās* (latent tendencies) and *karmāśayas* (latent deposits of past actions).[38] One must get rid of these root and branch, and burn up the possibility of future life not only by ceasing to have any hankering after it but also by taking steps to destroy its conditions. In this matter the *yogin* must go against the inclination of the natural man whose constant prayer is that he may continue to live and not be destroyed—a continuation of phenomenal existence that embraces both this life and the life hereafter.[39] He must not even aspire after a higher form of existence like that of gods or disembodied beings (*videhalīnas* and *prakṛtilīnas*);[40] for even these are born

apathy towards the spiritual. The Yoga reiterates in II. 15 the Buddhistic dogma that all is ultimately painful.

[37] *Y. S.*, II. 14; IV. 7.

[38] *Y. S.*, II. 4. See also I. 50-51; IV. 9.

[39] *Y. S.*, II. 9; IV. 10.

[40] *Y. S.*, I. 19; also III. 51. We have a classification under III. 51 of *yogins* into *prathama-kalpika*, the beginner whose practice of *vairāgya* is showing signs of success in the form of knowledge of other minds; *madhubhūmika*, the one who has set his heart upon conquering the world of external objects and his sense-organs and who is described in *Y. S.*, I. 48 as one who, by hearing the scriptures (*śravaṇa*), consideration of their intent through thinking or inference (*manana*), and reflecting upon their object through contemplation (*nididhyāsana*), obtains the truth-bearing insight (*ṛtambharā prajñā*); *prajñājyotiḥ*, the one in whom after the conquest of elements and organs by practising constraint as laid down in *Y. S.*, II. 47 there has been effected an acquisition of all necessary means to uninterrupted progress towards passionlessness; and *atikrāntabhāvanīya*, the one whose sole object is to resolve the mind-stuff and whose present life is the last (as of the *anāgāmin* in Buddhism). The invitation of the gods is meant neither for the first class who are not yet objects of serious consideration nor for the third and fourth classes for they do not care for heavenly joys, but only for the second class who may in this way be deflected from their purpose by the attraction of heavenly joys. The third class is described as starting from *viśoka* state (*Y. S.*, I. 36). The fourth class is possessed of the seven stages of insight as described in *Y. S.*, II. 27. After the fourth stage, at which thinkables end, there remain three stages of *cittavimukti* only; that is why it is called *atikrāntabhāvanīya*, for the cause of release has been known and nothing else remains to be known. The parallelism of these four classes of *yogins* with *yatamāna, vyatireka,*

and dissolved, and birth in *any* form is bondage. Brāhmaṇism, Buddhism, and Jainism are singularly unanimous on the point that attaining a higher form of phenomenal existence is not the ultimate objective of a spiritual aspirant.

### THE PROCESS OF RIGHT COGNITION

Now, the indispensable condition of all spiritual advance is the cultivation of dispassion or detachment (*vairāgya*)—not in a spasmodic fashion but in a systematic way (*abhyāsa*).[41] A person must be habituated to discriminative knowledge, and this habit can be established only by long practice, with no exception on any pretext, and with faith in its utility and efficacy ; in fact, the Yoga gives the same direction for the formation of habit as William James does.[42] In spiritual matters, a further condition is the cultivation of a spirit of detachment which in its advanced form takes the shape of loss of interest in both seen and revealed objects (*dṛṣṭānuśravikaviṣaya*)[43]—in sensible objects like women, food, drink, power, etc. and in revealed objects like heavenly joys and states of disembodied existence. The Yoga system advises control of affections as the indispensable condition of the disappearance of the phenomenal world. So long as we retain interest in any object, we are bound to notice its presence and feel the effects of that knowledge ; even subliminal cravings are to be checked by suitable means to ensure perfect freedom. The process starts with a desire that the senses should not stray into the fields of their normal activity: this is the condition of the striving (*yatamāna*). The next stage is represented by the knowledge that interest in certain objects has ceased but not in others: this is the condition of differentiation (*vyatireka*). The third stage is attained when interest in sense objects has completely ceased, but there still lingers a residual anxiety in the mind (whence it is called one-organed, *ekendriya*). Students of abnormal psychology will readily remember cases of anxiety-neurosis (and anxiety-hysteria) where the knowledge of the originating cause has disappeared from conscious memory and yet the affect appears in the form of anxiety. It is only when this stage is crossed and the state of detachment from seen and unseen delectations arises that the condition known as control (*vaśīkāra*), which is the highest form of lower detach-

*ekendriya*, and *vaśīkāra* is not perfect, but in *vaśīkāra vairāgya* there is the same apathy towards heavenly (and worldly) joys as in the stages beyond *madhubhūmika* (see *Y. S.*, I. 15). For the literal use of *prakṛtilaya*, see *Sāṁ.-kār.*, 45.

[41] *Y. S.*, I. 12-14; *B. G.*, VI. 35.

[42] *Y. S.*, I. 14. See James, *Principles of Psychology*, I. pp. 123-7.

[43] *Y. S.*, I. 15. See *Sāṁ.-kār.*, 2.

ment (*aparavairāgya*), is said to have been attained.[44] Beyond this stage is *paravairāgya,* highest detachment, in which complete indifference even to the elements of nature (*guṇas*) is reached because of self-knowledge; and this discriminative knowledge becomes the cause of salvation only when it is never disturbed or broken (*aviplavā*)[45] by a return of the consciousness of the subject-object or the agent-patient relation.

Side by side with the control of the emotional aspect of mental life there goes on a transcendence of crude cognitions in a progressive fashion. Every phenomenal cognition implies three factors, namely, the knower (*grahītṛ*), the process of knowledge (*grahaṇa*), and the object to be known (*grāhya*)—a trinity which noumenal knowledge wholly transcends.[46] The *citta* or mind-stuff has a tendency to identify itself with the object which it cognizes when its fluctuations are weakened; if its activities were absolute in character, then there would be no possibility either of improvement or of final liberation. Hence the importance of fixing the mind-stuff upon the right object, for what a mind thinks it tends to become. The Vedāntists say that the knower of Brahman becomes Brahman; the Yoga admits the truth of this proposition to this extent that in phenomenal cognition it is an advantage to fill the mind with proper objects of contemplation, for the mind tends to empty itself (*svarūpaśūnya*) and reflect the character of the object (*arthamātranirbhāsa*) with the development of concentration.[47] When the *yogin* is asked to concentrate his mind on some dispassionate soul (*vītarāgaviṣaya*), as, for instance, on Buddhas and Jinas in Buddhism and Jainism respectively, or on Īśvara, the omniscient and eternally free Lord and Instructor of the whole world, in Hinduism,[48] the hope is entertained that by so doing he would rise at least partially to the height of his ideate and speedily bring about his own salvation. Similarly, if the Upaniṣads could compare the state of dreamless sleep to the intuition of the Absolute, because in that condition all externality and duality disappear,[49] the Yoga system could advise the novice to take dream (where external knowledge is at an end and only internal knowledge persists) and sleep (where both external knowledge and internal knowledge are at an end) as objects of concentration, for in that case the cessation of mental fluctuations, as in those condi-

[44] *Tattvakaumudī* on *Sāṁ.-kār.*, 23; *Y. S.*, I. 15. See Vijñāna Bhikṣu, *Yogasārasaṅgraha,* II. See Brill, *Psychanalysis,* p. 89 f. (esp. p. 99).

[45] *Y. S.,* I. 16; II. 26; III. 9-12.

[46] *Y. S.,* III. 47 (with *Vyāsabhāṣya*).

[47] *Y. S.,* I. 43.

[48] *Y. S.,* I. 23, 37.

[49] *Bṛ. U.,* II. 1. 15-17; *Chā. U.,* VI. 8. 1; VIII. 3. 2; *Pra. U.,* IV. 4. See Ranade, *A Constructive Survey of Upanishadic Philosophy,* p. 125; also Deussen, *The Philosophy of the Upanishads,* p. 248 f., 297 f.

tions, would be easily attained.[50] In this way the mind can use any physical events or operations as objects;[51] the one principle that cannot be made the object of concentration is the self, which is always the subject, though not in the phenomenal sense of being the possessor (ego) of states or objects. Even God and other spirits are therefore possible objects of phenomenal cognition, but not so the soul itself, for in absolute cognition the soul loses all sense of duality and becomes isolated (*kevalin*).[52]

## THE STAGES OF CONCENTRATION

It has already been remarked that the path to liberation lies through the fields of Nature herself—that the soul uses the phenomena of Nature themselves to conquer her finally. The process of conquest consists in the different kinds of knowledge in the *citta* corresponding to the different kinds of Nature's manifestations. Thus, the ordinary mind is filled with contemplations of the grosser aspects of Nature—the products of the *mahābhūtas* which Prakṛti evolves last. Using a word which is common with Buddhism but not entering into such niceties of distinction as Buddhism does regarding the different kinds of intellection (*mano, citta, vedanā, viññāna, saññā,* etc.),[53] the Yoga calls this stage of knowledge *savitarka samādhi*—here the mind synthesizes its impressions and ideas into the percept of a gross object like a cow or a jar and keeps itself fixed thereon.[54] In this stage all the elements of perceptual knowledge, namely, the sound (*śabda*) or the name, the meaning (*artha*) conveyed to the mind, and the actual object (*vastu*) are all rolled up together so that the experience is as much a mental as a physical fact.[55] The duality of subject and object is, in its full significance, present in this cognition, and the mind does not rise here above the relativity which all concrete knowledge implies, the knowledge of one object being dependent upon a contrast with that of others.* Now this gross cognition can be superseded either in respect of the objective content or in that of the elements involved. Thus, when the three elements of sound (in the case of auditory cognition), meaning, and

[50] *Y. S.,* I. 38 (the *Tattvavaiśāradī* points out that the sleep must be of *sāttvika* quality, namely, such as is accompanied by the memory on waking that we had slept well). Sleep itself, however, is a hindrance as it means the predominance of the *tāmasa* quality. In Buddhism also torpor is condemned, although it was permitted to the *arhat* to take a periodical repose. (C. A. F. Rhys Davids, *Bud. Man. of Psy. Eth.,* p. 312, with footnote 2).

[51] *Y. S.,* I. 39.

[52] *Y. S.,* II. 18, 20, 25; III. 50; IV. 34.

[53] See C. A. F. Rhys Davids, *Buddhist Psychology,* Ch. III; S. Z. Aung and C. A. F. Rhys Davids, *Compendium of Philosophy,* p. 12 f., p. 94 f.; C. A. F. Rhys Davids, *Bud. Man. of Psy. Eth.,* pp. lxiii-lxxxii.

[54] *Y. S.,* I. 42. The term is found in the *Nikāyas* in the sense of attention applied (C. A. F. Rhys Davids, *Bud. Psy.,* p. 97, 110; Aung and Rhys Davids, *Comp. of Ph.,* p. 95; see esp. Rhys Davids, *Bud. Psy. Eth.,* p. 10, f.n.l. where the distinction between *vitakko* and *vicāro* has been carefully drawn).

[55] *Y. S.,* I. 42.

object intended are reduced to the last, i.e. when the mind understands the nature of objects in a direct fashion without the help of words or psychical doubles, we reach the stage of *nirvitarka samādhi*.[56] Words often tend to conceal the real nature of an object and also to produce the illusion of a sensible content (as in the case of negative words), whence the mental state called *vikalpa* follows.[57] It is necessary to rise above the complication of knowledge by verbal and meaning factors and to get a direct unverbalized knowledge of things, such as is possessed by babes and deaf-mutes:[58] when this is accomplished the *savitarka* stage is superseded by the *nirvitarka* stage and knowledge about things is transcended in a direct acquaintance with them.

But the *yogin* must go beyond this stage of gross content altogether and try to grasp the subtle elements of Nature (*tanmātras*) in their true essence. Here also the first stage is characterized by verbal complications as in the case of gross objects and it is only at the end that the mind grasps the nature of the subtle things without these complications. The two stages here are respectively called *savicāra* and *nirvicāra*, reflective and super-reflective, in contrast with *savitarka* and *nirvitarka*, contemplative (or deliberative) and super-contemplative, because while the latter types deal with objects whose existence is a matter of ordinary experience, the former types deal with objects whose existence can only be indirectly proved, so far as ordinary minds are concerned.[59] It is claimed, however, that the *yogins* are able to know even these subtle things directly after they have acquired certain powers by the practice of meditation. We are told, for instance, that in *savicāra samādhi* the *yogin* acquires the power of knowing such subtle things as atoms (which are invisible to ordinary persons till three binary atoms have formed a *trasareṇu* or the minimum visible magnitude), space, time, air, *manas*, and even the laws of morality by direct experience.[60] The list varies from system to system, but there is a general agreement that the obstacles that prevent the grasp of subtle and supersensible things in the case of

[56] *Y. S.*, I. 43.

[57] *Y. S.*, I. 9.

[58] On the whole subject of *nirvikalpa* (indeterminate) and *savikalpa* (determinate) perception, see Sinha, *Indian Psychology*: *Perception*, II (p. 31 f); Nalini Kanta Brahma, *Philosophy of Hindu Sādhanā*, IX.

[59] The term *savicāra* is found in Buddhism in the sense of sustained attention (see the references given above in f.n. 54). *Y. S.*, I. 44. The object of *savicāra samādhi* is said to be everything subtle of the external order inclusive of Pradhāna or Prakṛti, but not the self which also is subtle (*Vyāsabh.* on the *sūtra*). This would make a partial cross-division of the objects as other *samādhis* also have some of these subtle things as objects of their thought. See Sinha, *Ind. Psy.*: *Perception*, p. 348 f.

[60] See Sinha, *Ind. Psy.*: *Perception*, Ch. XVIII for the distinction between yogic perception and other forms of supernormal consciousness like *ārṣajñāna*, *siddhadarśana*, and *prātibhajñāna* (*Y. S.*, III. 32-3).

ordinary men do not operate in the case of the *yogins* who can see through the non-spiritual character of even the subtle manifestations of Nature. An instructive parallel to the distinction between *savitarka* and *savicāra* is the Kantian distinction between forms of intuition and categories of the understanding—the former being apprehended direct and therefore requiring only exposition, and the latter being known only indirectly and therefore requiring deduction ; to a *yogin* both the gross and the subtle are matters of direct knowledge, though to the ordinary individual the one is sensed and the other inferred. In the *nirvicāra* stage the *yogin* gains a direct non-conceptual non-verbalized knowledge of these subtle things.[61]

But even this stage is transcended when the *yogin* passes on to the *sānanda* stage. After he has discovered that neither the gross nor the subtle things of Nature are really final objectives and that identification with neither in a state, technically called *samāpatti* (a term probably borrowed from Buddhism),[62] where the object alone seems to exist and the self-reference is almost lost, is conducive to the realization of the true self, the *yogin* passes on to still more subtle forms of Nature to discover if the self could be found there. There is some difference of opinion about the things that should be included within the class of 'subtle objects', but the general tendency is to include within it everything of Nature, exclusive of the gross objects of sense, in which the elements of *rajas* (activity) and *tamas* (inertia) preponderate.[63] This leaves the sense-organs, which are the products of *ahaṅkāra* under the influence of the *sattva* (purity, balance) element, and also *buddhi*, and possibly also *ahaṅkāra* itself if we take the alternative view that it is not out of *ahaṅkāra* but out of *buddhi* direct that the objective series of *tanmatras* and *mahābhūtas* and the subjective series of *ahaṅkāra* and the sense-organs developed on parallel lines.[64] In *sānanda samādhi* the *yogin* may be supposed to gain an insight into the nature of these subjective or, rather, illuminating principles, with the exception of *buddhi*, which Nature evolves. We may, in fact, think that in *sānanda samādhi*, as Vācaspati Miśra holds, there is an identification

[61] *Vyāsabh.* on *Y. S.*, I. 44.

[62] See Rhys Davids, *Bud. Psy.*, p. 114.

[63] *Y. S.*, I. 45.

[64] There is some divergence of view about the process of evolution from *buddhi* or *mahat* to the organs of perception and action, *manas* and the *tanmātras* and also about the element that predominates in each case. The *Sāṁkhya-kārikā* (*śls.* 22, 24) upholds the classical view and most of the commentators accept the same. The other view is represented by Vijñāna Bhikṣu who derives the parallel series from *buddhi* (see Radhakrishnan, *Ind. Ph.*, II. p. 269, f.n. 3). This seems to follow *Vyāsabh.* on *Y. S.*, II. 19, but the commentators on the *Y. S.* are not unanimous on this point. For a thorough discussion of this matter, see Dasgupta, *St. of Pat.*, p. 60 f.

with the *grahaṇa* or means of knowledge just as in *savitarka* and *savicāra samādhis* there is an identification with the *grāhya* or objects of knowledge.[65] But the real difficulty is to understand why the term *ānanda* (and sometimes also *nirānanda* to indicate the super-*ānanda* condition)[66] should be used. Do we have here the psychic process that is designed to get rid of *rāga* and *dveṣa* that attend the knowledge of the phenomenal world and of which the residual effect remains in the form of anxiety when the object-consciousness disappears? In that case there would be some sort of relation between the five *kliṣṭa* states and the five kinds of *samādhi* (including the highest), although even then there would not be a strict one-to-one relation, as *savitarka* and *savicāra* would jointly correspond to *abhiniveśa*; *rāga* and *dveṣa* would jointly have *sānanda* as corresponding; and *sāsmita* and *asamprajñāta* would correspond to *asmitā* and *avidyā* respectively. But the statement that the states of the five *kleśas* are suppressed by *dhyāna* lends colour to the supposition that a correspondence with the five types of *samādhi* was intended in some way.[67] The other supposition, namely, that the affective residues of cognitive states are intended, cannot be altogether barred out, and we may believe that before the self finds out that no kind of cognition, not even the sense of personal identity, is really self-knowledge, it has to rule, first of all, the affective self-feeling out of court. The tendency, for instance, to identify the self with coenaesthesis, organic sensation or the feeling arising out of the proper or improper functioning of the bodily system, must be abandoned, for the self can have nothing to do with anything that is of the nature of a disturbance and that makes for clinging to mundane existence through its hedonic effects.[68] In the *sānanda* state this identification with the psychical accompaniments of vital functions is effected only to be transcended in *sāsmita samādhi*. It is also likely that by *sānanda samādhi* was intended the attention paid to the stream of awareness as such, as distinct from the objects revealed therein and the self-consciousness attending it. This would mean that the mind could attend to its own subjective states without reference to the objects of the physical world which they originally revealed to the spiritual novice. This does not explain the term *ānanda* but would satisfy Vācaspati Miśra's division of *samādhi* into three classes of which the second has

[65] See *Vyāsabh.* and *Tattvavaiśāradī* on *Y. S.*, I. 41.
[66] See Sinha, *op. cit.*, pp. 349-50.
[67] *Y. S.*, II. 11.
[68] The difficulty of this interpretation is that the vital airs are not separately recognized in the Sāṁkhya system, although their existence is taken for granted and in the *Yoga-Sūtra* directions about their control are to be found. Vijñāna Bhikṣu takes *ānanda* in the sense of bliss due to the influx of *sattva* quality and denies that there is also a *nirānanda samādhi*. See Dasgupta, *Yoga as Ph. & Rel.*, p. 153.

reference to the process of awareness, provided we do not mean by *grahaṇa* the sense-organs but the process of thought that apprehends.[69]

But the *yogin* can go further. He may transcend both the object and the process of thought and fix his attention on the consciousness of self itself. We have already seen that this self-consciousness is only Phenomenal, for here there is a reflection of the Puruṣa in the Janus-like *buddhi* whereby an illusory self-sense is generated in the first evolute of Prakṛti, namely, *buddhi* or *mahat*. Nature is so transparent in *buddhi,* owing to the preponderance of the element of *sattva,* that the self has great difficulty in dissociating itself from the consciousness of self, the 'I' from the 'me', the transcendental self from the phenomenal ego. *Buddhi* and *ahaṅkāra* are the two principles which closely operate together in producing individual centres of cognition, affection, and conation ; and although they require the help of the sense-organs to come into contact with the external world, they are sufficient by themselves to generate, or at least to conserve, a sense of private ownership of ideas and actions. *Buddhi,* like the *nous* in Plotinus, supplies the principle of intelligibility to Prakṛti which, like the One or Being of Plotinus, would remain unmanifested (*avyakta*) without its aid. But intelligibility in general becomes particularized through *ahaṅkāra* or ego-making principle, which canalizes intelligibility into individual channels and lays the foundation of personal ownership. In the *sāsmita samādhi* the self concentrates on the sense of personal cognition and effort only to transcend that state also.[70] It discovers that the sense of personal identity is also phenomenal and depends upon the compresence of Prakṛti and Puruṣa—the former supplying through *buddhi* and *ahaṅkāra* that medium in which alone Puruṣa could produce an image of itself and a sense of personal identity. But this is the stage hardest to overcome, for here the identity with the real self is so close that most people stop here, thinking that the final stage has been attained. As a matter of fact, the *Yoga-Sūtra* refers to two classes of beings—the *videhalīnas* and the *prakṛtilīnas*—both belonging to the *bhavapratyaya* class or the class of beings who are born without organic encumbrances like our own,

[69] Nāgoji Bhaṭṭa thinks that by *grahaṇa* are to be understood three distinct classes of sense-organs. We may mean either the different kinds of senses possessed by different kinds of beings, both sessile and moving, or the sense-organs as ordinarily understood, or *buddhi* and *ahaṅkāra.* The first would be the cosmic, the second the gross, and the third the subtle meaning of the term. See his commentary on *Y. S.,* I. 41.

[70] There is similar difficulty about the significance of the term *asmitā.* We may mean by it either the principle which because of its *sāttvika* character almost takes the form of the self (which interpretation would make *buddhi* the object of concentration) or a Puruṣa who is eternally free (i.e. God) or has become free (i.e. *muktapuruṣa*). See Nāgoji's commentary on *Y. S.,* I. 41; also Dasgupta, *Yoga as Ph. & Rel.,* p. 153; Sinha, *Ind. Psy.: Perception,* p. 351.

and possessing a natural capacity to know themselves if they would shake off the little ignorance that keeps them from salvation.[71] The *yogin* is an *upāyapratyaya* or one who has acquired his discriminative knowledge by adopting proper means ;[72] but he is not in any way inferior to the above two classes of beings, for he can win his salvation by going beyond the stages of *sānanda* and *sāsmita samādhis* in which these classes are held fast.[73] It is not enough to renounce the world or practise austerities—the *yogin* must gain complete insight into the distinction between his self and the phenomena of the physical world, and thereby win his freedom, if he wishes to avoid the condition in which the gods or some other types of beings, caught in the finer meshes of Nature, are at present. He must know that no amount of introspection or knowledge through *buddhi* would ever give a knowledge of the noumenal self, for in the empirical condition the self can be *inferred* from the operations of *buddhi* but never *experienced* directly—we get the 'me' or the object-self but never the 'I' or the subject-self as this can never be objectified without absorbing material factors like *buddhi, ahaṅkāra,* etc. Extremes have a tendency to meet, for the Sceptics, the Behaviourists, and the Patañjalites are at one so far as the value of introspective knowledge is concerned, as all deny its validity for the purpose of self-knowledge ; but while the Sceptics and the Behaviourists would say that the self is non-existent, the Patañjalites would say that the self requires some other method of knowledge to be known in its true essence.

It is evident that after the *savitarka* stage we are dealing with matters that are more or less supernormal, for the ordinary man can have no direct experience of the subtle elements or the organs of knowledge or the *buddhi* in which the *sattva* element has completely subordinated the other elements of *rajas* and *tamas.* When therefore these four kinds of meditation are called *samprajñāta samādhi,*[74] we are to understand by the term the kind of knowledge in which the duality of subject and object is present, though the object may vary from gross things to subtle, and even so-called psychical, entities, and the cognizer may be a novice in the art of concentrated thinking or a spiritual adept. It is instructive to compare this Yoga scheme with the Buddhistic system of *jhāna* (*dhyāna*), for it would show not merely that the practical part of the mind-training was similar but also that the term *sānanda* may have been borrowed from Buddhistic sources and then its

[71] *Y. S.,* I. 19.
[72] *Vyāsabh.* on *Y. S.,* I. 20.
[73] *Ibid.*
[74] *Y. S.,* I. 17. Later writers divided Yoga into four classes—Mantra-yoga, Laya-yoga, Haṭha-yoga, and Rāja-yoga. See *Yogatattva U., Yogaśikhā U.,* I. (To these are added Bhāvanā-yoga and Sahaja-yoga in *Yogaśikhā U.,* V.) The four stages of Yoga in this later literature are called Ārambha, Ghaṭa, Paricaya, and Niṣpatti.—*Ibid.,* V; also *Śiva Saṁhitā,* III. 29 and V. 169 f. (Rājādhirāja-yoga).

origin forgotten. In the *Anupada-Sutta* (Series-Discourse) occurs the following seriation of the concentrated states:

'For instance, *bhikkhus*, Sāriputta, aloof from sensuous desires, aloof from bad ideas, enters into and abides in First Jhāna, wherein attention is applied and sustained, which is born of solitude and filled with zest and pleasurable feeling. And the presentation in that First Jhāna, to wit, thinking applied and sustained (*vitakka, vicāra*), and zest and pleasurable feeling (*pīti, sukha*) and singleness of object (*citt'ekaggatā*), and contact, feeling, perception, volition, consciousness (*citta*), desire (*chanda*), choice, effort, mindfulness, indifference, adaptation of attention (*manasikara*)—these are for him serially determined ; these, as they arise, are for him things understood, and as they are present and as they depart, are for him things understood.'[75]

A similar seriation is to be found in other places too. Here, for instance, is another description of 'right concentration':

'When aloof from sensuous ideas, aloof from evil ideas, he enters into and abides in First Jhāna, wherein attention is applied and sustained (*sa-vitakka, sa-vicāra*), which is born of solitude and filled with zest and pleasant emotion ; when next, from the subsiding of attention applied and sustained, he enters into and abides in Second Jhāna which is inward tranquillizing of the mind, self-contained and uplifted from the working of attention, is born of concentration, full of zest and pleasurable emotion ; when next, through the quenching of zest, he abides with equal mind, mindful and discerning, experiencing in the body that pleasure whereof the Aryans declare: "Happy doth he abide with even, lucid mind," and so enters into and abides in Third Jhāna ; when next, by putting away both pleasant and painful emotion, by the dying out of the joy and misery he used to know, he enters into and abides in Fourth Jhāna, that utterly pure lucidity and indifference of mind, wherein is neither happiness nor unhappiness—this is the training of the higher consciousness.'[76]

We may very well believe that the Buddhistic ideal of realizing the non-permanent character of the ego finds its parallel in the yogic ideal of transcending the *asmitā* stage. Both the systems hold that the stream of thought which is responsible for the generation of the ego-sense must be stopped, even though an ultimate divergence of views becomes noticeable when the question of a transcendental self arises. The Buddhist transcends the ego-stage only to realize *nirvāṇa* and the *yogin* goes beyond the empirical ego to realize the noumenal self.

The Yoga analysis practically stops here and we pass on immediately

[75] See C. A. F. Rhys Davids, *Bud. Psy.*, p. 97.
[76] *Ibid.*, p. 110; see also Warren, *Bud. in Trans.*, p. 288.

to *asamprajñāta samādhi* or concentration where the object has been reduced to mere disposition (*saṁskāra*) and where therefore knowledge involving the duality of subject and object has ceased.[77] But there are indications in the *Yoga-Sūtra* itself that other stages of the soul's growth were once known, and possibly for these it is best to turn to Buddhistic literature from which most probably the stages were borrowed. We have already referred to the four trances (*jhāna*); but here are some more stages of knowledge which spiritual advancement possesses serially. Thus it is described of Buddha that after he had instructed his disciples, on the eve of his decease, to work out their salvation with diligence—

'The Blessed One entered the first trance; and rising from the first trance, he entered the second trance; and rising from the second trance, he entered the third trance; and rising from the third trance, he entered the fourth trance; and rising from the fourth trance, he entered the realm of the infinity of space; and rising from the realm of the infinity of space, he entered the realm of the infinity of consciousness; and rising from the realm of the infinity of consciousness, he entered the realm of nothingness; and rising from the realm of nothingness, he entered the realm of neither perception nor yet non-perception; and rising from the realm of neither perception nor yet non-perception, he arrived at the cessation of perception and sensation.'[78]

In the *Visuddhi-magga* we are told[79] that a limit of time may be set to this condition by the concentrated mind, provided that the termination of life, or respect for the Order, or a summons from the teacher does not interfere, and that when a person rises from this condition he completes the process of never-returning (i.e. he will not be reborn after the end of this life) or attains the full stature of sainthood and his mind is thereafter inclined to *nirvāṇa,* which is also described as isolation. The distinction between a dead man and a man who has entered on the cessation of perception and sensation is that in the latter bodily *karma,* vocal *karma,* and mental *karma* all cease and become quieted, but vitality does not depart, the natural heat does not subside, and the senses do not break up as in the former case.[80] But the person in this condition effects a threefold deliverance—he passes from a knowledge of the conditioned to that of the unconditioned, from a state of desire to desirelessness, and from the sense of falseness of the ego to the sense of the empty.[81]

[77] *Y. S.*, I. 18, 50. For *asamprajñāta samādhi,* see Sinha, *op. cit.*, pp. 342, 352.

[78] See Warren, *Bud. in Trans.*, p. 109. It is to be noticed, however, that Buddha passes into *nirvāṇa* directly from the fourth trance.—*Ibid.*, p. 110.

[79] *Ibid.*, pp. 385-6.

[80] *Ibid.*, p. 389.

[81] *Ibid.*, p. 378.

THE STAGES OF SANCTIFICATION

Echoes of these are to be found in the *Yoga-Sūtra,* for we are told that it is possible for the *yogin* to realize a sense of escape from the trammels of the body in the state of attention (*dhāraṇā*) called *mahāvideha,* which may be either relative (*kalpita*) when the knowledge of the body from which escape has been effected persists, or absolute (*akalpita*) when even this knowledge drops out.[82] We are also told that a *yogin* attains the infinity of consciousness in the state called *viśokā* (or *jyotiṣmatī*—a term reminiscent of the Buddhistic *arciṣmatī,* a condition in which the residues of ignorance and passion are burnt up by practices conducive to the perfection of *bodhi*).[83] There is also a reference to the condition of mind in which there is a sense of the body being expanded to infinity (*ananta-samāpatti*) and which favours fixity of posture (*āsana*).[84] It is true that the finer distinctions of the Buddhistic *arūpa-jhāna* in which the individual passes over more or less into a cataleptic condition[85] are not so nicely drawn in the *Yoga-Sūtra,* but the general outlines are the same and even the graduated sense of nearing the goal is present in both the systems. Thus in the doctrine of *prajñā* or insight, which is described as sevenfold and as advancing by stages to the highest (*prāntabhūmi*), we are told that a *yogin* passes through the four stages of *kāryavimukti* (release of insight from effects) and the three stages of *cittavimukti* (release of mind-stuff) as soon as the defilements due to impurity disappear and discriminative knowledge arises.[86] He has a knowledge that the things to be escaped have been thought out, that the causes that produce the things to be avoided have dwindled away, that the escape has been perceived through restricted mentation (*nirodha-samādhi*), that the means of escape, namely, discriminative knowledge, has been cultivated. These four stages, we may suppose, come after the *vaśīkāra* stage has been attained in the path of concentration. The stages of *cittavimukti* do not depend upon effort but represent the progressive stages of dissolution of the objective or phenomenal order after the proper subjective condition has been attained. They are that the jurisdiction of the intelligence-stuff is at an end, that the *guṇas* are

[82] *Y. S.,* III. 43.

[83] *Y. S.,* I. 36. See Suzuki, *Out. of Mahā. Bud.,* p. 316.

[84] *Y. S.,* II. 47. The traditional interpretation is that the mind is to be fixed on the Serpent King on whose hood the earth rests steadily. For the juxtaposition of *samādhi* and *samāpatti* in Buddhistic literature, see Suzuki, *Studies in the Laṅkāvatāra-Sūtra,* pp. 74, 75.

[85] For which see Aung and Mrs. Rhys Davids, *Comp. of Ph.,* pp. 64, 90 ; Mrs. Rhys Davids, *Bud. Man. of Psy. Eth.,* p. 71 f.

[86] *Y. S.,* II. 27, with *Vyāsabh.* In both Buddhism and Jainism also a double stage of the liberation process is to be found—*pudgala-nairātmya* and *dharma-nairātmya* in the former and freedom from *bhāvabandha* and *dravyabandha* in the latter. The Vedāntic equivalents would be *jīvanmukti* and *videhakaivalya.* The meanings are, however, not identical. For a different enumeration of the seven *yogabhūmis,* see *Yogavāsiṣṭha Rāmāyaṇa,* III. 118. 2-16; VIa. 120. 1-8; VIa. 126. 12-73. For a description of the *jīvanmukta,* see *Varāha U.,* IV.

being dissolved into their ground which also is disappearing, that the soul has passed out of relation with the *guṇas* and become isolated (*kevalin*) and pure (*amala*). The *yogin* in this condition is called fortunate (*kuśala*) and it is implied that he possesses a knowledge of the stages through which he has passed on his way to liberation, though the last three stages are more or less automatic after discriminative knowledge has been established.[87] These stages are not identical with the ten stages of a Bodhisattva's perfection (*daśabhūmi*) in Mahāyāna Buddhism ;[88] but the fact that the Buddhistic tenth stage, *dharmamegha,* turns up without context in the *Yoga-Sūtra*[89] shows that the Yoga manual possibly knew also of these stages, perhaps in a vague and distorted way, and used only the last stage in its scheme of liberation. Similarly, the word *āvaraṇa* to indicate the veil which keeps the soul from its freedom is probably more technically used in Jainism and conveys a similar sense in the *Yoga-Sūtra* also ;[90] but the Jaina term *guṇasthāna(ka)* to indicate the stages of spiritual progress[91] corresponding to the *daśabhūmis* of Buddhism was not accepted. The moral discipline of the three systems is more or less uniform because the soul's impediments are identical, but the psychological analysis is different in each owing to the different philosophical presuppositions of the three systems. Still, it appears that Buddhism and Yoga move in a similar atmosphere of thought, possibly because both had a background of Sāṁkhya philosophy. The similarity becomes greater if the *vibhūtis* or magical powers are taken into consideration and also the objects and methods of meditation ; but as these are partly extra-psychological, we need not bring out the similarity by detailed comparison. Both believed in a complete transcendence of discursive reason and in the attainment of a state of cognition to which empirical mind could lay no claim.

What happens to the soul after the *kuśala* condition cannot, from the nature of the case, be described, for the conditions of empirical knowledge all disappear then and the self regains its proper nature. Although described as witness (*sākṣin*), seer (*draṣṭṛ*), and knower (*jñātṛ*) of states, the transcendental self is really known only indirectly by a kind of implication so long as the condition of empirical knowledge persists.[92] Nature has evolved to ensnare and liberate the self ;[93] the progressive knowledge of the divergence of Nature and spirit is owned by the self with the help of *buddhi*. But all vicissitudes of knowledge, feeling, and conation leave

[87] *Vyāsabh.* on *Y. S.,* II. 27.
[88] For which see Suzuki, *Out. of Mahā. Bud.,* p. 313 f.
[89] *Y. S.,* IV. 29.
[90] Mrs. Sinclair Stevenson, *The Heart of Jainism,* pp. 132-3.
[91] For which see *Ibid.,* p. 185 f.
[92] *Y. S.,* II. 20.
[93] *Y. S.,* II. 18.

the sense of self unaffected; as the impurities fall off, the realm of the knowable begins to shrink without affecting the sense of the knower. All these imply that there is a self behind the states; but as the states are inessential to its existence, inasmuch as they might be suppressed altogether, the self must be construed as a spiritual essence which is experience itself without the attributes and limitations of empirical personality. Language was not devised to indicate this spiritual condition—hence the mystery of the self's nature remains ever unsolved to those who are in the empirical plane. All that we are permitted to know is that in that condition the fluctuations of consciousness are at an end, the sorrows of life have all disappeared, the residues of the moral life (good or bad) have all been burnt up so far as future embodiment is concerned. The Yoga system did not acknowledge the possibility of knowing that one more life remained to work off the fruits of action, as Buddhism did in its doctrine of the once-returner (*sakṛdāgāmin*); for it denied that after the saving knowledge had dawned there was any chance of rebirth, though in its doctrine of sevenfold insight it did admit a knowledge of the dissolution of the material conditions of the bound soul. Buddhism itself acknowledged that such knowledge was transcendental (*lokuttara*) and was higher than that experienced in the *kāmaloka,* the *rūpaloka,* and the *arūpaloka,* but it also held that the consciousness of the never-returning and that of the *arhat* were higher in the scale than the consciousness of the once-returning.[94]

### OBSTACLES TO CONCENTRATION

We may now leave these transcendental states aside and turn to the more immediately useful materials furnished in the *Yoga-Sūtra* to bring about the complete cessation of mental states. A careful analysis was made of the impediments to concentrated thinking and moral earnestness, and practical steps to overcome them were laid down. As is natural, the obstructions to meditation come in for fuller treatment than the aids and, even in the list of accessories, inhibitions figure quite prominently. It may be presumed that the Yoga as well as Buddhism knew of the usual methods of facilitating concentration by choosing the right time, place, and circumstances. The *Śvetāśvatara Upaniṣad,* the *Maitrāyaṇi Upaniṣad,* and the *Kaṭha Upaniṣad* (and the *Bhagavad-Gītā*) show Sāṁkhya-Yoga leanings in a systematic way;[95] but some of the characteristic *yoga* practices can be traced back to much earlier literature and the psychological processes

[94] See B. C. Law, *Designation of Human Types* (*Puggala-Paññatti*), pp. 26-27; Aung and Mrs. Rhys Davids, *Comp. of Ph.*, pp. 88-91.

[95] See Deussen, *Ph. of the Up.*, p. 246 f., 382 f.; also Ranade, *op. cit.*, pp. 182-90.

involved in contemplation and concentration were quite familiar phenomena before the *Yoga-Sūtra* systematized them.[96]

The obstacles to concentration were classified under different heads:[97]

(*a*) Sickness

It was laid down that the humours of the body, the secretions and the sense-organs were to be kept in proper order before *yoga* could be satisfactorily practised. In later Yoga works, like the *Haṭhayoga-pradīpikā,* it was mentioned in fact that *yoga* itself kept the body in a healthy condition.[98] Various indications about the progress of the mind towards *yoga* were found in the proper functioning of the different systems of the body. In the Haṭha-yoga minute prescriptions about ridding the body of all impurities were laid down[99] and the results attained were heightened sensibility, increased control over the activities of the body (including levitation, immersion in solids, walking on fluids, etc.),[100] and even the power of voluntary death. Continence and restraint of various kinds were as much in the interest of the body as of the mind and were accordingly prescribed. Over-indulgence and improper diet were tabooed for the same reason and fasting and austerities, in so far as they did not endanger life, were recommended.[101] When *yoga* is established the powers of clairvoyance, clairaudience, etc. are obtained, and also the knowledge of past, distant, and future things.[102] In one word, the absence of bodily infirmity would include the disappearance of all those impediments that limit the operations of the mind in time and space on account of bodily defects, diseases, and decays. Concentration cannot thrive when the body refuses to act as a pliant tool in the hands of the *yogin* and sets up organic disturbances. How, for instance, is a *yogin* to assume a fixed seat or posture when he is restless with fever, or fix his mind when he is in a delirious condition?

(*b*) Listlessness ; idleness ; languor

Closely related to infirmity is the heaviness of the body due to the preponderance of phlegm, or of the mind-stuff on account of the preponderance of the *tamas* element. When the mind is *unwilling* to stir, it is a case of idleness ; when it is *unable* to stir, it is a case of languor (*styāna*).[103]

[96] See Dasgupta, *Yoga Ph.,* p. 42 f. *Yoga* magical practice is mostly associated with the *Atharva-Veda* and in a minor fashion with the *Yajur-Veda.* See Keith, *The Religion and Philosophy of the Veda and Upanishads,* pp. 56, 81 (f.n.3), 492 (f.n.4); also Dasgupta, *Hindu Mysticism,* Lectures I and III.

[97] *Y. S.,* I. 30. Cf: *Tejobindu U.,* I; *Yogatattva U.*

[98] *Haṭhayoga-pradīpikā,* II. 20, 78 (Panini Office Edition).

[99] *Ibid.,* II. 22 f.

[100] *Y. S.,* III. 39, 42, 45.

[101] *Y. S.,* I. 60-65.

[102] *Y. S.,* II. 39; III. 16, 18, 25, 41.

[103] *Vyāsabh.* on *Y. S.,* I. 30.

So it is not enough to possess the capacity of concentration—one must actually will to exercise that capacity. A *yogin* may fail for lack of drive just as he may fail for lack of energy.

(*c*) Doubt ; heedlessness

It is not enough to possess the will and the energy to achieve concentration: one must also hold fast to a single object and persevere in the attempt to grasp it completely. The lack of definiteness gives us doubt (*saṁśaya*), where the mind is assailed with alternative thoughts and the necessary faith in the sole efficacy of the ideate is absent. Heedlessness (*pramāda*) is a lack of reflection upon the means of attaining concentration:[104] here there is no doubt about the object of knowledge, but steps are not taken to bring about the concentration by the adoption of appropriate means.

(*d*) Failure and instability in attention

It was found, however, that in spite of their willingness and application some could not attain a particular level of concentration. These could not make any progress in their spiritual quest. The explanation of this type of distraction is not forthcoming in the *Yoga-Sūtra,* but possibly it is due to congenital impediments or subconscious opposition. In its comprehensive scheme the Yoga system repeatedly draws attention to the necessity of taking the residues of our past thoughts and actions into consideration, and we may very well suppose that the past takes its vengeance on the present by obstructing progress.

It may so happen, however, that a position is won with effort, but very soon it is lost again. It is not enough to secure an advance—it is necessary to retain it also. In spiritual matters, not to advance is to recede ; and so effort is necessary to maintain positions by trying to go beyond them. The tendency to slide back to an inferior position, which does not require much effort to retain it, is a danger which always besets the path of the spiritual aspirant. Hence continual effort is needed to keep up one's attainments in the spiritual domain. A *yogin* should never be satisfied with anything less than total suppression of the modifications of the mind-stuff, or even the intermediate stages attained would slip out of his grasp.

(*e*) Worldliness ; erroneous perception

One of the gravest impediments is moral defect in the shape of greed or addiction to objects of sense. If the purpose of *yoga* is to draw the mind away in the interest of the spirit from thoughts and impulses leading to the recognition of the material world, it is obvious that excessive

[104] *Vyāsabh.* on *Y. S.,* I. 30.

fondness for the world of sensibility would obstruct the effort to detach oneself from empirical thinking. The *yogin* must therefore cultivate not only a habit of thought but also a habit of action conducive to the attainment of the maximum spiritual height. He must control his feelings as well as his thoughts and actions. So long as the desire to enjoy persists, no amount of intellectual effort to fix the mind on higher things would succeed ; and as *vairāgya* or dispassion will not thrive under such a condition of worldly attachment, the suppression of the mental states would not be brought about.

Hence the root-cause of all distraction must be eradicated by cultivating true knowledge and abolishing all false or illusory knowledge. Without an adequate knowledge of the principles of reality and the distinction between self and not-self, all effort to get rid of mental fluctuations would be futile. Hence we come back to the old position that at the root of all distraction stands man's imperfect knowledge, and so the removal of distraction and the removal of ignorance are one and the same problem. Many have failed to obtain salvation because they mistook the acquisition of certain powers or the appearance of certain agreeable mental conditions as the attainment of *samādhi*. Many have also been tempted to deviate from the main purpose of attaining isolation by their quest of magical powers (*vibhūtis*) ; and many have transferred their attention from the end to the means, as for example when the *haṭhayogins* of later times perfected the technique of bodily control, they desisted from the attempt to know themselves. The *Yoga-Sūtra* warns the learner to beware of these pitfalls and to forge ahead with the proper objective without being distracted by irrelevant considerations.[105]

In addition to the nine distractions mentioned above, namely, sickness, languor, doubt, heedlessness, listlessness, worldliness, erroneous perception, failure to attain a particular stage of concentration, and inability to keep it when attained, the *Yoga-Sūtra* refers to certain other obstacles to concentration. These are (a) pain proceeding from the mind itself, the external world, and the gods, (b) despondency owing to the non-fulfilment of desires (the passions being included within pain), (c) unsteadiness of the body, and (d) breathing (inspiration and expiration).[106] They accompany the distractions proper and disappear when the mind-stuff is concentrated. It is obvious that the *Yoga-Sūtra* itself initiated that inquiry into the bodily conditions of attention which attained some amount of scientific

[105] See, for instance, *Haṭhayogapr.*, IV. 97, where the happiness of Rāja-yoga is preferred to *mukti*.

[106] *Y. S.*, I. 31.

precision in later Yoga literature. We have here the rudiments of physiological psychology of which traces are to be found in the Upaniṣads also.[107]

### THE AIDS TO CONCENTRATION

Now each kind of distraction is to be met by an antidote of its own, though it is not unlikely that the distractions and their remedies are mutually related among themselves. The *yogāṅgas* (helps to *yoga*) represent the method of getting rid of the distempers of the soul in a progressive fashion. Thus, if bodily infirmity, unsteadiness of the limbs, and breathing upset the mind and render concentration difficult or impossible, these must be controlled and eradicated. Cleanliness (*śauca*) of the body, as of the mind, is therefore necessary for concentration.[108] Then again, the *yogin* must learn to control his limbs—he must try to sit straight like the trunk of a tree (*sthāṇu*), with the spine, the neck, and the head in one line, and assume certain postures (*āsana*) that are favourable to concentration.[109] The *Yoga-Sūtra* knows nothing of the later prescriptions about *mudrā* (pose of fingers, hands or body) or its Tāntric use (as in the *Dhyānabindu Upaniṣad,* for instance) and *nyāsa* (touching the various parts of the body) which came in the wake of Tāntricism and theism. The *nyāsa* in which the different muscles of the body are brought into exercise by rotation looks almost like a physical drill ; but the idea that the whole body becomes suffused with divine energy and the devotee becomes one with his god[110] saves it from degeneration into a mere physical exercise and invests it with a deep spiritual significance. The *mudrās,* however, cannot be so easily spiritualized and were probably imitative gestures or magical symbols in their original forms and were later on invested with esoteric meaning. The *Yoga-Sūtra* which believed in immobility could not consistently advocate the use of these modes of moving the body as they would disturb the attention. For the same reason it could not recommend the practice of the eighty-four *āsanas* of Haṭha-yoga, for many of these would have contravened the Yoga ideal of *āsana* as steady and easy in character.[111] Nevertheless, the *Vyāsabhāṣya* mentions a few, showing that many of the forms were well known and modelled on the postures of different types of

[107] *Vyāsabh.* on *Y. S.,* II. 32.
[108] See *B.G.,* VI. 13.
[109] See Nalini Kanta Brahma, *Philosophy of Hindu Sādhanā,* p. 320.
[110] For *mudrās* see *Gheraṇḍa Saṁhitā,* Lesson II; *Haṭhayogapr.,* III. Mantra-yoga consists in reciting *mantras* in honour of different deities along with touching different parts of the body where they are supposed to be located for the time being.
[111] *Y. S.,* II. 46. See *Gher. Saṁ.,* Lesson II; *Haṭhayogapr.,* I. 19 f. As contrasted with Haṭha-yoga the *yoga* taught in the *Yoga-Sūtra* is called Rāja-yoga, though Bahiraṅga-yoga or *yoga* with external or bodily aids like *āsana* and *prāṇāyāma* anticipates Haṭha-yoga practices.
[112] *Vyāsabh.* and *Tattvavaiśāradī* on *Y. S.,* II. 46. See in this connection *Triśikhibrāhmaṇa U.* for a description of some of the important *āsanas.*

animals.[112] The *Yoga-Sūtra,* however, recommends the practice of controlled breathing (*prāṇāyāma*) with the ultimate object of suspending it for as long a period as possible.[113] The breathing, both in and out, should affect as small an area as possible; its frequency should be diminished; and its duration should be expanded. In this way the body will breathe as few a number of times as possible and in a progressively shallower manner till it is able to hold the breath for a fairly long period without any risk of asphyxiation.[114] That the autonomic system could be controlled through the slender connection with the nervous system was a great discovery of the Yoga system[115] and it still retains its title to the sole possession of the technique to bring that about.

The Tāntric system developed at the same time a method of controlling the different plexuses (*ṣaṭcakra*)[116] and indulged in physiological speculations suited to the purpose; but the *Yoga-Sūtra* limited itself almost entirely to the practice of breathing without, however, elaborating the system of nerves (*nāḍi*) to any great extent, and laid down the suspension of breath as the objective of all spiritual aspirants. The idea that controlled breathing cleanses the system and that the elements of the body are thereby rid of all impurities (*bhūtaśuddhi*) came later;[117] originally breath was controlled because it disturbed the attention and because the control of breath not only made the mind attentive but also scoured away the *karma* that veiled discriminative knowledge.[118] Still, even in the *Yoga-Sūtra* an exaggerated importance given to breath-control for purposes of concentration and ultimate salvation is noticeable.[119] This may be reminiscent of the Upaniṣadic view that man is continually offering sacrifice to the gods through breathing (called *Pratardana* sacrifice after King Pratardana, who taught this doctrine)[120] and that all the scriptures were breathed out by the Absolute Being:[121] in fact, in later literature we are told that when inhaling, a man makes the sound *saḥ,* and when exhaling he emits the sound *haṁ,* and in this way he is unwittingly repeating the formula (*ajapā japa*) that the Jīvātman is identical with the

[113] *Y. S.,* II. 50. For *prāṇāyāma* see *Gher. Saṁ.,* V. For a similar Buddhistic belief, see Warren, *Bud. in Trans.,* pp. 354-6.

[114] *Y. S.,* II. 51. See also Warren, *loc. cit.;* also Dasgupta, *Yoga as Ph. & Rel.,* pp. 146-7.

[115] See Lickley, *The Nervous System,* pp. 30-31.

[116] See N. K. Brahma, *op. cit.,* pp. 289-90; A. Avalon, *Tantra of the Great Liberation* (*Mahānirvāṇa Tantra*), pp. lvii f.; *Dhyānabindu U.; Śiva Saṁhitā,* V. 56-131.

[117] N. K. Brahma, *op. cit.,* pp. 319-20. See *Darśanopaniṣad,* Secs. V and VI in this connection.

[118] *Y. S.,* II. 52. See *Chā. U.,* I. 3. 5.

[119] *Y. S.,* II. 52, 53. The *Brahmavidyā U.* goes to the length of calling the last five *yogāṅgas prāṇāyāmas.*

[120] *Kauṣītaki U.,* II. 5. This is the *Ajapā-haṁsa-vidyā* of *Dhyānabindu U., Haṁsa-vidyā* of *Brahmavidyā U.* and *Haṁsa U.*

[121] *Bṛ. U.,* II. 4. 10; *Maitri U.,* VI. 32.

Paramātman (*so'haṁ* or *haṁsaḥ*) without intermission.[122] That the regulation of breath had a therapeutic effect on the bodily system and increased the beauty and longevity of the person practising it was not the primary motive of *prāṇāyāma* in the *Yoga-Sūtra,* though perfection of body (*kāyasampad*), including beauty, grace, power, and compactness as of the thunderbolt, was regarded there also as a supernormal power (*vibhūti*) acquired by the *yogin* in the course of his progress towards concentration.[123] It is interesting to note that austerities (*tapas*) play a very small part in the *Yoga-Sūtra,* though they are regarded as a form of *yoga* (Kriyā-yoga)[124] and form one of the five observances (*niyama*);[125] this is an index of the attitude towards mortification of the flesh practised much more widely at an earlier time. Similarly, the Vedic sacrifice (*yajña*) practically disappears as a mode of spiritual progress, though the *Bhagavad-Gītā* admitted its utility even when it depreciated its value.[126] It is likely that the Yoga shared with the Sāṁkhya an abhorrence of sacrificial cruelty and readily adopted the Buddhistic and Jaina prescription of non-injury (*ahiṁsā*) as the cardinal tenet of spiritual emancipation.[127] Besides, after castigating bodily movement as an impediment to concentration, it could not logically back the Vedic mode of attaining liberation through sacrifice as it involved a lot of manipulation and movement. On the other hand, the Upaniṣadic formula of *Om* as the mystic syllable *par excellence* proved attractive because its monotonous repetition had the effect of bringing about concentration, if not stoppage, of thought; so it was made the subject of meditation and was also regarded as the most natural expression for Īśvara (God).[128] Like James, the *Yoga-Sūtra* discovered that the most intimate nature of the attentive process was the control of the body and that attention was more a function than a producer of bodily adjustment.[129]

But mere bodily control is not enough to bring about the cessation of the mental process. The senses are assailing the soul through the operations of the *buddhi,* and unless the mind withdraws from the senses or unless the senses are otherwise rendered inoperative, the disturbance to the soul will continue. Hence the practice of withdrawal (*pratyāhāra*) of

[122] *Gher. Saṁ.,* V. 84 (this is called *kevalakumbhaka*); see also *Haṭhayogapr.,* II. 72-4. See in this connection *Pāśupata-Brahmopaniṣad.*

[123] *Y. S.,* III. 46; also *Tattvavaiśāradī* on *Y. S.,* III. 37. See *Haṭhayogapr.,* II. 78. See *Yoga-cūḍāmaṇi U.* in this connection.

[124] *Y. S.,* II. 1. For Kriyā-yoga, see Dasgupta, *Yoga as Ph. & Rel.,* p. 142 f.

[125] *Y. S.,* II. 32.

[126] *B. G.,* IV. 33; XI. 48. See in this connection *Śiva Saṁhitā,* V. 2-5.

[127] *Y. S.,* II. 30, 31. See *Dīgha Nikāya, Kūṭadanta Suttanta* (*Sacred Books of the Buddhists,* II. pp. 160-85).

[128] *Y. S.,* I. 27. Cf. *Amṛta-nādopaniṣad* for the use of *Om* in meditation; also *Amṛta-bindūpaniṣad, Dhyānabindu U., Nādabindu U., Brahmavidyā U., Yogacūḍāmaṇi U.*

[129] James, *Principles of Psychology,* I. p. 435.

the senses must be resorted to.[130] The Yoga system does not recommend the plucking out of any sense, if that were possible, nor does it advise mutilation of any organ of knowledge or action ; for unless the thoughts are controlled, the mere disappearance of any sense-organ will not smooth the path to salvation. When the organs of sense cease to connect themselves with their proper objects, they imitate the mind-stuff itself which is not in direct contact with the objects and is naturally undifferentiated in respect of its contents.[131] There was some difference of opinion, it seems, about the exact meaning of the term 'mastery of the organs', but all agreed that complete mastery was synonymous with singleness of intent followed by loss of interest in objects of sense, whether this itself was or was not followed by the disappearance of the panorama of the external world.[132] In fact, insight and detachment are synonymous so far as objects of sense are concerned, and the whole yogic prescription can be put in the formula *'Contemplate, concentrate, conquer'*. In the second and third books of the *Yoga-Sūtra* we are told of the various powers (*vibhūtis*) that are acquired by concentrating on this or that object. While to the novice these powers prove intoxicating and he revels in their practice, the adept is advised to treat them as mere signs of the development of the spirit and to pass on to the stage of conquest of the organs of sense. It is not enough to know the things of the world in all space and time or to acquire the various perfections (*siddhis*) that enable one to dominate the objects as one pleases.[133] It is necessary to transcend that stage altogether and to realize the essential non-spiritual character of the world of matter. This is achieved by loss of interest in worldly things consequent on the mastery of the senses. The mutability of mind is most dependent on the presentations, and restriction of these is the first step towards realizing the cessation of the mental states. Representations depend on presentations, and presentations depend upon the interests of life. Ultimately therefore knowledge becomes a moral problem, for people know in order to act in the world for purposes of self-aggrandizement and enjoyment.

How then is interest in the world to be abated? Here we come upon the formula which is common to Hinduism, Buddhism, and Jainism—in fact, to all philosophies that condemn worldly pursuits without any excep-

[130] *Y. S.*, II. 54. See Mrs. Rhys Davids, *Bud. Psy.*, pp. 82-3, for similar Buddhistic preaching.

[131] *Y. S.*, II. 54.

[132] *Vyāsabh.* on *Y. S.*, II. 55.

[133] *Y. S.*, II. 39; III. 18, 25-9, 41-2, 45. These are called *abhijñās* or psychic faculties in Buddhistic literature (Suzuki, *St. in the Laṅk. Sūtra*, p. 383). Cf. *Ākaṅkheyya-Sutta* of the *Majjhima Nikāya* (see Warren, *op. cit.*, p. 303) and *Sāmañña-phala-Sutta* of the *Dīgha Nikāya* (*Sacred Books of the Buddhists*, II. pp. 88-89). See Aung and Mrs. Rhys Davids, *Comp. of Ph.*, p. 63; also Mrs. Rhys Davids, *Sākya or Buddhist Origins* for *iddhis* and *abhijñās*. See also *Yogaśikhā U.* for the *siddhis*.

tion. It is to concentrate on the abominable aspects of the attractive things of the world. Here, for instance, is a specimen from Buddhism[134] about the type of thought that one ought to indulge in if one wishes to avoid being attracted by physical beauty:

'For as the body when dead is repulsive, so is it also when alive; but on account of the concealment afforded by an adventitious adornment, its repulsiveness escapes notice. The body is in reality a collection of over three hundred bones, and is framed into a whole by means of one hundred and eighty joints. It is held together by nine hundred tendons, and overlaid by nine hundred muscles, and has an outside envelope of moist cuticle covered by an epidermis full of pores, through which there is an incessant oozing and trickling, as if from a kettle of fat. It is a prey to vermin, the seat of disease, and subject to all manner of miseries. Through its nine apertures it is always discharging matter, like a ripe boil. Matter is secreted from the two eyes, wax from the ears, snot from the nostrils, and from the mouth issue food, bile, phlegm, and blood; and from the two lower orifices of the body faeces and urine, while from the ninety-nine thousand pores of the skin an unclean sweat exudes attracting black flies and other insects.'

'Accordingly, it is on account of the concealment afforded by this adventitious adornment that people fail to recognize the essential repulsiveness of their bodies, and that men find pleasure in women, and women in men. In reality, however, there is not the smallest just reason for being pleased. A proof of this is the fact that when any part of the body becomes detached, as, for instance, the hair of the head, hair of the body, nails, teeth, phlegm, snot, faeces, or urine, people are unwilling so much as to touch it, and are distressed at, ashamed of, and loathe it. But in respect of what remains, though that is likewise repulsive, yet men are so wrapped in blindness and infatuated by a passionate fondness for their own selves, that they believe it to be something desirable, lovely, lasting, pleasant, and an Ego.'

Here is the same theme treated in earlier literature:[135]

'Just as if, O priests, there were a double-mouthed vessel full of various sorts of grain, to wit, śāli-rice, common paddy, beans, pulse,

[134] Warren, *Bud. in Trans.*, pp. 298-9; also p. 242, where occurs the following passage: 'When this body comes into existence, it does not arise in the midst of nymphaeas, nelumbiums, lotuses, and water-lilies, etc., nor of jewels, pearl-necklaces, etc.; but ill-smelling, disgusting, and repulsive, it arises between the stomach and the lower intestines, with the belly-wall behind and the backbone in front, in the midst of the entrails and mesentery, in an exceedingly contracted, ill-smelling, disgusting and repulsive place, like a worm in rotten fish, carrion, or rancid gruel, or in a stagnant or dirty pool or the like.' See also *Maitri U.*, I. 3; II. 4. (Deussen, *Ph. of the Up.*, pp. 284-85).

[135] See Warren, *op. cit.*, pp. 359-60.

sesame, and husked rice; and some intelligent man were to open it and consider its contents, saying, "This is śāli-rice, this is common paddy, these are beans, this is pulse, this is sesame, this is husked rice;" in exactly the same way, O priests, a priest considers this body upwards from the soles of the feet, and downwards from the crown of the head, enclosed by skin, and full of all manner of uncleanliness, saying, "There is in this body hair of the head, hair of the body, nails, teeth, skin, flesh, sinew, bone, marrow of the bones, kidneys, heart, liver, pleura, spleen, lungs, intestines, mesentery, stomach, faeces, bile, phlegm, pus, blood, sweat, fat, tears, lymph, saliva, snot, synovial fluid, urine." '

Let us continue the theme a little further in order to show the final attitude towards the things of sense.[136]

'Just as a man might have a wife beloved, delightful, and charming, from whom he could not bear to be separated for a moment, and on whom he excessively doted. If he then were to see that woman standing or sitting in company with another man, and talking and joking with him, he would be angry and displeased, and experience bitter grief. But if subsequently he were to discover that she had been guilty of a fault, he would lose all desire for her and let her go, and no longer look on her as "mine". From that time on, whenever he might see her engaged with any one else, he would not be angry or grieved, but simply indifferent and neutral. In exactly the same way the ascetic by grasping the constituents of being with the reflective insight becomes desirous of being released from them, and perceiving none of them worthy of being deemed "I" or "mine", he abandons all fear and joy in regard to them, and becomes indifferent and neutral. When he has learnt and perceived this, his mind draws in, contracts, and shrinks away from the three modes of existence, the four species of being, the five destinies in rebirth, the seven stages of consciousness, the nine grades of being, and does not spread out, and only indifference or disgust abides.'

The *Yoga-Sūtra* calls this thinking *pratipakṣabhāvanā* (thinking of the opposite) and advocates this method of weeding out one kind of disposition by cultivating the converse disposition through thought.[137] People will not lose interest in things or withdraw their gaze from them so long as they do not find the silliness and the unworthiness of the process of being attracted by objects of sense. It is only thus that attachment (*rāga*) can cease. Who would care to have connection with other bodies when

[136] Warren, *op. cit.*, pp. 376-77.

[137] *Y. S.*, II. 33, 34. The Buddhists call it *aśubhabhāvanā* (thinking of the evil side) and regard it as the negative supplement to the four positive contemplations of *maitrī* (friendliness), *karuṇā* (compassion), *muditā* (joy), and *upekṣā* (indifference), called *brahmavihārabhāvanā*.

he remembers with what difficulty and perpetual care his own body can be kept clean?

But this implies the power of keeping the mind fixed on one subject till a habit and a disposition grow up. The *Yoga-Sūtra* lays down a progressive scheme of fixation of attention in order to avoid distraction. Thus the mind could be fixed on any visible part of the body like the navel or the tip of the nose or of the tongue or, later, on some hidden constituent of it like the heart-lotus (*hṛdayapuṇḍarīka*) or the light within the head (*mūrdhajyotis*) after fixation on external objects has been practised.[138] The binding of the mind-stuff to one place in this way is called *dhāraṇā* (fixed attention)[139] and is intended to bring about a kind of auto-hypnotism without external suggestion. The effect of such concentration is a similarity of presentations (*ekatānatā*), and when this is achieved the mind is said to have attained *dhyāna* (contemplation)—a condition of mind which is characteristic in the meditation on divine nature.[140] When the knower almost loses himself in the object, the ultimate goal of the process of concentration is reached, namely, concentration (*samādhi*). The distinction of these three (*dhāraṇā, dhyāna,* and *samādhi*) is so small that the *Yoga-Sūtra* calls the three together constraint (*saṁyama*)[141] and lays down that in proportion as constraint becomes stable, concentrated insight (*samādhiprajñā*) becomes clear.[142] These three represent the direct aids to conscious concentration (*samprajnata samadhi*)[143] as compared with the other five aids, namely, *yama* (to be presently explained), *niyama, āsana, prāṇāyāma,* and *pratyāhāra,* which may therefore be called indirect aids. But even they are only indirect aids to super-conscious or seedless concentration (*asamprajñāta* or *nirbīja samādhi*), for, according to *Vyāsa-bhāṣya,* this can be brought about by other means also ; and these other means, according to Vācaspati, include contemplation of God.[144]

### THE CARDINAL VIRTUES AND THE SUBLIME MEDITATIONS

Before we consider that final condition of the mind, let us turn for a moment to the practical conditions of withdrawing one's self from all

[138] *Vyāsabh.* (and Nāgoji Bhaṭṭa) on *Y. S.,* III. 1.
[139] *Y. S.,* III. 1.
[140] *Y. S.,* III. 2; see also Vācaspati on *Y. S.,* III. 1. For *samādhi,* see *Y. S.,* III. 3.
[141] *Y. S.,* III. 4.
[142] See *Vyāsabh.* on *Y. S.,* III. 5.
[143] *Y. S.,* III. 7.
[144] Vācaspati on *Y. S.,* III. 8; also *Y. S.,* II. 45. For the relation between *Īśvarapraṇidhāna* and the *yogāṅgas,* see Dasgupta, *Yoga as Ph. & Rel.,* p. 145.
The classical number 'eight' of *yogāṅgas* was varied in some of the later Upaniṣads, e.g. *Tejobindu U.* mentions fifteen, *Amṛtanāda U.* five, *Dhyānabindu U.* six, etc. Vedāntic and theistic influences also began to make their appearance. For elaborate descriptions of the *yogāṅgas* according to later speculations, see *Triśikhibrāhmaṇa U., Dhyānabindu U.,* and specially *Śāṇḍilya U.*

activities that increase the range of thought. The *Yoga-Sūtra* agrees with Buddhism and Jainism that men's minds are constantly swayed by thoughts of expanding the self at the cost of others. Thoughts of injury, deceit, unlawful gain, sex, and greed toss the soul from object to object and keep up the stream of thought and activity. It is very necessary for the *yogin* to control these wild propensities of the mind by cultivating habits of non-injury (*ahiṁsā*), truthfulness (*satya*), non-stealing (*asteya*), continence (*brahmacarya*), and non-acceptance of gifts (*aparigraha*),[145] as also contentment (*santoṣa*).[146] The first five make up the abstentions (*yama*) while the last falls under observances (*niyama*). So long as mental control does not include these in their widest denotation, the mind is sure to go after the things of the world and to pile up the fruits of unholy action. Hence the sage must cultivate the habit of putting himself in the position of his intended victims and in this way get rid of unsocial, perverse, and immoral thoughts. As an example, we are told to rejoice at the happiness of others (*maitrī*), to pity those in distress (*karuṇā*), to take delight at the virtuous deeds of our fellowmen (*muditā*), and to practise indifference towards the vicious (*upekṣā*):[147] it is only thus that one can get rid of jealousy at the material and spiritual advancement of others, hatred and anger towards sinners, and indifference towards the poor. The main object of all mental discipline is to uproot all dispositions that have a tendency to sprout into overt thoughts and aspirations. If we could establish a sufficient amount of disposition towards restriction of mental states, the mass of disposition towards emergence of states tends to dissolve and the mental states become gradually restrained with the development of the power of restriction.[148] But the *Yoga-Sūtra* takes care to point out that a good disposition is as bad as a bad disposition in so far as the ultimate object of Yoga is concerned; for dispositions form a kind of residual mental existence, and the purpose of Yoga is to get rid of mental existence altogether.[149] When presentations and dispositions lose their difference, when the past, the present, and the future are not distinguished, when the intensity of mental states does not vary and qualitative changes disappear altogether from consciousness, then and then only can the *yogin* be said to have almost attained his object. Singleness of intent (*ekāgratā*) is the nearest approximation to this condition; so the cultivation of a

[145] *Y. S.*, II. 30. In the Buddhistic list abstention from alcoholic drink takes the place of *aparigraha*. See *Saṅgīti Suttanta* in *Dīgha Nikāya* (*Sacred Books of the Buddhists*, IV. p. 225).

[146] *Y. S.*, II. 32, 40.

[147] *Y. S.*, I. 33. See Mrs. Rhys Davids, *Bud. Man. of Psy. Eth.*, p. 65 f.; *Bud. Psy.*, p. 95. These constitute the four meditations of the sublime abodes (or states)—*brahmavihārabhāvanāni*, or the four 'infinitudes' (see *Sacred Books of the Buddhists*, IV. p. 216).

[148] *Y. S.*, III. 9. See Dasgupta, *Yoga as Ph. & Rel.*, pp. 155-56.

[149] *Y. S.*, I. 51; III. 50; IV. 34.

disposition of monoideism is essential for the destruction of that tendency towards dispersiveness which makes for mental flow and spiritual bondage.[150]

## THE PLACE OF GOD IN YOGA

The Yoga proceeds on the liberal principle that different natures can achieve their object by concentrating on different things. The theistic bent is brought out by the admission that one of the quickest ways of getting rid of obstructions is to fix the mind on God, for men become Godlike in freedom from defilement (*udayavyaya*), hindrance (*kleśa*), multiplicity (*dharmādharma*), and accidents (*jātyāyurbhoga*) when they become devoted to Him.[151] It is true that God is introduced in a rather irrelevant way in the first book of the *Yoga-Sūtra* and the continuity of the discourse would not be affected if *sūtras* 23 to 29 were omitted altogether. It is perhaps also true that by calling devotion to God a *yoga* of action (Kriyā-yoga) a lower plane was assigned to it in relation to the *yoga* of knowledge (Jñāna-yoga)—a position understandable by reference to the Sāṁkhya system in which knowledge is accepted as the only method of salvation. It is also true that this devotion appears only as one of the observances (*niyama*) along with cleanliness, contentment, austerities, and study. But it is not improbable that the rise of the theistic religions of Śaivism and Vaiṣṇavism some time before the Christian era made it almost obligatory to accord a place to devotion in the Yoga scheme; and if we believe that the *Yoga-Sūtra* underwent revision at theistic hands, we can understand why devotion to God should be regarded as being able to bring about unaided the highest kind of *samādhi* and also why the study of sacred literature should produce communion with the chosen deity.[152] It should be made clear, however, that the Yoga system had no intention to preach identification with and dissolution in God (or Brahman) as the ultimate condition of the finite soul, for, as Mādhavācārya points out, that being the express purpose of the Mīmāṁsā (Vedānta) system, the Yoga system would then be simply doing over again the same task.[153] Even when God is meditated upon, the

[150] *Y. S.*, III. 11.

[151] *Vyāsabh.* and *Tattvavaiśāradī* on *Y. S.*, I. 29. The word *Īśvarapraṇidhāna* occurs four times in the *Yoga-Sūtra,* namely, in I. 23, II. 1, II. 32, and II. 45. Dasgupta thinks that the meaning of the word is not uniform in the *Yoga-Sūtra,* for whereas in I. 23 it stands for 'love, homage and adoration of God', in later portions it means 'bestowal of all our actions upon God'.—See Dasgupta, *Yoga as Ph. & Rel.*, pp. 142-3, also p. 161.

[152] *Y. S.*, I. 44. See *Bhojavṛtti* on *Y. S.*, I. 23. Sectarian gods make their appearance in later Yoga Upaniṣads like *Yogaśikhā U.*

[153] *Sarva-darśana-saṅgraha* (Abhyankara's Ed.), pp. 346-47. Later Yoga Upaniṣads had Vedāntic leanings, e.g. *Tejobindu U.*, IV, VI; *Yogaśikhā U.*, LV; *Varāha U.*, II.

The following quotation from the *Laṅkāvatāra-Sūtra* is interesting: 'By tranquillity is meant oneness, and oneness gives birth to the highest Samādhi, which is gained by entering into the womb of the Tathāgatahood, which is the realm of supreme wisdom realized in one's inmost self.'—See Suzuki, *St. in the Laṅk. Sūtra,* p. 85; also pp. 121 and 201. On page 148 occurs this passage which is also interesting: 'Srotāpatti-phala, Sakṛdāgāmi-phala, Anāgāmi-

ultimate purpose is to stop the flow of mind in its conscious and subliminal aspects and to bring about the cessation of the modifications of the thinking principle. This alone explains why the Yoga manual can be, and has been, used even by those who do not believe in the reality of God.

The Yoga can therefore be best described as a manual of psychological ethics, to use the words of Mrs. Rhys Davids, intended for developing the powers of the mind with the ultimate object of seeing through the futility of exercising them in spiritual interests. Once it is recognized that the soul is different from matter in all its forms, unconscious and pseudo-psychical, there will be no inclination to attend to the objects of Nature or to indulge in any kind of thinking, feeling, or action. The soul is above all opposite modes of awareness (*dvandvātīta*) and relativity of subject and object. It is non-modifiable (*apariṇāmin*) and in it thinking and being coincide.[154]

### LATER DEGENERATIONS

The Yoga admitted, however, that Nature could be dominated by the sage before being annulled. The risk was not foreseen that the search after powers (*vibhūtis* and *ṛddhis*) would prove a snare or that the means of bringing about concentration would usurp the righful place of the end to be achieved. The newly discovered power proved intoxicating at the end and the various processes of posture (*āsana*), gesture (*mudrā* and *nyāsa*), and breathing (*prāṇāyāma*) were practised for the sake of acquiring powers over the body and also with a view to controlling the forces of Nature or transgressing her laws. In Buddhistic literature the exercise of such powers was prohibited;[155] but even there miracles abound and moving through space is not infrequent.[156] The many stories about the performance of miracles even by petty saints, to be found in sectarian religious literature all over the world, confirms the suspicion that spiritual power is seldom understood in terms of illumination and ethicality alone. While the

phala, and Arhattva—they are all perturbed states of mind. Sometimes I speak of the Triple Vehicle, sometimes of the One Vehicle, and sometimes of No Vehicle; all these distinctions are meant for the ignorant, for men of inferior wisdom, or even for the noble-minded. As to the entering into the ultimate truth (*paramārtha*), it goes beyond dualism. When one is abiding where there are no images (*nirābhāsa*), how could the Triple Vehicle be established? All kinds of Dhyāna, Apramāṇa, Arūpya, Samādhi, and the Extinction of Thoughts—they do not exist where there is Mind itself (*cittamātra*).'

[154] Dasgupta, *Yoga as Ph. & Rel.*, pp. 148-9, 152, 155, 163.

[155] For the ten *iddhis* in Buddhism, see Aung and Rhys Davids, *Comp. of Ph.*, p. 61; also Warren, *op. cit.*, 303 f. See also *Sāmañña-phala Sutta, Kevaddha Sutta* and many other places in the *Nikāyas*. The performance of magical feats was prohibited in Buddhism and Buddha refused to perform magical feats to win disciples.—See *Pāṭika Suttanta* (*Sacred Books of the Buddhists*, IV. p. 8); also *Brahmajāla Sutta*.

[156] The miracle at Śrāvasti and the ascent to Tuṣita Heaven are the most notable superhuman feats; but there are many other magical wonders performed by Buddha and his disciples. See, for instance, *Pāṭika Suttanta*.

*Yoga-Sūtra* thought that powers were incidentally acquired by a *yogin,* the popular mind demanded that they should be deliberately gained. It is time to remember once more that the object of Yoga psychology was to teach the way to self-knowledge and that to this everything else—including devotion to God—was subsidiary. For the same reason devotion to the teacher did not develop into the *guru*-cult of later esoteric religions and yogic practices.

The Yoga system of achieving salvation is a bold man's creed; and although there is theistic reference in this system, the ultimate effect of all process of thinking does not differ very much from that in Buddhism and Jainism where the theistic implication is absent. The gods figure as colourless in this system as in the heterodox schools and they are shown as inferior to the sage in all these schools of thought.[157] The Yoga system, like Buddhism, insists on certain fundamental traits for achieving success in spiritual culture. These are *śraddhā,* faith in the efficacy of concentration, *vīrya,* increased effort or energy arising out of that belief, *smṛti,* mindfulness or capacity to call up the desired object before the mind repeatedly by that energy, *samādhi,* concentration of the mind on a single object with a view to stopping all dispersiveness, and, lastly, *prajñā,* insight into the nature of things by concentration.[158] This list, with various additions, is to be found in Buddhistic enumeration also and apparently comprised those factors which were regarded as indispensable for narrowing down thought to a single object.[159] They are not processes but faculties which the individual must possess in order to obtain discriminative knowledge.

Here our imperfect study of a great subject ends. It is our considered opinion that the Yoga psychology cannot be properly understood without constant reference to the much fuller analysis of Buddhism on which very probably the Yoga system largely drew. Within the Sāṁkhya framework the Yoga introduced the theism of orthodoxy on the one hand, and the psychological analysis of the heterodox systems, especially Buddhism, on the other. It is not unlikely, however, that Yoga, Jainism, and Buddhism, which move in an identical atmosphere of intense moral discipline and individualistic spiritual progress, had before them an earlier handy manual

[157] See the writer's article on 'The Polite Atheism of Indian Philosophy' in *The Dacca University Studies*, I. 11. pp. 206-8.

A distinction is drawn between Īśvara (Supreme Godhead) and *devāḥ* (male deities). The *yogin* takes the former as an optional object of meditation, but not the latter whom, in fact, he wants to excel in spirituality.

[158] *Y. S.*, I. 20. Dasgupta includes these, as also *abhyāsa* and *vairāgya,* within *yogāṅgas* (*Yoga as Ph. & Rel.*, p. 135).

[159] See Warren, *op. cit.*, p. 335; *Sacred Books of the Buddhists,* IV. pp. 228, 236; Mrs. Rhys Davids, *Bud. Psy. Eth.*, pp. 15-18; Aung and Mrs. Rhys Davids, *Comp. of Ph.*, pp. 176, 180.

or prototype upon which they all drew and which they elaborated in accordance with their respective philosophical positions and religious beliefs. This would partially explain the large fund of common ideas and even identical expressions that is to be found in these systems of thought.

# 5

## NYĀYA-VAIŚEṢIKA

### INTRODUCTORY

ALTHOUGH in the earliest stages of their inception the schools of Nyāya and Vaiśeṣika held independent positions both in epistemology and metaphysics, it was recognized from the very beginning that the two schools had very much in common and their differences were of minor importance. The later fusion of the Vaiśeṣika metaphysics with the Nyāya epistemology was not an arbitrary or unnatural attempt at a *rapprochement,* but was dictated by an inner logical necessity of giving a complete philosophy of realism, with the deficiencies of each being made good in a well-rounded synthesis. It should be clearly recognized that Gautama's *Nyāya-Sūtra,* even with the *Bhaṣya* of Vātsyāyana and the *Vārttika* of Uddyotakara and the *Tātparyaṭīkā* of Vācaspati Miśra, does not give as full and free a consideration of the metaphysical issues as is found in the Vaiśeṣika system. Though the professed objective of both the systems is to provide a clear-cut formula for the achievement of salvation or freedom from the limitations of personalized existence, and the entire philosophical enquiry is dominated by this ultimate motive, the detached study of philosophical problems on their own merits does not suffer from a lack of speculative interest ; and particularly in the course of its development the purely philosophical interest comes to occupy more and more an importance of overmastering magnitude, and we feel tempted to believe that the ultimate problem of salvation is forgotten or pushed into the background, at any rate for the time being, in the zeal of philosophical speculations. Of course, the question of salvation is a problem of paramount importance and constitutes the justification and ultimate *raison d'être* of philosophical enquiry. Philosophy in India has never been a mere speculative interest irrespective of its bearing on life. Perfection in knowledge was believed to culminate in perfection in life, although the conception of perfect life was not uniform or identical. It will not be a fair attitude to condemn the philosophical enquiries of India as unspeculative or unfree because the goal was of a practical nature. Philosophic conviction was the necessary correlate of practical perfection in the life of the soul, and knowledge of truth necessarily resulted in the true freedom of the aspiring soul. The goal loomed large on the philosophical horizon, but it was recognized that there was no short cut or easy walk-over to it. The full price had to be paid in the shape of unfaltering philosophic realization of the ultimate mysteries of existence achieved through a rigorous moral discipline ; and mere academic and intellectual satisfaction accruing from philosophical studies was considered to be of value only in so far as it was calculated to bring about the happy consummation.

In his very first aphorism Akṣapāda (Gautama) states that salvation is the *summum bonum* and the ultimate objective of a spiritual aspirant, and the achievement of this highest perfection and complete freedom is possible through a proper understanding of the real nature of sixteen topics, viz. (1) proofs or sources of authentic knowledge, (2) the objects of authentic knowledge, (3) doubt, (4) the end or objective, (5) example, (6) approved conclusions, (7) members of a syllogism, (8) corroborative reasoning, (9) determinative conviction, (10) discussion with a view to discovery of truth, (11) sophistical argument, (12) wrangling or purely destructive argumentation, (13) fallacies, (14) quibbles, (15) false analogical arguments, and (16) clinchers or points of defeat. It is not possible here to discuss the exact value of every one of these topics, which are discussed in all their bearings in the original work and further and further developed in the later exegetical literature which has centred round it. But it will be apparent from a bare specification of the names that, barring the first and second topics which cover the epistemological and metaphysical positions of the system, the remaining topics are possessed of a subsidiary value and by themselves have very little philosophical importance. The first topic refers to the approved sources or instruments of valid knowledge, which are subsequently specified to be of four distinct types, viz. perception, inference, comparison, and verbal testimony. The question of cognitive instruments and valid cognition has from the very beginning received an elaborate treatment, and the *Tattva-cintāmaṇi* of Gaṅgeśa, which forms the main foundation of Navya-Nyāya, is almost exclusively devoted to a consideration of this topic alone. The latter-day developments in Navya-Nyāya in Navadvīpa are accordingly of the nature of epistemological enquiries, and the interest in metaphysics is purely of a subsidiary character.

In fact, the metaphysical interests of Nyāya philosophy even in the *Sūtra* and *Bhāṣya* periods occupy only a subordinate place, and the main energies are directed to questions of practical importance, such as the proper guidance of philosophical debates. The problems of psychology, ethics, metaphysics, and epistemology are all discussed incidentally, and the purely logical and philosophical aspects are not sharply distinguished. Theoretical logic is pronouncedly under the domination of practical logic, and this gives us an idea of the development of pure philosophy from an inchoate beginning to the clear-cut logical divisions which took place much later. It is only in the *Tattva-cintāmaṇi,* the *magnum opus* of Gaṅgeśa, that we find that Nyāya philosophy has shaken off the incubus of extra-logical influence. But here the metaphysical problems are given scanty treatment, and the interests are mainly confined to pure logic and epistemology. In the lucubrations of the Navadvīpa school this tendency is further accentuated, and, practically speaking, the divorce of epistemology from metaphysics is found to be complete. Of course, in the later manuals of a syncretic character attempts have been made to effect a synthesis of metaphysics and epistemology, and the rapprochement of Nyāya and Vaiśeṣika is almost complete. From the very beginning it is pronouncedly felt that Vaiśeṣika categories are presupposed throughout by Akṣapāda, and the doctrine of the atomic structure of the material world is admitted *totidem verbis.*

Vātsyāyana speaks of the Vaiśeṣika categories in terms of approval and justifies the Nyāya enumeration of the objects of cognition (I.1.9) on the ground of their special relevancy to the achievement of salvation. The enumeration is said to be not an exhaustive statement of all the categories of being or thought, but only to relate to those objects the knowledge of which is essential to the achievement of absolute freedom and the ignorance of which perpetuates bondage. This very vindication shows the spirit and the attitude to purely philosophical problems, viz. that the interest is more practical than theoretical. The Vaiśeṣika philosophy on the other hand stands in a better position, being directed to a critical evaluation of the world of reality, both subjective and objective, though it is not less emphatic than the Nyāya in its professions to show the unerring way to salvation. It is therefore not at all a matter of regret that in the course of their development the Nyāya and Vaiśeṣika schools were welded into one system, and this only shows the growing clarity of logical vision and the courage of conviction of later philosophers, which enabled them to rise superior to false considerations of prestige and allegiance and to produce a well-rounded, compact, and consistent philosophy. The prestige and honour which Nyāya philosophy enjoys at the present day are entirely due to this happy synthesis of Vaiśeṣika metaphysics and Nyāya epistemology, which made this branch of philosophy fuller, richer, and more consistent. The Vaiśeṣika philosophy is poorer in its epistemological interest and is pre-eminently metaphysical, and, contrariwise, Nyāya is pronouncedly lacking in its metaphysical interests and its strength lies in its logical and epistemological contributions. A combination of the two was a logical necessity.

## A SURVEY OF ITS EPISTEMOLOGY

We now propose to give a running survey of the development of the epistemology of the Nyāya-Vaiśeṣika school. It cannot be expected that any justice can be done to the subject, dealt with here as a side issue, when volumes can be written on it. But a student of general philosophy will have some idea of the development of thought that took place in this school. It is unthinkable how from the inconspicuous scrappy beginnings adumbrated in the *Sūtra* of Gautama, Nyāya logic and epistemology have come to occupy the position of universal recognition and undisputed authority. The latest contributions of the Neo-logical schools of Mithilā and Navadvīpa present a formidable array of facts and arguments, which scare away even a bold student. Nyāya philosophy grew in its strength and volume in consequence of its fight with rival schools, pre-eminently Buddhistic schools. Gautama's epistemology and logic as developed by Vātsyāyana in his *Bhāṣya* were mercilessly attacked by Diṅnāga, and their prestige suffered a rude shock. This gave the occasion to Uddyotakara to write his *Nyāyavārttika*. Uddyotakara in the course of his comments criticized Vasubandhu and Diṅnāga and defended the Nyāya position. Dharmakīrti, Dharmottara, and others took up the challenge and showed the weakness and inadequacy of Uddyotakara's defence. Next came Vācaspati Miśra who again gave replies to the animadversions of the Buddhist philosophers, and the defence of the Nyāya school of thought was carried forward by Jayantabhaṭṭa, Śrīdhara, and Udayana. After Udayana we do not hear of any rival Buddhist philosopher who caused trouble to orthodox systems. Even a casual survey of the works of these writers will convince the reader how keen and acute was the fight that was carried on between the two rival schools of thought.

The result was precision of definitions in which every word, nay, every particle, was duly measured and had to be defended. Nyāya in one sense came to be regarded as the science of definitions, the importance and necessity of which are now coming to be recognized in modern European philosophy on account of the attacks of the neo-realists of Europe and America. Every concept has been accurately defined, and there is no room for doubt or speculation as to the meaning and purpose of the philosophical arguments. Clarity of thought and accuracy of expression have become the characteristic features of works on Nyāya philosophy, and of other schools as well owing to the preponderating influence of Nyāya speculations on the course of philosophical thought of India. The uninitiated complain of the undue waste of skill and ingenuity on the elaboration of definitions, and of the attention devoted to the consideration of linguistic problems. Although the interests of verbal accuracy may have been pushed too far in some cases, the results on the whole have been salutary. The room for misunderstanding due to careless expression has been narrowed down to the minimum, and a course of discipline in Nyāya is a sure propaedeutic for philosophical accuracy. It is not a matter of surprise therefore that the scholarship of a student of Indian philosophy, of whatever school it may be, is looked upon with scepticism unless he can produce a proof of his acquaintance with the Navya-Nyāya speculations.

Udayana is the greatest exponent of Nyāya philosophy in modern times. In fact, he can be looked upon as the pioneer of the new school. Gaṅgeśa in his *Tattva-cintāmaṇi,* the *magnum opus* of the new school, has adopted the main substance of his work from the writings of Udayana. But the greatest achievement of Gaṅgeśa consists in the marshalling of the arguments of all previous writers in his work with an accuracy and ingenuity which evoke spontaneous admiration. In a short compass he gives us the best and ripest fruits of the labours of the past masters, and focusses the attention of the student on the most fundamental and characteristic contributions of the school. Naturally, this work alone has come to monopolize the attention of later students and commentators. Gaṅgeśa's main purpose is to treat of the four *pramāṇas—pratyakṣa* (perception), *anumāna* (inference), *upamāna* (comparison), and *śabda* (verbal testimony). In the first part dealing with *pratyakṣa,* he has discussed all the relevant problems associated with the epistemology of perception—its source, conditions, and results. The division of perceptual knowledge into indeterminate and determinate has received a thorough treatment, and the rival schools of thought, pre-eminently that of Prabhākara, have been relentlessly criticized. The disappearance of the schools of Buddhist logicians had rendered the refutation of the Buddhist positions a matter of abstract academic interest only, and energy and attention were mainly directed against the school of Prabhākara, who had close affinities with the Buddhist philosophers in regard to certain fundamentals. The most outstanding contribution of Gaṅgeśa in his *Pratyakṣakhaṇḍa* is, however, found in his dissertation on the problem of truth and validity of knowledge (Prāmāṇyavāda). In this chapter the positions of Kumārila, Prabhākara, and Murāri Miśra, who were advocates of the theory of self-validity of knowledge (Svataḥprāmāṇyavāda), have been thoroughly discussed and criticized, and the Nyāya position of Parataḥprāmāṇyavāda, which believes in the correspondence theory of truth and ascertainment of truth by verification, has been established. Much ingenuity has been spent in the formulation of a definition of truth consonant with the positions of the three philosophers who had sharp differences on the nature of knowledge. Then again, the problem is bifurcated into a twofold issue, viz. (1) the origin and source of validity (*utpatti*) and (2) the ascertainment of the same (*jñapti*). The Mīmāṁsist maintains that knowledge and validity are two necessary correlates and have their origin in self-identical conditions ; and as regards the discovery of truth, it is effected by the self-same instrument of the discovery of knowledge. Knowledge is self-revealing according to Prabhākara, and so truth too will be self-certified. Kumārila thinks that knowledge is imperceptible and its ascertainment and discovery are made by the help of inference. The validity of knowledge too will be discovered by the self-same instrument, viz. inference. Murāri Miśra holds knowledge to be revealed by introspection and so likewise its truth. Gaṅgeśa criticizes these three positions as absolutely untenable on the ground of contradiction of experience. If all knowledge was self-validated, there would be no occasion for doubt or misgiving, and this doubt is dispelled only by means of verification by another piece of knowledge. Of course, there is scarcely to be found a single novel argument, and Udayana has given all these in his works. But new issues have been raised, and the whole problem has been studied afresh.

## INFERENCE

It is in the chapter on inference (*anumāna*) that Gaṅgeśa and the later writers have shown their best ingenuity. The conditions of inference have been thoroughly analysed and explained. Inference is defined to be the judgement produced by the knowledge of the minor premise qualified by the knowledge of the universal proposition, the major premise, which states the connection between two terms in their universal reference. This universal connection is termed *vyāpti,* and a long discussion of the concept of *vyāpti* and its diverse definitions is undertaken. The possibility of the knowledge of the universal proposition, in one word, induction, receives a thorough treatment, and the position of the sceptics is shown to lead to self-contradiction and impossibility of practical life. A thorough exposition of each of these problems will require a separate article, and so we content ourselves with only indicating the lines of enquiry that have been pursued by later logicians. It should be observed in this connection that the later developments of logical speculations were necessitated by the hostile criticism of Nyāya concepts and definitions by Śrīharṣa, Citsukha, and other Vedāntists, who revelled in demonstrating the absurdity of the realists' attempts to explain the actual world in terms of reality. Gaṅgeśa came after Śrīharṣa and took upon himself the task of vindicating the orthodox Naiyāyika standpoint. Whether and how far he has succeeded in his self-chosen undertaking it is very difficult to say with any amount of certitude. The quarrel between the Naiyāyika realist and the Vedāntist dialectician has not come to an end and will perhaps never come to an end, because they represent two diametrically opposite standpoints and attitudes of thought. The value of the contributions of the Naiyāyikas should not be judged by the numerical strength of their adherents and followers, but by other standards. There is scarcely a characteristic Nyāya doctrine which has not been challenged by other philosophers. But this does not detract from the merits of Nyāya speculations. The chief value of Nyāya philosophy consists in its contributions to method and terminology, which have been invariably adopted by all other schools of thought. The consequence has been that whatever school of thought one may follow and whatever may be one's philosophical predilections and convictions, one must speak in the language of the Naiyāyikas.

### THE PSYCHOLOGICAL CONDITION OF INFERENCE—PAKṢATĀ

Before we proceed to the next topic, viz. verbal judgement as a cognitive proof, it is desirable that we speak of some of the speculations on the conditions of inference and fallacies, which will be regarded as original contributions in the sphere of logic. We have observed that inference is produced by the combined knowledge of the universal proposition (*vyāpti*) and of the minor premise (*pakṣadharmatā*). The minor premise states that the probans (middle term), which is stated to be essentially related to the probandum (major term) in the major premise, exists in the subject of inference (the minor term). But there is a preliminary condition which must be fulfilled in order that inference as a psychical process may follow as a natural consequence from the premises mentioned above. This condition is called *pakṣatā*—the essential character of the subject; and it is defined to be the absence of a previous conviction that the subject is possessed of the probandum as an accomplished fact. This, however, requires some elucidation. Now, inference as a vehicle of knowledge aims at proving the existence of the probandum (*sādhya*) in the subject on the strength of the existence of the probans (*hetu*), and this knowledge is the objective and *raison d'être* of inference as a means of proof. If, however, there is a previous knowledge of the conclusion, inference will be entirely superfluous and uncalled for, as it will have no scope for its own. So the preliminary condition of inference is that the subject (*pakṣa*) must not have been known to be possessed of the probandum before it is inferred. But the previous knowledge of the conclusion is not found to operate as a bar to inference, provided there is a positive desire to prove it by inference. A man may actually perceive fire and smoke in a place ; still he is at liberty to prove the existence of fire on the basis of the existence of smoke, provided he feels the urge of a desire to prove by inference what he knows by perception. Previous knowledge of the conclusion is a bar only when it is not accompanied by a desire for inference. Desire for inference alone is not the universal condition of inference, since there are cases of spontaneous and unpremeditated inference, as for instance, when we infer the rise of a cloud from hearing a roar of the cloud or the clap of thunder. Nor, again, can doubt of the issue, i.e. the existence of the inferable predicate in the subject, be regarded as the condition, as it is not infrequently observed that inference takes place without a previous doubt of the issue. The full definition of the character of the subject (*pakṣatā*) as the universal condition of inference can thus be propounded to be the absence of previous conviction of the existence of the inferable predicate in the subject, provided there is not a desire to prove it by inference. The legitimate subject of inference (*pakṣa*) is accordingly one which is not judged to be possessed of the inferable predicate (probandum) antecedently to the inference. The occurrence of the predicate is to be proved by inference, and that is the conclusion aimed at. But if the conclusion were forestalled, there would be no scope for inference. The consequences of this complex condition are observed in the following cases: (1) Inference is permissible where there is no previous conviction of the predicate in the subject irrespective of the presence or absence of a desire for inference ; (2) inference is permissible where there is a desire for inference irrespective of the presence or absence of the previous conviction of the conclusion ; (3) inference is not permissible where there is previous conviction together with the absence of a desire for inference.

## PREVIOUS KNOWLEDGE OF THE CONCLUSION DEBARS INFERENCE—WHY ?

Now a question arises, Why should previous knowledge of the conclusion operate as a bar to the realization of inference? Knowledge of the predicate *per se* cannot be believed to preclude a second knowledge of the same, since there is such a thing as continuous repetition of knowledge of the self-same object. Nor can it be believed to preclude inferential knowledge, since an object, though perceived, can be known again by inference. The answer is that previous knowledge acts as a bar to subsequent knowledge having reference to the self-same object only if it prevents the emergence of a desire for that kind of knowledge. Now, knowledge may be of a general or specific character, and desire for a general sort of knowledge is satisfied by any kind of knowledge, perceptual, inferential or the like. It is not possible to maintain that a desire for knowledge as such can be satisfied only by the possession of all possible kinds of knowledge, simply because this contingency even with regard to a single object is not possible of attainment, and if this impossible condition is insisted upon, the result will be an impossibility of the satisfaction of any desire for knowledge. It must therefore be admitted that desire for knowledge as such is satisfied by any kind of knowledge. In the case of desire for a specific kind of knowledge, it can be satisfied by the possession of that kind of knowledge alone. A man may feel called upon to prove a thing by inference for his own or other people's satisfaction, though there may be a perceptual knowledge of the same, if there is a demand for inferential proof either felt by himself or urged by another person. So previous conviction of the conclusion debars an inference when there is no subjective or objective demand for specific inferential knowledge, but only a knowledge of the predicate in general is aimed at. Desire is satisfied by the attainment of the object aimed at. Now, a man may desire to have a pen, and any pen may satisfy him. But if the desire is for a specific kind of pen of a specific make and quality, the desire will not be set at rest if he is provided with a pen other than the one that he desires. Thus, previous knowledge of the conclusion cuts at the very root of inferential knowledge if the knowledge desired is of a general, unspecified kind. But it will prove no obstacle to inference if the previous knowledge is other than inferential and if inferential knowledge alone be the objective.

Now, it easily follows as a corollary from the foregoing observations that previous knowledge acts as a bar only by removing the psychological condition of knowledge, viz. desire for the same; and in so far as it exercises a hostile influence on this psychological condition, it comes to be regarded as an obstacle to inferential knowledge. This law, however, holds good only in the case of inference and not in the case of perceptual or verbal knowledge. The reason is that perceptual knowledge is not conditioned by desire, but by the compresence of the conditions of perceptual knowledge, e.g. the presence of the object, the fitness of the sense-organ, the alertness of the percipient, and so on. In verbal knowledge also desire has no function, and it never fails to materialize if there is a knowledge of the sentence. In inference too the law of obstruction holds good only if the previous knowledge is on all fours with the inferential knowledge aimed at; but if there is an additional element in the subsequent knowledge, the former will not operate as a bar. In other words, the two pieces of knowledge must be in no wise different in content or, to be precise, the previous knowledge must not be deficient in content in reference to the subsequent one. Accordingly, if there is previous knowledge of the predicate in a particular individual, it will not bar out the inference of the same in all individuals of the same class. To take a concrete example, our knowledge that Tom, Dick, Harry, and many other men are mortal will be no obstruction to our inference of mortality with reference to the whole class of men, because the subsequent knowledge is wider in its content and reference than the previous one. But if there be a previous knowledge in a universal reference, the inference of the predicate either in a particular individual or in the class as a whole will be ruled out.

### THE SUBJECT-MATTER OF INFERENCE

An interesting problem may be raised in this connection. What is the subject-matter of inference, what is the nature of the conclusion? Is the predicate only the object of inference, or the predicate as related to the subject, or the relation of the two *in abstracto*? Now, the predicate alone cannot be the objective of inference, as the predicate in and by itself is known in our knowledge of the universal proposition. The subject too is known by other means of proof, perception and the like. The relation *in abstracto* is unmeaning nonsense, and even the relation between the subject and the predicate in the concrete cannot be supposed to be the objective. If it were so, the conclusion would be expressed as 'there is a relation between the subject, say man, and the predicate, say mortality'. It must be admitted therefore that the objective of inference is the entire judgement in which the subject and the predicate are held together by a relation. The subject and the predicate along with the relation binding them together are equally objects of inference—to be precise, the conclusion is a unitary judgement in which the subject and the predicate merge their individuality and become integral parts of an organic whole. Thus, when a person infers fire in a hill on the evidence of the smoke, the subject-matter of inference is neither fire nor the hill in isolation, but the judgement 'the hill is possessed of fire'. The hill is actually perceived, though fire is not ; still the whole situation, the hill and fire together, is the object of inference, and it would be an error of judgement to suppose that the hill is known by perception and fire alone by inference.

### PERCEPTION AND INFERENCE

We discover in this situation an interesting psychological law, which can be formulated in the following terms: 'In a situation where the conditions of perception and inference are present alike, inference will prevail over perception if the object to be cognized is different in each case.' In the present case, the object of perception is the hill and the object of inference, admitted on all hands, is fire. Here the conditions of inference overrule and prevail over those of perception, and the resultant knowledge (the hill is possessed of fire) is to be accepted as inferential in character. If this law be not admitted, no case of inference will be possible where the subject is an object of perception. In other words, our knowledge would be cognizant of the hill alone and fire would never be inferred, the conditions of perception being stronger than those of inference. So the above law must be accepted under pain of absurdity. Moreover, no inference whatever will be possible if the law formulated is not accepted. Now, inference is caused by the combined knowledge of the universal proposition and the minor premise, which can be expressed as the knowledge of the subject possessed of the probans in its necessary universal relation to the probandum (the predicate). This synthetic judgement (*parāmarśa*), if we may be permitted to coin a new expression, is the immediate cause of inference—that is to say, of the knowledge of the conclusion. Now, when this synthetic judgement arises in the mind, there is an equal possibility of this knowledge leading either to inference or to introspective knowledge of itself. According to the Naiyāyika the existence of a thing, be it a brute physical fact or a psychical phenomenon, can be attested by knowledge of the same, and the knowledge of a psychical fact, be it a cognition or a feeling or conation, is styled mental perception or introspection (*anuvyavasāya*). The condition of introspection is the presence of a psychical phenomenon in the soul and the association of the mind with the latter. Now, inference is effected immediately by the synthetic judgement. Thus, when the synthetic judgement emerges into being under the stress of the knowledge of the premises, the conditions of inference and of introspection (which is a species of perception) are invariably found to be present. It is to be decided which of the two kinds of knowledge, inference and perception, will have the chance to come into being. If the conditions of perception are thought to be of superior strength, the introspection of the synthetic judgement as the object will invariably be the resultant knowledge, and inference as a psychical fact will be reduced to an impossible fiction. But this is opposed to the deliverance of psychology. The law formulated above saves the situation.

Again, 'in a situation where the conditions of inference and perception are alike present and the object to be cognized is self-identical, the conditions of perception will prevail over those of inference and the resultant knowledge will be perception.' The impugnment of this law will lead to absurdities. To take a concrete example: a person finds himself in a puzzle when he cannot make out in a dimly lighted place whether the object standing ahead is a human being or an inanimate post. On closer and minuter observation he discovers that the object is possessed of hands and feet, and he at once decides that it is a human being, as hands and feet are characteristic of a human being alone and absolutely incompatible with an inanimate post. In this circumstance the condition of perception, viz. the contact of the visual organ with the human being, and that of inference, the synthetic judgement comprehending the existence of the probans—the possession of hands and feet as the invariable concomitant of humanity in the object standing in front—are present alike and the resultant knowledge may be perception or inference, but not both, being mutually contradictory. The object to be cognized is, however, the same, viz. a human being. If we are to declare that the knowledge at issue is inference, we shall have to accept the conclusion that perceptual knowledge after a doubt is impossible. But if we consult the deliverance of our experience, we must adjudge it to be perceptual. So also with regard to the corrective knowledge which arises after an illusion. The law formulated at the beginning of the paragraph states this fact and helps us to emerge from a quandary. But one important fact has not yet been stated. Both the laws are subject to a proviso in their operation. The first law rules supreme if there is not a positive desire for perceptual knowledge at work. If the latter is found to operate, it will swing back the pendulum and the result will be perception and not inference. In the second law also the presence of a desire for inference will operate as a counteracting condition, and the condition of inference thus reinforced will push the condition of perception to the wall and will eventuate in an inference. So both the laws are to be qualified by a rider to the effect that they hold true, provided there is not a desire for the opposite kind of knowledge.

## FALLACIES

We have dealt with the problem of *pakṣatā* and we now propose to deal with fallacies (*hetvābhāsas*), on which the Indian logician has furnished the evidence of his penetrating insight and critical observation. The study of fallacies in standard works on logic has been a favourite and useful pursuit from very old times both in Europe and India. Perhaps the necessity of exposing fallacies in the arguments of the opponent preceded the systematic and scientific study of logic as a separate science and discipline. In India we find that the distinction of fallacies of reason, which are strictly of a logical character and value, from the aberrations which resulted from inadvertence and sophistical motives, was clearly recognized even in the *Sūtra* period. Many of the fallacies treated of in standard works on European logic are not fallacies of inference, and they have been set apart in a different category by Indian logicians. The *nigrahasthānas* (grounds of defeat) are rightly believed to form a wider class, which comprehends logical fallacies (*hetvābhāsas*) in their scope as a particular variety, and were never confounded with purely logical aberrations. The fallacies, which have been called fallacies *in dictione* by Aristotle and which have their origin in ambiguity of language, are not regarded as fallacies proper by Indian logicians, and they have been judiciously placed under the head of *chalas* (quibbles). Many of the fallacies of the *extra dictionem* variety also are not regarded as fallacies of reason, and they may be placed either under the head of quibbles or that of *nigrahasthānas,* which are symptomatic of other than logical delinquency. The fallacy of *ignoratio elenchi,* which consists in proving a conclusion other than what is intended, will be subsumed under the head of *arthāntara,* a variety of *nigrahasthānas,* which serves to show that the arguer has no clear grasp of the issue. *Hetvābhāsas* or false reasons are precisely those fallacies in middle terms which when discovered are found to have no bearing on the conclusion sought to be drawn. A study of fallacies in a work on logic is justified on the ground that it contributes to the discovery of truth or defeat of the opponent by creating a habit of mind to avoid or to discover the flaws in our reasoning.

A *hetvābhāsa* is defined to be a false probans, the discovery of which works as a deterrent towards inference ; in other words, it is what makes inference impossible and illegitimate. A *hetvābhāsa* may be regarded either as a false reason (*hetu*) or as a defect vitiating the reason. Whichever view may be taken of the nature of a *hetvābhāsa,* the undeniable fact remains that the concept of *hetvābhāsa* (which will henceforward be rendered by us as fallacy) does not extend to any defect or shortcoming of a personal nature and stands strictly for those objective defects alone which obstruct the process of inference. We have seen that previous conviction of the conclusion is an obstacle to inference, and, according to the definition, it should be regarded as a case of fallacy. An argument, in which the probandum is admitted to be true by the opponent, is dismissed by the remark that it is wasted labour to prove what is not disputed or what is obvious. It is a case of *siddhasādhana,* i.e. of a reason proving what needs no proof, being too well-known. Though it may look like a fallacy, it is not so in reality. It is a defect, because it is concomitant with the third fallacy. The third fallacy, as we shall see, frustrates inference by making the synthetic judgement, which is the invariable antecedent condition of inference, impossible of realization. *Siddhasādhana* indicates that the requisite character of a logical subject is wanting, because it is already known to be possessed of the probandum. Inference is possible only in respect of a logical subject; and if it be absent there can be no legitimate minor premise, and hence no synthetic judgement will be available. Thus, previous knowledge of the conclusion becomes a bar to inference, not in its own independent capacity, but because it involves the fallacy of the unproven probans. What is true of *siddhasādhana* is also true of a conditional probans (*sopādhikahetu*). It is not an independent fallacy, but a concomitant of the first fallacy. The definition, however, covers the accredited cases of recognized fallacies, which, according to the Naiyāyika, are of five different types, viz. (1) *anaikāntika* (the inconclusive probans lacking invariable concomitance with the probandum), (2) *viruddha* (the contradictory probans which is invariably concomitant with the absence of the probandum), (3) *asiddha* (unproven probans), (4) *satpratipakṣa* (the counterbalanced probans), and (5) *bādhita* (the contradicted probans). We propose to consider how far these varieties of fallacies fulfil the terms of the definition. The inconclusive (*anaikāntika*) probans thwarts the process of inference by violating the universal concomitance (*vyāpti*), which is one of the conditions of inference. The frustration of inference may be direct or indirect through the violation of the conditions of inference. Now, the conditions of inference are (i) the universal concomitance of the probans with the probandum; (ii) the subsistence of such probans in the subject—which is expressed in the minor premise. The combined product of these two premises is the synthetic judgement (*parāmarśa*) which immediately leads to inference of the conclusion. If by reason of any defect the synthetic judgement fails to materialize, the conclusion will not follow and a deadlock will be the result.

(1) The first type of fallacy (*anaikāntika*) admits of three subdivisions, viz. (i) the common (*sādhāraṇa*); (ii) the uncommon (*asādhāraṇa*); and lastly, (iii) the inconsequential (*anupasaṁhārī*). (i) The common inconclusive probans is one which is found to co-exist with the probandum (*sādhya*) and the absence of the probandum (*sādhyābhāva*) alike. It violates the condition of necessary universal concomitance, which is fulfilled when the probans is found to be invariably concomitant with the probandum and to be absent in a locus wherein the probandum is absent. In other words, the concomitance must be attested both in agreement and difference. The common inconclusive fallacy is illustrated in the following argument: 'Word is imperishable, because it is a cognizable fact.' The concomitance of cognizability with imperishability is not necessary

and does not exclude the opposite possibility. Even perishable things are cognizable. So the probans 'cognizable' is inconclusive, being common to perishable and imperishable things alike. It is fallacious because it obstructs inference by violating the condition of necessary concomitance. (ii) The fallacy of uncommon inconclusive probans thwarts inference by thwarting the ascertainment of the concomitance in agreement, which is a necessary condition of inference. 'Word is imperishable, because it is a word.' 'The hill is possessed of fire, because it is a hill.' These arguments are illustrations of the aforesaid fallacy, because the concomitance between the fact of 'being a word' and 'being imperishable' or 'being a hill' and 'being possessed of fire' is not capable of being ascertained outside the subject, and the necessity of the existence of the probandum in the subject is debarred by doubt. (iii) The inconsequential inconclusive probans arises when the subject is the totality of existent things, and the probans and the probandum are absolute universal concepts, as for instance in the argument, 'All things are nameable, because they are cognizable.' There is no case left over where the concomitance between the probans and probandum can be tested, as all existents have been included in the denotation of the subject. This sub-species of fallacy, however, has been a subject of heated controversy, and Gaṅgeśa succeeds in vindicating this fallacy on the psychological ground of failure of a knowledge of universal concomitance, the failure being due to the absence of an accredited example where the concomitance can be ascertained.

(2) The contradictory probans (*viruddha*), being invariably concomitant with the contradictory of the probandum, contradicts the cognition of the necessary concomitance of the probans with the probandum and thus thwarts inference by removing one of its conditions.

(3) We now propose to discuss the third class of fallacy called *asiddha* (unproven). It admits of several subdivisions, varying with the terms of the syllogism that may be unproven. (i) The subject may be a fiction and this would involve the fallacy of the *unproven subject* (*āśrayāsiddha*). The argument, 'The golden hill is possessed of fire, because it is possessed of smoke', is abortive, inasmuch as no synthetic judgement cognizing the presence of smoke-concomitant-with-fire in a fiction is possible, while this judgement is invariably the immediate cause of inference. (ii) There may be a case of *unproven probans* (*svarūpāsiddha*) where the probans is known to be non-existent in the subject, as in the argument, 'The lake is on fire, because it is possessed of smoke.' The probans 'smoke' does not exist in the subject 'lake', and this affords an illustration of the fallacy of unproven probans. (iii) There may be a case of *unproven probandum* (*sādhyāsiddha*), as in the argument, 'The hill is possessed of golden fire, because of smoke.'

The fallacious character of the unproven probans and the unproven probandum is evidenced by the failure of the synthetic judgement owing to the absence of the probans in the subject in the former and the absence of the probandum in the latter. The synthetic judgement has for its constituent terms the probans, the probandum, the concomitance between them and the subject as qualified by such probans ; and the absence of any one of these factors will make the judgement, and through it the inference, an impossibility. The same consequence arises when the probans is qualified by a fictitious or superfluous attribute. Hence 'golden smoke' has no probative value and even 'blue smoke' is no proof of fire, as concomitance with fire is understood in 'smoke' in its simple character of being smoke and not 'blue-smoke'. The probantia under discussion are regarded as fallacious, as they preclude the knowledge of concomitance, and through this failure the synthetic judgement (*parāmarśa*) and inference (*anumiti*) are rendered impossible.

(4) The counterbalanced probans (*satpratipakṣa*) is one which is vitiated by a counter reason advanced in a separate argument to prove the contradictory of the thesis sought to be proved by it. To take a concrete instance, the argument, 'Word is imperishable, because it is amorphous like space', is counterbalanced by the argument, 'Word is perishable, because it is a product like a jar'. The first probans 'amorphous' is contradicted by the second probans 'product'. The result is a deadlock, as one probans is offset by another and consequently no inference is possible. The difference between the contradictory and the counterbalanced probans is this that the opposite thesis is proved by a second probans advanced in a supplementary argument in the fallacy of the counterbalanced probans, whereas in the former fallacy the self-same probans proves the opposite thesis and is further instrumental in proving the incompetence of the arguer in employing a probans to prove a thesis, which proves the reverse of it.

(5) We have now to deal with the last-mentioned fallacy called *bādhita* (contradicted). This fallacy arises when the absence of the probandum in the subject is ascertained by means of other evidence. Thus, for example, when a person would like to argue, 'Fire is not-hot, because it is a substance and all substances such as water, earth, and air are known to be not-hot', the probans employed will be a contradicted probans. Fire is known to be hot by direct perception, and this directly contradicts the inference. The general definition of fallacy applies to this case *a fortiori*, as it thwarts inference directly. In fact, the contradicted probans and the counterbalanced probans are cases of direct fallacy, as they thwart inference proper ; and the other fallacies are indirect, as they frustrate inference only

by thwarting the instrument (*vyāptijñāna*) or its operation in the shape of the synthetic judgement (*parāmarśa*).

This fallacy, however, is not admitted by the Buddhist and Jaina logicians as a fallacy of probans; they would rather believe it to be a case of false probandum (*pakṣābhāsa*). Others, again, have contended that this is not an independent fallacy and the failure of inference is due to the presence of other fallacies. Thus, for instance, if the probans is found to be non-existent in the subject, the fallacy would be a case of 'unproven probans'. If it is existent in the subject, it will be a case of inconclusive probans, as the concomitance of the probans with the probandum will be found to be absent in the subject itself by means of perception and the like. The Naiyāyika meets these contentions by appeal to psychology. The sense of contradiction is different from that of non-concomitance. Again, when a person argues the presence of odour in the earthen jug at the very moment of its origination, the fallacy becomes a case of purely 'contradicted probans'. A substance remains divested of its attribute at the moment of its origin and comes to be vested with it only in the second moment. The probandum 'odour' is predicated of the earthen jug at the moment of its origin, and this is contradicted by the law of causality —the jug being the cause of odour cannot synchronize with the effect.

## IMPORT OF WORDS AND PROPOSITIONS

The Naiyāyika, again, has his own contribution to the study of linguistic problems. Language has been studied in India both in its phonetic and semantic aspects. In the realm of semantics, so far as the logical value of import of terms and propositions is concerned, the grammarians, the Mīmāṁsakas, and the Naiyāyikas have each their own views, which are in sharp conflict with one another. There is a discussion of the expressive powers of words, of the objects denoted, of the meaning of the suffixes, the syntactical relations, and the resultant verbal judgement. It will be exceedingly cumbrous if we attempt to give an account of these speculations in English. But it must be stated, to guard against a possible misunderstanding, that these linguistic enquiries have not only achieved results which throw light on the structure of the Sanskrit language, but have also led to the discovery of universal laws which will apply to all the languages of the world. Though the syntactical structure of languages varies, the laws of combination of the meanings will apply *mutatis mutandis* to all languages. To take an example, 'Here is a blue cup' (*atra nīlaghaṭo'sti*), the syntactical relation of the adjective 'blue' to the substantive 'cup' is designated as *tādātmya* (denotational identity with connotational difference). The 'blue' does not denote an object different from the 'cup', so the relation is one of non-difference of denotation. The individual words have their specific individual meanings, but the relations of these meanings, which cement them into one unitary judgement, are not expressed by the component words, but by dint of their juxtaposition in a sentence in obedience to certain laws. These laws are called *ākāṅkṣā* (mutual expectancy), *yogyatā* (relevancy), and *sannidhi* (proximity both in regard to place and time). If only the adjective 'blue' were uttered, it would not give a complete meaning, and there would be an expectation for another term, viz. 'cup'. This capacity for giving rise to expectation in a human mind constitutes one of the cementing bonds of individual terms, by reason of which they produce a judgement in a rational mind. The second law of relevancy is also a necessary condition. We cannot speak of a 'cold fire', because the meanings are incongruent and irrelevant. The separate articulation of the individual words after long intervals will not give rise to the verbal judgement. So these three laws must be satisfied before there can be a consistent proposition. The syntactical relations, however, are understood only if the terms in a proposition fulfil the conditions noted above. So these relations are the import of the whole sentence. The whole, though made of parts, has a distinct individuality and a function distinct from that of the component factors. The meaning of a verbal proposition cannot be necessarily known by any other instrument of knowledge, say, perception or inference, so far at any rate as the hearer may be concerned, and hence the necessity of postulating a separate means of cognition, viz. verbal testimony (*śabda*). This is of course not the universally accepted position. The Vaiśeṣikas and the Buddhists do not admit the logical necessity of verbal testimony as a separate instrument of knowledge, and they would fain include it under the head of inference or perception. The result has been an interminable tangle of polemics, into which the space at our disposal prevents us from entering.

### COMPARISON

Comparison (*upamāna*) is a special kind of *pramāṇa,* and there is a difference of views between the Naiyāyika and the Mīmāṁsaka both in regard to its nature and function. The Naiyāyika thinks it necessary to requisition the aid of this cognitive instrument when a person has to affix a verbal label to an unknown entity from analogy. To take an instance, a person is told that there is a wild animal called *gavaya* which closely resembles a cow. It so happens that the person so informed goes into a forest and actually sees a *gavaya,* and then recognizing its close resemblance to a cow, he recollects the words of his informant and at once concludes that the animal is a *gavaya.* The designation of the animal as *gavaya* is made possible only by means of *upamāna,* a separate source of knowledge, and neither by perception nor by the recollection of the informant's testimony. Whatever may be its logical value, which has been challenged by rival philosophers, it must be admitted that comparison as a proof has such a limited scope and its achievement is so meagre that it can be safely dispensed with in a scheme of epistemology. The centre of interest is found in the other three *pramāṇas,* of which again *anumāna* and *śabda* have come to monopolize the entire attention of later students.

### THE PLACE OF GOD IN THE NYĀYA-VAIŚEṢIKA SŪTRAS

It will not be possible within the limits of this paper to discuss all the metaphysical problems that have been broached in the *Sūtra* and elaborately developed in the subsequent exegetical literature. We propose to deal with the following fundamental problems: the position and nature of God and the relation of God to the individual souls and the world. The *Nyāya-Sūtra,* like the cognate *Vaiśeṣika-Sūtra,* postulates the ultimate reality of atoms as the material cause of the world and God as rather the organizer and engineer of the world-order. The world-process proceeds in cycles, and so far as its cyclic existence is concerned it is without a beginning and is coeval with God. The individual souls are eternal entities dating from a beginningless time and so have a parallel existence with God and the world. The Nyāya-Vaiśeṣika school is in this matter of beginningless creation fully in agreement with other Indian schools of philosophy. In fact, the doctrine of beginningless existence of the individual souls together with the cyclic world-process is a fundamental postulate of most of the schools of Indian philosophy, and it deserves to be examined whether this doctrine is sanctioned by logical necessity or is an unreasoned dogma, uncritically accepted without question. A detailed examination of this problem will not be relevant to our present enquiry, and we must content ourselves only with showing that this conception is neither absurd nor unnecessary. Unless we accept the position of unqualified scepticism or absolute illusionism, we have to admit the existence of a timeless entity, be it God or time or atoms or the individual souls. It is generally accepted in Western philosophy that the soul is immortal ; its immortality is, however, not clearly defined as existence through all time, but rather as existence after death. If the soul is denied pre-existence and is believed to come into being with the birth of the present body, it becomes difficult to believe in its endless future existence. It is a truism that things that have a definite origin are liable to destruction. And so unless we are prepared to accord a timeless existence to the soul, it will not lie in us categorically to assert its immortality. Again, God at any rate is believed to be a timeless entity; and, if God is by nature an active principle, His activity too will be coeternal with His being, and it must express itself in the process of creation or destruction, and whatever may be found to be reasonable to predicate of God in the way of His activity must be supposed to exist through all time. Then, again, the individual selves, who are *prima facie* supposed to have a somewhat independent existence apart from God, cannot be supposed, without giving rise to absurdities, to have begun their career from a definite point of time. If they are supposed to be created by God in time and as such to be destitute of a pre-existence, no proof can be put forward to establish their immortality, which is the accepted position of most of the philosophers of Europe, barring of course the materialists and sceptics. It is refreshing to find that Dr. McTaggart is a staunch believer in the pre-existence of the self, and he has proved his thesis by arguments which are not liable to be easily assailed. But to the problem of immortality we shall have to advert in the course of our enquiry, and we now propose to deal with the position of God in the *Nyāya* and *Vaiśeṣika Sūtras*.[1]

### NO MENTION OF GOD IN THE SŪTRAS

It is a matter of surprise that in the enumeration of the objects of authentic knowledge (I.1.9.) there is no specific mention of God, and in the proofs adduced for the existence of a unitary soul-entity as distinguished from the psychological processes, there is not the slightest allusion to God either as a supreme soul *primus inter pares* or as a separate category. We also miss any reference to God in a most expected quarter. The Nyāya and Vaiśeṣika schools are zealous advocates of the supreme authority of the Vedas in the matter of religion, and though they do not believe either in the eternity of word-essence or the uncreated character of the Vedas as the Mīmāṁsaka does, there is no explicit statement of God as the author of Vedic revelation in the *Sūtra*. This seems curious, inasmuch as the authority of verbal testimony, not excepting the authority of the Vedas, is derived from the veracity and infallibility of the speaker or writer. In the *Bhāṣya* of Vātsyāyana too there is no clear reference to the divine authorship of the Vedas, although Vātsyāyana is a staunch believer in the existence of God. In the *Vaiśeṣika-Sūtra* (II.1.18) the authorship of the Vedas is attributed to persons of superior wisdom, who are said to be possessed of the power of direct intuition of supersensuous things spoken of in the scripture. In the aforesaid work (IV. 5. 1-4), again,

[1] For a somewhat elaborate treatment of the problem the reader is referred to my article entitled 'Immortality of the Soul or After-life' published in the Centenary Number of the *Udbodhana,* the Bengali organ of the Ramakrishna Math.

the Vedic sentences are said to be the product of intelligent persons who had first-hand experience of the facts. Now, there is no decisive evidence, so far as the wording of the *sūtras* is concerned, which can enable us to conclude that the *Vaiśeṣika-Sūtra* definitely and clearly assigns a place to God in its scheme of metaphysics. The evidence of the *Nyāya-Sūtra* too, we shall see, is not more definite, and there is room for speculation that these systems were, at any rate in their period of inception, without definite predilections or commitments in favour of God. The *sūtras* 19-21 of chap. IV, sec. 1, in the *Nyāya-Sūtra* are the only textual passages which allude to God as the creator of the world. But the first *sūtra,* which speaks of the inadequacy of the individual's *karma* (moral actions) as the causal principle and makes God the creator of the world, is treated of as the *prima facie* view, which is rejected in the next *sūtra.* The third *sūtra* in the present context is interpreted by Vātsyāyana as establishing the necessity of God's agency. The whole discourse can be summed up in the following words: The actions (*karmas*) of men are not the self-sufficient cause of the world, and so for the creation of the world we must postulate the agency of God. The answer to this contention is that this position cannot be maintained. If the actions of men were immaterial and God alone was the sufficient cause of the world-order, there would be no *raison d'être* for moral activity. But we cannot conceive that results can take place without previous deeds. The third *sūtra* '*Tatkāritatvādahetuḥ*' has been interpreted by Vātsyāyana in the following way: 'The actions of men are by themselves incapable of producing their fruits, but these are directly made fruitful by the agency of God. So the previous argument is inconsequential.' The results of this discourse, as interpreted by the scholiast, seem to establish the fact that for the creation of the world God's agency is indispensable, as it is God alone who can dispense the rewards and punishments proper to men's actions in previous lives. Men's actions are not self-sufficient to produce their results, which are realized in the creation of the world only because there is an omniscient and omnipotent Being behind them as the judge and ordainer of the fruits. So actions too are contributory factors to creation, but the direct agency is in the hands of God.

But this is not the only possible interpretation. The *vṛttikāra* has given an alternative explanation which entirely dispenses with God's agency and seeks to explain the failure of men's actions as due to the absence of previous merit (*adṛṣṭa*). The divergence of interpretation, which is made possible by the cryptic language of the *sūtras,* leaves room for honest doubt whether the admission of God into the architectonic plan of Nyāya-Vaiśeṣika metaphysics is strictly demanded by a logical necessity. Moreover, the introduction of this question of God's agency into the discussion of the origin of the world is made by way of incidental reference in the *Nyāya-Sūtra* and cannot be regarded as clinching the entire dispute. The purport of the *Sūtra* seems to be to wage a crusade against those theories which denied the efficacy of *karma* and hence the moral foundation of the world-order. But in spite of the fact that the *Sūtra* literature is obscure and non-committal on this vital issue, the later Nyāya-Vaiśeṣika literature, beginning with Vātsyāyana and Praśastapāda, down to the latest developments in the Navadvīpa school, is noted for its staunch defence of God's existence against the attacks of atheistic schools, and the Nyāya-Vaiśeṣika school has rightly come to be respected as the masterful champion of theism. We therefore propose to consider the contributions of these writers to the evolution of the theistic doctrine in this school.

## RECOGNITION OF GOD IN THE SCHOOL

Vātsyāyana holds that God is a soul *primus inter pares,* although distinguished from ordinary souls by reason of the absence of moral defect, error, and inadvertence and the eternal presence of superabundant righteousness, pure knowledge, and supernormal powers, by virtue of which He is capable of creating the world by a mere fiat of the will. He is the shelter of all creatures and protects all beings like an affectionate father. He is possessed of eternal knowledge of all things. God is not a simple existent without any characteristic, as an uncharacterized entity is only a conceptual fiction. Vācaspati Miśra gives voice to a possible objection to the possession of superabundant mercy by God on the score of the presence of undisputed suffering and pain in the created world. The usual explanation of the inequalities in the world-order by reference to the unequal values of the past actions of individual souls is but a poor defence, inasmuch as these actions are not self-productive of their results, and if God abstains from dealing out the fruits of actions, the world-order would be destitute of the imperfections and limitations that are unfortunately ruling rampant. Vācaspati answers the objection with his usual boldness. Although God is all-powerful and there is no limit to His mercy, He cannot subvert the moral laws, which are by their nature immutable. God's omnipotence is subject to the supremacy of the moral law, and the moral law is rather the law of His own being and also of the being of individual selves. There can be no escape from the consequences of moral actions except by enjoyment thereof. Man remains unfree so long as he is not absolved from the bonds of actions, good or bad, and the creation of the world is solely motivated by the supreme desire of God to create opportunities for the individual selves to work off the load of their actions. Suffering is not an unmitigated evil. It serves to make men feel disinclined towards the things of the world and helps them to realize the vanity of worldly pleasures. This detachment and disinclination is the condition precedent for all spiritual progression, as it induces man to contemplate the means of escape from the worries of transmigration, and he finds the means in the philosophic realization of the true nature of the self and the world and their mutual relationship. So suffering is a blessing in disguise.[2] Unalloyed pleasure on the other hand would make a man forget the highest interests of life and its true mission, and degrade him to the rank of the lowest brute. Suffering is thus a propaedeutic discipline and a necessary preparation for the achievement of the highest goal, viz. unfettered freedom, the *summum bonum* of life.[3]

### MOTIVE OF CREATION

Another difficulty is raised, Why should there be a will to creation at all? All activity is normally motivated by some ulterior purpose of satisfying a need either in the way of acquisition of an advantage or avoidance of an evil. In the case of God no such motive can be supposed to set free an activity, as He is *ex hypothesi* free from all disadvantages and is self-sufficient and self-satisfied. A God with an unsatisfied want would be a contradiction in terms. It has been maintained that God engages in creative activity in a sportive mood. Creation is but a game and pastime with Him, and no question of motive therefore can be urged as necessary. But Uddyotakara refuses to be convinced by this argument, as even play is not a motiveless activity. It is resorted to only with a view to enjoyment of the pleasure which is derived from it, and also because abstention from play causes uneasiness to those who are lovers of it. But such a contingency cannot be conceived to be possible with reference to God, because He is absolutely free from all shades of uneasiness and worry. The theory of playful activity therefore cannot be regarded as a satisfactory explanation of God's creative impulse. The second theory that God's creative activity is inspired by a desire for demonstrating His infinite powers and glory in and through the inconceivable varieties and complexities of the created world does not seem to stand a better chance of success. The question arises, Why should He be eager to give a demonstration of His glory? Certainly God does not gain any advantage from

[2] *Nyāyakandalī,* p. 53.

[3] Cf. But he that creeps from cradle on to grave,
Unskilled save in the velvet course of fortune,
Hath miss'd the discipline of noble hearts.
W. R. Sorley's *Moral Values and the Idea of God,* p. 346.

His adventure, nor do we conceive of any possible loss on His part if He ceases from this enterprise. If any advantage or disadvantage could accrue, God would be a lesser God—in other words, would cease to be God. What then is the explanation? No explanation can be offered beyond positing that it is God's nature to do so. Cosmic activities are an essential part of His being, and Godhood minus cosmic functions is an unintelligible fiction. It may be interesting to observe in this connection that Gauḍapāda too, in his *Māṇḍūkya-kārikā,* has summed up these views in a couplet and drawn the same conclusion with Uddyotakara that it is the essential nature of God to engage in creative activities, as no motive can be alleged with reference to one who has no unsatisfied want. There can be no questioning again with regard to ultimate facts and constitution of things. It is absurd to interrogate about the nature of even material objects as to why they should behave in the peculiar way they do and not otherwise. God is a dynamic principle, and His dynamism is manifested in His cosmic activities; and no room is left for speculation as to why God should be dynamic and not be quiescent and inactive. The ultimate nature of things can be understood only from observation of their behaviour and not *a priori.* So no question of motivation is either legitimate or profitable.

But the opponent raises another objection. Granted that God is dynamic by His very constitution and nature, but this would make His activity a perpetual necessity, since one cannot resist one's nature, and perpetual cosmic activity would make the periodic dissolution of the world-process an impossibility. Moreover, there would be simultaneous creation of all objects, but this is opposed to our experience. Things are produced on a graduated scale, and the process of creation and dissolution, of distribution and redistribution of causal energies, is attested to be the ruling order by scientific researches and popular experience as well. Uddyotakara in reply observes that this objection would be insurmountable if the ultimate principle were conceived to be a blind force without intelligence and prevision. But God is an intelligent principle and creates those things for which He thinks that there is an occasion and necessity; and His cosmic activities, although not compelled by an external necessity, are conducted and guided by a moral self-urge which takes the direction best calculated to bring about the deserts of actions accumulated by individual souls, in pursuance of intrinsic spiritual laws which have their seat in the fundamental morality and the spiritual nature of God and the souls and are unfolded in the spatio-temporal order of the universe. So no such consequences are possible.

### GOD AND THE MORAL ORDER

God, again, is the supreme ruler of the universe, and this supremacy is coeternal with His being. His powers are infinite and unlimited. Ordinarily, power is acquired by virtue of moral excellence, which again is achieved by moral exertion and activities. If God's powers are coeternal with His own being and, as such, not acquired by religious merits or moral activities, then the universality of the moral law would be untenable, as God would be placed above its jurisdiction. But this should not cause a difficulty. If the moral law is to be an eternal ruling principle, it must be found to exist in its perfection as a *ne plus ultra* somewhere, and it is found in God. The moral law is supreme because God is supreme and the law is but the manifestation of His being. In the case of individuals their powers are but the outcome of moral and spiritual excellence, which too is actually acquired, no doubt, but this achievement is made possible by the eternal moral perfection that is in God. If the supremacy of God were the product of acquired moral excellence, the unobstructed supremacy of the laws of morality would be an impossibility and a chimera, a consummation that might be piously hoped for but never possible of realization. Moreover, the hypothesis of acquired perfection and acquired supremacy in God would be tantamount to a denial of God and the eternity of divine justice, and the result would be a negation of the moral foundation of the world-order.[4]

### GOD AND THE WORLD-ORDER

The previous arguments have served to make it clear that God may be a plausible existent, but no proof has been adduced to establish the existence of God as a matter of logical necessity. Is there any logical proof of God? Is it absolutely necessary that we must admit His existence, and can the world-order not be explained except on this hypothesis? We propose to consider the logical proofs that have been advanced by the philosophers of this school. Now, we are familiar with three different classes of existents. In the first place, there are objects which are obviously known to be products of intelligent and thoughtful agents, such, for instance, as palaces, gates, walls, pens, chairs, and tables. In the second place, there are existents which are admitted by a general consensus of opinion to be destitute of any author and as such to be eternal existents, such, for instance, as atoms and space. In the third place, we meet with existent facts which are susceptible of being suspected as made by some intelligent agent, viz. the body, the mountain, the sea, the tree, and other such objects. The doubt of intelligent authorship legitimately arises

[4] *Nyāyavārttika,* p. 464.

with regard to the last-mentioned category of objects on account of their striking similarity with objects of the first class and also on account of the divergence of views among philosophers of rival schools. There is no categorical evidence for the absence of intelligent authorship either. It is certainly true that no man has seen them to have been produced by an intelligent author, but absence of perceptual evidence is no proof of the absence of an intelligent author, as such an author may legitimately be supposed to be invisible like atoms etc. Absence of perceptual evidence can be regarded as proof of absence of the object only when the latter is amenable to perception and not otherwise. In the case of the body, the tree, the mountain, etc. they are known to have a definite origination in time and to have been non-existent before their origination. Who has brought them into existence? It can legitimately be inferred that they have been brought into existence by an intelligent maker who had knowledge of the material causes and the process of production, just as palaces and roads are built by a knowing person. Both these sets of phenomena are seen to come into existence at a definite point of time and they evince the same intelligent plan and teleology. Why, then, should one set of phenomena be supposed to come into existence independently of a maker and not the other set, although we find very little difference between them so far as the teleological character of their construction and their definite origination in time are concerned? But it may be objected that the origination of the grand phenomena of nature—the mountain, the sea, the forest, the river, and so on—is not definitely perceived by any man whose testimony may be accepted as proof. In the circumstances how can an origin be positively predicated of these objects, even if it is allowed that origination is proof of an intelligent agent? The answer is that objects which are capable of being divided into parts cannot be supposed to be ultimate existents; and as the process of division and analysis shows the constituent factors, they must be supposed to have come into existence by means of a previous integration and combination of the component factors. And none but an intelligent being could bring about such a combination with a view to the result. This is certainly the case with regard to productions of arts and crafts. Why should there be a difference in the case of natural objects, though the same intelligent planning of means to ends is observable in them also? It should be admitted then that objects which are seen to be possessed of parts arranged according to a purposive plan must have been made by some intelligent maker.[5]

[5] *Vide Tātparyaṭīkā*, pp. 602-3; *Nyāyakandalī*, pp. 54-5.

It has, however, been contended that this teleological argument is futile as it leads to self-contradiction. Even if it is granted that the world has an agent who is possessed of intelligence and forethought, there is no escape from antinomies. The reason is that all knowledge is produced by an impact on our organic sensibilities; and if the ultimate author of the universe be possessed of a psycho-physical organism, all his cognitions would be contingent events, and so he could not be regarded as omniscient. Moreover, all his cognitive activities would be subject to the limitations of sense-faculties, and he would not be able to envisage the super-subtle causes of the world and so would not be the creator. If it is supposed that God is independent of a physical organism, it will be extremely difficult to imagine how He can have knowledge at all, and, still further, how He can operate upon the atoms, the ultimate constituents of the material world. If you deny a bodily organism to God, you will have to deny all intelligence and purposive activity on His part; and to think that He has an eternal body associated with Him will lead to absurdities, as an eternal body is as impossible as an eternal world. And if He is possessed of a body of limited dimension, it will be liable to origin and destruction; and furthermore, He will not be in touch with all matters lying outside the body. If sense-organs are added to the organism, all the cognitions and volitional activities will be as transitory as ours. The result will be that an unthinking and unintelligent God will have to be posited, and this will be an absurdity. Nor can we suppose that God is entirely unassociated with a physical organism and is possessed of eternal intelligence, eternal desire, and eternal will, because there is absolutely no warrant for this supposition, as all knowledge and volitional activity are seen from experience to be contingent on the possession of a nervous system and cerebral functions, which are sought to be denied of God. God thus becomes a chimera and a fiction of the imagination, whether we affirm a physical organism with a cerebral system and nervous organization or we deny the same of Him. It is better therefore if we desist from the supposition that the world-order has an intelligent author.

### THE BEARING OF THE BODY UPON PSYCHICAL ACTIVITIES

In reply to these charges the philosophers of this school have pointed out that the opponents have failed to appraise the relation of the body to the psychical activities at its proper worth and to observe that voluntary activities are not in any way contingent on the possession of a physical organism, although from a surface view of things this may seem to be the necessary condition. What is the condition of voluntary activity

—the association of the physical organism or the influence exerted by an active principle possessed of relevant causal efficiency? The mere association of the physical organism is irrelevant to volitional activity, as we do not find any such activity when a person is indifferent or in deep sleep, in spite of the fact that the physical organism is present intact. So we must set down voluntary activity to the exertion of an active agent possessed of causal efficiency irrespective of his association with a physical organism, which has been found to have no bearing upon it. If the possession of a physical organism be a necessary condition for the exercise of voluntary activity, we cannot explain how the agent can control his own body, as the help of another bodily organism cannot be obtained for the purpose. It can be contended that even in the controlling of the body the presence of the body is an essential condition. Yes, but the body is not present as the condition, rather it is the object of the controlling activity, and similarly in the case of God's activity the object to be operated upon is present in the shape of the atoms which are the constitutive principles of the material world. But it has been further urged that the controlling activity that is exercised upon one's own bodily organism is made possible by dint of a desire and volitional urge, and this desire and the volitional urge are seen to occur only in association with a bodily organism and not in its absence. So the presence of the bodily organism must be admitted to be the condition of these psychical activities, which are admittedly the internal springs of the physical control; and thus the bodily organism will be the indirect condition of all physical controlling movements. The presence of the physical organism is thus to be set down as the necessary condition of all voluntary activity, and if God is *ex hypothesi* destitute of any such organism, the exercise of voluntary controlling activity will be impossible. But this argument too is not convincing. Even if it is admitted that the medium of the physical organism is a necessary condition for the emergence of psychical activities, for which there is no proof beyond the matter-of-fact evidence that we have no experience of a psychical activity except in association with a body, which may be a mere accident, still it may be legitimately maintained that the causal efficiency of the physical organism with regard to bodily movements is not proved, although its bearing on such psychical activities as desire and volitional urge may be left a moot question. The controlling of the bodily organism and its movements and activities is urged by a purely psychical force without any assistance from the bodily organism, barring the fact that it is present as the object to be operated upon. The very fact that the spirit can control and activate an inanimate object simply by dint of a desire and voluntary exertion without any assistance from any bodily organism, should clinch the proposition that 'all effects are the products of an intelligent agent'. But it may be contended that the emergence of desire and volition is contingent upon a bodily organism, and for the emergence of these psychical activities at any rate, God will stand in need of a physical organism. Yes, the contention may have some plausibility with regard to those psychical activities which are events in time, but with reference to eternal psychical facts it has absolutely no force and no bearing. Nor is there any logical incompatibility in the supposition that God's cognition, desire, and volition are eternal verities, uncaused and unproduced. Of course, these psychical phenomena are always observed to be transitory events in our experience, but that is no argument that they cannot be eternal in any substratum. Such qualities as colour and taste are ordinarily perceived to be transitory, but they are admitted to be eternal verities in atoms. The transitoriness or permanence of qualities is relative to the substrata in which they are found. So psychical attributes too may be permanent fixtures just like the physical attributes of colour etc., and there is no inherent logical absurdity in this supposition.

## GOD'S KNOWLEDGE AND WILL ARE ETERNAL

The permanent existence of these necessary psychical activities in God has been shown to be plausible, and we think it possible to prove it by a *reductio ad absurdum*. The arguments of the opponents have failed to shake the foundational universal proposition that whatever is possessed of an origin has for its author an intelligent agent ; and once the origination of the world-process is admitted, the inference of an intelligent author becomes irresistible. And if an intelligent author of the universe is established as a matter of logical necessity, the nature of his intelligence and volitional activity will be determined in conformity with his authorship. They will have to be admitted to be of such a character as not to be in conflict with his cosmic activities. The cosmic activities presuppose an intelligent agent who has a direct knowledge of the materials and the *modus operandi* necessary to bring about the universe. Certainly this knowledge of all existent facts extending over all divisions of time cannot be a contingent event, as in that case God will have to be assumed to be ignorant of whatever has happened in the past and so will have no agency in that regard. If His knowledge is as transitory as ours, it will have no application to the future, and so God will not be the controller of the future course of events. If, however, it is supposed that God has an infinite series of cognitions, volitions, and desires, produced in regular succession and all these have reference to all things, possible or actual, still we shall have to admit a number of psychical acts which are absolutely without any similarity to our psychical activities. It will be simpler and more convenient to suppose that God's cognitive activity is one and eternal and so also the other psychical activities. The admission of God as an author of the universe will necessitate the postulation of eternal psychical activities which are necessary for the creation, superintendence, and control of the universe. These attributes are consequential to God's cosmic functions, and to seek to refute the existence of God on the ground of the impossibility or improbability of these attributes will be a roundabout procedure, without any logical validity. If you expect to deny God with any show of plausibility, you will have to prove either that the universe does not presuppose an intelligent maker or that it is existing as a finished product for all eternity, which is the position of the Jainas and the Mīmāṁsakas. If, however, the positions adumbrated cannot be maintained with any semblance of logic, the admission of God and of His consequential attributes and powers will follow as a matter of indisputable logical necessity. The opponent, who builds his destructive logic on the apparent absurdity of the consequential attributes of God, has only to be reminded that his generalization that psychical attributes cannot be eternal is based upon purely empirical data and does not bar out the contrary possibility by a *reductio ad absurdum*. We have, however, seen that the eternal existence of relevant psychical activities in God follows as a corollary from the nature of the universe, which becomes unintelligible unless an omniscient and omnipotent creator and ruler is postulated.

### THE INDIVIDUAL SELF IS CENTRAL TO CREATION

We now propose to discuss certain other consequential problems before bringing this dissertation to a close. The main ground of the proof of God has been shown to be teleological, and this teleological argument again is ultimately based upon the argument of the moral law—the law of Karma. The *raison d'être* of creation is found in the moral necessity of providing the rewards of actions done by individual souls in their previous lives; and so in the philosophy of the Nyāya-Vaiśeṣika school, and of all schools of Indian thought which believe in creation, the individual self holds a prerogative position of honour, since the entire creation is believed to centre round him and to provide only the stage on which the drama of his destiny will be played. God has no destiny and no personal mission. He is only the judge and ordainer of moral deserts; in other words, He has only a judicial and executive duty which

He discharges out of an irresistible sense of justice to uphold the supremacy of moral laws, and we have seen how God's justice is tempered with mercy. But a question of logical difficulty raises itself in this connection, viz. the relation of God with individual selves whose destiny is guided by Him. The merits of individuals inhere in the individual souls ; and if God is to operate upon these merits, it has to be shown how God comes into relation with these. The individual selves are held to be ubiquitous substances, and so also is God. It has been held by some thinkers that two ubiquitous substances may be related by way of uncaused conjunction ; and if this relation is accepted, we can explain the relation of God with individual selves as one of uncaused conjunction, God being connected with the individual souls for all eternity and, through this, with their merits. But this relation of uncaused conjunction is not universally admitted, and so another relation acceptable to all has been propounded by Vācaspati Miśra. The individual selves are connected with the atoms, as they also are eternal entities ; and these atoms are connected with God. So God and the individual selves are connected through the medium of atoms. Even indirect relation is of service for causal operations. Here also the relation of God to individuals may be explained either through atoms or through the mind, both of which are eternal existents and are eternally conjoined with God. So we see that the relation of God and individuals is not logically inconceivable, although it is not possible to give any definite judgement as to the peculiar extension of the relation, whether it is of unlimited extension or of limited extension. The question is inspired by idle curiosity and does not have any metaphysical importance. It is sufficient that a relation is logically conceivable, and the question of extension and the like appears to be based upon irrelevant analogy of spatial relations of material bodies, which cannot be pushed too far.

## GOD'S ACTIVITY IS ETERNAL

Another question may be raised. Granted that God is the creator of the universe, but then He may take a holiday and retire from the cosmic functions, which may take their destined course under their own laws. What argument makes you suppose that God will be the eternal controller and guide of every detail of the world-process? The answer is that the same necessity which makes God's activity inevitable in the past is present throughout the world-process. The blind forces of nature cannot be self-guided, and for their control and guidance the supervision of an intelligent being is necessary. The movements of natural forces, the elements, the atoms, and so on are perpetually going on and they are meant to serve some purpose; and who makes their movements fruitful and who again imparts activity to them but God? So God is an eternal living force and the eternal judge and ordainer of the moral order, but for whose intervention and guidance the world would fall to pieces like a piece of rotten cloth.

### PLURALITY OF GODS IS A METAPHYSICAL IMPOSSIBILITY

But a question arises, Is a plurality of Gods possible? No, there is but one God and one God alone. Why should a plurality of Gods be postulated at all? If one God is impotent to bring about the world-order or to maintain discipline, a number of Gods with different functions allotted to them may be necessary and we shall have a republic of Gods and not absolute monarchy. But are these Gods omniscient? If they are not omniscient and omnipotent, they will be as impotent and helpless as we mortals are, and so they will not be equal to the task of creation and control of the world, which requires just these attributes. The result will be a failure to explain the world-order. If they are omniscient and omnipotent one and all, it is logically simpler and more economic to postulate the existence of one such God, for He will be able to discharge the cosmic functions alone and unaided. Apart from considerations of simplicity and logical economy, the postulation of a number of equally omniscient and omnipotent Gods will lead to insoluble complications. There is no certitude that they will act in unison and accord for all time, and there may arise occasions when they may differ. The result will be an unrelieved anarchy and confusion. If, however, it is supposed that these Gods will be guided by the counsels of one among them who will be the President, a *primus inter pares,* just as we see in the systems of democratic government, then, again, the President will be the virtual God and the supreme ruler, if his mandate is obeyed by all. If it is supposed that these omniscient Gods will never have occasion for dispute, since they will all be persuaded of the wisdom of a particular line of action and will therefore act in complete agreement, then of course none will be the ruler of the universe and so none will be God. But why should we at all believe in such a republic of Gods—what logical necessity is there which will make us bless the theory? Absolutely no case can be made out for this hypothesis, and so we must reject it without hesitation or scruple. Polytheism as a philosophical doctrine is absolutely an illogical and superfluous hypothesis, and it should be clearly recognized that India never favoured this doctrine either in theory or in practice, though unsympathetic critics, owing to their ignorance of the inwardness of Indian religious practices, have maligned the people of India and their religion on this ground.

## RELATION OF THE INDIVIDUAL WITH GOD

We shall conclude our dissertation by adverting to a question of supreme importance. It is a truism that the Nyāya-Vaiśeṣika school staunchly believes in the infallibility of Vedic religion, and its allegiance is not confined to the ritualistic portion of the Vedas alone, but extends to the Upaniṣads also, although this school follows its own interpretation of them. The Nyāya-Vaiśeṣika school does not believe in monism, and its philosophy can be characterized as uncompromising pluralism. The relation of individual souls to God is neither one of pure identity nor one of identity in difference, but one of absolute and unqualified otherness. The relation of God to the individual selves is not internal but strictly and purely external. God is alluded to as being in the position of a father to the suffering souls, and His cosmic activity has been spoken of as inspired by considerations of justice and mercy alike. The supreme solicitude of God for the deliverance of suffering creatures from the meshes of transmigration is also alluded to in clear and unambiguous language in the *Bhāṣya* of Vātsyāyana. But man's relation to God is not clearly emphasized in the ancient literature. It is only in the works of Udayana that we find this topic broached. Udayana begins his *Nyāya-kusumāñjali* with an impassioned salutation to God, and in the course of his writing he speaks of the worship of God as instrumental in the achievement of salvation and enjoyment of heavenly bliss, whichever may be sought for by His devotees. He goes on to state that philosophical speculation is a kind of worship of the Deity and has its supreme justification and fulfilment only in so far as it leads the enquiring soul to surrender himself to God's protection and mercy. We are tempted to believe that the predominance of the devotional attitude in subsequent Nyāya literature is entirely due to the influence of Udayanācārya. It is remarkable that Vardhamāna took great pains to reconcile this statement of Udayana with the orthodox Nyāya position that salvation is achieved by an unerring realization of the true nature of the self, and this supreme saving knowledge is effected by proper understanding of the sixteen topics only. There is no room for love of God or worship of God or knowledge of God as an instrument of salvation. Vardhamāna therefore was at great pains to bring it into line with the central position of the Nyāya philosophy, and he succeeds by making knowledge of God contributory to self-realization. But Udayana in the concluding passages of the *Nyāya-kusumāñjali* emphatically maintains that worship of God is essential for salvation, and his pleadings and advocacy of the necessity and logical possibility of self-surrender and meditation on God are unsurpassable for their devotional ardour, impassioned enthusiasm, and moral fervour. A better and more successful advocacy of theism is difficult to conceive.

The *Nyāya-kusumāñjali* will remain, we may be permitted to remark without exaggeration or partisan spirit, one of the best works on theism in the whole of world literature, noted alike for its spiritual earnestness and logical consistency. The philosophical literature of India, and not only of the Nyāya-Vaiśeṣika school, would have been *pro tanto* poorer and weaker if Udayana had not been born to enrich it by his masterly contributions.

# 6

# NAVYA-NYĀYA

## THE SCHOOLS OF INDIAN LOGIC

MM. Dr. Satish Chandra Vidyabhusan introduces three broad divisions into the schools of Indian logic, namely, ancient, mediaeval, and modern. According to him ancient Indian logic deals with the sixteen categories, *pramāṇa, prameya,* etc., comprising such heterogeneous elements as the doctrine of salvation, birth, death, and the nature of the soul. Mediaeval logic, on the other hand, concerns itself with one category only, *pramāṇa,* and touches upon the others only so far as is necessary for its proper elucidation. Inference, a kind of *pramāṇa,* which was briefly noticed in ancient logic, receives full treatment from the mediaeval school. *Prameya,* the object of knowledge, is rejected on the ground that it is useless, in works on logic, to treat of the soul, birth and death, topics which are comprised in this category. Mediaeval logic is therefore termed *pramāṇa śāstra,* the science of right knowledge.

Vidyabhushan has not given us any clear definition of what he understands by modern logic. He holds that in the early writings of the modern school there was some attempt to combine the categories of the Nyāya and the Vaiśeṣika, but later modern logic has selected only one topic, *pramāṇa,* to the exclusion of the remaining fifteen topics of the ancient school. Modern logicians reject the division of the *pramāṇa* into the subdivisions prescribed by the Buddhists and the Jains, and accept the orthodox division of *pramāṇa* into four. They also take note of certain Vaiśeṣika categories, which are discussed along with the theory of perception. But the main emphasis is on the formal accuracy of linguistic expression.[1]

Mm. Dr. Ganganath Jha thinks that the modern school has freed itself from the groove of the *Nyāya-Sūtra* and betaken itself to the rigid course of strict reasoning. Udayana is the pioneer of this school, which has reached its consummation in the *Tattva-cintāmaṇi* of Gaṅgeśa. Dr. Jha, however, suggests that there is one criterion which serves to demarcate very clearly the Prācīna from the Navya Nyāya. The later Naiyāyikas (logicians) do not concern themselves much with metaphysics as such, but remain satisfied if they can arrive at correct definitions; *lakṣaṇa-pramāṇābhyāṁ vastu-siddhiḥ* is their dictum, and to *lakṣaṇa* and *pramāṇa* alone they turn.

[1] *History of Indian Logic,* pp. 158, 402, and 403.

By this criterion, then, we shall be justified in dividing Nyāya into three schools: (1) Prācīna or old, represented by Gautama and his commentators; (2) Madhyama or mediaeval, represented by the Jaina and the Bauddha writers, who, though confining their attention to the *pramāṇas,* do not devote themselves entirely to the verbal accuracy of their definitions; and (3) Navya or modern, which deals only with *pramāṇas* and *lakṣaṇas*; and even here, the concentration is mainly on the verbal *lakṣaṇas* or definitions of things. It has to be borne in mind that, in point of time, there is constant overlapping in this division.[2]

Dr. A. B. Keith in his short review of the *Tattva-cintāmaṇi* holds that in it 'the doctrine of the theory of knowledge is presented in a definitive form freed from intermixture with the miscellany of contents of the Sūtra [*Nyāya-Sūtra*], and placed in a position to confront the attacks of the Buddhists and the Jains'.[3] Dr. Keith intends to convey the idea that there is no cardinal difference between the ancient and the modern logicians—only the novel technique of language confers upon the band of logicians headed by Gaṅgeśa the epithet 'modern'. Dr. S. Radhakrishnan hints at a change of outlook in modern Nyāya, and suggests that the modern Naiyāyika pays exclusive attention to *pramāṇas* or the means of knowledge and the theory of definition and discards altogether the question of *prameyas* or the objects known.[4]

Let us now review the remarks of the great scholars on the characteristic features of modern logic. Gaṅgeśa's *Tattva-cintāmaṇi* is a work on epistemology and logic. Can we expect him to discuss all the metaphysical questions in that treatise? If he does not, can we blame him for leaving aside metaphysics? But, as a matter of fact, Gaṅgeśa does discuss many metaphysical questions which have a bearing upon the theory of knowledge. He is a methodologist. His logic is not metaphysics. Therefore, it is not to be expected that he will pay particular attention to metaphysical problems in his logic. It is a truism that Gaṅgeśa and his followers are very particular about the accuracy of their definitions. But this accuracy presupposes a thorough knowledge of the things defined. Moreover, if Gaṅgeśa, realizing the vastness of the scope of epistemology, does not append it to a metaphysical treatise, does he do anything wrong or does he express his antipathy to metaphysics? He takes for granted the metaphysics of his predecessors, and every chapter of his work is full of their metaphysical findings. His dissertations on universals, negation, *manas,* sense-organs, inherence, and God should not be overlooked.

[2] *Sadholal Lectures,* pp. 266-8.
[3] *Indian Logic and Atomism,* p. 34.
[4] *Indian Philosophy,* II. pp. 40-2.

Gaṅgeśa's treatment really paves the way for sound metaphysics. Sound epistemology and logic should precede metaphysics. The stable universe of realities should be based upon the solid rock of the data of our experience. We should observe facts and discover laws and, on the basis of observation, construct our metaphysical edifice. Mystic intuition should not be the only source of metaphysics. Gaṅgeśa does not minimize the importance of mystic intuition, but at the same time he does not give a free hand to it in the matter of philosophical speculation. He laid the foundation of the revised metaphysics of the Vaiśeṣika school by making some attempt to revise the Vaiśeṣika categories in the light of the new theory of knowledge, but left the unfinished task to be completed by his successors.

Modern logic gradually emerges from the seed of free thinking sown by Gaṅgeśa. The younger Vācaspati Miśra places equal reliance upon the authority of perception and of the Śrutis, and holds that the truth of perception cannot be cancelled by the authority of a Vedic passage simply because the latter is held to possess a superior authority. Śaṅkara Miśra is bold enough to discard the authority of any Vedic passage that contradicts the truth of valid perception. This attitude towards the authority of the Vedas constitutes the line of demarcation. The neo-logicians prefer to be guided by the evidence of perception and inference, though in transcendental matters they do not intend to interfere with the authority of the Vedas.[5]

Raghunātha Śiromaṇi and other such free thinkers do not hesitate to subject the traditional theories to severe criticism and to bring about fundamental changes in the structure of Vaiśeṣika metaphysics, if sound perception and inference demand such a change. The ancient writers failed to raise their voice against the *sūtrakāras*. Whenever they tried to introduce a new idea, they did it with the help of some other authority or adopted some device to avoid the unpleasant task of disowning the authority of their masters. Vātsyāyana's *anvīkṣā* is based upon perception and the Āgamas,[6] whereas the *tarka* of the modern logicians is based upon perception alone. The modern logicians may be indebted to the Bauddha and the Jaina thinkers for this free thinking, but, be it said to their credit, they have not allowed themselves to be carried away completely by the speculations of the latter. They keep their minds open but at the same time cherish a profound and deep-rooted love for the tradition they are born and brought up in.

[5] *Bheda-ratna*, p. 65 and *Khaṇḍanoddhāra*, pp. 30 and 34.
[6] *Nyāya-bhāṣya*, p. 4.

VALID KNOWLEDGE

Valid knowledge lies at the root of every sound system of metaphysics. Is valid knowledge possible? The Naiyāyikas answer that it is possible, because the validity of knowledge is ascertained by subjecting it to an adequate test. This problem has a history behind it. The *sūtrakāras* take the possibility of valid knowledge for granted and do not closely examine their assumption. Nāgārjuna and his followers hold a sceptical view about the existence of valid empirical knowledge. The Naiyāyikas and Mīmāṁsakas join issue with the sceptics. The resulting contest forms an important chapter of epistemology. Gaṅgeśa's *Tattva-cintāmaṇi* does not embody the earlier phase of the debate. Among the modern works on logic, the *Nyāya-kaustubha* has only a passing reference to the starting point of the problem.[7] Gaṅgeśa represents a more advanced stage. At this stage, the argument revolves round the point whether the validity itself is intrinsic or extrinsic. He subjects the theories of intrinsic validity of knowledge propounded by the Bhāṭṭa and Prābhākara schools to severe criticism. He also refers to the attempted synthesis of the opposing views worked out by the Jains and criticizes it also.

The two main charges against the extrinsic character of the validity of knowledge are: (1) if an act of consciousness does not carry with it the conviction that it is valid, then no activity or movement of the cognizer can follow from it, and (2) if an act of consciousness does not bear the stamp of validity on the face of it, then the process of proving its validity can stop nowhere.

Gaṅgeśa meets the arguments of his opponents thus. He holds that an assurance of the validity of an act of consciousness is not necessary for physical activity. The mere absence of invalidity is enough for the purpose. He means to say that the ascertainment of validity is not the essential condition of human activities. Assurance of the validity of an act of consciousness comes later. In other words, our voluntary movement does not necessarily presuppose the determination of the validity of an act of consciousness which conditions such a movement.

The second charge has some force in it. If we judge it from the theoretical point of view, then the problem remains insoluble. But human nature is satisfied if a man takes only a few correct steps to prove the validity of his initial consciousness. Suppose a person sees water from a distance, moves towards the water, obtains it, and quenches his thirst therewith. Does a doubt as to the validity of his initial perception arise in his mind afterwards? It is an ultimate element in human nature that man is satisfied

[7] *Nyāya-kaustubha*, pp. 31-2.

with a solution which, from the purely theoretical point of view, might be incomplete.

Gaṅgeśa holds that a perceptual judgement reveals its object in the form, 'This is so-and-so' and not, 'I know this is so-and-so', since the function of a judgement is to lead to action, and it is too much to assume that a judgement must be self-conscious in order to discharge its own function. If an act of consciousness reveals itself as an object of itself, then one and the same act of consciousness would become both a subject and an object. Besides, if we are sure of the validity of our awareness, then how can a doubt arise at all in our minds? The Bhāṭṭas hold that consciousness is imperceptible but inferred, and that its validity is also inferred along with it. Let us explain the several steps that are taken to infer our consciousness. 'This is a jar' is the first judgement.[8] It only reveals the jar, but we do not know that we know the jar. Then cognizedness is produced in the jar. The cognizedness is known by us in the form that this jar is being known. Then we recollect the induction that whenever the property of cognizedness is produced in an object, there is a process of knowing to produce it. This process of knowing, being itself an activity of our self, defies direct knowledge. Now we deduce from the above the existence of an activity of consciousness which has a bearing upon the judgement that the jar is being known.

Again, does what is directly grasped and not subjected to doubting fall on the subject judged or thought about? Price says, 'Now plainly what is genuinely intuited, if it comes within the sphere of judgement of all, must always fall on the subject judged about. It is what is given, as opposed to what is discovered in or attributed to the given.'[9]

Gaṅgeśa's answer would be different. His analysis of perceptual consciousness is this. He admits that perceptual consciousness is not discursive but intuitive. In the perceptual act there is neither wandering nor questioning, though it is an *actus*. He hints at the activity of such an act. In the indeterminate (*nirvikalpaka*) stage of perception a subject or determinandum alone is not held before the mind, but the prospective subject and the prospective predicate are both presented to it, though they stand unrelated. The act of determinate perception which follows in the wake of the indeterminate perception ties them together by a bond of relation. The relation itself proceeds from one term and flows towards another. Two or more terms thus related form a judgement. Each term has a distinct position in a judgement. The very direction of a term in a judgement makes it what it is, either a subject or a predicate. Determinate

[8] *Nyāya-kaustubha*, p. 34.
[9] *Perception*, p. 162.

perception is an *actus* in the sense of relating or joining together two terms, but not in the sense of questioning. In the initial stage of a determinate perception we take for granted the reality of the predicate of a subject.

The other part of the problem of validity is how validity is imparted to an act of judgement. Udayana has elaborately discussed this problem in *Nyāya-kusumāñjali* and has shown that the validity of a judgement owes its existence to a special positive condition which is technically called *guṇa*. Gaṅgeśa has discussed the problem still more elaborately and cited many crucial instances which help to prove the thesis of Udayana.

Gaṅgeśa in his *Tattva-cintāmaṇi* does not deal with one of the most fundamental problems, viz. the nature of consciousness. Is consciousness presentative or representative? Udayana hints at it in his *Ātma-tattva-viveka*. Raghunātha in his commentary on it includes some discussion of the problem but puts forward the conclusion of the Nyāya school that consciousness is presentative. None of them have thoroughly discussed all the hypotheses of representative consciousness. The Sāṁkhyas, the Buddhists, and the Advaitins mainly subscribe to the hypothesis of representative consciousness. Regarding the nature of consciousness, all admit that an act of awareness reveals an object. Is this awareness at the same time aware of itself? The Naiyāyikas put this question to their actual experience and answer it in the negative. Diṅnāga and others hold that whenever an awareness reveals an object, it must, as the ground of its knowledge, have awareness of itself. The Prābhākaras come forward with a similar hypothesis. They hold that whenever an act of consciousness takes place, it enjoys itself and reveals the knower and the known. Gaṅgeśa subjects the hypothesis of triplicate perception to severe criticism. He establishes after a lengthy discussion that an act of awareness and its introspection are two discrete events and should not be fused together. Kumārila holds that an act of awareness can never be a direct object of awareness. An act of awareness operates upon its object and produces cognizedness on it. That is why the objectivized object is revealed. An act of awareness is only inferred by means of its invariable effect of cognizedness.

Gaṅgeśa has not discussed the hypothesis of transcendental consciousness. He has also not paid much attention to the nature of the relation holding between consciousness and its object. Gadādhara in his *Viṣayatā-vāda* has done justice to this problem of subject-object relationship. Every act of consciousness, he says, has a necessary reference to its object. Consciousness having no such reference is unthinkable. Therefore the implication of this hypothesis is that the hypothesis of transcendental consciousness is untenable, since every event of consciousness has a necessary reference either to a particular object or set of objects, while transcendental consciousness, if it is in any way related to objects, must be related to all objects at the same time. Transcendental consciousness should always be omniscient. The subject-object relation (*viṣayatā-sambandha*) is external. The objects are independent of the act of consciousness and the knowing mind. Consciousness, like a word, is also related to a past or a future object. Each word is related to the object denoted by it ; it was so, and it will be so. In this case, a relation subsisting between the two terms (the person and his name) holds good even if one of the two terms be absent. An act of consciousness is similarly related to its objects.

Consciousness is formless. Hence, terms like ideas and concepts do not find a place in the Nyāya epistemology and logic. We are aware of individuals and universals, and common properties of many individuals. We do not know objects through images, but our consciousness directly refers to objects lying outside the act itself. In our dreams we do not perceive such images as forms of our consciousness, but our consciousness refers to extra-mental objects. The dream-objects do not exist in the real world and are constructed by our imagination by means of constituents which are real.

## DEFINITIONS OF TRUE KNOWLEDGE

Gaṅgeśa scrutinizes a good number of definitions of true knowledge. We shall here discuss only five theories indicated by the definitions of 'truth'.

(1) The Novelty Theory: True knowledge is such as grasps a novel object only (i.e. an object not cognized before). The Mīmāṁsakas and others subscribe to this view. Gaṅgeśa differs from these thinkers and asks them whether a series of perceptions focussed upon one and the same object is true. The object as experienced cannot be held to change along with its relation to the different minute elements of time, since the minute elements of time (*kṣaṇas*) themselves escape our notice. Thus the object of such a series of perception lacks novelty. To say that the first perception of the series is true and the others, though having the same character, are untrue is absurd. Therefore the novelty theory is untenable.

(2) The Pragmatic Theory: True knowledge is such as leads to successful action. This theory bears a close resemblance to the view that 'the true is the efficient'. Gaṅgeśa rejects this definition with the remark that some true knowledge does not offer an incentive to action. The upholder of this theory may urge that what is capable of stirring up successful action is called true knowledge. But when we perceive an object and satisfy ourselves that our perception is not false, we move to have it. We proceed, assuming the truth of our knowledge. Any piece of knowledge,

however, cannot stir up our action, which always presupposes the validity of its basic knowledge. Therefore the pragmatic theory of truth is not tenable.

(3) The Coherence Theory of Truth: An experience is said to be true when it coheres with another experience. It means that the object revealed by the experience in question is the same as revealed by another experience. Gaṅgeśa points out that this definition is wide enough to be applicable to a mistake as well. Two persons may mistake a piece of rope for a snake. Is their erroneous perception true?

(4) The Theory of Non-contradiction: The popular view is that an experience of an object is true when it is not contradicted. Such a definition presupposes contradiction, but the nature of contradiction has not been scrutinized. Contradiction implies the true knowledge of the negation of the object in question. The implied meaning of contradiction amounts to this, that the experience of an object is true when its negation is known to be not true, and the experience of the negation of an object is true when the object negated is known to be not true. Therefore the definition in question involves a vicious circle.

Similarly, the Advaita theory of objective non-contradiction is open to objection, though Gaṅgeśa has not touched upon it.

(5) The Theory of Accordance: The Naiyāyikas now ask, 'What is truth?' and 'What is falsehood?' They are not asking how a man can know whether a proposition is true or false. They hold that truth is correlative to falsehood. They frame a theory of truth which leaves enough room for falsehold. What they mean to say is that it is the statements or propositions, and not the facts of the world, that are true or false. In other words, truth and falsehood are only properties of propositions, judgements, and statements. From the above statements it follows that the truth or falsehood of a judgement depends upon what lies outside the judgement itself. The Naiyāyikas also hold that in order to make provision for falsehood it must be admitted that truth or falsehood is not a property of such forms of consciousness as are related either to a single object or to two or more unrelated objects. Truth or falsehood applies neither to the indeterminate perception of their school nor to the mystic intuition of the soul. Thus, the *nirvikalpaka* perception of the Buddhist schools (intuition of a real particular), in spite of its vividness, is neither true nor false from this standpoint. The Naiyāyikas further hold that if falsehood is to be duly allowed for, then the possibility of knowledge by complication cannot but be admitted. The senses, unaided by some cognition, cannot produce erroneous judgements. The sense stimulus initiates the formation of these judgements. Hence they are perceptual. The predicate of an

erroneous judgement is supplied by a previous event of consciousness. The connection of the senses with the object of that event of consciousness is established by means of the transcendental contact in the shape of memory consciousness. Whenever our senses come into contact with an object, an erroneous perception does not instantaneously arise. There are certain elements in a sensed object which provoke our memory of some other object. Our sense-organ becomes united with the constituents of two objects. By the process of perception these constituents are combined and presented to us as a concrete object. Thus, a judgement of error owes its existence to a complicated process in which a sense-organ and an act of consciousness co-operate to bring about a judgement of error. The implication of this theory is that the objective constituents in a judgement are identical with the real elements in the universe, but the order of the elements in the judgement does not reflect the order of the object complex referred to, and the knower forgets that the elements in the judgement are knitted together into one complex whole by complication.

The subject itself (the self that experiences) is not a constituent of the subjective complex. It merely arranges the objects of its consciousness and puts them in a certain order. The initial non-relational consciousness develops into relational consciousness. It is now called a judgement. If the objects referred to by the terms which constitute the judgement are identical with the elements in the object complex, and if the relation between the terms of the judgement reflects that between the constituents of the complex object, and the direction of the relation in both cases is the same, then it is held that the judgement accords with the complex object. Some of the upholders of the view that consciousness is representative hold that no object is directly cognized, but its form is only seized by consciousness. The others hold that an object is grasped only when it becomes merged in the mode of intellect. In any case, the so-called object becomes the content of consciousness. The object which is cognized becomes included in our consciousness. But it is a truism that we make false judgements. If our judgement does not accord with its corresponding complex object, it is false.

Gaṅgeśa now discusses the character of illusory consciousness. The Prābhākaras hold that illusory consciousness is not a judgement. It owes its existence to the non-apprehension of difference (*akhyāti*) between two distinct forms of knowledge, viz. perception and memory. Let us take an example of illusion, 'This is silver'. We perceive 'this' and remember 'silver'. When we fail to find out the difference between the perception and the recollection there, the two acts of consciousness, being undifferentiated, assume the form, 'This is silver'. The illusion, 'This is silver', is really made up of two pieces of consciousness but is never a judgement, since no object can make itself appear as something else.

Gaṅgeśa in his *Anyathā-khyāti-vāda* subjects this view to severe criticism. He holds that the evidence of introspection is unquestionable. The introspection of illusory consciousness reveals the fact that illusory consciousness is a judgement. Knowledge that determines our movement is always a judgement. Illusory consciousness determines our movement. Therefore illusory consciousness is a judgement. The Naiyāyikas, of course, admit that memory plays an important part in the production of an illusory judgement. What is the exact nature of this judgement of illusion? Is it a judgement of perception? Gaṅgeśa answers in the affirmative. But an act of perception owes its existence to some contact with a sense-object. The subject 'this' of the judgement of illusion may come into contact with the sense-organ, but the predicate 'silver', being a remote object, can never be united with the sense-organ. Gaṅgeśa points out that normal contact does not condition this perception, but a transcendental one does. The memory of 'silver-ness' discharges the function of the required contact. Thus perceptual illusion takes place. If we do not object to the perceptual character of a judgement of recognition, then why should we not agree to accept the existence of perceptual illusion? He does not discuss the other theories of illusion. In the *Nyāya-kaustubha* five theories of illusion have been thoroughly discussed. The most fundamental conclusion of the Nyāya theory of illusion is that the subject of the judgement of illusion is never misapprehended but only the predicate is mistaken. It follows from this conclusion that the very possibility of hallucination is ruled out.

### DOUBT

We may now turn to an analysis of doubt. The distinguishing characteristic of doubt is that it is always a judgement, i.e. relational. It is always indefinite or vague and marked with uncertainty. Two irreconcilable predicates are alternately ascribed to one and the same subject, and consequently there is constant hovering between these two predicates. A familiar example of it is, 'Is yonder object a post or a man?', which is an instance of disjunctive judgement.

There is much difference of opinion between the ancient and the modern logicians regarding the nature of a disjunctive judgement. According to the ancient logicians, the alternative predicates may be either positive or negative terms. Some modern logicians lay emphasis upon the point that one of the predicates must be positive and the other must be its negative, i.e. must involve the contradictory negation of the positive term. The ancient logicians hold that a disjunctive judgement may also be illustrated in the form, 'It is a cow or a horse', whereas the modern logicians hold that the illustration of a disjunctive judgement must always be in the form, 'It is, or is not, a cow'.

The subject of a judgement is characterized by its predicate. The subject has the property of being characterized, which is technically called *viśeṣyatā*. The predicate has the property of characterizing, which is technically called *prakāratā*. These two properties are correlative. According to some, each *viśeṣyatā* has only one corresponding *prakāratā*. According to Gadādhara, the subject of a disjunctive judgement is one, but it has two *viśeṣyatās* (properties of being characterized). Jagadīśa holds that a single disjunctive judgement may contain any number of alternative predicates and that the lowest limit of the predicates must be two. He also adds that there is no law that there must be only two predicates and that one must be contradictorily opposed to the other. But, according to him, there is no bar to a negative alternative predicate.

Rakhaladasa Nyayaratna invites our attention to one important point, viz. that the incompatibility of the predicates of a disjunctive judgement must be apprehended; for disjunction presupposes a previous knowledge of negation, either contrary or contradictory.

According to the Naiyāyikas, a disjunctive judgement is always perceptual. The author of *Ratna-koṣa* admits also the existence of a non-perceptual disjunctive judgement. The modern logicians insist that the perception of the subject is one of the necessary conditions of a disjunctive judgement and that the subject of this judgement is never doubted.[10]

## MEMORY

We shall now discuss the nature of memory. Is memory a form of valid knowledge? All the ancient logicians—Vācaspati Miśra, Jayanta Bhaṭṭa, Udayana, and others deny validity to it, since it only refers to such objects as have been experienced before, and does not add to our stock of knowledge by new discoveries.

Gaṅgeśa argues in a different manner and arrives at the same conclusion. His argument is as follows:

(1) Experience and memory generated by it refer to the same object. Memory is expressed in a peculiar language, e.g. 'I remember that jar'. The demonstrative pronoun 'that' is an empty word. It represents no distinct object. It only indicates its genesis from impressions. An object is perceived as present together with its qualities. The perceived object

[10] Vide *Kevalānvayi-ṭīkā* of Gadādhara, *Pakṣatā-ṭīkā* of Jagadīśa, *Vividha-vicāra* of Rakhaladasa Nyayaratna, and *Nyāya-kaustubha*.

naturally suffers a great change when it is remembered. Therefore the object which is remembered, not being endowed with the qualities of the original percept, cannot yield valid knowledge. Therefore memory cannot but be false.

(2) It may be urged that an immediate experience and memory do not refer to the same object. Memory refers to an event in the past, while an immediate experience refers to an object in the present. How does memory acquire its reference to past time? Since an immediate experience reveals an object as present, how can memory, which follows from it, reveal the same object as past? Therefore memory *per se* is false.

(3) Memory, being a form of consciousness, should reveal its object as present. No object that is recalled by memory should be presented to consciousness as past. Therefore memory, which points to its object as a past event, is always false.

Jagadīśa, Viśvanātha, and others hold that memory may be true if it makes a true representation of its object. It refers to an object in the past, and if it does so correctly, then it must be true. But they do not meet all the points raised by Gaṅgeśa.

### SUBJECT-OBJECT RELATION

The ancient Naiyāyikas hold that a state of consciousness has its corresponding object. An objectless consciousness is a fiction. Udayana is the pioneer logician to have discussed the problem of the specific relation between consciousness and its object. He holds that the relation in question is *viṣayatā,* which is a kind of *svarūpa-sambandha. Svarūpa* relation does not require the aid of any other relation to unite the two correlative terms. The specific nature of the *viṣayatā-sambandha* is that it is one of the relations capable of producing relational knowledge without the aid of another relation. Mahādeva explains in his *Nyāya-kaustubha* that by *viṣayatā-sambandha* Udayana means consciousness in its essence.

Gaṅgeśa has incidentally discussed the problem of *viṣayatā-sambandha,* but other modern logicians take up the problem in detail. According to them, *viṣayatā* is a distinct external relation but is not a *svarūpa* relation. They argue that if *viṣayatā* be a *svarūpa* relation, then it will be either consciousness itself, or the object itself, or both consciousness and its object. If the relation of *viṣayatā* be not distinct from the act of consciousness itself, then an act of perception which grasps two independent objects together will turn out to be a false one. Suppose we simultaneously perceive a cow and a horse. The logicians hold that the objects characterize our consciousness. If these objects are not related to that act of perception by a number of distinct relations, but by a single relation of *viṣayatā,* then that event of perception cannot assume the form of the copulative judgement, 'This is a cow and this is a horse'. These two objects, when analysed, are many in number, viz. an individual cow, the universal of cowness, and their relation, and an individual horse, the universal of horseness, and their relation. Many objects are thus related to the same act of perception by a single relation of *viṣayatā*. If this relation is identical with that act of perception, then how can we arrange these objects in their proper order in our perception? In the above case a cow would not have been perceived only as a cow, but also as a horse, and the horse would not have been perceived only as a horse, but also as a cow, since only the difference in the nature of the relation of *viṣayatā* can determine a predicate in its proper place in a judgement. Moreover, if the relation of *viṣayatā* be identical with the event of consciousness, then why should not the two predicates in the above copulative judgement simultaneously qualify each of the two subjects contained therein? Therefore the first alternative cannot be entertained.

The second alternative is also inadmissible. If the *viṣayatā* had been identical with the object itself, then the true judgement, 'This is a jar', would not have been distinguished from a false judgement, since the *viṣayatās* of the true judgement, 'This is a jar', and that of the false judgement, 'This is a cloth' (when a jar is mistaken for a cloth), are one and the same, the objective basis of both the judgements is one and the same, viz. a jar.

The third alternative is also defective. If the *viṣayatā* relation had been both consciousness and its object, then it would have involved irrefutable contradiction in cases like the judgement, 'A jar has a universal'. The universal in question belongs to the *viṣayatā* relation when it is identical with its object, but when it is identical with consciousness the universal which belongs to the object cannot belong to it. But the *viṣayatā* in question maintains its numerical identity, and hence it has and has not the universal in question at the same time, which is absurd.

The modern logicians conclude that the relation of *viṣayatā* is a distinct one. It admits of four types: the first relates indeterminate perception with its object, the second relates a judgement with its predicate, the third relates a judgement with its subject, and the fourth relates a judgement with its copula. These *viṣayatās* are respectively called *nirvikalpakīya, prakāratā, viśeṣyatā,* and *saṁsargatā*. Some hold that introspection has a special type of *viṣayatā;* but others object to this supposition.

Some logicians classify the relation of *viṣayatā* under two heads: the first relates itself with two isolated objects, e.g. the *viṣayatā* relation of an indeterminate perception; and the second relates itself with related objects, e.g. the *viṣayatā* relation of a determinate perception. Some logicians hold that there is also conational *viṣayatā* (the relation of *viṣayatā* obtaining between desire and its object), which is also a distinct relation like the relation of *viṣayatā* mentioned above.

### PERCEPTION

We shall now try to select some of the essential elements of Gaṅgeśa's doctrine of perception and present them to our readers. Gaṅgeśa's contention is that perceptual consciousness does not, on the face of it, bear the stamp of immediacy. Immediacy is not a universal inherent in the individual perceived. The essence of ordinary perception is that it is generated by the sense-organ. Gaṅgeśa defines perception as that which is not produced by the instrumentality of cognition. In order to be consistent with the theological doctrine of his school that divine intuition is eternal, he could not but frame a negative definition, which fulfils all the logical conditions of a sound definition but does not enlighten us very much.

The problem of true perception has been mainly approached from three different points of view. A section of the Buddhists holds that true perception is determined only by its object. When imagination contributes nothing to the body of perception, it is called *nirvikalpaka* perception, which roughly corresponds to the term sensation of Western psychology. The Prābhākaras find the true character of perception in its immediacy. Perception is direct awareness. The Prābhākaras also believe that some forms of consciousness may be partly direct and partly indirect. The ancient Naiyāyikas believe that every form of consciousness is determined by its object, and that consciousness does not reveal its own specific nature, viz. mediacy or immediacy. Hence perception, according to them, is generated by the instrumentality of a sense-organ. Gaṅgeśa holds that sense-organs play the part of an instrument in the production of perception in a common human being. Knowledge by complication, recognition, and other similar forms of awareness, though not direct in the literal sense of the term, are declared to be perceptual by Gaṅgeśa, since they all cannot but depend upon the instrumentality of sense-organs for their coming into being. The import of his theory is that if sense-stimulus remains active and operative in the production of a particular consciousness, then it is perceptual.

Perception admits of two classes, viz. non-relational and relational. The *nirvikalpaka* perception of this school is neither sensation nor intuition. It has only a logical existence. We cannot dispense with it since perceptual judgements presuppose it. Gaṅgeśa invites our attention to a special feature of determinate perception which none of his predecessors mentioned. He holds that in a perceptual judgement some terms should be not only related, but also qualified ; but some terms remain unqualified and indeterminate.

In the perceptual judgement, 'This is a jar', an individual jar is only qualified by the universal of jarness; but the universal itself remains unqualified. In the negative perceptual judgement, 'There is no jar on the spot', the spot is qualified by the negation of a jar, and the negation is also qualified by the universal of jarness, which itself remains unqualified. Thus every determinate perception is partly indeterminate, but the subject of all determinate perception must be qualified.

The objects of perception are as follows: (1) substance, (2) attributes, (3) action, (4) the relation of inherence, (5) universals, and (6) negation. Perceptible objects alone are perceived, and experience teaches us that objects are perceptible. Gaṅgeśa also treats of various kinds of sense-object contacts. He points out in this connection that only the fit sense-object contacts lead to perception. He justifies the postulation of the relation of *samavāya*. It cannot be equated with the relation of *svarūpa*. Gaṅgeśa subjects to criticism the thesis of Kumārila that negation is not sensed but is known mediately in and through the privation of cognition. As against the Prābhākara school he maintains that negation is objectively real.

Gaṅgeśa seriously considers the thesis of introspection of the ancient logicians, who assume it as a settled fact. The Buddhists and the Prābhākaras give a rude shock to this assumption. In no ancient work of the Nyāya-Vaiśeṣika school has the problem of introspection been attended to. It is Gaṅgeśa who fully discusses the problem of introspection. If consciousness is not self-conscious, how can it reveal an object? This is a knotty question that threatens the very nature of consciousness. Moreover, if we are aware of our awareness of an object by a distinct act of inner perception, then a never-ending series of inner perceptions would arise, and we should only be confined within the circle of the series of introspections arising from a single object, and would not be able to transcend it. Thus the Prābhākaras hold that every act of awareness is of triple character. It illuminates its object, the act itself is lived through, and the subject, the self, is also revealed as the subject of that act of awareness. The perceptual judgement of the form, 'This is a jar', does not occur; but it assumes the form, 'I know that this is a jar'. The Prābhākaras hold that nature should be held responsible for the peculiar feature of consciousness that it becomes both the subject and the object at the same time.

Gaṅgeśa controverts the theory that every act of awareness is self-conscious. He points out that the theory is not based upon sound experience. Moreover, logic does not demand that every act of awareness should be self-conscious in order to regulate our activities. The judgement, 'This is silver', is competent enough to lead us to activity. The so-called verb 'to know', implied in awareness, does not reveal the character of a verb, viz. activity, since activity as qualifying our awareness is not an object of introspection. Gaṅgeśa also makes the point that no awareness can intuit itself as its own object. Every object of direct awareness contains the sense-object contact that produces the direct awareness. In awareness the object does not contain such sense-object contact. Therefore an awareness cannot be intuited by itself as its own object. An object of perception always conditions its perception. Gaṅgeśa also points out that there is no hard and fast rule that we are always aware of our awareness.

### PERCEPTION AND REALISM

We shall now show the distinction between the theories of perception as advanced by Western and Indian realists. Western realists mostly hold that sensa are directly sensed and material objects are indirectly known. We are not aware of sensa and material objects in the same sense. Indian realists hold that a material object is not known through the medium of sensa. The sensa, as defined by the modern realists of the Cambridge school, constitute the surface of a material object. Indian realists of the Nyāya school hold that one of the conditions of the true perception of a material object is the contact of one of our sense-organs with many such surfaces of a material object. If the contact is exact, then the material object, the whole, of which the surfaces are parts, is directly perceived. They draw no distinction between sensation and perception, and say that if sense-data are not inseparable parts of material substances, then no material object can be perceived. The Naiyāyikas hold that the material object is a whole. It expresses itself in and through its parts. The whole, which is constituted of many parts, inheres in each of its parts. The sense-organ, when it is connected with a surface or surfaces of a material object, is also connected with the whole. A percipient perceives only sounds, odours, and tastes, but not the substance in which they inhere. By vision and touch only the percipient perceives both the material substance and its qualities capable of being visualized and touched. The perceptual judgement that the jar which is seen is the same as that which is touched points to this conclusion. So, the theory of perception of the Naiyāyikas bears a close resemblance to that of naive realism.

### ILLUSION

Let us now see how the Naiyāyikas solve the problem of illusion. They say that an absent object is also connected with the sense-organ by means of some form of consciousness, say memory. The piece of rope by some of its properties excites the memory of a snake in our mind. The object of memory is connected with our eyes by means of supernormal contact. Our eyes, thus connected with the object of memory, produce the visual perception of a snake. There is no discernible difference between a normal perception and perception produced by supernormal contact. The Naiyāyikas do not prove this hypothesis but simply assume it. If their assumption is worth accepting, then their realism stands, otherwise it falls to the ground.

The import of the Nyāya theory of illusion is that the subject of a judgement of illusion is never wrongly cognized, but only the predicate is misread. As it stands, the theory maintains that we directly perceive a number of substances, some of their qualities, actions of perceptible substances, universals, the relation of inherence, negation, difference, etc. The whole, i.e. a material substance, is directly perceived, and the self, the spiritual substance, is also directly known by means of introspection. The Naiyāyikas ignore hallucination and interpret all such cases in terms of illusion. If hallucination is an undeniable fact, then the Nyāya theory of realism cannot be tenable. No modern logicians have taken proper notice of hallucination, which has been explained in terms of illusion.

## INFERENCE

People learn from experience that the existence of an object is a sign of the existence of some other object. The sign may either precede or follow the other object or may coexist with it. The sudden swelling of the small rivers of a hill region is the sign of a heavy rainfall in the immediate past. The appearance of a dark cloud is a sign of rainfall in the immediate future. A rise in the body temperature is a sign of fever. Earlier logicians have arranged these signs and brought them into a logical order. The sign may be a cause or an effect, or something other than a cause or an effect. A section of earlier Naiyāyikas revises the arrangement of the sign, and lays emphasis upon the invariable association of the sign with some other thing marked by the sign. This process of knowing, through a perceived sign, some other object that is not perceived, is called inference. Inference, though based upon perception, carries us beyond the sphere of perception and contributes much to the extension of the sphere of our knowledge.

We are now to solve the question whether such an extension of knowledge through inference is valid beyond doubt or is subject to it. Gaṅgeśa holds that not any and every doubt, but only such as have a practical bearing on our lives, can invalidate an inference. Human life has two aspects; (1) the speculative and (2) the practical. The principle of induction does not fully satisfy the speculative aspect of the human mind, but is an unavoidable necessity for its practical aspect. Gaṅgeśa thinks that logic has a close bearing upon the practical side of human life and therefore the principle of induction cannot be dispensed with. He further shows that an inference which is based upon sound experience informs us of what is not experienced. The very hypothesis that no inference is valid presupposes the validity of the principle of induction. Again, an inference itself cannot invalidate it, since nobody can have recourse to an inference without assuming the very validity of the principle of induction.

The ancient Naiyāyikas have made desperate attempts to prove the validity of the principle of induction by means of *tarka,* i.e. the method of *reductio ad absurdum,* but have failed to notice the most fundamental character of the principle of induction. The so-called general laws, such as the law of causality, are all dependent upon the principle of induction and cannot contribute to the proof of the validity of the basic principle of induction. Gaṅgeśa realizes the true nature of the principle of induction and attaches no importance to *tarka* as a method of proving the validity of the principle of induction.

According to the logic of the Nyāya school, the truth of the inductive principle is not self-evident. Experience cannot supply us with a key to its validity. Therefore the only alternative is to prove its validity in an indirect manner, viz. by means of silencing the opponents with the refutation of their arguments. He has done this admirably. He has devoted many chapters to a thorough treatment of *vyāpti,* the invariable coexistence of *probans* with *probandum.* His definition of *vyāpti* clearly points to the fact that he takes note of the relation of coexistence, but not of antecedence or consequence, as an essential element of *vyāpti.*

Inferential knowledge is that which is generated by the instrumentality of the knowledge of *vyāpti.* Inferential knowledge is neither mere deduction nor mere induction but a combination of both. Indian logicians take note of both formal consistency and material validity.

Nyāya recognizes two types of inference, viz. inference for convincing oneself and that for convincing others. The first type represents discovery and verification ; and the second, demonstration. The first involves three limbs or steps, whereas the second consists of five.

The essential elements in an inference are as follows:—(1) *pakṣa,* the subject of an inference, (2) *sādhya* (*probandum*), what is to be established as existing in the subject of inference, (3) *hetu* (*probans*), the invariable sign of *sādhya,* and (4) *vyāpti,* the invariable association of the *hetu* with the *sādhya.* First we should describe the actual logical process which leads to inferential knowledge. We perceive a mark (*hetu*) as existing in a *pakṣa,* the subject of inference. We remember the relation of invariable concomitance subsisting between *sādhya* and *hetu.* Then we know that the *hetu* which exists in the *pakṣa* is invariably associated with the *sādhya* in question. The remembrance of *vyāpti* becomes active and operative when the above knowledge is produced by the joint work of the perception of *hetu* and the remembrance of *hetu's* invariable association. The complex judgement, which is an embodiment of knowledge by complication, is called a *vyāpāra,* i.e. the actual operative procedure of *vyāptijñāna.* This complex judgement in question is called *parāmarśa.* Let us take an example. A man sees smoke on a mountain. He remembers the relation of invariable concomitance holding between fire and smoke. The invariable concomitance is discovered by him on the basis of observation of positive examples where smoke is associated with fire and non-observation of negative examples, i.e. no case of its dissociation from fire has been noticed. Now the perception of smoke on the mountain and the memory of the invariable relation subsisting between fire and smoke result in a complicated judgement that the mountain contains smoke which is associated with fire. This judgement, if it be not suspended in its operation, gives rise to the inferential knowledge that the mountain has fire.

The Naiyāyikas also hold that a reliable sign of the most common type of inference has five characteristic features, viz. (1) the sign must belong to the subject of inference, (2) it must belong to positive examples, (3) it must be absent from the negative ones, (4) its presence must not be gainsaid by a counter argument, and (5) the absence of the sign must not be definitely ascertained. These five characteristic features, however, do not necessarily belong to all reliable signs.

The Naiyāyikas classify inferential knowledge under three heads according to the nature of *sādhyas.* The first type of *sadhyas* has both positive and negative examples. It is called *anvaya-vyatireki anumāna.* The hill is fiery because it is smoky. Our kitchens furnish us with the positive examples. Lakes etc. constitute the negative ones. Water and fire are incompatible with each other. Lakes cannot therefore contain fire. The second type of *sādhyas* has only positive examples, no negative ones being available. The jar is knowable because it is nameable. Every object in the universe is knowable and hence no negative example is available. Such an inference is called *kevalānvayi anumāna.* The third type of *sādhyas* has only negative examples and no positive ones. The earth is different from other substances because it has smell. The earth in its entirety being the subject of inference, no positive or parallel examples are available. Such an inference is called *kevala-vyatireki anumāna.* Gaṅgeśa criticizes the rival theory of the Mīmāṁsakas, who refute the threefold division of *anumāna* and hold that only those *sādhyas* are inferred which have both positive and negative examples. He thinks that *tarka*—the method of *reductio ad obsurdum*—contributes much to the justification of an induction, since it removes the doubts which encompass it.

Gaṅgeśa elaborately treats the fallacies (*hetvābhāsas*). He pays closer attention to material fallacies, their definition, classification, and illustration. Gadādhara's *Sāmānya-nirukti-ṭīkā* is a classical work on fallacy. Gaṅgeśa's treatment of *upādhi* (conditional inference) is also very exhaustive. He is the first logician to discuss elaborately why an *upādhi* is a source of logical error. He keeps up the traditional view of the Nyāya school and establishes that *upamāna* cannot be included in inference. He also draws a distinction between the *upamāna* of the Nyāya school and that of the Mīmāṁsā school. The former does not result in the knowledge of resemblance. It serves to identify the meaning of an unfamiliar term by means of the knowledge of resemblance to a familiar object.

### ŚABDA: VERBAL TESTIMONY

The ancient logicians such as Vātsyāyana and Praśastapāda hold that the great sages are the authors of the Vedas. But the post-Kumārila thinkers of the Nyāya-Vaiśeṣika schools hold that God is the author of the Vedas. This view is consistent with their doctrine of God as the ordainer of the moral universe. If laws come later, how can God administer justice? If laws are framed by the sages, how can God judge cases before the framing of laws? The words of authoritative persons are also a distinct source of valid knowledge. Gaṅgeśa in his *Śābdaprāmāṇyavāda* establishes that verbal knowledge is indirect, but neither inferential nor analogical.

Who is an authoritative person whose words are infallible? The modern logicians hold that a person whose knowledge of the meaning of a sentence is exact is reliable. The change in the meaning of *āpta* (authoritative person) means a good deal. But the new meaning has not been fully utilized by the modern logicians.

Now, let us see how a sentence communicates its meaning to others. The knowledge of the words in a sentence plays the most important part in the communication of the meaning of the sentence. The intervening process which leads to the communication of meaning is the knowledge of the meaning of words, the constituents of the sentence in question. But this is not in itself sufficient. It requires the aid of other auxiliary conditions, viz. the knowledge of the syntactical relation among words and of their relation to their meanings, non-contradiction among the objects denoted by the words, the close proximity of the correlative terms, and the purport of the statement conveyed by the words. One cannot read the mind of another person, but still the purport of a statement is objectively determined by the context in which he speaks and by other factors. The term *'saindhava'* means (i) a horse and (ii) salt. But when a man takes his meal and says, 'Bring *saindhava'*, the intention of the speaker is read from the circumstances, and it is understood that the term *'saindhava'* denotes salt and not a horse.

If words are not expressive of meaning, they cannot convey the syntactical relation among their meanings. The power of expression in words, called *vṛtti,* is twofold, viz. (1) *śakti* or the expressiveness of such meaning as is invariably understood whenever the word is uttered, and (2) *lakṣaṇā* or expressiveness of such unusual meanings as follow from the reading of the intention of the speaker. The sentence, 'Protect the pot of curd from the crows', does not convey the sense that the pot should be protected only from crows and not from other creatures that may spoil the curd in question. The rhetoricians hold that words have also the power of suggestion (*vyañjanā*). The logicians hold that *vyañjanā* is not a distinct *vṛtti* but is included in *lakṣaṇā*. *Lakṣaṇā* admits of a twofold division, viz. *jahat-svārtha* or the secondary meaning sacrificing the original meaning, and *ajahat-svārtha* or the secondary meaning inclusive of the original meaning.

Significant words are of four different types, viz. (1) *yaugika*—a word having the etymological meaning, e.g. *pācaka* signifying the agent of cooking (the root *'pac'* signifies the act of cooking, and the suffix means the agent) ; (2) *rūḍha*—a word having only the technical or conventional sense, e.g. *vipra* meaning a Brāhmaṇa (this meaning does not follow from its etymology); (3) *yogarūḍha*—a word having both the etymological and conventional meanings, e.g. *paṅkaja* meaning literally that which springs up from mud, but signifying only a special kind of object, viz. a lotus ; and (4) *yaugikarūḍha*—a word having alternatively both the etymological and conventional meanings, e.g. *udbhida* meaning (*a*) etymologically, that which comes out piercing the earth, i.e. a tree or a shrub, and (*b*) conventionally, a kind of Vedic sacrifice.

The modern logicians have dealt with stems and their inflexions, roots and their suffixes and prefixes, their voices, tenses, and moods, relations between words, etc. so exhaustively that it seems almost impossible to improve upon them. For example, they have discussed elaborately the meanings of the ten tenses current in Sanskrit grammar with all their nice shades of meaning. They have paid much attention to the meaning of injunction, e.g. *vidhiliṅ,* which signifies that the means to be adopted should lead to the desired (good) goal, should not tend to evil consequences, and must be practicable. The *Vyutpatti-vāda* of Gadādhara is honoured even by the eminent grammarians of the Pāṇini school. Raghunātha Śiromaṇi's *Nañ-vāda* is a classical work in which both the logical and the metaphysical import of negative sentences have been elaborately discussed.

### ONTOLOGY OF THE MODERN LOGICIANS

The critics generally hold that the contribution of the modern logicians to ontology is nil. But if the works of these logicians are studied attentively, it will be seen that Gaṅgeśa has followed the traditional ontology, while Raghunātha Śiromaṇi has revised the traditional ontology to a great extent. The innovations suggested by the latter are as follows:—(*a*) God is the seat of eternal bliss and consciousness, but has no material property. (*b*) Time and space are not distinct substances, but are identical with God. (*c*) The sky is not a distinct substance. God is the inherent cause of sound. (*d*) The internal organ (*manas*) is not a distinct substance. It is identical with the triad (molecule) of any one of the four elements. (*e*) The assumption of atoms and dyads is baseless. The triads constitute the limit of division of elements. Raghuṇātha discovers a number of objects which cannot be classed under the seven categories of the Vaiśeṣikas. They are as follows: (1) *svatva,* possession, (2) *śakti,* capacity for producing an effect, (3) *kāraṇatva,* the essential property of a cause, (4) *kāryatva,* the essential property of an effect, (5) *saṁkhyā,* number, (6) *vaiśiṣṭya,* the relation of the qualifier to the qualified, (7) *viṣayatā,* the subject-object relation, and (8) the relation of inherence, which is not one but many.[11]

Veṇidatta in his *Padārtha-maṇḍana* suggests a new classification of the categories accepted by the modern logicians. All the positive reals come under four heads: (1) substance, (2) quality, (3) action, and (4) property (*dharma*). The substances are of nine kinds. This particular number of the different types of substances has the approval of the Vedas. The types of qualities are nineteen in number. Action is only of one kind, viz. *gamana* (movement). The properties admit of various types, viz. *kāraṇatva* etc. Relations have no separate metaphysical existence and are not different from the terms related. They are the very *svarūpa* of the relata.

Viśvanātha holds in his *Bheda-siddhi* that the types of reals accepted by the Naiyāyikas refuse to come into the closed box of seven categories. This is a summary statement of the ontological conclusions of the modern logicians.

Rakhaladasa Nyayaratna in his *Tattvasāra* has made a number of contributions to the ontology of the modern logicians. The most basic change suggested by him is that our soul (Jīvātman) is not distinct from

[11] See *Padārtha-tattvanirūpaṇa*.

*manas*, the internal organ.[12] He reviews the new hypothesis of Raghunātha that *manas* is a triad of an element, e.g. air, and establishes that *manas* is a distinct class of substance and is atomic in size. All the specific attributes which are asserted to belong to the soul inhere in the *manas*.

Rakhaladasa makes a broad division of all reals into two types, viz. positive and negative. According to him, the positive reals come under six heads, viz. (1) substance, (2) quality, (3) action, (4) inherence, (5) non-inhering (*upādhi*) universals, and (6) universals. He thinks that all the newly discovered reals come under the non-inhering universals. The negative reals are of four kinds: (1) destruction, (2) pre-negation or the negation of an object prior to its coming into being, (3) the negation of an object qualified by a relation, and (4) the negation of the identity of an object. Rakhaladasa also mentions that some modern logicians discard the hypothesis of pre-negation. He classifies the substances under six different heads, viz. (1) earth, (2) water, (3) light, (4) air, (5) God, and (6) *manas*.

The modern logicians have done a great service to the defence of pluralism by their close re-examination of the refutations by the Advaita philosophers. Panchanana Tarkaratna in his *Dvaitokti-ratna-mālā* undertakes the task of completing the unfinished work of his predecessors. He closely examines all the arguments of Śaṅkara put forward in his *Brahma-Sūtra-bhāṣya* and adequately meets them all. He also shows that the purport of the Upaniṣads is in favour of pluralism. The conclusion of the rational theology of the modern logicians is that God is an inference. They thus re-establish, in a more subtle manner, the old conclusion of Vātsyāyana, Praśastapāda, and Udayana.

## ETHICS

The modern logicians keep up the ethical doctrine of the ancient masters. The moral goal of life is *mukti*. Logic and ontology are means to this end. True knowledge of the self delivers us from the initial erroneous knowledge, viz. the confusion between the body and the soul, which is the source of all evils. Erroneous knowledge which is very deep-rooted moulds our habit of thinking. Superficial true knowledge cannot cope with this persisting blunder—the basic tragedy of human life. It requires rigid discipline and a life of meditation to prepare the way for receiving the deep impressions of true knowledge. Gadādhara in his *Mukti-vāda* reviews the moral goals of the different philosophical schools. He elaborately discusses the problem whether the moral goal is eternal bliss

[12] *Manasām eva caitanyaṁ na tu jīvāntarasthitiḥ.*

or the absolute negation of all sorrows. He expresses his opinion in favour of the second alternative. He also discusses the problem whether the intuition of the soul, or that of God, is the source of final emancipation. Raghunātha sticks to the first alternative, others to the second. Gadādhara disobliges none, but makes a happy synthesis. He does not cast aside the *paurāṇika* view of *mukti,* but assigns a place to it.

To conclude this discussion of the main points of Navya-Nyāya, we may sum up as follows:

The modern logicians shed light to a great extent on the difficulties of language. Traditional language cannot keep pace with the evolution of thought. We cannot express the new concepts without possibilities of ambiguity and confusion of terms. It is a fact that 'language in general is evolved at a comparatively low level of experience, and there is no vocabulary capable of expressing any great degree of subtlety of discrimination'. An epoch-making evolution of language is due to the modern logicians. Almost all the branches of Sanskrit literature, viz. philosophy, grammar, law, rhetoric, etc. are indebted to Navya-Nyāya for the expression of their subtle thoughts. The study of Navya-Nyāya has become as essential as that of Sanskrit grammar.

The study of Navya-Nyāya helps to sharpen our intellect and promotes a better understanding of problems and their solution ; it awakens keen insight and develops the critical faculty ; it champions the cause of commonsense ; and it is a truism that the power of analysis steadily increases if one undergoes the discipline of Navya-Nyāya.

The modern logicians lay the greatest stress on free thinking and recognize the pre-eminent value of direct observation and reasoning. They labour to re-establish realism and empirical logic in their former position, and to evolve a new philosophy of grammar which is capable of offering a challenge to the *Mahābhāṣya* of Patañjali.

It must, however, be admitted that the range of study of the modern logicians is not very extensive. They do not always take pains to study the standard works of the rival schools. The early modern logicians are thoroughly acquainted with the works of the Mīmāṁsā school, but most of them are ignorant of the Vedānta systems and of Jaina thought. In most cases their knowledge of the rival schools is not first-hand. Most of them are not alive to current topics. The source of their information is very limited. The modern logicians are in the dark about the different branches of Indian science. It is for this reason that they could not bring about a revolution in ontology. They have glorified perception, but shirked drawing its logical conclusions. Like other philosophers they often lack the historical sense. They think that social and political laws are divine. That is why they could not stand above the influence of tradition in spite of their love of freedom. Thus their search after truth has not been thorough and complete.

The contribution of the modern logicians to ethics is not worthy of their attainments. They keep up the traditional view that the goal of life is the absolute cessation of all sufferings. The path of asceticism is recommended for reaching the destination. The pivot of the ethical doctrine is the law of Karma. Have they carefully examined this law? Does not the law of Karma presuppose the atomic structure of a society? The individuals of a society are so many atoms each of which moves in its own way. Though referred to in ancient literature, the *karma* of groups of men has been ignored by the modern logicians. They have not dealt with the problem raised by Śrīharṣa, how a disembodied soul, which is no better than a piece of stone, can be the goal of human aspiration.

The theology of the Nyāya-Vaiśeṣika school is not in touch with practical religion. The modern logicians have made no improvement upon it, since they fail to remove the anthropomorphic idea of God. God, according to this school, is the great king-cum-engineer-cum-tutor. Moreover, the Naiyāyikas handle God as a machine to solve all difficulties. They hold that God has no feelings, but at the same time assert that an individual soul attains to *mukti* through His grace.

In the Nyāya-Vaiśeṣika system of thought there are no watertight compartments for epistemology, logic, psychology, ethics, theology, metaphysics, etc. It is naturally expected that these different sciences would therefore be harmoniously blended together into an integrated system of thought. But, as a matter of fact, there is a wide gulf between the ethics and theology of the Nyāya-Vaiśeṣika school. The goal of ethics is self-realization. If one sincerely and constantly practises meditation upon the self, then the virtue arising out of such meditation will surely lead one on to the direct intuition of the soul as a substratum. This mystic vision of the soul will surely dispel basic ignorance and lead on to final emancipation. Divine worship has no part to play in the attainment of the moral goal. Raghunātha Śiromaṇi lays emphasis upon the exclusive necessity of self-realization. Thus God becomes divorced from the real ethics of the modern logicians. God is an inference, whose existence is considered necessary for the creation, preservation, and destruction of the universe. God has been thus converted into little more than a *deus ex machina,* the function of which seems to be to solve the difficulties felt by the modern school. Gadādhara has made some attempt to bridge the gulf that separates Nyāya ethics from its theology, but is not sufficiently sure of his own ground to take a firm stand against the views of Raghunātha. He suggests that divine grace can grant us self-realization, but he does not uphold the view that divine grace is the only source of self-realization. Divine grace cannot in fact lead directly to final emancipation. Self-realization is its necessary condition. Therefore God is not an integral part of Navya-Nyāya ethics.

The defect of the modern logicians is that they have failed to infuse the spirit of discovery into their students. They have sharpened their intellect, but have not taught them to apply it to life's problems. They look like soldiers who constantly sharpen their weapons, but fail to appear in time of need. In addition, they have failed to touch upon the secondary ends of human life, arrange them in a hierarchy, and correlate them to the highest end. In short, they are divorced from real life and tend to live too much in a world of abstraction.

# 7

## PŪRVA-MĪMĀṀSĀ

THE great sage Jaimini is the author of the *Mīmāṁsā-Sūtra* (aphorisms). There is a difference of opinion among scholars as to his identity. Whether he is the disciple of Vyāsa mentioned in the *Mahābhārata* or some other person is a controversial question. Two *ṛṣis,* Bādarāyaṇa and Bādari, are mentioned in Jaimini's *Mīmāṁsā-Sūtra,* and Jaimini is mentioned in Maharṣi Veda-Vyāsa's *Śārīraka-Sūtra.* But none of these texts clearly indicates the relationship of teacher and disciple between Vyāsa and Jaimini. Though this led to a controversy among Western scholars, yet Śabara Svāmin, the famous commentator of Jaimini's *Mīmāṁsā-Sūtra,* while explaining the use of the word 'Bādarāyaṇa' in *sūtra* I.1.5, says that it is used here to denote that Bādarāyaṇa's opinion is also the same ; and by this the opinion expressed in the *sūtra* has been strengthened and not opposed.

According to Śabara Svāmin therefore, it is clear that Bādarāyaṇa was respected by Jaimini, and his name is mentioned to show that the intrinsic validity or self-evidence of knowledge as advocated in the *sūtra* has the sanction of Bādarāyaṇa also and is therefore valid.

Though it is not clearly mentioned that this Bādarāyāṇa is Maharṣi Veda-Vyāsa, the author of the *Mahābhārata* and the teacher of Jaimini, yet on the authority of this hint of Śabara Svāmin, ancient Indian scholars have accepted the relation of teacher and disciple between Veda-Vyāsa, who is mentioned as Bādarāyaṇa, and Jaimini.

It is not necessary to enter into this controversy here for the study of our subject. The *Mīmāṁsā-Sūtra* embodies the results of discussions regarding ritual practice, the beginnings of which are found in the Brāhmaṇas, and which have subsequently descended in a long course of tradition. The teacher's name is often cited to support the doctrines set out, as in the *Kauṣītaki* and the *Śatapatha Brāhmaṇas.* The collection of *mantras* in the Saṁhitās and the accounts of sacrifices in the Brāhmaṇas presented points of divergence, and the order in which the offerings were to be performed was determined by reasoning. The order in the Saṁhitās and the normal sequence of actions had greater weight than the order in the Brāhmaṇas. The person by whom a particular action had to be performed, when not specified, was determined by logical argument. Nyāya was hence an early name for Karma-Mīmāṁsā. The Dharma-Sūtras, e.g. of Āpastamba and Baudhāyana, employ arguments akin to those of the Mīmāṁsā, though the language differs, and hence Jaimini's rules may not have existed in their present form at the time.

The object of Jaimini's *Mīmāṁsā-Sūtra* is to explain the meaning of the Vedas. The Vedas directly or indirectly indicate what *dharma* or virtue is and what *adharma* or vice is. They do so in order that persons may practise *dharma* and abstain from *adharma*. The *Mīmāṁsā-Sūtra* therefore should not be regarded as a commentary on the Vedas like other *bhāṣyas,* but its function is to explain how to arrive at the real meaning of the Vedas which is acceptable to the wise. Every student of the book should remember well that its main object is to lay down and explain in detail rules for removing doubts and thus arriving at the real meaning of the Vedas.

The Vedas come under the proof known as *śabda-pramāṇa.* The Pūrva-Mīmāṁsā has considered at great length whether *śabda* or verbal authority is itself a *pramāṇa.* The conclusion is that like perception (*pratyakṣa*), inference (*anumāna*), etc. it also is a form of proof. Ordinary words, however, are of two kinds: some words uttered by man may be regarded as true (*pramāṇa*), while others may be regarded as untrue (*apramāṇa*). Whether the assemblage of words in the Vedas may be taken as true *in toto* is discussed in detail in the *Mīmāṁsā-Sūtra,* and the result is that the Vedas have been accepted in their entirety as authoritative. The first part of this paper aims at briefly discussing those reasonings which are used by the Mīmāṁsakas to arrive at this conclusion.

## AUTHORLESSNESS OF THE VEDAS

Before entering into this discussion it is essential to find out what the Mīmāṁsakas understand by the term 'Veda'. They regard the Vedas as self-revealed (*apauruṣeya*), that is to say, they have not been written or composed like the *Rāmāyaṇa* and the *Mahābhārata* by man. Had they been so written, then the author of the Vedas, like Vālmīki and Veda-Vyāsa, the authors respectively of those two books, would have been remembered by us. The Vedic teachers and disciples have maintained a continuous chain of the study of the Vedas from time immemorial, but nobody ever heard the name of the author of the Vedas. From this it may be inferred that there was no author of the Vedas, because in that case some one or other of these people would have heard his name. It is therefore the unanimous conclusion of the exponents of the Mīmāṁsā philosophy that the Vedas must be regarded as self-revealed, since there is no remembrance from time immemorial of any special man as the author of the Vedas. The purport of what Śabara Svāmin says in order to arrive at this conclusion is as follows:

'We must not think that someone has connected the Vedic words with their meanings in order to give currency to the Vedic rites and ceremonies. This relation is self-evident. Had there been any man who connected the Vedic words with their meanings and introduced the Vedic rites, then at the time of performing such rites the performer must have remembered the author. This remembrance of the connection between the author and the user of the text is absolutely essential to the fulfilment of the aim and object of such performance. For instance, Pāṇini coined the word *vṛddhi* for certain vowel modifications. If we remember him when we hear this word, then only we know that the word *vṛddhi* denotes such and such, and can use it according to the method invented by him and obtain the appropriate result. But when we do not remember the word as a definition of his, we do not ascribe to it any such meaning, nor use it according to his rules, nor get the result thus obtainable. Similarly, a *ṛṣi* named Piṅgala, who is the author of the science of prosody, takes *ma* to denote any group of three consecutive long syllables. When we remember him, we take *ma* to denote a word containing three such long syllables, e.g. Vaiśālī, and use it in metrical compositions and get the desired result. But when we do not think of it as a technical term used by Piṅgala, it fails to suggest to our minds any such group of syllables, e.g. Vaiśālī, and we do not use *ma* according to the rules of prosody. It follows therefore that unless a sect becomes extinct we always remember the author and user of the technical terms current in the usages of that sect. This is the general rule. It is now clear that had the Vedas been created by any man and the rites depending on them been first performed by him, then we should always have remembered the author. As we cannot understand the meaning of Pāṇini's aphorism *'Vṛddhiryasyācāmādiḥ . . . .'* (I.1.73) and cannot apply it unless we know the meaning of his other aphorism *'Vṛddhirādaic'* (I.1.1.), so we should be unable to follow and apply the Vedas. But our actual experience is quite contrary to this. We do not know of any author or originator of the Vedic rites and ceremonies ; yet we have been performing them continually from the beginning. Hence it cannot be established by any direct proof that someone conceived the relationship between the Vedic words and their meanings and introduced the Vedic rites of his own free will, and thus was the creator of the Vedas.'

Kumārila Bhaṭṭa, the famous author of *Ślokavārttika,* an explanatory treatise on Śabara Svāmin's commentary, explains the passage quoted above thus: 'The study of the Vedas has always been dependent on previous study ; for this study is carried on through words, as the present system of Vedic study will show.'[1]

[1] *Ślokavārttika, Vākyādhikaraṇa,* 336.

This conclusion of the Mīmāṁsakas regarding the self-revealed character of the Vedas is not accepted by the Naiyāyikas. According to them, the Vedas were made and revealed by Almighty God as the source of all happiness and prosperity for the first race of men created in this land. It should not, however, be understood that He composed the Vedas anew as a set of books; but that He only revealed the Vedas which existed in the previous cycle (*kalpa*). This He did in the previous cycle also. Hence there is no author of the Vedas except God.

Ācārya Udayana, the author of *Kusumāñjali,* says on this point: 'What is "Veda"? Every word cannot be called "Veda". Words denoting unseen things cannot be called "Veda", because the words of an impostor are not regarded as "Veda". The words of Maharṣi Manu and others about virtue and vice and other unseen things are not regarded as "Veda". Hence the reply is that those words which cannot be traced to any other source and which are accepted by the wise as authority constitute the Vedas. It cannot be said that the words which have come down to us as the Vedas originated from perception and other proofs. Nor can it be said that they sprang from the error of an ignorant person or the imposition of a cheat; for then they would not have been accepted as authority by the good and the wise. The view of the Mīmāṁsakas that the chain of teachers and students from time immemorial is the source of the Vedas is also not tenable, because at the time of dissolution (*mahāpralaya*) such a chain cannot exist.'

Ācārya Udayana has clearly said that the source of the Vedas cannot be the perception or inference of any human being like ourselves, because the supernatural subject-matter of the Vedas is unintelligible to a man with human reasoning. The argument that someone without understanding it rationally has ascribed his own imaginary meaning to it and has introduced it for some selfish motive is also not sound; for there is no proof that the results of the actions mentioned in the Vedas are not attainable. And as they have been regarded as authority by the wise (*śiṣṭa*) and sages (*mahājana*), their author cannot be an ignorant person or a cheat.

His criticism of the Mīmāṁsaka view deserves careful consideration. He says, 'Like the words used by us, the Vedas also are composed of words and hence they have been made by someone. The argument of the Mīmāṁsakas that there is no author of the Vedas, since the memory of such an author is not handed down to us, is also not valid, because the scriptures themselves declare the divine origin of the Vedas. Says the Smṛti: "Then the Vedas came out of His mouth. Thus in the beginning of each cycle different Vedas are composed"; and "I have composed the

Vedānta and I am the knower of the Vedas".[2] And the Śruti: "From that God have sprung all offerings of oblations as well as the *Sāman, Ṛc,* and other Vedas."[3] Such remembrance also is current among the students of the Vedas. It may be urged that these are laudatory words designed to praise the Vedas and not to establish their divine origin. But this does not stand the test of reason. There being no rule laid down in the Vedas that the author must be remembered, the priests did not remember the author while performing the rites, and a time came when the author was totally forgotten; but that does not prove that there was no author at all. If words must be regarded as authorless (*apauruṣeya*) when there is no remembrance of the author, then if the name of Kālidāsa be forgotten, *Kūmāra-sambhava* also should be regarded as authorless—a view which nobody would accept.'

But the Mīmāṁsakas have not accepted the divine origin of the Vedas as believed by the Naiyāyikas. Their reasons for rejecting the Naiyāyika view are briefly given below.

It has already been shown above that, in the opinion of the ancient Mīmāṁsakas like Śabara and Kumārila, there is no reliable evidence to show that someone composed the Vedas in the beginning and introduced the Vedic rites. Moreover, it is admitted by the Naiyāyikas also that though the Vedic rites have been current among the learned and the wise at all times throughout the length and breadth of India, yet there is no evidence to show when and by whom these were introduced first. On these arguments the Mīmāṁsakas base their belief in the authorlessness of the Vedas.

How man was first created on this earth has been explained in different ways by different learned men, who do not agree among themselves. This was done in the past, this is done at the present time; but there is no explanation which has been accepted by all. Those who seek to postulate the existence of the author of the Vedas on the ground that a sentence (*vākya*) must be the creation of man, should admit that the first creator of the Vedic sentences must have been a man; for it is not possible for any other creature to create them. It is common knowledge that it is beyond the power of any other creature to compose a sentence consisting of words made up of vowels and consonants. It is clear therefore that the first author who composed these sentences was a man. It must also be admitted in this connection that that man had the knowledge of the technique of combining words into sentences to convey the desired meaning. If it be so, it may be asked how that first man acquired the knowledge of words and the things they signified. We find that one who frames a

[2] *B.G.*, XV. 15.
[3] *Ṛ.V.*, X. 90. 9.

sentence learns the words and their meanings and their mode of combination from some one else before one can compose a sentence intelligible to others. Hence the existence of the author clearly indicates the existence of a previous author of the words and their meanings. Otherwise it is impossible to frame a sentence to express one's feelings or ideas. We do not come across any deviation from this rule. If this be an established rule for composition by man, this rule must also be observed in Vedic composition.

No theory or conjecture propounded by scientists and philosophers from time to time about the origin of the first man or the mode of his use of words or formation of society has received universal acceptance ; and no sane man can hope to find a consensus of opinion in this respect. On the other hand we find at the present time among those who perform Vedic rites that the student learns them from his teacher who in his turn learnt them from his own teacher, and so on. This continuous chain has come down to us from time immemorial. No reliable evidence is before us to show that this chain was actually broken at any time in the past. Hence this eternal continuous chain of the teacher and the taught is the bed-rock of the belief in the authorlessness of the Vedas.

Considerations of space compel us to be brief here. Those readers who are interested in the subject and want to know more details are referred to *Śabara-bhāṣya* and Kumārila's *Ślokavārttika.*

### VALIDITY OF THE VEDAS

Granting that the authorlessness of the Vedas has been accepted, how can the authority (*prāmāṇya*) of the Vedas be established? Take for example a local rumour regarding the abode of an evil spirit in a particular banyan tree. Nobody knows who first gave currency to this report ; the people of the locality, however, have known it for a long time as being handed down from father to son. But is it reasonable to accept it as valid on this ground? There are hundreds of such stories current among us ; but should we take them as valid? Similarly, though there has been an unbroken chain of teachers and disciples of the Vedas, yet is it reasonable to accept the Vedas as authority on this ground?

In reply to this the Mīmāṁsakas say that one should first understand clearly the axiomatic nature of authority. Correct knowledge is called truth (*pramā*) and incorrect knowledge is called error (*bhrama*). Every item of knowledge is not correct and hence not truth. The question, however, is how one should discover what is truth. Different answers are given to this question by different schools of philosophy. According to the Nyāya and Vaiśeṣika schools, the correctness or incorrectness of knowledge cannot be found out at once. If, after proper investigation, we find that the senses through which the knowledge has come are in a reliably sound condition, then we infer that the knowledge gained is correct. When, for example, the eye sees an object under normal conditions, we conclude that the knowledge obtained is correct (*pramā*). If such knowledge comes from abnormal causes or is based on insufficient data, we know that it is an error. This is the view of the Naiyāyikas and other philosophers who accept extraneous evidence (*paratah-pramāṇa*) as the source of knowledge.

The Mīmāṁsakas say in reply that the above argument cannot bear scrutiny. For the circumstances under which the vision of an object takes place have been assumed to be true or favourable for correct vision without any proof that they are really so. To prove that they are really favourable, normal, or sound, one must prove that their causes are sound and correct; and this process would continue *ad infinitum*. We are thus landed in the haze of imagination; the practical result of such a process is the impossibility of ascertaining the truth of the knowledge in question. Suppose that a man is sitting somewhere in the thick darkness of a new-moon night. A sudden flash of lightning reveals a tiger in front of him with jaws wide open. As soon as he sees the animal, he runs away in bewilderment without caring for any proof whether the sight of the tiger is real or only an illusion. Still less does he care for the favourability, suitability, or soundness of the causes which led to the terrible ocular experience. He believes in the presence of the beast more firmly than any truth proved by anybody and attempts to escape by running away from it. It is clear from this that the power of judging the correctness of the knowledge acquired is inherent in our nature. That is why man has always carried on his practical affairs accordingly in all ages and will do so in future. It must be admitted by all therefore that knowledge does not depend for its validity on the subsidiary knowledge of the soundness of its causes. Knowledge is self-revealed and its correctness (*pramā*) self-evident, and on this self-evident correctness are based all the actions of man.

Though the proof of its correctness is inherent in knowledge itself, no one admits that there can be no error at all. Though we naturally and automatically accept the validity of knowledge by intuition, yet on occasions we question the validity of knowledge under compulsion, and at times we do oppose, criticize, reject, and declare it to be an error. But when are we compelled to do so? We do so when we find that the knowledge in question is opposed to or sublated by another piece of knowledge which has already been proved to be true; or when we find that the causes from which the knowledge has sprung are faulty and consequently unable to produce the correct knowledge. In short, we reject a newly acquired piece of knowledge as error for two reasons: first, when it is contradictory to what has already been proved to be true ; secondly, when the cause of the knowledge is found faulty. The faults or defects of the cause of knowledge are briefly shown below.

Knowledge is of two kinds, direct (*pratyakṣa*) and indirect (*parokṣa*). Knowledge acquired through the perception of the senses is called direct knowledge, and knowledge gained from inference or verbal authority (*śabda-pramāṇa*) is called indirect knowledge. If the eye is weak or affected by jaundice or any other disease, the knowledge acquired through it cannot be free from error. Thus the degree of error in the knowledge is proportional to the weakness or defect of the sense-organ through which the knowledge is gained.

The means or sources of knowledge are called the *pramāṇas,* and they are six according to the school of Bhaṭṭa, i.e. Kumārila. These are direct perception (*pratyakṣa*), inference (*anumāna*), verbal authority (*śabda*), analogy (*upamāna*), presumption (*arthāpatti*), and non-perception (*anupalabdhi*). *Pratyakṣa* results from the immediate contact between sense and its object. It is objective, i.e. it is conditioned by the object, and is not subjective, i.e. comprising the knowledge and the knower, for these two are not reflected or revealed therein. Prabhākara omits the sixth. Non-perception, according to him, is negation and is identical with its locus and not a separate category.

In inference the object of knowledge, being mediate or remote, is inferable. The knowledge and the knower, i.e. the subject, are, however, directly cognized. In the view of Prabhākara, ordinary, i.e. secular, verbal testimony has no independent validity as a source of knowledge. For it is included in inference, being an index to the import of the speaker. Vedic texts like injunctions, however, are valid means of proof. In this view perception alone has validity as proof. In both views, validity as proof consists in communicating knowledge unapprehended before and otherwise not contradicted. Memory, which has as its content what was cognized before, is not an independent source. In all kinds of cognition or forms of knowledge there is revelation of the proof, the probandum, and the prover. In direct perception all the three are immediately cognized. In inference and the rest the object alone is inferable. The prover and the proof are in them also directly cognized. The operation of inference etc. therefore refers to the object portion only.

The cause of indirect knowledge is *vyāpti-jñāna,* or the knowledge of the invariable concomitance of two things. If it is not correct, the inference drawn from it is sure to be erroneous. Thus even when a word is faultless, the indirect knowledge of its meaning, which is based on the word itself, is regarded as an error, if the man using it is unable to pronounce it correctly or is careless or deceitful.

According to this rule, if the indirect knowledge derived from the Vedic words be regarded as erroneous, then we are compelled to admit that there is some fault in the Vedic words themselves, or there is some knowledge in this world higher than what is derivable from the Vedic words.

In reply to the above the Mīmāṁsakas say that there is no possibility of the knowledge springing from the Vedic words being tainted with the faults mentioned above. From the Vedic words we understand that those who want to go to heaven should perform certain sacrifices like *jyotiṣṭoma, darśa-paurṇamāsa, agniṣṭoma,* etc. We do not find any contradictory proof, namely, that eternal happiness in heaven is not derivable from these sacrifices. Heaven cannot be proved by any evidence that can be used by men. Similarly, we have no strong reason to think that after death a happy life in heaven is not possible. Therefore there is no strong contrary reason to prove the knowledge of the duty of performing Vedic sacrifices as erroneous. Next, the doubt that the authority of the Vedas must be rejected owing to faults like error, carelessness, defect in the sense-organ, deception, etc. in the author or the propounder of the Vedas, is also not reasonable ; for it has been shown above that so long as this doctrine is not refuted by strong reason and evidence, the knowledge of the supernatural meanings derivable from the Vedic words and the self-evident truth inherent in them cannot be discarded. If the existence of the author of the Vedas be proved, then only the possibility of his faults like error etc. is imaginable. Since the Vedas consist of words which have come down from time immemorial, and since there is no author of the Vedas, their axiomatic authority stands unassailable. This is the sum and substance of the Mīmāṁsaka view regarding the authorlessness and self-evident authority of the Vedas.

Though the monistic Vedāntins accept the self-evident authority of the Vedas, yet they do not believe in the Mīmāṁsaka theory about the authorlessness of the Vedas. According to them, the Vedas have been naturally revealed without any effort, like respiration from the eternal, pure, wise, and ever free God at the beginning of the new cycle, and as such their self-evident authority cannot be rejected.

An interesting point to note is the difference of opinion between the earlier and later schools of the Mīmāṁsā. The latter do not agree to the arguments adopted by Jaimini, Śabara, and Kumārila Bhaṭṭa to establish the self-evident authority of the Vedas without postulating God and admitting His authorship of the Vedas. The later Mīmāṁsakas like Prabhākara, Khaṇḍadeva, Gāgābhaṭṭa, and Āpadeva do not hesitate to assert that the author of the Vedas cannot be any one but the omniscient and omnipotent God ; more than this, they declare in unequivocal terms that the existence of an omniscient and omnipotent God and His authorship of the Vedas have been proved beyond any shadow of doubt with the help of the Vedas themselves.

### MĪMĀṀSĀ—ITS MEANING AND SCOPE

It is necessary here to know the exact meaning of the word *mīmāṁsā*. It means the reasoning which has to be adopted in order to understand the connotation of a word or a sentence. The interconnected words and sentences which teach the method of such reasoning constitute what is called Pūrva-Mīmāṁsā. The epithet *pūrva* is added because it deals primarily and exhaustively with the method of reasoning regarding the rites which form the *pūrva* or earlier portion of the Vedas. It is also known as Karma-Mīmāṁsā, since it seeks to find out the real nature of these rites and the results accruing from their due performance. Hence, it is necessary for every student of this philosophy to remember that the subject-matter of this system is the study of the Vedic rites.

Acts are divided into two classes—ordained and forbidden. *Darśa-paurṇamāsa, agnihotra, jyotiṣṭoma,* etc. are ordained acts. Drinking wine, killing a Brāhmaṇa, etc. are forbidden acts. The Pūrva-Mīmāṁsā discusses at length, in the light of the Vedic texts, the nature of the Vedic rites, their primary and secondary character, their priority and posteriority in the matter of performance together with their results and purposes, and also the particular sense or method in which a Vedic injunction, positive or negative, is to be interpreted to bring about the desired result. This, in short, is the aim of the Mīmāṁsā philosophy. A detailed discussion on the above points is not possible in this short article. We therefore proceed to a consideration of some of those features which account for the high esteem in which this philosophy has ever been held in India, and which constitute its contribution to the development of the religious life of the country.

### VEDIC INJUNCTIONS

The Mīmāṁsaka school has given an elaborate analysis of the origin of the religious motive or the impulse to pious conduct and a minute consideration of the effects, immediate and mediate, of the Vedic injunctions.

An injunction or *vidhi* urges and leads a person to acts which may be (1) regular, imperative, or obligatory (*nitya*), (2) necessitated by occasions (*naimittika*), and (3) optional, i.e. performed with a view to obtaining some boon or worldly good (*kāmya*). In the Bhāṭṭa view, all these three kinds of action, being within the scope of injunctions, constitute *dharma*. According to Prabhākara, an injunction impels a person to the first two kinds, i.e. regular and occasional only. For it tends to generate the impulse in a person who through sloth and the like does not engage in such acts; and the authority of the injunction lies there. In optional action a person acts from his own desire or attachment. Hence the *vidhi* carries no inducement to such action. But an injunction signifying the relation of means and end between sacrifice and heaven desists at that point and intends nothing further. Hence it neither induces a person to do nor dissuades him from doing an optional act and therefore pertains neither to *dharma* nor to its opposite. Reprehensible acts like the eating of *kalañja* or the performance of *śyena,* a sacrifice to injure another being, comprised as they are within prohibitions, constitute demerit in this view.

The Mīmāṁsakas recognize two kinds of energy in injunctions for this purpose—verbal and actual. Verbal energy is the special function which conduces to a man's impulse. It inheres in an inspirer like the preceptor and is a wish or an intention of the form, 'Let him be induced to do it', conveyed by the *liṅ,* i.e. the imperative in the verb. It is expressed as an incitement, inducement, or mandate. In the Vedas, which are impersonal in origin, the injunction cannot be the intention of any person and hence is construed as an operation conducive to a person's inclination which resides in the imperative in the Vedic text. It ensues immediately after the hearing of the injunctive text, 'Sacrifice in order to attain heaven', and is seen in such an attitude as this, 'I am urged by the Vedic imperative'. It is called *bhāvanā* since it conduces to the production or being (*bhavana*) of the human impulse, and, as inhering in the Vedic words, it is called verbal. Hence it follows that the verbal energy is a peculiar transcendental function which lodges in the imperative in an injunctive sentence. Certain Mīmāṁsakas like Maṇḍana Miśra hold that *śābdī bhāvanā* or verbal energy is a special property which resides in the intended import of the verb and is of the nature of a means or instrument or the desired result. But this exposition is not accepted by all.

Actual energy, on the other hand, is the operation pertaining to the performer of sacrifices and the like, and tending to the production of the result. The character common to both the kinds is a special function of incitement which conduces to the effecting of that which is to be. This is signified by the predicative portion. Propositions like 'shall sacrifice', 'shall offer oblation', 'shall donate' imply the result, the operation leading to it, and exertion necessary for the purpose. Of these the result and the operation tending to it are connoted by the verb and the effort is signified by the predicative mood. Mīmāṁsakas like Pārthasārathi hold the predicative to denote exertion in general. Some, like Someśvara Bhaṭṭa, take it to signify the special exertion itself. This is the actual energy, and it produces the result through the sense of the verb. It is called actual, since it directly produces the result. All Mīmāṁsakas consider this special effort or operation as the main part of the significance of predication and hold all the other elements to be connected with it. The conclusion of the Mīmāṁsakas is that this exertion or operation causes performance of the sacrifice, and through that the invisible potency, and through that the result. And in their view this *apūrva* or invisible potency is an entity which is of the highest worth and most necessary and unavoidable.

## MAN'S NATURE AND GOAL

Though very little has been said in this system about the real nature of the self of man, who alone is entitled to perform the ordained acts such as sacrifices (*yajña*), offering of oblations in the consecrated fire (*homa*), and charity (*dāna*), we shall briefly discuss this subject from the standpoint of the Mīmāṁsakas.

Like other dualistic schools of philosophers such as Naiyāyikas and Vaiśeṣikas, the Mīmāṁsakas believe in the separateness of the self (Jīvātman) from the body, senses, and mind, and look upon special properties like intelligence, will, and effort as the natural attributes of the self.

There is no specific mention, however, of the real nature of the Jīvātman in the *Mīmāṁsā-Sūtra* of Jaimini. Śabara Svāmin, the commentator of this book, makes only a passing reference to it in his commentary, but even that is not his own. He only quotes some earlier commentator whose identity has not yet been determined. Some are of opinion that the commentator was his teacher Upavarṣa. But there are reasons to disbelieve this assumption.

There is no clear mention of the Jīvātman as either infinite or of the size of the body or atomic, either in the original *Sūtra* or in Śabara's commentary. Later Mīmāṁsakas, however, accepting the Naiyāyika view, regard it as all-pervasive like ether.

Āpadeva and Laugākṣi Bhāskara hold on the authority of the *Bhagavad-Gītā* that a sacrifice performed in honour of Īśvara or Govinda produces the highest good. In later treatises of the Mīmāṁsā school, Vedāntic texts are adopted at some points. The commentator Guṇaratna considers Jaimini to have accepted the doctrine of Māyā. This attribution is not altogether without the sanction of ancient text and tradition. In the *Vedānta-Sūtra* Jaimini's views appear in a twofold light as upholding Mīmāṁsā texts as well as subscribing to certain undoubted Vedāntic doctrines, e.g. the attainment by the departed soul of Brahman endowed with the qualities set forth in the *Chāndogya Upaniṣad* (VIII. 7). If Jaimini upheld one set of doctrines, the later exponents of the Mīmāṁsā like Prabhākara and Kumārila have to be regarded as sifting and retaining those of the traditional school to the exclusion of whatever did not pertain to this store.

From such Vedic texts as 'This is he, the performer of sacrifices, who attains heaven thereby', the Mīmāṁsakas conclude that heaven is the *summum bonum* of human life. There is, however, no indication in the works of Jaimini, Śabara, and Kumārila as to whether this heaven (*svarga*) is identical with bliss, or it is a place where happiness unalloyed with pain or grief can be enjoyed. Later Mīmāṁsakas understood the term in the latter sense. But most of the Mīmāṁsakas maintain that heaven does not mean anything but bliss. In support of this view they cite the following saying of the *ṛṣis*: 'That happiness which is not mixed with sorrow or eclipsed by any other mental state, which has no cessation, and which is available for the mere wish, is heaven (*svarga*).'

Śabara Svāmin has openly declared that this heaven cannot be enjoyed on this earth. To attain it one must leave the body behind. According to him, people offer oblations and perform sacrifices with the desire of attaining heaven; but when it is not possible to realize heaven in this body, the faithful performer of these sacrifices is forced to believe that this body is not the soul; for heaven cannot be attained unless this body is destroyed, though people spend huge sums of money and undergo many hardships in performing sacrifices with the desire of going there.

The self-revealed Śrutis clearly say that the performance of sacrifices, the offering of oblations, and charity are the means of attaining heaven. But since the present body is not capable of enjoying it on this earth, the soul must be encased in a suitable body for the purpose. It must therefore be admitted by all who have faith in the authority of the Vedas that there is the eternal soul as an entity distinct from this body. This is the conclusion of Śabara Svāmin.

There is no clear indication in the *Mīmāṁsā-Sūtra* or the commentary of Śabara about the possibility of emancipation (*mokṣa*) of the self. Kumārila Bhaṭṭa, who was the immediate predecessor of Śaṅkarācārya, states in his *Ślokavārttika* that emancipation (*mokṣa*) is the supreme end of the self. But his emancipation does not include happiness. The real nature of emancipation is the perfect extinction of sorrow. Kumārila has no hesitation in discarding the view that the realization of the bliss of the soul is the real nature of emancipation.

Although admitted by later Mīmāṁsakas, *mokṣa* or emancipation is not, as in the Vedānta, of the nature of final and absolute annihilation of objective existence. For, in this view, objective existence has ultimate reality. Sacred texts signifying unreality import that it is not destined to endure eternally. Hence objective existence, though real, undergoes destruction of connection with the perceiving ego or self. Threefold is the connection of the self with the objective world, namely, through the body, the senses, and their objects. The body is the basis of enjoyment or experience, agreeable or otherwise. The senses are the seats of enjoyment. The contents of enjoyment are form, taste, smell, etc. Enjoyment is direct experience comprising pleasure, pain, and the like. The ego or *puruṣa* is bound by these three. This bondage is called *saṁsāra*—the evanescent cycle of existence. The permanent cessation of the three is *mokṣa* ; ultimate or permanent cessation is the destruction of the body, the senses, and their objects created before, and their non-emergence afresh. These two processes terminate pleasure and pain. Such extinction is due to the extinction of *dharma* and *adharma,* right and wrong, worthy and unworthy conduct, merit and demerit. The termination of *dharma* is effected by the enjoyment of the fruits of merit or piety already acquired. And extinction of *adharma* or impiety or demerit ensues from the performance of 'obligatory' and 'occasional' duties. Among these effects of causes, non-performance of the optional acts and the avoidance of the prohibited acts lead to no results. If only the 'obligatory' or 'regular' duties and those entailed by certain occasions are performed, sin is avoided, and no cause leading to the creation of a body arises ; hence the previously acquired body being lost, the soul remains without a body. This condition is designated as release or *mokṣa.* This release cannot be attained merely through knowledge of the self. Therefore all who desire emancipation have to strive to attain the bodiless selfhood by the aforesaid process.

The Mīmāṁsakas do not believe in the absolute dissolution (*mahā-pralaya*) of this world. They say that this universe has existed as it is from eternity, and there is no proof that this eternal religion of the Vedas and its adherents belonging to the three castes will ever be totally extinct. From Kumārila Bhaṭṭa downwards the Mīmāṁsakas have propounded this view with great force. The above Mīmāṁsakas believe that man can never acquire omniscience without the help of the Vedas. We can know of supernatural things only through the Vedas, as did Manu and other great sages.

In the Mīmāṁsā philosophy, work recommended by the scriptures has been declared to be the source of all blessings. It is through such work that man can fulfil his desires and at last attain to emancipation, which is equivalent to the extinction of all misery and sorrow. The Mīmāṁsakas do not believe that knowledge divorced from ritualistic work can enable a man to rise to the full stature of his being. Man is born to do this kind of work. Renunciation of this work, in other words, the non-performance of ordained acts, instead of doing him any positive good either in this world or in the next, plunges him into a sea of troubles and sufferings here and hereafter. The Mīmāṁsakas proclaim that it is a pity to be born as man in this world if the individual fails to perform ordained actions.

The validity of these injunctive texts of several kinds rests on their promulgating the rituals which they prescribe. And the explanatory texts, read in conjunction with them, are commendatory of the prescribed acts. An injunctive text aims at inducing a person to some specific act. Such a person through dislike or sloth may not desire to engage in an act which involves exertion. And in that case the entire Vedas which aim at such performance lose their use or purpose. Hence the Vedas seek to praise such performance in order to produce the inclination of people to them through their liking for them. This praise is done by the explanatory sentences which are read by the side of the injunctive texts. Hearkening to such praise, men in whom the liking has been produced perform the acts with zeal and obtain the boon. Hence the main function of the explanatory texts is to rouse a sense of the commendable nature of the acts. The Upaniṣads mostly belong to this category ; for, by propounding the imperishability of the soul engaged in such and such an act and its enjoyership of fruit thereof, they commend these acts to competent persons. They have no independent authority of their own.

### POTENCY OF SACRIFICE

The Mīmāṁsakas have attempted to answer the question how a remote result, say, the attainment of heaven, is obtained by an action such as a sacrifice, which belongs to and in fact ceases in the present. Injunctive texts ordain that the fruits, namely, heaven and the like, should be achieved by sacrifices such as *darśa-paurṇamāsa*. And this implies that the sacrifice is the means to the fruit, viz. heaven. A sacrifice is of the nature of an action which is very soon lost. Hence the instrumentality of the sacrifice to the fruit which is to take place at a distant time is hardly possible. To establish this instrumentality, which is propounded by the Śruti, between sacrifice and heaven, an invisible potency is admitted which issues from the sacrifice and which endures till the fruit is generated and which resides in the soul of the sacrificer. This is called *apūrva*. It ceases on producing the result. It is also otherwise called merit or demerit. It is recognized also by the Naiyāyikas. But these Mīmāṁsakas being expounders of *karma* or ritualistic duty, all their reasoning turns on this *apūrva* and is as such fully approved by others. It is a power in the sacrifice. Although of the nature of a potency inhering in the sacrifice, it is presumable on account of the result. And it is presumed as existing in the locus or receptacle where the result is produced, i.e. in the soul of the sacrificer. Unless this is admitted, actions like sacrifice can have no causal connection with their result. In the absence of such a link men of prudence would have no disposition to perform them. And such disposition failing, the Vedas as a whole would have no use or purpose. And they would be open to objections of fraudulence etc. To avoid such objections *apūrva* must needs be admitted. This *apūrva* is to be presumed as of many kinds, such as subsidiary or pertaining to minor acts (*aṅgāpūrva*), contributory or flowing from each one of a set (*utpattyapūrva*), the result of the whole performance as a single unit (*phalāpūrva*), the final or the immediately preceding factor (*paramāpūrva*), etc. Otherwise, the parts also coming to an end as soon as they are performed, can have no connection with the principal, the result of which occurs after a long interval. Failing such connection, the parts would have no value as being ancillary to the main or whole which they benefit. And therefore the incidental *apūrvas* also are necessary and admissible.

## GOD AND DEITIES

To preclude the possibility of slackness in ritualistic work, the Mīmāṁsakas give more importance to the ordained acts, namely, sacrifices etc., than to the deities to whom these sacrifices, accompanied with the offering of oblations, are offered. The deities occupy a secondary place in this system ; nay, it even denies their existence as something separate from the *mantras*. The duty of performing ordained actions throughout life is emphatically enjoined in this school of philosophy, which defines this duty and classifies it. The Mīmāṁsakas hold that a knowledge of the innumerable ordained actions which a man has to perform throughout life is obtainable from the Vedas only and not from any other source or authority. They cite the following Vedic story to give an idea of the extent and depth of this great ocean of knowledge, the Vedas: 'There was a famous sage named Bharadvāja. By dint of penance he attained a long life of three hundred years, during which time he led a celibate life, performing the ordained Vedic rites and studying the Vedas. At last he was crippled with age and was confined to bed. One day Indra himself came to him and said, "Bharadvāja, if I extend your life by a hundred years more, what will you do with it?" He replied, "I shall utilize it in the same way as I have done so far." Whereupon Indra showed him three large mountains that he had never seen, placed before him a handful of dust from each and said, "Bharadvāja, the three mountains that you see are the three Vedas—*Sāman, Ṛc,* and *Yajus* ; they are eternal and endless ; what you have collected from your teacher and from the study of the Vedas by observing celibacy is equal only to these three handfuls of dust ; the endless remainder still lies unexplored before you. Come, learn from me the real import of the Vedas. They are the source of all knowledge." So saying Indra initiated him into the mysteries of the worship of that fire which is connected with the sun as a means to the attainment of Vedic knowledge. Bharadvāja worshipped it properly and obtained eternal life in heaven' (*Taittirīya Brāhmaṇa*, III. 1. 11).

There is an elaborate discussion in Śabara's commentary on whether the deities have forms. The Mīmāṁsā philosophy emphatically maintains that man can get all his desires fulfilled by performing properly and at the proper time the rites enjoined in the Vedas, and the question whether the gods have bodies or not need not trouble him, as it is immaterial to his purpose. Students of this philosophy should always remember the purport of the system, without which the study will be fruitless.

Śabara Svāmin, while establishing the Mīmāṁsaka theory of the eternal nature of sounds (or words), has refuted Sphoṭavāda in his commentary. According to the Sphoṭavādins—the grammarians and philosophers—words (i.e. sounds) like *gauḥ, aśvaḥ,* etc. are elementary sounds without any component parts ; *g, au,* and *ḥ* are not considered parts of *gauḥ*. But Śabara Svāmin says that *gauḥ, aśvaḥ,* etc. are not elementary sounds ; *gauḥ* is nothing but a combination of *g, au,* and *ḥ* ; hence the word is not elementary, but a combination of the successive letters of which it is composed. Therefore no word is conceivable as elementary, as the Sphoṭavādins would have it. There is, besides, no proof in support of their view. In this connection Śabara quotes Upavarṣa as follows: 'Bhagavān Upavarṣa says that *gauḥ* is formed by combining *g, au,* and *ḥ*.'

Jaimini has not mentioned in his work anything about the existence of the omniscient, omnipotent, and all-merciful God, the creator, preserver, and destroyer of the universe. Śabara Svāmin and Kumārila are also silent on this point. But the later exponents of this system, viz. Khaṇḍadeva and Gāgābhaṭṭa, have clearly expressed their views on this point. They declare unhesitatingly that it is not the object of this philosophy to deny the existence of the benevolent God, but to explain the real nature of the Vedic rites and ceremonies and other allied topics. They opine that about God and salvation the Pūrva-Mīmāṁsā system has nothing new to add to what has been so exhaustively discussed in the Uttara-Mīmāṁsā or Vedānta. Hence there is no reason to conclude that Jaimini, Śabara, and Kumārila did not believe in the existence of God or salvation.

# 8

## MATERIALISTS, SCEPTICS, AND AGNOSTICS

IT is well known to students of Indian philosophy that the original *sūtra* works of the materialists, sceptics, and agnostics of India are now lost to us. To be compelled to rely exclusively for a certain doctrine or way of thought on its presentation by its avowed opponents is not the safest way of understanding it. Opponents are seldom found free from prejudices and personal predilections. *Pūrvapakṣas* or the opponents' views are almost invariably presented in an inadequate and unsympathetic manner, so that no sound judgement as to their proper philosophical worth can be easily formed. If one notes how the doctrines of the Sarvāstivādin Buddhists, the Pāśupatas, and the Pāñcarātras have suffered at the hands of Śaṅkarācārya, it would be clear that the study of a certain system from its presentation by its opponents has to be undertaken with a proper appreciation of these difficulties. An attempt has been made here to collect from different sources fragments of actual statements by the founders and propounders of different schools of the materialists, sceptics, and agnostics of India. *Kusumāñjali, Nyāyamañjarī, Advaita-brahmasiddhi, Vivaraṇa-prameya-saṅgraha,* and numerous other works by orthodox writers, Hindu and Jain, Sanskrit and Prakrit works, and Buddhist Pali works, all contain a good deal of useful information on these schools. But these are only fragments of the original works of these schools now irrevocably lost to us. The *pūrvapakṣas* or views of opponents, in which form they appear in subsequent literature, have been studied in the light of, and interpreted consistently in the spirit of, the fragmentary texts yet preserved of the earliest exponents of the systems.

Viśvakarman speaks of a class of thinkers who are 'enwrapt in misty cloud' (*nīhāreṇa prāvṛtaḥ*) and 'with lips that stammer' (*jalpya*). The subsequent thinkers speak of *avidyā* or ignorance and *vicikitsā* or perplexity. *Saṁśaya* or doubt is another term which is met with in this connection in subsequent literature (*Mu. U.*, II. 2-8). The Muṇḍakas and the Vājasaneyas use the term *avidyā* in the sense of anything which is not transcendental knowledge (*parā vidyā*) or the knowledge of Brahman (*Brahma-vidyā*), and anything which is not conducive to ideal self-realization. The word *vicikitsā,* according to Āsuri, means a mental state (*Bṛ. U.,* I. 5. 3.). In the *Kaṭha Upaniṣad* (I. 20) the word has been used in the sense of philosophic doubt as to man's existence after death: 'Some say he exists; others, he does not.' These latter are no doubt the sceptics and agnostics of ancient

India. Viśvakarman had evidently in mind (1) those hymn-chanters who doubted the existence of Indra (*Ṛ.V.*, VIII. 89. 3), (2) Parameṣṭhin, who saw no possibility of knowing any cause or reality beyond the original matter (*Ṛ.V.*, X. 129. 6-7), and (3) Dīrghatamas, who was ignorant of the nature of a first cause (*Ṛ.V.*, I. 164. 6). In subsequent literature we find that the Kenīyas were of opinion that the know-all does not know at all, while the know-nothing knows everything (*Ke. U.*, II. 3). And, as stated above, some sages, according to the *Kaṭha Upaniṣad,* doubt the existence of man after death (I. 20). Scepticism and agnosticism are the expressions of a free mind that refuses to accept traditional wisdom without thorough criticism. In this respect the materialists of ancient India are very closely related to the present-day sceptics and agnostics. However minor their position may be in the field of philosophy, they are, no doubt, the fathers of free and independent thinking in India.

Bṛhaspati Laukya or Brahmaṇaspati, who may be termed the founder of Indian materialism, first embodied his views about the origin of the world in the hypothesis that in the beginning being came out of non-being (*Ṛ.V.*, X. 72. 2)—*asataḥ sadajāyata,* that matter is the ultimate reality. Parameṣṭhin treated matter as the ultimate reality as Bṛhaspati did, but disavowed all possibility of knowledge of the ultra-material substratum, if there were any. He refused to extend his metaphysical inquiry beyond matter. Bṛhaspati was a materialist. Parameṣṭhin was a sceptic. But they were inter-related. Subsequently Mahāvīra speaks of the Aṇṇāniyās, who pretend to be intelligent but are in fact unfamiliar with truth and have got rid of perplexity or puzzlement (*vitigicchatiṇṇā*). These Aṇṇāniyās are ignorant teachers who teach ignorant pupils and speak untruth without proper investigation of knowledge (*Sūtrakṛtāṅga,* I. 12. 2). These ignorant teachers seem to be the agnostics of ancient India. Subsequently Bṛhaspati of the Cārvāka school is pictured as an agnostic of this type. The close relation between the agnostics of the *Sūtrakṛtāṅga* and the materialists of the Purāṇas cannot be ignored.

In the Buddhistic records (*Mahāvagga,* I. 23. 24) Sañjaya, who maintains a sort of indifferent or neutral attitude towards such problems of metaphysical speculation as those which are concerned with the first cause, the final cause, future life, retribution, and so forth, is best known as a sceptic. According to Sañjaya, the same philosopher tends to be an agnostic and a sceptic. When he freely confesses his inability to know the ultimate beginning and end of things, which is virtually the same as admitting that these are unknown and unknowable, he is an agnostic. When he doubts or hesitates to admit the correctness of all bold assertions about matters beyond human cognition, he is a sceptic. What we find in the teachings of Dīrghatamas, Parameṣṭhin, the Kenīyas, and the Kaṭhas is represented by the agnostics and the sceptics.

Vyāsa (in his commentary on the *Yoga-Sūtra,* I. 30) does not determine the nature of the psychological relation between scepticism and agnosticism. In the commentary of Vācaspati on the *Yoga-Sūtra* the point has been properly thrashed out. According to Vācaspati, doubt and false knowledge do not differ much from each other, and yet the former is separately mentioned with a view to specifying its precise signification as the touching and evading of both sides of a question. Indeed in this respect doubt may be regarded as a subhead of false knowledge.

These earliest attempts cannot properly be called philosophical systems. They are more like fingerposts of philosophical tendencies. After a long course of development they became systematized. Amongst these systems of Indian philosophy materialism can be counted as very old. Some go so far as to regard it as the oldest and adduce, among others, the following reasons in support of their opinion. It is a fact that all other schools of thought try to refute the truths established by this school, which shows its priority. It is also a fact that the word *darśana* in its primary sense means perception ; in its secondary sense it means the Śāstra (scripture) which is considered to be as good an authority as perception. This emphasis on perception reminds us of the materialists, and there are scholars who maintain that the word first originated with the followers of Bṛhaspati. It was from them that it was borrowed by other schools. This fact induces them to establish the priority of this *darśana* to all others. Some scholars are even bold enough to declare that the materialistic school is the only original school of philosophy ; all other schools originated simply for the sake of refuting and destroying this school, whose teachings, according to them, were detrimental to the best interests of mankind. Others, again, say that it may be as old as other schools of philosophy, but not older. Materialism is preached nowhere as a doctrine of philosophy except as a reaction against some accepted but, in its view, perverted ideas or practices. The materialists of India, namely Bṛhaspati and his followers, do not pretend to lay down a constructive system of philosophy of their own. They try to refute the foolish orthodoxy of other schools. This, in their opinion, proves that the system of Bṛhaspati cannot be the first system ; it is rather the last. It raises objections against the views of all other systems, and therefore presupposes their existence.

But all systems of philosophy are the growth of years, nay, of centuries. The different systems of philosophy, as now known, are rather the latest summing up of what has been growing up among many generations of isolated thinkers, rather than the first attempts at a comprehensive treatment.

A large mass of philosophical thought must have existed in India long before there was any attempt to divide it into well-defined systems of philosophy. But such a growth must have required a great length of time. So it is probable that during that long period the views of one system had been continually discussed in others and modified in the light of criticisms, till at last they reached the forms we find them in. It is not improbable that the Lokāyata school was the first system of philosophy to be developed when other schools were yet mere tendencies and had not taken shape as systems. Thus, although as tendencies almost all philosophical thoughts are contemporaneous, as systems they belong to different ages.

Originally, the school of Bṛhaspati aimed at *vitaṇḍā* or destructive criticism and tried simply to refute the views of other schools, without having any constructive element to suggest or any positive theory to propound. This negative aspect finds expression in the Vedas themselves. From the earliest Vedic times there were people who denied the existence of even the Vedic deities. The Vedic hymns pointedly refer to scoffers and unbelievers. Those hymns which are traditionally ascribed to Bṛhaspati, the son of Loka, contain the first germs of protest against a mere verbal study of the Vedas and emphatically declare that a man who tries to understand them is far superior to the mere reciting priest. The celebrated hymn on frogs is a satire, says Prof. Max Müller, upon Vedic priesthood or, better, upon the system of hymn-chanting. Yāska clearly tells us that those who merely memorize the texts without knowing their meaning do not see the real form of the Vedas, and that such people are deluded, inasmuch as the way to attain the *summum bonum* is not revealed to them. In various Brāhmaṇas mere knowledge of a performance has been mentioned as having the same effect as the performance itself. Jaimini, recording this conflict of views, devotes an entire chapter in his *Mīmāṁsā-Sūtra* to drawing the conclusion that study consists not only in learning by heart the letters of the Vedas, but also in clearly understanding their spirit. Traces of an opposition to the religion of the Vedas appear in the Vedas themselves as well as in later works. In the *Aitareya Āraṇyaka* we find, 'Why should we repeat the Vedas or offer this kind of sacrifice?' Later on, the very authoritativeness of the Vedas was questioned. Opposition was the only function of the followers of Bṛhaspati, and they did it from the very beginning of their career. They opposed the Vedas and the practice of repeating them mechanically.

But all these represent only the negative aspect of the Bārhaspatya system, which therefore appeared to be incomplete. To remedy this, in its second stage, in explaining how an event or product takes place, it accepted the doctrine of *svabhāva* (nature). This doctrine maintains that 'the effects are self-existent and are produced neither by different things as causes nor by themselves, inasmuch as no cause can be discovered for the filaments of the lotus or the eye-like marks on the peacock's tail. If it cannot be found, it certainly does not exist. Such is the case with this diversified universe. Similarly, feelings like pleasure, pain, etc. have no cause, because they appear only at times'. This doctrine of *svabhāva* had been in existence in an independent form. In the course of time it came to be affiliated to the Bārhaspatya system, which thus became the earliest representative of the extreme form of Svabhāvavāda. From this time the rejection of the causal principle and of the good and evil consequences of actions formed its most important features. The product comes into existence without any cause. The materialistic view held that the existent was born of the non-existent. The *Śvetāśvatara Upaniṣad* enumerates some of the most popular theories current at the time in explanation of the origin of the universe, and naturalism is one of them. Bṛhaspati, with a lofty enthusiasm, flung away the fetters of religion, so that he might be freely righteous and noble. Some of the verses of the Vedic hymns ascribed to him are quite edifying. Whatever may be said of his followers, his own teachings were of an elevated character. Bṛhaspati had many followers, and all of them were independent thinkers raising objections against the current superstitions. It is perhaps for the liberties he took with the gods that Bṛhaspati was regarded as their teacher. But this state of things changed; a reaction against the school of Bṛhaspati set in, for which its negative attitude was perhaps responsible. The Vedic literature posterior to the Mantras is disfigured by anecdotes in which the pious sages poured out their wrath on the heads of those early oppositionists, viz. Bṛhaspati and his followers. The *Taittirīya Brāhmaṇa* relates an interesting anecdote, which runs as follows: 'Once upon a time Bṛhaspati struck the goddess Gāyatrī on the head. The head and the brain were smashed to pieces. But Gāyatrī was immortal and so did not die. Every fragment of her brain remained alive.' Some scholars find an allegory behind this: Gāyatrī is the symbol of Hinduism; Bṛhaspati tried to destroy it by introducing opposition. But Hinduism is eternal, it was not destroyed. In the *Maitrāyaṇī Upaniṣad* we find another anecdote: Bṛhaspati assuming the form of Śukra brings forth false knowledge for the safety of Indra and for the destruction of the *asuras*. By it the *asuras* are taught that good is evil and evil is good; and they say that this new law which upsets the Vedas should be studied. Here Bṛhaspati is painted as a deceiver, a hypocrite. The *Mahābhārata* records a story of this period, relating how Bṛhaspati, the sceptic, had a long discussion with Manu, one of the founders of the sacrificial cult, and was in the end converted to the latter's view-point. The worst that is said of Bṛhaspati's teaching is that it is drawn from a study of the female intellect which is full of subtlety and deceit! The *Viṣṇu Purāṇa* records that a number of demons, in ancient times, began to practise severe penances according to the injunctions of the Vedas. This caused great apprehension to Indra. At his prayer Māyāmoha was created, and he preached to the demons the pernicious doctrines of Bṛhaspati, not for their benefit, but for their destruction. Thus they became enemies of the Brāhmaṇas, gave up their austerities, and were averse to the study of the Vedas. Then, as they had strayed from religious observances, Indra killed them. Almost similar is the account recorded in the *Padma Purāṇa*. Human institutions prosper through opposition. As a reaction against the opposition of Bṛhaspati and his followers, the Vedic schools strove to popularize the Vedic creed of life by means of the most elaborate and thoroughgoing expositions. Opposed by the strong advocacy of the orthodox, the Lokāyatikas returned with the affiliation of naturalism (Svabhāvavāda). Neither of these two doctrines accepted the good or evil consequences of actions. The Lokāyata school, which had so long been a tendency only, now formed a philosophical system. Thus originated the first *darśana,* the Lokāyata.

## EPISTEMOLOGY

Perception was emphasized in this newly built system. So far the Bārhaspatyas had not admitted any authority whatsoever. Now in its new shape, the school accepted the authority of perception. The principle of causation was rejected, because it was not supported by sensuous perception. Mere perception of two events which stand isolated and self-contained is not sufficient to establish between them a causal relation. 'To ascertain whether a given antecedent condition has the character of a true cause, it is really necessary to find out with certainty the elements of invariability and of relevancy involved in such a notion. But this certitude can never be arrived at.' Universal propositions cannot be established by our limited perceptions. Perception presupposes actual contact of the object with the perceiving organ and is thus necessarily confined to the present. It is a case of here and now ; it does not extend to the past or the future, and is thus unable to establish the universal connection of things. In other words, sense perception can give us only particular truths. But the knowledge of particular facts cannot give us knowledge that is universally true. Therefore perception cannot give us universal relations. Nor can they be established by inference alone. For the inference which yields a universal relation as its conclusion cannot work unless it presupposes another universal connection as a necessary pre-condition of its possibility, and that again another, and so on. In other words, the process of reaching a universal conclusion involves infinite regress. Thus even inference in itself is not sufficient to produce a universal proposition. Nor is the universal relation supplied by verbal testimony ; for the validity of any testimony is itself ultimately based upon inference. Comparison is equally unable to establish a universal relation ; it only establishes the relation between a name and something that bears that name, e.g. the application of the already learnt name *'gavaya'* to an animal that looks like but is not a cow (*gau*). Now such relation between the name and the named is a particular relation, while we are here in search of an unconditional universal relation. Thus the universal relation, which is indispensable to all inference, is not given by any of the so-called sources of knowledge. Therefore universal relations cannot by any means be established. As inference is not possible without universal connection, and universal connection is unattainable, the Lokāyata system in its earlier stages discarded inference as a source of knowledge.

It rejected ether as an element, because ether cannot be known by perception, and it maintained that the four elements, viz. earth, air, fire, and water, were the original principles of all things. These elements in their atomic state, when mixed together in a certain proportion and according to a certain order, became transformed into an organism.

Consciousness is a function of the body and is an indispensable factor for its manifestation. Consciousness does not inhere in particles of matter. When these particles come to be arranged in a specific form, in a manner not yet scientifically explicable, they are found to show signs of life. Consciousness is inseparable from life. Our thinking power is destroyed with the dissociation of the elements whose combination produced it. Consciousness is produced from the body which is endowed with life or vital air. When the body perishes no consciousness can remain ; it must perish also. So there is nothing to transmigrate. The body, consciousness, and sense-organs are transitory. The mind is the product of a combination of elements sustained in a peculiar state, like intoxicating power generated by fermenting of rice-grains. The four elements, when combined, produce or manifest the mind ; there is no other reality than they. The instinctive movements and expressions of new-born babies are as much due to external stimuli 'as the opening and closing of the lotus and other flowers at different hours of the day or night, or the movement of iron under the influence of loadstone. In the same way the spontaneous generation of living organisms is frequently observed, as in the case of animalcules which develop in moisture or infusions, or of maggots or other worms which grow in the constituent particles of curds and the like and which begin to live and move in so short a time'. It is an indisputable fact that sensations and perceptions can arise only in so far as they are conditioned by a bodily mechanism. But it would not be so, were not the body the receptacle of consciousness. The properties of particular preparations of food and drink, conducive to the development of intellectual powers, afford another proof in favour of the fact that consciousness is a function of the body. As contraction is the function of muscles, so are thoughts, feelings, etc. the functions of the brain. The mind therefore has no substantial reality of its own ; it springs out of the vibrations of the molecules of the brain. When the molecular activity of the brain sinks below a certain level, consciousness disappears and the mind ceases to exist, as for example in sleep. When it rises again above a certain degree, consciousness reappears. The conscious life is not a life of continuity. It is coming out of and sinking again into unconscious elements. The hypothesis of a continuous stream of consciousness is a myth of divines and theologians.

One may object that since the body is declared to be the agent of all actions, it should be held responsibe for their natural consequences. To this the reply of the Lokāyatikas is that their system does not admit the existence of consequences of good or evil actions. The particles which form the body are always in a state of flux ; and the body which performs an action at one moment does not continue at the next to feel its reaction. It is, on the other hand, undeniable that the body suffers change. According to this school, the experience of pleasure and pain comes by chance. This is sought to be refuted by others as follows: The theory of matter is unable to account for the facts of memory and recognition. Reason demands that memory and the original experience which gives rise to it should be referred to one and the same conscious subject. But this is possible only when the subject is fundamentally an unchangeable entity. This objection is met by the Lokāyatikas in the following manner: The traces left by previous experiences are capable of being transmitted from the material cause to its direct product, an analogous instance being the transference of the odour of musk to the cloth in contact with it. But the general answer of this school to every question is that everything happens through the influence of *svabhāva*. It is *svabhāva* or a law of nature that consciousness is a function of the body and therefore the body is the self.

## METAPHYSICS

The Lokāyatikas deny past and future births, as there is no reality existing before birth or after death except the four primary elements, and the mind is the product of these. So it cannot be maintained that the mind at death passes on to another body. Minds must be different in different bodies. The consciousness of a body which has already perished cannot be related to the new body which comes into being. One mind cannot produce another mind after total annihilation. The theory that the foetus is endowed with consciousness is untenable. For consciousness presupposes sensation through the sense-organs, all knowledge being posterior to and derived from experience. And the sense-organs do not function in the foetus. Since no power or quality can exist without a subject, consciousness cannot persist when the body perishes ; it must perish with the body. If it be urged that past, present, and future births are nothing but particular conditions of the stream of consciousness which, according to the Vedicist, is eternal, the Lokāyatikas would say that the chain of consciousness is not an entity, and a condition that can be predicated only in respect of an entity cannot be proved with regard to it. A future existence of an entity that is non-existent cannot be predicated. This is how the Lokāyatikas reject the existence of future and previous births.

They also maintain that there is no soul apart from the body. If there be any soul, it is only the living principle of all organisms. It exists so long as the body exists, and ceases to exist when the body goes out of existence. It is the body that feels, sees, hears, remembers, and thinks. When one says, 'I am stout', 'I am lean', 'I am dark', one evidently means the body. Stoutness, leanness, or darkness attaches only to the body. Phrases like 'my body' are only metaphorical, the possessive case-ending having the same meaning as in 'Rāhu's head' (Rāhu, the demon of eclipse, being only a head). Just as a knave might induce an innocent person to accept glass and other such worthless materials in exchange for precious stones, so has the Śruti misled the innocent devotee and made him believe that the soul is distinct from the body, thus displacing his inborn, and therefore right, belief that the body and the soul are identical (Dehātmavāda). As nothing answering to the soul exists after death to go to the next world, there is no necessity to admit the existence of such a place.

With the denial of *karma* this school denies the existence of the mysterious universal agency called fate (*adṛṣṭa* or *daiva*). It denies the existence of merits and demerits acquired in a previous existence. In answer to the objection that fate must be admitted as the cause of the differences and determinations of the phenomenal world, Bṛhaspati's followers bring forward the doctrine of *svabhāva* or spontaneous generation of things according to their respective natures. Religion is as harmful as opium ; prayer is the hope of men who are weak and lacking in the will-power to do anything ; worship is an insincere practice to save oneself from the tortures of hell ; and prophets are the greatest liars among men. The Vedas are no authority, for they contain *mantras* (formulae) which do not convey any meaning whatsoever; some are ambiguous or absurd or contradictory, and some repeat what is already known. Between certain portions of the Vedas we find discrepancies and contradictions; cases are not rare where a line of action prescribed by one text is condemned by another. Again, they speak of results that are never realized. If it were possible for the sacrifices to make one reach heaven after their performance has ceased, the performer himself has perished, and the ingredients have been used up, then the trees of a forest, burnt down by fire, might as well produce abundant fruits.

Religious exercises and ascetic practices are merely a means to livelihood for men devoid of intellect and manliness. A *putreṣṭi* sacrifice, performed for the birth of a child, may not be followed by that event. When a child is born, the knaves say that it is due to the power of their incantations uttered in the course of the rite; and when a child is not born, they explain it as being due to the rite being incomplete in some way or other. The priests say that a beast slain in a sacrifice goes to heaven. Then how is it that they do not kill their own old fathers in a sacrifice in order to send them directly to heaven? If the offerings in a funeral ceremony can produce gratification to beings who are dead, then in the case of travellers, when they start, it is needless to give them provisions for the journey. All these ceremonies are prescribed by the Brāhmaṇas as a means to their livelihood and are worth no more than that. Hence the endeavour to propitiate the gods through religious ceremonies—to satisfy them by prayers—is vain and illusive. Religion is the invention of persons desirous of deceiving their fellowmen in order to further their own selfish interests. There is no particular place named heaven; even the Vedas themselves doubt the existence of a world beyond. If a man goes to another world after death, why does he not come back, drawn by the love of his friends and relatives? When once the body is reduced to ashes, how can it go to the other world? When an evil person dies, everything ends there; he does not enter into a region of pain or of darkness unrelieved by a single ray of light. That God is the judge of our actions also does not stand to reason, because in that case partiality and cruelty on His part would be inevitable. If He visits us with the evil consequences of our sins, He becomes our enemy for nothing. Therefore it is better not to have a God than to have a cruel and partial God. There is no such being as God, the supreme author and governor of the world, an omniscient spirit; the senses cannot reach Him. *Adṛṣṭa* (fate), the principle of causality, and inference are all denied. The Vedas reveal no signs of infallibility. So how can we ascertain that an all-knowing, all-pervading, and all-powerful spirit exists? Nature, and not God, is the watchword of this school.

ETHICS

The Vrātyas, who were Aryans of previous and later migrations or Aryanized racial stocks, were incorporated into this sect. They too, like the Lokāyatikas, challenged everything, including the caste system, the sacrifices, and the Vedas, and were the bitter opponents of orthodox Brāhmaṇism. Strengthened by the support of these Vrātyas, the Lokāyatikas exhorted people to strain every nerve to work out their immediate earthly welfare instead of running after heaven, *kāma* or the fulfilment of desire being considered the *summum bonum* of human life. The result of this movement was an inspiration for freedom—freedom for the individual as well as for society, for woman as well as for man, for the poor as well as for the rich. The wonderful result of this struggle for freedom is also visible in the rise of the Buddhist culture. Buddha's views against the Vedic sacrifices, the memorizing and fruitless repetition of the Vedic *mantras,* the caste system, the authority of the Vedas and the worship of the deities, the magic rites and the ascetic practices—all have their counterparts in the views of the Lokāyatikas. It is perhaps because Buddhism was greatly influenced by the Lokāyata school that we find in later accounts of this system the doctrines of Buddha and Cārvāka almost amalgamated as in Jābāli's exhortation to Rāma in the *Rāmāyaṇa* (II. 108) and the name Cārvāka sometimes applied to Buddha. India seethed with free thinking, and Buddha was the product of this freedom. No man ever lived so god-less, yet so god-like a life as he did. The *Viṣṇu Purāṇa* has a record of this stage of the school. It refers to a sect of people of very ancient origin who were free to live wherever they liked, unworried by conventions, pure at heart and blameless in action. Virtue or vice they had none ; they lived in an atmosphere of perfect freedom in which men could move without the fear of transgressing conventional dogmas of religion and social usage. But the votaries of the mundane were not satisfied merely with social and religious freedom ; politics became incorporated into the Lokāyata school, which ignored *ānvīkṣikī* (metaphysics), *trayī* (Vedas)—in fact everything that dealt with the supersensuous—and appreciated *daṇḍanīti* (politics) and *vārttā* (economics) as the only branches of knowledge deserving special cultivation. The earthly king became the only God. So long *kāma* or pleasure had been considered to be the only good of human life ; now *artha* or material advantage was added to it. As the Lokāyatikas captured the hearts of the cultured as well as the common people, all concentrated on working out their immediate earthly welfare. The result of this movement was the propagation of different arts and sciences.

Vātsyāyana mentions some sixty-four names of Indian fine arts which flourished probably in this period of Indian materialism ; so does the author of *Lalita-vistara*. Kambalāśvatara, who is mentioned by Śāntarakṣita in his *Tattva-saṅgraha,* Pāyāsi, whose views are recorded in the oldest known Buddhist and Jaina works, Ajita Keśakambalin, and many other materialists also wrote their works on materialism during this period. The *Sāmañña-phala-Sutta* preserves the following record of Ajita's view: 'There is no such duty as the giving of alms, or the performance of sacrifices, or the making of offerings. Good and evil deeds produce no results, and there is no such thing as this world or the next. There is neither father nor mother, nor beings springing into life without them. There are no recluses or Brāhmaṇas who, having realized the meaning of both this world and the next, make their wisdom known to others. A human being is made up of four elements. When he dies, the earth element in him returns to the earth, the fluid to the water, the heat to the fire, and the airy element to the air. Four bearers remove his dead body till they reach the burning ground ; men utter forth his eulogies, but there his bones are bleached and his offerings end in ashes. The talk of gifts is the doctrine of fools. It is an empty lie, mere idle talk, when men say there is a prophet there. Fools and wise men alike, on the dissolution of their body, are annihilated ; after death they are not.' This Ajita flourished during the lifetime of Buddha. Up to that time politics had not yet been taken up by the Lokāyatikas ; so there is no trace of it in the teachings of Ajita. Kṛṣṇa Miśra gives an almost perfect account of the doctrines of the Lokāyata school of his time: 'Lokāyata is always the only Śāstra. In it, only perceptual evidence is authority. The elements are earth, water, fire, and air. Wealth and enjoyment are the objects of human existence. Matter can think. There is no other world. Death is the end of all.'

The success of the Lokāyata system ended in corruption. Extreme freedom gave birth to licentiousness. Supreme bliss was transformed into sensual pleasure, the enjoyment of which in its gross form became the only end of human life. The elevated teachings of Bṛhaspati were metamorphosed into the eroticism of his followers. Let us enjoy pleasure alone, they said. It is the only thing which is true and good. The only reasonable end of man is enjoyment. We know pleasure is never pure, never free from pain. But because the pleasure is mixed with pain, should we therefore reject life? Should we fling away sheaves of paddy, rich with the finest white grains because they are covered with husk and dust? Should we refrain from plucking lotuses because there are thorns on the stalks? Shall we not eat fish because they have bones and scales? Should we exclude rice from our meals only for the trouble it gives in husking? Who will not soothe his mind and body in ambrosial moonlight, though there are spots on the moon? Shall we not enjoy the pleasant breeze of summer because there is a little dust in it? Should we not prepare food for fear of beggars? Unmixed happiness is not available in this world, yet we cannot overlook the least enjoyment. The only goal of life is our own pleasure. We should fully enjoy the present ; to sacrifice the present for the future is unwarranted and perilous. The present is ours ; the past is dead and gone ; the future is doubtful. The present is all that we have ; let us make the most of it.

With this credo the Lokāyatikas of that remote period of Indian history preached and practised an extreme form of hedonism. At this stage Indian materialism received the additional designation of Cārvāka. The word means 'entertaining speech'. 'While you live, drink ; for once dead, you can never return.' 'As long as he lives, let a man live happily ; even borrowing money, let him drink ghee.' The propagation of this cult was the first step towards the downfall of the Lokāyata system.

At this stage of Indian materialism the Buddhists and Jains came to the field of philosophy to preach their doctrines. At their first appearance they claimed to be successors of the old heretics, i.e. the followers of Bṛhaspati, by directing their attacks mainly against the doctrines relating to sacrifices as actually preached and practised in the Vedic school. They became, like the Lokāyatikas, very popular for the time being, as the minds of the people were still under the sway of materialistic doctrines. But as time went on, the state of things began to change. The Cārvākas came to know what these newcomers really were. They led the opposition against the orthodox Buddhists and Jains, as they had previously done against the Vedicists. The result was that the Lokāyatikas were opposed both by the Vedicists and by the Buddhists and Jains. By this simultaneous attack they were for the first time pushed into a corner. The philosophers of the Vedic schools now became very strong; aided by the idealist doctrines of the new heretics, they stood as successors of the sages of old, and repelled the attacks on their eternal principles. As time passed, one Vedic school after another opposed the heretics, both old and new. They opposed the materialistic views of the old heretics and the anti-Vedic doctrines of the new.

The frontal attack was delivered by Nyāya and Vaiśeṣika. Gautama adduced very strong arguments against the theory of Dehātmavāda (which preaches that the body is the self) held by the old heretics and established the theory that the soul is different from the body. Kaṇāda made an endeavour to refute the theory of Svabhāvavāda or the naturalism of the old heretics, by propagating the theory that the diversity of creation cannot be due to nature, which is unconscious. The diversity, he said, is produced from the atoms, which are unconscious, through the will of God acting in agreement with the doings of men's previous births. Sāṁkhya and Yoga joined the fray in a different manner. Kapila, who is regarded by some as representing the oldest trend of philosophy, formulated his arguments in favour of dualism, for which the field had perhaps been already prepared. Then came Patañjali with his system of Yoga, designed to establish the existence of God. Through the influence of these teachers, the mass mind was inclined towards belief in the spiritual nature of the soul and in transmigration. Jaimini made a direct attempt to establish by argument that the Vedas were infallible and authoritative ; that *karma* or action was more powerful than even God, if there were any ; and that for the sake of purification of the mind the performance of rites was indispensable. When, under the influence of Jaimini, the minds of the people had been prepared for the performance of duties enjoined by the Vedas and for conceiving the soul as spiritual, and the influence of anti-Vedic doctrines and tendencies had, for the time being, almost worn off, Vyāsa came to the field and preached his idealistic philosophy. Lokāyata, being thus opposed by these powerful adversaries, wavered and leaned towards idealism. This stage may be called the second or middle stage of its downfall, when under the Suśikṣita Cārvākas it admitted gradually the identification of the self with the sense-organs, the vital principle, and the mind, shaking off its old doctrine of the identity of the self with the body. The first view, in which the self is identified with the sense-organs, is based on the fact that consciousness and bodily movements follow the initiative of the senses and that the judgement expressed in 'I am blind', which shows this identification, is universally accepted as valid. Opposed further by the idealists, it maintains that the vital principle is really the source of intelligence, for on it the senses depend for their existence and operation. When this view too was attacked, its sponsors maintained that consciousness was a quality of the mind ; the other organs were only the means of indeterminate sense knowledge. It was the mind that introduced the element of determinateness. Moreover, the mind by its power of volition controlled the outer organs and might persist and function even when the latter were absent. Therefore the mind was the true self. All these have been recorded by Sadānanda in his *Advaita-brahmasiddhi.* He speaks of four different materialistic schools, the chief point of contention among whom is the conception of the soul. One school regards the soul as identical with the gross body, another with the senses, a third with the vital principle, and the fourth with the organ of thought. Again, the Lokāyata views had so far maintained that perception was the only source of knowledge. Now, being severely attacked by its opponents, who maintained the authority of inference, it showed for the first time a leaning towards admitting inference as a source of knowledge.

At first it said that for practical purposes probability was sufficient. At the sight of smoke rising from a spot we have a sense of the probability of fire, and not of its certainty; this is enough for all practical purposes, and there is no need to assume the existence of a distinct kind of evidence called inference. When further pressed, this school accepted inference as a means to right knowledge, since it was useful in our daily life. But it rejected the form of inference proposed by the Buddhists and others as being impracticable for daily use. In other words, it divided inference into two classes—one class referring to the future and the other to the past. It accepted the second and rejected the first, the inference about what has never been perceived, as for example, the future world, God, and the soul. Purandara lived in this period and was an advocate of the Cārvāka school. Śaṅkara, the commentators Kamalaśīla and Abhayadeva, Jayanta (the author of *Nyāyamañjarī*), and the unknown author of the *Sarvamata-saṅgraha* record his views. Being further pressed, this school accepted, at this stage, even ether as an element—a fact adverted to by Guṇaratna. The extremists of the Cārvāka school (Dhūrta Cārvāka) denied the causal relation of an object or event and held the view that things came into existence by themselves. But the progressive Cārvākas (Suśikṣita Cārvāka), on the contrary, were found, in this stage perhaps, to be inclined to accept *svabhāva* or nature as the cause of this universe, though *svabhāva* itself was believed to have no cause, no antecedent. This was referred to by Śāntarakṣita in his *Tattva-saṅgraha.* And it was in this stage that the progressive Cārvākas drifted to the refined hedonism of Vātsyāyana.

As they were supported by the Buddhists and Jains in their attack on the Vedic sacrifices, the old heretical oppositionists again became powerful. They received their general name of *nāstika* in this period. Vedic rites proper were gradually pushed into the background. New scriptures of the Vedic schools were in preparation, fully adapted to the needs, tastes, and tendencies of the changing times, but not entirely divorced from all connection with the Vedas. Voluminous works were written to satisfy varying temperaments. But elements of different nature were expressly visible in these schools. By way of compromise with the old heretical school, whose influence still predominated in the country, they included and adopted the popular doctrines regarding indulgence of the senses, and, as successors of the idealist schools, they gave them an esoteric purpose and thus modified them to some extent. Since that time, viz. the period of the great Hindu revival after the fall of Buddhism, India has been popularly Vedic, i.e. Paurāṇika and Tāntrika, in her outlook, though the Cārvāka system must have been a force to reckon with even so late as the time of Haribhadra, Guṇaratna, Śāntarakṣita, Kamalaśīla, Siddhasena, Abhayadeva,

Kṛṣṇa Miśra, Śrīharṣa, Jayanta, Sadānanda, Mādhavācārya, and others, who have criticized its theories in their works. It was Śaṅkarācārya and his school who did not even consider the Cārvāka school to be a system of philosophy. The great reaction against Cārvākism was started by Mādhavācārya who pronounced the Cārvāka system to be the lowest system of philosophy and scored a most decisive victory over it. Through lapse of time the original works of the Bṛhaspati school, the extreme materialistic system, either perished owing to natural causes or were destroyed by its powerful rivals. The Buddhistic and Jaina schools, being idealistic in essence, did not meet with total annihilation. As to the materialistic school, it may be that for a considerable time its views became more and more feeble and unpopular until it lost independent existence and was absorbed by the rival schools.

PART II

# THE VEDĀNTA

# 9

## BRAHMA-MĪMĀṀSĀ

### THE OPENING SŪTRAS

THE *Brahma-Mīmāṁsā* (the *Vedānta-Sūtra* of Bādarāyaṇa) beginning with the *sūtra* (I.1.1) *'Athāto Brahma-jijñāsā'* (Now therefore the inquiry into Brahman) and ending with the *sūtra* (IV.4.22) *'Anāvṛttiḥ śabdāt anāvṛttiḥ śabdāt'* (No return, so the scripture declares) is regarded by Śaṅkara, Ānanda Tīrtha (Madhva), Vallabha, and Vijñāna Bhikṣu as distinct from and independent of the *Karma-Mīmāṁsā* (the *Pūrva-Mīmāṁsā* of Jaimini). The several commentators on the *Vedānta-Sūtra* interpret the word *atha* differently. Vijñāna Bhikṣu and Ānanda Tīrtha take *atha* in the sense of indicating the beginning of the subject. Vallabha holds that the particle is used merely to signify the auspicious. Śaṅkara considers that *atha* means 'after acquiring the four *sādhanas* (requisites)', which are indispensable for beginning the study. According to the schools of Śrīkaṇṭha, Bhāskara, and Rāmānuja, the two *Mīmāṁsās* are one. The *Uttara-Mīmāṁsā* must be considered to be only a continuation of the *Pūrva-Mīmāṁsā,* and so the word *atha* implies the antecedent inquiry into *karma.* The point of difference is that the Jñāna-karma-samuccaya-vāda (the doctrine of the synthesis of *jñāna* and *karma*), adopted by Bhāskara, is not followed by Śrīkaṇṭha and Rāmānuja, who are of opinion that *karma* has an instrumental value in the inquiry into Brahman as generating knowledge. Like Śrīkaṇṭha and other teachers, Śaṅkara also recognizes the instrumental significance of *karma* ; but he considers that it is not an invariable rule that the inquiry into *karma* should precede the inquiry into Brahman in the present life, as it suffices if *karma* has been performed in previous births. Hence he holds that those who have taken to *sannyāsa* immediately after the *brahmacarya* stage are competent to inquire into Brahman even before the inquiry into *karma.* In the opinion of Śrīkaṇṭha and others, however, for those who become *sannyāsins* direct from the Brahmacaryāśrama, the performance of *karma* is not essential, since the possession of the virtues of *śama, dama,* etc. will qualify them for *Brahma-vicāra.* All the schools are unanimous in holding that, during the period of inquiry, the duties of one's particular *āśrama* should be followed. But according to Śaṅkara, the inquiry into Brahman should invariably follow the acquisition of the four requisites, whether the aspirants are householders or *sannyāsins* or those who do not belong to any *āśrama* or are even *devas.* The view of Śrīkaṇṭha and others is that *karma* or work is essential for householders, while *sannyāsins, devas,* or those who do not belong to any *āśrama* can for the same purpose practise the virtues of gift, austerity, etc., as the case may be.

### SUPREME REALITY AND ITS REALIZATION

The commentary of Śrīkara closely follows the commentary of Śrīkaṇṭha. But according to Śrīkaṇṭha, Sadāśiva is the supreme Soul, while Rāmānuja and Ānanda Tīrtha regard Nārāyaṇa as the supreme Soul. To Śrīkara and to Vijñāna Bhikṣu the supreme Soul is Brahman, not particularized by any name.

The subject to be inquired into is held to be the same by all these schools. It is Brahman, though conceived under different names and forms. All, except Śaṅkara, hold that the egoity of the pure individual self (*śuddha-pratyagātman*) remains and persists even in the state of *mokṣa* or liberation. They hold that liberation does not mean the destruction of this egoity. Śaṅkara, however, insists that 'I' does not mean the real self but the self mixed with the non-self. The real individual self is beyond the three states of waking, dream, and sleep, and is absolute consciousness which is also the nature of Brahman. Hence the Jīva is really one with Brahman. Śaṅkara further holds that egoity is destroyed in the state of *mokṣa,* but the self survives, this being the purport of the Śruti. Philosophers other than Śaṅkara think that none will desire *mokṣa* if in that state the ego becomes non-existent. But according to Śaṅkara, what is destroyed is not the essence of the ego which is the self, but the ego-consciousness as something distinct from Brahman. While others believe that the realization of the truth of the *mahāvākya 'Ahaṁ Brahmāsmi'* (I am Brahman) will have no meaning if the 'I' does not persist as such in *mokṣa,* Śaṅkara holds that *aham* here refers, not to the 'I' persisting in its distinction from Brahman in the state of *mokṣa,* but to what was distinct from Brahman prior to realization. In this view, the ego-sense is a form of bondage, which one should struggle to break. According to Śaṅkara, Śrīkaṇṭha, and others, the inquiry into the *sādhana* connoted by *atha* in the *sūtra 'Athāto Brahma-jijñāsā',* is dealt with in the third chapter on *sādhana,* while the inquiry into Brahman is the subject of the first and second chapters. This view is accepted by other schools also, the only difference being that the particle *atha* is not held by them to signify 'after the acquisition of the *sādhanas* (the four requisites)'.

The knowledge connoted by 'desire to know' (*jijñāsā*), according to Śaṅkara, includes and extends up to realization, i.e. the direct experience of Brahman, which is the fruit of the inquiry. Others hold that the knowledge in question is the same as that denoted by words such as meditation etc. or, in other words, the knowledge is equivalent to a vision and is of the nature of devotion. This being so, Śaṅkara holds that the word *draṣṭavya* (to be seen) in the Śruti beginning with *'Ātmā vā are draṣṭavyaḥ'* (The Ātman is to be seen) denotes the result, while other systems hold that it is indicative of *dhyāna,* which is almost on a par with realization (*darśana-samānākāra*). All the commentators agree that the two equivalent texts *'Ātmā vā are draṣṭavyaḥ'* (The Ātman is to be seen) and *'Tad vijijñāsasva tad Brahma'* (Inquire into that, that is Brahman) constitute the subject. The only difference among the commentators in this matter is that according to Śaṅkara, Ātman and Brahman are one and the same, while other schools think that the word Ātman in its primary meaning denotes the Paramātman, the supreme Self.

### MATERIAL AND EFFICIENT CAUSES

All the systems hold that the *sūtra* (I.1.2.) *'Janmādyasya yataḥ'* (From whom proceeds the origin etc. [of this universe]) defines Brahman. The unanimous opinion of all the commentators is that the doctrine of the Sāṁkhya that Prakṛti transforms itself, and the doctrine that Hiraṇyagarbha is the efficient cause of the universe do not constitute the purport of the Vedānta. Hence all hold that this *sūtra* rejects the theistic and the atheistic Sāṁkhya view as well as the doctrine of Hiraṇyagarbha being the efficient cause. But Ānanda Tīrtha and Vijñāna Bhikṣu take this *sūtra* to mean that Brahman is merely the efficient cause of the universe, while the other commentators hold that Brahman is both the material (*upādāna*) and the efficient (*nimitta*) cause.

Bhāskara and Vallabha accept the view that, though Brahman is without parts, the cosmos is the transformation of Brahman. Hence, according to them, Brahman Itself is the material cause of transformation, while Vijñāna Bhikṣu holds that Prakṛti alone is transformed, though Brahman too, being the locus of Prakṛti, may be said to be the material cause. Śrīkaṇṭha, Śrīkara, and Rāmānuja are of opinion that, even though Prakṛti alone is immediately transformed, Prakṛti and Brahmaṇ are inseparable, both being related as the body and its indweller (Prakṛti being the body of Brahman). Hence they accept the view that Brahman is the material cause, since Brahman too is transformed together with Prakṛti.

The monists hold that the *sūtra* does not directly refer to the ultimate Brahman, but is intended to explain the origin etc. of the universe by referring to the creative agencies of the Saguṇa Brahman which is an adjunct of the Nirguṇa Brahman. This is according to the Vivaraṇa school which considers both Brahman and Prakṛti as material causes, the former being *vivartopādāna* (material of apparent or illusory transformation) and the latter *pariṇāmopādāna* (material of real transformation). Prakṛti is transformed as the cosmos, while Brahman only apparently manifests Itself as the cosmos. But according to Vācaspati Miśra (*Bhāmatī*), Brahman is the *upādānakāraṇa* (*vivartopādāna*), Prakṛti being only the *nimittakāraṇa*. In this view there is no *pariṇāma* or transformation, but only a *vivarta* of Brahman or appearance brought about by *avidyā*. Bhāskara and Vallabha agree in holding the view of the direct transformation of Brahman. Rāmānuja refutes this view in his commentary on the *sūtra* (I.4.23) *'Prakṛtiśca pratijñā-dṛṣṭāntānuparodhāt'* (Brahman is also the material cause, the view not being contradictory to the propositions and illustrations). Also in the beginning of the *adhikaraṇa* entitled *Īkṣati* (on account of consciousness attributed to the first cause [Pradhāna is not the first cause, as it is against the scriptures]) he refutes the view that Prakṛti alone is transformed.

Śaṅkara, Śrīkaṇṭha, and others consider that the reason given in the above *sūtra 'Prakṛtiśca'* etc. for Brahman being the material cause holds good for Its being non-different, as is shown in the *sūtra* (II.1.14) *'Tadananyatvam ārambhaṇaśabdādibhyaḥ'* (Its non-difference is proved by words like origin etc.). Śrīkaṇṭha and others hold that the non-difference relates to the twin elements, viz. that which is transformed and the process of transformation, being united in the causal relation ; one being the effect and the other being the cause and both being real. But Śaṅkara is of opinion that Brahman is the direct material cause (*vivartopādāna*) and appears to transform Itself, because the cosmos is superimposed on Brahman. He also holds the view that the cosmos cannot exist apart from and without Brahman. In his system therefore Brahman alone is real, and the cosmos is an appearance of Brahman as Its effect. In the phenomenal stage, Brahman *appears* as the appearances ; but upon the dawn of realization the *appearances* disappear in Brahman, and *abheda* (distinctionlessness) of Brahman means the unreality or non-existence of an *other*.

## AUTHORITATIVE SCRIPTURES

In all the schools the Śāstra is accepted as the final authority. In the system of Vallabha the *sūtra* (I.1.3) *'Śāstrayonitvāt'* (The scriptures being the means of right knowledge) is but the concluding portion of the *sūtra* (I.1.2) *'Janmādyasya yataḥ'*. Hence according to him, the *sūtras* up to (I.1.4) *'Tat tu samanvayāt'* (But that is established, because it is the main purport of Vedāntic texts) constitute three *sūtras*. According to others, there are four *sūtras* here. These *sūtras* are regarded by all schools as summing up the whole essence of the *Brahma-Mīmāṁsā*.

According to Ānanda Tīrtha, the word Śāstra means the Vedas ; and the *Pañcarātra* and the other Āgama Śāstras have no authority. Rāmānuja also agrees with this view. But Śrīkaṇṭha holds that the Pāñcarātra etc., with the exception of the Pāśupata system, have no authority. According to Vijñāna Bhikṣu, these, except the ancient Sāṁkhya, are all not authorities. Vallabha holds that the Vedas, the *Bhāgavata,* and the *Gītā* alone possess primary authority. Almost all commentators are unanimous in the view that the meaning of the *samanvaya sūtra* is that Brahman is the main purport of all the Vedāntic texts. Vallabha alone considers the meaning of this *sūtra* to be that Brahman is the cause on account of Its all-pervasive nature.

### OTHER TOPICS IN THE FIRST CHAPTER—SAMANVAYA

All the commentators agree that the rest of the *samanvaya* chapter (first chapter) deals with the inquiry into Brahman as that to be known or meditated upon, as also with the refutation of the Sāṁkhya doctrine of Prakṛti being the sole cause, and the theory of the Jīva being the cause.

All, except Śaṅkara, hold that all the topics (of the first chapter) deal with Brahman with attributes. Śaṅkara makes a distinction and says: The seventh topic of the first *pāda* of the first chapter deals with the *Chāndogya* passage (I.6.6) *'Atha ya eṣa antarāditye hiraṇmayaḥ puruṣo dṛśyate hiraṇyaśmaśruḥ'* (Now that golden person who is seen within the sun, with a golden beard) etc. The first topic of the second *pāda* of the first chapter treats of the *Chāndogya* passage (III.14.2) dealing with *'Manomaya puruṣa'* (He who consists of the mind) etc. These two topics and those dealing with Vaiśvānara are the four topics that discuss Brahman with attributes, while all the other topics are concerned with passages regarding Brahman without attributes.

All schools agree that the chapter on *samanvaya* is concerned with the elucidation of doubtful passages in the *Kaṭha, Praśna, Muṇḍaka, Taittirīya, Bṛhadāraṇyaka, Chāndogya, Śvetāśvatara,* and *Kauṣītaki Upaniṣads.* Ānanda Tīrtha would add certain other Upaniṣads also. In respect of the Upaniṣads not referred to above, there is no doubt about their significance and the specified canons of interpretation should be applied to their texts.

### THE SECOND CHAPTER—AVIRODHA

Śaṅkara considers that, of the Sāṁkhya, Yoga, Vaiśeṣika, Saugata (Buddhist), Jaina, Pāśupata, and Pāñcarātra systems, the Sāṁkhya, Yoga, Pāśupata, and Pāñcarātra are acceptable in certain respects and not in others (i.e. those portions that are inconsistent with the Vedānta are to be rejected), while the other systems are to be totally rejected. Śrīkaṇṭha and Śrīkara hold that, in the Pāśupata system, only the Tāmasa Pāśupata is to be rejected. Rāmānuja accepts the full authority of the Pāñcarātra. So does Ānanda Tīrtha, but rejecting the Śākta theory of it. Though Vijñāna Bhikṣu follows Śaṅkara in every respect, he thinks in this connection that only the modern Sāṁkhya and Yoga are to be rejected and not the ancient ones.

Non-difference between cause and effect is the main thesis of this Śāstra. In the theory of Bhāskara and Vallabha, the effect is a transformation of Brahman Itself. Śrīkaṇṭha, Śrīkara, and Rāmānuja consider that it is the transformation of the body of Brahman. Vijñāna Bhikṣu says that Prakṛti as located in Brahman is transformed. According to Śaṅkara, Prakṛti and Brahman are both material causes. None of these accept the Sāṁkhya theory that Prakṛti existing independently is modified into the effect. The theory of cause varies in the two wings of Advaita. One is identical with that of Vijñāna Bhikṣu in holding that Prakṛti is located in Brahman, and it is that which undergoes transformation and becomes the *upādānakāraṇa.* The followers of Vācaspati Miśra and others regard Īśvara as only a *nimittakāraṇa* and not as the *upādānakāraṇa.* This view is identical with the Pāśupata theory rejected in the second *adhyāya.*

All the schools affirm that the ultimate cause, Īśvara or Brahman, however called, is the controller (*niyāmaka*) of the effect. Bhāskara, Śaṅkara, and Vallabha hold that the cause and effect being identical (the cause being in Śaṅkara's theory the substratum in which the effect appears by superimposition), Brahman Itself is the *upādānakāraṇa* and is therefore the *niyāmaka* of the effect. According to Rāmānuja, Śrīkaṇṭha, and Śrīkara, the controllership of Brahman in respect of effect (*niyāmakatva*) arises from the *śarīra-śarīrin* relationship in which, though in theory Brahman in Its entirety must be held to be the material cause, it is the bodily (*śarīra*) aspect of Brahman alone which operates as such. Ānanda Tīrtha also regards Brahman as *niyāmaka,* but does not accept the *śarīra-śarīrin* relationship between Brahman and the universe. His followers, however, consider that their view is not very different from Rāmānuja's, that Brahman being the *nimittakāraṇa* of the world obviates the need for an *upādānakāraṇa.*

The Advaita is distinguished from other systems in holding that Brahman without attributes is the supreme Reality and is non-different from the individual soul. All other systems have it that Brahman with attributes is the supreme Reality and is different from the Jīva. According to the Dvaita system, Brahman being merely the efficient cause, the Jīva is totally different from Brahman and Jīvas are themselves different from one another. Śrīkaṇṭha and others hold that though Jīvas are different from one another, they form the body of, and are inseparable from,

Brahman. According to Bhāskara and Vallabha, the Jīva and Brahman are at one and the same time different and non-different from each other, while according to the Advaita, they are completely one as absolute Consciousness, the apparent difference in the phenomenal order being due to superimposition. Though according to Pariṇāmavāda also the effect appears to be different from the cause, the difference and the relation and the relata are considered, as in Śāktavāda, to be real, while Śrīkaṇṭha holds that the difference is real and the relation unreal. Thus have been summarized the views of Śaṅkara, Śrīkaṇṭha, Bhāskara, Rāmānuja, Ānanda Tīrtha, Vallabha, and Vijñāna Bhikṣu on the purport of the second *pāda* of the second chapter.

According to Vallabha, the *sūtras 'Tat tu samanvayāt'* (I.1.4), *'Prakṛtiśca pratijñā-dṛṣṭāntānuparodhāt'* (I.4.23), *'Pariṇāmāt'* (I.4.26), *'Na vilakṣaṇa-tvādasya tathātvañca śabdāt'* (II.1.4), *'Kṛtsnaprasaktir-niravayavatva-śabda-kopo vā'* (II.1.26), etc. deal mainly with the transforming cause and give a particularly consistent and significant meaning. If we accept the theory that Brahman is merely the efficient cause, these *sūtra*s treating of Brahman as the material cause will have no significance. It will be irrelevant to hold that these refute over again the Sāṁkhya view. The same reason holds good regarding the view that Prakṛti being the body, Brahman is the material cause, or the view that Brahman is the material cause through *vivarta* or apparent transformation; the word *pariṇāma* in the *sūtra 'Pariṇāmāt'* does not fit in with the views cited above. The *sūtra 'Māyā-mātrantu kārtsnyena anabhivyakta-svarūpatvāt'* (III.2.3) has been explained by the *sūtra 'Vaidharmyācca na svapnādivat'* (II.2.29). By the word *mātra* in the *sūtra* beginning with *'Māyāmātram'* is refuted the view that Brahman is the cause of dream experiences, and by the *sūtra* beginning with *'Vaidharmyācca'* is shown the distinction from the waking experience. Thus the system of Vallabha, which holds that dream experiences are due to the transformation of Māyā without Brahman as the material cause, Brahman being the material cause of the waking experiences, is the only consistent and significant one.

Śrīkaṇṭha, Rāmānuja, and Śrīkara hold the following view. The topic of the Inner Ruler (*antaryāmin*) mainly deals with Brahman, having as its body the insentient and the sentient (nature and the individual souls). The topic *'Aṁśo nānāvyapadeśāt'* (II.3.43) treats of the Jīva as a part of Brahman. The topic *'Jño'ta eva'* (II.3.18) concludes with the *sūtra 'Jagadvyāpāra-varjam'* (IV.4.17) and shows that there is the sameness of bliss in the state of *mukti*, but the Jīva does not possess the powers of creation, conservation, and destruction like Brahman. In all the systems, except the Advaita, the subject begins with the definition of Brahman as the cause of the universe and is followed by *'Ānandamayo'bhyāsāt'* (I.1.12) and other *sūtras*.

According to monism, many passages in the first chapter, viz. on *samanvaya*, deal with Brahman without attributes. The topic of *'Tadananyatvam'* (II.1.14) treats of Brahman being the material cause through *vivarta* which has been established by the topic *'Prakṛtiśca pratijñā-dṛṣṭāntānuparodhāt'* (I.4.23). In the *sūtra* (III.2.3.) *'Māyāmātram'* etc. (The dream world is mere illusion), the words *'kārtsnyena anabhivyaktisvarūpatvāt'* (because its nature is not manifest with the totality of the attributes of reality) give the reason. All the unambiguous and undiscussed passages bear a consistent Advaitic meaning.

All the commentators think it their duty to help their followers by construing the Vedānta passages referred to in the *sūtras* in accordance with their systems. This is due to their devotion to their own systems. It is expected that each should follow, as far as he can, the course of life consistent with the system to which he belongs.

According to dualism, the knowledge that is conducive to *mokṣa* is the knowledge of the fivefold difference, namely, the difference between (1) one Jīva and another, (2) Jīva and Brahman, (3) one insentient and another, (4) insentients and the Jīvas, and (5) insentients and Brahman. The Jīva is atomic in size and dependent (on God for his action) and is essentially knowledge and the substratum of knowledge; though all Jīvas are similar in the state of liberation (*mukti*), all being servants of the supreme Self, still there is inequality in bliss amongst them. The *avatāras* (incarnations) and the *vyūhas* (emanations) are parts of the essential nature of Brahman and, as His instruments, are the cause of the universe. The system of Śrī Caitanya, being predominantly devotional, is almost similar, the only difference being that it regards Śrī Kṛṣṇa as the supreme Self as in the Bhāgavata school, whereas in dualism proper Nārāyaṇa is regarded as the supreme Self. Thus, between these two schools, there is but a difference in the name of the supreme Reality. This system totally rejects the view that the universe is unreal or that the Jīva is identical with Brahman. It follows that the universe has the same degree of reality as Brahman.

All schools accept Māyāvāda in one form or another. According to Śaṅkara, Māyā, which is called Prakṛti, possesses the twofold power of concealing Brahman (*āvaraṇa śakti*) and manifesting the universe as Prakṛti (*vikṣepa śakti*). Others deny the *āvaraṇa śakti* of Māyā and assert that it has only the *vikṣepa śakti*. The theory of the unreality of the world, seen in the Advaita, is a logical consequence of attributing the *āvaraṇa śakti* to Māyā, by which the *prapañca* (phenomenal order) is to be traced to superimposition on Brahman caused by Māyā. Upon the dawn of the knowledge of reality (*tattvajñāna*), *ajñāna* disappears; and with it the *āvaraṇa* and *vikṣepa śaktis* of Māyā, together with the phenomenal appearance, disappear; and Brahman alone remains as the sole Reality. But for others who maintain that Māyā has *vikṣepa śakti* only, Prakṛti will abide even at the end and so will not disappear even when *tattvajñāna* arises.

In systems like Viśiṣṭādvaita, the views are very similar to what has been stated regarding dualism. But there is this peculiarity. Viśiṣṭādvaita does not accept the difference between Jīva and Brahman, and the insentient and Brahman; for, being inseparable, they are non-different. Hence only three differences are admitted, viz. amongst Jīvas themselves, amongst insentients themselves, and between Jīvas and insentients, and they are all real as is the fivefold difference in Ānanda Tīrtha's system. Advaita also speaks of the three kinds of difference; but here they are not real, they are only empirical. The reference to *bheda* in the *sūtras* in different contexts is, according to Śaṅkara, to be understood in the empirical sense only, when the Jīva is associated with the sense of egoity; but according to others, it is ultimate and absolutely true. The fivefold difference is not accepted by the Viśiṣṭādvaitins. In the state of liberation there is merging in Brahman. There is neither inequality in bliss nor complete identity with Brahman, as is maintained by pure non-dualism. There is another difference too, viz. that they admit Brahman to be the material cause, directly or indirectly, as stated above.

In all systems, except Advaita and Dvaita, knowledge is an essential attribute of the Self, being its inseparable concomitant (*apṛthaksiddha-viśeṣaṇam*), and it is eternal; it only contracts and expands.

In Advaita and Dvaita, knowledge is not an *attribute* of the Self but is a transformation of *antaḥkaraṇa* (the inner organ, mind), as in the Sāṁkhya. The *antaḥkaraṇa-pariṇāma* inheres in the Ātman and has equal reality with it, according to Dvaita. Advaita considers both *antaḥkaraṇa* and its *pariṇāma* as ultimately unreal, as both are the results of superimposition on the Ātman. All schools agree in holding that the Ātman is of the nature of pure consciousness. Such consciousness is to be equated with pure *jñāna*. The Ātman in itself is the substrate and substance of such *jñāna*. It is *jñāna-svarūpa*. This substantive *jñāna* has a distinguishable adjunct which inheres in it by way of inseparable concomitance like the glow in a flame. This may be considered a form of adjectival *jñāna*, *dharmabhūtajñāna,* which, as mentioned above, contracts under the influence of *avidyā* expressing itself as *karma,* or expands when the taint of *karma* and the resulting *avidyā* are removed. It is this expanded *dharma-*

*bhūtajñāna* or the transformation of mind, i.e. *antaḥkaraṇa-vṛtti,* that can alone destroy *ajñāna,* in whatever form, either as, according to Advaita, concealing nescience or as, according to other systems, tainting *karma*. Thus this kind of *dharmabhūtajñāna* in its expansive character and *ajñāna,* which makes for contraction, are opposed to each other. But the *svarūpa-jñāna* which is pure consciousness in its substantive being will be unaffected by *ajñāna,* which may reside in it and conceal it till the *akhaṇḍā-kāra-sākṣātkāra,* or the absolutely expansive nature of *dharmabhūtajñāna,* is attained. So, according to Advaita, the *akhaṇḍākāra-vṛtti* (the sense of infinite expansion) alone is the enemy of *ajñāna,* but not *svarūpajñāna,* and this provides the answer to the objections raised regarding the locus and the removal of *ajñāna*.

Regarding the third part of the second chapter, all agree in holding that earth, water, fire, air, and ether have been created according to the order mentioned in the Śruti. By this is explained also the dissolution of these elements, which is in exactly the reverse order of the process of their creation. But according to Śrīkaṇṭha, the order of the process of dissolution is not the purport of the text, but only the order of the creation of the elementals, which follows the order of the creation of the elements.

The creation of the Jīva is due to the adjuncts and is only apparent and not real ; all commentators agree that the Jīva is really eternal. Śrīkaṇṭha and others, however, hold that there are not two *adhikaraṇas* (topics) which prove this, but only the *sūtra 'Carācara-vyapāśrayastu'* etc. (II.3.16), which is construed by Śaṅkara and others as treating only secondarily and metaphorically of the creation of the Jīva. The ultimate connotation of all the texts, according to Śrīkaṇṭha, Rāmānuja, and others, is to lead to the supreme Self. This being so, all the commentators, except Ānanda Tīrtha, are of opinion that the *sūtra 'Nātmā'śruternityatvācca tābhyaḥ'* (II.3.17) refutes the creation of the Jīvātman. Ānanda Tīrtha holds that this *sūtra,* like the *sūtra 'Asambhavastu sato'nupapatteḥ'* (II.3.9), refutes only the creation of the supreme Self.

Almost every commentator admits that the Jīva's nature is knowledge, and it is also the locus of knowledge. There is, however, this difference among the schools. Both Advaita and Dvaita hold that knowledge as an attribute pertains to the mind (*antaḥkaraṇa*) and is transient. According to other systems, knowledge is an attribute of the Self and is eternal. But Ānanda Tīrtha holds that the *sūtra 'Jño'ta eva'* assumes that the Jīva is the substratum of knowledge as an attribute ; and he supports the view of its dependent origination, it being a reflection of Brahman. Śaṅkara, however, holds that the conception of the Jīva as the substratum of knowledge is due to the adjuncts. Hence, the *sūtra 'Jño'ta eva'* merely supports the view that the Jīva's very nature is knowledge. The word *jña* is interpreted by him to mean intelligence. The *sūtra 'Jño'ta eva'* is held by Śaṅkara to constitute a separate independent *adhikaraṇa* complete by itself. Other commentators, however, hold that the *adhikaraṇa* is composed of fourteen or fewer *sūtras* beginning with *'Jño'ta eva'*.

All, except Śaṅkara and Bhāskara, think that the *sūtra 'Jño'ta eva'* supports not only the view that the Jīva is the substratum of knowledge, but also that it is atomic in size. Ānanda Tīrtha is, however, alone in holding that the *sūtra 'Vyatireko gandhavat'* (II.3.26) shows that the Jīva has many forms and that the text read by him as *'Atattvamasi'* shows that the Jīva is different from Brahman. But Śaṅkara is of opinion that the *sūtra 'Utkrāntigatyāgatīnām'* (II.3.19) raises a doubt as to the Jīva's being atomic and concludes that the Jīva is by nature one with Brahman and all-pervading. It is only atomic through its adjuncts. The Jīva's being an agent or a part of Brahman is also due to its adjuncts. Others, however, think that all these are predicated of the Jīva's own real nature and not of its adjuncts.

Almost all commentators agree in accepting the creation of the elements and the elementals as well as the idea of the Jīva's dependent activity and its eternity. Śaṅkara's view is as follows: The Jīva is not atomic but all-pervading. Its nature is absolute knowledge. Its agency, like its self-hood (*jīvatva*), is due to superimposition, hence phenomenal and not real; its being a part is also not real but superimposed.

Thus, in effect, there are two opinions, viz. that the Jīva is different from Brahman and that it is one with Brahman. According to Ānanda Tīrtha, the Jīva is ever different from Brahman. So he holds that texts like *'Pṛthagupadeśāt'* (II.3.28), which treat of the identity of Jīva and Brahman, are to be taken in a secondary sense or as figurative. These *sūtras* are introduced for the purpose of refuting the view of the inseparability of Jīva and Brahman. In this matter the views of Śrīkaṇṭha and Rāmānuja do not differ in the least from the above opinion. The commentary of Śrīkara also holds the same view. Though Ānanda Tīrtha accepts the view that Brahman means Nārāyaṇa, he holds that Nārāyaṇa has the fivefold *vyūha* (emanation), viz. Pradyumna, Aniruddha, Vāsudeva, Saṅkarṣaṇa, and Nārāyaṇa. He also says that there is the utmost difference between the Jīva and Brahman.

Proceeding to the topic of ether, in explaining the *sūtra 'Antarā vijñānamanasī'* etc. (II.3.15), Vijñāna Bhikṣu deals, like Rāmānuja, with the proposition that by the knowledge of the One everything is known. He, however, admits the continuity of Brahman and *ākāśa,* maintaining the permanence of ether in the subtle form, and its origination in the gross form.

That Brahman is with parts is treated by Vijñāna Bhikṣu chiefly in the topic on parts, as in systems other than the Advaita. According to this school, the *sūtra 'Asambhavastu sato'nupapatteḥ'* (II.3.9) is explained as dealing with Prakṛti being eternal, while the *sūtra 'Tadabhidhyānādeva tu talliṅgāt saḥ'* (II.3.13) discusses the question of Brahman being the sustaining cause of the universe. The *sūtra 'Jño'ta eva'* (II.3.18) is supplementary to the *sūtra 'Nātmā'śruternityatvācca tābhyaḥ'* (II.3.17) proving that if the Jīva is not eternal, its instinctive actions such as sucking its mother's milk etc. will go against reason. The *sūtras* beginning with *'Utkrāntigatyāgatīnām'* (II.3.19) are, however, treated by him, as by the Advaitins, as stating the *prima facie* view of the Jīva being atomic. The *sūtra 'Pṛthagupadeśāt'* (II.3.28) is the view of the author of the *sūtras* on the matter showing that the Jīva is all-pervading. Vijñāna Bhikṣu considers that the meaning of the *sūtra* is that the intellect etc., which are adjuncts different from the Jīva, are atomic. In other matters he follows the Advaita view with the difference that in the beginning of the topic of the Jīva as agent, as also in the interpretation of the third *pāda,* his view is similar to Rāmānuja's.

Vallabha follows Śaṅkara's view almost wholly in his commentary on the *sūtra 'Carācara-vyapāśrayastu'* etc. (II.3.16). Only he is of opinion that the *sūtra 'Jño'ta eva'* shows that sentience belongs to the substratum. Though the Jīva is identical with Brahman in its sentience, it has no independent existence apart from Brahman, but exists only as a part of Brahman. Thus alone can the topic of the Jīva being an aspect be relevant. Its being an aspect is a primary fact as held by Vijñāna Bhikṣu and others. According to this view, the *sūtra 'Tadguṇasāratvāt'* etc. (II.3.29), dealing with the non-difference between the Jīva and Brahman conveyed by *'Tattvamasi'* (That thou art) and other scriptural texts, is to be understood in a secondary sense as in the Dvaita system. As regards the topics of the Jīva being an agent and being atomic etc., Vallabha follows Rāmānuja.

Bhāskara accepts the view of Vallabha as regards the question of Brahman's undergoing transformation by Its own nature. Only he maintains that the Jīva is all-pervading and non-different from the Paramātman. In other respects his view is similar to that of Śaṅkara.

## THE THIRD CHAPTER—SĀDHANA

In the third chapter dealing with *sādhana,* the views of allied systems are similar. As regards the first *pāda* of this chapter the views of all systems are similar in the discussion of the topic of the Jīva's passing out at death and its return at birth, though there is a difference of opinion with respect to the number of topics dealt with. Ānanda Tīrtha considers that the *sūtra*

*'Api ca sapta'* (III.1.15) also supports the existence of an eternal hell. In other systems there is similarity regarding such points as the descent of the Jīvas through the 'path of smoke'. Ānanda Tīrtha stands alone in holding the view that the Jīvas may enter hell and remain there permanently. The commentators all agree in holding that this topic of the ascent and descent of the Jīva is considered to subserve the practice of *vairāgya* (non-attachment).

Vijñāna Bhikṣu thinks that the *sūtra 'Api ca sapta'* (III.1.15) does not merely treat of the ascent and descent of the Jīvas to heaven and hell respectively, but also of the seven Jīvas inhabiting seven planes. He is also an exception in considering that this order of ascent and descent of the Jīvas does not hold good in the case of insects born of sweat, dirt, etc. as well as in the case of Nandīśvara, Nahuṣa, and others. He bases his view on the *sūtras 'Na tṛtīye tathopalabdheḥ'* (III.1.18), *'Smaryate'pi ca loke'* (III.1.19), and *'Darśanācca'* (III.1.20). In all other respects his view agrees with that of all the other commentators.

Vallabha is of opinion that the main purport of the first *pāda* of the third chapter is to show the necessity of attaining another body to receive knowledge, and not merely to instil *vairāgya* (non-attachment) into the heart of the Jīva, as other commentators hold. The main topic here is the meditation on the 'five fires'. He considers that, viewed in this light, the *sūtra 'Yoneḥ śarīram'* (III.1.27) is a fitting conclusion, as it treats of the fruit of the 'five oblations'. The discussion of the paths, which is introduced in the course of this *pāda,* is supplementary to the meditation on the 'five fires'. Non-attachment arises incidentally from the discussion of the topic of the 'path of smoke'. The order of attaining another body applies to those who follow the ordinary path. The *sūtra 'Na tṛtīye tathopalabdheḥ'* (III.1.18) shows that this order does not hold good in the 'path of Puṣṭi' (the particular path of the grace of God propounded by Vallabha). Vijñāna Bhikṣu agrees that birth need not be occasioned solely by the natural procreative process. He does not refer, however, to the Puṣṭi-mārga. According to him, *tapas* (austerity) is the cause of birth other than by the natural process. Both Vallabha and Vijñāna Bhikṣu agree in holding that the Śruti text *'Jāyasva mriyasva'* (Be born and die) discusses birth other than by ascent and descent, the difference being that Vijñāna Bhikṣu holds that such a birth applies to insects as well as to Nandīśvara and therefore includes the case of Droṇa, Dhṛṣṭadyumna, Sītā, Draupadī, etc. who were born by other than the natural process. All commentators agree in holding that sinners go to the abode of Yama, sacrificers go through the 'path of smoke', and those who meditate on the 'five fires' go through the 'path of light'.

It is held by almost all the commentators that the second *pāda* of the third chapter is introduced for the purpose of investigating the meaning of *Tat tvam* ('That' and 'thou') of the *mahāvākya 'Tattvamasi'* (That art thou). Vallabha alone holds that this part discusses the fitness of the Jīva for salvation. He follows Śaṅkara in considering that the first topic treats of the illusory nature of dream experiences, the Māyā of Īśvara (the Lord) being the sole material cause of dreams independent of Brahman. But there is this difference between the two systems. According to the Advaita, both Īśvara and Māyā are the material causes, while Vallabha holds that Māyā alone is that cause. Śrīkaṇṭha and Rāmānuja agree in holding that the experiences in dreams, as those of the waking state, are created by Īśvara. They hold that the word *māyā* in *'Māyāmātram'* is used to express wonder. Vijñāna Bhikṣu is of opinion that dreams are a particular modification of the mind capable of being grasped by the intellect. According to Ānanda Tīrtha, Īśvara creates the things seen in dreams by His own will, taking as material the previously experienced impressions, or, in other words, it is these impressions that are reflected in dreams. In all systems except those of Śrīkaṇṭha, Rāmānuja, and Śrīkara, dreams are differentiated from the waking state. All agree that it is the possession of the three states of waking, dreaming, and deep sleep that constitutes the characteristic of the Jīva. In the Advaita system the investigation of the conditions under which dreams occur is undertaken to refute the reality of the three states and to illustrate the Jīva's persistence therein. Vallabha disagrees with this view.

All commentators concur in holding that the topic *'Na sthānato'pi'* etc. (III.2.11) is for the purpose of investigating the nature of *Tat* (That), the supreme Brahman. According to the Advaita, however, the topic really treats of Brahman without attributes, and the topic *'Prakṛtaitāvattvam'* etc. (III.2.22) is introduced to elaborate the same idea by means of other Śruti texts. The *sūtra 'Paramataḥ setūn'* etc. (III.2.31) introduces a different and independent topic. But other commentators consider that the three constitute only one topic, which is introduced for the purpose of establishing that Brahman is with attributes. According to the Advaita system, the nature of Brahman can only be indicated, while other systems have it that the nature of Brahman is conveyed by the natural, explicit meaning of the words given and does not go beyond it.

All commentators are of opinion that the third *pāda* treating of attributes is for the purpose of determining the particular attributes or qualities needed for particular forms of meditation. According to Vallabha and Bhāskara, the fourth *pāda* supports the theory of the simultaneous practice of *jñāna* and *karma*. Other systems consider that *karma* subserves *jñāna* which brings about *mokṣa*. But there is the difference of view that, according to the Advaita system, the good deeds done in previous births also conduce to bringing about *jñāna*. Śrīkaṇṭha and Rāmānuja consider that good deeds are directly helpful in bringing about *mokṣa*, while according to the Advaita system, good deeds only co-operate with other factors in generating *jñāna* which leads to liberation. Systems other than Advaita hold that the *jñāna* referred to here is of the form of *upāsana* (meditation) connoted by the word *bhakti* (devotion). The Advaita system understands by *jñāna* the direct experience or realization of the indivisible Brahman. All systems agree in accepting *sannyāsa* as being prescribed by the scriptures. Vallabha, however, considers that in the path of Puṣṭi neither *sannyāsa* nor *karma* is necessary. In his opinion the fulfilment of the duties of each stage of life (*āśrama*) applies only to those who tread the Maryādā path. Regarding other subjects in this *pāda* all the systems agree.

## THE FOURTH CHAPTER—PHALA

The subject of the fourth chapter is the inquiry into the result or the fulfilment of knowledge. According to Vallabha, the first topic deals with rebirth due to the effect of *karma*. Other systems consider that this topic deals with the *sādhana* of the repeated hearing of the Śruti and other primary *sādhanas* leading to the fulfilment of knowledge. Vallabha holds that the topic is an inquiry into the *sādhana* and not into the result. Others have it that it is only an inquiry into the result, as the hearing (of the Śruti) is a mediate effect. Vijñāna Bhikṣu thinks that the subject dealt with in this *adhikaraṇa* is the practice of meditation on truth in the form of the control of the modifications of the mind, which leads to liberation here and now.

Vijñāna Bhikṣu thinks that the *sūtra* '*Ātmeti tūpagacchanti grāhayanti ca*' (IV.1.3) shows the nature of the Jīva to be that of Brahman, regarded as the Ātman. In his view, though the Jīvatman is sentient, it becomes insentient by the will of God, as has been described in the *Mokṣadharma* section of the *Mahābhārata*. The sum and substance of his view is that the self is to be regarded as Brahman. This is also the view of Śrīkaṇṭha and Rāmānuja. The sole difference is that, according to these systems, the Jīva is not insentient at the time of meditation. According to Vallabha, as a result of the performance of work in the spirit of dedication to God, the Lord, being the Self of all, makes the individual self follow the path of *jñāna* or *bhakti*. But the commentaries of Śrīkaṇṭha and Śrīkara follow Rāmānuja in this respect. Though they agree that the Jīva is the body of Brahman, yet the Jīva in the body of the supreme Self is not insentient like the body of the Jīva. According to them, the supreme Self possesses two bodies, the *cit* (the self) and *acit* (the universe). In the system of Advaita, however, the Jīva is non-different from Brahman, and the real nature of the Jīva is therefore Brahman. Bhāskara thinks in this connection that the Jīva is a particular power of Brahman, and the knowledge of the 'I' or the 'Self' as Brahman conduces to *mokṣa* because of the non-difference between the power and its possessor. Hence we see that all agree that the knowledge of Brahman as a means to *mokṣa* is the subject dealt with here, though they differ in detail. All agree that the meditation on symbols does lead to *mokṣa*. In the same way all systems agree that in meditating on symbols, it is not the symbol as such that should be meditated upon, but Brahman represented by the symbol.

With the dawn of knowledge, all *karmas,* past and future, except the *prārabdha* (that which has started functioning), are destroyed. This is held by all except for a slight difference in the case of Vallabha, Ānanda Tīrtha, and Vijñāna Bhikṣu. Vallabha holds that the *prārabdha* has no effect for one who follows the Puṣṭi-mārga. Vijñāna Bhikṣu says that the *prārabdha karma* does not function, as is evidenced by the case of Māṇḍavya and others. Ānanda Tīrtha holds that by knowledge, which is termed *upāsana* (meditative approach to the Divine), good deeds done without desire are not destroyed.

In the *sūtra 'Bhogena tvitare kṣapayitvā sampadyate'* (IV.1.19) the word *sampatti* is regarded by Vallabha as meaning the attainment of a divine body after the destruction of the gross and subtle bodies. Vijñāna Bhikṣu regards it as a state of merging, connoted by the term inseparability, as in the case of a river entering the ocean. Śrīkaṇṭha, Śrīkara, and Rāmānuja regard *sampatti* as meaning merely equality in bliss expressible by the term *avinābhāva,* i.e. the individual self not existing apart from the Paramātman. The Advaita system holds, with Bhāskara, that *sampatti* is the attainment of the state of God. The difference here between the two systems is that, according to the Advaita, the Jīva does not exist as such apart from Īśvara ; while according to Bhāskara, the Jīva exists in its own nature as the power of God. In all systems, except the Advaita, the ego or 'I' connotes the Jīva. According to the Advaita, the ego is the non-self, the real and primary nature of the Jīva being consciousness without the mind (*antaḥkaraṇa*). In the theory which upholds the existence of many Jīvas, the *Īśvarabhāva,* or the state of being God, persists till *mukti.* The real *mukti* or liberation, according to the Vivaraṇa school of the Advaita, is pure consciousness in which all Jīvas are merged and liberated. In other schools of Advaita it is consciousness without adjuncts, as in the Bhāmatī school of Vācaspati, which holds the view that ignorance is manifold; while the author of *Prakaṭārtha* accepts the view that even Īśvara is only a reflection of Brahman. This essential difference among these schools is noteworthy.

Śaṅkara and Vijñāna Bhikṣu think that the first *pāda* of the fourth chapter treats of the liberation of those whose knowledge of the Nirguṇa Brahman is ripe, as this *pāda* ends with the consideration of *sampatti*. Others, since they do not accept the Nirguṇa Brahman, are of opinion that there is no state of liberation other than the consummation of the knowledge of the Saguṇa Brahman, i.e. Brahman with attributes. It is only in the Advaita system that the word *sampatti* in the primary sense of being one with the Nirguṇa Brahman is accepted. According to the other systems, it is only a partial union. Vijñāna Bhikṣu and the Advaita system both hold that those whose knowledge of Brahman with attributes is ripe reach liberation gradually. Vallabha considers that the text *'Atra Brahma samaśnute'* (*Bṛ. U.*, IV.4.7; *Ka. U.*, VI.14) applies only to those who follow the Puṣṭi-mārga. So in his system, as in the Advaita, the primary meaning of *sampatti* is unrestrained. Nevertheless, since he accepts the difference between the Jīva and Brahman, and since he holds that only the divine form created by God's *līlā* is like Brahman, this is what is meant here by the text 'attaining Brahman'. Hence *sampatti* is only relative or secondary and not absolute or primary.

The second *pāda* of the fourth chapter, according to the Puṣṭi system of Vallabha, discusses the question of what happens to the gross and subtle bodies, consisting of organs of sight, speech, etc., when the state of Brahman is reached, and concludes that they are dissolved completely even here in the case of those who follow the Puṣṭi-mārga, while as regards those who follow the ordinary Maryādā path or the path of knowledge, each of the sense-organs is dissolved in its respective element. Therefore it is the ascent of such souls alone that is dealt with in this *adhikaraṇa*. After the dissolution of the gross and subtle bodies, these souls, by the *līlā* of God, get divine bodies and enjoy bliss through those bodies; and they also suffer intense pain when separated from the Lord, though even that pain or sorrow is one form of happiness. These ideas are detailed in Vallabha's commentary. Vallabha holds that the *sūtra 'Pratiṣedhāditi cenna śārīrāt spaṣṭo hyekeṣām'* (IV.2.12) denies only the sorrow caused by *karma*, and not the pain of separation from the Lord, in the case of those following the Puṣṭi-mārga, because in his system the order of ascent applies only to those who follow Jñāna-mārga or the path of knowledge. It is clear that this path of knowledge is different from the Jñāna-mārga of the Advaita. The path of knowledge, as defined by Śrīkaṇṭha, Rāmānuja, Śrīkara, Ānanda Tīrtha, and others, is also different from the path of knowledge as understood in the Advaita system. Another difference is that, according to Vallabha, what appears as *saṁsāra* to those who follow the path of knowledge does not contain any element of misery in the case of those who follow the Puṣṭi-mārga. Śrīkaṇṭha and others accept only the Maryādā-mārga and hold that in the state of *mukti* or liberation the disembodied individual self remains non-separate from Brahman. This is the view of all systems except the Advaita, which alone holds that when the individual soul attains liberation and reaches the state of Brahman, it does not remain apart from It either in its own nature as the Jīva or as consciousness.

Ānanda Tīrtha holds that all the *devas* up to Hiraṇyagarbha and even the liberated souls dissolve in Brahman through the will of the supreme Self. Though the passing away of the knowers of Brahman is similar to that of others, the former pass out of the body by the door of the top of the heart lighted by the grace of God; and their passing away does not take place in *dakṣiṇāyana* or during the time when the sun journeys towards the south. This is how Ānanda Tīrtha explains the second *pāda* of the fourth chapter.

According to Ānanda Tīrtha, the third part of the fourth chapter discusses the nature of the 'path of light'. In this view he is at one with the others, except that he holds that the superhuman person (on this side of *Brahmaloka*) who guides the ascending soul is the primary *prāṇa*—God, and none else. And this God, the chief *prāṇa,* leads one to the supreme Brahman and not to the Kārya (derived or lower) Brahman, inasmuch as the soul worshipped Brahman without any symbols. Others are led to the Kārya Brahman. The Advaita system says that the 'path of light' leads only to the Kārya Brahman and not to the supreme Brahman. When one attains the supreme Brahman, however, there is no need to go anywhere, because it is established in the second part of the third chapter that one attains Brahman even here without migrating. In discussing the Dvaita systems, the question arises, If the gods can reach Brahman without transmigration, as Ānanda Tīrtha maintains, why should there be this rule that the 'knowers' among men should depend on migration to reach the state of *mukti*? This remark applies to the systems of Rāmānuja and others who think that Hiraṇyagarbha and the dwellers of that *loka* do not need to migrate in order to attain liberation.

Vallabha agrees with Rāmānuja and others as regards those who follow the Maryādā-mārga. He thinks, however, that those who follow the Puṣṭi-mārga do not need to go by the 'path of light', and do not require the guidance of a supernatural being to reach Brahman. They attain Brahman directly and here on earth without the mediation of anyone. This is an essential difference between Vallabha and others. It is to be noted that systems other than the Advaita consider the abode of Prajāpati to be the abode of Kārya Brahman and so regard the nature of Parabrahman as the same as that of *Brahmaloka,* which is different from the abode of Prajāpati. The Advaita, on the other hand, holds that the Kārya Brahman is different from Prajāpati but is not altogether free from the adjunct of ignorance, and hence must be considered different from the supreme Brahman in which there is not the slightest touch of *avidyā.*

We shall now summarize the substance of the fourth *pāda* of the fourth chapter. Vallabha says that the first topic therein deals with the state, after reaching Brahman, of one who follows the Maryādā-mārga. Such a person, by the grace of God, appears in a form created by the *līlā* of Brahman, and that manifestation is in the abode of Brahman and not here, whereas a follower of the Puṣṭi-mārga attains manifestation here. Vijñāna Bhikṣu generally follows the theory of Rāmānuja. But there is this difference. Those who worship Brahmā, Viṣṇu, and others, worship symbols. They attain the *Kārya-Brahmaloka* of the respective deities they worship. Those who worship the Kāraṇa Brahman, however, really attain Brahman. This can be done only through *samādhi.* There is no movement involved as to another plane. When the bondage is removed, the all-pervasive character reveals itself. Kārya Brahman, according to him, is Brahmā, Viṣṇu, or Rudra. The followers of Puṣṭi-mārga also adopt the same view. In the Advaita too it is no movement from one state to another, but the revelation of the identity of the Jīva and Brahman upon the dawn of *tattvajñāna,* and whatever is not of the nature of the Nirguṇa Brahman must be held to be Kārya Brahman. For interpreters other than Vijñāna Bhikṣu and Vallabha, the attainment of the Kāraṇa Brahman implies a process and a progress.

Vijñāna Bhikṣu holds that the attainment of the state of Brahman consists in becoming pure consciousness by being freed from all adjuncts. The Jīva is inseparable from Brahman like a river from the ocean. The attainment of the powers of Brahman occurs just before liberation, and that is reached in a particular state of *samādhi* even before liberation. He says that in the state of liberation Brahman-consciousness, which is beyond the three *guṇas,* and the Jīva-consciousness remain inseparable. It is, according to Vallabha, the grace of God that endows the Jīva with the enjoyment of all lordship when it realizes Brahman ; for he holds that the Lord is the means as well as the end, and that the path of Puṣṭi is quite different from the path of transmigration. The view of Vijñāna Bhikṣu is similar to that of Vallabha as regards the enjoyment of all bliss either without a body or with a body created by will. According to the system of Śrīkaṇṭha and others, the liberated person, being inseparable from Brahman, attains the powers of lordship pertaining to Brahman. According to the Advaita system, liberation means attaining the state of Brahman, that is, being pure Consciousness. All are at one in holding that those who attain to the Saguṇa Brahman, i.e. Brahman with attributes, acquire all the powers of Brahman except that of controlling the universe. Vallabha thinks that the liberated person is similar to Brahman only in the enjoyment of bliss without having any worldly activity.

### NIMBĀRKA'S INTERPRETATION

In the philosophy of Nimbārka the three categories of Brahman, *cit,* and *acit* form the central topics of discussion. This is indicated in the first *sūtra* itself, *'Athāto Brahma-jijñāsā'*. Here the *jijñāsu* (inquirer) is *cit,* the *jijñāsya* (object of the inquiry) is Brahman, and the motive for *vicāra* or inquiry is the desire to get rid of *ajñāna,* which is ignorance of the nature of Brahman and whose cause, Māyā, is the stuff of *acit.* In this respect there is similarity between Rāmānuja and Nimbārka, except that according to Rāmānuja, *akṣara* (immutable) refers to the *muktātman* or the released soul, but in Nimbārka's view it refers to Prakṛti. Both these commentators hold that the Jīva refers to the individual ego, and each ego is different from every other. It is of the nature of *jñāna,* but is yet the locus of the attributive consciousness or *dharmabhūtajñāna.* It has the qualities of a doer and enjoyer. The Jīva is *aṇu* (atomic) and the *vibhutva* (ubiquity) that is predicated of it is due to its participating in the immanent *śakti* of Brahman from which it is inseparable (*abhinna*).

The Bhedābheda relation between the Jīva and Brahman is established by different commentators in different ways. To the Advaitins, the *bheda* refers to *vyāvahārika daśā* (phenomenal state) and the *abheda* to *pāramārthika daśā* (absolute state). For Rāmānuja, *śarīra* connotes *bheda* and *śarīrin* connotes *abheda* in the *śarīra-śarīri-sambandha.* Bhāskara says the Jīva's *bheda* from Brahman is due to the action of the *upādhis* or limiting adjuncts while the *abheda* refers to Brahman as *śakti.* Nimbārka's theory of the Bhedābheda relation takes its stand on the analogy of the sun and its effulgence, conveying the equal validity of unity and difference. The Jīva is both self-subsistent and dependent on Brahman, Brahman being the *niyāmaka* (controller) and the Jīva the *niyamya* (controlled). As self-subsistent it is *abhinna,* non-distinct from Brahman, but as *niyamya,* it is distinct, indicating its *bheda* (distinction).

The *mahāvākya 'Tattvamasi'* which expresses the identity between the Jīva and Brahman is variously interpreted by different commentators. We have dealt with the views of others; Nimbārka's solution is a little novel. He holds that the *niyamya* is secondary to the *niyāmaka,* as the *śakti* is secondary to the possessor of the *śakti* in the *śakti-śaktimat* relation. So the Jīva by its *niyamyatva* has only a dependent reality, and the *tvam* is to be understood in its secondary meaning as *niyamya.*

According to Śaṅkara, those Śrutis which deny difference, the *bheda-niṣedha* Śrutis, show that difference is not ultimately real, but has only phenomenal reality. According to the Dvaitavādins, *bheda* alone is primary ; and the *abheda* texts are to be understood as in *'Tadguṇasāratvāt'*, in terms of similarity between the Jīva and Brahman, and also as an aid to concentrated meditation on Brahman free from dispersal and distraction according to the *niṣedha* Śruti *'Neha nānāsti kiñcana'* (there is no many). The *bheda-niṣedha* (repudiation of distinction) Śrutis are intended to deny the absolute and self-sufficient independence of the Jīva and *prapañca* (phenomena) apart from Brahman and to emphasize their dependence on Brahman. In Rāmānuja's view, apprehensive cognition is the Jīva's *svarūpa* (essential nature) and is *dharmabhūta* (adjectival). But there is no *śarīra-śarīrin* relation between this cognition and the Jīva. Nimbārka, however, applies the same relation as subsists between cognition and Jīva to that between Jīvas and Brahman. The difficulty in the concept of *śarīra-śarīrin* relation between the Jīva and Brahman is that the Jīva as Jīva has a *śarīra* (body) of its own, of which it is the *śarīrin* (the possessor), and if it is looked upon as the *śarīra* of Brahman which is the *śarīrin,* the *śarīra* of the Jīva must in effect be also the *śarīra* of Brahman. In the stage of *mukti,* in the Viśiṣṭādvaitic view, every soul acquires a transcendental body, an *aprākṛta śarīra,* and the same problem of the relation between this *aprākṛta śarīra* of the Jīva and Brahman's *śarīra* constituted of Jīvas will persist. In any case, one body cannot be the body of another. If the soul loses its body, either *prākṛta* or *aprākṛta,* then it loses its distinctiveness from other Jīvas and from the Absolute. Nimbārka says that the Jīva is referred to as *śarīra* only as the *niyamya* of Brahman and so the śarīrahood of the Jīva is not to be understood literally, but only in so far as it is the field of activity of Brahman's *śakti.*

Like Rāmānuja, Nimbārka too does not accept anything like Nirguṇa Brahman. Brahman can be Saguṇa only and possesses an infinite number of auspicious qualities. It is free from imperfections of the material qualities or *heya guṇas* (undesirable qualities) of Prakṛti. It is *ānandamaya* (blissful) ; and the creation, preservation, and dissolution of the world and also the conferment of *mukti* are all due to It. In creating the Jīva and leading it through transmigration, the *kāraṇaśakti* (causal power) of Brahman brings about the effected Jīva, which re-acquires its former consciousness in association with its individual body and according to its antecedent *karma.* Brahman is both the *nimittakāraṇa* (efficient cause) and the *upādānakāraṇa* (material cause). As the *nimittakāraṇa,* Brahman associates the Jīva's *anādikarma* (beginningless series of actions) lying dormant in the *pralaya* (dissolution) stage with the *cetana* (consciousness) of the Jīva and endows it with *bhoktṛtva* (enjoyership). Brahman's being the *upādānakāraṇa* (material cause) means that the *śakti* and the *kārya* which are in Brahman in subtle forms are manifested in a gross manner in the Jīvas and in the *prapañca* (universe).

*Mukti,* according to Nimbārka, is the gift of Brahman in response to the *bhakti* of the Jīva. All the auspicious qualities of Brahman are acquired by the released soul except those pertaining to the creation etc. of the world. There is resemblance with Brahman in the transcendental enjoyment. It is a case of *sādharmya* (similarity of nature) only and not absolute identity with Brahman.

Referring to the condition of the Jīva in *mukti* in the context of the *sūtra 'Avibhāgena dṛṣṭatvāt'* (IV.4.4), Nimbārka says that the soul perceives Brahman as non-contradictory to *bheda* and as non-distinct from itself. This is different from Bhāskara's view that in *mukti* the difference due to limiting adjuncts disappears and the essential non-difference between the Jīva and Brahman (*svābhāvikābheda*) remains. On the topic of Brahman's being *upāsya* and needing a body to be the object of worship, Nimbārka follows Rāmānuja and says that Brahman's body is of a transcendental nature, i.e. *divyamaṅgala vigraha* (divine auspicious body).

With regard to the relation subsisting between Brahman on the one hand and the Jīva and *jagat* on the other, Nimbārka holds that these latter are the real *pariṇāma* of Brahman Itself and not of Its *śarīra* or qualities. The *pariṇāma* of Brahman (holding as It does the Jīva in the form of subtle consciousness as *aṁśa,* part), into the *sthūla* Jīva with consciousness in the gross state, arises from the expansion (*vikāsa*) of the Jīva's inherent *jñāna.* But the Jīva is not originated like the *sthūla prapañca,* which is the effect of the *svarūpa-śakti-pariṇāma* of Brahman. Thus the Bhedābheda relation is established by virtue of the *sthūla cit* and *acit,* the *sūkṣma cit* and *acit* being all *aṁśas* of Brahman understood as Its *svarūpa-śakti.* Then it is easy to see how if the one, viz. Brahman, is comprehended, everything else becomes known.

## BALADEVA'S INTERPRETATION

Baladeva, the author of *Govinda-bhāṣya* on the *Vedānta-Sūtra,* refers to Brahman as Hari and to the Bhāgavatas, whether bound or free, as Haridāsas. In this he follows the tradition of Ānanda Tīrtha. But unlike Ānanda Tīrtha, he says that Brahman is both the efficient and the material cause of the universe. The Bhedābheda relation between the Jīva and

Brahman, according to him, is in the manner of the relation between a *daṇḍa* (stick) and a *puruṣa* (man). *Puruṣa* is different from *daṇḍa,* but he is one with it as *daṇḍin* (possessor of the stick [Baladeva's commentary on the *sūtra* II.1.13]). So also the Jīva and *prapañca* are different from Brahman, but become identical with Brahman as *jīva-prapañca-viśiṣṭa* (qualified by the aspect of manifestability as Jīva and the world). Baladeva agrees with Rāmānuja and Nimbārka in postulating the reality of the *prapañca,* but he does not adopt Rāmānuja's view of the *śarīra-śarīrin* relation or Nimbārka's view of the *śakti-śaktimat* relation. He does not adopt the Advaitic theory that the *prapañca* is unreal. He comes very near the views of Ānanda Tīrtha and Vijñāna Bhikṣu in the matter of the relation between *prapañca* and Brahman. But he differs from Ānanda Tīrtha when he says that Brahman as *niyāmaka* (controller) is *upādānakāraṇa* (material cause), which is also the view of Vijñāna Bhikṣu (MSS. of the Oriental Manuscript Library of Madras, No. 2990 and No. 3297).

In addition to the three principles (*tattvatraya*) of *cit* (soul), *acit* (matter), and Īśvara (God) in Rāmānuja's theory, Baladeva posits two others, namely, *kāla* and *karma*. Īśvara is omnipresent, but the Jīva is atomic. Both are *cidrūpa* (of the nature of consciousness), and both are *jñānāśraya*—being the locus or support of *dharmabhūtajñāna* (knowledge as quality)—their relation being like that of the sun and its lustre. Īśvara and Jīva can be referred to by the expression *aham*. When it is said that the Jīva and *prapañca* are the *pariṇāma* (transformation) of Brahman, what is meant is that it is Prakṛti and *sūkṣma cit* (subtle consciousness) that undergo *pariṇāma* as *prapañca* and Jīva respectively and not Brahman. This *viśeṣaṇa* (capacity or process of qualification), according to Baladeva, is inseparable (*avinābhūta*) from Brahman. Brahman is both the *nimitta* and the *upādānakāraṇa*. Brahman as the locus of the subtle *cit-acit-śakti* is *nimittakāraṇa*. When it is qualified by the *sthūla* (gross) *cit-acit-śakti,* it becomes the *upādānakāraṇa* (I.4.26). When the *dharmabhūta* of the *sūkṣma cit* undergoes expansion caused by the adjunct of *śarīra,* it becomes *kārya* Jīva. *Acit* is the *bhogya* (enjoyed) and the Jīva is the *bhoktṛ* (enjoyer). The *adhikaraṇa* of the second *adhyāya* (II.2.42-45), which according to Śaṅkara relates to Pāñcarātra, is according to Baladeva, as also Nimbārka, a criticism of Śākta-mata (II.3.27). *'Pṛthagupadeśāt'* is understood by Ānanda Tīrtha to convey the absolute difference between the Jīva and Brahman. Baladeva, however, takes it to mean only the mutual difference between the several Jīvas. The *adhikaraṇa* beginning with *sūtra* II.3.42 is taken by all, except Ānanda Tīrtha and Baladeva, to mean that Jīvas are *bhinnāṁśas* (dissociated parts) of Brahman and the *avatāras* (incarnations) are *svarūpāṁśas* (integral elements) of Brahman. In the *sādhanādhyāya,* Baladeva prescribes *bhakti* as the *mukhya sādhana* (primary method) for the attainment of Brahman. Commenting on the first two *pādas,* he explains that *vairāgya* (detachment) in relation to the world and attachment to Hari are the means of salvation.

In the state of *mukti* the Jīva retains its consciousness of being a Haridāsa and preserves its separateness as such from Brahman. In this, Baladeva is one with Ānanda Tīrtha and differs from Rāmānuja and Nimbārka, for the Jīva in *mukti* retains its *bheda* consciousness and does not feel its identity with Brahman.

Thus a host of problems like the relation of God and His attributes, the nature of knowledge, the constitution of the material world, the relation of the soul to knowledge, etc. were mooted and discussed with marvellous thoroughness, which excite the admiration of all lovers of speculation even to this day. The Vedānta teachings have an all-pervasive influence on the life and literature of India ; and its destructive criticism of rival schools and constructive scheme of philosophical thought, with their bearings on practical life, are still matters of aesthetic delight, ennobling sentiment, and intellectual satisfaction.

# 10

## ESSENTIALS OF VEDĀNTA

### WHAT DOES VEDĀNTA MEAN?

VEDĀNTA is knowledge that has for its aim the solution of the mystery of all existence. In a sense every man has an explanation of the universe known to him, though it cannot be said that he has solved all the doubts that have presented themselves. What the Vedāntin, however, does is to make a systematic, nay, the most comprehensive inquiry possible. From time immemorial Indian thinkers fully recognized the fact, so often overlooked, that a man can grasp only what he has the capacity to think about or perceive, and that the same truths are viewed in a variety of ways according to different stages of intellectual development or different mental attitudes or tastes. The Indian or Vedāntic philosophers have in view this fact when they present their solution in a number of ways. This feature causes not a little confusion in the minds of those who approach Vedāntic literature from the modern Western or Westernized standpoint. Some have taken it to be religion and some, mysticism. Others have thought that it is theology or scholasticism. And yet others have considered it to be the rudiments of scientific thinking. A few, however, believe that it is a philosophic interpretation of the universe. All these views are both correct and incorrect ; for Vedānta is all these. Vedānta attempts to sum up the whole of human knowledge, as far as possible. It considers every kind of human knowledge or experience to be a step on the ladder. At one stage it is religion, at another it is mysticism, and so forth. It recognizes even atheism or agnosticism as a step. It takes a bird's-eye view of all sciences and arts also. It ignores or discards nothing of human experience. At its highest stage Vedānta is *pure* philosophy. It seeks not an imaginary or hypothetical, but a verifiable or true explanation of the whole of existence.

That Vedāntic thought made great progress in the past is generally acknowledged. But whether it has kept itself abreast of the recent advances in science and philosophy is doubted by many. For latterly it only helped to produce a colossal literature in theology and scholasticism or to drive men to mysticism. It was left to Sri Ramakrishna Paramahamsa and Swami Vivekananda to present Vedānta in a manner suited to the modern mind. They have shown that Vedānta includes and implies all stages and varieties of human experience and knowledge, and that it is not opposed to the latest developments of science and philosophy.

## OF WHAT USE OR VALUE IS VEDĀNTA?

Vedānta is a treasure of which no conqueror can deprive India but of which she can freely give to all mankind, thereby enriching not only the receiver but also the giver. It actually and truly blesses him that gives and him that takes, inasmuch as it seeks, as the goal of all existence, universal or supreme good (*parama puruṣārtha*). While every religion and every school of mysticism vouchsafes its joys or satisfactions only to the individual or individuals entering its fold, Vedānta seeks, without stooping to proselytization, the good of all men, nay, of all beings, and that in the highest degree, though at first sight such an objective appears too ambitious to be within actual human reach. Further, whereas every religion promises the highest good or bliss after death, Vedānta aims at realizing such good in this world. In this respect, its object conforms in the strictest sense to the laws of verification known to the most modern scientist.

Vedānta naturally starts with an inquiry into the nature and the means of satisfying human cravings or desires, which, when not satisfied, beget sorrow or suffering. Many a Western critic has misunderstood this feature of Vedāntic inquiry, characterizing it as a pessimistic philosophy. But it only starts with such universal facts as best stimulate the spirit of inquiry. What distinguishes Vedānta from all other human pursuits is that it does not rest till it attains the goal of universal good by eradicating all sorrows. This it seeks to reach by probing the mystery of existence. It may not be possible for everyone to reach what is called the ultimate truth or to bring about the highest good. To the extent men approach this truth do they achieve and promote universal good. Therefore great souls seek to help humanity in attaining supreme knowledge (*Brahmajñāna*), which is inseparable from universal good, the goal of Vedānta.

## WHO IS QUALIFIED TO MAKE THE VEDĀNTIC INQUIRY?

The first condition to be satisfied by a seeker after the highest truth is that he must possess the requisite competency. Now, there are different degrees, or, as it is sometimes thought, different views of the same truth. There are, as already said, truths of religion, mysticism, science, and different philosophic schools, marking the steps so far reached. But the peculiarity of Vedānta lies in the fact that it comprehends all of them and aims at the highest or all-unifying truth. He who is satisfied with any particular kind or degree of truth other than the highest, and is not eager to get at the latter, is not qualified to make the Vedāntic inquiry. The seeker after this end should possess the strength and determination needed to continue till the goal is reached. He must be able to command perfect concentration or one-pointedness (*ekāgratā*) of mind. Such concentration means the complete elimination of all personal preconceptions (*ahaṅkāra* and *rāga*). These disciplines are made possible in the modern world in science, provided the determination to reach the very end is persistent, which unfortunately is absent in most scientists. The scientist often lacks this determination, because he fears he may have to forgo some of the things he is most attached to in the world. To give an instance, some eminent scientists, though they see at times that the causal relation is no more than one's own intellectual conception or an idea, cannot yet rise above the belief that it somehow inheres in the objects themselves. These men think in this way because of their attachment to the world. It is when their minds can rise above this causal complex, freeing them from its coils, that they can get at the Vedāntic point of view. Nor is the scientist able to rise to that pitch of complete detachment which demands greater sacrifices (*vairāgya*) than are commonly made. The old Indian discipline which combined *yoga* (mental control) and *vicāra* (inquiry) has fallen into disfavour. The modern Hindu student of philosophy is prepared for *vicāra* alone without the necessary *yoga,* which demands the acquisition of many moral qualities. The Indian philosophic preparation for the pursuit of truth is known as *sādhana.* As this course of preparation is slow and gradual, men are made to pass through the stages called religion, theology, scholasticism, and mysticism, including a taste for art, before they attempt *śāstra-vicāra* or what is known as inquiry on scientific lines. At this stage, lest they should feel discouraged, men are made to think that they are near the goal. They are therefore made to discard doubt and rely solely upon faith. The pursuit known as *philosophic* inquiry (*tattvārtha-vicāra*) marks the last step. Vedānta is often interpreted as signifying only this last stage, though in reality it covers the whole field of human knowledge including this last step which is its most distinguishing feature.

Philosophy commences when one sees the fallacy of relying upon authority or tradition, including scriptures or the testimony of others, however extraordinary. Philosophy, further, repudiates all mystic attitudes or ecstatic visions which manifest themselves in such expressions as 'I know', 'I have seen', or 'I have felt', and cannot rely upon them as absolute truth without testing them.

When one is thus qualified, that is, after one is able to eliminate all personal preconceptions either by rigorously applying the scientific method or by undergoing full yogic discipline, one may embark upon the rational interpretation of existence, i.e. philosophic inquiry. Men at the helpless or child stage have to rely upon the help of others, and have therefore to begin with some kind of belief, suited to their own temperaments, in an unseen or more powerful Being, or in some existence after the death of the body, or in the reality of the objective world. At this stage the mind, finding satisfaction in what it attains, clings to it. But when it grows in vigour it begins to doubt and ask for proofs. Doubt is dangerous, as the *Bhagavad-Gītā* points out, inasmuch as it tends to unsettle the mind. It must be got rid of at least by dogmatic faith. Faith is the sheet-anchor of such minds. But to those who possess the strength and capacity to think acutely, doubt is a stimulus to further inquiry. As the *Nāsadīya-sūkta* or the *Uddhava-Gītā* indicates, doubt is the mother of knowledge. Philosophy first develops the thirst to emancipate oneself from the slave mentality of relying upon tradition or authority or upon one's own unverified knowledge. Since this emancipation is a gradual process, every man is in one sense a philosopher, to the extent to which he is able to pursue truth. Religion and mysticism seek to live in a world of faith and vision, whereas science and philosophy try to live in a world of verified facts.

## THE NATURE OF THE TRUTH OF VEDĀNTA

All systems of philosophy, wherever found or developed, are but approaches to the common end or summit of Vedānta, which is the end of all knowledge. This end or goal of Vedānta is thus described: It is that which being known, everything becomes known, and which being attained, nothing else remains to be attained. The urge or impulse to attain to this goal manifests itself in the earliest stages as efforts to satisfy cravings or wants and to overcome fears, all of a physical character. In the higher stages it seeks to satisfy all intellectual as well as spiritual wants and overcome fears of all kinds. To attain the former, men make use of religion and science, and to attain the latter, they pursue philosophy, especially Vedānta. Vedānta therefore does not despise religion or science but seeks their co-ordination. All disciplines from religion upwards tend to purify, sharpen, or make one-pointed, the *buddhi* or reason—not the intellect, as so many writers on Vedānta say. But it should not be thought that one can straightway start the study of philosophy before this capacity to 'depersonalize' (efface the ego) is attained.

Such a seeker has to be warned against a serious error into which men often fall in the attempt to recognize truth. All men naturally love truth and seek it. And satisfaction is thought to be the index of truth. But a Socrates dissatisfied knows more of truth than an unthinking person satisfied. It is the seeker's satisfaction that determines the truths of religion, mysticism, theology and, not unoften, of science also. A Max Planck or a Bertrand Russell prefers to stick to the causal relation merely because it gives him satisfaction. The theologians and scholastics, who wrangle over logical or grammatical interpretations, rely finally upon personal satisfaction, which evidently varies. The test of the highest truth in Vedānta consists in the inconceivability, and consequently the impossibility, of difference in it. Mere satisfaction, joy, or bliss experienced by one is no criterion of *truth* in Vedānta. The two must go together, though truth alone is sought.

### WHAT IS EXISTENCE?

Vedānta studies all experience by first analysing it, as is most commonly done, into two factors, the knowing agency (*kṣetrajña*) and the known or knowable world (*kṣetra*), which are, roughly speaking, similar to the mind and matter of European thought. The correspondence, however, is but a rough one. For, in the West, philosophers do not seem as yet to have analysed mind and matter, or subject and object so completely as the Vedāntins have done. The knowing factor does not include, in Vedānta, the contents of mind, such as thoughts, feelings, and ideas which are treated as mind in Europe and America. They are treated as the known or the object in India, and are put into the same category as percepts. Vedānta recognizes two classes of objects, mental and physical, i.e. internal and external. The witness (knower) is thus separated from what is witnessed (known), i.e. the entire panorama of the physical and mental worlds. The reason for such an analysis is that the two factors belong to distinct categories. The seen or known is inconstant, whereas the witness only sees the changes and is as such constant.

### THE PRACTICAL SIGNIFICANCE OF THIS DIVISION

Such men as are struck by the impermanence of the objective world, and particularly of this physical body, seek the comfort and support of religion, theology, mysticism, or the like. Such others as cling to the objective world, believing it or at least its changes to be real because of the pleasure they yield, are realists, and many of these are scientists. They do not ignore the objects known as mental. Only they rely most upon the seen or known, internal or external. Those few, on the other hand, who investigate both mind and matter, i.e. the witness and the witnessed—the subject (knower) and the object (known)—and seek the absolutely real, are philosophers. They do not fall back upon mere intuition or imagination, as do the first group, nor do they ignore any part of the mental factor, as do the second group, or take the known world to be real because it is a source of pleasure to them. What the philosopher seeks, according to Vedānta, is not comfort or joy, but truth. He who knows the truth of all existence is said to attain supreme knowledge, which is seen to comprehend the universal good.

### WHAT DO WE MEAN BY THE WHOLE OF LIFE OR EXPERIENCE?

This is in fact the central problem of the philosophy of Vedānta. European and American philosophy is based upon the data of the waking state, in other words, of a fraction of experience, while Vedānta takes all the three states of waking, dream, and deep sleep, or the whole of experience, into consideration. Western philosophy, again, takes the waking data as the standard of reality, and with this standard it evaluates the experience of dream and deep sleep ; whereas Vedānta places all the three states on the same level and inquires into their worth as reality. The philosophic conclusions of the West cannot therefore attain a view of the whole truth. Vedānta is the only road leading to it, for it considers the whole of experience.

Without going into detail, it will suffice here to say that the study of the three states leads one first to the fact that the entire world of the waking state is as much a creation of the mind as the world of dreams ; and as both the worlds disappear in deep sleep into the mind, the entire objective world of the waking and dream states is unreal or illusory. They *appear* to be real for the time being. Vedānta is neither realism nor idealism, but unrealism so far as the objective world goes, and Ātmanism so far as the substance in itself is concerned ; for the whole world of mental creation emanates from and returns to the mind. The knowledge that everything is Ātman cannot be attained unless one rises above the mere thought or concept of Ātman, and lives or has one's being identified with everything, the all.

### THE GOAL OF VEDĀNTA

The true test of the worth of Vedānta lies in its bearing on life here and now, and not in any speculative hypothesis or any intellectually constructed system. The only question is, Does Vedānta explain the whole of life, and at the same time help the realization of universal good in actual life? These are not two separate questions but are the obverse and the reverse, so to say, of the same question. Generally people view the highest good as the supreme bliss in this or in some future life, taking the individual standpoint, and rest satisfied with it. This is religion or mysticism. Though, as religion, Vedānta starts with the welfare of the individual, yet it does not stop till the whole of mankind, nay, the whole world of life, is embraced in its conception of the highest good. Man is not happy unless he has the satisfaction of possessing as much as possible of what is outside him. At first he seeks wealth and all the means of happiness which are outside him. He wants wife, friends, and neighbours, or society ; and he feels that their joy or sorrow is his joy or sorrow. In a word, he feels that their well-being constitutes his well-being. He next learns that man's good and the good of other creatures are interdependent. Vedānta goes a step further and says that the good of even the plant world involves the good of man. In fact, Vedānta points out that what constitutes the body of man also constitutes in different combinations the material world. What constituted the human body a minute ago is now part of the body of entities outside, and *vice versa.* His body is food for others as other objects are food for him. In fact, this exchange is so continuous that it is impossible to say whether there is anything that can be called one's own at any time. It is a vain belief or delusion to think that there exists permanently anything separate as one's own body. Similarly, the individual mind is made up of the thoughts or ideas of a man's parents, neighbours, and ancestors, nay, of the world known to him. Nowhere in the mental world of the individual can a line be drawn to indicate what is exclusively his own. His passions and feelings and cravings came to him with his body from his parents, i.e. inherited from his ancestors.

Next, as regards what is called the self. Everyone refers to his self as 'I'. What is the characteristic of this 'I'? What is its general mark? It must be the common factor or feature of all the 'I's with all their differences. Eliminating the latter, which change with every man and every moment, the common feature of 'I' is the only permanent factor known. In a word, individuality cannot be defined as a permanent feature. Whatever exists permanently is the universal only. 'The One remains, the many change.' Individuality is a notion which, when inquired into, lands us in the universal, the all. The firm conviction that the One is the all, attained by constant and deep inquiry into the meaning of life in all its aspects, is the goal of Vedānta. This attainment is impossible unless one constantly looks into one's own life and actually sees in it the all.

### WHY IS PHILOSOPHY CONSIDERED SO DIFFICULT?

The fact that there exist so many schools and systems, differing from, and sometimes even hostile to, one another, and the most disheartening fact that the number is multiplying every day, makes one seriously doubt whether there can be any philosophy that will be universally or absolutely true. It may be asked whether after all it is not wiser to avoid this wild-goose chase, if some kind of mysticism or religion will not give one the peace of mind or joy that one needs in life. This great maze of thought regarding ultimate reality is due, says Vedānta, to the circumstance that men confine themselves only to the experiences of the waking state in which man's valuation of truth depends upon his intellect. So long as he is guided by the intellect, philosophies will only multiply and be more a hindrance than a help in attaining a final solution. All philosophical wranglings, so often met with, are of the intellect. To such intellect-ridden minds, religion or at best *yoga* or mysticism is the best antidote. In fact, the best philosophers of modern and ancient Europe, who have soared to some of the highest peaks of the intellect and have written the most admirable works, have lost themselves finally in some kind of mysticism. But Vedānta teaches that the real solution is to be sought not in the intellect, nor in mere intuition or ecstasy, but in reason which takes the all of life into consideration. It is therefore said, 'In reason seek thou shelter'. It is the whole of life with which reason is concerned. In other words, it is this knowledge of *kṣetra* and *kṣetrajña* that is the subject-matter of reason, and not the knowledge of matter alone, nor of mind or of spirit alone, that the intellect addresses itself to, and that multiplies systems, perhaps to the weariness of mankind.

## THE BEST GUIDE TO PHILOSOPHY

There is a time-honoured conviction held by the Hindu that the best exposition of the philosophy of a man is the life lived by him. It is therefore insisted that association (*saṅga*) with holy men is indispensable. Where this is not possible, a study of their lives is the next best course. Now, it is evident from what we know of the greatest Vedāntins, from Śrī Rāma, Janaka, and Śrī Kṛṣṇa down to Śaṅkarācārya and Ramakrishna Paramahamsa, that they did not, after their philosophy had ripened, hide themselves in mystic contemplation in caves and forests or sit statue-like on river banks or mountain tops, but wore themselves out working with all their might for the world around them, wherever the call came from. Such was the way in which they sought the fulfilment of the object of their existence. Before realizing the highest truth, they did have recourse to all the disciplines known as religion, mysticism (*yoga*), and studies of various kinds, even inquiries along different lines. But all these were dropped when they reached the world of philosophic truth.

# 11

## PHILOSOPHY OF THE ADVAITA

PHILOSOPHY of the Advaita is the title under which the metaphysics of the Vedānta will be treated here. The system of thought characterizing the Upaniṣads or the final portion of the Vedas is known as the Vedānta. It is philosophy in the sense that it makes an inquiry into truth and reality; but, unlike pure speculation, the truth it reveals is not a theory liable to modification with the advance of scientific knowledge but is positive and ultimate, verified and verifiable. Being the science of reality, it avails itself of all the sources of knowledge, viz. experience and intuition, and embraces all states and conditions through which life passes or is supposed to pass. Non-dualism denies that number can enter into the constitution of reality.

The Vedānta owes its significance to its unique attitude towards life, which it views from an angle of vision altogether its own. While others concentrate their attention on the world before us, which is taken to comprehend all the reality that we can know, and while sleep and dream-experiences are utilized to explain the phenomena of waking life, the Vedānta proposes to deal with life as it manifests itself in all the three states and so determines the nature of reality as a whole. The two view-points differ fundamentally. In the one, the waking world represents all our real interests, and sleep and dream are gently put aside as the mere appendages of waking. But in the other, each of the states is given a right place and is invested with equal significance; the man contemplating them easily rises to a condition in which his individuality and limited views are automatically shed, and the time-place-change-ridden world ceases to molest him. In the one case, we are hopelessly merged in a mysterious world which baffles all efforts to solve the enigma; in the other, the results are so grand that they exceed all expectations. Besides, in speaking of sleep and dream our intellect, which can grasp things only as external objects, plays a trick with us which we never suspect. Though they are independent of waking, we yet reduce them to the terms of waking. When did he sleep? How long?—are questions which hide the contradictions they involve. They are not like questions relating to waking acts, such as, When did he come? How long did he stay? In the latter case the acts are placed in waking time, and quite correctly. But we extend the same form of expression to sleep and dream, though these are *not* waking acts and hence cannot be measured in terms of waking duration. When did he sleep?—is a plain contradiction, for it would mean, At what point of waking time did he sleep?—implying thereby that sleeping is a waking act! Similarly, the states are not external things which we cognize by means of our intellect. They are known to us as immediacies by intuition. We intuit sleep and dream, and, what is more surprising, we intuit our waking also. For, consider the dilemma—Do we wake first and then perceive the world, or do we perceive the world and then wake to it? The latter conception is self-contradictory, since perception presupposes waking. The former is equally untenable as the order in which the acts take place—waking, perceiving—requires a basis of time, and waking time would commence before waking! It is thus evident that the sequence of the states in which we naively believe is no sequence in one time order. If it were otherwise, the states would be continuous, and their difference in character would be an inexplicable puzzle. Dream-events would then have to be placed in waking time and space, leading to a grotesque confusion by no means removable. A man lying on his bed would have to account for his being suddenly transported to a scene and surroundings thousands of miles away. Time cannot be inserted between state and state, and only the spirit remains to connect them. Thus the study of the states cannot be carried on solely through the intellect, which is bound by time and space, but through the aid of intuition.

We shall now deal with the analysis of the three states as effected by the Vedānta. Śaṅkara, its greatest exponent, has systematized the teachings of the Upaniṣads in his comments on the *Brahma-Sūtra*. In his comments on the *Brahma-Sūtra*, the Upaniṣads, and the *Bhagavad-Gītā*, we find a rational, consistent, and exhaustive treatment of all the problems of truth and reality as they arise in the course of his exposition of Vedic monism.

## WAKING EXPERIENCE

In the introduction to the *Brahma-Sūtra*, Śaṅkara, imbued with a truly scientific spirit, discusses the foundation of empirical life. We can discover in him no traces of theological or scholastic leaning. 'Subject and object—the self and the non-self—are so radically opposed to each other in notion and in practical life that it is impossible to mistake the one for the other.' After this grand beginning he adds, 'Yet we find that the mistake is universal, and we can never trace it to its source; for in our common life we cannot do without this initial error'. Without identifying the self (subject) with the non-self, viz. the body, the senses, and the mind, we could not describe ourselves in terms strictly applicable to the latter. We could not say, 'I am lean or stout', 'I am walking or sitting', 'I am blind or deaf', 'I feel, I perceive or act'. Hence we unconsciously confound the pure subject or the witnessing consciousness with its own objects ; and, conversely, we confound the ego with the witness, whereby the real unattached character of the pure consciousness is lost sight of altogether. Admittedly this is due to a fundamental illusion on which all our waking activities are based ; and to attain to truth and reality we must, realizing this illusion, rise above it by means of a rational inquiry. Reason which points out the illusion must also be competent to release us from its hold. Śaṅkara is not alone in drawing our attention to the illusory nature of empirical life. Plato, Kant, and Hegel adopt the same view, and in recent times, Bergson, equipped with all the knowledge of modern science, arrives at the same conclusion. The intellect, he says, disguises reality, misrepresents it, and presents to us a static world, while reality is pure movement, change, or a wider consciousness. According to both Śaṅkara and Bergson, the illusion is necessary to practical life, though none the less it is an illusion. Śaṅkara does not favour the reality of the idea as against that of the object. The testimony of consciousness itself establishes their distinctness. While the idea is admitted to be real, this reality can be maintained only by contradistinguishing it from that of the object. Still the reality of the idea and the object cannot be held to transcend the state in which both are experienced. In other words, their claim to reality is valid *within* the state, not beyond. This is a philosophical view that disposes of the dream-experience also. If we are true to consciousness, if consciousness is true to us, the objects and notions of dream are presented as indisputably real at the time, and are discovered to be illusions only after dreaming gives place to waking. We cannot suppose that waking experience can survive waking any more than dream-experience can survive dreaming. For that would be self-contradictory. Waking life may thus seem to be reduced to a long dream ; but, as Locke would say, 'Even then the thinker and the critic being equally involved in the dream, their mutual relations remain the same as if the condition was one of waking'. Hence the external world with its multiplicity of other minds and objects, and the internal world with judgements, feelings, and volitions (like the ego cognizing them and engaged in action and enjoyment) are all on one level of reality which correlates them. It is wrong therefore to imagine that the Vedānta is solipsistic, that while it concedes reality to the ego, it denies it to the non-ego.

Nevertheless, this does not conflict with the fundamental principle of Śaṅkara that practical life is made possible only by the spontaneous ascription of the qualities of the subject to the object, and *vice versâ*. For the reality of the experience of each state is ineluctably confined to it, the reality is such only for the state, is only relative, not absolute. That waking life taken by itself is a mystery teeming with endless contradictions in whatever way we view it, and that the armies of scientists and philosophers, carrying on an incessant fight with nature to discover the matrix from which things originate and grow, are faced with an ultimate *ne plus ultra* in all their investigations, are unquestionable facts to which all human researches testify. The very categories of thought are so many riddles; substance, quality, action, the universal, the particular, relation, space, time, causality, change—these are a phalanx of grenadiers whom every thinker has had to encounter in a close fight, of which the issue has remained doubtful to this day.

To find the ultimate truth in the universe itself is a hopeless task, but to peer through it and detect the reality that it disguises is the first duty of every rational thinker. For, situated as we are, our view of the world can be only external, and we must proceed from knowledge to knowledge which can never be final, since it cannot be of an object as it is in itself, but as it is known. We shall now examine the dream-state with two or three preliminary remarks.

Waking or dreaming is not a state in the strict sense of the term. A state implies change occurring in the soul or the object. When we compare waking with dreaming, the soul assumes the position of a witness of the two, and no change can be allowed in the witness. The two states seem to offer themselves successively for trial, but as they are not events in one time series, their sequence is an illusion. Neither can we suppose a change in the objective order which would demand a continuity of the same time series. Moreover, we labour under the disadvantage of having to judge from our memory of dreaming, which cannot be called up to confront us as a present experience, and this memory is itself of a strange character. Memory ordinarily refers to the past—a past time moving backwards infinitely from the present moment at which it terminates, that is to say, to a continuous time flow related to the present. Dream-experience, however, does not belong to this time series, and cannot be included in its past. Again, just as we cannot know when waking begins, so we cannot know when dreaming begins, for both seem to be uncaused. A cause connects one event with another of the same time order and the cause of a state would have to be inside the state, so that to transcend the state in order to discover its cause would be not merely illogical but impossible. Further, the soul as the witness of the two states intuits both, and that is how we know both. Hence, the witnessing character of the soul claims special consideration. It behaves as an entity free from attachment to the bodies, the minds, the sense groups, and the percepts of the contrasted states, and becomes a metaphysical element which can be realized only as the 'I', but with the 'I' divested of the egoity of waking or dreaming. While it is difficult and impracticable for us to eliminate in waking this witness from the ego complex, and the witness might seem to be a mere abstraction, our ability to remember dreams and appropriate it to ourselves proves that nature makes for us the analysis which we are unable to do for ourselves. She does this in virtue of the undeniable fact that the witness is the reality, the essence of our being. In discussing sleep, we shall come upon another feature of the witness which then passes off into pure consciousness.

## DREAM-STATE

From the waking point of view, a dream is a typical case of illusion, or rather hallucination. Admittedly without an external ground a whole world rises into view, and no suspicion is aroused that we are hoaxed. Scene after scene follows, originating feelings and acts with the stamp of genuineness. We are actors in the drama, playing fantastic parts, enjoying and suffering we know not how or why. There is no limit to the grotesqueness of the pageantry, overleaping the bounds of waking possibility. Yet at the time there is no surprise; everything looks natural. We take things at their face value. All the elements of waking are reproduced: time, space, change. In the very midst of the drama, we might jerk into waking, and, behold, it was all a dream! The usual explanation offered is that the impressions formed on the waking mind remain latent in the background of the unconscious and suddenly gain scope for activity, manifesting themselves in the shape of dream-experience. Sleep is the region of the unconscious, and we are then admitted behind the scenes to the sight of how the impressions, in their various kinds and degrees, act and react upon one another in the deeps of our nature. No impression apparently ever dies, and when it is denied adequate scope in waking, it obtains it in dreaming, which is a realm of life for the latent impressions. Space and time are creations of the mind, and the relation of cause and effect is improvised. The intellect suspends its censorship and our critical faculties are laid to sleep. Such is the dictum of waking reason. But this theory of impressions loses sight of the fact that if the theory be right, an impression has to be endowed with the power to create a world of realities at a moment's notice, rather, without any notice at all. If the mind by a fiat can create actualities, where is the need or place for matter which is the object of absorbing study for a scientist? How can this indispensable factor of life be brushed aside so lightly? If the reality of matter in waking life depends on our belief in our close observation and experimentation, how is our involuntary belief in the reality of our dream-occurrences to be accounted for? How can we take two contradictory attitudes towards life, the one solipsistic and the other realistic? This explanation is therefore suicidal and demolishes the very foundations of science. We can, besides, never notice the beginning or the origin of a dream. All our notions of propriety are outraged, without still engendering any surprise in us. Our consciousness which guides our judgement suddenly turns capricious, and one who lies down in Calcutta might find himself in a moment, as it were, in London. A single moment might expand into days and years. The dreamer might be transformed into a bull, a goat, or an insect. And the learned explanation is belated. It comes after the illusion is over, for there are no certain marks or characteristics by which we can identify a dream as such at the time. In truth, a dream cannot be defined ; otherwise we could not fail to detect the trickery when it repeated itself a second time ; but a man's, even a philosopher's life must include dreams to his dying day, and nature's power to delude is irresistible, supreme. A dream can indeed mimic all the features of waking, but one element remains triumphant and beyond its utmost power to touch, and that is consciousness. All the rest is plastic in the omnipotent hands of the dream ; consciousness alone defies its tactics and remains an unruffled witness of its whims.

We have hitherto viewed dreaming as an object of the waking mind, as an external object. We shall now examine it from within, by placing ourselves sympathetically in its midst. This is properly to judge a dream as a dream without the waking bias. Dreaming now appears to be a perfect replica of waking. A world is unrolled before us ; we never notice its suddenness or its incongruity with waking ; on the contrary it comes with all the impress of waking. Time, space, and change are inevitably present. No element of life is missed—other minds, natural scenes, familiar faces and objects, the earth below, and the star-studded sky above. Memories and emotions stream in, giving birth to strange conations. We converse with gods and ghosts. Sometimes the future is foreshadowed. We acquire new powers, occupy new positions ; nothing is impossible. We fly without wings and fall from hill-tops down, down through endless space. Nevertheless, we believe that all is real and nothing shocks us. After waking we condemn dreaming as an irrational, self-contradictory, and unreal illusion, and resolve to be no more befooled. But in the next dream there is the same masque enacted and the same helplessness on our part to detect it, and this is repeated without end to our eternal chagrin through all our living days. It will not do to brush aside this aspect of life as a mere phantasy. And on what is the claim of waking to reality based? Evidently on its own pronouncement. If so, is not a dream entitled to equal reality according to its own pretensions? If it is objected that waking is never stultified whereas a dream is, the answer is, How can a state which is accompanied with a sense of waking stultify itself while it continues? A state which is believed to be waking can never be conceived as liable to stultification while it lasts. A dream proper is never known to be such at the time. A stultified state appears as a past dream, and the present is *ever* waking. Thus a sympathetic examination of dreaming leads to the conclusion that it is a rival state as real as waking; and owing to the indeterminable discrepancy between the two in the time flow, added to the unconscious and timeless interval between, they must be adjudged of equal independence, as different realms of reality of which they are expressions. The word 'interval' used above is inadequate, but is meant to denote what is timeless. For if a time interval were imagined, it would connect waking and dreaming and make them a single continuous state, which would militate against all experience. Waking time rules waking and stops with it, and dream-time is coeval with a dream.

We are now free to consider the results obtained at this stage of our inquiry. The examination of the dream-state was made possible only by our individuality being laid aside. The mind and the body constitute our personality, and our individual life depends on our connection with them. These two factors can hardly be supposed to be identical in both waking and dreaming, as our experience is to the contrary. So are the two worlds distinct. In setting the states side by side in our study, we have mentally disentangled ourselves from both and have attained to an attitude in which, free from the trammels of individuality, we comprehend the two manifestations of reality as undivided wholes—an attitude quite different from that in which we think of the waking world. In the latter case the world is not seized as a whole, since, as our object of attention, it is separated from ourselves and placed right against us in thought. We conduct our examination of the dream-state, not as one ego contemplating the other, but as the soul divested of its egoity altogether. The simple experience denoted by the words, 'I dream', raises us to the level of the witness and above that of the ego. The soul is thus proved to be an entity at the back of the mind, taking its stand as the metaphysical basis of life. The soul thus sheds its individuality and becomes universal spirit, beyond the region of *meum* and *tuum*. The mind perceives the world, while the soul or spirit intuits both waking and dreaming, projects both, and absorbs both. The difficulty that perplexes the inquirer, viz. 'When I am sleeping, is there not a world outside in which simultaneously there are other minds awake and active, whom I rejoin when I awake? How does my sleep affect the real affairs of the world which go on uninterrupted for all *my* changes of state?'—this difficulty now vanishes. For the individuation implied in *my* sleep and the waking of *others* ceases when the comparative view of the states is taken. This is possible only with the individuality dropped. Moreover, the world, composed of other minds and matter, with which waking connects me and from which sleep releases me, is strictly bound up with waking, and to aver that my waking or my waking world persists when I am sleeping is not only illogical but inconceivable. The world has no status outside of my waking. Solipsism or subjectivism is easily transcended, for the witness is no ego and reality attaches to the former alone. Thus we have arrived at an entity which is the universal basis of life, which is all life, beyond time, change, and individuality. Why then should we examine sleep? For the simple reason that it is the primary state without which waking and dreaming would be impossible. We dream in sleep and wake from sleep.

Meanwhile we shall advert to some philosophical problems which receive their solution from our inquiry so far. The question of perception dissolves itself. The spirit manifests itself as matter and mind, which appear as the correlated elements of experience in each state. Their metaphysical basis is one, and this affinity in their source accounts for their mutual adaptiveness. The spirit as mind perceives spirit as matter. The puzzles of realism and idealism evaporate. For the principle on which we explain waking perception must apply equally to dreaming perception. If in the one case our knowledge is real, so must it be in the other. No purpose is served by affirming or denying the reality in either.

### DREAMLESS SLEEP

We commonly think that deep sleep is a state of absolute unconsciousness. What can we know of it? In answering this question, we must bear in mind that waking, dreaming, and deep sleep are states that we intuit and that cannot create any conceivable break in life. They are known as immediacies and are not observed externally. Hence our knowledge of them is more intimate and perfect, less liable to error or misunderstanding, than that of objects. I see a chair, and my notion of it agrees with that of several other minds, and practical life is pivoted on such agreement. But as to what a chair is in itself apart from my perception generates a problem which has endlessly exercised the intellect of scientists and philosophers. Our knowledge of objects must be infinitely progressive, because we cannot know them as we know or realize our own feelings and sensations. The very structure of the intellect precludes the contrary. But this habit has so grown upon us that we forget the limitations of our power to know and instinctively believe that that knowledge alone is true which we acquire by observation and experiment. We call it scientific.

The states which cannot be so handled we are prone to ignore as not allowing of the scientific method of approach. Now, there must be something fundamentally wrong in this attitude, since the states are the *sine qua non* of life—the elements of which it is made up. The world which is the theatre of our activities, enjoyments, and ambitions, with its comic and tragic sides, is unfolded to us in only one of them. In the other there is a mimicry of it, and in the third it is conspicuous by its absence. Experimental psychology, which presumes that the nature and the capacity of mind can be accurately known and measured by 'behaviour', cannot go to the root of the matter. The scientific description of sleep from our observation of the condition of the sleeper's body is, in the words of the Upaniṣads, to beat the ant-hill and imagine the snake inside to be killed.

We have found that the entity that connects waking and dreaming is not the ego of either state, but the witness or the spirit which is free from individuality. We have now to ascertain the principle which pieces together all the three. We have first to tackle deep sleep. This is produced in three or four ways. First, in the natural manner; secondly, by means of drugs like chloroform; thirdly, by the practice of mental concentration known as *yoga*; or fourthly, through devout meditation. The nature of the experience, however, does not vary, for in each instance the mind that alone can detect difference ceases to operate. As the sleep which comes to us naturally every day is the only form familiar to us universally, and as even the *yogins* cannot help sleeping, a close study of sleep is rendered possible to all, and obviates the necessity of studying the other forms. Though fancied to be a mere blank, a state of unconsciousness, we shall presently realize that it is the home of reality, the temple of God, and the true nebula giving birth to both mind and matter. It is the treasure-house of all truths; and in spite of our prepossessions we shall know it as the rock basis of life.

To begin with, we have to dispose of the common notion that sleep is unconsciousness. This evidently is a serious misapprehension. For conscious beings as we are, though we may have a notion of unconsciousness, the notion when examined will be found to have no content. A notion is formed in consciousness, and the latter cannot conceive its own absence while it is there to testify to itself. Unconsciousness cannot be a link in the chain of life, and we could never speak of sleep if it did not constitute an integral element of conscious life. So it is not a mere idea. A person complaining of sleeplessness does not suffer from an inability to form the idea. As Wildon Carr observes: 'When we say that a man is unconscious in his sleep, we do not mean by unconsciousness a complete absence of consciousness, as when we say that a stone is unconscious. We mean that the consciousness which is present is blocked or hindered from being effective. Rouse a man from his sleep . . . and consciousness returns.' Besides, the statement, 'I was unconscious during sleep', contradicts itself. For how can you say that you were unconscious unless you were *conscious* of your unconsciousness? If one retorts, 'I know now that I was unconscious', his position is not improved. How can you now refer to or describe a past occurrence unless it was part of your experience? And an experience of a conscious being presupposes consciousness at the time of the experience as well as at the time of recollection. Further, the memory of sleep points to it as a period of felicity or bliss essential to life. It is thus futile to argue that sleep is a period of absolute unconsciousness. We can never be *aware* of such a state. We cannot own it or describe it as thus and thus.

'I was aware of nothing, neither of myself nor of the world'—this is how a man roused from deep sleep describes it; and thereon hangs the whole possibility of metaphysics as a positive science. If a man says he was aware of nothing, he must have been *aware* of this awareness. Do what we may, we cannot rid ourselves of awareness in some form or other. 'I was not aware of myself or of the world'—this disposes of the ego and non-ego in sleep, and discloses their eternal concomitance. I was not aware of the non-ego, because I was not aware of the ego. Just as the presence of the one necessarily demands and depends on the presence of the other, the absence of the one must spell the absence of the other. In waking we perceive the world, because there is the ego to perceive it. In sleep we are aware of neither, because neither is present. To suppose an outside world flourishing all the same by the side of the sleeper is not to the point. It is illogical. The world persisting is obviously the waking world connected with the individual sleeper, which is cognized by the waking critic; but the sleeper has shed his individuality when he has passed into sleep, into pure spirit, and no world can attach itself to spirit. For the world is seen to be concomitant with the individual ego, and it is the mind, the senses, and the body that individuate spirit. When, however, these shackles of determination are flung off as in sleep, still to hold that the world exists in relation to spirit is neither rational nor consonant with experience. The world comes and goes with the waking state; and as I can change my states, so I can, when I move into the next state, switch off the world (which is my cumber in waking) along with the ego, its counterpart. The recognition of this truth requires some clear thinking, as the mind and the present ego act as clogs impeding the higher view revealed by intuition.

What then is the awareness characterizing deep sleep? It is not one craving an object and an ego. It is not of the subject-object variety that we are familiar with in waking and dreaming. It is what the Vedānta calls the transcendental or pure consciousness. We shall call the other the empirical consciousness, and the life predominated by it the empirical life. We shall now more closely examine sleep as pure consciousness. In the first place, it is a state of absolute unity. In the absence of time and space there is no room for change or plurality. Rāmānuja indeed believes in the persistence of the ego, and some other thinkers in that of the non-ego also, then in a latent condition. But evidently they are wrong. For we have seen how the entity which alone links up waking and dreaming as the witness, is already divested of egoity, and our present examination of sleep is rendered possible only by the persistence of the same witness in sleep also, that is to say, of the witness divested of the psychic set (mind and senses) and the physical body, which are the individualizing elements. Time ceases to operate outside of the states and is absent from sleep. Hence the ideas of latency or patency which are confined to the sphere of a time order are inapplicable to the contents of sleep. We carry over to sleep our waking bias when we conceive multiplicity in a potential condition in it, and we forget that it is an independent state to be judged and understood by itself and not to be translated into the terms of the others whereby we should forfeit the advantage of a new experience. There is neither a potential world in sleep nor an actual world beside the sleeper.

In the next place, it is not a state *in* which pure consciousness abides, but is itself pure consciousness. The popular view that it is a state is due to a misapprehension of its true nature which a careful analysis can alone reveal. For it is timeless and changeless, and to call it a state under the circumstances is a misnomer. The witness has transformed itself into pure consciousness, for without it we could have no knowledge of sleep. But its report of the non-existence then of the ego and the non-ego shows that it has assumed the rôle of pure consciousness. It is hence clear that the witness of the ego and the non-ego in the other states is also the witness of their absence, and that the witness and pure consciousness are identical. A mirror reflects objects presented to it, but in the absence of objects it ceases to be a reflector, though the power to reflect is ever inherent in it.

In the third place, the states are independent expressions of reality, so many wholes in which reality manifests itself; for, being free from time and space, it is indivisible. For the same reason, not only waking and dreaming are each a whole, but every one of their constituents is such. The plurality perceived within a state stands as an obstacle to our recognition of the indivisibility of reality, 'standing undivided amidst beings, yet appearing as divided' (*B.G.*, XIII.17). But in sleep we have pure consciousness, presented as the whole which is the master-key with which we have to unlock the doors of the other states. The metaphysical nature of the latter is thus revealed as pure consciousness which determines the value and the nature of the rest.

### REALITY, WITNESS, BRAHMAN, AND GOD

Having analysed the states we are in a position to discuss those philosophical questions which obtain a final solution in the light of the Vedānta. First, what is reality? Since the three states exhaust all life and experience, reality is that which invariably accompanies the states and persists in the midst of and in spite of the varying contexts. It is thus seen to be pure consciousness which pervades all life, whose nature is such as to make even an idea of its non-existence unthinkable. In defining reality as that whose non-existence cannot be conceived or imagined, Śaṅkara identifies it with pure consciousness or the witness, not subject to change. For the witness of change cannot change. Pure consciousness is not merely the reality, but the all. Its remaining single and secondless in sleep, its indivisibility, and its ubiquity through life show that it is the radical principle on which hang the wholes, waking and dreaming. It includes its manifestations, it is all-inclusive. This knowledge is the truest, the highest that we can or need possess. It is the absolute truth, relating as it does to the all-inclusive reality, and from this standpoint it is clear that Bradley was right in declaring that truth and knowledge merge in reality. The authority of the Vedas which unfold this truth becomes unquestionable.

One may imagine that the methodology of the Vedānta, which eschews external observation and experiment, is defective, inasmuch as it fails to throw light on the nature of the world. This is a mistake. In studying the inner life, we rise above its manifestations, and get at the very root from which the ego and the non-ego of the states branch out. Yet the relation is not organic but metaphysical. Reality does not develop by a process in time into waking and dreaming, but seems directly to manifest itself as the latter. There are no intermediate stages. Reality does not bring into being what was *non est,* but apparently becomes its own 'other', for even while appearing as the objective world, it remains an undiminished whole. And the advantage of the inner analysis lies in this that it discloses reality no less than our identity with it. It is we before whom the states are furled and unfurled, it is we who are resolved in sleep into pure consciousness, which like a canopy covers the whole of life. It is our self that co-ordinates the states. Placed beyond time and generating the time flow of each state, it is immortal, and by immediate experience we know it to be perfect bliss. This is the highest being which the Upaniṣads call Brahman. It gives being to the objects and occurrences of the states as well as to the states themselves, and this imparted being is real within each state. A state and its contents mutually determine their own reality, but as a manifestation this reality is not ultimate. The contents of the state as much as the states themselves, when viewed as separate from pure consciousness, fade into nothing. They are mere abstractions, void of reality. Again, reality as the eternal witness cannot rightly be treated as an object, and number and quality which apply to objects cannot be predicated of it. Being an immediacy, it allows of no doubt, hypothesis or predication concerning its nature. It is not transcedent, but transcendental. It is the Absolute, bearing no relation to any other. For in the absence of time and space no relation can exist between reality and its manifestations, since the terms of the relation cannot meet on the same level of reality.

The question how the world arose is altogether inadmissible. Causality works only in time, and the waking world must find its cause in waking which circumscribes the sphere of causation. Neither can we ask why we wake and dream—for we intuit the states ; and those intuitions, being the prius of our mental and bodily activities, are primary and so beyond the pale of time and causation. We can now indeed turn our minds forwards and backwards ; but when we approach the question of the origin of the state that brings forth the mind, we realize our limitation and are struck dumb. Waking limits the sphere of causation. This, however, does not affect our conclusions. Pure consciousness being the all, waking and dreaming can only be its expressions, no less than the worlds which they bring into view. Their fugitiveness and contingency mark them as realities of the second or subordinate degree.

We shall now advert to another interesting point of inquiry. What is the nature of pure consciousness or the witness? Is it, as pure being, a concrete or an abstract idea? If it is abstract or empty of all contents, it cannot give rise to the states or to their worlds, for nothing can come out of nothing. If on the contrary it is concrete, it already contains in solution all the elements that afterwards crystallize into creation, in which case the unity is not an undiluted absolute, but a real complexity in a subtle condition, and non-dualism is a mere web of fancy and so also are the various degrees of reality. This objection has been raised by Hegel against the Vedānta from a total misconception of its position. The pure consciousness of the Vedānta is neither an idea nor an object. It is the witness which converts everything else into an object, and is known to us more intimately as our self than any object can possibly be. It cannot be classed in any of the categories of thought as these are products of thought, and no category can precede consciousness which it presupposes. Thus the dilemma whether pure consciousness is an abstract or a concrete idea is meaningless. To treat it as an object would be to do injustice to its nature. But not to be an object is not to be nothing. It is more real than any other, because it is our own self whose reality is a primary datum with us, a truth we start from, before we ascertain the reality of other things. To question its reality is to question whether we live. The Vedānta does not trace the world to the Absolute either directly or indirectly. Its truth is based on facts of experience. In sleep we find pure consciousness without a second, and in waking and dreaming the worlds unroll themselves before us, in addition to pure consciousness. Since this view exhausts all reality, we can legitimately suppose only that the second element in the states, viz. the world, is but the original pure consciousness appearing without loss of integrity as the object to itself. As there is no change in it, this second element appearing as an alien must be a delusion. It is not alien. Thus to resolve all into pure consciousness is the highest function of reason. It is wrong to derive waking or dreaming from sleep. All three are independent of one another, and the temporal relation of posterior or anterior is the creation of our own time-ridden mind. There is no time to connect them. Only a comparative survey of the states enables us to assess their metaphysical value.

Two important considerations force us to recognize this truth. First, the notions of 'I', the subject, and consciousness are peculiar in their nature and inhibit plurality in strict thinking. We cannot conceive two 'I's, two subjects or two consciousnesses, unless these are turned into objects. This radical fact no pluralism can explain. Secondly, why we believe even illusions to be real at the time baffles all psychology, and is rendered intelligible only in the light of the truth that as we are real we can never experience unreality, neither perceive nor conceive it. In this manner we transfer in every instance our reality to the object of knowledge. Both the 'I' and the world bear on them the sure proofs of their origin in pure consciousness. The 'I' cannot be pluralized and the world is out there only for a cognizing consciousness. This concomitance of the world with consciousness must point to a common source of both in which they have their kinship.

As children fear darkness, says Schopenhauer, so do people fear annihilation. Exactly similar is the fear of Brahman, devoid of qualities and individuality. But the fear must be overcome, if we are to face facts and not indulge in comforting fancies. Is there, however, cause for fear? Gauḍapāda remarks: 'They conceive fear in what is free from all fear' (*Māṇḍūkya-kārikā*, III. 39). How then is this repugnance to Brahman to be accounted for? In the first place, when we try to comprehend It, we require It to be described in terms of what we know in waking life, that is to say, in empirical terms. It must be presented as an individual person with power, wisdom, and mercy, in short, as the God of theology who alone can hear our prayers, hasten to our help, absolve us from our sins, and be our saviour. But our experience of sleep stultifies all these features and compels us to conclude that Brahman cannot be described in familiar terms, though this does not amount to saying that It is nothing. Our whole nature revolts against such a view, and we cannot conceive nothing. Our self surely is not nothing. On the contrary, the aim and object of manifestation would seem to be the objective realization of the greatness of Brahman as expressible in names and forms. The ideas of power etc. displayed in life must be traced to Brahman, and we cannot define or describe It in other terms. To make It acceptable to our empirical conception, even personality must be imposed on It. Thus the interpretation of sleep as a negation of all that we know is but a natural criticism from the view-point of waking. It is an external view. In itself, it is a unity consisting of consciousness and bliss and divested of all alien elements. Since such is our essence our opposition to it is futile.

Those that cannot make up their minds to accept the unadulterated truth, are free to regard Brahman as clothed with attributes which manifestations suggest and justify. In fact, dreaming and waking are nature's comments on sleep. All the power, mental, physical, and moral, that they display, all the goodness, mercy, and wonder that we discern in them, must be ultimately traced to pure consciousness, though these manifestations do not affect it in the least. Says the *Bhagavad-Gītā* (X. 41): 'Whatever is glorious, good, beautiful, and mighty, understand thou that to go forth from a fragment of my splendour'. Metaphysically there is no evil as there is no alien, though from the empirical view both are real and give rise to ethics. Theology contemplates reality clothed with attributes, though it does not realize the true basis on which its faith must eternally stand. The Vedānta supplies that basis. God then is not fictitious, but is the real of reals. Our faith in Him is not without its fruit, for life is Brahman, and no unreality can be smuggled into It. Still the path of reason is distinct from that of faith. While knowledge removes the fetters of ignorance immediately, faith steeps us endlessly in dualistic life in which perfect peace cannot reign, from which contradictions cannot be banished. The dualities of common life are appearances whose essence is the One.

Ethics is the eldest born of the Vedānta. As the interests of the individual are secured by the relation of the soul to God as one of self to self, so the ends of morality are ensured by the recognition of the same self in others. The *Gītā* declares (XIII. 28): 'He that sees the one ruler existing everywhere cannot injure another who is his own self, and so attains the highest goal'. And the goal is harmony and peace. The sense of individuality and the seeking of individual interests are wrecked on the rock of universal identity, the refusal to perceive any other entity than Self or Brahman, which is the all and includes all. Theology which emphasizes distinctions can neither enjoin aimless self-denial nor ensure God's sympathy. For, if God and the souls are essentially distinct, their interests may collide and never be identical. On the contrary, he who realizes his oneness with God, the all-inclusive Being, triumphs over his narrow views induced by a sense of individuality, and can find no evil in life that does not ultimately tend to confirm his conviction. To set the seal on it, he becomes pure in thought, word, and deed, which are its inevitable forms of expression. 'Vedānta', says Paul Deussen, 'is the greatest support to morality'. It fixes the standard of right and wrong and explains the instinct imbedded in us in the form of the categorical imperative or the preference of the good over the bad.

### ETHICS, AESTHETICS, METAPHYSICS, AND MYSTICISM

The aesthetic feeling or the sense of the beautiful is due to a temporary suppression of individuality and objectivity, to an unconscious realization of oneness. This can never be explained by pluralism. Culture, training, and personal predilections are contributory factors. But the effect, viz. annihilation of 'otherness', would be impossible if the 'other' were absolutely real. The aesthetic delight is a metaphysical experience, bringing to light the essentially blissful nature of spirit. For beauty is externalized bliss.

In accounting for the second element in life, the Vedānta propounds a theory. Brahman manifests Itself as the world in order to obtain an objective view of Itself. It suffers separation into the subject and the object, and through eternal change It contemplates Its own inexhaustible nature. Self-expression is for self-realization. Brahman works assiduously in the person of the scientist to ransack all corners of nature to make them intelligible. Hence the progress of science is bound to be unlimited. The Vedāntic spirit supplies the most powerful stimulus to the cultivation of science in all departments of life. While the truths so discovered cannot be final, owing to the ceaseless change that rules the universe, they can never affect the Vedāntic truths which envisage all the three states and relate to a sphere transcending time. The reader will carefully remember that the Vedānta has fulfilled its function when it has established the one reality, which is all-inclusive and which resolves everything into itself leaving no remainder. The doctrines of Māyā and *avidyā* are offered only to help the aspirant to rise to the plane of the absolute oneness, for the appearance of an outstanding second element might operate on him as a hold back. When this is reached, however, there is no worry with a second.

The eschatology of the Vedānta is among its dogmatics. It concerns the fate of unenlightened souls ; and as its pronouncements are neither verifiable nor refutable, they must be tested only by the moral principles they involve. On the one hand the soul is eternal, and on the other its embodiment must continue while it remains ignorant of its true nature. Hence the doctrines of Karma and rebirth are formulated to determine its course through its spiritual evolution. Heaven and hell are described as places in which the souls of the dead experience joys and sufferings respectively in consequence of their deeds in life—'according to acts and culture' (*Ka.U.*, V. 7)—and not as reward or punishment. Migration from body to body continues until enlightenment occurs, which puts an end to further migrations and brings about release. God as our truest friend guards and guides the soul through all its wanderings and can never desert it, for He is its very self. His solicitude for its well-being never ceases till it is safely landed on the shore of deliverance. No soul is left to perish in the waters of *saṁsāra* (transmigration). Sin which arises from attachment to non-self creates a distance between us and our very self, God. Prayer, meditation, and worship bring about communion, and facilitate approach. Those that lean on faith must pass through a very strict discipline in life, practising self-control, celibacy and renunciation, devotion and service, worship and meditation. Through the grace of God so obtained and through special experiences they receive enlightenment leading to release. A Vedāntin cannot decry these means warranting a pure and disinterested life, for he alone can truly appreciate the adamantine basis on which they rest.

We shall now briefly consider the doctrines of Māyā and *avidyā*, which, as we have seen, have no place in the strict system of truth.[1] Māyā is the power with which Brahman is regarded as invested in order to account for the phenomenal life. The term is also used to indicate the phenomena. The contradictions which run through all empirical life point to its unreality by itself and demand a basic reality to make it effective. The belief in objects, taken by themselves, comes to us naturally and is due to *avidyā* or ignorance of the truth. Empirical life endowed with an existence independent of God is common delusion, the source of all evil. In truth, Brahman neither creates nor destroys. It is above change and time and is beatitude itself. In the strictest sense we are Brahman. Much of the unpopularity of the Vedānta is due to the reckless manner in

[1] For a fuller idea see the writer's *Vedānta or the Science of Reality*.

which the truth is expounded. The idea that all is Brahman is inspiring, while the notion that all is Māyā or illusion is to most people disconcerting, paralysing. The *Bhagavad-Gītā* refers to the absolute and the relative phase of the same reality: 'Without any of the senses, shining with all sense faculties; unattached, supporting everything; and free from qualities, enjoying them' (XIII. 14). The one is the transcendental, and the other the empirical view.

The reader who has so far followed the Vedāntic reasoning will readily perceive that the question of a cause never arises with regard to Māyā or *avidyā*. Māyā is a theoretical concession to the *avidyā*-ridden soul to satisfy its craving for an explanation of the world, and *avidyā* or ignorance must in all cases be traced to the absence of inquiry. The order of evolution is fixed and immutable: first, *avidyā* or ignorance, and then intellection. Causation cannot precede ignorance, for it presupposes intellection. Knowledge is the implacable foe of ignorance which it completely destroys.

There is an impression that the Vedānta is mysticism and that the latter is the culmination of its teaching. The two, however, are wide and distinctly apart. The Upaniṣads no doubt deal largely with *upāsanās* or meditations which aim at the experience of mystic oneness and the ecstasy resulting from it. This is evidently meant for those who avoid discussion and reasoning. In the Vedānta the rational portion stands out more prominently, and the methodology is based on it. The distinction between the two is radical and far-reaching. Mysticism seeks private experience by conscious effort, while the Vedāntic reason builds on universal experience. Although philosophy must throw light on all kinds of human experience, its truth cannot be drawn from special experiences, however rare; for the latter are not within the lives of all. The Vedānta aims at knowledge of truth; mysticism at ecstasy.

In contemplating life we seem to be spectators of a strange drama, a play of shadows in the shape of the states enacted before us. The actors and the scenes are ourselves transmuted, without the least loss of our integrity. So long as we take the shadow for substance, we are merged in joys and sorrows, in birth and death. When we remember that it is but a shadow and that reality can cast no shadow, the play now known to be an illusion deceives us no more, and the states rolling and unrolling themselves before us fool us no longer. We are left to admire the greatness of Brahman, which can project such scenes and withdraw them into Itself, leaving no trace behind.

ŚRĪ ŚAṄKARĀCĀRYA
*Courtesy : O. C. Gangoly*

# 12

## THE PHILOSOPHY OF ŚAṄKARA

Of all Indian thinkers Śaṅkara is perhaps the most misunderstood, although it can be said without any fear of contradiction that throughout his extensive writings he has nowhere been ambiguous. He combined profundity of thought with clarity of expression—a combination rare in philosophical writings. It is curious therefore that such a writer should be so much misunderstood. This may be due to the fact that his philosophy tolerates no human weakness and requires its followers to sever connection with all that is dear to the heart. Our attachment to worldly objects is so deep-rooted that we do not willingly part with them, even for the sake of truth. It is possible therefore that our worldly-mindedness unconsciously obscures our vision, and we try to interpret things in a manner that fits in with our own beliefs and likings.

### THE ABSOLUTE AND THE INDIVIDUAL SELF

Śaṅkara's unflinching logic led him to the supra-rational (and not to the irrational). He starts with the view that the essence of reality must be its absoluteness: it must remain ever the same, unconditioned by time, space, and causality.[1] It follows from such a conception of reality that the human intellect, conditioned and varied as it is, has not the remotest chance of ever comprehending it in its entirety. Hence revelation is the only source of knowledge regarding the ultimate reality of the universe. Nevertheless, Śaṅkara fully appreciates the value of reasoning in an inquiry into the nature of reality. He says that in matters of philosophical inquiry, unlike discussions on *dharma* (duty), perception, inference, and other human evidences are as indispensable as the Śruti. But only such arguments are to be tolerated as are not independent of the Śruti but supplement it.

The world abounds in evil, and suffering seems to be the lot of every individual. The Naiyāyikas (logicians) have gone so far as to declare that there is no pleasure in the true sense of the term in any worldly affair; there is only misery which is foolishly accepted as pleasure. Everybody desires to attain happiness and avoid misery. In fact, all our endeavours are directed towards that end. Desire for salvation is a desire to get rid of all kinds of misery, which truly constitute our bondage. But how to attain a perfect state of happiness?

[1] See *Adhyāsa-bhāṣya, Brahma-Sūtra*.

In order to root out suffering it is proper to investigate its cause. How do we account for the wrongs of which the world is full, and the apparently undeserved sufferings which befall its inhabitants? If suffering be a result, it can only be the outcome of our own acts. It is illogical to hold that A suffers for the fault of B. So orthodox philosophers maintain that every individual reaps the consequences of his own deeds, whether performed in this life or in former lives. Most intimately connected with this doctrine of the pre-existence of the soul is the universally accepted law of Karma. Nothing can be lost. The law of Karma in the moral world is the counterpart of the law of the conservation of energy in the physical world. Whatever a person may do, he must some day feel its consequences. But it is also evident that the consequences of all our actions are not experienced in this single life. Every action bears fruit, but it requires a suitable time and environment for its fulfilment; till then it remains a latent force (*adṛṣṭa*). So if life has continued from eternity, the store of our *karma* must necessarily be inexhaustible, for while part of it is being spent through experience (*bhoga*), fresh *karma* is being added. Hence it is clear that the wheel of *karma,* once set in motion, will gather momentum at every turn, and there will be no escape from sufferings, which are the inevitable result of action, until such action is brought to a standstill.

But how can the ever-revolving wheel of *karma*—the cause of birth and death—be stopped? It is idle to think that the eternal store of *karma* can be exhausted through experience. Philosophers of whatever school are emphatic in their declaration that this can be effected only by knowledge. The followers of Śaṅkara hold the following view.

Every individual works, and by the law of necessity has to reap the consequences of his actions. But we must see if it is in the very nature of an individual to work. If so, it is evident that there could be no escape from it at any time, and the cycle of births and deaths would consequently go on unhampered, and no salvation would be possible. If an individual is essentially a *kartṛ* (doer), he will ever remain so, for he cannot go against his nature ;[2] and as in the normal state of things work can have no end, salvation is out of the question. On the other hand, if it can be proved that the individual is not essentially a *kartṛ,* and hence not a *bhoktṛ* (enjoyer), then and then only would salvation be possible.

That the Ātman is immutable and indestructible is declared by the Vedānta to be a self-evident truth. Were it changeable, there would remain none to witness or cognize the changes. Again, none can deny his own existence, for he who denies would surely exist and therefore be the

[2] *Upadeśa-sāhasrī,* II. 89.

Ātman. It is evident therefore that the Ātman is neither the body nor the senses nor the mind, inasmuch as all these are in a state of flux. It may be noted that the *ahaṅkāra* (ego) is in existence only in so far as it is understood with reference to events. Is there anything underlying the *ahaṅkāra* which might be supposed to exist independently of all mental activities? If so, that might be accepted as the Ātman, the reality, the everlasting and unchanging essence of the individual, inasmuch as it is unaffected by psychic or physical changes and at the same time forms the noumenon of which all mental and bodily changes are phenomena. But the difficulty of discovering it is apparent. Apart from the Śruti, the only other means of recognition at our disposal is the mind. But the mind, being itself phenomenal and having inherent limitations, can have no claim to comprehend the Ātman. Further, anything discovered with its aid must necessarily be coloured by it. It is impossible to comprehend anything unaffected by the psychic process.

Śaṅkara shows that the subject (*viṣayin*) can never be the object (*viṣaya*). The 'I' can never be anything other than the 'I'. When I say that I have known myself, what I have actually known is not the self but something other than it. Whatever becomes an object of knowledge becomes, by that very fact, something other than the self. So the knower is unknowable. The body, the *manas* (mind), the *buddhi* (intellect), and the *ahaṅkāra* (ego) are all objects of knowledge, are variable, and are not therefore the Ātman. Rationally speaking, the subject can never be the object, yet it is a habit of human nature—a necessity of thought—to transfer the essence and qualities of one to the other and to identify the one with the other.[3] In fact, all our actions, both mental and physical, are possible only on the assumption that the Ātman is identical with either the mind or the body or with both. It is evident therefore that our ordinary conception of the 'I' is altogether wrong and that the true 'I' is neither the body nor the mind and is as such unknown and unknowable. But this should not be taken as a message of despair. The Ātman ever remains the subject, and cannot become the object. So an individual is in essence the Ātman, never affected by mental and bodily changes, which are all extraneous.[4]

This is the true nature of the Ātman, which is neither the *kartṛ* nor the *bhoktṛ* and is in reality ever free. To think that Ātman is in bondage is wrong, and is due to sheer ignorance of its essential nature. The Ātman is falsely identified with the *anātman* (non-self), and hence the bondage.

[3] See *Adhyāsa-bhāṣya, Brahma-Sūtra.*
[4] *Ibid.*

Bondage is therefore not real.[5] It exists only so long as one fails to realize the unaffected nature of the Ātman, and identifies it with the non-self. As soon as the true Ātman is discovered, the illusory bondage disappears. So says the Śruti: 'All knots of the heart are cut asunder, all doubts are dissolved, and all *karmas* are ended, when the highest Brahman is realized as one's self' (*Mu. U.,* II. 2. 8). So salvation is no new state of existence, it is no acquisition.

### MĀYĀ

Having once accepted the authority of the Śruti as unquestionable and final, Śaṅkara did not flinch from its inevitable consequences. His adherence to Vedic authority is so complete that he would not tolerate any compromise, even when his interpretation of Śruti came in conflict with experience. Such a contradiction he explained away by boldly declaring that 'Brahman alone is real, the world is false, the individual is Brahman and nothing else'—which sums up very accurately the fundamental doctrine of his philosophy.

The Śruti says, 'Thou art That' (*Tat tvam asi*). The individual (Jīva) is to be regarded as perfectly identical with the absolute Brahman. and Śaṅkara takes Brahman to be essentially *nirguṇa* (without any attribute), *niṣkriya* (without any activity or movement), *niravayava* (without any parts), *nirupādhika* (unconditioned and absolute), and *nirviśeṣa* (having no distinguishing element in it, a simple homogeneous entity). Even the words *sat, cit,* and *ānanda,* he says, do not imply any quality or differentiation in the being of Brahman, but what they simply mean is pure being, pure consciousness, and pure blessedness, each implying the others.[6] Now the Jīva is evidently just the reverse of all this. How could it then be identical with Brahman?

Again, the world, which is always in a state of flux, is said to have the self-same Brahman as its cause (*kāraṇa*), both material (*upādāna*) and efficient (*nimitta*). In what sense could this phenomenal world be spoken of as emanating from, subsisting in, and finally merging in the absolute Brahman? How could the non-relational Brahman be linked with the relational world, a world containing the individual Jīvas as well? Śaṅkara says that in no way could this impossibility be made possible. And ultimatcly it must be held that the world is not, nor did it ever exist, neither will it exist in future. The only truly existing thing is Brahman, and all else is naught. So Gauḍapāda in the *Māṇḍūkya-kārikā* (II. 32) says, 'There is neither dissolution nor creation, neither a person in bondage nor any

[5] *Upadeśa-sāhasrī,* XII. 17; *Brahma-Sūtra-bhāṣya,* IV. 3. 14; *Taittirīya-bhāṣya,* I.
[6] See *Taittirīya-bhāṣya,* I, where the subject is elaborately discussed.

spiritual aspirant, neither any seeker after liberation nor one that is liberated—this realization is the highest truth'. Now, this negation of the world of time, space, and causality in the being of Brahman, the ultimate Truth (*paramārtha-satya*), is itself an attempt to reconcile the apparent contradiction between the Śruti and experience. But any such attempt at reconciliation would be tantamount to bringing down the Śruti within the realm of logic, whereas the importance of the Śruti depends not upon its rationality, but upon its authority. So all such attempts would go against the very spirit of the Śruti. Yet so long as we are what we are, that is, slaves of rationality, the absolute self-sufficiency of the Śruti can make little appeal to us; a rational explanation of the contradiction becomes necessary, and that is the task of the philosopher.

Śaṅkara explains it by what is known as Māyā (illusion) or *adhyāsa* (superimposition), the principle of unifying contradictions—contradiction between the self and the non-self, the ego and the non-ego, the subject and the object, the cause and the effect, Brahman and the world. Contradictions, as we know, can never be reconciled. But no experience is possible unless and until they be *somehow* unified. Māyā is therefore the principle that mysteriously unifies contradictions and is as such inexplicable and indefinable (*anirvacanīya*). In other words, it is the principle of identification of contradictions or the principle that makes a thing appear as what it is not.[7] You take a rope to be a snake; this is *adhyāsa*. You take Brahman to be the world; this too is *adhyāsa*. In reality there is no snake, no world, and there should not be any superimposition; the one cannot be the other. Yet it is the inherent nature of man to identify truth with falsehood. This principle of *adhyāsa* therefore is such as has no reason to exist, and yet is most indispensable for all human affairs. It is the law that regulates all our actions and all our movements; nay, it is the law that makes the world what it is. Although it is indefinable, yet it is no abstraction and has a most concrete existence so far as the phenomenal world is concerned.

The Vedāntins have discussed the problem of error very thoroughly and have come to the conclusion that illusions are due not so much to the knowledge of the object this way or that as to the absence of the knowledge of the object as such.[8] This want of knowledge (*ajñāna*), however, must not be understood to be a mere negation of knowledge. It is not an *abhāva*, but a *bhāvarūpa* (a positive entity), although from the standpoint of Brahman, the ultimate Reality, its existence is altogether denied.

Now the Jīva can be said to be identical with the featureless

[7] See *Adhyāsa-bhāṣya, Brahma-Sūtra; Praśna-bhāṣya,* I. 16; *Māṇḍūkya-kārikā-bhāṣya,* I. 9.
[8] See *Siddhānta-leśa-saṅgraha.*

(*nirviśeṣa*) Brahman, only if his Jīvahood be held to be a mere appearance—in other words, if Jīvahood is taken to be a mere superimposition upon Brahman and, as such, false. Śaṅkara actually holds this view and says that it is Brahman that appears as the Jīva through ignorance or superimposition (*adhyāsa*).

Again, Brahman can be called the cause of the world, only if the world be taken to be a mere appearance, a superimposition—in other words, if Brahman be taken to be the ground (*adhiṣṭhāna*) of the world-illusion. The rope does not lose its ropeness even when it is mistaken for a snake. Brahman certainly cannot be said to transform Itself into the world. It only *appears* as the world because of *adhyāsa*.

From what has been stated above it follows that the world is a figment of Māyā, a mere appearance. But an appearance cannot have, even temporarily, an existence independent of that of which it is the appearance. The Sāṁkhya holds that the world is an evolution (*pariṇāma*) of Pradhāna, which, it says, is a self-existing, independent principle. But matter by itself is inert (*jaḍa*), devoid of sentiency, and its movement towards the evolution of an ordered world is simply unthinkable. The Vedāntic Māyā, on the other hand, is said to be an entirely dependent principle. It can be conceived only in reference to pure being and pure consciousness. Brahman being the only reality, nothing can be conceived without being related to It.[9] Māyā therefore by itself is not sufficient to account for this phenomenal world. So the Vedāntins do not hold Māyā to be the cause of the world. Rather it is said that Brahman is the cause or ultimate ground of the world. But when Brahman is said to be the cause of the world, It must necessarily be supposed to be conditioned (*sopādhika*); absolute (*nirupādhika*) Brahman can have nothing to do with the world. And the *upādhi* (condition) that conditions Brahman as the cause is Māyā.

## LEVELS OF TRUTH

So the world has no absolute reality (*pāramārthika satyatva*). It has an apparent and relative reality. The world-perception goes on unimpeded till one realizes what one really is, that is Brahman. Idealists deny reality to external objects. Śaṅkara is not prepared to attribute reality even to mental events; but he maintains that so long as Brahman is not realized, that is, so long as the empirical world continues to be perceived, both the external and the internal world are to be accepted as facts, neither more nor less. Hence the world too has a reality of its own, which, as distinguished from absolute reality, may be called *vyāvahārika satyatva,* that is, reality as far as it is necessary for all practical purposes. The objects of a

[9] See *Māṇḍūkya-kārikā-bhāṣya,* I. 9.

dream, although known as false on awakening, are real within the limits of the dream. Similarly, the world is also relatively real and is said to be false (*mithyā*) only when knowledge dawns. It should be specially noted that although the world is false, yet it is not altogether non-existent (*alīka*) like the son of a barren woman. Śaṅkara is even prepared to grant some reality to the *rajju-sarpa* (the snake in the rope), which he calls *prātibhāsika satyatva* (seeming reality) as distinguished from the other two kinds of reality.

The Vedānta of Śaṅkara stands for the theory of Vivarta, as against the theories of Ārambha (of the Nyāya) and Pariṇāma (of the Sāṁkhya), in any of the following senses of the term: (1) Vivarta may be defined as the appearance of a higher reality as a lower one, as for example, when the transcendental (*pāramārthika*) Reality (Brahman) appears as the empirical (*vyāvahārika*) reality (the world), or when an empirical reality, say a rope, appears as a seeming (*prātibhāsika*) reality (a snake); (2) Vivarta is the appearance of *cit* (consciousness) as *jaḍa* (the non-conscious); (3) Vivarta is that state of the cause, usually known as effect, which is neither different from nor identical with the cause, and as such is inexplicable. It will be noted that the arguments adduced by the Ārambhavādins[10] and the Pariṇāmavādins[11] are equally weighty, although they hold contradictory views—the former taking the effect to be different from the cause, and the latter taking the effect to be identical with the cause in substance. Śaṅkara, however, does not accept or reject either of these views. He says that all that can be said with any amount of certainty is that the effect has no existence independent of the cause, and that which has no existence by itself cannot be said to have any reality in the true sense of the term. So the effect neither is nor is not; for if it were absolutely non-existent, no activity would be induced. The world we see before us is neither real nor unreal, nor both real and unreal. Hence it may be logically termed as really indefinable (*anirvacanīya*). This is the fundamental position of the theory of illusory appearance.

### VIEWS IN BRIEF

We may conclude by briefly noting the findings of Śaṅkara in his study of the Vedānta:

1. Knowledge or consciousness absolute is the reality that is Brahman. Brahman is *nirguṇa, nirviśeṣa,* absolute consciousness. It is one, indivisible, without a second, having in Itself no *bheda* (difference)—either *sajātīya, vijātīya,* or *svagata.*[12]

[10] Those who hold that an effect is something newly created, e.g. the Naiyāyikas.
[11] Those who hold that the effect existed in its cause, e.g. the Sāṁkhyas.
[12] Meaning respectively the difference 'within the same species' (as between two trees),

2. The Jīva is essentially the same as Brahman and is therefore self-illumined, unlimited, and ever free. Its limitedness and all its consequent effects are due to *upādhis* or conditions, which, again, appear through *avidyā* (nescience) and as such are unreal. Eliminate the *upādhis*; the apparent duality at once ceases, and the Jīva no longer retains separate identity. The sense of personality is bondage, that of universality is freedom. To be Brahman is not the extinction of the individual, rather it is the expansion of one's individuality into the infinitude of Brahman. The Jīva is always Brahman—during bondage the *upādhis* screen this truth; in the state of freedom it shines forth as Brahman—as what it always is; nothing new happens.

3. Brahman simply *appears* as the world (including individuals as well) through *avidyā*. The world has a phenomenal reality, but no reality of its own. *Avidyā* too is no entity separate from Brahman, but is indefinable and negligible.

4. Brahmanhood is realized by the knowledge of the absolute identity of the Jīva and Brahman. The dictum *Tat tvam asi* reveals this identity. *Mukti* (liberation) is nothing but the realization of this identity. It is quite possible even in this body, that is, even while living (*jīvanmukti*).

5. Permanent bliss can never be a result of work. It is directly attainable by knowledge (*jñāna*), and once enlightenment has been obtained, no work is necessary. But till then all prescribed works must be scrupulously performed, as these certainly help towards realization.[13]

Last of all, we may appeal to the readers of Śaṅkara to bear always in mind the following two fundamental principles of his philosophy for a clear understanding of his position:

1. That although he does not really admit kinds of truth, yet for the sake of convenience he speaks of (i) *pāramārthika* truth attributable only to Brahman, (ii) *vyāvahārika* truth attributable to the objective world, and (iii) *prātibhāsika* truth attributable to the illusions of an individual so long as they last.

2. That (i) from the standpoint of Brahman, Māyā is *tuccha* (negligible)—the question of its existence or non-existence does not arise, (ii) from the standpoint of strict logic, Māyā is *anirvacanīya* (inexplicable), i.e. it logically fails to explain any relationship between Brahman and the objective world, (iii) from the standpoint of common experience Māyā is *vāstava* (real), the very life of the world.

'between different species' (as between a tree and a cow), and 'within itself' (as between the branches, leaves, etc. of a tree).

[13] See *Brahma-Sūtra-bhāṣya* on I. 1. 4, IV. 1. 16; *Upadeśa-sāhasrī*, I. 6. 26, etc.

# 13

## THE ADVAITA AND ITS SPIRITUAL SIGNIFICANCE

THE illusoriness of the individual self is apparently the central notion of Advaita Vedānta. Every vital tenet of the philosophy—Brahman as the sole reality, the object as false, Māyā as neither real nor unreal, Īśvara as Brahman in reference to Māyā, *mokṣa* (liberation) through knowledge of Brahman and as identity with Brahman—may be regarded as an elaboration of this single notion.

### ADHYĀSA AND SPIRITUAL DETACHMENT

An illusion, unlike a thinking error, excites wonder as it is corrected. One's apprehension of something as illusory involves a peculiar feeling of the scales falling from the eyes. To be aware of our individuality as illusory would be then to wonder how we could feel as an individual at all. As we are, it is indeed only in faith, if at all, that we accept the illusoriness of our individuality. But even to understand the position, we have to refer to some spiritual experience in which we feel an abrupt break with our past and wonder how we could be what we were. A person behaves as though he believed he were his body, and although he never explicitly says that he is his body, he never also ordinarily feels detached enough from the body to wonder how he cannot yet get rid of the belief. The notion of *adhyāsa* or the false identification of the self and the body would never occur to a person who has no experience of himself as a spirit and of the object as distinct from the subject, as another person is from oneself. It is only one who felt such a distinction of the self and the body that would wonder at his own implicit belief in their identity. He can take the identity to be illusory, only if he feels it to be impossible and cannot yet deny its appearance. Vedānta starts with the notion of *adhyāsa* and presupposes such an experience of spiritual detachment from the body, including the empirical mind.

We can conceive this spiritual condition as a deepening of the form of moral consciousness in which we not only repent of our past actions, but find it hard to imagine how we could perform them. In this consciousness, our past being is felt not only to be strangely alien to us, but as an intellectual absurdity, as apparently at once subjective and objective, at once I and me. One at best thinks of one's body as me and not as I; but in repentance, unless it is a senseless whipping of a dead horse, one is aware of the self that is castigated as not merely me but also as I; not only as a thing of the past, alienated or objectified, but as still tingling with subjectivity. In the further stage, in which the past appears unintelligible, this past I is not only sought to be disowned, but is cognitively viewed as a sort of you (*yuṣmad*) that is yet I (*asmad*), a contradiction that yet appears. This alienated I which is not mere me is the individual self, and it is on this spiritual plane, and not lower, that one is cognitively aware of one's individuality. One is aware, however, here of the individual self as a contradiction, or as somehow at once true and false, true as the unobjective subject and false in so far as it appears as another I (you), as at once me and I. The notions of the individual self, of the individuality or me as false, and of the eternal self as the I that is never me, are born in one and the same spiritual consciousness.

The individuality is understood as me, i.e. as the illusory objectivity of the subject and not merely illusory identity with the object taken as real. The identity of the self and the not-self has the form of the self, being in fact the embodied self and not the conscious body. The individual self means the self feeling itself embodied, the embodiment being only a restrictive adjective of the self ; and the illusoriness of the embodiment is the illusoriness of the body itself and not merely of the self's identity with it. The idea of the object, in fact, as distinct from the subject, is derived from the idea of the embodiment, which itself is born in the consciousness of the individual self as false in respect of its individuality.

### TWO ILLUSIONS

There is, however, a complexity. The me is taken as illusory not primarily because it is objective, but because the individual self already appears to itself false in so far as it takes itself to be an objective subject, to be a sort of you which is at once me and I. As the individual self is felt to be false, it is realized that the I cannot be me ; but this does not prevent the me or the body from appearing as I. There are apparently two illusions—of the I appearing as you (objective subject) and therefore also as me (object), and of the you appearing as I. In the spiritual consciousness in which a person wonders how he could be what he cannot be, he corrects the former illusion, but not the latter, for unless the past self were still present, there could be no sense of intellectual absurdity. His past self (you) is still somehow he, though he sees he cannot be that self. Under the first illusion he is aware of the me or the body as only felt, as his embodiment or limiting character ; and the correction is his realization that such a body was only his individual illusion. In the other illusion that continues, the body appears to be a substantive fact, distinct from him and yet as somehow he. With the correction of the first illusion, he sees that this appearance also should be illusory, but he still does not actually disbelieve it. Hence it is that he wants this illusion to be dissipated and meantime realizes that it is not his individual illusion, but a cosmic illusion, the dissipation of which would mean for him realization of the body and the entire world, of which it is the point of reference, as illusory.

To be conscious of oneself as individual or me is to be conscious of the me as illusory and of the subject or I as the truth. The me is the prototype of objectivity, and to feel it to be illusory is to be aware of the possibility of objectivity itself being illusory. We take a particular object to be illusory only as we believe in the objective world, but we could never conceive the illusoriness of the world itself unless we started with the illusoriness of the me. Were it not also for this starting illusion, an illusory object would not be conceived, as it is conceived in Advaita philosophy, namely, as *anirvācya,* as an unassertable that is yet undeniable. The illusion of a snake being corrected rouses wonder. Wonder should mean that this (rope) being a snake is a contradiction that yet was presented, but there is apparently no actual consciousness here of a contradiction presented as such, viz. of this being at once snake and rope. The spiritual consciousness of one's illusory individuality is, however, explicit consciousness of the contradiction of the self having been believed as not-self. It is the illusion of the individuality therefore that suggests the theory of objective illusion called Anirvācya-khyātivāda.

### THE CONCEPT OF MĀYĀ

This brings in the concept of Māyā or the principle of illusion as what cannot be characterized either as real or as unreal. It is primarily the illusion through which the self believes (in willing and feeling) that it is an individual. As this belief persists even when the individual sees that the self cannot be individual, the individuality appears neither as real nor as unreal, for if the belief were removed, there would be no individual self to see the unreality of individuality. The principle of individuality, then, is prior to the individual's actual consciousness of himself as individual and of this world as his experience (*bhoga*) ; and as yet this individuality is what cannot be real, it has to be taken as the cosmic principle of illusion. Māyā is the principle of individuality, the beginningless nescience that the individual self has to conceive as positively conditioning his individual being as also his subjective ignorance. To the individual there are many individuals, and so Māyā may be taken as the corpus of the many beginningless individualities. Again, as the world is understood as the system of experiences of the individual self, which apart from the self are but empty distinctions and forms, *nāmā-rūpa* as they are called, Māyā may be characterized as the manifold of *nāmā-rūpa*—the name and form—which has no self-identity and yet is undeniable.

### BRAHMAN AND ĪŚVARA

This last conception of Māyā, however, is intelligible only through the conception of Māyā as the cosmic principle of illusory individuality. As cosmic, it has to be understood in reference to the unindividual self or Brahman, though only as what is not Brahman. Brahman has, however, no necessary reference to Māyā ; He can be, but need not be, understood as what is not Māyā. Understood as what is not Māyā, or as it is figuratively put, as shining against Māyā without being identified with it, or as a master using this principle as his servant, He is Īśvara, the Lord of the individual selves and the Creator of the world. The world is understood as the system of the experiences of the selves, and as they believe themselves to be individuals so far as they will, the experiences are to be taken as their *bhoga* accordant with their *karma.* Īśvara then is conceived as actualizing their *karma* into their *bhoga* or experience, and thus manifesting the manifold of *nāma-rūpa,* which as experienced is just this world or *jagat.*

Īśvara has different relations to the individual selves and to the world. He is the Creator of the world, but not of the selves, the notion of creation of souls being foreign to all Indian philosophy and not to Advaitavāda only. Creation is understood as manifestation in the soil of Māyā. Brahman in a sense becomes the world without losing His transcendence. The world is an absolute appearance, at once real and unreal, real as Brahman, the cause that continues in the effect, and unreal as alienated from Him. It cannot, however, be said similarly that Brahman becomes the Jīva ; the Jīva is Brahman and only views himself as other than Brahman, the otherness being no absolute appearance, but only the content of his wrong belief. As explained, however, the principle of illusion itself has to be taken by the Jīva as cosmic, and hence, though his individuality is not an absolute appearance, Brahman in relation to him appears absolutely as Īśvara.

Īśvara in Advaita Vedānta is conceived as an absolute emanation from Brahman, though He has been sometimes erroneously supposed to be Brahman as merely viewed by the Jīva in reference to himself and the world. This reference to himself and the world is not his thinking only ; that creative thought (*īkṣā*)—'Let me be many', etc.—belongs to Brahman and is not simply referred to Him allegorically by the Jīva. At the same time this manifold that is manifested by Him is manifested as (partially) unreal, as already 'in the jaws of death', as in fact as much retracted as created. Hence His creativity is like that of the magician ; as the creativity of absolute appearance, His freedom or *śakti* is neither absolutely real nor unreal, and this is just how the cosmic Māyā is characterized.

As absolutely free in respect of creation as Brahman Himself, with this absolute freedom or Māyā *śakti*—a determination that means no restriction of His being—Īśvara is not only not a false idea of the Jīva, a mere symbol adopted for his *upāsanā* (worship), He is not also an absolute appearance like the world. Īśvara is as much unconstituted by Māyā as Brahman, and both are characterized by the same epithets—*nitya-buddha-śuddha-mukta* (eternal, omniscient, pure, free). Īśvara has a dual form, as wielding Māyā *śakti* and thus immanent in the world (*vikāravartin*), and as dissociated from it, transcendent (*triguṇātīta*) and merging back into Brahman. As transcendent, Īśvara is conceived as what is not Māyā, as determined not by Māyā but by freedom from Māyā, as other than the world that is put forth by Him as an appearance, while Brahman is understood without reference to Māyā and the world. The current conception of Brahman and Īśvara as the higher God and the lower God appears to be a fallacious exaggeration of this simple distinction.

## MOKṢA AND ITS MEANS

Brahman is the eternal Self that has not only no positive determination, but has not even the negative determination of consciously rejecting positive determination. He is indeed characterized as Sat (existence), Cit (knowledge), and Ānanda (bliss), but these are not determinations, being each of them the unspeakable Absolute viewed by us as beyond the determinate absolutes Sat, Cit, and Ānanda formulated by our consciousness. The individual self has not only to correct for himself his subjective illusion of individuality, not only to wait for the cosmic illusion of individuality to be corrected, but also to contemplate all correction to be itself illusory. He has to contemplate *mokṣa* not as something to be reached or effected or remanifested, not even as an eternal predicament of the self, but as the self itself or the *svarūpa* of Brahman. The self or the absolute is not a thing having freedom but is freedom itself.

The individual illusorily thinks he is not free and wants to be free. To his consciousness, accordingly, there is the necessity of a *sādhana* or discipline to attain freedom. This discipline to him must be such as will lead him to realize that his bondage is an illusion and that he is eternally free. To know the truth about himself can be the only way of attaining freedom, and the discipline therefore is primarily that of knowing (*jñāna*) and secondarily that of willing and feeling (*karma* and *bhakti*). The latter is in the first instance helpful as a preparation for knowledge, as securing the spiritual attitude in which the inquiry into spiritual truth can start.

In reality it is more than mere preparation, since with the progressive transparency of the mind effected through any discipline, the truth begins to shine in, though it may not be in the intellectual way. Knowledge that is demanded for freedom is spiritual being rather than the detached consciousness of a spectator, being knowledge of the self not as distinct from but as one with the knowledge. The spiritual being that is secured by *karma* and *bhakti* cannot therefore be very different from *jñāna*. The clarity of spiritual being is implicitly or explicitly the clarity of knowledge.

Vedānta is primarily a religion, and it is a philosophy only as the formulation of this religion. All religion makes for the realization of the self as sacred, but the religion of Advaita is the specific cult of such realization understood explicitly as self-knowledge, as sacred knowledge, and as nothing but knowledge. Without rejecting any other *sādhana,* it prescribes knowledge as its distinctive *sādhana* and regards it as self-sufficing and requiring no supplementation (*samuccaya*). The self is to be known—accepted in the first instance in faith, which as confirmed, clarified, and formulated by reason would be 'inwardized' into a vision. This work of reason is philosophy, which is thus not only an auxiliary discipline, but an integral part of the religion and its characteristic self-expression.

### UNIVERSAL OUTLOOK

Advaitism as religion and philosophy in one is at once individualistic and universalistic in its spiritual outlook. Religion is nothing if not individualistic; it is an 'inwardizing' of one's subjective being, a deepening of one's spiritual individuality, this being the unspoken inner function even of a religion with the salvation of all as its professed objective. Philosophy on the other hand is essentially universalistic in its attitude, presenting a truth that is for all, and is not merely a mystic experience of the individual philosopher. As an explicit religion, Advaitism insists on the conservation of one's spiritual individuality or *svadharma,* while implicitly as philosophy, it recognizes the *svadharma* of everyone else as absolutely sacred, being in this sense the most catholic and tolerant among religions. Again, as an explicit philosophy, it takes every individual self as the one self or reality; and at the same time as an implicit religion, it denies the world that is common to all and retires into the solitude of subjectivity. In either aspect it appears to combine the boldest affirmation with the most uncompromising denial.

### PRACTICAL IDEALISM

Advaitism stands for a strong spirituality, for efficient practice of idealism, for unworldliness that is neither sentimental nor fanatical. It not only asserts the detachment of freedom of the self from the world, it boldly denies the world, though it does not take even the illusory object to be merely imaginary (*tuccha*). So too, while it prescribes *nivṛtti* or renunciation of the world in spirit, it demands that it should be practically and methodically achieved through such discipline as is suited to the *adhikāra* or actual spiritual status of each individual, and may not involve even in the case of the highest *adhikārin* a literal adoption of the hermit's life. While the spirit is taken as the only reality, the object is understood not as absolute naught, but as absolute appearance, as a necessary symbolism of the spirit. Logic, law, and the revealed word itself are all in this sense symbolism—unreal in themselves and yet showing the reality beyond. The object has thus to be accepted in order to be effectively denied. One has to be a realist to outgrow realism. It is for the strong in spirit to attain the self, and strength consists not in ignoring but in accepting facts—accepting the conditions of the spiritual game in order to get beyond them.

Advaitism aims at the absolute freedom of the self, freedom from all relativity, including the relativity of good and evil. Freedom from law is, however, to be achieved by the willing of the law, by the performance of one's moral and spiritual duty without desire—desire not only for pleasure but even for spiritual merit, and by merging one's individuality in objective or institutional spiritual life which represents a *yajña* or the sacrificial concert of gods and men. It would imply the strenuous cultivation of a dispassionate serenity of soul and the strength that it implies to keep out illusions and stand unruffled in one's subjective being.

## TOLERATION

Toleration is to Advaita Vedānta a religion in itself; no one who realizes what any religion is to its votary can himself be indifferent to it. The claim of a religion on its votary is nothing outside the religion and is itself as sacred to others as the religion is sacred to him. While then an individual owes special allegiance to his own religion or *svadharma*, which chooses him rather than is chosen by him, he feels that the religion of others is not only sacred to them but to himself also. This, in fact, is the practical aspect of the Advaitic view of all individual selves being the one self. The oneness is not contemplated in the empirical region, and there is no prescription of universal brotherhood in the sense that the happiness of others is to be promoted as though it were one's own happiness. There is indeed the duty to relieve distress, but such work is to be performed as duty rather than as a matter of altruistic enjoyment, the dry detached attitude of duty being consonant with the spirit of the religion of *jñāna*. The brotherhood that is practically recognized in this religion is the brotherhood of spirits realizing their *svadharma,* the *dharma* of each being sacred to all. If, then, in this view it is irreligious to change one's faith, it is only natural to revere faiths other than one's own. To tolerate them merely in a non-committal or patronizing spirit would be an impiety, and to revile them would be diabolical. The form in which the truth is intuited by an individual is cosmically determined and not constructed by him, and the relativity of truth to the spiritual status of the knower is itself absolute. Even the illusory object in this view is a mystical creation (*prātibhāsika-sṛṣṭi*), the three grades of reality that are recognized—the illusory, the relational, and the transcendental—being in fact grades of this absolute relativity.

## RESPECT FOR INDIVIDUAL DIFFERENCES

The doctrine of *adhikāri-bheda* is an application of this epistemological notion of absolute relativity to the specifically religious sphere. The difference of *adhikāra* or spiritual status is not necessarily a gradation ; and so far as it is a gradation it does not suggest any relation of higher and lower that implies contempt or envy. The notion of *adhikāra* in fact means in the first instance just an acceptance of fact or realism in the spiritual sphere. It is a question of duty rather than of rights in this sphere ; and a person should be anxious to discover his actual status in order that he may set before himself just such duties as he can efficiently perform in spirit. It is a far greater misfortune here to over-estimate one's status than to under-estimate it. A higher status does not mean greater opportunity for spiritual work, since work here means not outward achievement, but an 'inwardizing' or deepening of the spirit. Again, from the standpoint of toleration, one not only respects the inner achievement of a person admitting an inferior status, but can whole-heartedly identify oneself with it ; the highest *adhikārin* should feel it a privilege to join in the worship of the humblest. There is aristocracy in the spiritual polity ; spiritual value is achieved by the strong and is much too sacred a thing to be pooled. At the same time every individual has his sacred *svadharma* and has equal opportunity with everyone else to realize or 'inwardize' it.

The merit of Advaitavāda lies in having explicitly recognized that spiritual work is this 'inwardizing', the deepening of faith into subjective realization, the striving after self-knowledge. This work can start from any given point, any spiritual status or situation that happens to be presented. Men are intrinsically higher and lower only in respect of this inner achievement. The problem of altering traditional society, of equalizing rights in order to create opportunities for self-realization, has accordingly a subordinate place in the Advaitic scheme of life, being recognized mainly negatively as the duty of abstaining from acts of conscious injustice. This scheme of life would view with positive disfavour iconoclasm in any shape or form, any violent tampering with an institution that is traditionally held to be sacred ; but it would not also apparently require one to vitalize artificially such an institution if one believes—not by hearsay, but after loyally trying to work it—that it is moribund or dead. Spiritual realism would demand both reverence for and dissociation from what was sacred. One sacred custom can only be superseded by another sacred custom, the former being either reverently allowed to die a natural death or incorporated in an ideal or symbolic form in the latter. There is no room in Advaita religion for the duty of profaning one god for the glorification of another.

The idea of hustling people out of their reverence in their own spiritual interest would be scouted in this religion as a self-stultifying profanity. Social life and tradition are viewed as sacred, as a *yajña* being performed through the ages, the sacredness being the shine of the one Self, the shadow of Eternity. It is the life of the gods, and we can help it best by merging into it, by realizing it as our subjective life. This subjective realization may sometimes come spontaneously, but so far as it can be effected by *sādhana,* it can be effected by each individual for himself. He can indeed help others in the work by education, but he can educate only in the measure he has himself realized this life. He can wish and pray that others' self-realization might be expedited ; but for an *ordinary* person to suppose that he can and ought to energize and vitalize other spirits is, to the religion of Advaita, a delusion and a curious mixture of arrogance and sentimentality.

## AN INTEGRAL PART OF HINDUISM

Much of what is attributed here to Advaitavāda is the implied creed of Hinduism and Hindu society. This philosophy is the most satisfying formulation of the distinctive spirit of Hinduism, and in this sense it may claim to be a synthesis of other systems of Indian philosophy, which all seek to formulate this spirit ; and it has also explicitly influenced the historical evolution of Hinduism. As it is not only a formulation of the religion, but is itself the religion in the simplified and unified form of the realization of subjectivity or self-knowledge, it is sometimes characterized as a rationalistic religion ; and there is a tendency to isolate it in the abstract and to interpret it as disowning all Vedic and post-Vedic worship and ceremonial. But the abstract cult of self-knowledge derives its whole meaning from the concrete religion of worship and ceremonial, and is recognizable as a religion only as its concentrated essence. It represents a protest against the concrete religion only so far as the latter resists 'inwardization' ; but it implies no rejection but only an interpretation of the concrete religion. The Advaitin would whole-heartedly join in the traditional worship and would be false to himself if he professed contempt for it, though he would recognize that the contemplation of the abstract significance is itself a part of the worship and at a certain stage may be the whole spiritual activity.

The contemplation that is demanded is more than mere philosophic thought, being a specific enjoyment of the thought as sacred and representing a new stage of spiritual consciousness. The truth has to be felt as a self-revelation, as a light that shows itself. Light is a sacred symbol, not a mere metaphor, from the contemplation of which the Vedāntic conception of the self itself may be taken to have emanated.

The Advaita discipline of *jñāna* is primarily a protest against the discipline of *karma,* of moral (and ceremonial) activity which is apt in all ages to be taken as a self-sufficing religion. The discipline of *karma* is important as a preparatory chastening of the soul, but taken as a religion by itself, it is understood to work against the attainment of *mokṣa.* To will is to energize in *ahaṅkāra* (egoism), even though it be willing without desire, the specific willing to deny will, to sacrifice one's individuality. At the same time, such willing without desire tends unconsciously to dissolve the *ahaṅkāra,* though the tendency requires to be confirmed by *bhakti,* by the dedication of the spiritual merit of the willing to the Lord, or by the feeling of merging oneself in the cosmic *yajña,* the symbol of the life divine. All good willing means self-purification, and although it requires to be superseded so far as it involves *ahaṅkāra,* the supersession is itself effected through willing in an attitude of detachment, in the implicit consciousness of the self being beyond *ahaṅkāra.* Hence Advaitism, far from encouraging a premature quietism or renunciation of *karma,* positively prescribes *karma,* though rigorously as a duty and not for gain, and conceives it possible even for one who has risen above morality to perform *karma* in *lokānugraha,* for the education of others and for the conservation of the social order.

The religion of *jñāna,* however, is in no sense a protest against the religion of *bhakti.* To it the higher stages of *bhakti* at any rate not only mean soul-clearing, but also involve the enjoyment of the truth in one's being. It is indeed demanded that the felt truth may be self-revealed as known truth, but this knowledge is itself understood as an intuition which amounts to ecstasy and does not in any sense mean a supersession of *bhakti.* Although *bhakti* implies individuality, it represents the individual's joy in surrendering his individuality. The *bhakta* may feel his individuality restored through the Lord, but that is a mystery of divine life with which the Advaitin would not dally. The individual's own achievement terminates with the surrender of individuality.

# 14

## POST-ŚAṄKARA ADVAITA

If Śaṅkara is both the solid base and the highest pinnacle of the magnificent range of the Advaita Vedāntic thought, the post-Śaṅkara Advaitins like Sureśvara, Vācaspati, Prakāśātman, Citsukha, Madhusūdana, and others are undoubtedly the other massive peaks. Although Śaṅkara has spoken in unmistakable terms of Brahman as the one cause of the world, of Māyā or *avidyā* (nescience) as an indeterminable entity which is the root of the manifold world, and of the identity of Brahman with individual souls (Jīvas), yet there are points in Śaṅkara's writings which admit of diverse interpretations. The main points of difference among the interpreters of Śaṅkara are the nature of causality of Brahman and Māyā, the nature of the dissolution of Māyā (*avidyā-nivṛtti-svarūpa*), the nature of individual souls, and certain other technical matters of the Advaita Vedānta, such as the 'obligatoriness' of listening to the Vedāntic texts (Upaniṣads). Some of the later interpreters of the Advaita Vedānta differ about the nature of the objective world. The theory of Vedāntic solipsism (Dṛṣṭi-sṛṣṭi-vāda), formulated by Prakāśānanda in the sixteenth century, was, according to Vidyāraṇya's account in *Vivaraṇa-prameya-saṅgraha*, originally started by Maṇḍana Miśra (about A.D. 800), a powerful Vedāntin and probably a contemporary of Śaṅkara.

### MAṆḌANA'S INDEPENDENT APPROACH

Maṇḍana's work on the Vedānta, called *Brahmasiddhi*, was commented on by not less than four commentators, namely, Vācaspati, Anandapūrṇa, Śaṅkhapāṇi, and Citsukha. It is evident from its contents, that *Brahmasiddhi* is an independent interpretation of the Advaita Vedānta that does not tally in many points with the interpretation of Śaṅkara or Sureśvara. So even if Maṇḍana was the same person as Sureśvara,[1] he must have written *Brahmasiddhi* before becoming Sureśvara, a disciple of Śaṅkara. *Brahmasiddhi* of Maṇḍana is the first of the four renowned '*siddhis*'—works bearing the word '*siddhi*' at the end of their titles, the other three being *Naiṣkarmyasiddhi* of Sureśvara, *Iṣṭasiddhi* of Vimuktātman, and *Advaitasiddhi* of Madhusūdana. The work is divided into four chapters, the first of which is *Brahmakāṇḍa*, dealing with the nature of Brahman as one and immutable, as pure consciousness and bliss. Brahman as bliss is not merely the

[1] Scholars like Prof. Hiriyanna and Mm. Kuppuswami Sastri hold them to be two different persons.

negation of pain as some hold it to be, but is positive bliss. The bliss is both knowable and unknowable ; or rather, it is neither unknowable nor knowable. If it were unknowable, that would render everything unknowable, for it is Brahman that imparts knowableness to everything else. Besides the definition of Brahman as bliss would be meaningless. Nor is it knowable like an object, as Brahman is never an object. Such is also the position of the knower self. It may be remarked that here, in *Brahmasiddhi,* we get the basic idea of the later developments of the definition of *svaprakāśa,*[2] which is an important point stressed by the post-Śaṅkara Advaitins. Such self-shining positive bliss is connoted by the word Ānanda. Thus, pure bliss or pure consciousness (Cit) is the nature of Brahman, which is immutable. Again, this Brahman is identical with Akṣara (the Word), the Śabda Brahman of the Śabdādvaitins. Maṇḍana, who accepted the theory of *sphoṭa* advocated by Bhartṛhari and others, tried to harmonize the doctrine of the Śabdādvaita with the Brahmādvaita of the Advaitins —'The word is Brahman, the word is all'. This is indeed a peculiar feature of Maṇḍana's Advaitism. Māyā or *avidyā* (ignorance, nescience) which is neither identical with nor different from Brahman, neither existent nor non-existent, is capable of being annihilated.[3] This *avidyā,* which obscures the true nature of Brahman, has for its support (*āśraya*) the individual souls, and not Brahman as some others maintain. Thus *avidyā* has Brahman for its object (*viṣaya*) and individual souls (Jīvas) for its support (*āśraya*). But the Jīvas, again, being essentially one with Brahman and superimposed by *avidyā* (or *kalpanā*), depend on *avidyā* for their existence. The objection of *itaretarāśrayatva* (mutual dependence), which is evident, has been answered in two ways. Firstly, Māyā by itself, being an inconsistent entity, can never be free from the charge of inconsistency.[4] Secondly, accepting the position of the Avidyopādānabhedavādins (who maintain that *avidyā* is the stuff of the world diversity), it may be said that both *avidyā* and the Jīva being beginningless, their logical interdependence is acceptable. The Jīvas move in bondage through *avidyā,* but as reflections of Brahman on *avidyā* they are essentially identical with Brahman.[5] Verbal knowledge of the contents of the Vedāntic texts, which is mediate (*parokṣa*), cannot produce perception of the reality (*Brahma-sākṣātkāra*) and liberation, unless the proper *vṛtti* (mental image or modification) is formed through constant meditation.

*Avidyā,* according to Maṇḍana, is of two kinds: *agrahaṇa* (non-appre-

[2] *Brahmasiddhi,* I.
[3] *Ibid.,* I.
[4] *Ibid.,* I.
[5] *Ibid.,* I.

hension) and *anyathā-grahaṇa* (misapprehension).[6] Meditation is indispensably necessary to uproot the *saṁskāras* (residual impressions) produced by this second kind of *avidyā*.[7] The nature of the dissolution of nescience has been mentioned in some places (*Brahmasiddhi*, III) as identical with *vidyā*, which is a positive entity. This positively contradicts the statements of some later Advaitins ascribing the Bhāvādvaita theory to Maṇḍana on the ground that he admits at least two negations—*avidyādhvaṁsa* (destruction of ignorance) and *prapañcābhāva* (disappearance of manifestations) as irreducible reality which is neither identical with Brahman nor annihilated by the realization of Brahman. Bhāvādvaita means a type of non-dualism which excludes the duality of positive entities, but does not exclude the existence of negatives like *avidyādhvaṁsa* and *prapañcābhāva*. The position of the objective world is not very clear in the text of *Brahmasiddhi*. If the Jīvas with their individual *avidyās* be the stuff of the world, then the world becomes an object of *dṛṣṭi-sṛṣṭi* (creation of individual perception) and different for each individual. This is at least how Vidyāraṇya understands Maṇḍana, though he speaks of Brahman as creating the world like a magician (*māyākāra*)—a view which militates against Dṛṣṭi-sṛṣṭi-vāda. Śaṅkara and his followers hold *karma* to be only an indirect or remote cause (*ārādupakāraka*) of realization through the production of *vividiṣā* (desire for realization), and never a direct cause or means of realization. Nor can *karma* be co-ordinated with *jñāna* to produce liberation. Maṇḍana also emphatically denies the co-ordination of *karma* with *jñāna*,[8] but he differs from the Śaṅkarites in attributing a little higher position to *karma*.[9] Maṇḍana's view of *jīvanmukti* (liberation in life) is also somewhat different from that of the Śaṅkarites. A *jīvanmukta* or a *sthitaprajña* is still a *sādhaka* (aspirant), and not a *siddha* (perfected one)[10] who has totally annihilated *avidyā*, for the body must fall with the total annihilation of *avidyā*.

## THREE POST-ŚAṄKARA SCHOOLS

Three lines or schools of the Advaita propounded by Śaṅkara were set up by Sureśvara and his follower Sarvajñātmamuni, Padmapāda and his commentator Prakāśātman, and Vācaspati and his followers. They have also made an attempt to explain the realistic tendency of Śaṅkara with regard to the objective world, as against the idealistic view of the Vijñānavādins (Buddhists). Again, all of them, except Vācaspati, have given

[6] *Ibid.*, III.
[7] *Ibid.*, I.
[8] *Ibid.*, I.
[9] *Ibid.*, I.
[10] *Ibid.*, III.

prominence to the Vedāntic *mahāvākyas* (great sayings) as the means to the realization of Brahman, by holding that not only the senses but words (*śabda*) also have the capacity to produce perception in certain cases. Again, all of them have supported the theory of illusory transformation (Vivarta-vāda) according to which Brahman is the object (*viṣaya*) of ignorance (*avidyā*) which it obscures and makes fit in some way to be the cause of the world. Another important point of agreement is that there cannot be any obligatory injunction (*kartavyavidhi*) with regard to *Brahmajñāna* (knowledge of Brahman). Actions (*kriyā*), being dependent on will, may be commanded by injunctions. But a right cognition depends mainly on the object and not on our will or action, which is subject to injunction. So there cannot be any obligatoriness or injunction with regard to *jñāna,* or for that matter *Brahmajñāna.* This view of the Advaitins carefully excludes the possibility of intrusion of *apūrva* (subtle action-residue) and *karma* (rites) into the final step of realization, for if liberation (*mokṣa*) were a result of *jñāna* and *karma,* it would be mutable like other effects of *karma* and therefore would not be the *summum bonum.*

## THE SCHOOL OF SUREŚVARA

Sureśvara's famous works are *Naiṣkarmyasiddhi, Bṛhadāraṇyaka-bhāṣya-vārttika,* and *Taittirīya-bhāṣya-vārttika. Naiṣkarmyasiddhi* has at least five commentaries, the earliest of them being *Candrikā* by Jñānottama and *Bhāva-tattva-prakāśikā* by Citsukha. The most important commentaries on the *Vārttika* works are by Ānandajñāna (or Ānanda Giri), though *Bṛhadāraṇyaka-bhāṣya-vārttika* has other commentaries also. *Bṛhadāraṇyaka-bhāṣya-vārttika* by Sureśvara is a great independent work though written as an interpretation of the *Śaṅkara-bhāṣya* on the *Bṛhadāraṇyaka Upaniṣad. Sambandha-vārttika* itself, which is only an introduction to the whole work, deals with the relation of Vedic duties (rites) to the realization of Brahman, and contains more than 1,100 verses of great philosophical depth and subtlety.

According to Sureśvara, Brahman is the only reality (Sat), the substratum of the world. Pure Brahman is the material cause of the world. But as Brahman is unchangeable, it is through Māyā that such world appearance, such transformation of Brahman, has been made possible. Māyā is thus only a secondary or mediate cause of the world. Yet it pervades creation. From the standpoint of the absolute Reality, neither Māyā, nor creation exists ; but from the practical standpoint of the ignorant Jīvas, Māyā exists in Brahman, the only reality and possible support.[11]

[11] *Sambandha-vārttika, 'Avidyā'syetyavidyāyāmevāsitvā prakalpyate, Brahma-dṛṣṭyā tvavidyeyaṁ na kathañcana yujyate.'*

There is no other reality, positive or negative. Everything else, which appears as different, is but a superimposition on that pure Brahman which is identical with pure consciousness (Cit) and bliss (Ānanda). This superimposition (*adhyāsa*) is possible through Māyā or *avidyā* which veils the true nature of Brahman and makes It appear as the subtle and the gross world. This *avidyā* has Brahman both for its *viṣaya* (object) and for its *āśraya* (support).[12] Brahman is the only possible support or locus of *avidyā,* because everything else, including the individual souls (Jīvas), being the effects of *avidyā,* cannot be the support of *avidyā.* Sarvajñātmamuni, a follower of Sureśvara, has enunciated this theory of Sureśvara in clear terms in a famous verse in his work *Saṁkṣepa-śārīraka.*[13] By maintaining Brahman, and not the Jīvas, to be the locus of *avidyā,* Sureśvara has carefully opposed the tendency towards subjective idealism. Again, when realization of Brahman is produced by the Vedic texts, *avidyā* disappears and is reduced to Ātman.[14] Thus cessation of *avidyā* is not a separate negative reality, but is identical with Brahman. Unlike Maṇḍana, Sureśvara maintains that the Vedic texts are capable of producing immediate cognition of the self as Brahman. Sureśvara repudiates the necessity of meditation (*dhyānābhyāsa*) or repetition (*prasaṅkhyāna*) as a means of producing immediacy (*aparokṣatva*). This view of Sureśvara and others is called Śabdāparokṣavāda. He has also refuted the theory (maintained by Maṇḍana) that *avidyā* is of two kinds, stating that *avidyā* must be one, because it has only one supreme Self for its object and support.[15] In the *Bṛhadāraṇyaka-bhāṣya-vārttika* he has also emphatically rejected the *anyathā-khyāti* theory regarding the nature of error, and has established the theory of *anirvacanīya-khyāti,* which was accepted by all the later Advaitins.[16] As

[12] *Sambandha-vārttika, 'Kalpyāvidyaiva matpakṣe sā cānubhavasaṁśrayā.'*

[13] *Saṁksepa-śūrīraka,* I.

[14] *Sambandha-vārttika, 'Ato manottha-vijnana-dhvastā sā'pyetyathātmatām.'*

[15] *Bṛhadāraṇyaka-vārttika, 'Dvaividhyaṁ cāvidyāyā na ca yuktyāvasīyate, aikātmya-mātra-vastutvādavidyaikaiva yujyate.'*

[16] With regard to error different schools of Indian philosophy hold different theories which play an important part in epistemology. The most prominent of these theories are: (i) *sat-khyāti* of the Rāmānujites, (ii) *ātma-khyāti* and *asat-khyāti* of the Buddhists, (iii) *akhyāti* of the Mīmāṁsakas, (iv) *anyathā-khyāti* or *viparīta-khyāti* of the logicians (the Nyāya and the Vaiśeṣika schools), and (v) *anirvacanīya-khyāti* of the Advaitins.

According to the *akhyāti* theory of the Mīmāṁsakas, in an error there is only an *akhyāti,* i.e. an omission of knowledge but no commission or mistaking of any kind. In an error like 'This is silver', there are two separate cognitions, the one perception and the other remembrance. The part 'this is' refers to the perception of the present object, and the part 'silver' is a remembrance of 'silver' perceived elsewhere. The two cognitions are separate and not connected. Non-apprehension of this separateness (*asaṁsargāgraha*) of the two different cognitions and their objects is the only defect in an error, but there is no sort of misapprehension, i.e. taking one thing for another (*anyathāgraha*).

The Naiyāyikas and the Vaiśeṣikas oppose this theory and hold that there cannot but be some misapprehension or taking one thing for another in any act of error. Error means an 'otherwise' (*anyathā*) apprehension (*khyāti*) of something, i.e. to know something to be other than what it actually is. The actual shell is perceived to be a piece of silver. The

a strict follower of Śaṅkara, he has also ignored the *sphoṭa* and the Śabdādvaita doctrine of Maṇḍana. The Jīvas, according to Sureśvara, are but reflections of Brahman (*cidābhāsa*) on individual *antaḥkaraṇa* (*avidyā* as mind with its *saṁskāras*). Reflection on the product of *avidyā* (i.e. mind) is Jīva, and the reflection on the causal *avidyā* is Īśvara.

But this reflection (*pratibimba*), according to Sureśvara, being different from the original (*bimba*), is a false phenomenon (*ābhāsa*) ; and this has earned for the theory a new name, viz. the Ābhāsavāda, as contrasted with the Pratibimbavāda of Maṇḍana, Prakāśātman, and others, which holds reflection to be real in its aspect of identity with the original, though not real in the form of reflection. So, it is the pure Cit that runs into bondage through the *ābhāsa* (reflection) and is liberated with the destruction of the *ābhāsa*. According to the Advaitins, it is the unchangeable self or the witness (*sākṣin*) in us which perceives the changes and transformations of mind, because the empirical self (*pramātṛ*), which is none other than the mind with reflected consciousness (*cidābhāsa*), cannot perceive its own changes. Many later Advaitins regard this *sākṣin* as an entity distinct from Īśvara and the Jīva, though ultimately they are all admitted as one with Brahman. But according to Sureśvara, the supreme Self (Īśvara) as *sākṣin*, perceives all the mental changes and the ignorance in the Jīvas.

Sureśvara holds *karma* to be only a means to the purification of mind. *Karma* is useful and possible only until *vividiṣā* (desire for knowledge) originates, when one is to give up *karma* and take to *sannyāsa* before resorting to *śravaṇa* (hearing of the Vedānta from competent persons), the prime means of realization. This is a strong antithesis to the Mīmāṁsakas and others who advocate *jñāna-karma-samuccaya* (synthesis of Vedic duties and knowledge of Brahman) as a means of final emancipation. This also refutes Maṇḍana's view which holds *karma* to be a direct means to realization. In *Sambandha-vārttika* Sureśvara forcefully rebuts the '*aikabhavika*' doctrine of some Mīmāṁsakas according to which if one can refrain from actions prompted by desire of the fruits (*kāmya*) and those prohibited (*niṣiddha*) by the scriptures, and carefully perform the obligatory ones (*nitya*) which destroy the results of previous *karmas,* one may achieve liberation, after exhausting one's fructifying (*prārabdha*) *karmas* by reaping their results in

silver visualized there is but a distant piece of silver brought there through an extraordinary contact called *jñāna-lakṣaṇa-sannikarṣa*.

According to the Advaitins, such an extraordinary contact is illogical and untenable. But the perception of 'silver' in error must have some present 'silver' as its object, because in perception the object requires to be present. Therefore the illusory 'silver' is a new creation which can neither be called really existing nor altogether non-existing or a combination of both; hence it is of an indeterminable nature (*anirvacanīyotpatti*) and apprehension of that kind of indeterminable objects (*anirvacanīya-khyāti*) constitutes an error.

the present life. It is *jñāna* that is necessary to remove ignorance and achieve emancipation which is already in the soul (*siddha*)[17] and has not to be produced (*sādhya*).

Sureśvara, as a follower of Śaṅkara, has strongly supported the latter's *jīvanmukti* doctrine. In *Naiṣkarmyasiddhi* and *Bṛhadāraṇyaka-bhāṣya-vārttika* he has elaborately discussed this doctrinal point, and concludes that the body should not necessarily fall immediately after realization of the unity of Ātman and Brahman and annihilation of ignorance.[18] He has also refuted the Bhāṭṭa and Prābhākara schools of Mīmāṁsakas with regard to the meaning of *vidhi* (injunctory suffixes). According to them, *bhāvana* (urge) and *kārya* or *niyoga* (unique results of actions) are respectively held to be the meaning of *vidhi*. But according to Sureśvara, *iṣṭasādhanatva* (its capacity to bring about the desired result), and not any *bhāvana*, is what is meant by a *vidhi*.[19] In this respect he is at one with Maṇḍana.

### SARVAJÑĀTMAN—A FOLLOWER OF SUREŚVARA

Sarvajñātman has systematically formulated the views of Śaṅkara and Sureśvara. His only known work is *Saṁkṣepa-śārīraka*, which has many commentaries, the chief ones being those of Nṛsiṁhāśrama, Rāma Tīrtha, and Madhusūdana. With regard to the causality of pure Brahman, the mediate causality (*dvāra-kāraṇatva*) of Māyā, the nature of the cessation of *avidyā*, and the support of *avidyā*, Sarvajñātman's views are the same as Sureśvara's. He strongly and elaborately supports the theory that *śabda* (Upaniṣadic texts) can produce direct and immediate cognition of Brahman.

Māyā (nescience), according to Sarvajñātman, is one and not many. It pervades all the individuals (Jīvas) and it continues to exist even after a single individual's ignorance is destroyed through realization, just as a universal (*jāti*, e.g. cowhood) pervades all the existent individuals and is not affected by any change in their number.[20] The Jīvas are reflections of Brahman on *antaḥkaraṇas* (minds) while the reflection of Brahman on Māyā (*avidyā*) is Īśvara. Māyā, through its *āvaraṇa śakti* (concealing power) and *vikṣepa śakti* (transforming power), makes it possible for Brahman, its only object and support, to appear as the Jīva, Īśvara, and the world.[21] In the state of dreamless sleep, he holds, the pure self as bliss is directly perceived by the Jīvas through some subtle functioning of *avidyā*, thus

[17] *Taittirīya-vārttika*, I.

[18] *Bṛhadāraṇyaka-vārttika*, *'Samyagjñānasamutpattisamanantarameva ca, śarīrapātaḥ kasmānnetyetaccāpahastitam.'*

[19] *Sambandha-vārttika*, *'Ataḥ samīhitopāyatayā vastvavabodhayan abuddhaṁ prerako vedo jñāpanā preraṇā matā.'*

[20] *Saṁkṣepa-śārīraka*, II. 132.

[21] *Ibid.*, I. 20.

differing from Sureśvara, who denies any such functioning of *avidyā* in that state.

*Karma* is accepted as but a remote cause of liberation. A *jīvanmukta* has to wait for the fruition of his *prārabdha* which remains with *avidyāleśa* (trace of ignorance), and after that he attains final emancipation (*kaivalya*), which is immediate oneness with Brahman and not a departure (*gati*) to any heaven beyond. Sarvajñātman's exposition of the meanings of the Vedāntic texts like *'Satyaṁ-jñānam-anantam'*, *'Ahaṁ Brahmāsmi'*, *'Tattvamasi'* is of great skill and exactness. According to him, the Pariṇāmavāda (theory of real transformation) is a theory of lower grade and a step to the highest truth of the Vivartavāda (theory of apparent transformation).[22] He suggests that for practical purposes the Vedānta admits Pariṇāmavāda, which, if deeply analysed, leads to the Vivartavāda and to the realization of Brahman as the only reality.

## THE SCHOOL OF PADMAPĀDA

Next to the school set up by Sureśvara comes the one started by Padmapāda and subsequently elaborated by his famous commentator Prakāśātman (*circa* A.D. 1200) in his *Pañcapādikā-vivaraṇa.* His chief work is *Pañcapādikā* which is a commentary on the *Catuḥsūtrī-bhāṣya* (including *Adhyāsa-bhāṣya*) of Śaṅkara, i.e. on Śaṅkara's commentary on the first four *sūtras* and on his introduction thereto. *Pañcapādikā* has another commentary by Ānandapūrṇa, but not so renowned as Prakāśātman's, whose name the term *Vivaraṇa-prasthāna* (*Vivaraṇa* line of interpretation) bears. *Vivaraṇa* was commented on by Akhaṇḍānanda (A.D. 1350) in his *Tattvadīpana,* and by Nṛsiṁhāśrama (sixteenth century) in his *Pañcapādikā-vivaraṇa-prakāśikā.* Govindānanda (sixteenth century) followed the *Vivaraṇa* line in interpreting *Śaṅkara-bhāṣya* in his *Ratnaprabhā.* Vidyāraṇya (fourteenth century) wrote his *Vivaraṇa-prameya-saṅgraha,* dealing with the Vedāntic problems on the lines of *Pañcapādikā-vivaraṇa.* Rāmānanda (seventeenth century), a disciple of Govindānanda, also strictly followed the *Vivaraṇa* line in his *Vivaraṇopanyāsa,* which is a commentary on the *Śaṅkara-bhāṣya.* Most of the independent works on the Advaita Vedanta, subsequently written, followed the *Vivaraṇa* line in their interpretations.

*Pañcapādikā* of Padmapāda is divided into nine chapters called *varṇakas,* each of which deals with different problems of the Advaita Vedānta. The first *varṇaka* is mainly engaged in explaining the *Adhyāsa-bhāṣya* of Śaṅkara, where he inquires into the nature and the cause of *adhyāsa* (erroneous superimposition). Irrational and indefinable ignorance

[22] *Ibid.,* II. 61.

(*anirvacanīyā avidyā*) is the material cause of superimpositions and of the world appearance.[23] The word *mithyā* in Śaṅkara's commentary means *anirvacanīyatā* and not *apahnava* (negation). But by calling *avidyā 'jaḍātmikā avidyāśakti'* (a force of material nature) and by holding *avidyā* to be the material cause of the world appearance, Padmapāda has attributed more substantiality to *avidyā* than have Śaṅkara and Sureśvara. Prakāśātman, his commentator, has further emphasized this point by proving *avidyā* to be a positive entity (*bhāvarūpa*). The *avidyānumāna* (inference of *avidyā*) in the *Vivaraṇa*, which has often been cited by the later Advaitins, proves the positivity of *avidyā*, though *avidyā* is directly perceived as such by the *sākṣin*[24] and requires no inference to prove its existence. Being something of a positive nature, *avidyā* is capable of being the material cause of *adhyāsa* and of concealing the true nature of Brahman as infinite bliss. Māyā, Prakṛti, *avyākṛta, avyakta, tamas, śakti*, etc. are synonyms for this positive *avidyā*. When the power of concealing (*āvaraṇa*) is predominant, ignorance is called *avidyā*, and when the power of projection or transformation (*vikṣepa*) is predominant, it is called Māyā.

*Avidyā* rests on pure Cit (Brahman), though practically it affects the Jīvas who are constituted by the *āvaraṇa* power of *avidyā*. Thus, Brahman is both the *viṣaya* and the *āśraya* of *avidyā*. Hence, it is evident that in many respects the Vivaraṇa school of thinking had its origin in the Vārttika school of interpretation, though it has also made much original contribution to the interpretation of the Advaitic thought. According to *Pañcapādikā*, Brahman is the root cause (*mūla-kāraṇa*) of the world, being the ground of all apparent transformation (*vivarta*).[25] But it is with Māyā that Brahman is the material cause of the world. As Brahman is unchangeable (*avikārin*), it is actually Māyā which is the material cause (*vikāri upādāna*). Brahman may be called the *avikāri upādāna* in the sense of being the ground. *Vivaraṇa* is more clear on this point when it holds that Brahman together with the power of the indeterminable Māyā is the cause of the world, both material and efficient. Unity of the material (*upādāna*) and the efficient cause (*nimittakāraṇa*) of the world, which is a common doctrine with the Advaitins, is thus maintained by *Vivaraṇa*. Prakāśatman puts forward three alternative explanations with regard to the causality of Brahman. The first is that Brahman and Māyā are the cause of the world jointly, like two threads twisted in a rope. Secondly, Brahman, which has Māyā as Its power, is the cause of the world. Thirdly, Brahman being the support of Māyā, which is the actual *upādāna* of the

[23] *Pañcapādikā*, I.
[24] *Pañcapādikā-vivaraṇa*, I.
[25] *Pañcapādikā*, I.

world, is the cause of the world.[26] The Jīvas, according to Prakāśātman, are but images of Brahman reflected on *avidyā* as *antaḥkaraṇa* (mind) and *saṁskāra* (mind in a causal condition). The reflected images, according to Padmapāda and Prakāśātman, are not different from the original (*bimba*) Brahman and are therefore real as Brahman,[27] though not real in the form of reflected images. This theory of reflection is called the Pratibimbavāda as contrasted with the Ābhāsavāda of Sureśvara. But Īśvara is not a reflection, as Sureśvara holds, but Brahman in the aspect of being the original (*bimba-caitanya*) of reflections which constitute the Jīvas. *Avidyā,* being supported by Brahman, manifests itself as two powers, knowledge (*jñāna-śakti*) and activity (*kriyā-śakti*). As *jñāna-śakti* it manifests itself in the *antaḥkaraṇa* as *manas* (mind), *buddhi* (intellect), and *ahaṅkāra* (egoity), and as *kriyā-śakti* as the *prāṇa* (vital force). It is in association with these that the pure self is falsely regarded as the Jīva, the *kartṛ* (doer of actions) and *bhoktṛ* (enjoyer of experiences).

Later epistemological developments, which are found in *Vedānta-kaumudī* of Rāmādvaya (A.D. 1300) and in *Vedānta-paribhāṣā* of Dharmarājādhvarīndra (A.D. 1600), have their foundation and starting point in the writings of Padmapāda and Prakāśātman. Immediate perception (*aparokṣa*) of an object, according to Padmapāda, is its contact with consciousness[28] through the transformation of *antaḥkaraṇa* which has the natural power of being connected with consciousness.[29] The *antaḥkaraṇa* (mind), says Prakāśātman, goes out to the position of the object and is transformed into its likeness, connecting the object with the consciousness limited by the *antaḥkaraṇa.* Though there is some manifestation of objects (*arthaprakāśa*) in indirect cognitions like inference and others, there is no immediacy in them for want of such contactual relation of *antaḥkaraṇa.* Thus the pure self (Ātman) with the limitation produced by the transformation of *antaḥkaraṇa* (or the ego with the consciousness limited by it) is the knower (*pramātṛ*).[30]

Another original contribution of Padmapāda and Prakāśātman is their definition of falsity (*mithyātva*) attributed to this world (*prapañca*) by the Advaitins. According to Padmapāda, the world is false in the sense that it is different both from what is *sat* (existent) and what is *asat* (non-existent). Anything that is neither existent nor non-existent is false. Prakāśātman explains this definition and adds two others, viz. (1) whatever is destroyed by true knowledge is false; and (2) whatever can be negated

[26] *Pañcapādikā-vivaraṇa,* I.
[27] *Pañcapādikā,* I.
[28] *Ibid.,* I.
[29] *Pañcapādikā-vivaraṇa,* I.
[30] *Ibid.,* I.

for all time on its own ground or support where it was known to exist, is false. The first is simple, but the second needs a little elucidation. An illusory 'silver' (*śukti-rūpya*) which is false, is always absent and therefore can be negated on its own support, the oyster shell (*śukti*). In the subsequent understanding, 'It is not silver', the illusory 'silver' is negated for all time (past, present, and future) on the very shell where it was known to exist. The world appearance is false to the Advaitins in the sense that with the final realization of Brahman it is negated on its own ground (Brahman).

With regard to points like the nature of the cessation of *avidyā,* the nature of final emancipation (*mukti*), the efficacy of *karma* in the scheme of liberation, and the capacity of *śabda* (Vedic sentences) to produce immediate cognition of Brahman, the Vivaraṇa school has accepted the views of the Vārttika school of interpretation. As regards the injunction *'śrotavyaḥ'*, the Vivaraṇa holds the view of *niyama-vidhi* of *vicāra* (discussion), which requires that one must persist in holding discussion on Brahman. The first *sūtra* of the *Brahma-Sūtra 'Athāto-Brahma-jijñāsā'* also suggests that one should hold discussions on Brahman for the purpose of *jñāna* (realization). The word *jijñāsā* means *vicāra* by implication (*lakṣaṇā*) and not the desire to know, for a desire cannot be commanded by an injunction. Another important point is that there is no antagonism between *avidyā* and self-shining Brahman,[31] which is the locus and the revealer of *avidyā* (*ajñānāvabhāsaka*). It is the knowledge of Brahman (*Brahmajñāna*) which is antagonistic to and destructive of *avidyā.* Though *avidyā* is one, the Jīvas are many owing to the plurality of *antaḥkaraṇas* which are the adjuncts of the Jīvas. Prakāśātman holds a long discussion on the theory of reflection (Pratibimbavāda) which he supports in preference to the Avacchedavāda (the theory of limitation) which he refutes with sound arguments that have been accepted by most of the later Advaitins.

## THE SCHOOL OF VĀCASPATI

Vācaspati Miśra (*circa* A.D. 840) who is renowned as an independent commentator on all the systems of philosophy (*sarvatantra-svatantra*), is the author of *Bhāmatī,* the most celebrated commentary on the *Śaṅkara-bhāṣya* of the *Brahma-Sūtra.* Besides his celebrated commentaries on *Sāṁkhya-kārikā, Yoga-bhāṣya, Nyāyavārttika, Vidhi-viveka,* etc. another work of his, on Advaita Vedānta, is a commentary on Maṇḍana's *Brahmasiddhi,* viz. *Tattva-samīkṣā,* the text of which is not available yet. He attempted to maintain his loyalty to Maṇḍana's views, as far as he could harmonize them

[31] *Pañcapādikā, 'Ato na cidāśrayatva-virodhaḥ.'*

with Śaṅkara's. Vācaspati's admission of the Jīvas as the support of ignorance, of the incapacity of *śabda* to produce immediate cognition, and some other views are a direct heritage from Maṇḍana. The most celebrated commentary on *Bhāmatī* is the *Vedānta-kalpataru* by Amalānanda (thirteenth century), on which there are again two commentaries, *Kalpataru-parimala* by Appaya Dīkṣita (A.D. 1550) and *Ābhoga* by Lakṣmīnṛsiṁha (seventeenth century). There are also many other commentaries on *Bhāmatī* like *Ṛjuprakāśikā, Bhāmatī-vilāsa,* etc. which are all included in the *Bhāmatī-prasthāna* (the *Bhāmatī* line of interpretation). Svayamprakāśānanda (A.D. 1600), who is the author of a commentary on the *Brahma-Sūtra,* called *Vedānta-nyāya-bhūṣaṇa,* also belongs to this school. According to Vācaspati Miśra, Brahman is the material cause of the world, not as the locus of nescience but as the object of nesciences supported by individual souls, Māyā being only an accessary cause. According to some interpreters (e.g. Madhusūdana in his *Siddhānta-bindu*), Vācaspati's view is a type of subjective idealism, the Jīvas, with *avidyā* abiding in them, being the material cause of the world, which is different for each individual. But Amalānanda has refuted such interpretation in his *Kalpataru.* In *Bhāmatī* (I.4.23) Vācaspati clearly states that Brahman (Īśvara) is both the material (*upādāna*) and the efficient cause (*nimitta*) of the world. Of course the word Brahman here means Brahman which is particularized by being the object (*viṣaya*) of the nesciences. It is, according to Vācaspati, Īśvara who is the one pole of the nesciences, the other pole being the Jīvas, the supports (*āśraya*) of the nesciences. Appaya Dīkṣita also states clearly in his *Siddhānta-leśa-saṅgraha* that, according to Vācaspati, Brahman, who is the object of the nesciences, is the material cause of the world and *avidyā* is only an accessary (*sahakārin*). Amalānanda also holds *ajñāna* to be an accessary when he states nescience to be *nimitta* or the *bīja* in moulding the world (*jīvājñānaṁ jagadbījam*).

This interpretation militates against the Dṛṣṭi-sṛṣṭi-vāda (Vedāntic solipsism), which holds the Jīva with its nescience to be the material cause and creator of the world appearance, which does not exist outside the perception of the Jīva (or Jīvas).

But there are certain elements in Vācaspati's views which tend towards some sort of idealism. His advocacy of the plurality of nescience and of the Jīvas as the loci of nesciences leads to the plurality of the world—a different world for each Jīva. Thus for the different Jīvas there are different worlds, though they are similar to a great extent. It is owing to this similarity that the experiences of different individuals are similar, though the objects are different.

*Avidyā* or *ajñāna,* according to Vācaspati, cannot abide in Brahman which is of the nature of knowledge (*vidyā*).[32] It must be supported by the locus of the *jñāna* (cognition) by which the *ajñāna* is to be destroyed. Thus the Jīvas, being the loci of *jñāna,* are also the loci of *ajñāna.* Nescience, being the adjunct which separates the Jīvas from Brahman, cannot be one, as Padmapāda and Sureśvara hold. There must be a plurality of nesciences supported by the different Jīvas. The charge of mutual dependence does not stand, as both the Jīvas and the nesciences are beginningless. When the ignorance in one soul is sublated by the realization of the true nature of the soul, the nesciences in other souls still remain to limit in them the unlimited Brahman, to make them feel like separate entities moving in bondage. Thus, Vācaspati is more inclined to the theory of limitation (Avacchedavāda) with regard to the appearance of the Jīvas. But, in *Bhāmatī,* Vācaspati has described the Jīvas as reflections also. On this point his view may be regarded as syncretic as in the case of Śaṅkara. But Appaya Dīkṣita, in his *Parimala,* holds that Vācaspati is in favour of the theory of reflection, which, according to him, is the final import of the *Brahma-Sūtra.*

In the introductory verse of *Bhāmatī,* Vācaspati refers to two kinds of the indeterminable *avidyā.* One is the psychological *avidyā* in the form of *bhrama-saṁskāras* (error impressions) ; and the other is the primal, positive *avidyā*[33] which produces these beginningless series of delusions and *saṁskāras.* The latter is called *mūlāvidyā* or the *kāraṇāvidyā* (primal nescience) which produces the former which is *tūlāvidyā* or *kāryāvidyā* (derivative nescience). These derivative individual ignorances are removable by the cognition of the true or real objects, while the primal nescience is destructible only by the realization of its object, viz. Brahman. This duality of *avidyā* and the plurality of the primal nescience are the distinctive features of Vācaspati's philosophy. Though the dissolution of nescience is not different from the only reality (Brahman) which is already in us, yet it is to be achieved anew, just like an acquired but forgotten treasure.

Due performance of rites is necessary to purify the intellect and thereby kindle the desire for realization (*vividiṣā*). Thus *karma* is a remote cause (*ārādupakāraka*) of knowledge and liberation. In this he accepts the view of Sureśvara. But where he distinctly differs from Sureśvara, Padmapāda, and others, is regarding the means to the final realization. *Śabda* (Vedic texts), according to Vācaspati, can never produce immediate cognition (perception). It is the mind or the intellect (*buddhi*), purified and stimulated by meditation, which produces the final intuition

[32] *Bhāmatī,* I. 4. 3.
[33] *Kalpataru,* I. 3. 30.

or knowledge of Brahman, though the Vedic texts help the mind to a great extent. Immediate cognition, mental or external, requires a sense-organ to produce it ; and the mind is the sense-organ which produces the final perception of Brahman. This view also is a heritage from Maṇḍana and is opposed to the views of the author of *Vivaraṇa* and others who do not hold the mind to be a sense-organ or the means (*kāraṇa*) to the final realization. The dictum *'śrotavyaḥ'* does not mean any sort of obligatoriness, as others hold, because it is not at all an injunction (*vidhi*), though it has the semblance of an injunction. It cannot be a *vidhi,* as it is but a restatement (*anuvāda*) of what we can know by our common sense.

## VIMUKTĀTMAN'S VINDICATION OF ADVAITA

*Iṣṭasiddhi* is the third of the four celebrated *siddhi* works. *Iṣṭasiddhi* by Vimuktātman (tenth century) is perhaps the first work of the Advaita Vedānta which adopted the method of establishing non-dualism predominantly by refuting others' views (*khaṇḍana*) and also by strongly maintaining the indeterminableness (*anirvacanīyatva*) of Māyā[34] and all its products. It has also displayed great mastery over the art of dialectics. Later on these special features were greatly developed by Śrīharṣa (twelfth century), Citsukha (thirteenth century), and others renowned as great polemics in the Advaita Vedānta. According to Vimuktātman, Brahman, who is of the nature of consciousness (*anubhūti*) and infinite bliss, is the canvas on which the illusory world has been painted. Brahman is the ground cause and Māyā is the stuff of the world. The world is an apparent transformation (*vivarta*) of Brahman. *Anubhūti* is the ultimate reality. It is the eternal, pure consciousness. Everything else, which is illumined by it, is matter (*jaḍa*) and mutable. But this difference between the illumining principle (*dṛś*) and the illumined (*dṛśya*) is also empirical and illusory. Difference (*bheda*) is not the intrinsic nature of entities.[35] But if *dṛśya* (matter) is not different from *dṛś* (conscious principle), it is also not identical with *dṛś,* which is the eternal, ultimate reality. Thus, matter is neither different nor non-different from the reality. It is indeterminable (*anirvacanīya*). Refuting the different theories of error—*ātma-khyāti, akhyāti, anyathā-khyāti,* and *asat-khyāti,* Vimuktātman vindicates the theory of *anirvacanīya-khyāti* which holds the object of error to be an illusory creation (*prātibhāsika*), private to each self, but not a subjective mental creation. It is indeterminable as existent (*sat*) or non-existent (*asat*), like *avidyā* and *bhrama* (error).[36] His view regarding *avidyā* is that it is

[34] *Iṣṭasiddhi,* I.
[35] *Ibid.,* I.
[36] *Ibid.,* I.

supported by Brahman which is the only possible support of *avidyā,* because everything else, being itself a superimposition of *avidyā,* must imply some other support.[37] The content (*viṣaya*) of *avidyā* is also none other than Brahman (Cit), because the knowledge of Brahman can destroy only that ignorance which has Brahman for its content. Unlike other Advaitins who hold that in *jīvanmukti* ignorance is totally destroyed by *Brahmajñāna,* though owing to the *karma* momentum (*saṁskāra*) the body persists, Vimuktātman holds that a trace of ignorance (*avidyā-leśa*) also remains with the *prārabdha* which holds the body till final emancipation (*videhamukti*) is attained.

The most distinctive feature of Vimuktātman's view is regarding the nature of the cessation of *avidyā.* At first he holds it to be an entity of a fifth kind, other than *sat, asat, sadasat,* and *anirvacanīya.*[38] Cessation of *avidyā* cannot be *sat* (real), as such a view would hurt Advaitism. It cannot be *asat* (non-existent), as then it would be never achieved. It cannot be both *sat* and *asat,* these being contradictory. Nor can it be *anirvacanīya* (indeterminable), as it is the negation of the *anirvacanīyā avidyā.* Thus it must be of a fifth category other than these. But in the last chapter of *Iṣṭasiddhi,* where Vimuktātman deals with this problem exclusively, he admits the cessation of nescience to be as indeterminable as nescience itself. The destruction of the false entity must also be false. Everything other than Brahman is false and indeterminable.

### ĀNANDABODHA'S VIEWS

Ānandabodha (eleventh century) is the author of three works, viz. *Nyāya-makaranda, Nyāya-dīpāvalī,* and *Pramāṇa-mālā,* of which the first is the most celebrated. In this he refutes the multiplicity of selves as advocated by the Sāṁkhya philosophy and the apparent difference of objective entities. Differences are not in the nature of things. Everything other than Brahman is false owing to its being perceived (*dṛśyatva*). This *dṛśyatva* has been accepted by the later Advaitins as a probans (*hetu*) to infer the falsity of the world. Ānandabodha adds a new definition of falsity as being different from the real (*sadbhinnatvaṁ mithyātvam*). *Avidyā,* which is neither negative nor positive, is supported by Brahman. Thus, *avidyā* is positive in the sense that it is non-negative. He has proved uncompromisingly that cessation of *avidyā* is an entity of a fifth category. It cannot be *sat* like Brahman or *asat* like the hare's horn, or *sadasat* which is contradictory, or *anirvacanīya* which implies *avidyā.* Brahman is self-shining consciousness. Consciousness, which is one and unlimited, is

[37] *Ibid.,* VI.
[38] *Ibid.,* I.

called cognition when limited by objects as its adjunct. When the adjunct (object) falls off, the consciousness remains as a homogeneous whole, which is the self-shining supreme Self.

## TENTH AND ELEVENTH CENTURY ADVAITINS

The tenth and eleventh centuries produced more writers on Advaitism; but their works contain very little that is original. One of them, Gaṅgāpurī Bhaṭṭāraka, the author of *Padārtha-tattvanirṇaya,* is known for his view that Brahman is the changeless stuff (*apariṇāmi upādāna*) and Māyā the mutable stuff (*pariṇāmi upādāna*) of the world. It is for this reason that both existence (*sattva*) and insentience (*jāḍya*) are found to persist in the world. Another is the author of *Prakaṭārtha* or *Prakaṭārtha-vivaraṇa,* a commentary on the *Śaṅkara-bhāṣya* of the *Brahma-Sūtra.* He has drawn a line of distinction between Māyā and *avidyā.* Māyā, which is the material cause of the world, is one and all-pervading. *Avidyā* is the limited part of Māyā; it is the individual ignorance, different for each soul. The reflection of Brahman in Māyā is Īśvara, and the reflections of Brahman in individual *ajñānas* are the Jīvas. Thus Māyā and *avidyā* (ignorance) are the conditions or adjuncts of Īśvara and the Jīva respectively. The epistemological principles enunciated by Padmapāda and Prakāśātman were greatly developed by the author of *Prakaṭārtha.* He defines cognition as a transformation of the mind which manifests consciousness. The mind, which is made predominantly of the cognitive element (*sattva-pradhāna*), is extended like a stream of light to an object and is transformed into the likeness of the object. The self-shining consciousness is reflected upon the transformed mind, revealing the mind with the object. Thus it is the union of the object with the self-luminous consciousness that leads to its perception. Such union does not occur in the case of mediate cognitions like inference etc., because there the transformation of the mind takes place within, without any actual contact with the object. Rāmādvaya and others were much influenced by the views of the author of *Prakaṭārtha.*

In the eleventh century, one Kulārka Paṇḍita propounded his peculiar modes of logical syllogism, called the *mahāvidyā anumāna.* Citsukha, Amalānanda, Ānandajñāna—all refer to these *mahāvidyā* syllogisms in their writings. Bhaṭṭa Vādīndra, an Advaitin of the thirteenth century, wrote his *Mahāvidyā-viḍambana* evidently to refute the *mahāvidyā* syllogisms. Opposition to Advaitism came also from the Viśiṣṭādvaita schools of the Vedānta associated with the names of Srīkaṇṭha and Rāmānuja. The Advaita doctrine of indefinableness (*anirvacanīyatva*) was losing ground before the vehement efforts of the logicians, whose main purpose was to prove that whatever is knowable is definable and real.

## ŚRĪHARṢA'S POLEMICS

Śrīharṣa (twelfth century) was the author of many works of diverse interests, some of which have been mentioned in his *Naiṣadha-carita*. But his celebrated philosophical work is *Khaṇḍana-khaṇḍa-khādya* which literally translated means 'the sweets of refutation' or 'the tonic of refutation'. The work aims at establishing the pure self-shining consciousness (Brahman) as the only reality by refuting all arguments put forward by the Naiyāyikas and the Vaiśeṣikas to support the reality of the *pramāṇas* (the means of valid cognition) and the *prameyas* (the objects of valid experience). Śrīharṣa attempts to prove that all empirical experiences and their objects are but conventional relative truths, having no ultimate reality in them. This negative method of destructive criticism (*khaṇḍana*), originally started by nihilistic Buddhist philosophers like Nāgārjuna, Candrakīrti, and others, was first avowedly applied by Śrīharṣa in the field of the Advaita Vedānta and was followed by Citsukha, Ānanda Giri, and others. Though mainly occupied in refuting the definitions of the logicians, Śrīharṣa has also criticized some views and definitions of the Mīmāṁsakas and the Buddhists. He admits the similarity of his philosophy to that of the nihilists (Śūnyavādins) ; but he promptly points out the difference too, saying that while the Buddhists hold everything to be indeterminable and false, the Brahmavādins (Vedāntins) hold knowledge (*vijñāna*) to be self-evident and real ;[39] that while the former hold that the world does not exist outside cognition, the latter assert that the world, though indeterminable as *sat* or *asat*, is different from cognition.

Śrīharṣa proceeds to refute the categories (*padārthas*) established by the Nyāya and Vaiśeṣika philosophies. According to them, it is by testimony (*pramāṇa*) and definition that the categories or things are established (*lakṣaṇa-pramāṇābhyāṁ vastusiddhiḥ*). The reality of *pramāṇa* (the means of right cognition) is untenable, because *pramā* (right cognition) and its means (*karaṇa*) are indeterminable.[40] *Pramā* cannot be defined as knowledge of the real nature of an object, because the real nature is not determinable. Nor can right cognition be defined as correspondence of the cognition with its object,[41] because such correspondence, which means similarity, is also impossible to be determined. Similarity in certain points may be found even in the case of errors. All other possible definitions of *pramā* like proper discernment, defectless experience, uncontradicted experience, etc. are all untenable. Instrumentality (*karaṇatva*) is also indefinable, as is the operative function (*vyāpāra*) which is said to

[39] *Khaṇḍana-khaṇḍa-khādya*, I.
[40] *Ibid.*, I.
[41] *Ibid.*, I.

constitute the definition of the instrument (*karaṇa*). Thus Śrīharṣa refutes being (*bhāvatva*) and non-being (*abhāvatva*), the general categories of the logicians, on the ground that *bhāva* cannot be defined as existent by itself, because *abhāva* also exists. If *abhāva* is defined as negation of *bhāva*, *bhāva* is no less a negation of *abhāva*. The Nyāya definition of *dravya* (substance) as *guṇāśraya* (the support of qualities) or *samavāyi-kāraṇa* (inhering cause) is also untenable. Even a quality like colour is known to be the support or the inhering cause of qualities (viz. number) when we think of one colour or two colours. After refuting the Nyāya definitions of quality (*guṇa*) and universals (*sāmānya*), Śrīharṣa refutes the Nyāya concepts of relation like *ādhāratva* (subsistence) and *viṣaya-viṣayi-bhāva* (subject-object relation). The definition of cause as immediate antecedent is also faulty, since no cause other than the causal operation (*vyāpāra*) is immediately antecedent. He refutes the definitions of perception, inference, invariable concomitance (*vyāpti*), and other allied matters. The definitions of all the different fallacies have also been refuted. It must be understood that by refuting the definitions, Śrīharṣa has only denied the ultimate reality of things or the categories, but not their practical value. He does not deny the apparent difference of things,[42] nor the practical validity of the *pramāṇas*.[43] Perceptions, being concerned with and limited to present individual things, are not competent to negate the universal ultimate reality of oneness. Thus Brahman alone is the reality, the world of difference being all indeterminable.

### CITSUKHA'S ELUCIDATIONS AND REAFFIRMATIONS

Śrīharṣa's work, *Khaṇḍana-khaṇḍa-khādya,* has many commentaries of which those by Ānandapūrṇa and Śaṅkara Miśra are the most current. Citsukha, who was a prominent follower and commentator of Śrīharṣa, probably lived in the earlier part of the thirteenth century. He is the author of many important commentaries, such as *Bhāṣyabhāva-prakāśikā* on the *Brahma-Sūtra-bhāṣya* of Śaṇkara, *Abhiprāya-prakāśikā* on Maṇḍana's *Brahmasiddhi, Naiṣkarmyasiddhi-ṭīkā* on Sureśvara's *Naiṣkarmyasiddhi,* and the commentaries on Ānandabodha's *Nyāya-makaranda* and Śrīharṣa's *Khaṇḍana.* But his most important independent work is *Tattva-pradīpikā* or *Citsukhī* which was commented on by Pratyagbhagavat in his *Nayana-prasādinī.* In this work, Citsukha exerts himself not only to refute the Nyāya and Vaiśeṣika categories as Śrīharṣa has done, but also to establish some of the fundamental points of the Śaṅkara Vedānta by carrying out a subtle analysis and interpretation of them. He interprets the Advaita

[42] *Ibid.,* I.
[43] *Ibid.,* I.

concept of the self-luminosity (*svaprakāśatva*), the concept of the Self as consciousness, the nature of *avidyā,* the nature of falsity (of the world), the nature of illusion, realization of Brahman, *jīvanmukti,* final liberation, and such other points.

The Vedāntic concept of self-luminosity was elaborately analysed by Citsukha and formally defined as that which, without being an object of cognition, can be immediately experienced or intuited. This definition does not apply to anything other than the Self which is self-luminous consciousness. It is only the Self that is clearly distinguished by this definition, as the Self is not an object of cognition, being consciousness itself. If it were cognized like an object, it would require another consciousness to reveal it, and would thus involve a vicious unending series. On the other hand, if this Self were not self-effulgent, the world would turn blind, there being nothing to reveal it. This definition also excludes the Buddhistic concept of self-revelation, which implies revelation of consciousness by itself (*svaviṣayatva*), which, according to the Vedāntins, is a contradiction, as it holds the same thing as subject and object simultaneously. The Self is of the nature of consciousness as it is also immediate without being the object of any cognition.[44] Citsukha gives his definition of falsity as the non-existence of things in that which is supposed to be their stuff or locus.[45] The falsity (*mithyātva*) of illusory silver is its non-existence in the mother of pearl which is considered to be its locus. The world is also false, i.e. it does not exist in its locus Brahman, though it exists empirically. Citsukha proves the falsity of the objective world (*dṛśya*) also, by showing the inexplicability and falsity of the subject-object relation.

*Avidyā* or *ajñāna* is a beginningless positive entity. It is called positive only in the sense that it is not negative. It is not the negation or absence of knowledge. Ignorance is not perceived by any sense process but is directly perceived by the self-shining consciousness (*sākṣin*). Just before the cognition of an object there is ignorance covering the object which is then experienced by the *sākṣin* as having been unknown (*ajñātatayā*). Thus all things are objects of the witnessing consciousness (*sākṣin*) either as known or as unknown.[46] The *sākṣin,* according to Citsukha, is none other than the pure Brahman which is in the Jīva as its unchanging background. Citsukha explains error as the experience of a false presentation of an indeterminable nature (*anirvacanīya-khyāti*). He refutes the Prābhākara theory of *akhyāti* which means that in error there is only a mental omission (*asaṁsargāgraha*) and not an act of commission. He refutes time (*kāla*)

[44] *Citsukhī,* I.
[45] *Ibid.,* I.
[46] *Ibid.,* I.

as a separate category, as there is no testimony to prove it. Such is also the case with space (*diś*). Our knowledge of space depends on a sense of relativity. The numbers two, three, etc. are also mental constructions. Things are by themselves one and single. Thus Citsukha refutes the categories of Nyāya and Vaiśeṣika, like *dravya, guṇa,* etc. to prove the indefinableness and falsity of the world. On fundamental points such as the nature of *avidyā,* the nature of its cessation,[47] the support of *avidyā,* the state of *jīvanmukti,* etc. he has accepted and supported the views of his predecessors like Sureśvara and others. He accepts, however, the view of Vimuktātman that there are as many nesciences as there are cognitions.

## FOURTEENTH CENTURY CONTRIBUTIONS

Ānandajñāna or Ānanda Giri (fourteenth century) who is well known to the Vedāntins as a commentator on all the *bhāṣyas* of Śaṅkara, is also a polemical writer in the line of Śrīharṣa and Citsukha. In his *Vedānta-tarka-saṅgraha* he tries to refute all the Vaiśeṣika categories like *dravya, guṇa, bhāva, abhāva, paramāṇu, jāti, samavāya,* etc. In his conclusions and in his interpretations of the Advaita Vedānta, he has followed his predecessors Ānandabodha and others. *Avidyā* or *ajñāna,* which is an indeterminable false entity, must be the stuff of this false world. *Ajñāna* is one and is supported by Brahman.

The most celebrated author of the fourteenth century is Vidyāraṇya Mādhava, brother of Sāyaṇācārya (the great Vedic commentator), who wrote *Pañcadaśī, Vivaraṇa-prameya-saṅgraha, Jīvanmukti-viveka, Śaṅkara-digvijaya,* etc. besides his renowned philosophical compilation *Sarva-darśana-saṅgraha.* He also wrote *Bṛhadāraṇyaka-vārttika-sāra,* a summary of Sureśvara's *Bṛhadāraṇyaka-bhāṣya-vārttika.* He followed the line of Prakāśātman (*Vivaraṇa*) in his interpretations. His most popular work is *Pañcadaśī.* In its fifteen chapters Vidyāraṇya deals with different Vedāntic topics of metaphysical and spiritual importance. At the very outset he establishes consciousness as a changeless, undivided, self-luminous entity which neither rises nor sets. Even in dreamless sleep there is an abiding consciousness which stands as witness to the dreamless state, as is proved by the subsequent remembrance of that state. It is the eternal self. This self is of the nature of bliss, because it is the most beloved among all things. Our worldly experiences of pleasure would have been impossible if this self as bliss had been completely obscured or completely unobscured (revealed). It is *avidyā* that obscures the infinite bliss and makes us what we are. Vidyāraṇya differentiates the self (*svayam*) from the ego (*aham*),

[47] *Ibid.,* IV.

stating that the former (*svayam*) is common to all persons (first, second, and third) while the latter (*aham*) is not so, being confined to the first person only. Unlike Sureśvara and Sarvajñātman, Vidyāraṇya holds the *sākṣin* to be a fourth kind of the one consciousness, the three others being Brahman, Īśvara, and the Jīva. In a separate chapter he deals with the nature of the *sākṣin* as the substratum (*adhiṣṭhāna*) of the illusory imposition of the two kinds of bodies, the gross and the subtle, of which it is the unchanging witness. Vidyāraṇya draws a line of distinction between Māyā and *avidyā* which are adjuncts to Īśvara and the Jīva respectively. Both Īśvara and the Jīva are reflections of Brahman.

Another important figure in the fourteenth century is Rāmādvaya, the author of *Vedānta-kaumudī* and its commentary *Vedānta-kaumudī-vyākhyāna*. This work is celebrated for its contribution to epistemological speculations as well as for its merits in interpreting the Advaita conclusions. Later in the seventeenth century, Dharmarājādhvarīndra wrote his *Vedānta-paribhāṣā* with similar epistemological discussions, which differed from Rāmādvaya's on some points. In defining right knowledge (*pramā*) Rāmādvaya has accepted the theory of correspondence. A cognition which corresponds to its objects is a right one. This is quite different from the definition given by Dharmarāja, with whom right knowledge must have for its object what was previously unknown and what cannot be contradicted. Thus, Rāmādvaya's definition is more realistic than that of Dharmarāja. The pure consciousness limited or conditioned by the *antaḥkaraṇa* (mind) is the knower (*pramātṛ*), and it, being connected with the object through mental modification (*vṛtti*), becomes one with the object-consciousness (i.e. consciousness limited by the object). Thus both the subject and the object, being connected in the same cognitive function (*vṛtti*), are revealed in the cognitive consciousness connected as 'This is known by me'.[48] *Vṛtti* (cognitive operation) breaks through the veil of *avidyā* which covers every object superimposed on consciousness by *avidyā*. Thus, unlike the view of Ānandajñāna, there are as many *ajñānas* or *ajñāna* veils as there are cognitions, each cognition removing only one *ajñāna*. The problems of the origination of validity in knowledge and the awareness of validity have also been discussed by Rāmādvaya and Dharmarāja. Validity (*prāmāṇya*) is produced in a cognition spontaneously (*svataḥ*), i.e. it is not derived from any source other than the conditions of a cognition. Awareness of the validity is also spontaneous, i.e. every cognition is known as valid if it is not invalidated by subsequent knowledge

[48] *Vedānta-kaumudī*, '*Vṛtterubhayasaṁlagnatvācca tadabhivyakta-caitanyasyāpi tathātvena mayedaṁ viditam iti saṁśleṣa-pratyayaḥ.*'

of a defect (*doṣa*). But the invalidity (*aprāmāṇya*) of a cognition is produced by defects (distorting elements) and is known by a subsequent knowledge (inference etc.).

### PRAKĀŚĀNANDA'S SOLIPSISM

One of the most striking figures among the post-Śaṅkara Advaitins is Prakāśānanda (fifteenth century or the earlier part of sixteenth century) who propounded in his *Vedānta-siddhānta-muktāvalī* (commented upon by Nānā Dīkṣita) the doctrine of Dṛṣṭi-sṛṣṭi-vāda or Vedāntic solipsism, the germs of which are to be traced to the writings of Gauḍapāda, Maṇḍana, Vācaspati, and even to some statements of Śaṅkara.[49] While in the hands of Śaṅkara's followers the false world was growing more and more real with Māyā as its material cause, Prakāśānanda's doctrine was a strong blow to the growing Vedāntic realism. To Śaṅkara and his followers, the world is as real as the subject (mind). But to Prakāśānanda the world is nothing more than its perception (*dṛṣṭireva sṛṣṭiḥ*). Everything other than Brahman is perceptual (*prātibhāsika*), having no existence outside perception (*ajñātasattva*). *Avidyā* (nescience) is one, and there is only one Jīva who feels bondage through ignorance in this world, which exists only in his perception and only at the time of his perception. There is no grade of existence called *vyāvahārika* (phenomenal). The world should be regarded as false and *prātibhāsika* as the 'shell-silver' (shell mistaken for silver). *Avidyā* (ignorance) has both for its support and its object the pure Self which, having achieved individuality (*jīvabhāva*) through the adjunct of ignorance, conceives this universe, consisting of gods, animals, etc., all being as imaginary as in a dream. The seeming plurality of Jīvas is due to the plurality of bodies. The one infinite Self, which is of the nature of self-luminous consciousness and bliss, has imagined itself to be a worldly Jīva through its own ignorance.[50] When, again, this Jīva hankers after freedom, it resorts to the prescribed means of *śravaṇa* etc., all imaginary as in a dream, and regains its real state of freedom by destroying its ignorance. Then, of course, no other Jīva or the world remains. Thus, Prakāśānanda supports Ekajīvavāda (the 'soleity' or oneness of the Jīva) as the basis of his extreme form of subjective idealism (Dṛṣṭi-sṛṣṭi-vāda).

With regard to the causality of Brahman and *ajñāna*, he holds *ajñāna* to be the cause (stuff) of the world, because Brahman being unchangeable cannot be a cause. Brahman is said to be the cause of the world only due

[49] *Bṛhadāraṇyaka-bhāṣya, 'Kaunteyasyaiva Rādheyatvavat avikriyasya . . . ātmanaḥ anādy-avidyāvaśāt jīvabhāvaḥ.'*

[50] *Vedānta-siddhānta-muktāvalī, 'Eka eva ātmā paripūrṇaḥ svayamprakāśānandaikasva-bhāvaḥ svājñānavaśāt jīvaḥ . . . .'*

to Its being the ground or locus of *avidyā*.[51] The world is only an apparent transformation (*vivarta*), a seeming duality experienced by Brahman. In reality the world does not exist, hence it cannot be experienced at all. The theory of transformation is also a plea put forward for the satisfaction of the ordinary intellect. From the view-point of the Upaniṣads, Māyā and the world are as non-existent (*tuccha*) as is the hare's horn. He also refutes the theory of *jīvanmukti* on the ground that no *prārabdha* (*karma* that has begun to bear fruit) or trace of ignorance can persist after self-realization. A Vedānta teacher, though he is an illusory production and not a *mukta* (liberated), may instruct and lead to truth, just as the Vedas do.[52] He speaks of the ultimate reality as neither dual nor non-dual, but as pure Self of the nature of compact consciousness.

### APPAYA DĪKṢITA OF THE BHĀMATĪ SCHOOL

Appaya Dīkṣita (sixteenth century), a versatile scholar and a syncretic Advaita writer, is the author of a large number of books of which *Vedānta-kalpataru-parimala* (a gloss on the commentary on *Bhāmatī*) and *Siddhānta-leśa-saṅgraha* (a compilation of the views of the different interpreters of Śaṅkara Vedānta) are held in high esteem. Though a strong supporter of the Advaita interpretation of Śaṅkara, he also wrote the commentary *Śivārkamaṇi-dīpikā* on Śrīkaṇṭha's Śaiva commentary on the *Brahma-Sūtra* in which he has supported the doctrine of the qualified Brahman, Śiva, as the highest entity. He says that the main interest of the Advaitins is in establishing the one undivided Ātman and not in explaining the facts of the empirical world.

### MADHUSŪDANA, THE DIALECTICIAN AND SYNCRETIST

The most towering figure among the later post Śaṅkara Advaitins is Madhusūdana Sarasvatī (sixteenth century) who wrote a large number of works, the chief among them being *Advaitasiddhi, Advaita-ratna-rakṣaṇa, Vedānta-kalpa-latikā,* besides his commentaries like *Siddhānta-bindu, Saṁkṣepa-śārīraka-sāra-saṅgraha,* etc. But his masterpiece is *Advaitasiddhi,* the last word yet on the Advaita philosophy, which enabled Advaitism to withstand successfully the vehement attacks from the great logician and dualist Vyāsa Tīrtha, the author of *Nyāyāmṛta*. *Advaitasiddhi* has at least three commentaries, the chief being the *Laghu-candrikā* by Brahmānanda Sarasvatī. Vyāsa Tīrtha refutes the definitions and arguments of falsity presented by the Advaitins. So at the very beginning of *Advaitasiddhi,*

[51] *Vedānta-siddhānta-muktāvalī, 'Brahmājñānāt jagajjanma Brahmaṇo'kāraṇatvataḥ, adhiṣṭhānatva-mātreṇa kāraṇaṁ Brahma gīyate.'*

[52] *Vedānta-siddhānta-muktāvalī, 'Kalpitopyupadeṣṭā syāt yathāśāstraṁ samādiśet.'*

Madhusūdana refutes the objections of *Nyāyāmṛta* and strongly supports all the five definitions of falsity enunciated by his predecessors, viz. (i) difference from both the existent and the non-existent, (ii) the character of being negated on its own ground, (iii) the character of being negated by a right cognition, (iv) the appearance of something on the locus of its non-existence,[53] and (v) the character of appearing as existent, though different from the real. Falsity does not mean non-existence like that of the hare's horn, which never even appears to exist nor serves any purpose. Yet it is different from the reality which is eternal and unchangeable. The world appears to exist where it does not really (absolutely) exist. The probans (*hetu*) put forward by the Advaitins to infer the falsity of the world is also faultless. Objectivity of cognition (*dṛśyatva*), insentience (*jaḍatva*), and limitation (*paricchinnatva*) are correct and sufficient proofs to establish the falsity.

Another contention of Vyāsa Tīrtha is that if the falsity (of the world) be correct, non-dualism will be disturbed. If the falsity be incorrect, the world becomes real. To this Madhusūdana's answer is that *dṛśyatva* being the determinant of falsity, falsity, being knowable, is as false as the known world. Reality and falsity, having no coexistence anywhere, are contrary entities ; but they are not contradictory, so that the negation or falsity of the one may not go against the existence or reality of the other. Both reality and falsity are absent in the non-existent (*asat*) like the hare's horn, just as both the contraries cow-hood (*gotva*) and horse-hood (*aśvatva*) may be negated in an elephant. Thus both reality and falsity with regard to the world are false, as both of them are empirical and cognizable (*dṛśya*). With the knowledge of Brahman both of them are negated. The world appears to be real (*sat*) only because it is superimposed on the real Brahman as its ground. It is the reality of Brahman that is perceived in things, in cognitions like *'san ghaṭaḥ'* (the jar exists).

Madhusūdana supports many of the conflicting theories separately and independently, implying thereby that any of the theories may be resorted to in explaining the indeterminable false world, the main interest of the Advaitins being in the one absolute Brahman. Thus he analyses and accepts the unity as well as the plurality of the Jīvas, the unity as well as the plurality of nesciences, Brahman as well as the Jīva as the locus of nescience, the objectivity of the world as well as the Vedāntic solipsism (Dṛṣṭi-sṛṣṭi-vāda), and so on. He prescribes the different theories for different Vedānta students according to their fitness (*adhikāra*). Himself a *bhakta,* he could easily harmonize *bhakti* with the Advaita doctrine of

[53] Mentioned in *Citsukhī* as an alternative.

attributeless Brahman. Thus, just after the chapter where he strongly affirms the formlessness of Brahman, he indulges in a highly emotional description of his deity Kṛṣṇa who, he says, is the 'highest' known to him.

### OTHER DEVELOPMENTS

Kāśmīraka Sadānanda (seventeenth century) who was a great polemic and refuter of all the antagonistic doctrines and systems of philosophy, shows, like Madhusūdana, a syncretic spirit with regard to the theories of reflection and limitation in defining the Jīva, supporting both of them and stating that these theories do not much concern the Advaitins. In his excellent work *Advaita-brahmasiddhi,* Sadānanda supports Ekajīvavāda (the theory of one Jīva) and Dṛṣṭi-sṛṣṭi-vāda as the chief and final Vedāntic conclusion.

Besides the authors and interpreters discussed above, there has been, in almost every century, a galaxy of Advaita writers who wrote commentaries and independent treatises on Advaita Vedānta. Mention may be made of *Vedānta-nyāya-bhūṣaṇa* by Svayamprakāśānanda and *Vārttika* by Nārāyaṇa Sarasvatī which are commentaries on the *Śaṅkara-bhāṣya* of the *Brahma-Sūtra.*

### DISTINCTIVE FEATURES OF ADVAITISM

Advaitism is not idealism, as the term is generally taken to mean. It is rather 'Brahmanism', if the term is allowed. Not only the objective world, but the subjective also is a superimposition (illusory construction) on the subject-object-less pure consciousness which is Brahman. Fully conscious of the impossibility of explaining the manifold world by one attributeless Brahman, it refers to Māyā, an indeterminable false principle, which must be the cause of the indeterminable world appearance and the cause of errors and falsities. It is only Māyā that explains all facts and phenomena, which are also indeterminable when thoroughly analysed and examined. Māyā is a neither-existent-nor-non-existent entity, and therefore does not affect the non-dualism of the absolute reality, Brahman. It is the source of relativity—time, space, and causality. It does not exist at all from the standpoint of the Absolute, though it is indeterminable (*anirvacanīya*) from the standpoint of reason. Pure Consciousness (Cit, Brahman) is the absolute ground which cannot be doubted or denied.

Advaitism has proclaimed the freedom of the soul of man and discovered its immense potency and possibility. By declaring the individual soul (Jīva) as Brahman, it has placed the soul above everything else. Although theistic, Advaitism has shifted the centre of gravity of Indian thought from an external God to the soul of man. In addition to its sublimity and uniqueness, Advaitism is 'an accommodating doctrine' (Nirvirodhavāda), as the great master Gauḍapāda calls it. It can accommodate all, placing each in its proper place in the panorama of world thought, leading all to the ultimate reality of Oneness. It is this spirit of accommodation and synthesis which places the Vedānta on a glorious pedestal and claims for it the status of the world philosophy of the future.

# 15

# PHILOSOPHY OF THE BHĀGAVATA

THE *Bhāgavata* purports to be only one among the various Saṁhitās or compilations which have been handed down by word of mouth in the form of folk-songs, ballads, hymns, and instructions, current among the masses as well as among kings. The compiler of the *Bhāgavata* takes Śrī Kṛṣṇa's life and teachings as the quintessence of all scriptures. Though the book deals with the five topics which characterize the Purāṇas, its main and central theme is God. The stories are meant only to illustrate the principles and way of life of the Paramahaṁsas or people who see God in everything and renounce all worldly ambition for the sake of the enjoyment of the love and service of man as the highest manifestation of God.

## PHILOSOPHICAL OUTLOOK

The *Bhāgavata* is a gospel of divine life and not a text-book of systematic philosophy as ordinarily understood. Its philosophy is based upon the actual direct experience of the absolute Reality attained in the first instance by Śrī Kṛṣṇa in a state of superconsciousness and afterwards corroborated by the similar experiences of a host of his disciples. This actual direct experience of the absolute Reality is known as *vijñāna* and the rational philosophy built on it as *jñāna*.

This philosophy has its theoretical as well as its practical aspects, known respectively as Brahmavāda and Bhāgavata Dharma. From the standpoint of *vijñāna* it is admitted by all teachers that Bhagavat is the only absolute, independent Reality; and *dharma,* the means of realizing Him through complete surrender to His grace. Both the aspects are non-dualistic from the standpoint of *vijñāna*, and dualistic from that of the relative knowledge gained in the other three states, viz. of waking, dream, and dreamless sleep.

The essence of this philosophy is that Brahman or Ātman is the only absolute Reality and that the whole universe, including body, mind, and ego, is only an expression in name and form of this Reality and as such has no independent existence of its own. This view of the absolute Reality must, however, be distinguished from pure pantheism. In the latter, God fully exhausts Himself in manifestation as the universe. He is not limited or affected by the phenomenal universe according to the *Bhāgavata.* He exists beyond phenomena and even in their absence. This transcendence and immanence of God must also be distinguished from those of Western theism. Whereas in the latter, God, man, and the world are always different and separate, the theism of the *Bhāgavata* insists that all these are one in *vijñāna,* where there is no other real entity to be transcended or to be immanent in. The transcendence and immanence of God are predicated only in relative consciousness.

The *Bhāgavata* accepts four *pramāṇas* as aids which point out this ultimate essence of the universe, viz. perception, inference, the tradition of the spiritual experience of saints, and the Śrutis. All these merely point to the essential reality of the non-dual Brahman only. They are primarily capable of proving only the unreal and ephemeral nature of the phenomena experienced in the three normal states of consciousness. They can never actually prove the existence of Brahman, but only help to remove misunderstandings. Brahman is self-effulgent and self-evident and requires no proof. Even the Śrutis are incapable of describing or proving Brahman. It exists as the very stuff and substratum of phenomena and can actually be experienced by any practised, concentrated, and pure mind, by an analysis of the three states. Such an analysis shows that there is an inner witness of these three states which remains unchanged even in the midst of the change of states, and which alone can explain the fact of memory of the three states. Every act of normal knowledge therefore involves also the knowledge of this pure Consciousness. It is this pure Consciousness or Cit that constitutes the real essence of Sat, the cause and support of the universe.

This basic, essential, and absolute pure Consciousness, as realized in *vijñāna,* is described in the text as the Paramātman, Pratyagātman, Brahman, Puruṣottama, Akṣara, Turīya, Bhūman, etc. as in the Upaniṣads. The *Bhāgavata* calls it also by such other names as Kṛṣṇa, Vāsudeva, Nārāyaṇa, Hari, etc. It is, however, beyond words and thought and free from all attributes and limitations. It can be grasped or experienced only when all obstructions are removed. It can be correctly characterized, if at all, only negatively in terms of the *neti, neti*—'not this, not this'—of the Upaniṣads. It is that which is beyond Māyā and therefore absolutely inexpressible by any thought, word, or activity. The text uses all these negative descriptions of the Absolute, only to give the reader at least some idea of the final goal of all spiritual endeavours.

From the standpoint of normal consciousness, however, this Absolute is described positively as an impersonal super-person, the creator, maintainer, and the final refuge of the whole universe of mind and matter. He is its material, efficient, final, and first cause, present in His entirety and in undiluted glory in every atom of the universe, regulating every thought, feeling, and activity from inside and outside, without Himself being in the least affected by the world process or phenomena. He is the parent, teacher, friend, and the Lord of the universe, wielding the infinite power, Māyā, and yet ever gracious in bestowing upon His devotees all the fruits of their actions according to their deserts, and leading them to the ultimate goal of union with Himself. He is the embodiment of infinite beauty, love, and bliss, of the highest goodness, holiness, and truth, and is the source, ground, and goal of all values. He takes whatever form His devotees desire to worship Him in, though at the same time He continues to be formless. He is therefore also described as the highest and the twenty-sixth among the *tattvas.* Form is sometimes described as being attributed to Him only by the ignorance of man for purposes of devotion, and sometimes as actually assumed by God, just as He assumes the form of any other object. At other times, again, these two ideas are combined in a more comprehensive doctrine according to which the formless, attributeless God assumes different forms and attributes through His own Māyā in order to bless the devotees according to their desire. Even the devotees themselves transcend these names and forms in their highest spiritual experience, and God shows His form to the devotees only temporarily and withdraws it afterwards. The emphasis of the text is on this personal God with form as more suited to love, devotion, and worship.

One such favourite ideal form of God and His attributes is described in the text symbolically on the basis of the experience of saints, and the symbolism is explained. The personal God in this particular form is not merely an abstract imaginary entity but a concrete being. All their heart's worship, love, and adoration were showered upon Him alone. The psychological necessity of understanding the unknown only in terms of the known, the ontological fact of all creatures being in essence only God, the Śruti statement of the identity of Brahman with a realizer of Brahman, the traditional practice of worshipping the *guru* and men of realization as God, Śrī Kṛṣṇa's express declarations and demonstrations about His own divinity, the religious faith that God Himself is the only *guru*, and spiritual experiences of the saints in which God appeared to them only in the form of Kṛṣṇa according to their desires and in which they merged into and emerged from the Absolute in *samādhi*—all these justify the conviction of the saints and devotees that not only was Kṛṣṇa God, but God was none else than Kṛṣṇa. In fact, it is only in response to the desire of the devotees of Kṛṣṇa to purify themselves by listening to His glories that the *Bhāgavata* was composed and narrated. The doctrine of *vyūhas,* wherein not only Śrī Kṛṣṇa but also His relatives were deified, shows how God was conceived only in terms of Kṛṣṇa. The transplantation of even the earthly Vṛndāvana to the celestial regions and the idea of God enjoying His eternal dance with the *gopīs* there point to the same conclusion. It also explains why all the incarnations are treated as only *avatāras* of Kṛṣṇa.

No doubt this personal God is sometimes called Viṣṇu, but the Viṣṇu of the *Bhāgavata* is only an idealized form of Kṛṣṇa and is thus entirely different from the Viṣṇu of the Vedas. Though this aspect is not unknown to the text, it gives Viṣṇu a higher status as one of the trinity, functioning as preserver and protector and as identical with the Absolute in His highest state. As the highest personal God, one with the Absolute, Viṣṇu is identical with the Śiva of the Śaivas. The same sages are represented as devotees of both Viṣṇu and Śiva. Rudra and Viṣṇu are themselves described as vying with each other in recognizing themselves in each other.

### BHAGAVAT AND AVATĀRA

Bhagavat is one of the central concepts of the text. Etymologically it means 'one who possesses or has realized *bhaga*', which, derived from the root *bhaj,* implies, true to its Vedic sense, 'the gracious Lord', 'the adorable One', who loves to bless His devotees with the recovery of their lost inherent divinity. Hence it is applicable to all *ṛṣis* and holy men possessing the required virtues of imparting grace to fallen humanity. Nowhere in the Śrutis is the word used as the name of God Himself. And the *Bhāgavata* is true to this tradition as is amply borne out by its usage of the term throughout the text. But it has extended the application of the term to both the personal God and the Absolute ; and therein lies its uniqueness. But since it has been imitated by all theistic literatures of the land, this has come to be regarded as the sole meaning of the word.

Although the same divine man is often termed Bhagavat and *avatāra,* there is a slight difference in the connotation and implication of the two words. In the latter concept, it is God that is seen as a person for purposes of love and worship, whereas in the former, it is a human being that is deified and worshipped as God. The *avatāra* is Bhagavat, but Bhagavat is not necessarily an *avatāra.* While any Jīva can become a Bhagavat by effort, an *avatāra* is not a Jīva but a special manifestation of God. The word *avatāra* has been used in the religious literature of the Hindus in a number of senses, the most widely accepted being, however, the sense of descent—the *avatāra* is one who brings down the kingdom of heaven on earth. There is a difference, according to the *Bhāgavata,* between an ordinary man of realization and an *avatāra.* The former is only a Jīva, whereas the latter is God Himself. While the former represents the ascent of man to Godhood, the latter represents the direct descent of God to humanity. While the birth of the former is the inevitable result of his *karma,* the birth of the latter is the result of free choice. While the Jīva takes up the body only for his own sake, the *avatāra* incarnates only for the sake of saving others. Whereas the former's body is still under the sway of his *prārabdha karma,* the latter has no such *prārabdha* at all. If God's manifestation as the universe and His omnipotence and grace are once admitted, there is nothing unreasonable in supposing that He can also assume a special and unique form as an *avatāra,* fully retaining consciousness of divinity from His very birth. Though it is sometimes said that the purpose of the *avatāra* is the destruction of evil-doers, the so-called destruction is only a poetical and allegorical description of the destruction of their wickedness by purifying their minds for the purpose of redeeming them. So, along with the virtuous, even the wicked are saved by being restored to their natural form. The real object of an *avatāra* is therefore only to protect all by placing before them an aborable object wherein the glories of God are fully manifested and to which worship can be offered spontaneously. It is only the *avatāra* that sees both the Absolute and the manifested world simultaneously and can teach the world about the Absolute. Even the highest Vedāntic truths would have remained but theories, had not God appeared as man and actually demonstrated how they could be put into practice and perfection attained here and now.

Historically, the *avatāra* is a man of realization engaged in the service of the world. Many of the *avatāras* such as Sanatkumāra, Nārada, Nārāyaṇa, Kṛṣṇa, Pṛthu, Ṛṣabha, and Paraśurāma were actually the *ṛṣis* (seers) of Vedic *mantras.* Even the apparently sub-human or semi-human *avatāras* were originally only certain *ṛṣis* of ancient days carrying the names of their clans, some of these clans themselves being named after their totems. Thus we find various *ṛṣis* of Vedic *mantras* named after animals, birds, and fish, such as Ṛṣabha, Śunaka, Śvetāśvatara, Sarpa, Kapota, Śyena, Pataṅga, Matsya, etc. Many of the miracle stories and myths about some of their achievements might have been originally only local traditions current among these clans, which were later given a spiritual colour and absorbed into stories of the *avatāras.*

The number and sequence of the *avatāras* seem to have changed in the course of time. Thus the earlier texts mention only ten, whereas the *Bhāgavata* mentions about forty of them by name and believes that the *avatāras* are innumerable, like thousands of streams issuing from the same lake, overflowing its banks. In fact, it also forecasts future *avatāras.* It enunciates the general law that no part of the world need suffer at any time for want of a saviour, as God is always ready to manifest Himself, at the right time and place, to restore spiritual equilibrium, wherever and whenever it is too violently disturbed. Some of these *avatāras* are called *kalās* or digits, some *aṁśas* or smaller parts, and others *aṁśāṁśas* or fractions of parts, according to the degree of divine manifestation. While some are considered to be the actual birth of God, others are regarded as having only the divine afflatus or *āveśa* temporarily. Kṛṣṇa is considered to be the most perfect of all the *avatāras,* and all the others, only partial manifestations of Kṛṣṇa Himself.

### PURUṢA

Whereas the concepts of Bhagavat and *avatāra* are post-Vedic, the concept of Puruṣa is as old as the *Ṛg-Veda.* All attempts to understand man in terms of the material universe must prove futile, as the objective universe can never be known without the help of consciousness, which, however, is self-evident and self-effulgent. The highest and purest form of this consciousness is available only to man. Having no direct knowledge of anything except himself, whatever knowledge of the external world he has, is, according to the principle of apperception, only in terms of himself. Philosophically as well as scientifically, it is a fact that the external universe, if any, can only be known indirectly in terms of the sensuous and mental reactions produced by it. Therefore only this pure consciousness constitutes the essential reality of man as well as of the universe. This the text calls the real Man or Puruṣa or Puruṣottama, manifesting Himself objectively as the individual and the universe ; and Kṛṣṇa is the same as this Puruṣa or Puruṣottama.

Progressive understanding of one's own essential nature facilitates a corresponding understanding of the universe also. When man considers himself to be only a physical body, he correspondingly regards the universe as constituted only of material sense objects. When he comes to know the mind as the more essential reality of himself, the body itself being only an idea, the whole universe also seems to him to be only mental in nature, being waves in the cosmic mind. When, as a result of the philosophical analysis of the three mental states, he finds pure consciousness to be the essence of both body and mind, and consequently knows himself only as the Ātman, he finds the whole universe also to be essentially the same Puruṣa who spontaneously projects the world out of Himself. Self-knowledge thus leads to God knowledge. The concept of Puruṣa is thus helpful in facilitating the understanding of the identity of man, God, and nature, which is the central theme of the *Bhāgavata.*

The universe, thus pictured as an organism and invested with a body, mind, and soul, is conceived of only as a magnified edition of the *avatāra.* The Puruṣa is described in various contexts almost in terms of the *Puruṣa-sūkta.* The cosmic forms of Vāmana and Kṛṣṇa, revealed to Bali and Yaśodā respectively, illustrate this. This Puruṣa is none other than God who has covered Himself with His own Māyā, just as a spider covers itself with its own web. He is the infinite, which has finitized itself only to regain its original infinity through an equal and opposite reaction in the form of world process. He has a subtle, seed form, called Brahmāṇḍa, and a manifested form, the variegated universe. The Puruṣa is the material cause of the universe, the trinity representing the efficient cause. This belief in the bifurcation of Godhead into the material and efficient aspects from the standpoint of causality, and a further subdivision of the efficient aspect into the trinity on the basis of the difference in functions and *guṇas,* is very helpful in understanding the unity of Godhead and the divinity of the universe.

### MĀYĀ

While the concept of Puruṣa emphasizes the reality of the universe as existing only in God, the concept of Māyā lays emphasis on the unreality of its phenomenal aspect as divorced from God. Māyā does not exist in *vijñāna* (self-knowledge). This is poetically described as Māyā feeling shy to face the Absolute. It is said to be *sat* in relation to the phenomenal universe but *asat* in relation to the Absolute. As time, space, and causality exist only within Māyā, no sort of causal relation can be predicated between the Absolute on the one hand and Māyā and its products on the other. The world can be causally related only with Māyā or the personal God, as all of them belong to the same plane of consciousness. The statement of this relationship is called Satkāryavāda according to which it is the cause itself which is manifested as the effect, and the effect exists in a potential form in the cause before manifestation. If therefore the personal God is the cause of the universe, the universe as the effect is also God Himself. If, on the other hand, it is only Māyā that has evolved into this universe, then, too, since Māyā is only a power of God, God is the final basis and support of all names and forms.

The personal God is the wielder of this inscrutable power by means of which He evolves Himself into this variegated universe without being affected by this modification. Māyā is thus not only not in perpetual opposition to God, like Satan or Ahriman, but is actually a helpmate and is, in its ultimate essence, one with Him. To show this intimate and subordinate relation of Māyā to God, it is called *'devī'.* This power has two aspects, *avidyā* and *vidyā.* By the former it deludes the Jīva, and by the latter it redeems him from the bondage and suffering caused by such delusion. Bondage and freedom occur only within the realm of Māyā and depend respectively upon the impurity and purity of the mind.

Within Māyā, everything is relative; and in everything there is an element of good and evil, as none is entirely free from the effects of the three *guṇas*. There is nothing absolutely good except the Absolute. Relative good consists in approximation to the ideal of life set by such men of realization as Kṛṣṇa, and evil is only a deviation from this ideal. But evil is not ultimate, as, in the last analysis, evil also is only a form of the Absolute.

The universe of waking experience is as unreal as that of a dream. Sometimes a distinction is made between *jagat,* the universe of God's creation, and *saṁsāra,* that created by the human mind, the former being considered to be more permanent than the latter. But even God's universe is ultimately impermanent and ephemeral, since it appears and disappears in regular periodic succession in the course of aeons. The whole universe along with the personal God and His *loka* disappears in *ātyantika pralaya* (final dissolution).

Māyā has three ingredients or strands—*sattva, rajas,* and *tamas.* The whole universe is a product of the permutation and combination of these three when their equilibrium is disturbed by the will of God, who Himself remains inactive like a magnet, itself at rest, inducing movement in iron filings. This evolution is said to be set in motion sometimes by the *avidyā śakti* of Māyā, and sometimes by the Lord's power as *kāla* or time, *svabhāva* or nature, and the *karma* of individuals. *Kāla* is the cause of the agitation of the *guṇas, svabhāva* of changes of form, and *karma* of birth. These are not really different from God, but they manifest themselves directed by His wish. Evolution takes place in two stages, primary and secondary. Various categories or *tattvas* are involved in it in the first stage. These are differently enumerated and classified by different *ṛṣis* in varying orders of evolution. The text accommodates all these as reasonable. In thus periodically evolving into the universe, God provides a stage for the various deluded souls to gather experience by reaping the fruits of their accumulated actions. Thus by realizing the ephemeral nature of the world and finally turning to God as the sole refuge, they gradually work out their own salvation. Though this may seem to imply that all creation will come to a stop if and when all souls attain *mukti,* such a possibility is ruled out as the souls are infinite in number and are inexhaustible. Moreover, the world process is only an expression of the inherent playful nature of God and hence cannot cease altogether.

The world process appears to the devotees as only a *līlā* of God, where He is the only actor in the drama, playing all the rôles. *Līlā* is not to be taken in the sense of a pastime or play or sport, as there cannot possibly be any motive or necessity for Him to resort to them. It only suggests that He has no special purpose, and that He is not constrained by any external agency or desire. His activities are only a spontaneous overflow of the fullness of His own bliss like the activities of a man of realization. It also suggests the effortlessness, ease, and pleasure with which He undertakes activities, and complete independence of others for help. The pleasure of the Lord is in the activity itself and in the redemption of struggling souls. He is personally unattached to any of these, and hence His activity is called '*yogamāyā*'.

No doubt this Māyā appears to be inconsistent and self-contradictory, but this inconsistency itself is its crowning glory, since it drives the normal mind to seek the reality beyond itself. It is only *vijñāna* that can really explain how the world is only an illusion or a mystery. Hence we find that, when Vidura questions Maitreya about the illogicality of Māyā, the latter coolly accepts it and directs Vidura to go beyond Māyā and attain the superconscious experience of the Absolute for himself, when alone all doubts would be finally set at rest.

## LOVE DIVINE

The practical philosophy of the *Bhāgavata* aims at the development of an all-round perfection of personality through a synthesis of various spiritual practices, approved by scriptures, which have to be cultivated with effort by aspirants, but which are found in saints as the natural external expression of their perfection. Due recognition is given to each man's tastes, capacities, and qualifications ; and each is allowed to begin practice with whatever he feels to be the most congenial. But it is insisted that as the practitioner advances in spiritual life, he should not neglect the correcting, steadying, and purifying influence of the proper use of all his faculties.

While it is thus liberal in its views in this matter, it specially favours the emotional and volitional approaches as more effective, easy, and natural to the ordinary man, and as open to all, irrespective of caste, creed, colour, age, or sex. Anyone who reads the text is at once struck by the supremely important place it gives to love and service, without prejudice to knowledge or ritual. Without love, everything else is considered useless and ineffective. With love, the others are not necessary, but they come of their own accord. Mere dry *jñāna* (knowledge) or ritual is only a waste of energy like pounding the husks of grain. Love as an emotional relation between two individuals certainly has no place in superconsciousness where there is no duality. But love in its purest and highest form is only the enjoyment of absolute bliss when all duality is transcended. Even in ordinary love the ideal seems to be the complete union and merging of the lover and the beloved into one, where there is complete self-effacement and identity of interests. Human love is only a higher expression of the reaction against the action of Māyā in splitting up the one into the many and in making the infinite finite.

As in human love, both God and the devotee are eager to rush into each other's arms. Thus two aspects of love are dealt with in the text—God's love for man and man's love for God. The first is divine grace and the second is *bhakti*. God is even more anxious about the welfare of His creatures than they themselves are, like a cow anxious about the welfare of her new-born calf. His grace is perennial, spontaneous, and impartial, as it is His very nature. The very names Hari and Kṛṣṇa are suggestive of this grace, as they mean by their derivation one who is eager to take away the sins, miseries, and ignorance of devotees and to steal their hearts. This grace is not merely theoretical, but a fact experienced by all devotees who feel how at every step of their spiritual progress they have been helped by God.

The whole world process is an expression of this grace, as it affords opportunities to souls in bondage to work out their own salvation. The *avatāra* is an especial expression of this grace, before which even the law of Karma loses its inexorability. Though grace triumphs finally, it works only through the law of Karma in the intermediate stages of man's evolution, and is often rendered temporarily ineffective by the obstacles created by bad *karma*. Even God, though omnipotent, has to wait till the time is ripe to show His grace by enabling man to wipe out his own *karma*.

Like God's grace, man's love for God is inherent and perennial, though temporarily dormant, as both are phases of the same attempt to reunite. Love develops only when obstacles to its manifestation are removed by congenial surroundings and proper spiritual practices. These spiritual practices constitute the lowest variety of *bhakti* known as *sādhanā-bhakti, vaidhī-bhakti,* or *maryādā-bhakti,* and may be undertaken even in childhood. Although of the form of *karma,* they are called *bhakti* only by courtesy, as they are intended only as devices for the manifestation of love. When love actually appears, there is no further necessity for such practices. When this love first manifests itself, it is, however, in many cases contaminated by the *guṇas* of the mind and is therefore classified as *sāttvika, rājasika,* or *tāmasika* according to the predominance of the particular *guṇa*. When the mind becomes perfectly pure and free from all *guṇas,* it is called *nirguṇā, aikāntikī, ahaitukī, ātyantikī,* etc. In this stage love flows towards God spontaneously and uninterruptedly like the flow of a river into the ocean or the movement of a piece of iron towards a magnet. It is called *kevalā* (unmixed) or *śuddhā* (pure) when traces of *jñāna* and *karma* are so dim as to appear completely absent. When *jñāna* and *karma* are patently associated with this love, it is called *jñāna-miśrā* or *karma-miśrā*. One who has reached this *nirguṇā bhakti* is still conscious of a difference between himself and God. He is then called a *mahā-bhāgavata*. When, as a result of superconscious experience, the lover enjoys the natural bliss of the realization of his identity with the Absolute, his bliss expresses itself in the form of love and service for the whole of creation as God. One who has attained this final stage of *bhakti* has reached the status of God Himself, which is variously described as *Bhagavadbhāva, Brahmapada,* or Viṣṇu's *paramapada,* and the devotee is called a *bhāgavatatama, bhaktatama, sattama, paramabhakta,* or *bhāgavatottama*. This highest love itself is called *parā bhakti*. This *parā bhakti* is not the fruit of any *karma* at all, as it is only the perfect manifestation and expression in life of the natural bliss of the soul and is one with *mukti*. It is the same which is known as *vijñāna* in terms of the intellect and *paramadharma* in terms of the will.

The object of *bhakti* may be the personal God or *avatāra* or the whole universe. Of these, love and devotion to the *avatāra* or saint is the easiest and sweetest, as he can be grasped not only in thought and imagination, but also by the senses. Two forms of this love are described, one based on actual contact between the devotee and the *avatāra,* and the other based on their separation. The latter is more powerful than the former in cleansing the mind and in facilitating meditation. Kṛṣṇa therefore advises the *gopīs* to profit by their separation from him, which is deliberately engineered by him only to strengthen their pure love. Various types of this love are portrayed in the stories of the devotees of Kṛṣṇa, viz. *śānta, dāsya, vātsalya, sakhya, kānta* or *mādhurya*. This love for the saint should not be confused with ordinary attachment for other beings. Whereas attachment is selfish, love is always selfless. It makes all the difference whether the love and meditation are on a worthy object or on an object with debasing attributes. This explains how even the apparently sexual love of the *gopīs* was transmuted into pure *bhakti* by the fact of its being directed to an *avatāra* like Kṛṣṇa. The fact that even men like Uddhava aspired to have the same love for Kṛṣṇa shows that it could not have been of a sexual nature. Their contact with Kṛṣṇa made them purer and purer and, in the days of long separation after he left Vṛndāvana and with the spiritual instruction given by him through agents and in person, their love ripened into *parā bhakti*.

A special feature of this emotional relation is the doctrine that even such emotions as hatred and fear may be sublimated and transmuted into love. Some passages go to the extent of saying that hatred is even superior to love. But, when studied with other statements which condemn hatred, these are seen to be mere poetic exaggerations to show how much easier it is to purify oneself by love when God is so gracious as to save even those who hate Him. It is not the hatred that saved them but the intense meditation that resulted from such hatred. The stories are given only to illustrate how God is gracious to *bhaktas* (devotees), even though they chance to hate Him sometimes on account of the predominance of temporary *rajas* or *tamas*. Their contact with the saint or *avatāra* led to their sin being wiped out, and they benefited by His grace, impartially bestowed on enemies and friends alike. The statement that it was because of Prahlāda's *bhakti* that Hiraṇyakaśipu was saved shows that the latter also benefited by his son's holy company.

## SERVICE

Pure love naturally expresses itself as service. The service of the ideal personal God is more symbolic and mental than actual, but the saints of the world can be actually served in person. This service gradually expands in scope until it includes the service of the whole world as God. This concept of service is rooted in the philosophical idea of the universe as a cosmic person and also in the factual identity of everything with God. All elements of nature as well as human society are really forms of one's own self and of God—limbs of the cosmic person.

We therefore find selfless service considered to be one of the highest of all kinds of worship of God. A man of realization sets an example to others in being always engaged in the service of the world, especially the poor and the distressed. Kṛṣṇa tells Nanda, his foster-father, how the service of all beings down to an outcaste and a cow is superior to mere ritualistic worship, and he demonstrates the same in his own life. Prahlāda condemns those pious men who run away from the world seeking their own spiritual welfare, and says that he prefers to spend his life in the service of others even risking his own salvation. Referring to Śiva's drinking poison to save the world, it is declared that the highest form of worship consists only in the selfless service of the world as God. This ideal of service is to be distinguished from ordinary conceptions of social service, for in these one does not get the spiritual benefit of seeing God in everything. Service may be negative or positive in character. Even if one cannot help others, one should strive, as far as possible, not to injure them by obstructing their spiritual development. The best kind of positive service is the removal of such obstacles. Since the chief obstacles are ignorance and selfishness, spiritual and moral help which removes these is the highest form of service. Even wicked people are not outside the scope of service, though the service in such cases may often take the form of punishment.

To the *Bhāgavata* the motherland is a special object of reverence and worship, than which there is no holier symbol of God. Bhāratavarṣa (India), named after Bharata, is not a mere geographical unit but the mother of civilization and the very embodiment of moral and spiritual culture. It is the land of *ṛṣis* and *avatāras,* of holy places of pilgrimage, of purifying rivers and forests, of saintly kings who renounced their kingdom to seek God. Compared to it, heaven itself is contemptible, and the gods themselves are said to be hankering to be born on this sacred soil where they can easily attain the final goal of life. It is a land full of holy associations, its river-banks, woods, and hills reminding its people of the hermitages where saints and spiritual aspirants lived a life exclusively devoted to the spirit and to the service of the spirit. Patriotism is thus synonymous with love for God and the universe, and is not a parochial, racial, or national sentiment.

The whole *varṇāśrama dharma* (scheme of duties according to castes and stages of life) is a vindication of man's right to grow to the highest heights of spiritual realization. It recognizes only character and conduct as a test of greatness, and not birth. He only is a *dvija* whose mind is cultured through moral and spiritual practice. A devotee, though of low birth, is superior to one who is a Brāhmaṇa only by birth. In fact, the greatest of devotees and saints, those who are themselves the promulgators of the *Bhāgavata,* do not belong, by birth, to the so-called higher castes at all. The social service expected of each one is dependent upon individual qualifications, hereditary as well as acquired. *Varṇāśrama dharma* is planned to provide everyone with the opportunity to give his best for the good of society as worship to God.

The principle of *svadharma* (class duties), which is the corner-stone of this organization of society, ensures to every individual member of any class the opportunity to convert his social service into an act of worship unhampered by others. The State is given the right to use force only against those who are engaged in interference with the freedom of others, and against external enemies who threaten the freedom of the State. The use of force in defence of the freedom of the individual or the State is not only not considered *hiṁsā* or violence, but is actually treated as *ahiṁsā* or non-violent service. Soul-force, no doubt, is the best defence against any encroachment, as is so convincingly demonstrated by Prahlāda in his stand against his tyrannical father. But where the enemy is too callous, even physical force has to be used, though mercifully, when all other means fail. This explains Kṛṣṇa's insistence on Arjuna's fighting even with his own kith and kin and *guru,* and his inducing Yudhiṣṭhira to utter a white lie in order to eliminate Droṇa. He who punishes the wicked and the supporters of wickedness only worships God thereby, but by meting out unjust punishment he goes to hell. Those who kill animals, even in a sacrifice, go to hell, as well as those who exploit others for their own pleasure. Any help rendered to another because of blood or race relationship or in return for services rendered or in expectation of future return, cannot be regarded as service. Service is free giving from fullness of the heart in order to make the world free and happy and to enable it to progress towards its high spiritual destiny.

### WORSHIP

Religious emotion consists not merely in love but also in reverence. Whereas in the former there is a sense of equality between the lover and the beloved and, sometimes, even of the inferiority of the object of love, as in the case of Yaśodā's love for Kṛṣṇa, reverence is felt only towards an object that is superior. Worship is the external expression of this reverence, as service is of love. Worship can therefore be offered only to him whom one adores and reveres. Any ritual which does not provide a proper stimulus and opportunity for the exercise of religious emotion does not deserve the name of worship, even if sanctioned by the scriptures. The company and service of men of realization constitute the most efficacious environment and means for the development of *bhakti*. At the beginning of his religious life a man has his parents or teacher as a substitute towards whom reverence is natural. But very often the reverence inspired by them may remain only as a sort of attachment and subservience. To avoid this danger, symbolic representations of a saint or God, called *pratimās,* are prescribed as constant objects of worship, thereby spiritualizing the emotion of reverence. Books dealing with the inspiring lives of saints and sages and places associated with them, as well as institutions like temples which are meant solely for glorifying God and spiritual life, also serve as suitable stimuli. The text also allows the worship of inspiring objects of nature, termed *pratīkas,* such as the sun, the river Gaṅgā, and the Himālayas. The essence of all such worship, according to Prahlāda, is renunciation and self-surrender to God. According to Nārada, it is continuous remembrance of God by any means available. While the former emphasizes the negative aspect of all spiritual practices, viz. *tyāga,* the latter emphasizes the positive aspect, viz. *yoga.* But Kṛṣṇa emphasizes both these aspects and adds that the essence of all worship consists in self-control and, in thought, word, and deed, looking upon all beings as God. According to others, constant repetition of the names of God accompanied by meditation is the most efficacious in the *Kaliyuga* (Iron age).

Ritualistic worship is only a help for the cultivation of this higher worship. But it is necessary for most people, if not for all. To think of

God, however, there must be a form, and various forms are provided in the text. These forms may be worshipped internally in the heart or externally in images. In either case the worshipper has to meditate on the form as one with his own self. All such worship involves the service of the image or symbol exactly as the worshipper would honour God or a saint if either of them came to his house in person.

The text has also some valuable suggestions to give regarding the various aspects of worship. A real devotee does not pray to God for anything for himself, for he is quite sure that the omniscient Lord knows what is best for him. God does not really stand in need of being petitioned for His grace. Prayers are meant only for self-purification. The essence of prayer is a craving for the love and service of God and His creatures, and for freedom from selfish desires and attachments, as indicated by various typical prayers given in the text. The devotee need not expect all his foolish prayers to be granted ; and God, in His mercy, grants only those that are spiritually beneficial. The objects to be offered in worship should be such as are considered valuable from the worldly standpoint and which are likely to create attachments. All the fruits of worship are to be surrendered at the feet of the Lord. Places of pilgrimage have their value only on account of their association with saints ; and therefore worship of saints is preferable to pilgrimages, as it is the saints that really constitute the *tīrtha.*

## LIFE AND LIBERATION

Kṛṣṇa says that the Deity manufactures various types of bodies in the course of organic evolution for the purpose of manifesting Himself, and it is only in the human body that He could do so in all His glory. Even heavenly beings are said to be anxious to be reborn as men to get the opportunity of realizing their true divinity. Among man's special endowments are free will, creative activity, and the capacity to understand and achieve the goal of life. As vestiges of the previous stage of evolution cling to him in the form of *tamas* and *rajas,* his inherent *sāttvika* nature is clouded, and his freedom of will and creative activity are rendered sterile. The purpose of free will is fully served only when the ego is completely surrendered to God and divine grace is allowed full play. Fate or destiny is only the result of the working of free will in the past, and so it cannot stand in the way of the same free will in the present or in the future.

The highest goal of life is called *mukti.* Negatively, it is a state where all bondages are annulled and an unhampered freedom felt ; positively, it is the achieving, rather the getting back, of the natural divinity or the bliss and perfection of the soul, as of a lost 'treasure trove'. The freedom is from Māyā and its delusions—ignorance, doubt, misery, fear, egoism, passions, desires, attachments, and a sense of difference—which constitute the impurity of the mind. It is also freedom from *karma* and its effects, the *saṁsāra* with all its hordes. The achievement of perfection consists in the experience of oneness with God and His universe, enjoyment of undiluted bliss, disinterested love and service of the world, and realization of one's true nature. *Mukti* is also further explained in terms of the three functions of the mind. In terms of the intellect, it is called *parajñāna* or *vijñāna,* in terms of emotion *parā bhakti,* and in terms of the will *paramadharma.* Of these, the text attaches the greatest importance to the *parā bhakti* aspect.

*Mukti,* as described above, can be achieved only by the superconscious experience of the Absolute. As such an experience is possible in this very life, it is called *jīvanmukti.* But those, who have not had this experience, and who are afraid of losing their individuality in such an experience, prefer the blissfulness of *mukhyā bhakti* or *nirguṇā bhakti,* where the difference between Jīva and Īśvara is still retained. This bliss of *mukhyā bhakti* is also an actual experience of these devotees. The intimate union with the personal God is called *sāyujya.* Some of the devotees, however, enjoyed this highest felicity merely by living in the same place as Kṛṣṇa; others, like the *gopīs* and Kubjā, in his company; others, when they acquired the same perfection of character as Kṛṣṇa by following in his footsteps; and still others, when they acquired the same divine powers as demonstrated by Kṛṣṇa in his life. Naturally, in the course of their meditations on the personal God also, they obtained the type of felicity which they aspired after. These four types are called respectively *sālokya, sāmīpya, sārūpya,* and *sārṣṭya.* Though each is considered by the devotee concerned to be the highest goal, it can be seen on critical examination that these are only progressive steps towards *parā bhakti.* When Kṛṣṇa became the personal God, the latter's Māyā of pure *sattva* became his *loka.* Since this Māyā and the personal God are, in the final analysis, the same Absolute, Vaikuṇṭha is the Absolute itself pictured objectively, and, since Śakti and Brahman are not different from each other, both of them are called by the same name 'Vaikuṇṭha'. Vaikuṇṭha is pictured concretely in terms of the earthly Vṛndāvana. The eschatological description of the *devayāna* or the path of the soul to Vaikuṇṭha is only an objective, allegorical picture of the various stages of the subjective progress of the soul in devotion and enlightenment. The description of Vaikuṇṭha and the mention of the fact that the devotee finally merges, together with the personal God, into the Absolute at the time of the final dissolution, show that the highest goal is nothing more than the realization of identity with the Absolute in superconsciousness.

It would seem, however, that some of the devotees apparently consider *bhakti* to be a separate and superior goal of life. A closer study of the text as a whole will, however, reveal that the *mukti* to which *bhakti* is considered superior cannot be *parā bhakti*. These passages refer only to cases of individual preference in people of an emotional temperament who naturally value emotional satisfaction through love and service more than the death-like absorption in *samādhi* aimed at by other *yogas*. These passages only eulogize the *bhakta's* absolute freedom from all desires, even the desire for *mukti*.

*Dharma* is accepted as a goal only because it is a means to *mukti*. It is not merely a code of conduct which ensures and conserves the stability of society, nor a code of laws or morals as understood by law-givers and sociologists to whom society is all in all and whose idea of its welfare is confined merely to the worldly prosperity of its members. Nor does it mean religious merit supposed by the ritualists to accrue from the mere performance of scriptural duties, entitling one to more intense and enjoyable sense pleasures in another world called *svarga*. Even *siddhis* or supernatural powers are said to be only obstacles in the path of spiritual progress. *Dharma* consists of only those practices that help to develop the *sattva-guṇa* leading directly to divinity. This, especially, is called the Bhāgavata Dharma as Bhagavat or God is the root as well as the fruit, the alpha and the omega, of the *dharma*, as it is based on the truth that the whole universe is the Lord Himself. The attainment of *svarga* is only a temporary transfer from mundane life and is subject to the vicissitudes of *saṁsāra*. Vaikuṇṭha, on the other hand, which is the abode of spiritual bliss in the love and service of God Himself, is attained through devotion and is more permanent. In the cosmography of the *Bhāgavata*, Vaikuṇṭha, occupies a region beyond the three *lokas* and forms a part of *Satyaloka* or *Brahmaloka*. Whereas *svarga* is attained through the *pitṛyāna* (the path of the manes), Vaikuṇṭha is attained through *devayāna* (the path of the gods). Spiritually, *svarga* is not a world at all, but only a state of mind. It is only the development of *sattva* and the resulting enjoyment of the bliss of God at the stage when one has not yet transcended the relativity of the three *guṇas*, whereas Vaikuṇṭha represents the fuller enjoyment of the same bliss after transcending the *guṇas*. Rituals, however, are not objected to, if they do not involve sacrifice of life, and if performed as worship of God without desire for their fruits. If properly performed, they lead to a stage when ritual itself is transcended through *bhakti*.

*Artha* or wealth does not itself deserve to be considered a goal of life at all. It is condemned not only as a great obstacle to spiritual life, but as a great source of trouble, worry, and anxiety even in worldly life. One should not therefore aspire to amass wealth even on the plea of its being sanctioned by the scriptures. It is tolerated, however, if it is in any way really helpful to the practice of *dharma*. Although a person may therefore own enough to maintain the health of himself and his dependants, he should be careful not to be attached to his possessions and should cease to earn more when the bare needs have been met.

*Kāma* or desire for sense enjoyment is the greatest of all obstacles to spiritual life. Amongst these, the pleasures of sex and the palate are the most powerful and dangerous. Their control is the *sine qua non* of spiritual life. It is impossible to control sex through enjoyment, which leads only to greater craving. Passion can be conquered only by avoiding all kinds of sex indulgence and developing love of God. Those who are engrossed in domestic happiness cannot sufficiently benefit by the instructions of saints or the scriptures. The married couple cannot escape misery or secure real happiness. Even good sons, like Śuka, are only a source of anxiety and grief to their parents when they leave home in search of God; a bad son may be preferable, as he may evoke *vairāgya* (detachment) in them as in the case of Aṅga. One should not therefore hanker after a child, for, after all, he is only a deluding bondage which causes various kinds of trouble. Ṛṣabha therefore advises parents, if they care for God's grace, not to drag down their children to the householder's life like their own. Nārada advises spiritual aspirants to practise *brahmacarya* (celibacy) even against the advice of elders and parents. It is not wrong even to go against those teachings of the scriptures which apparently advise one to discharge one's debt to the ancestors by marriage and the production of children, for he who takes refuge in God has no such debts to discharge. All demigods, *pitṛs,* etc. are really only forms or limbs of God and are therefore satisfied when God is pleased. Of all the stages of life, the *sannyāsin's* is the highest, being the culmination of all the others, and the householder himself is expected to treat the *sannyāsin* with the highest respect and honour. Once, however, a little taste of the love and bliss of God arises, the spiritual aspirant will no longer be able to remain a householder.

### THE IDEAL PHILOSOPHER

We thus see that the philosophy of the *Bhāgavata* is intensely practical and affects all aspects of life. A thorough understanding of this philosophy can be had only by a study of the lives of the great philosophers presented in it. They come from all walks and stages of life, from all classes of society, from both sexes, and from all age-groups. But the greatest amongst them all is Śrī Kṛṣṇa, who, according to Swami Vivekananda, is the first great teacher in the history of the world to discover and proclaim the grand truths of love for love's sake and duty for duty's sake. Born in a prison, brought up by cowherds, subjected to all kinds of tyranny by the most despotic monarchy of the day, and derided by the orthodox, Kṛṣṇa still rose to be the greatest saint, philosopher, and reformer of his age. All the greatest sages and the most immaculate saints of his time pay him divine honours ; they consider him the best and most perfect among the spiritual men of the age, and with one voice acclaim him as divinity manifest on earth, looking up to him for light and guidance. To them, he is not only a *vibhūti* (an especial divine manifestation), *vyūha* (the fourfold expression of Puruṣottama), *bhagavattama* or *avatāra,* but also the personal God and even absolute Reality. In him we find the ideal householder and the ideal *sannyāsin,* the hero of a thousand battles who knew no defeat, the terror of despots, sycophants, hypocrites, sophists, and pretenders, the master statesman, the uncrowned monarch, the king-maker who had no ambition for himself. He was a friend of the poor, the weak, and the distressed, the champion of the rights of women and of the social and spiritual enfranchisement of the Śūdra and even of the untouchables, and the perfect ideal of detachment. In him, again, we find the perfect harmony of *jñāna, bhakti,* and *karma*—of head, heart, and hand. The philosophy of such a man cannot but be an inspiration to all who study it, and the *Bhāgavata* which records and illustrates his teachings is, in the words of Sri Ramakrishna, 'sweet as cake fried in the butter of wisdom and soaked in the honey of love'.

## 16

## THE VIŚIṢṬĀDVAITA OF RĀMĀNUJA

VIŚIṢṬĀDVAITA is a philosophy of religion; and therefore it gives a synthetic view of the spiritual experience of God or Brahman. It affirms the Upaniṣadic truth that by realizing Brahman everything is realized. Mere philosophy is a theoretical speculation on the nature of Reality, and its conclusions are not final. More often than not, the philosopher is stranded on the shores of scepticism. Reason is the instrument that philosophy employs. But Reality or Brahman can only be intuited and not inferred by reason. If, however, speculative philosophy is barren owing to the inadequacy of reason, 'a faith that has not passed the test of reason is blind'. Spiritual experience by itself is subjective and lacks definiteness and universality. Hence arises the necessity in religion for the application of the critical method of philosophy.

### A RATIONAL RELIGION

Vedānta is what may be called a rationalistic religion, or a religion satisfying the demands of reason. It is not mere speculative thought nor is it a faith in dogmas. The spiritual truths that constitute it are revealed in the Vedas (Śruti), realized by the *ṛṣis* (seers) in their mystic intuition of Brahman, and justified by reason or critical intelligence (*yukti*). Revelation is supersensuous and supra-rational: it concerns itself with what is beyond the perception of the senses and the power of reasoning, but it is not antagonistic to experience and reason. Otherwise, it would be a dogma deduced from a mere faith, which is hostile to the spirit of philosophic inquiry. Vedānta as a true philosophy of religion avoids the two extremes of blind faith in authority and belief in the omnipotence of reason. Faith in what is revealed in the scriptures has to be verified by intuition or personal experience, and intuition should conform to the rational demands of certainty and universality. It is reason that mediates between faith and intuition, and makes the truths of revelation realizable and those of intuition intelligible. In expounding the nature of Reality according to Viśiṣṭādvaita, Rāmānuja harmonizes the claims of revelation, intuition, and reason. His genius for synthesis is evidenced in his liberal interpretation of the term 'scriptural authority'. He accepts as the word of God not only the Vedas, but also the *Pañcarātra*; and the utterances of the Āḷvārs are ranked by him as being equally authoritative. The real proof of the being of God is the being in God. Rāmānuja applies this

ŚRĪ RĀMĀNUJĀCĀRYA

pragmatic test of verifiability to prove the authoritativeness of the *Pañcarātra* and the sayings of the Āḷvārs. Brahman is absolutely true, good, and blissful. These eternal values—truth, goodness, and bliss, which are enshrined in the Vedas, are declared in the *Pañcarātra* as well, which is therefore, according to Rāmānuja, a direct revelation of God and a synopsis of spiritual truths which can be verified pragmatically from personal experience. Consequently, the *Pañcarātra* as the word of God is as valid as the Vedas. The Āḷvārs are specialists in religious experience ; and in their Tamil utterances they have recorded their experience of God. Since they are the seers of the truth, their sayings are also as trustworthy as the Vedic verities. The eternal spiritual truths of Vedānta are universally verifiable and are therefore authoritative. Viśiṣṭādvaita recognizes the verifiability of the Vedic truth in spiritual experience. The supreme Sat (existence) is one, though its seers call it by various names. Āḷvārs or mystics may express it psychologically in various ways. The Vedāntic liberality consists mainly in the harmony it effects between revelation and realization, and the invitation it extends to humanity to experience the beatitude of Brahman.

Viśiṣṭādvaita relies on the valid knowledge given in sense perception, inference, and revelation, and affirms the truth that Brahman is the ground of all existence and the goal of all experience, the first and the final cause of all things. The true synthetic insight into this philosophy and religion is afforded by the Upaniṣadic text *'Brahmavid āpnoti param'*—the knower of Brahman attains the Highest (*Tai.U.*, II.1). This text exhibits the unity of the threefold system of Vedāntic wisdom known as *tattva* or philosophic apprehension of Reality, *hita* or the moral and spiritual methods of knowing it, and *puruṣārtha* or the knowledge of Reality which is the *summum bonum* of life. *Tattva* is the ultimate knowledge of Brahman as the immanent ground of all existence ; *hita* is the moral and spiritual means of realizing Brahman ; and *puruṣārtha* is the attainment of Brahman which is the home of eternal values like truth, goodness, and beauty.

*Tattva* is a consideration of reality under the aspects provided by the three regions of philosophic knowledge, viz. epistemology, ethics, and aesthetics. Considered under these aspects, reality has three essential attributes which, in Viśiṣṭādvaitic terminology, are known as *ādhāratva, vidhātṛtva,* and *śeṣitva* (the qualities of being the ground, the supporter, and the whole). According to Rāmānuja, reality is determinate and can be defined by stating its essential qualities. The Upaniṣads declare Brahman to be real (*satya*), self-conscious (*jñāna*), infinite (*ananta*), sinless (*apahatapāpman*), and blissful (*ānanda*). Brahman is the Absolute that is good, true, and blissful. It is the source and sustenance of all ; and all things, *cit* and *acit,* exist for Its satisfaction.

## EPISTEMOLOGY

From the logical and metaphysical point of view, Brahman is defined as real (*satya*), conscious (*jñāna*), and infinite (*ananta*). In Rāmānuja's epistemology, knowledge, in all its levels of sense perception, inference, and spiritual intuition, is valid and is an affirmation of reality ; and his theory of *dharmabhūtajñāna* or consciousness as an attribute, as distinct from substantive consciousness, avoids the defects of realism and idealism. Realism insists on the reality of the external world and of external relations, and thus saves knowledge from the perils of subjectivism. But it creates a gulf between thought and things, which it is unable to bridge. Idealism, on the other hand, reduces things to thought, defines reality as a mental or spiritual construction, and saves knowledge from the perils of materialism. But its constructions are likely to be purely subjective. The theory of *dharmabhūtajñāna* states the reality of the subject-object (*cit-acit*) relation. *Cit* and *acit* can be distinguished by logical thinking, but they cannot have independent existence. Their relation is eternal ; and Brahman expresses Itself in their intimate relationship. Both *cit* and *acit* (sentient and non-sentient beings) connote the Absolute and are parts of It. They exist eternally but are not external to Brahman, the supreme Sat or Existence. *Dharmabhūtajñāna* has a threefold function: it can know things as they are in reality ; it is self-luminous ; and it can reveal the Absolute. It is thus a vital link between *cit* and *acit,* Īśvara and nature, self and God. At present, it is cribbed and cabined by the imperfections and limitations imposed by *karma* ; but when it is purified, it can break the bonds of finiteness, expand into infinity, and bring about an immediate intuition of God. Finite knowledge is now confused and fragmentary ; but it can be perfected, and then it becomes clear and whole. Finite consciousness has thus really an infinite possibility ; it can perceive *acit* or matter as it is in its entirety, recognize the self as the centre and source of consciousness, and realize the Absolute as the all-self which is the ultimate subject of all knowledge. Every judgement thus refers ultimately to the whole of Reality or Brahman. Even the negation of certain attributes in Brahman has a positive import, and the well-known negative definition of Brahman as 'neti, neti' (not this, not this) brings out only the impossibility of an adequate description of Brahman in terms of finite categories ; it does not mean the denial of finite things or beings. It negates the finiteness of the Infinite and not the finite itself. Predication is the essence of reality. It is possible to state what reality is or has, and the Upaniṣadic predicates like *satya, jñāna,* and *ananta* are attempts to define the metaphysical nature of Brahman.

## METAPHYSICAL CONCEPTION OF BRAHMAN

The metaphysical conception of Brahman as real (*satya*), conscious (*jñāna*), and infinite (*ananta*) brings out the truth of Viśiṣṭādvaita that Brahman *is* and *has* reality and self-consciousness and is infinite. The universe of the sentient (*cit*) and the non-sentient (*acit*) has its ultimate source or ground in Brahman and derives its essential nature and function from Brahman, which is known as the indwelling self (*antaryāmin*) of all beings and the real Reality within all of them. *Cit* and *acit* exist, but they have their meaning and value only in the universal spirit that is their immanent self. There is difference in denotation but identity of content between Brahman on the one hand and *cit* and *acit* on the other. The purity and perfection of Brahman are not affected by the perishing nature of Prakṛti or matter (*acit*) and by the moral imperfection of the finite self (*cit*). The world of nature really serves as an environment for the liberation of souls.

Brahman is the Sat without a second, which wills the many and differentiates Itself into the manifold of sentient and non-sentient beings. This view does not deny the plurality of existents. What it denies is only the sense of plurality. The Sat is the all-inclusive unity or the Absolute that imparts substantiality to all beings and thus sustains their existence and value. Though Brahman is the ground of all changes, It in Itself does not change. While *acit* undergoes modifications in its essential nature, and while the intelligence of souls is subject to contractions and expansions on account of their *karma*, Brahman is entirely free from these alterations and alternations. Hence Brahman is defined as 'the real of reals' (*satyasya satyam*). Likewise, the term 'higher than the highest' used of Brahman in the Upaniṣads refers to the supreme Self which is the home of all eternal values. Brahman is not only real; It is also intelligent (*jñāna*). It is the Self underlying all, and the ultimate subject of experience. While It abides within the sentient and the non-sentient, It is not touched or tainted by their imperfection. When the Upaniṣads define Brahman as knowledge, it refers not merely to consciousness, but also to self-consciousness, because any act of consciousness presupposes a self. Brahman is therefore referred to as 'the light of lights'. It illumines the suns and the stars, and is the inner light of the individual self. *Acit* is devoid of consciousness, but it exists for a conscious subject. *Cit* is and has consciousness, and it is distinguishable from *acit,* but is not independent of it. Brahman, which is the super-subject of all experience, is distinguishable from the finite self and the world of matter or non-sentient things, but cannot be divided from them. The attribution of infinitude (*anantatā*) to Brahman, while denying the finiteness of the Infinite, does not deny the reality of finite beings. The infinitude that is predicated of Brahman is not that infinity which refers to the last term in a spatio-temporal series. Nor does it mean either bare endlessness or negation of the finite. The true infinite is infinite of its own kind and is therefore absolute. The Absolute is self-related ; but it is not out of relation with the finite. The infinite enters into the finite and communicates its character to it. But at the same time it does not lose its purity. When the Upaniṣad employs the term 'not this', it does not deny the world. What it denies is the limited nature of Brahman. Negation is not absolute negation. No judgement of quantity brings out adequately the infinity of perfections belonging to Brahman. When we define the Absolute as the true reality and the subject of all experience, we do not reduce the infinite to an infinite number of attributes. Every attribute no doubt refers to reality. But when we say that the world of self and non-self constitutes the nature of Brahman, we do not mean that the self is a mere adjective which brings out the quality or nature of the Absolute. The self has not only an adjectival nature ; it has also a substantive being. It exists, but it derives its meaning from the infinite or supreme Self which is the ground of all existence. Thus from the metaphysical point of view, Brahman may be defined as real (*satya*), conscious (*jñāna*), and infinite (*ananta*). It is the supreme Sat which sustains all beings as their ultimate ground. It is the all-self which is the true subject of all experience. It is the absolute, self-related super-subject. While the world of the intelligent and the inert is caught up in the vortex of a ceaseless change, Brahman remains immutable and infinite.

The conception of the Absolute as the all-inclusive reality thus satisfies the philosophic quest for unity. The metaphysical mind seeks to reduce all experience to a systematic unity in terms of such relations as whole and part, substance and attribute, cause and effect. The whole is defined as the universal that pervades the parts and gives them a meaning. Hence it is regarded as an identity that persists in and through difference. Employing the relation of substance and attribute, Viśiṣṭādvaita regards all beings as depending upon and deriving their substantiality from Brahman. The Sat or the substance is the subject, or the all-self that explains the nature of consciousness. Consciousness is ever a relation that exists between a perceiving or thinking subject and an object that is perceived or thought of, and Brahman as the super-subject not only *is* consciousness but *has* consciousness. The idea that Brahman is the cause of all things, again, does not imply that creation is an act having a beginning in time. The universe of the living and the non-living is an eternal cyclic process with *pralaya* (dissolution) and *sṛṣṭi* (creation) alternating with each other. In *pralaya* the world remains latent as a real possibility; and *sṛṣṭi* is the actualization of what is possible. The entire creative process is the self-expression of the Absolute. God reveals Himself in creation. The logical idea of cause cannot be sundered from the ethical concept of purpose. The process of nature and the progress of man can be explained only as the self-actualization of the divine will. Brahman as the Sat without a second wills the many and becomes the manifold of sentient and non-sentient beings; and the purpose of the cosmic process is to provide an opportunity for the Jīva or finite self to realize its divine destiny.

## ETHICAL CONCEPTION OF BRAHMAN

The philosophic intellect no doubt strives to reduce the whole of experience to a single unity; but it fails to satisfy the demands of the moral consciousness. The Sat without a second may be the logical highest; but it is indifferent to the deeper ethical values of human life. The definition of Brahman has therefore to be restated in the language of moral philosophy using such terms as the ruler and the redeemer. God is not only the ground (*ādhāra*) of the universe, He is also the controller (*niyantṛ* or *vidhātṛ*) of those that are to be controlled (*vidheya*). What logic perceives as the supreme Self or Puruṣottama possesses an infinity of moral perfections. The Upaniṣad points out the ethical character of the Absolute when it attributes to it such a quality as *apahatapāpmatva* (sinlessness). The Mīmāṁsaka insists on the meticulous performance of the rites prescribed in the Vedas. The Vedic imperative insists more on the performance of duty than on the knowledge of the deity who is the source of all good. Vedanta, on the other hand, regards the knowledge of Brahman as more important than the performance of *karma*. The good, according to the Vedas, is the attainment of heavenly pleasures, which, according to Vedānta, are evanescent and have no intrinsic value. The supreme good, according to Vedānta, is the apprehension of Brahman and the consequent attainment of eternal life and everlasting bliss. The supreme good of Brahman cannot be bartered away. Brahman alone, which is the inner and immortal ruler, ever holy and perfect, can impart Its eternality and blissfulness to the finite self. To the logical intellect, Brahman is immanent in all beings as their inner ground; but ethics refers to Its transcendental eminence and holiness. Although It is the pervading unity of all beings, It is not perverted by the evils, errors, and imperfections of the universe. The Lord is the righteous ruler of the world dispensing justice according to the deserts of each Jīva. The theory of Karma does away with the notion of an omnipotent God who rules the world by an arbitrary fiat of His will. Īśvara is righteous and absolute good, and there is no caprice or cruelty in the divine nature. The goodness of God as the creator of creatures functions through the moral freedom of man, and hence there is really no contradiction between the infinite might of God and the moral freedom of man. Īśvara is not an absentee God who makes the world and lets it go. Nor is He identical with the created universe. If whatever is be divine, then there would be no need for release (*mokṣa*). While being immanent in the universe, God also transcends it. The idea of immanence guarantees the intimacy of union between God and the finite self ; and the concept of transcendence justifies the absolute infinity and perfection of the Godhead and inspires religion, reverence, and humility. The imperfections of the universe do not affect the absolute goodness of God. The responsibility for these imperfections is traceable to the moral freedom of the finite self. The existence of evil and sin without doubt derogates from the goodness of God. But it is a sacred mystery, and wisdom consists in abolishing evil rather than in accounting for it. The finite self has the freedom either to grow into the goodness of God or lapse into wickedness and vice.

## THEORY OF KARMA

The theory of Karma is the application of the law of cause and effect to moral experience. It brings to light the inner working of the righteousness of God and affirms the impossibility of predicating arbitrariness and cruelty of the divine nature. The problem of unmerited suffering does not really affect the omnipotence of God. Justice consists in the equitable apportionment of rewards and punishments according to the nature of the *karma* of each Jīva. In this manner divine righteousness realizes itself by making the finite self the cause of its own destiny. *Karma* on the psychological level implies that every action must have its effect in the form of *saṁskāras,* good or bad, according to the law of retributive justice. What a man sows he reaps ; and not even the gods can alter the course of the moral law. In its ethical aspect, the law of Karma affirms the freedom of the self. Freedom is a real possibility, and the Jīva can control its moral propensities imbedded in its psychological equipment (*sūkṣma śarīra,* subtle body) ; the individual can make or mar his future. But, on the religious level, the law of Karma is not all-powerful. The incessant urge to evil and the ever increasing burden of sin implicate the self in the endless cycle of *saṁsāra* (transmigration). *Avidyā* (nescience) and *karma* form an endless cycle, and their effect cannot be removed by death or retribution. *Mukti* (liberation) would be impossible if divine justice functioned through the mathematical rigour of the law of Karma.

Therefore ethical religion requires that the legal conception of *karma* should be transformed into the religious idea of redemptive love ; *kṛpā* or the grace of God transfigures the rigorous law of Karma and becomes the ruling principle of religion. The contrast between the holiness of God and human culpability and sinfulness would leave no hope of salvation unless the saving grace of God mediates between the two and transforms the ruler into a *rakṣaka* (saviour) ; *karma* then becomes an attitude of absolute self-surrender. From this angle of vision, even the law of retribution or *daṇḍana* has redemption as its inner motive. Punishment for sin is born of God's mercy. Redemption is the central motive of divine incarnation. *Avatāra* (incarnation) is the entry of divine love into cosmic history in its critical moral situations in order to arrest the progress of sin. Overpowered by mercy and tenderness, God realizes His godliness by saving the sinner and seeking the saint. The idea of *avatāra* does not imply any kind of limitation or self-limitation. It shows the infinite creative power of love. From this point of view even *pralaya* and *sṛṣṭi* are merely expressions of the divine will to redeem all beings. When the universe is steeped in sin and sensuality, the Lord in His infinite mercy suspends for a while the cosmic process and thus deprives the self of its instruments of evil ; this is *pralaya*. *Sṛṣṭi* affords a fresh opportunity to the Jīva to pursue the path of duty and ascend to the world of grace.

### AESTHETIC CONCEPTION OF BRAHMAN

The idea of God as ruler and redeemer does not remove the contradiction between *karma* and *kṛpā*. Retribution and redemption do not and cannot coexist. While the law of requital does not inspire any hope of *mukti* or salvation, the law of redemption leads to divine arbitration. The dualism between *karma* and *kṛpā* cannot be overcome by ethical religion. The seriousness of the moral consciousness and the reality of the sinfulness of sin fail to bring out the spontaneity and freedom of the divine life. The defect is removed by the aesthetic philosophy of God as the beautiful. The Upaniṣad defines Brahman as the effulgent One that illumines suns and stars and as the inner beauty, different from the finite self. Brahman is the infinite beauty ; and the cosmos is the expression of the creative urge and spontaneity of the divine will to be beautiful. Brahman is no doubt beyond Prakṛti (matter) and its *guṇas* (attributes). It is in truth partless (*niravayava*) and attributeless (*nirguṇa*). But in order to draw away the finite self from its ugly career of *saṁsāra,* It assumes a spiritual form of surpassing beauty. The absolute Sat becomes the divine alchemist by the magic of Its love (*ātma-māyā*) and transforms Itself into the cosmic beauty that pervades the whole universe and into the beauty that resides in the heart of all beings. But it is the beauty inherent in the incarnation of the Lord that really brings out the aesthetic meaning of reality. The Lord of splendour takes delight in sporting with the finite self with a view to transmuting it into its own nature. The world is really beautiful ; but it is mistaken to be ugly by the finite self owing to its feeling that it is identical with the body.

## THREE CONCEPTIONS HARMONIZED

Viśiṣṭādvaita gathers up the conclusions reached in metaphysics, ethics, and aesthetics, and presents them in their true perspective by its own distinctive theory of God as Brahman and the universe as the *sarva* (all). Metaphysics defines the nature of the Absolute or the cosmic ground by means of the relation of *ādhāra* and *ādheya.* Brahman is the Sat without a second that sustains all existence ; It is the Self which is the true subject of all experience ; It is the true infinite which is immanent in the finite and transcends it. Brahman is thus real (*satya*), conscious (*jñāna*), and infinite (*ananta*). Ethical philosophy refers to Brahman not as the ultimate ground but as the absolute good, and defines the relation between God and the world in terms of Īśvara or *niyāmaka* (ruler) and *niyamya* (ruled). The supreme Sat becomes Īśvara or the moral ruler of the universe and its redeemer. Aesthetic philosophy defines the Absolute as the beautiful and the blissful. These determining qualities of Brahman as employed by the Upaniṣads are usually stated in Western thought as the eternal values of the true, the good, and the beautiful housed in the Absolute. Each attribute of Brahman expresses the infinite perfection of God in its own way ; but it does not exhaust the nature of Brahman. The relation of *śarīra* and *śarīrin,* the body and the soul, formulated by Viśiṣṭādvaita as existing between God and the world of sentient and non-sentient beings, brings out the synthetic co-ordination of these ultimate values. The Jīva as the essential and eternal self is distinct from the body ; but as the *śarīrin,* it makes the body live, controls and co-ordinates its functions, and uses it as an instrument for its own satisfaction. In the same way, Brahman is the *śarīrin* or soul of the universe, because It is the source and sustenance of all beings in the world, and because the functioning of the cosmos is an expression of Its satisfaction or *līlā.* The relation of body and soul harmonizes the three relations stated already, viz. the relations of *ādhāra* and *ādheya* (support and the thing supported), *niyāmaka* and *niyamya* (the controller and the controlled), *śeṣin* and *śeṣa* (the lord and his servant). The relation of *ādhāra* and *ādheya* is from the point of view of metaphysics which defines Brahman as real (*satya*), conscious (*jñāna*), and infinite (*ananta*). This relation emphasizes the inner unity of reality. The relation of *niyāmaka* and *niyamya* brings out the transcendental goodness (*apahatapāpmatva*) of God and His redemptive impulse. The relation of *śeṣin* and *śeṣa* satisfies the highest demands of ethics and aesthetics by defining God as the supreme Lord for whose satisfaction the world of *cit* and *acit* lives, moves, and has its being. The relation of body and soul combines all the three together and serves as an analogical representation of a spiritual truth. Spiritual truths are only spiritually discerned. The intuitions of the infinite cannot be adequately grasped by the intellect. Reality is essentially spiritual, and the sensuous setting employed by the intellect only serves to bring out the inadequacy of explaining super-sensuous truths by metaphors from sense perception.

## DEVOTION AND ITS GOAL

The finite self is not a self-subsistent entity existing by its own right. It is really an organ of the Absolute, drawing its sustenance therefrom and serving as a willing instrument for Its cosmic purpose of redemption while life pulsates through every cosmic part and determines its form and function. That God is the life of all life is the central idea of Viśiṣṭādvaita. In its practical aspect it insists on the idea of God as redemptive love and lays down the path of *bhakti* (devotion) or *prapatti* (self-surrender) as the means to the attainment of eternal bliss. He who desires release (*mumukṣu*) specializes in spiritual quest, and the nature of this search is elaborated by Rāmānuja in his scheme of Karma-yoga, Jñāna-yoga, and Bhakti-yoga. The *Śrī-bhāṣya* insists on a sevenfold culture of mind and body (*sādhana-saptaka*)[1] as a preparatory discipline to *bhakti*. The discipline consists of physical and mental purity, performance of the duty relating to one's own station in life, freedom from elation or depression, and the practice of ceaseless meditation on God. The Jīva, owing to its feeling that it is identical with the body, seeks the pleasures of sensibility in this world and in *svarga* (heaven). It is caught up in the endless cycle of births and deaths in the sub-human, human, and celestial worlds. This is bondage or *bandha*. *Mokṣa* consists in the attainment of freedom from the shackles of *saṁsāra* by seeking the redeeming love of God. The first step in the building up of *bhakti* is the practice of duty for duty's sake (*niṣkāma-karma*) without looking either for subjective pleasure or for objective utility. The Jīva attains self-sovereignty and is no longer bound by the attractions of the pleasures of sense. When the Jīva sheds its body-feeling and attachment, it realizes its own nature as Ātman or the soul as

[1] *Viveka* (abstention), *vimoka* (freeness of mind), *abhyāsa* (repetition), *kriyā* (works), *kalyāṇa* (virtuous conduct), *anavasāda* (freedom from dejection), and *anuddharṣa* (absence of exultation).

different from Prakṛti or matter; when the false self or Prakṛti is removed, the real spiritual self is realized. Karma-yoga thus finds its consummation in Jñāna-yoga or the method of self-realization. But the latter is only a half-way house to devotion. In self-realization the Jīva is stranded in solid singleness (*kaivalya*) ; it is self-centred and not God-centred. Bhakti-yoga recognizes the need for shifting the centre from self-consciousness to God-consciousness. The spiritual joy or serenity (*śānti*) that arises on the level of the state of the single soul should be replaced by the religious consciousness that God is the source and centre of all finite life, and that all selves gravitate towards God. This knowledge enables the Jīva or the ego to renounce its egoity (*ahaṅkāra*) and resign itself absolutely to the will of God. Ethical religion thus undergoes a gradual transformation from the idea of *niṣkāma-karma* to the concept of service to God. Acts with selfish ends are first transmuted into those without ulterior motives. The rationale of *niṣkāma-karma* is the recognition that the Jīva is the Ātman and not Prakṛti. The next step in the process of transmutation is the conversion of *karma* into *kaiṅkarya* or consecrated service to God and humanity. Every kind of work is thus transformed into worship of God.

## MYSTICISM

While the ethical religion of Rāmānuja lays stress on the ideal of absolute self-surrender to the will of God, it is his mysticism that brings out clearly the nature of God as love and the character of *bhakti* as intense yearning for communion. The mystic has a genius for God ; and he is sustained by the indwelling love of God who is the very life of his life. When the finite self is freed from its 'selfism' by a process of self-annihilation or self-stripping, it is caught up to God and develops an infinite longing for His love. This infinite longing of the mystic (*mumukṣu*) can be satisfied only by the infinite. The sense of sin as the failure of the finite self to obey the will of God is traceable to the sense of alienation from God and the forgetfulness of its home in the infinite. The self somehow forgets its divine destiny and is stranded in the world of *saṁsāra.* When its spiritual sense is awakened, it thirsts for God ; and the agony of separation experienced by the mystic at this stage is recorded in such outpourings of the religious heart as the *Gopī-Gītā,* the sayings of Nammāḻvār, and *The Gospel of Sri Ramakrishna.* Spiritual hunger can be satisfied only by the realization of God. In the state of separation the self loses colour and warmth, and even the sense-organ pines for the light of God. Without Him, life itself becomes a burden. The intensity of this yearning is accompanied by physiological symptoms like sleeplessness, suspension of physical activities, and bodily deterioration. Mentally there is a gradual wasting away in desperation, resulting in spiritual inanity and blankness. The Lord of love is likewise seized by soul-hunger; and scorning His heavenly aloofness and infinite glory, He invades the mystic's soul and longs for union with him. In the ecstasy of the unitive experience that follows, the agonies of the dark night of the soul are forgotten, and its separative existence is swallowed up in the ocean of bliss that is Brahman. The soul is then ravished out of its fleshly feeling and soaked in eternal ecstasy. In the unitive experience the self is deified, and there is a new inundation of vitality resulting from the consciousness of eternal bliss.

This unitive experience does not last long; and it is a feature of the *līlā* of love that there is an alternation between the bliss of union and the anguish of separation. But the elusiveness and evanescence revealed in the game of love do not satisfy the mystic's quest for the stability of eternal life. Owing to the hazards and hardships experienced in the spiritual adventure, the *mumukṣu* longs for the life everlasting that transcends the world of space-time. The body-self is only a particular mould of space-time and a concretized form resulting from *karma*. When the body made of *karma* is dissolved, the finite self sheds its mutability and becomes immortal. The freed soul has a vision of its divine destiny. It ascends to its home in the Absolute. He who knows Brahman attains the highest. This is the *summum bonum* which is sought by all beings. Even the process of nature is designed for the spiritual procession of the Atman. The realization of Brahman by all beings is the one increasing purpose running through the ages. *Mukti* is not only the immediate apprehension of Brahman, but also the attainment of His *paramapada* (supreme status) which transcends the empirical concept of space-time. Brahman is not only the whole or the holy, but is the home of the eternals and their values. *Mukti* as the integral experience of Brahman defies the logical understanding and cannot be adequately described or defined in logical terms, though it is often clothed in anthropomorphism. The self realizes its essential and eternal nature and is deified and thus attains the being of its being. Its consciousness, limited by *avidyā* and its result, *karma* in the empirical world of space-time, now expands into omniscience and cosmic consciousness. It is a state of unitary consciousness in which the self is immersed in the bliss of Brahman and its thought expires in enjoyment. Its will is effaced or fulfilled in the will of God, who is really the endeavour as well as the end of every act of service. The will to truth and goodness that is in God is eternally self-realized. Īśvara does not therefore require the help of man as a fellow-worker to fulfil His redemptive end. Spiritual service thus implies not the loss of will, but the merging of the finite in the infinite will. *Mukti* is on the whole freedom from the individualistic outlook and the attainment of divine vision and divine bliss. In that state the sense of separateness of the Jīva alone is abolished and not the Jīva itself, and the free and freed spirits form a community owing to the common nature of their deified attributive consciousness; and their freedom is expressed either in helping humanity to regain spiritual freedom or in the enjoyment of the bliss of divine communion.

### CATHOLICITY OF VIŚIṢṬĀDVAITA

Viśiṣṭādvaita guarantees God and salvation to all finite beings, human, sub-human, and celestial. It is therefore a religion of harmony and hospitality. It does not stop with affirming the fatherhood of God and the brotherhood of man. It goes a step further and asserts that God is the inner life and soul of all beings. Its idea of God as the soul of the world brings out the immanence of God in all beings, spiritual intimacy, and the goodness of God. As every Jīva is big with Brahman, the realization of the Absolute is a real possibility. The spiritual knowledge of the Jīva, as different from the embodied self and as gravitating towards God, affords a lofty view of the destiny and value of the finite self; and the view that God is immanent in all faiths for the purpose of cosmic redemption inspires the feeling that the God of all religions is ultimately one, though the seers and sects may give expression to Him in different ways.

ŚRĪ MADHVĀCĀRYA

# 17

## MADHVA'S BRAHMA-MĪMĀṀSĀ

### LIFE AND WORKS OF MADHVA

MADHVA was born in A.D. 1197 near Udipi on the west coast of India. With the permission of his parents he was initiated into monastic life by Acyutaprekṣa, a *sannyāsin* of Vaiṣṇava tradition, under the name of Pūrṇabodha or Pūrṇaprajña.

Śaṅkara had taught that Brahman is *nirguṇa* (attributeless) and that Māyā (nescience), as superimposed on Brahman, is the origin of the world. Madhva thought that this position was dualistic. Rāmānuja had taught that Brahman as *sūkṣma cidacid-viśiṣṭa* (having subtle consciousness and materiality as attributes) is the origin of the universe as it is experienced (*vyakta*). Madhva pointed out that so long as there is insistence on this *viśiṣṭa* character of Brahman, oneness of the ground is not attained and there still persists the question about the author of the *viśiṣṭa* character of Brahman. Madhva showed that Brahman is that which is the complete and independent ground of all that is other than Brahman. To expound this truth, Madhva wrote four *bhāṣyas*: (i) on the *Brahma-Sūtra,* (ii) on the opening passages of the *Ṛg-Veda,* (iii) on the ten philosophical Upaniṣads, and (iv) on the *Bhagavad-Gītā*. He also wrote expositions of the *Mahābhārata* and the *Bhāgavata,* ten treatises bearing on the inquiry into Brahman, and several other works in order to indicate that it is possible to make the whole life of man an expression of inquiry into Brahman (*Brahma-jijñāsā*). In all, Madhva wrote thirty-seven works.

Madhva's works exhibit a thorough unity of purpose. Each work serves as an interpretation of the others, so that all his works are finally different chapters or sections of a single work. This idea seems to have been fully recognized by his immediate followers who collected his works under a single title *Sarvamūla*. Jaya Tīrtha, the greatest of Madhva's commentators, at the opening of *Tattvaprakāśikā,* defines the character of his commentary as *'saṅgamyante guroḥ giraḥ'* (the teacher's statements are brought together).

### VEDAS, BRAHMAN, AND THE WORLD

Throughout his teaching Madhva lays special emphasis on epistemological considerations. Ontological ideas are only the implications of the epistemological positions. This is the significance of his defining Reality (*tattva*) in the sense of *prameya,* i.e. that which is presented by correct knowledge. In his search for the final implication of this truth he comes to the conclusion that in the last analysis there is one case of correct knowledge, viz. the knowledge caused by the Śruti, and one case of Reality which the Śruti presents as Brahman. What he defines as the Śruti may appear to be the same as what is commonly called the Vedas. But his position is profoundly different. If the Vedas are generally taken as a case of revelation or authority, for Madhva their validity lies in their being the only source of correct knowledge. He defines himself as *tyaktaveda,* uninfluenced in his thought by the Vedas in the sense of authority. While others fit truth to the Vedic sayings, Madhva fits the Vedic sayings to truth. It is this bold stand that distinguishes him as a Vedānta philosopher from Śaṅkara, Rāmānuja, and others.

Madhva's position that knowledge given by the Vedas is the only correct knowledge inevitably presupposes a careful examination and recognition of different levels of correctness, all pointing to the absolute character of the correctness of the highest knowledge, i.e. the knowledge given by the Vedas in the sense defined by him. Corresponding to these levels he points out different levels of reality with the single purpose of showing that all these levels necessarily point to one absolute Reality which the Śruti characterizes as Brahman and defines as *sarvottama,* the Supreme. Madhva defines *sarvottama* as *'Ekaḥ sarvottamo jñeyaḥ eka eva karoti yat'.* The meaning of the passage is: 'The Supreme is to be known as the independent doer (and independent maker of the doer), because It does and makes others do without depending upon anything else'. The whole expression stands for the idea that the creative activity of the Supreme presupposes or aims at absolutely nothing except Itself. His other expressions for the same idea are *para, parama,* etc.

Brahman is *sarvottama.* It is therefore not one among many truths. It is the Truth which includes all and transcends all. The world is Its creation and Its expression. Brahman is the giver of reality in all its aspects, which does not therefore exist apart from Brahman. For this reason the Śruti speaks of *abheda* (non-difference) between the two. But Brahman is ever transcendent. It is not lost in creation. Nor is It exhausted by it. Therefore the Śruti speaks of *bheda* (difference) between the two. *Bheda* in this context does not signify the independent character of the world, but only signifies the transcendent (*vilakṣaṇa*) character of Brahman.

Madhva shows that of *bheda* and *abheda,* to concentrate on either alone is the cause of *bandha* (misery). To concentrate on either *bheda* or *abheda* alone is to negate Brahman, the all-doer and the independent. To hold that *sarvottama* and the world are different, taking difference in the ordinary or general *darśana* (philosophic) sense as, for example, between a jar and a car, is to hold that the world is independent of *sarvottama*. Again, that which is not different from *sarvottama* and is affirmed to be *sarvottama* itself is in a logical sense independent of *sarvottama*. If *sarvottama* is the principle of the world, if it is the source of the very reality of the world, and for this reason it is *svatantra* (independent) and the world *paratantra* (dependent), then how can the world be not different from it?

Madhva notes that the Śruti does not lay stress on *bheda* or *abheda* alone. For the Śruti, *bheda* and *abheda* are not important; Brahman is the only important thing. He observes the absence of doership on the part of an individual self. Every case of doing affects the whole world. So every case of any doing is a case of all-doing. It is all-doing because it affects all things of the world. With each act of doing there is a fresh change. With every change there is a fresh disposition of the thing. With each disposition the thing is created in a new light, and all other things are disturbed, or modified, or determined in the corresponding degree. What appears as doing or as doer is the creation of *sarvakartṛ* (all-doer). That which is the author of all is *kartṛ* and *kārayitṛ*. By Its very nature It is independent (*asahāya,* i.e. *svatantra*). The Śruti defines It as *eka* (one). This implies that It is *advitīya* (without a second). There is nothing to determine It. It presupposes nothing. It aims at nothing. This is Its *pūrṇa* (complete) character. The Śruti therefore defines It as Brahman.

## BRAHMAN'S ALL-DOERSHIP AND INDIVIDUAL DOERSHIP

The thought of individual doership and individual doing is therefore a case of illusion; for Brahman is the all-doer. Its world is an absolute system and it requires no addition, no improvement, and no correction. To know this truth is to dedicate the whole life in all its aspects to Brahman. It is in fact to make the body and soul the complete work as well as the abode of Brahman's activity. Madhva notes that the *Īśa Upaniṣad* shows how the appreciation of the all-doership of Brahman does not make an individual self inactive but it makes the self full of activity. If the individual thinks that he is a free agent, then only there is the possibility of keeping still and not doing anything, because he is free to do anything.

Hence to think that an individual is the doer is to arrest activity. It is misery (*bandha*). Moral or religious teaching made on this basis, i.e. on the basis of individual doership, does not help the individual, because the whole thing ends in making the illusion of individual doership more and more confirmed, and consequently *bandha* more and more intense.

In illustrating this point Madhva considers the place of *karma* (moral activity) in the scheme of obtaining knowledge. He observes that *karma* is the result of knowledge. It is the spontaneous expression of knowledge. He means by knowledge the appreciation of the truth that Brahman is all-doer. Without this appreciation no *karma,* no moral activity, is worth recognizing. For without knowledge *karma* is the result of the illusion of individual doership. The so-called *karma* of this kind is a case of *ahaṅkāra* and *mamakāra.* It is the negation of Brahman, the all-doer.

Madhva considers that this defect vitiates all those philosophies that hold that *karma* is prior to knowledge on the supposition that it gives purity of mind (*sattva-śuddhi* or *antaḥkaraṇa-śuddhi*) that is the prerequisite of knowledge. He shows that *karma,* devoid of knowledge, makes one blind and opposed to knowledge. It is the possession of knowledge that makes one morally pure ; it is therefore moral purity itself.

Madhva holds that the realization of the absence of individual doership is the origin of all discipline that is really spiritual. This realization is, in other words, the recognition of the all-doership of Brahman. He means by all-doership (*sarvakartṛtva*) the state of doing all of all. This means that there is nothing in the world that subsists or endures by its own merit. In this sense he defines the world as *paratantra* (dependent) and Brahman as *svatantra* (independent). *Svatantra* is the self-established. That it is self-established implies that it is *guṇapūrṇa,* that in which every property is complete in the sense that it is never exhausted, never modified, even though it is the source of the same property that forms an aspect of the world. Some hold that Brahman is incomplete (Nyāya and Rāmānuja). Some others hold that it is attributeless (Śaṅkara and his followers). Against these positions Madhva shows that Brahman as incomplete presupposes Brahman as complete as its author ; similarly Brahman as attributeless presupposes Brahman with attributes as its author. The incomplete has its origin in the complete ; and the negative has its origin in the positive. Further, 'attributelessness' is unintelligible, as, in the absence of other attributes, attributelessness itself serves as an attribute. The Śruti defines Brahman as Viṣṇu. Viṣṇu in the Vedic sense is the creative principle. In recognition of this truth Madhva gives a ruling *'Brahma-śabdaśca Viṣṇāveva'* (the word Brahman in the Śruti is used only in the sense of Viṣṇu).

### ŚRUTI AS NITYA, NIRDOṢA, SVATAḤPRAMĀṆA, AND APAURUṢEYA

What is Śruti? Madhva's answer is that the Śruti is the language of Brahman. It is therefore present with reference to every idea of Brahman. Every case of knowledge is necessarily expressed by speech.

The knowledge of Brahman also has its own expression. This expression is the Śruti. The Śruti does not limit Brahman by speech. It is rather the process of finding out the expression for presenting the idea of the absolute completeness of Brahman. The Śruti as an expression of Brahman is present because Brahman is present. In this sense the Śruti is *nitya* (indispensable). To the extent that it is indispensable it is the expression of the fullness of Brahman. So even by implication it does not modify Brahman. It is in this sense defectless (*nirdoṣa*). Because it is *nitya* and *nirdoṣa,* it is its own standard, measure, or test. It is all-comprehensive. There is no case of knowledge that falls outside it. Its truth is therefore self-established (*svataḥpramāṇa*).

The truth that the Śruti is *nitya, nirdoṣa,* and *svataḥpramāṇa* implies that it is completely free from personal elements. To explain an expression by means of personal elements such as reliability (*āptatva*) is to determine it from outside. But the Śruti is *svataḥpramāṇa.* It is therefore *apauruṣeya* (impersonal). The Śruti is thus *nitya, nirdoṣa, svataḥpramāṇa,* and *apauruṣeya.* How is this to be found out? By means of inquiry (*jijñāsā*) consisting of understanding, reflection, and application (*śravaṇa, manana,* and *nididhyāsana*).

## JIJÑĀSĀ—ITS NATURE AND OBJECT

So there are two things to find out—the Śruti and Brahman. The Śruti is the source of knowledge (*pramāṇa*). Brahman is the object of this knowledge (*prameya*). So with regard to the highest truth both *pramāṇa* and *prameya* must be found out. To abstract one from the other is to negate both. The process of finding them out is *jijñāsā*.

Madhva holds that the language of *Brahma-jijñāsā* is the *Brahma-Sūtra* beginning with *'Athāto Brahma-jijñāsā'.* Without the *Brahma-Sūtra,* the Śruti and its meaning are not found out. Hence his philosophy or exposition of the Vedic thought is essentially *Brahma-mīmāṁsā,* i.e. *Brahma-jijñāsā.* His one aim is to understand the absolute completeness (*pūrṇatva*) of Brahman which is *sarvakartṛ,* i.e. *sarvasattāprada* (the giver of reality to all), being the origin, the principle of existence, and the only aim of all things that exist in different senses. Apart from Brahman, the truth of all, Madhva has nothing else in view. It is a mistake to think that he appeared to save the reality of the world against Māyāvāda, the position of Śaṅkara. To have interest in the reality of the world for its own sake is rather the attitude of the Cārvāka. Madhva really wanted to save the conception of Brahman against Māyāvāda itself. This incidentally required the establishment of the reality of the world, because if the world is unreal then there is no occasion to find out and conceive Brahman as the ground or principle of all that exists in terms of mind and in terms of matter. In the course of his thought, irrespective of reality or no reality of the world, he wants to understand Brahman defined as Ātman by the Śruti *'Tamevaikaṁ jānatha ātmānam ; anyā vāco vimuñcatha'* (Know only that which is Ātman ; abandon the talk of other things). Further, in the same context as he discusses the reality of the world he makes it clear that to hold that the world is *mithyā* (unreal) in the sense that Śaṅkara defines it leads to nihilism and thereby makes the problem of finding out its origin and so on a contradiction in terms. Neither the conception of *mithyā* nor the denial of the problem satisfies a philosophical mind. Further, after establishing the reality of the world so as to make the problem of finding out its origin inevitable and indispensable, he points out the richness of the world in terms of its *nitya* (permanent) and *anitya* (impermanent) character so as to illustrate and amplify the richness of the creative power.

Knowledge, according to him, is the *jijñāsā* itself. At every stage of the process of knowledge the conclusion arrived at is sound only in so far as it leads on to further *jijñāsā.* Thus he insists on an ever-growing process of *jijñāsā.* Just as *jñāna* is identified with *jijñāsā, karma* and *bhakti* also, according to him, are not what they are defined to be in the other *darśanas,* but they are in the Vedic sense different aspects of *jijñāsā* itself. *Karma* is the process of activity involved in, and made inevitable by, *jijñāsā. Bhakti* is the devotion to the subject matter of *jijñāsā,* both as its presupposition and as its result. He considers therefore that *jijñāsā* is the only kind of *tapas,* spiritual discipline.

## MADHVA'S APPROACH TO PRAMĀṆA

A careful study of Madhva's works reveals that he conducts the examination of *pramāṇa* (source of knowledge) in four stages in an ascending order. (1) The stage of *pramāṇa* as commonly understood: In continuation of the discussion started by the other *darśanas,* Madhva holds that there are finally three *pramāṇas—pratyakṣa* (perception), *anumāna* (inference), and *āgama* (scripture). The things that are presented by them are generally just those that common people readily believe (*anādikālato'nuvṛtta*) and that immediately appeal to the senses (*pratītisundara*). (2) The stage of reasoning: In the light of Madhva's teaching under *Śāstrayonitvādhikaraṇa, Ānandamayādhikaraṇa,* and *Samayapāda* of the *Brahma-Sūtra-bhāṣya,* two levels under this stage can be distinguished. The first is the level of different sciences, and the second of *darśanas.* At the scientific level *āgama* has no place that is exclusively important. If it is accepted, it is so only in so far as it makes *pratyakṣa* and *anumāna* leading. According to the usefulness of discoveries, different sciences become popular even to the extent of giving rise to the illusion that there is nothing apart from these sciences. *Darśanas* are mental constructions of a more subtle order finally based on *pratyakṣa* and *anumāna.* Sometimes *āgama* is given the place of exclusive importance even to the extent of making it more important and decisive than *pratyakṣa* and *anumāna.* Madhva says, it can be easily found out that every *darśana,* however admirable or transcendent (*alaukika*) it may appear to be, is after all an expression of *pratyakṣa* and *anumāna,* i.e. experience (*anubhava*) that is secular (*laukika*) in character. (3) The stage of *upadeśa* (instruction): In this stage the Śruti and the Smṛti are introduced to the student. The Śruti is impersonal (*apauruṣeya*) verbal testimony. Its validity is unquestioned. The Smṛti derives its validity from the Śruti. The student at this stage has realized the emptiness of empirical thinking and of the scientific and *darśana* ideas and several *āgamas* based on secular experience. He tries to rise above these stages. He feels that there is something noble and grand and transcendent in the ideas given by the Śruti and the Smṛti. (4) The stage of *jijñāsā,* inquiry (philosophy): In spite of the appreciation of the Śruti and the Smṛti, the student feels contradiction in the meaning and application of them. He can never reconcile the implications of the different Śruti passages, and the inter-relations of the Śruti, the Smṛti, and *anubhava.*

But the student of *Brahma-mīmāṁsā* is not in a position to consider mere appearance to be ultimate. At the present stage he has realized the uselessness of *upadeśa,* because after all it presents things that do not finally transcend the empirical, as it is the outcome of an individual thinking. To transcend the empirical was the reason why he was introduced to the Śruti and the Smṛti. The Śruti is *apauruṣeya* and the Smṛti is the shadow of the Śruti. Therefore nothing empirical enters into the Śruti as well as into the Smṛti.

What is that which is above all that is empirical and which is therefore expounded by the Śruti? To consider this problem is the process of *jijñāsā,* i.e. *Brahma-mīmāṁsā.* The meaning of *jijñāsā* in this connection cannot therefore be fixed according to a thinker's will. For the Śruti is *apauruṣeya* and *apauruṣeya* cannot be fixed by *pauruṣeya.*

In expounding these truths Madhva studies the significance of *apauruṣeya* and consistently with it fixes the character of *jijñāsā.* He notes that interpreting *apauruṣeya* in the sense of verbal meaning (*yathāśrutārtha*) is definitely wrong. He finally arrives at the conclusion that *apauruṣeya* is the language of the Creator of all in being self-conscious, i.e. in understanding Himself as the Creator of all. Though he means by *apauruṣeya* what is known as the Śruti, his idea of the Śruti has a profound significance. The Śruti, according to him, is the plan of creation. To understand the Śruti is therefore to understand the whole creation. In the language of the Śruti the creative principle is Nārāyaṇa. As the Creator He is defined as Vāsudeva. The Śruti illustrates the whole process of Śāstra as the process of Nārāyaṇa's understanding Himself as Vāsudeva. Madhva calls this whole principle, i.e. Nārāyaṇa understanding Himself as Vāsudeva, Bādarāyaṇa. In illustrating this point he shows that Bādarāyaṇa is the origin of the whole Śāstra. Śāstra consists of *nirṇeya* (that which is to be determined) and *nirṇāyaka* (that which determines); *nirṇeya* is the Śruti and the Smṛti. The origin of both is Bādarāyaṇa. Their real meaning must be understood only through a process of discipline. This process is the process of *jijñāsā*.

Bādarāyaṇa's *Brahma-Sūtra,* consisting of 564 *sūtras* in 223 *adhikaraṇas,* under four chapters, each with four quarters, presents the process of *jijñāsā*. That which is not *Brahma-mīmāṁsā* can never hope to conceive the absolute point of view. Again, Brahman understood is no longer *guṇapūrṇa* or Viṣṇu. If It is Brahman, then It lies beyond the sphere of understanding. To understand this truth, i.e. to understand Brahman as Viṣṇu, is the aim of *Brahma-mīmāṁsā*. To hold that Brahman is not understandable is to emphasize the knowledge of the ununderstandable as ununderstandable as expounded by the *Kena Upaniṣad 'Avijñātaṁ vijānatām ; vijñātamavijānatām'* (It is not known to those that know ; It is known to those that do not know).

Śāstra, according to him, consists of *nirṇeya* and *nirṇāyaka*. *Nirṇeya* consists of the Śruti and the Smṛti. It does not by itself help knowledge, because it has apparent contradictions. It is therefore *aparā,* inferior, i.e. it is not *vidyā* (philosophy). But these two must not be taken to be separate. Through the process of *jijñāsā, nirṇāyaka* becomes merged in *nirṇeya*. In this circumstance *nirṇeya* transcends its *nirṇeya* character, becomes one with *nirṇāyaka,* and presents its true meaning, Brahman. *Nirṇāyaka* is thus innate in *nirṇeya*. *Sūtra* is its expression. *Jijñāsā* is its form.

## THEORY OF KNOWLEDGE

Madhva notes that knowledge implies knower and the known. Without them knowledge is impossible. Attributeless knowledge is a contradiction in terms. Knowledge as an attribute, distinct from knower, i.e. *dharmabhūtajñāna,* does not bring out that the knower is of the nature of knowledge. The knower and knowledge are non-different. Yet knowledge can be spoken of as though it is different from the knower. Even Śaṅkara ought to admit this fact. Otherwise the conception, 'Brahman is *nirviśeṣa*', cannot be formulated. To hold that Brahman is inconceivable is a contradiction in terms. So everything that can be conceived is *saviśeṣa.*

Knowledge is by nature true. It is given as true. To make truth dependent with regard to its origin or its knowledge is never to arrive at it. In every circumstance, that which is given is the object of knowledge. The given is in time and space. This constitutes its reality. The non-given is unreal.

In certain passages Madhva explains that wrong knowledge is no knowledge. It is knowledge distorted. It consists in presenting the real as unreal, the existent oyster shell as non-existent silver, and the unreal as real, the self which is unreal as doer as real doer.

In every case of knowledge on the empirical level operation of two distinct sources is observed—the knowing self and the apparatuses through which it knows. The self in an operating capacity is called *sākṣin.* The others are sensory organs. The operation of the former forms the background for the operation of the latter. With reference to 'This is a jar' the jar as a particular is given by a sense-organ. The time in which the jar exists, its distinction from all other things, etc. are given by the *sākṣin.* Madhva studies these facts under *pramāṇa.*

Attributeless knowledge is a contradiction in terms. Attributelessness is itself an attribute. Further, knowledge as an attribute distinct from knower, i.e. *dharmabhūtajñāna,* does not bring out that knower is of the nature of knowledge. If knower is of the nature of knowledge, then knowledge cannot be a distinct attribute. Knower and knowledge are therefore only distinct expressions with regard to an identical entity. The disposition of this entity is such that without being different within itself it admits of usages of distinctions, knower, knowledge, substance, attribute, and so on.

Madhva defines *pramāṇa* as *yathārtha. Yathārtha* is that which grasps its object as it is. There are two kinds of *pramāṇa—kevalapramāṇa* and *anupramāṇa. Kevalapramāṇa* is knowledge. *Anupramāṇa* is the instrument (*sādhana*) of correct knowledge. Both knowledge and its instrument grasp their objects as they are. There are three cases of *anupramāṇa—pratyakṣa, anumāna,* and *āgama* corresponding to perception, inference, and verbal testimony. Madhva notes that these three *pramāṇas* are so comprehensive in their implication that they include all other so-called *pramāṇas,* namely, *arthāpatti, upamāna, anupalabdhi,* and so on.

*Pratyakṣa*: *Pratyakṣa* implies defectless sense-organ (*nirdoṣendriyaṁ pratyakṣam*). There are seven sense-organs—*sākṣin, manas,* and five sense-organs (eye, ear, nose, tongue, and skin). The last five are on the outward surface of the body. They operate when they are in contact with their objects on the one hand and on the other with *manas* which is an active entity in contact with the knowing self. Their operations characterize the waking state. *Manas* exists inside the body. It is an internal organ. It is the proximate cause of memory. It works through the impressions (*saṁskāras*) deposited in it as the result of the previous experiences of the knower. The knowledge caused by external sense-organs and memory consists of the modifications of *manas*. In the dream-state *manas* functions independently of external sense-organs on the basis of *saṁskāras*. These cases of knowledge are called *vṛttijñāna* and are owned by the knower as *mine* in its witnessing capacity. This capacity, i.e. the witnessing principle, is called *sākṣin*. *Sākṣin* is as enduring as the knower. It operates in sleep as well. It apprehends the knower as 'I' and pleasure, pain, etc. as what occur to 'I'. This apprehension forms the background of all cases of knowledge—*sākṣin* and *vṛtti*. *Vṛtti* knowledge may or may not be correct. The knowledge caused by *anumāna* and *āgama* is also *vṛtti* knowledge, because it is the work of *manas*.

*Anumāna* (inference): *Anumāna* is defectless proof giving rise to the knowledge of something relevant to it. It is based on the knowledge of *vyāpti* (unconditioned and invariable concomitance) between the proof and the proved and the fact that the proof is in a suitable position to give the knowledge of the proved. The basis for the determination of *vyāpti* may be *pratyakṣa, anumāna,* or *āgama*. Determination of *vyāpti* results from repeated observation of the 'togetherness' of the proof and the proved.

*Āgama*: *Āgama* is defectless verbal testimony. The defects of verbal testimony are stating what is irrelevant, stating what is sublated by *pramāṇas,* and so on. There are two cases of *āgama*—*apauruṣeya* and *pauruṣeya*. *Apauruṣeya* is the Veda. It is *apauruṣeya* because it is impersonal, and for the same reason the order in which the letters, words, and sentences are arranged in it never admits of change, if it is to continue as the Veda, i.e. if the meaning which it conveys is to be retained. *Pauruṣeya* is that which admits of change in the order in which letters etc. are arranged. *Pauruṣeya* becomes the source of correct knowledge only when it is consistent with the Śruti. *Apauruṣeya,* when it is recognized as *apauruṣeya,* is necessarily the source of the knowledge of Brahman.

The function of *pramāṇas*: Of the three *pramāṇas, pratyakṣa* presents things that are in contact with the sense-organs, in a clear and distinct manner. Vagueness pervades the things presented by *anumāna* and *āgama* in general. *Āgama* and *anumāna* based on *āgama* present both things that are perceivable and things that are not perceivable. But *āgama* as the Śruti has one speciality. The Śruti is *jijñāsā* in its complete sense.

For this reason, though, to start with, it gives rise to knowledge in a vague manner, as *jijñāsā* becomes more and more pronounced and comes to its perfection, the Śruti character of Śruti becomes realized, and there is consequently the *pratyakṣa* knowledge of the truth expounded by the Śruti. Madhva points out that the truth of this observation can be appreciated only through an intensive *Brahma-mīmāṁsā*.

*Kevalapramāṇa*: *Kevalapramāṇa* is the knowledge caused by *anupramāṇa*. Corresponding to the three cases of *anupramāṇa* there are three cases of *kevalapramāṇa—pratyakṣa, anumiti,* and *śābdajñāna*. Knowledge is never objectless. In the absence of an object external to it, it is its own object. Objectless knowledge is a contradiction in terms.

As has been already indicated, after a careful examination and analysis of experience, two types of knowledge are distinguished by Madhva: (1) knowledge caused by *sākṣin* and (2) knowledge caused by the other instruments of knowledge. He calls the former *svarūpajñāna* and the latter *vṛttijñāna*. *Svarūpajñāna* is self-conscious. In being conscious of itself it becomes conscious of the fact that it is correct (*yathārtha*). Further, the consciousness of time forms the very background of all mental activities as 'That is this' and so on. This illustrates how *svarūpajñāna,* i.e. the operation of *sākṣin* is present in *vṛttijñāna* as its basis.

*Vṛttijñāna* is a modification or state of *manas*. It is called knowledge because, like *svarūpajñāna,* it reveals its object. Even this is due to the fact that *svarūpajñāna,* being in contact with *manas,* gives it the power of reacting so as to give rise to what is called *vṛttijñāna*.

*Vṛttijñāna* may or may not be correct. In general cases it is correct. When it is correct it is known to be correct by the *sākṣin*. When it is incorrect the fact that it is incorrect is due to some defect in its condition. A person who has defective eyes mistakes an oyster shell for silver.

The ideas 'Knowledge is *yathārtha* (true)' and 'Knowledge is not objectless' are the expressions of the same truth. The fact that knowledge is occasionally wrong does not affect this truth. The percipient has a defective eye. His eye is in contact with a shell. Owing to some defect it does not apprehend the shell as shell but only as 'This shining thing'. As the thing is not apprehended as a shell, the perception of shining kindles the impression (*saṁskāra*) of another shining thing, silver. This impression operates on the whole of the circumstances. There is consequently the illusion, 'This is silver'.

If all the circumstances in which this illusion takes place are examined, then it is not difficult to see how the illusion presupposes correct perception of the shell as a shining something, correct perception of silver at a previous time so that there is the impression that shining is an attribute of silver, and so on. So though what a given thing is mistaken for is unreal, every case of illusion points to the fact that knowledge is *yathārtha* by nature and is therefore never objectless.

The importance of Madhva's analysis of *pramāṇa* consists in the following. Under *pratyakṣa,* his conception of knowledge caused by the *sākṣin,* in its implication, puts an end to all theories that on the one hand support subject-and-objectless knowledge such as *nirviśeṣa-caitanya* and on the other support the idea that knowledge is an accidental property of the self such as *jñāna* of the Nyāya-Vaiśeṣika and *dharmabhūtajñāna* of the Viśiṣṭādvaita. Under *anumāna,* Madhva considers two kinds—*sādhanānumāna* and *dūṣaṇānumāna.* The distinction between these two is psychological. They have respectively close reference to *siddhānta* (the position of the Śāstra) and *pūrvapakṣa* (that which opposes *siddhānta*). Under *āgama,* Madhva finally arrives at the conclusion that *Brahma-mīmāṁsā* is the only thing that gives rise to correct knowledge.

### EXPERIENCE AS THE STARTING POINT OF PHILOSOPHY

Any philosophy that does not start from experience is false. For the purpose of philosophy is to find out the explanation of experience. To deny the validity of experience as such, to posit some imaginary entity such as *vijñāna* (of the Yogācāra) or *cit* (of Śaṅkara) as the true case of knowledge, to deny the reality of the world, and to consider it to be *mithyā* are unwarranted. Again, to hold that the objects of the world are partly or wholly ultimate or enduring on their own merits is another extreme. All these ideas, however subtle, however philosophical they may appear to be, are different expressions of the negation of Brahman.

Madhva points out that the element of prepossession, which he calls *durāgraha* or *bhrānti,* is the basis of all these ideas. He asks the student of philosophy to take things purely objectively. Taken in this sense, things of the world are *vibhakta* (separated) and *vikārin* (changing). Every thing is *vibhakta.* It has its own individuality as against the other things. But its disposition changes with every change that takes place in the world. Madhva notes that this is the common feature of all the things of the world presented to us by the three *pramāṇas.* He studies the world in two aspects: (1) Things called *indriyas, arthas* (sense-organs and their objects), *manas, buddhi* (different aspects of intellect), self, and *avyakta,* the later ones being superior to the earlier ones; and (2) *Abhimānins* (presiding deities) that make these things function. Under these two heads Madhva brings material objects beginning with an insignificant object and ending with *avyakta* (non-manifested), the root matter of all, and spiritual entities beginning with the *cetana* (knowing self) of the lowest order and ending with *Śrītattva* or Lakṣmī, the highest *abhimāninī* of the whole universe consisting of *cetana, acetana,* and *abhimāni-devatās.*

## MADHVA'S REFUTATION OF MĀYĀVĀDA

*Prameya* is that which is the object of correct knowledge. It is the same as real (*satya*), according to Madhva. In the absolute sense it is Brahman. In arriving at this conclusion Madhva examines Śaṅkara's conception of *mithyā,* and against it he calls the world *satya.* At this stage the relative significance of these concepts may be noted. If *mithyā* is translated as unreal, then *satya* may be translated as real. But in the philosophical language real and unreal have different significances. Unreal may mean *asat.* But *mithyā* does not mean *asat.* According to Śaṅkara, *mithyā* is taken to mean *sadasadvilakṣaṇa,* that which is other than *sat, asat,* and *sadasat.* This conception is based on the supposition that the world is sublated (*bādhya*) by the knowledge of Brahman. Real may mean absolutely real. But *satya,* according to Madhva, as applied to the world other than Brahman, means *abādhya* (unsublated). He illustrates this point by showing that the world is *prāmāṇika* (given by *pramāṇa*), or *prameya* (being the object of correct knowledge). While Śaṅkara holds that Brahman alone is *abādhya,* Madhva shows that the terms *abādhya* etc. may be applied also to that which is relative, dependent, and non-absolute.

Madhva is prepared to admit that the world is *mithyā* or *sadasad-vilakṣaṇa* in any sense that does not modify that it is *abādhya, prāmāṇika,* and so on. But if *mithyā* means the negation of any of these ideas, if it means or implies something that makes serious thinking impossible, if it means something that makes the world or any part of it void of any ground, or if it means something that makes the ground of the world in any sense incomplete, relative, and dispensable either in thought or in deed, or something that makes it avoidable or dispensable, then he disavows that the world is *mithyā* or *sadasadvilakṣaṇa.* Against these ideas he shows that the world is *satya.*

Whether a thing is spirit or matter, three aspects may be distinguished in it—essence (*svarūpa*), the state of its being an object (*pramiti*), and function (*pravṛtti*). Every entity of the world is dependent in all these aspects. Further, the fact that a thing is real means that it is real in all these aspects. Madhva therefore calls these aspects three cases of *sattā,* existence. He notes that they are dependent in order to show that they are derived. Madhva shows also that if a thing is dependent in any sense, then it is necessarily dependent in every sense in which it may be considered.

The richer and more complex the function of a thing and the greater its causal efficacy, the greater is its relative character, the greater its dependence, and the greater the degree in which it points to the authorship of Brahman. It is on this principle that he fixes the gradation (*tāratamya*) of the entities of the world. The entities that point more to the authorship of Brahman come first in the order of the creation of Brahman.

Whether the world is, in some circumstances or other, recognized to be real, unreal, relative, dependent, independent, eternal, or absolute, it is essentially *paratantra,* dependent, i.e. it has only a derived reality, and its source is Brahman. It is the realization of this idea that brings about release from bondage. For it is this realization that makes one free from illusions. Brahman, the source of all, has essence, objectivity, and function. With reference to every aspect It is independent. Madhva calls the non-confusion or discrimination between the dependent and the independent *bheda* (difference). The dependent is the world. The independent is Brahman. This is the significance of his doctrine of *bheda* (Bhedavāda). He says, *'Tasya bhedaśca sarvataḥ adoṣatvasya siddhyartham'* (It is held that Brahman is distinct from everything else in order to maintain that It is defectless).

Further, to see that the world is dependent is to see that it is the work of the independent. To see further that Brahman is independent is to see that Its work is dependent. Considering finally that the dependent, because it is only derived, is no truth, Madhva insists on seeing that there is after all only one truth, viz. Brahman. The Advaita of the Śruti illustrates the independent character of Brahman. But Advaita, as applied to Śaṅkara's Vedānta system, means non-duality, and it has in view *mithyātva* of the world and *nirguṇatva* of Brahman. Madhva asks the student of Vedānta not to confuse these two ideas.

## CETANA, ACETANA, AND ABHIMĀNINS

Madhva's works on ontological problems are intended to show how Brahman is the only Reality. In one of his works, called *Tattvasaṅkhyāna,* he speaks of two ways of approaching Brahman. He says, *'Svatantram-asvatantrañca dvividhaṁ tattvamiṣyate'* (There are two ways of presenting *tattva* [truth], *svatantra* and *asvatantra*). Though apparently this passage seems to mean that there are two *tattvas,* a reading of the passage in the light of Madhva's own point of view, viz. Brahman as Viṣṇu, reveals a different truth. If *svatantra* means the principle of all, then *paratantra* means *svatantra* in operation.

Madhva comes to the conclusion that in the exposition of Śāstra the words that are ordinarily taken to mean things of the world really present *paramaiśvarya* (supreme lordliness), i.e. *svatantrecchā* (independent will), *līlā* being the overflow of *ānanda* of *ānandamaya,* Viṣṇu. So, the correct way of seeing the world is to see it as the expression of Brahman, as the illustration of *paramaiśvarya* of Brahman. The world consists of spirit (*cetana*) and non-spirit (*acetana*) with their *abhimānins,* beginning with Lakṣmī as the highest, and non-spirit consisting of the Vedas, space, time, Prakṛti, etc. as known by the *pramāṇas, pratyakṣa* and so on.

*Cetana* is that which knows. Knowledge in its highest form is knowledge produced by *Brahma-mīmāṁsā.* From the standpoint of this knowledge Madhva observes three types of *cetana.* (1) That to which this knowledge occurs. Occurrence of this knowledge is indicated by the disposition (*svarūpa*) of the individual *cetana.* This disposition consists of the states hankering after this knowledge, avoiding the circumstances which may lead to non-knowledge after seeing their defects, realizing that the only means for obtaining this knowledge is *Brahma-mīmāṁsā* under a preceptor who is *śrotriya* and *Brahmaniṣṭha,* i.e. who has understood or is devoted to Brahman as *śrutyukta* (considered and expounded only by the Śruti). This *cetana* is called *muktiyogya,* fitted to have *mukti.* (2) That disposition which is opposed to the disposition of the *muktiyogya* makes one *tamoyogya,* fitted to have *tamas,* delusion, destruction. (3) A doubtful disposition makes one *nityasaṁsārin,* fitted to have repeated births and deaths. Madhva holds that this *cetana* finally becomes *tamoyogya.* Madhva's final position is that *cetana* in its true sense is only *muktiyogya.* Brahman as knowledge and bliss forms the principle (*bimba*) of this *cetana.* This is the reason why a *cetana* becomes *muktiyogya.* As Brahman manifests Its *jñāna* and *ānanda* character more and more, the individual *cetana* comes to have more and more *jijñāsā* and with it *vairāgya,* and *Viṣṇubhakti* becomes more and more purified.

To enable an individual to have this knowledge, Viṣṇu has made it an organism consisting of *manas, buddhi, ahaṅkāra,* five *tanmātras* (elements in their rudimentary form), five organs of knowledge (eye, ear, nose, tongue, and skin), and five organs of action (speech, hand, foot, organ of excretion, and organ of generation) with consciousness (*cetana*) added to the rest. In some passages Madhva calls this organism Jīva. To make this organism operate, Viṣṇu gives it a gross body made of five elements (*bhūtas*). This is what we commonly call an individual knower. In this Madhva distinguishes three aspects—gross body, *liṅga* body consisting of the first eighteen items, and *svarūpa* body, consciousness itself. Of them the gross body is observed to come into existence and perish; but *liṅga* survives death and helps the next birth. Process in time and space is endless; but it has a beginning in Viṣṇu in that it is the product of

*Haricchā* (desire of Viṣṇu). Thus, according to Madhva, a beginningless (*anādi*) thing has its origin or beginning in Hari or Viṣṇu.

According to other *darśanas, cetana* is ever in its finished form. For example, Śaṅkara holds that the self is ever Brahman. Bondage is only superimposed on it; but the self is never affected by bondage. Similar is the position of all other *darśanas.* But, according to Madhva, during bondage *cetana* is ever in the making. Brahman as *jñāna* and *ānanda* forms the *svarūpa,* the principle of reality in *cetana.* Madhva calls this *svarūpa-bimba.* For the reason that Brahman as *jñāna* and *ānanda* is *svarūpa* of *cetana, cetana* is characterized by *jñāna* and *ānanda.* As Brahman, by Its independent will (*svatantrecchā*), manifests its *jñāna* and *ānanda, cetana* comes to have them. This means that it grows as *cetana.* When it is thus made an accomplished *cetana* it becomes liberated. Other *darśanas* hold that *ajñāna,* etc. are definitely opposed to the self. But Madhva shows that they are rather the elements that in different ways help the process of the growth of *cetana.* Madhva holds that no stage in this process is the work of the Jīva. The whole process with all its aspects is entirely the work of Viṣṇu.

Madhva distinguishes five kinds of *muktiyogyas—deva, ṛṣi, pitṛ, pā,* and *nara*—god, seer, manes, ruler, and man. To define them as *muktiyogya* signifies that those that are devoid of *Brahma-jijñāsā* do not deserve to be these beings.

*Acetana* is that which does not know. It consists of two aspects, positive and negative—*bhāva* and *abhāva.* The positive is that which is apprehended as existent at the first instant of its apprehension and the negative as non-existent. The positive are the Vedas, space, time, Prakṛti, and its products. The negative are the absence of an entity that precedes its production (*prāgabhāva*), the absence that follows its destruction (*pradhvaṁsābhāva*), and the absence that is always there like the horn of a hare (*atyantābhāva*). Just like *cetana, acetana* also is in every sense the work of Viṣṇu. Viṣṇu as existence (*sat*) is the principle (*bimba*) of every item of *acetana.*

The world of *cetana* and *acetana* is real because of Viṣṇu, because Viṣṇu as *sat* is its *bimba,* principle. That which is unreal is unreal because of *Haricchā* (will of Hari) that it should be so. Thus the unreality of the unreal is a positive property. Viṣṇu is the source of degrees of reality (*tāratamya*) also. *Acetana,* for example, is not as real as *cetana.* This is indicated by the absence of consciousness in *acetana* and its presence in *cetana.*

Madhva holds that every entity, *cetana* or *acetana,* in the world is, with regard to its reality and so on, governed by a supervising deity. He calls this deity *abhimāni-devatā. Abhimāni-devatās* are more real than those they supervise. Of these *devatās,* Vāyu is the *abhimānin* of vital principles and Lakṣmī of all *cetanas,* including Vāyu, as well as all *acetanas.* The author of the gradation of reality is Viṣṇu.

Most of these things are seen to have no beginning and no end in time. Some of them have beginning and end. Some of them have changes in some parts and no change in other parts. Each thing has its own individuality. Each is different from others. Every entity has therefore its place in the system of things. Even illusion has its own place. It has its own function to fulfil. Everything is justified in so far as it is active. Individual effort has its own place in the system of things. It is, in fact, inevitable. Without it an individual has lived in vain. Institutions, cultural, social, political, national, and universal, are the creations of individual efforts.

## BRAHMAN

Madhva notes that to define Brahman as *nirguṇa* (attributeless) or *kalyāṇaguṇa* (of auspicious qualities) has only empirical import. This is the defect of Vivartavāda and Pariṇāmavāda, however subtle they may appear to be. Brahman is *alaukika* (transcendent). As such It is ever doubted. It is therefore the object of never-ending inquiry. Empirical inquiry does not help the knowledge of Brahman. Inquiry is *Brahma-jijñāsā.* It finds out Brahman as the meaning of the Śruti. Without it the Śruti does not teach Brahman. With inquiry the Śruti is found to establish Brahman as the one single principle of creation, existence, destruction, law and order, knowledge and non-knowledge, bondage and release that occur to things, and *cetana* and *acetana* in various manners. Brahman is independent. All else is derived from It. As the maker of all It is in all. It is *bimba,* source. That which It makes is *pratibimba* (reflection), derived. It is different from the latter. The latter is not an illusion ; for, it is the work of Brahman. Brahman as the principle of all is not imagined. It is *śāstra-gamya,* established by *śāstra-jijñāsā.* Śāstra is that the truth of which is self-established. It is 'Veda' found out by means of *jijñāsā.* In this circumstance each word of the Veda has a complete and absolute meaning, viz. Brahman. In this capacity each word is in perfect harmony with the other words ; this is *śrutivākya-samanvaya.* Without this Brahman is not found out. Brahman thus found out is not *gauṇa* (relative). It does not involve dualism (*dvaita*). It is ultimate. Devotion to this Brahman brings about *mokṣa.* It is Ātman as expounded by the Śruti. From It come all names and forms and with them law and order. Its operation in every case is wonderful (*acintya* and *adbhuta*). It originates two orders of the world, *bimba* and *pratibimba. Bimba* is the source of the reality of the *pratibimba* (derived being). *Bimba* is Brahman Itself. It is complete (*guṇapūrṇa*), absolute (*nirdoṣa*), that which is known (*jñeya*), and that which is attained (*gamya*) in the thing. To understand the world as *pratibimba* or *paratantra* is to understand its principle, Brahman. This is to understand that there is no evil, no misery in the world. The world is the expression of the fullness of Brahman. Brahman is thus *ānandamaya,* bliss itself. Every thing becomes dear because of Brahman. To see this truth is to attain *ānanda,* Brahman.

### DISCIPLINE LEADING TO MOKṢA

In illustrating this point Madhva speaks of the fivefold difference (*pañcabheda*): the difference between Jīva and Īśa, the difference between Jīva and Jīva, the difference between *Jaḍa* (an inert body) and Īśa, the difference between *jaḍa* and Jīva, and the difference between *jaḍa* and *jaḍa.* He signifies by this that things must not be confused. Without due attention to these facts, to speak of unity leads nowhere.

Having established that reality is Brahman and *jijñāsā* (philosophy) is the only approach to it, Madhva considers how *jijñāsā* occurs. According to him, *karma* is no discipline ; for it arises from superimposing doership on the individual self that is a non-doer (*paratantra*). *Bhakti* in the usual sense is the negation of *jijñāsā.* Even *dhyāna* (meditation) that is independent of *jijñāsā* is the arrest of the intellect. An individual self is attracted by them when some preconception (*durāgraha*) is working in his mind. *Jijñāsā* occurs only to him who is free from all preconceptions. Madhva calls this freedom *vairāgya.* It is intellectual in character. It consists in realizing that things of the world, including even Lakṣmī, are *anitya* (non-enduring) and *asāra* (essenceless). The result of *vairāgya* is devotion to Viṣṇu. Only to one who has this disposition, *jijñāsā* or *Brahma-mīmāṁsā* occurs. To have this disposition or *jijñāsā* is not the individual's own making. When an individual is seen to have *jijñāsā,* it is an indication that he is having the *prasāda* (grace) of Viṣṇu. *Jijñāsā* is the process of *śravaṇa* (understanding), *manana* (reflection), and *nididhyāsana* (application). It expresses itself in two forms—study (*svādhyāya*) and teaching (*pravacana*). *Pravacana* or teaching is higher. It pleases Viṣṇu (*Viṣṇu-tuṣṭidaḥ*). It is the highest aspect of discipline.

### JĪVANMUKTI AND MUKTI

With *jijñāsā* without a break the truth that is mediately understood to start with, becomes immediately realized. This is called *aparokṣa.* This is the proper stage to teach philosophy, i.e. *Brahma-mīmāṁsā.* This is the state of *jīvanmukti.* At this state the individual is no longer distracted by the things of the world. Distraction is illusion (*pramāda*). It is the cause of bondage. Madhva says that bondage (*bandha*) is *pramādātmaka,* the result of illusion consisting in superimposing *kartṛtva* (doership) on the individual self. But at this stage, i.e. *jīvanmukti,* by means of *jijñāsā* the individual has realized Viṣṇu as the all-doer and himself as completely *paratantra.* He has seen *ekatva,* i.e. the *sarvottama* (supreme) character of Viṣṇu and is free from delusion (*moha*) and misery (*śoka*).

With *pravacana* the individual becomes more and more purified, i.e. the conviction that he is *paratantra* becomes more and more confirmed. This confirmation is the indication of the grace of Viṣṇu. As the result of this grace he finally becomes liberated (*mukta*). At the stage of *mukti* he is consciously living in *svatantra,* i.e. Viṣṇu, the principle of his reality. Viṣṇu is immortal. Therefore the individual has become immortal. Viṣṇu has become the dearest to him. He therefore enjoys the *ānandamaya* character of Viṣṇu. This enjoyment makes him merged in *ānanda* (bliss). The whole thing occurs as the result of the grace of Viṣṇu. Madhva points out that an individual can have only that much of *ānanda* as is consistent with the degree of *jijñāsā* he has at the stage of discipline. So even in *mukti* he speaks of gradation. He sees that gradation is the inevitable implication of the infinite richness of *Brahma-mīmāṁsā,* and as such it is an item of enjoyment on the part of the *mukta.*

The realization of one's self as *paratantra* brings *mukti* to the self. Madhva holds that this is essentially the process of *jijñāsā. Jijñāsā* is the process of Brahman's creative will. It is therefore the process of all aspects of *ānanda.* With *jijñāsā, cetana* becomes one, i.e. in complete harmony with the creative will. This is how it lives in Brahman. This is *Brahma sampatti.* With this, *cetana* sees that the whole process of bondage, discipline, and *mokṣa* with all their circumstances and aspects is the work of Brahman. This is what *Brahma-mīmāṁsā* signifies by defining Brahman as Viṣṇu. To contemplate this constitutes the *mukta's ānanda.*

## CONCLUSION

Madhva has thus in his exposition of *Brahma-mīmāṁsā* brought the monism expounded by the Vedas and the Upaniṣads to its culmination. His position is essentially Brahmavāda. His chief contribution to Indian culture, and, in fact, to world culture, consists in the following. He showed that philosophy is the only kind of spiritual discipline. He found out that the Śruti is not a mere verbal testimony but the expression of pure philosophy. He discovered that *Brahma-mīmāṁsā* is the highest form of philosophical thinking. He found out that the real cause of *bandha* (bondage) is superimposition of doership on the individual selves. He realized that man is really a doer only when he understands that he is *paratantra.* He saw that the only way of appreciating the highest truth as the only truth is the recognition of the reality and actuality of the world in a healthy sense. He showed that the highest truth must necessarily be absolutely complete with reference to every aspect of it (*guṇapūrṇa*), free from every kind of dependence (*nirdoṣa*), the real object in every object (*jñeya*), the goal of every endeavour (*gamya*), and the source of knowledge as such (*guru*). For this reason he calls this truth Nārāyaṇa ; and he makes it clear that an individual can have peace only when he has realized this truth. Not to realize this truth is to confuse it with the world and consequently to have misery and delusion (*śoka* and *moha*). This realization is possible only by an enduring process of study and teaching of philosophy, i.e. *Brahma-mīmāṁsā.* He emphasized that political, national, and social reconstruction in terms of this study only is the salvation of mankind. He showed that the very contemplation of these truths is the source of joy (*ānanda*). As the expounder of this Śāstra which leads to *ānanda,* he is called Ānanda Tīrtha.

# 18

## THE NIMBĀRKA SCHOOL OF VEDĀNTA

NIMBĀRKA, who was one of the five principal commentators on the *Brahma-Sūtra* of Bādarāyaṇa and the first systematic propounder of one of the five main schools of the Vedānta, was a Tailaṅga Brāhmaṇa. He is generally supposed to have flourished after Rāmānuja, in the eleventh century A.D., though no definite evidence is available on this point. He wrote a short commentary on the *Brahma-Sūtra,* entitled *Vedānta-pārijāta-saurabha* (the odour of the heavenly flower of the Vedānta). This commentary is very condensed and written in simple language. Its peculiarity is that the author makes no attempt whatsoever to refute the theory of any other commentator on the *Brahma-Sūtra,* such as Śaṅkara and others, or even, for the matter of that, to expound his own theories by means of appropriate arguments. In fact, it is doubtful whether his views would have been fully clear to readers but for the excellent commentary *Vedānta-kaustubha* on the *Brahma-Sūtra* by his immediate disciple Śrīnivāsa. Nimbārka was also the author of a small work of ten stanzas, called *Daśa-ślokī,* dealing with the three realities (*tri-tattva*)—Brahman (Kṛṣṇa), soul (*cit*), and matter (*acit*). It also is not properly intelligible without commentaries. Besides these, Nimbārka composed several other works, some of which are no longer extant.

### BRAHMAN

Like other Vedāntins, Nimbārka calls the highest Reality Brahman, literally meaning the greatest Being—one who is unsurpassedly great in nature and qualities—beyond any limit whatsoever. To Nimbārka, Brahman is a personal God, and not the impersonal Absolute of Śaṅkara. Nimbārka calls Him Kṛṣṇa or Hari. But while to other Vaiṣṇava Vedāntins, like Rāmānuja and Madhva, Brahman is Nārāyaṇa or Viṣṇu, to Nimbārka, as to Vallabha, He is Gopālakṛṣṇa (Cowherd Kṛṣṇa), accompanied by Rādhā.

Brahman is eternal, independent, omnipresent, omnipotent, and omniscient. He is the sole cause of the entire universe, but is without cause. He alone creates, maintains, and destroys the world of souls and matter. Brahman is thus both the material (*upādāna*) and the efficient (*nimitta*) cause of the world. Ordinarily the material and efficient causes are different from each other, e.g. the lump of clay is the material, and the potter with his instruments the efficient, cause of a clay jar. But in the case of world creation the two are one and the same, viz. the one Brahman, the omnipresent Being. The scripture (*Chā. U.*, VI.2.3) tells us that the universal Self, wishing to be many, transforms Himself into the form of the world. Thus, in so far as He transforms *Himself* into the world, He is the material cause; and in so far as He *transforms* Himself as such, He is the efficient cause of the world. Nimbārka himself does not explain clearly in what precise sense Brahman is both the material cause and the efficient cause of the world, seeing that Prakṛti, the primal matter, is ordinarily said to be the cause of all material objects. This has been clearly explained by Puruṣottama in his famous work *Vedānta-ratna-mañjūṣā*. He points out there that Brahman is the material cause of the universe in the sense that creation means the manifestation of His subtle powers of sentience (*cit*) and non-sentience (*acit*) in the form of gross effects. That is, during dissolution (*pralaya*), the entire universe of the sentient and the non-sentient returns to and remains in Him in a subtle state as His natural powers. Then, at the beginning of creation, Brahman manifests these powers (*cit-śakti* and *acit-śakti*) in the form of souls and Prakṛti; and from this Prakṛti, the primal matter, there is the gradual evolution of the entire material world.

Now, it may be asked here, how Brahman, who is entirely non-material (*ajaḍa*), can still possess an element of materiality (*jaḍatva*) or have non-sentience as one of His powers (*acit-śakti*). But there is nothing inconsistent or absurd here, if we properly understand the real implication of the Vedānta doctrine of *śakti*.

The sentient and the non-sentient (*cit* and *acit*) are among the numerous powers or *śaktis* of Brahman, and a power does not affect the real nature (*svarūpa*) of the thing possessing that power, e.g. fire has the power to produce smoke, but is not itself smoky. In the same manner, Brahman has the power to produce the non-sentient world, yet is not Himself non-sentient. Moreover, a power cannot vitiate or affect the thing itself. So the non-sentient world does not make Brahman imperfect when it returns to Him during dissolution (*pralaya*), for it surely does not return to Him in its gross, imperfect form, but simply inheres in Him as His subtle power. Again, Brahman is the efficient cause of the universe in the sense of transforming Himself into the form of the universe, there being no other external agent to fashion the world. And this act of transforming Himself, as explained by Puruṣottama, means to unite the souls, so long merged in Him, as His subtle power of sentience (*cit-śakti*), with their respective *karmas* and the instruments for experiencing them. In other words, He creates the world according to the past *karmas* of the individuals and thereby regulates the destiny of the souls according to strict justice.

Nimbārka succinctly refutes several objections against this doctrine of the causality of Brahman, and in this connection propounds the famous Vedānta doctrine of *līlā* or creation in sport, which, if rightly understood, is one of the best solutions ever offered of that very difficult philosophical problem of the why or the motive of creation.

Brahman is the creator, sustainer, and destroyer of the world. But He is not an external creator like the potter of the pot, but, being also its material cause, as stated above, is immanent in it, like clay in the pot. But He, the infinite Being, cannot be exhausted in a single universe. He pervades the universe, yet transcends it. Thus, Brahman is both transcendent and immanent, and, as such, the inner soul and essence of the world.

Thus, on the one hand, Brahman is the greatest of the great, high above the individual soul, the creator and controller of the world, its lord and ruler. But, on the other hand, He is the abode of infinite beauty, bliss, and tenderness, and is in sweet, intimate, and personal relation with the individual soul. He is essentially gracious to devotees and helps the deserving ones to attain salvation by enabling them to have a direct vision of Himself (*sākṣātkāra*). He also incarnates Himself on earth for their guidance.

Hence Brahman has two aspects—the majestic and the sweet. He is all-powerful yet all-merciful, transcendent yet immanent, all-pervading yet residing within the heart of man, a stern judge yet a gracious friend.

Brahman is thus essentially possessed of attributes (*saguṇa*). He is the abode of an infinite number of auspicious qualities, which, as we have seen, are broadly of two kinds, supreme majesty, omniscience, omnipotence, and omnipresence on the one hand; infinite beauty, bliss, love, and purity on the other. Sometimes, however, Brahman is also described as attributeless (*nirguṇa*). But this simply means that He is free from all inauspicious attributes as found in the world. It may be asked here, How can Brahman, the omnipresent Being, avoid having bad, worldly attributes as well, seeing that everything must exist in Him? As stated above, during dissolution (*pralaya*), the world exists in Brahman, not as it really is, but as a mere *śakti* or power. But during creation and the later period of subsistence (*sṛṣṭi* and *sthiti*) the world, with all its grossness and imperfection, must inhere and subsist in the same all-pervading Lord as part, element, or attribute. Hence Brahman must possess these infinitely bad qualities of the world, together with His supremely excellent ones. In fact, whatever is, is God—so evils and imperfections, too, must be in Him in the same way as virtues and perfections are. This fundamental problem of the relation between the all-good God and the undeniable evils of the world has not been tackled separately by Nimbārka. But this does not present any formidable difficulty, if we understand the real meaning of the Vedānta doctrine of the omnipresence of Brahman and the consequent relativity of evil. What are parts or elements from their narrow partial standpoint are not so from the standpoint of the whole. Thus, evils are evils only from the narrow human standpoint, but never from the standpoint of the all-pervading unity of the Absolute. Evils are thus relative—though not unreal, they are yet not absolutely real. It is, we think, to emphasize this transmutation of the separate imperfections of the parts in the whole that the Vaiṣṇava Vedāntins repeatedly emphasize the *nirguṇatva* of Brahman (of course, in a sense absolutely different from that of the Advaita Vedāntins). Brahman is all-pervading, yet *nirguṇa* or free from all ordinary material, unworthy, inauspicious qualities, because evils as evils lose their essence in Him. It may, of course, be asked here, Why is it only evil, and not good also, that loses its distinctive nature in God? The reply is that while evil is only relatively real, good is absolutely so. So, in the Absolute, it is evil that is dissolved, while good persists.

### CIT: THE JĪVA

The Jīva or the individual soul, according to Nimbārka, is essentially of the nature of intelligence (*jñāna-svarūpa*), and, as such, wholly non-material (*ajaḍa*). Hence it has to be carefully distinguished from the body, the sense-organs, the vital breaths, the mind, and *buddhi,* which are all material and non-sentient. Thus, the eleven organs (five external sense-organs, five organs of action, and mind, the inner organ) and the five vital breaths are but the instruments through which the sentient and non-material soul perceives, acts, and enjoys, and which are guided by it.

But the soul, according to Nimbārka, is not only knowledge, intelligence, or consciousness in essence (*jñāna-svarūpa*), but also a knower, i.e. an intelligent or conscious being (*jñātṛ* or *jñātṛtva-dharma-vat*) or, in other words, it is both knowledge in *essence* and has knowledge as its *attribute.* This, however, sounds rather self-contradictory. How can the same thing viz. knowledge or consciousness, be both the *essence* and the *attribute* of the very same soul? But really this insistence of the Vaiṣṇava Vedāntins on knowledge being both the *essence* and the *attribute* of the soul at the same time is neither without meaning nor self-contradictory. Inasmuch as either of these two alternatives by itself would present a difficulty, both must be taken to be true at the same time. Thus, if consciousness be only the *essence* of the soul, and nothing else be needed for its knowledge or consciousness, then the soul must know, from the very beginning, what it will know throughout its entire existence; and there cannot be, later on, any appearance or disappearance, increase or decrease thereof. But we know that this is an absurdity; for we are originally ignorant of a thing, then we gain knowledge about it; we have at first no perception of a thing, then we come to perceive it; we, again, have knowledge of a thing and then it ceases: we perceive a thing, then our perception ceases; our knowledge also increases or decreases: our perception becomes fuller or more perfect, or just the reverse. All these are facts of experience and cannot be denied. So, they prove definitely that something else is needed to explain such appearance and disappearance, increase and decrease, of knowledge in the soul. In other words, over and above being *consciousness in essence* passively, the soul is also a *conscious knower* actively, i.e. it possesses the *attribute of consciousness* which appears or disappears, increases or decreases, with regard to particular things according to circumstances. But it may be asked here, Why, then, insist on calling the soul *consciousness in essence* as well, instead of taking consciousness as its *attribute* only, which, as shown above, so very well explains the fact of its knowing and non-knowing, or its increase or decrease in knowledge? The answer is that this, too, will lead to another difficulty; for, if consciousness or knowledge be only an *attribute* of the soul and not also its *essence,* then, there being always a distinction between substance and attribute, the soul practically ceases to have consciousness as its *nature* and the distinction between the soul and a material object becomes one of *attributes* only, instead of being, as it fundamentally is, one of *essence* mainly. In fact, it is absurd to maintain that the soul is not consciousness in *essence,* that, in other words, it is a gross non-conscious material object, but has only the *attribute* of consciousness. So we have to admit that the individual soul is *both* knowledge *and* a knower; or, in other words, that knowledge is both the *essence* and the *attribute* of the soul. Consciousness being the *essence* and the *attribute* of the soul, it always remains a conscious knower even during the states of deep sleep (*suṣupti*) and salvation, in which latter case it is omniscient.

The individual, being a knower (*jñātṛ*), is also an active agent (*kartṛ*). All the scriptural injunctions presuppose the soul to be an agent. Further, it is the soul that controls the body and the organs, as stated above. This also proves the soul to be an active agent. The soul is an agent not only during its state of bondage, but also when it is free. Then its power to realize all desires and to move about at will is fully manifested.

The individual soul is an enjoyer (*bhoktṛ*) too. This is a necessary logical corollary of the above. For, if the soul be an active agent, a doer of *karmas,* it must also be an enjoyer, the reaper of the fruits thereof, good or bad. The soul is an enjoyer not only during its state of bondage in the world, but also when it gets rid of all *karmas* and becomes free. Of course, the freed soul does not experience the fruits of *karmas* like the soul in bondage, and its enjoyment does not lead to rebirths. But its enjoyment consists in being a co-sharer in the infinite bliss of Brahman.

Still, the soul is not an independent being, but essentially dependent on the Lord for existence, knowledge, activity, and enjoyment. Even when the soul is free, it remains wholly under the control of Brahman.

Thus, as regards its *nature,* the individual soul is knowledge in essence, and a knower, a doer, an enjoyer, dependent on God, and eternal.

Next, the *size* of the soul. It is atomic in size, as proved by the fact that the soul is said to pass out of the body through such small openings as the eye etc. But although the soul itself is atomic, its attribute of knowledge pervades the whole body; and that is why it is capable of experiencing the various states of the body, just as a small lamp in a corner can flood the entire room with its pervasive rays. Here, Nimbārka, in his usual succinct manner, takes pains to refute the doctrine of the all-pervasiveness of the soul. This would entail, he points out, either eternal perception or eternal non-perception on the part of the soul; for the all-pervasive soul must always be in connection with all objects and know them eternally; or, if it be not somehow in connection with them, there is nothing outside it to bring about such a connection.

Next, the *number* of souls. According to Nimbārka, there is an infinite number of souls, and it would be wrong to identify all these numerous souls with one another or with Brahman.

Finally, the *kinds* of souls. There are, broadly speaking, two kinds of souls, viz. souls in bondage and freed souls. The former are associated with material bodies and are subject to births and rebirths according to their own *karmas.* The latter get rid of all connection with *karmas* and *matter* and are thereby freed from mundane existence.

We may now briefly consider the different *states* of the soul in bondage. Such a soul has five different states, viz. waking, dream, deep sleep, swoon, and death. The state of waking has been considered above—then, the soul is a knower, a doer, and an enjoyer. During the states of dream and deep sleep, too, it remains a knower and an enjoyer, knowing and enjoying various dream objects created by the Lord. During the state of deep, dreamless sleep, too, the soul is a knower and an enjoyer, though, naturally, its knowledge and enjoyment remain more or less unmanifest then. The state of swoon is halfway between sleep and death, not identical with either of them. Finally, the state of death. Of this there are two kinds—that which leads to rebirth, and that which leads to liberation.

We may also refer briefly to the different *destinies* of the soul, viz.

heaven, hell, and salvation. There are, broadly speaking, two classes of souls in bondage: doers (*karmin*) and knowers (*jñānin*). The former, again, are of two kinds: pious workers and sinners. These three kinds of souls (pious workers, sinners, and knowers) undergo different destinies, attaining different ends through different paths. Thus, knowers go to the world of Brahman through the path of the gods (*devayāna*), not to return any more; pious workers go to the world of the moon (heaven) through the path of the fathers (*pitṛyāna*) to return to earth, according to their *karmas,* as higher forms of animals like men, cats, dogs, etc.; sinners go to the 'third place' (hell) to return to earth as the lowest forms of life like worms, snails, etc.

### ACIT: THE NON-SENTIENT

According to Nimbārka, *acit* is of three kinds: *prākṛta* or what is derived from Prakṛti, the primal matter, *aprākṛta* or what is not derived from Prakṛti, and *kāla* or time.

Prakṛti here is conceived to be just like the Sāṁkhya Prakṛti, the only difference being that it is taken to be wholly dependent on and under the control of the Lord, and not independent and self-sufficient like the Sāṁkhya Prakṛti.

Nimbārka himself does not tell us what precisely are the *aprākṛta* and *kāla.* But we get very good accounts of these in the *Vedanta-ratna-mañjūṣā* of Puruṣottama. He points out that just as Prakṛti is the stuff of the mundane world, so what is *aprākṛta* is the stuff of the celestial bodies, ornaments, and other objects of enjoyment, and also the regions of the Lord and the freed souls. *Kāla* is eternal and all-pervasive, the basic principle of the entire cosmic existence. But though the regulator and controller of everything, it itself is wholly under the control of the Lord.

### BRAHMAN, CIT, AND ACIT—THEIR RELATIONSHIPS

Thus, according to Nimbārka, there are three equally real and co-eternal entities: Brahman, *cit* (the sentient), and *acit* (the non-sentient). Brahman is the controller (*niyantṛ*), *cit* the enjoyer (*bhoktṛ*), and *acit* the object enjoyed (*bhogya*). The question is, What exactly is the relation between these three realities? In the first place, there is a real difference between Brahman on the one hand, and *cit* and *acit* on the other. Thus, Brahman is the cause, the soul an effect; Brahman is the whole, the soul a part; Brahman is the object to be worshipped, the soul the worshipper; Brahman is the object to be known, the soul the knower; Brahman is the object to be attained, the soul the attainer—and there is always a distinction between the cause and the effect, the whole and the part, the worshipped and the worshipper, the known and the knower, and the attained and the attainer. Again, Brahman is the inner controller, and dwells within the heart of the soul ; and the controller and the controlled, the dweller and the place dwelt in, are of necessity different. Further, Brahman is omniscient, omnipresent, and omnipotent, possessing the powers of creation, maintenance, and destruction of the universe, but the soul is infinitely small and does not possess these powers of creation etc., and further, it is wholly dependent on Brahman. Even the freed soul, which is similar to Brahman in other respects, differs from Him in the last two points. That is, it is neither omnipresent (being atomic in size) nor omnipotent (lacking the powers of creation etc. and being absolutely under the control of Brahman).

There are even more fundamental differences between Brahman and the universe. Brahman is the cause, the universe His effect. He is the whole, it is a part ; He is sentient, non-gross, non-material, ever pure ; the world is just the opposite. Hence the two must be different. Thus, there is an eternal, natural, and undeniable difference (*svābhāvika-bheda*) between Brahman on the one hand, and soul and matter on the other.

Yet just as this difference between Brahman and the other two realities is true, the non-difference between them is no less true. The souls and the world are effects of Brahman, and as such are different from Him, as pointed out above ; but they are also non-different from Him none the less for the same reason. The fact is that the cause and the effect, the part and the whole, are neither absolutely different nor absolutely non-different, but are both different and non-different. In essence the effect is the cause itself—so far it is identical with the cause ; yet the effect has its own peculiar form, attributes, and functions—so far it is different from the cause. The clay jar, the effect, is non-different from clay, the cause, for it is, after all, nothing but clay through and through. Yet it is also different from a mere lump of clay in form, attributes, and functions. The same is true of the relation between the whole and its part. The whole is immanent in a part—so far the part is identical with the whole ; yet the whole transcends the part—so far the part is different from the whole. Thus, the relation between Brahman on the one hand, and souls and matter on the other, is a relation of natural difference-non-difference. Hence Nimbārka's doctrine is called Svābhāvika-bhedābhedavāda.

### MOKṢA OR SALVATION

*Mokṣa* or salvation means realizing our essential similarity with the Lord. When the soul in bondage attains a direct vision of the Lord, it attains His nature and most of His attributes, and this is freedom from the cycle of births and rebirths and the consequent, infinitely miserable, mundane existence.

But such an attainment of the nature of Brahman (*tadbhāvāpatti* or *Brahma-svarūpa-lābha*) is only one element in *mokṣa*. The other equally important element is the attainment of one's own real and essential nature (*ātma-svarūpa-lābha*). The difference between Brahman and the soul, being natural and eternal, persists always—not only during the soul's state of bondage, but also during the state of release. Thus, the freed soul, too, like the soul in bondage, is both different and non-different from the Lord. Hence salvation does not imply any identity of God and soul, any annihilation of the individuality or personality of the soul. On the contrary, it means the full development of its real nature or personality. This implies the full manifestation of its real *nature* or *essence* as consciousness or intelligence through and through as well as of its real *attributes* of 'freedom from sins' (*Chā. U.*, VIII.1.5) and the rest. During its state of bondage, when the soul is associated with a material body, both its real *nature* and *attributes* are hidden, like the rays of a lamp inside a pot. Then, instead of being consciousness (*jñāna-svarūpa*) through and through and omniscient, it becomes subject to ignorance, delusion, and the like, and instead of being free from sins, it comes to be affected by all sorts of defects and impurities, and is subject to decay, death, and rebirth. But, when during the state of salvation, it becomes eternally free from matter, its true self shines forth in all its pristine glory.

Attaining the nature of Brahman means, as pointed out above, becoming *similar to* and never *identical with* Brahman. Similarity means neither absolute identity nor absolute difference, but *identity-in-difference*. The identity or non-difference between Brahman and the freed soul consists in the following points: first, as pointed out above, the freed soul attains the nature and attributes of the Lord. Thus, it is, like God, pure consciousness, bliss, and existence in essence (*saccidānanda-svarūpa*). Again, in attributes, like God, it is sinless, ageless, deathless, painless, free from hunger, free from thirst, capable of realizing all its desires, and capable of fulfilling all its resolutions (*Chā. U.*, VIII.1.5). It shares the bliss and enjoyments of Brahman, and is self-ruling, not under the control of any one except that of the Lord. Again, the difference between Brahman and the freed soul consists in the following points: first, even the freed soul is atomic or infinitely small in size, while Brahman is all-pervasive. Secondly, Brahman alone, and not even the freed soul, possesses the power of creating, maintaining, and destroying the world. Thirdly, Brahman is absolutely independent, but even the freed soul is under the control of the Lord, though not of any one else. The freed soul is identical with Brahman except in these points.

Thus, according to Nimbārka, salvation is a positive state of supreme self-development—of infinite knowledge and bliss; it is not a mere negative state of unconsciousness (as held by the Nyāya school) nor an absence of pain without the presence of bliss (as held by the Sāṁkhya school). Nimbārka, however, does not believe in *jīvanmukti* or salvation here and now, in the present physical world, while possessing a material body. He points out that after all is said and done, the essential nature and attributes of the soul cannot but remain veiled and obstructed so long as the body is there to affect them. For example, the soul's supreme knowledge and powers cannot in any way be manifested so long as it continues to possess a physical body; for then it has to know through the help of the mind and the sense-organs and act through the organs of action, and as the powers of all these organs are limited, the knowledge and powers of the soul itself become limited to that extent. Hence the real nature and attributes of the soul can be fully manifested only after death, only when it permanently gets rid of all connection with the physical body and the physical world. Thus, Nimbārka supports the doctrine of *videhamukti* or salvation after death.

### ETHICS: THE SĀDHANĀS

There are five *sādhanās,* or means to salvation, according to Nimbārka, viz. *karma* or work, *jñāna* or knowledge, *upāsanā* or meditation, *prapatti* or self-surrender to God, and *gurūpasatti* or devotion to the spiritual preceptor.

(1) *Karma,* according to Nimbārka, is not a direct means to salvation. When performed in a *niṣkāma* or selfless spirit, in accordance with the injunctions of the scriptures, it purifies the mind and thereby leads to the rise of knowledge, which leads to salvation.

(2) Salvation can be attained only through the right kind of knowledge regarding reality, i.e. Brahman and the self. Knowledge is not subsidiary to *karma,* yet *karma,* as pointed out above, prepares the mind for the ultimate rise of knowledge. Thus, first, the proper performance of the religious duties incumbent on one's stage of life (*āśrama-dharma*), performed not for any selfish gain (*sakāma*) but in an altogether disinterested spirit, purifies the mind and thereby expedites the rise of knowledge. Secondly, not only the external performance of sacrifices, but also the internal control of the senses is incumbent on one who desires knowledge and salvation. Further, the seeker after salvation should also possess the essential qualities of deep learning, childlike simplicity, unostentatiousness, profound thoughtfulness, and the gift of silence.

(3) *Upāsanā* or meditation is another essential means to salvation. There are, broadly speaking, three kinds of meditation, viz. (i) meditation on Brahman as one's own self, i.e. as the inner controller of the sentient; (ii) meditation on Brahman as the inner controller of the non-sentient; (iii) meditation on Brahman as different from the sentient and the non-sentient. According to Rāmānuja, *upāsanā* and *bhakti* are identical. But according to Nimbārka, *bhakti* is not a synonym of *upāsanā,* but implies a special kind of deep love for God.

(4) *Prapatti,* too, is taken by Nimbārka to be a special *sādhanā* or means to salvation. It means complete self-surrender or resignation to God. One who resorts to this means has to give up his narrow individuality and be dependent on Him alone in every respect. Then God will Himself lead him to salvation and eternal bliss. But it would be wrong to think that this kind of self-surrender means complete inactivity on the part of the devotee, for he has to exert himself to do what is liked by God and avoid what is disliked by Him. Then alone will he be favoured and helped by God. That is why *prapatti* has six factors, viz. goodwill towards all, absence of ill-will, faith in the protection of God, acceptance of God as saviour, a feeling of helplessness, and self-surrender to God. Thus love of God means love of mankind no less; and self-surrender to Him means ceaseless effort to follow the right path.

(5) *Gurūpasatti* or self-surrender to the spiritual preceptor, and not directly to God, is also taken by Nimbārka to be a separate *sādhanā.* Here, the *guru* will lead the devotee to God, and whatever is necessary for salvation is done for the devotee by the *guru,* just as the mother of a suckling child who is ill, herself takes medicine for curing her child.

Thus, Nimbārka speaks of five *sādhanās* or means to salvation. They all lead to salvation, either separately or jointly, and are to be resorted to by men of different castes, stages of life, inclinations, and capacities. The upper three castes are entitled to follow any of these, the fourth caste can pursue the last two only. Again, those who are confident of attaining salvation by their own efforts resort to the paths of work, knowledge, and meditation; those who are not, to those of self-surrender to God and self-surrender to the spiritual preceptor.

## THEOLOGY

In Nimbārka, the Absolute of philosophy and the God of religion merge into one; and the Being who satisfies the intellect as the only logical explanation of the world system and as One in whom all apparent contradictions are dissolved, also inspires the heart to direct its inborn feelings of love and devotion to Him as their only repository. The eternal relation between man and God, according to Nimbārka, is that between the worshipper and the worshipped. Even the freed soul, as we have seen, is different-non-different from Brahman, and is His worshipper and servant. But this relation is not one of fear and compulsion, but one of sweet intimacy, love, spontaneous devotion, and self-surrender. To emphasize this sweet personal relation between man and God, Nimbārka describes God as Gopālakṛṣṇa, accompanied by Rādhā and the *gopīs*, and engaged in play with them. Thus, Nimbārka is a prominent propounder of the Rādhā-Kṛṣṇa cult, one of the most popular and influential cults that ever flourished in India, which even today claims millions of adherents all over the country.

## AN ESTIMATE

Such, in brief, is the Svābhāvika-bhedābheda doctrine of Nimbārka. One of the fundamental problems of philosophy is the relation between the one and the many, unity and plurality, God and the world; and many different views have been advanced on this point. On the one hand, there is the strict monistic system or Advaitavāda of Śaṅkara which completely identifies the one and the many, i.e. asserts the one only and denies the many. On the other hand, there is the strict dualistic system or Dvaitavāda of Madhva which completely differentiates the one from the many, God from the world. In between these two, there are various types of theories which recognize both difference and non-difference between the one and the many and try to reconcile them. Here Nimbārka tries to solve this difficult problem in a new way of his own by accepting both difference and non-difference between God and the universe as equally natural and perfectly compatible.

The problems of the *why* and *how* of creation will, perhaps, never be satisfactorily solved. Thus, first, *why* should God, the all-perfect, ever-satisfied, self-sufficient Being, create another, the world? For all actions—and creation is an action—are due to some want, imperfection or unfulfilled desire. Here Nimbārka points out that creation is due not to any want on God's part, but to mere sport (*līlā*), arising out of the fullness of His bliss, perfection, and satisfaction. A person indulges in sport not because he is unhappy and dissatisfied, lacking something he wants to possess, but because he is perfectly happy and contented, and this happiness spontaneously expresses itself in play. Such is the case with the cosmic sport of the Lord. But this cosmic sport, though purposeless from the point of view of Brahman, is not so from the standpoint of the individual souls (Jīvas), as for them it serves a moral purpose. It is regulated by the law of Karma, the demand of justice, so that the universe created by God in sport is also created according to the *karmas* of the souls.

Secondly, in explaining the relation between God and the world, so created, Nimbārka brings in the analogy of the *cause-effect* relation. This *cause-effect* relation, according to Nimbārka, is a relation of *identity-in-difference*. Thus, the effect is *different* from the cause, because it has a peculiar individuality (i.e. special attributes and functions) of its own. Again, the effect is *non-different* from the cause, because it is but a transformation, a modification, of the cause, and is in essence nothing but the cause. The cause, on its side, is *different* from the effect, because the effect is not the whole of it, and it has a peculiar nature of its own that is not fully exhausted in the effect. Again, the cause is *non-different* from the effect, because it *is* the effect, so far as it goes. In the very same manner, Brahman, the cause, and the universe, the effect, are both different and non-different from each other. Brahman is *different* from the universe, because He is transcendent to it ; Brahman is *non-different* from the universe, because He is immanent in it. Thus, if we take difference and non-difference in this sense of transcendence and immanence, no contradiction is involved if we take both difference and non-difference to be equally and simultaneously true.

From the point of view of religion, too, Nimbārka's system has much to commend itself, emphasizing, as it does, a personal relation of love and friendship between God and man. While Rāmānuja emphasizes *aiśvarya-pradhānā bhakti* or a distant relation of awe and reverence, Nimbārka extols *mādhurya-pradhānā bhakti* or an intimate relation of love and friendship. Although religion begins in awe and reverence, it ends in love and most intimate fellowship. In this sense, Nimbārka has given us the last word, the inner core, the real essence of religion.

From the ethical point of view also, the system of Nimbārka manifests a commendable spirit of broad-mindedness and rationality. Nimbārka emphasizes not only the external performance of religious rites and rituals, but also, equally, the inner cultivation of the supreme qualities of self-control, purity, simplicity, and the like. He is of opinion that one need not give up the world to attain salvation. Even a householder, in the midst of his thousand and one mundane duties, can realize Brahman provided he performs them in a disinterested spirit. According to Nimbārka, it is the *spirit* with which one does one's duties that counts. Anyone who performs his duties in an unselfish spirit attains salvation, whether he is a householder or an ascetic.

Thus, the doctrine of Nimbārka has much to commend itself from the points of view of philosophy, religion, and ethics. Its most distinctive feature is that it strikes a happy balance between the rigid intellectualism of Advaitism and the effusive emotionalism of later dualistic schools.

After Nimbārka and Madhva, non-Advaitic Vedānta gradually reduces itself into an emotional form of religion. This kind of emotionalism cannot long sustain a rational mind; for sheer emotion is not sustainable for any length of time and soon tires the person. On the other hand, the over-dry intellectualism of philosophy, with no place for a personal religion, may be awe-inspiring, but it depresses the devotee, who desires to relax in a simpler and softer feeling of personal relationship. It is here that Nimbārka does the greatest service to mankind by pointing to a path which satisfies both intellect and feeling, head and heart, without over-emphasizing the one at the expense of the other.

ŚRĪ VALLABHĀCĀRYA
*Courtesy : G. H. Bhatt*

# 19

## THE SCHOOL OF VALLABHA

### INTRODUCTORY

THERE were several schools of the Vedāntic thought before Śaṅkarācārya (A.D. 788-820), and attempts have been made by scholars[1] to collect materials that might throw light on these pre-Śaṅkara systems. It is, however, not possible to get a systematic account of their views, and consequently the history of the Vedānta really begins with the system of Śaṅkarācārya. The earliest known critic of Śaṅkarācārya is Bhāskara (ninth century) who strongly attacks his doctrine of Māyā. Later on, a host of critics of Śaṅkara, such as Rāmānuja, Nimbārka, Madhva, and Vallabha, appeared one after another. These thinkers, who happened to be followers of the Bhāgavata school, could not accept Śaṅkara's interpretation of the basic texts, namely, the Upaniṣads, the *Gītā,* and the *Brahma-Sūtra,* and offered their own interpretations, thereby enriching the literature on the Vedānta. Moreover, the abstract philosophical speculations of Śaṅkara could not naturally make much appeal to the masses, who found sufficient spiritual food in the *bhakti* (devotion) schools of Rāmānuja and others. In other words, *jñāna* (knowledge) lost its previous hold and made room for *bhakti* which had been progressively gaining in strength.

### ŚUDDHĀDVAITA AND PUṢṬI-MĀRGA

Vallabhācārya (A.D. 1473-1531), a Tailaṅga Brāhmaṇa of South India, was born in a family with leanings towards Vedic rituals and the worship of Gopālakṛṣṇa. He made more than one extensive tour in India and came in contact with leaders of other religious schools. He showed exceptional ability in philosophical disquisitions, won the title of an *ācārya* (teacher) in the court of Vijayanagara, and found a good following in all communities. He spent most of his life in places like Banaras and Adel (about two miles from Allahabad), where he carried on his literary and religious activities. He tells us that, under the command of the Lord

[1] Mm. Kuppuswami Sastri, 'Ācārya Sundara Pāṇḍya', *Journal of Oriental Research,* Madras, I.5; 'Bodhāyana and Dramiḍācārya', *Proceedings of the Third All-India Oriental Conference,* p. 465. Prof. M. Hiriyanna, 'Bhartṛprapañca', *Indian Antiquary,* June, 1924, p. 77; *Proceedings of the Third All-India Oriental Conference,* p. 439; 'Brahmadatta', *Proceedings of the Fourth All-India Oriental Conference,* p. 787. Mm. Dr. P. V. Kane, 'Vedānta Commentators before Śaṅkarācārya', *Proceedings of the Fifth All-India Oriental Conference,* pp. 937-953. Mm. Vidhusekhara Bhattacharya, *'The Āgama-Śāstra of Gauḍapāda',* Introduction, pp. 103-113.

Kṛṣṇa, he devoted himself to the task of faithfully interpreting sacred texts, such as the Upaniṣads, the *Gītā,* and the *Brahma-Sūtra,* which had been misrepresented by Śaṅkara.[2] Vallabha has tried to show that these basic works teach beyond doubt the doctrine of Advaita (non-dualism), pure and simple, without any reference to what is called Māyā by Śaṅkara. The Advaita of the Upaniṣads is thus *śuddha* (pure), unalloyed with Māyā, both the cause and the effect being pure and one. Vallabha's system is therefore known from the philosophical point of view as Śuddhādvaita (pure non-dualism).[3] As the system, again, strongly emphasizes *puṣṭi* (divine grace) as the most powerful and unfailing means of enjoying the highest bliss, it is also known from the religious point of view as Puṣṭi-mārga (the path of divine grace).

### FOUR BASIC WORKS

Vallabha accepted four basic works as authority: (1) the Vedas, (2) the *Bhagavad-Gītā,* (3) the *Brahma-Sūtra,* and (4) the *Bhāgavata.* The order of these works, we are told, is most logical, as the doubts in each preceding work are removed by the one that follows. The doubts in the Vedas are therefore to be removed in the light of the *Gītā* ; those in the *Gītā* in the light of the *Brahma-Sūtra* ; and those in the *Brahma-Sūtra* in the light of the *Bhāgavata,* which has been aptly described as the ripe fruit of the wish-fulfilling tree, namely, the Vedas which have their root in the *Gāyatrī* verse (*R.V.*, III.62.10). The Upaniṣads and the *Brahma-Sūtra* may be classed together ; while the *Gītā* and the *Bhāgavata* form another group. Just as the *Brahma-Sūtra* is, in a way, a commentary on the Upaniṣads, the *Bhāgavata* is to be considered a commentary on the *Gītā.* But though these texts are arranged in two different groups, they are at the same time considered to be interconnected ; and attempts have been made to show how the *Bhāgavata* really explains and develops all the points of the *Brahma-Sūtra.*[4] In fact, every *sūtra* of the latter finds an exact and detailed parallel in the *Bhāgavata,* and so there is a complete harmony between the teachings of these two sacred texts. These texts are thus the highest authority in philosophical matters, and all other texts and the various means of proof, such as inference etc., are considered authoritative only in so far as they follow this highest authority. The *Bhāgavata,* which is a record of all the experiences of Vyāsa in meditation and which is therefore otherwise known as *Samādhi-bhāṣā* (the language of meditation), enjoys the most important position in the Śuddhādvaita system.

[2] *Aṇubhāṣya* on the *Brahma-Sūtra,* II.2.26; *Subodhinī,* I.1.1.

[3] The term is explained in two ways: (i) Pure non-dualism and (ii) Non-dualism of the two—cause and effect—which are pure.

[4] *Brahma-Sūtra* with *Śrīmad-Bhāgavata-bhāṣya,* Calcutta Oriental Series, No. 15.

## LITERATURE OF THE SCHOOL

Vallabha has written some works in the form of commentaries and some others as independent treatises for the elucidation of the teachings of the sacred texts. He tells us that he has written commentaries on the *Brahma-Sūtra,* the *Jaimini-Sūtra,* and the *Bhāgavata,* and has also composed some independent works.[5] Unfortunately, all his works are not available in a complete form. His commentary on the *Brahma-Sūtra,* called *Aṇubhāṣya,* is available only up to III.2.33, the remaining portion being supplied by his second son, Viṭhṭhalanātha.[6] Vallabha seems to have first written a more extensive commentary on the *Brahma-Sūtra,* which may be described as *Bṛhadbhāṣya* (long commentary),[7] and then made a summary of this in the form of what is known as *Aṇubhāṣya* (short commentary). The only available commentary on the *Jaimini-Sūtra* is on I.1.1 and II.1, and it begins with forty-two verses, which summarize the discussion of the *bhāṣya* on the first *sūtra.*[8] The commentary on the *Bhāgavata* called *Subodhinī,* as now available, is on the first three *skandhas* (books), a part of the fourth *skandha* (viz. six chapters and a portion [13 verses only] of the seventh chapter), the tenth *skandha,* and a part of the eleventh *skandha* (viz. four chapters and only one verse of the fifth chapter). There is also another important work called *Tattvārthadīpa,* popularly known as *Nibandha,* with Vallabha's own gloss called *Prakāśa,* which is divided into three parts known as *Śāstrārtha, Sarvanirṇaya,* and *Bhāgavatārtha.* The *Prakāśa* is complete so far as the first two parts are concerned ; but of the third part it is available only up to the thirty-third verse of the fourth section. Viṭhṭhalanātha tried to fill up the gap by supplying the gloss on the sections following, but unfortunately even his commentary is available only up to the 135th verse of the fifth section. *Śāstrārtha* discusses the content of the *Gītā* ; *Sarvanirṇaya* discusses different philosophical topics ; and *Bhāgavatārtha* explains the subject matter of the *Bhāgavata* in a very general way. Vallabha, following Bopadeva,[9] holds the view that he who makes a critical study of the *Bhāgavata* and realizes the fact that one and the same topic is discussed in all the seven different parts of the *Bhāgavata* enjoys liberation. These seven parts are Śāstras (scriptures), viz. *Bhāgavata* as a whole, *skandha* (branch, i.e. the 12

[5] *Tattvārthadīpa, Śāstrārtha,* 5.

[6] G. H. Bhatt, 'Double Authorship of Aṇubhāṣya', *Proceedings of the Fourth All-India Oriental Conference,* pp. 799-806.

[7] A portion of the commentary on the *Brahma-Sūtra,* III.1 and III.2.1-12, published in an old magazine, now defunct, *Puṣṭi Bhakti Sudhā* (Vol. V, No. 10 to Vol. VI, No. 6), was claimed to be a fragment of Vallabhācārya's *Bṛhadbhāṣya*; but the claim is unjustifiable as the printed text is a fake, written by some modern scholar.

[8] The available portion is published in the magazine *Puṣṭi Bhakti Sudhā,* Vol. V, No. 2; Vol. VII, Nos. 2-4.

[9] Bopadeva, *Harilīlā,* XII.17.

books of the *Bhāgavata*), *prakaraṇa* (topic), *adhyāya* (chapter), *vākya* (sentence), *pada* (word), and *akṣara* (syllable).[10] *Bhāgavatārtha* gives the meaning of the first four parts, while *Subodhinī* gives the meaning of the remaining three. Vallabha does not seem to have written independent commentaries on the Upaniṣads and the *Gītā*. He has, however, written small works, such as the sixteen treatises, *Patrāvalambana* etc., which are very helpful in understanding his system. The literary activities of his school have been carried on with great vigour up to the present day by his descendants and followers, who have produced a very rich literature, not only in Sanskrit but also in some of the vernacular languages of India, such as Hindi, Vraja, and Gujarati, and have exercised a great influence over millions of people in northern and western India.

## PHILOSOPHY: PARABRAHMAN

Vallabha has evolved his philosophy solely on the authority of the verbal testimony (*āpta*), and has thereby shown that dry logic has no independent place in the discussion of philosophical problems—an attitude which is responsible for his strong criticism of Śaṅkara. His philosophical views are as follows.

The highest entity is Brahman, which is Sat (existence), Cit (knowledge), Ānanda (bliss), and Rasa (sentiment). He is Pūrṇa (perfect) Puruṣottama (the best of beings), and is therefore personal in nature. He possesses many divine qualities, of which *jñāna* (experience) and *kriyā* (activity) are the most prominent. He also possesses contradictory qualities. He is devoid of worldly or material qualities, and the negation of qualities in Brahman, mentioned in the Upaniṣads, refers to the absence of material qualities in Him. He possesses a sort of body totally made up of *ānanda*. His *ānanda* is infinite. He is omnipresent and eternal. He is both *kartṛ* (agent) and *bhoktṛ* (enjoyer). For *līlā* (sport) He has created the universe out of Himself, and is thus both the efficient and the material cause of the universe which is naturally sustained by Him and absorbed in Him at the end. Although the world is full of people, both happy and unhappy, and comes to an end at particular periods, Brahman is not open to the charges of practising cruelty and creating inequality, simply because He has created the world out of Himself in *līlā*. Again, He does not undergo any change even when He transforms Himself into this world—a doctrine known as *avikṛtapariṇāma* (unchanged transformation). The *kriyā-śakti* (power of action) of Brahman is described in the *pūrva-kāṇḍa* (first or ritualistic portion) of the Vedas, while His *jñāna-śakti* (power of knowledge)

[10] *Tattvārthadīpa, Bhāgavatārtha,* 2; *Subodhinī,* I.1.1.

is described in the *uttara-kāṇḍa* (latter portion, i.e. the Upaniṣads). Brahman, the Lord, as associated with both *kriyā* and *jñāna śaktis* is, again, described in His grandeur in the *Gītā* and the *Bhāgavata*.

## AKṢARA

Next to and lower than, Parabrahman is Akṣara (immutable) or Akṣara Brahman. He possesses *sat, cit,* and *limited ānanda* (as against *infinite ānanda* of Parabrahman). He is the *dhāman* (abode) of Parabrahman. He appears in various forms according to the different aspects of the latter. He may appear as *Vaikuṇṭhaloka* when Parabrahman, the Lord, appears as residing in Vaikuṇṭha. He may appear as the *caraṇa* (foot) of the Lord when the latter appears in the form of *antaryāmin* (the inner controller) and also in the form of an *avatāra* (incarnation). He also appears as the foot in the *ādhidaivika* (celestial) forms of the Lord. The Akṣara is further described as the *puccha* (tail) of the *ānandamaya* (blissful) Lord, and is the *ādhyātmika* (corporeal) form of the latter. When the Lord wants to give *mokṣa* (liberation) through *jñāna,* He manifests four forms, viz. *akṣara, kāla* (time), *karma* (action), and *svabhāva* (nature). *Akṣara* then appears in the forms of Prakṛti (primal matter) and Puruṣa (soul) ; and this Prakṛti develops through different stages into the universe, and is therefore called the cause of all causes. The negative descriptions of Brahman in the Upaniṣads refer to this Akṣara Brahman which becomes the subject of meditation of *jñānins* alone.

*Kāla, karma,* and *svabhāva* are, like *akṣara,* different forms of the Lord inseparable from Him, and serve some purpose in the creation of the world. There are, again, twenty-eight *tattvas* (principles) which appear in the process of creation, viz. *sattva* (purity), *rajas* (activity), *tamas* (inertia), Puruṣa, Prakṛti, *mahat* (cosmic intelligence), *ahaṅkāra* (egoism), five *tanmātras* (subtle elements), five *mahābhūtas* (gross elements), five *karmendriyas* (organs of action), five *jñānendriyas* (organs of knowledge), and *manas* (mind). But though *akṣara, kāla, karma,* and *svabhāva* exist even before the creation of the universe, they are not included in this list of the *tattvas,* as they are general causes *inseparable* from the Lord. The twenty-eight categories are called *tattvas* as they represent in the world the causal capacity of the Lord.[11] The Lord, as the cause of the whole universe, expresses His causal capacity in the form of these twenty-eight categories which, in spite of the same nomenclature, have to be clearly distinguished from the categories of the Sāṁkhya system.[12] For instance, the three *guṇas* (qualities), which constitute the Prakṛti of the Sāṁkhya,

[11] *Tattvārthadīpa, Sarvanirṇaya,* 86.
[12] *Tattvārthadīpa, Śāstrārtha,* 94.

are distinct from Prakṛti in this system ; the *indriyas* (organs) are developed from the *rājasa ahaṅkāra,* and their *devatās* (presiding deities) from the *sāttvika ahaṅkāra* ; the *indriyas* and *manas* are atomic and eternal.

## SOUL

The Lord was alone, without a second, in the beginning of a cycle. He desired to be many for the sake of pleasure ; and as He desired, thousands of souls came instantaneously out of Akṣara Brahman like sparks from fire. In special cases the souls may emanate from the Lord Himself. The soul is thus an *aṁśa* (part) of Brahman and is eternal. With a view to enjoying sport, the Lord suppressed the element of *ānanda* (bliss) in the soul, and the soul consequently became subject to bondage and wrong knowledge. The soul is never created, nor does it ever die. It is only the body which is created and destroyed. As long as the soul is associated with the body, birth and death, which are the attributes of the body, are metaphorically predicated of it. The soul is atomic—it is neither omnipresent, nor does it vary in size according to the body it inhabits. It experiences everything in the body through its quality of *caitanya* (intelligence) which pervades the whole body. It knows, does, and experiences various things in the world ; but these qualities of the soul are, in fact, derived from the Lord. The soul is thus quite real, and not a product of nescience. The Lord, in order to bring about variety, which is essential for the sake of pleasure, makes the souls varied in nature. Consequently, the souls can be grouped into three classes, viz. (1) those that are busy with worldly matters, (2) those that follow the Vedic path according to the letter of the Vedas, and (3) those that worship the Lord out of pure love engendered only through divine grace. These three types are generally described as *pravāha, maryādā,* and *puṣṭi* respectively.

## THE UNIVERSE

The universe is the effect of Brahman and is real and non-different from Him. It represents the *ādhibhautika* (material) form of Brahman. The element of *sat* is manifest in it, while the other elements of *cit* and *ānanda* are latent. The Lord has created the universe out of His own self for the sake of sport (*līlā*) without suffering any change whatsoever, and is related to it as the spider is to its web. The origination, existence, and destruction of the world are entirely due to Brahman. The world of experience is completely different in nature from the world of dreams and is therefore not unreal like the experiences in a dream. The universe (*jagat*) is clearly distinguished from the unreal world (*saṁsāra*) caused by the *avidyā* (nescience) of souls. For the sake of diversity, the Lord makes the souls subject to His power of *avidyā* which is the root cause of the ideas of 'mine' and 'thine'. *Saṁsāra,* which is solely made up of *ahantā* (I-ness or egoism) and *mamatā* (My-ness or the idea of possession), has to be destroyed by means of knowledge, devotion, etc.

### PUṢṬI CONTRASTED WITH JÑĀNA AND KARMA

Three paths have been generally recognized as leading to *mokṣa,* viz. Karma-mārga, Jñāna-mārga, and Bhakti-mārga. The several schools of the Vedānta differ from one another in laying differential emphasis on the elements of *karma, jñāna,* and *bhakti.* According to the Śuddhādvaita system, the Lord manifests Himself in the five forms of *kriyā* (Vedic sacrifice), viz. *agnihotra, darśa-paurṇamāsa, paśuyāga, cāturmāsya,* and *somayāga,* in the *pūrva-kāṇḍa,* and in the form of *jñāna* in the *uttara-kāṇḍa.* He who performs the Vedic rites and obtains the knowledge of Brahman as described in the Upaniṣads, enjoys *mokṣa* in the form of divine joy. To such a man the Lord, described in the Vedic literature as possessing the six forms (the five of sacrifice and the one of *jñāna*) manifests Himself. He goes by the path of the gods (*devayāna*) and gradually attains *mokṣa* ; but if he happens to enjoy the special grace of the Lord, he gets *mokṣa* immediately after death. He who does not attain the knowledge of Brahman but performs the Vedic rites without any motive, pleases all the gods concerned in the sacrifices and enjoys *ātmānanda* (the bliss of the soul). The term *svarga,* used in this connection in the sense of *ātmānanda,* etymologically means 'that which is perfectly earned', or the happiness of the soul which is unmixed, eternal, and inferior only to the supreme divine joy which is the privilege of those who enjoy the favour of the Lord. But he who performs different sacrifices, simply with a view to fulfilling different desires, goes to the popular *svargaloka* (heaven), where he enjoys different kinds of happiness till his merit is exhausted, and then returns to the world of mortals to move again in the cycle of birth and death.

It should be further noted that he who attains the knowledge of Brahman and realizes that everything in the world is Brahman, is a real knower of Brahman. But he is absorbed in Akṣara Brahman, and not in Parabrahman or Pūrṇa Puruṣottama, because, as already stated, he meditates upon Akṣara Brahman and considers it to be the final stage of reality that has no higher. But if this knowledge of Brahman is associated with devotion, the knowing devotee is absorbed in Pūrṇa Puruṣottama. This stage is, indeed, higher than the stage of absorption in Akṣara Brahman. There is, again, another stage which may be described as the highest. When the Lord desires to favour a particular soul—and be it remembered that in showing His favour He is not guided by any other consideration than His own will—He brings out the soul from Himself, gives him a divine body like His own, and plays with him for all time. In this play, which is called *nitya-līlā,* the Lord, remaining subordinate to the devotee, gives him the pleasure of His company, which is generally known as *bhajanānanda* (the bliss of devotion) or *svarūpānanda* (the bliss of the Lord Himself) which is referred to in the *Taittirīya Upaniṣad,* the *Bhāgavata,* and other Purāṇas.

It is most interesting to note that this divine bliss is purely a gift of the Lord and cannot be obtained by any human effort. It is this very idea of the gift of divine grace that is called *puṣṭi* in the Śuddhādvaita system.[13] The best illustration of divine grace (*puṣṭi*) is found in the case of the *gopīs* of Vṛndāvana, who are rightly described as the spiritual teachers who have opened the path of *puṣṭi* to the world at large. Those who enjoy this divine grace automatically begin to love the Lord and look upon Him not only as their Lord, but as everything. The doctrine of regarding the Lord as everything is called *sarvātmabhāva* (all-in-oneness), which should be distinguished from the *sarvātmabhāva* (one-in-allness) of the *jñānins.* In the *sarvātmabhāva* of the *jñānins,* men of realization see Brahman in all things, while in the other case the devotees see everything in the Lord. The *gopīs* possessed this attitude in a remarkable manner, and Lord Kṛṣṇa had therefore to remain quite obedient to them. The experience of *svarūpānanda,* which is decidedly superior to that of *Brahmānanda,* is, according to Vallabha, the highest conception of *mokṣa,* the *summum bonum.* The Lord is full of *rasa* (sentiment), and out of the eight *rasas* (love, heroism, fury, humour, wonder, terror, pathos, and horror), *śṛṅgāra* (love) is the most prominent. As *śṛṅgāra* has two aspects, viz. *saṁyoga* (union) and *viprayoga* (separation), there are two stages in this *rasa* which the devotees enjoy. In the company of the Lord the devotees enjoy the happiness of union, while in His absence they suffer the misery of separation and think of Him all the time, so much so that they cannot see or experience anything but Lord Kṛṣṇa. According to some, the stage of separation is therefore superior to that of union.

### PUṢṬI AND MARYĀDĀ

Vallabha has clearly distinguished the Puṣṭi-mārga from the Maryādā-mārga. In the latter, an individual has to follow the dictates of the Vedas, and practise the different types of *bhakti,* such as *śravaṇa* (hearing) etc. until he begins to love the Lord, who, taking his efforts into consideration,

[13] For a fuller conception of *puṣṭi,* cf. G. H. Bhatt, 'The Puṣṭi-mārga of Vallabhācārya', *Indian Historical Quarterly,* IX, pp. 300-306.

grants him *sāyujya mukti* (mergence in His body). In the Puṣṭi-mārga, however, through the operation of divine grace only, one starts with loving the Lord and then practises *śravaṇa* etc. out of that love, and not with a view to generating it. The Maryādā-mārga is open only to the males of the first three classes, viz. Brāhmaṇas, Kṣatriyas, and Vaiśyas, while the Puṣṭi-mārga is open to all without reservation. This knows no distinction of sex, caste, creed, or nationality ; it is universal religion ; and this aspect is clearly borne out by literary and historical evidence. In short, whatever is done by the devotee of the Maryādā-mārga is done on the strength of the Vedic injunctions and in conformity with them, while the devotee of the Puṣṭi-mārga does everything out of his natural love and for the sake of the Lord.

Vallabha saw that his own times were most unfavourable to *karma, jñāna,* and Vedic or *śāstrīya bhakti,* and that people in general, and women and Śūdras in particular, had no chance of ameliorating their status from the spiritual view-point. The duties of the different *varṇas* (classes) and *āśramas* (orders of life) could not be satisfactorily discharged ; and the Vedas, though most effective in the past, had ceased to be so, not because they were useless, but because the people could not put the Vedic teaching into practice and perform sacrifices. The Ācārya has tried to show that over and above the paths of *karma, jñāna,* and Vedic *bhakti,* there is one more path, that of divine grace, which, if once enjoyed, makes our life divine. The doctrine of grace is clearly referred to in the Upaniṣads, the *Gītā,* and the *Bhāgavata* ; and although Rāmānuja and others admit it to be an all-saving factor, it must be said to the credit of Vallabha that the way in which he has dealt with this question is unique. The followers of the other Vaiṣṇava schools also believe in the power of divine grace, but their mode of worship is 'maryādic', as they look upon the Lord as the great awe-inspiring God, endowed with infinite qualities and possessing great powers. Their worship is not prompted by love, which is possible only through the grace of the Lord. The followers of the Puṣṭi-mārga, however, worship the Lord, not because He is the Paramātman or the highest Entity, but because they ardently love Him. The worship of these devotees is therefore *snehātmaka* (consisting of love) ; and the Lord who is thus loved and worshipped is called Gopījanavallabha (the beloved of the *gopīs*), a term which is very significant in the system. The *gopīs* are the pioneers in this line, and others who follow them enjoy the same divine bliss. The mode of worship that has been followed in this system up to the present day is based on the spirit of the *gopīs.* One who follows the Puṣṭi-mārga aspires to be a *gopī* and worships the Lord with that attitude. In fact, all souls represent the feminine principle and have the Lord as their spiritual husband.

## SPIRITUAL DISCIPLINE

As regards the daily life of a devotee of this type, the Ācārya tells us that he should first of all dedicate his own self and all his belongings, including all the members of his family, to Lord Kṛṣṇa, who appeared in the world for the uplift of people of all classes, and particularly those who are not in a position to attain *mokṣa* by their own efforts. There is a *saṁskāra* (sacrament) called *Brahma-sambandha* which has to be performed by the Jīva (soul) to re-establish the lost contact with the Lord, to remove thereby the weaknesses of his nature, and to qualify himself fully for worship. The devotee, after performing this sacrament, worships the Lord, making an unreserved use of his own body and property, and thereby destroys *saṁsāra,* which is of the form of 'I' and 'mine' (i.e. ego-centric). This sacrament can be performed by all persons irrespective of caste and creed. The unreal *saṁsāra* is thus removed by the dedication of the body and wealth to the cause of the Lord, and not by the renunciation of the world. We are told by the Ācārya that in the *Kaliyuga* formal *sannyāsa* (monasticism) without the spirit of renunciation is detrimental to spiritual progress, and that it is justifiable only when one is unable to bear the pangs of separation from the Lord. The Ācārya himself took *sannyāsa* in his last days, when he felt that he could not live in the absence of the Lord and that family life was an impediment to the highest bliss, which he wished to enjoy in the company of the Lord. The worship of the Lord requires the services of all members of the family, and they are promised the highest bliss that always results from worship or *sevā* (service). This mode of service makes the whole family free from worldly ties even when leading a householder's life, and their whole life becomes divine. If the head of the family finds that some of the members of his family are not supporting him in this, he is advised to leave them and pass his time in *sevā* quite alone. The highest form of *sevā* is mental ; in this stage the devotee thinks of the Lord alone.

The duties of the four *varṇas* and *āśramas* cannot be satisfactorily performed in modern times ; and if they are carried out mechanically, they fail to give any reward. When there is a conflict between the *Bhagavad-dharma* (the service of the Lord) and the *varṇāśrama-dharma,* a devotee of the Puṣṭi-mārga must choose the former: he may perform the duties of *varṇāśrama* when he finds leisure from his *sevā,* but under no circumstances at the cost of the service of the Lord. This is the real *ātma-dharma,* duty relating to the soul, while the duties of the *varṇas* and *āśramas* are simply duties relating to the body ; and of the Ātman and the body, the former is decidedly the superior.

It is thus obvious that a follower of the Puṣṭi-mārga devotes his own self and all his belongings to the Lord and passes his whole time in His service. He completely loses his independent existence in the world and cannot therefore possess any property. Whatever he requires for personal use, he first dedicates to the Lord and then makes use of with His permission. Since everything is dedicated to the Lord, the devotee cannot in any way exercise the right of ownership over anything. It is also impossible for a follower of the Puṣṭi-mārga to be immoral, for this path is based on renunciation, not enjoyment. Although its doors are open to all—men and women, people of the upper three castes and Śūdras, and even those who are morally fallen (*patita*) and seem to have lost all chances of spiritual uplift, it does not encourage immorality. It should not be looked upon as a licence for doing immoral actions without responsibility; it simply promises safety to all who would follow its doctrines. The essence of the Puṣṭi-mārga is to establish connection between the soul and the Lord, and this is possible in many ways. One may be constantly angry with the Lord and still get *sāyujya*. It is immaterial whether it is anger or jealousy or devotion or passion that serves as the connecting link; what is required is connection. It should, however, be noted that those who are connected with the Lord through love (*sneha*) enjoy the privilege of partaking in the *nitya-līlā* of the Lord and of enjoying *bhajanānanda*, while others simply get *sāyujya*. If for any reason this kind of *sevā* is not possible, one should not be disappointed. The Ācārya tells us that such a man should throw himself at the feet of the Lord and remain at His mercy. This method is called *prapatti* or self-surrender.

## THE DEITY FOR WORSHIP

The form of the Lord that is generally worshipped in this system is known as Śrī Govardhananāthajī, popularly called Śrī Nāthajī, who is the embodiment of the twelve *skandhas* of the *Bhāgavata*, and whose shrine is situated at Nathadwar in Mewar. In other words, Śrī Nāthajī represents the very form of the Lord which is taught by the *Bhāgavata*. The twelve *skandhas* of the work are identified with the twelve parts of Śrī Nāthajī's form, the tenth *skandha* which describes the *rāsa-līlā* being identified with the heart. The image of Śrī Nāthajī was, according to the traditions of the school, revealed to the Ācārya on the hill of Girirāja and was later on brought to Nathadwar.[14] It represents the highest form of the Lord known

[14] Vallabhācārya inherited from his father, Lakṣmaṇa Bhaṭṭa, the image of Madanamohanajī accompanied by Rādhā on one side and Lakṣmī on the other. This represents the form of Kṛṣṇa which is associated with the *rāsa-līlā*. In the course of time when Viṭhṭhalanātha divided his property amongst his seven sons, he gave each of them a *svarūpa* (image) for *sevā*. These are still worshipped in different places by his descendants. All the seven images are included in the perfect and original form of Śrī Nāthajī. The later writers

as Pūrṇa Puruṣottama. All other images represent the *vibhūtis* (powers) and the *vyūhas* (manifestations), and not the highest form. The worship of the Lord is called *sevā,* while that of the *vibhūtis* is called *pūjā.* The Śuddhādvaita system, again, accepts the four *vyūhas,* viz. Vāsudeva, Saṅkarṣaṇa, Pradyumna, and Aniruddha, with their respective functions of giving *mokṣa,* removing the burden of the world, creating, and establishing *dharma.* These *vyūhas* are inferior to Pūrṇa Puruṣottama, to whom belongs the privilege of lifting up even those who are entirely helpless. In the different activities of Kṛṣṇa one can easily determine, from the nature of His actions, whether the particular form assumed is the highest one or a *vyūha* or a *vibhūti.* The Ācārya has laid down the criterion for distinguishing one from another. Applying the criterion, he very emphatically recommends the *sevā* of Śrī Nāthajī, and this constitutes his originality. He is not indebted to any of his predecessors in his teaching of the Puṣṭimārga, and the belief that Vallabhācārya simply carried on the traditions of one Viṣṇu Svāmin is therefore untenable. [15]

## A NOTE OF WARNING

The Ācārya, when he placed before the world the conception of *puṣṭi* as illustrated in the *rāsa-līlā,* anticipated certain difficulties owing to misunderstanding and its evil consequences, and he therefore frequently sounded a note of warning. He tells us that the episode of the *gopīs* and the Lord is both real and allegorical. If it is taken to be real, it must be clearly borne in mind that there is no tinge of sensualism in the *rāsa-līlā,* even though its description in the *Bhāgavata* appears to be more or less worldly. Moreover, he who listens with devotion to this account of the *gopīs* and the Lord becomes free from all the pangs of the heart and enjoys bliss. Some of the verses written by Vallabha in this connection deserve careful study. If one is disposed to interpret the *rāsa-līlā* as allegorical, one can say with him that the *gopīs* represent the Śrutis, and when they are said to enjoy the company of the Lord, it simply means that the Śrutis teach only one thing and that is the Lord. The Ācārya has considered this most important question from all points of view and has asked his followers not to imitate the Lord, but to serve Him and hear the account of His doings. Nay, when he was on the point of leaving this world, standing on the Gaṅgā near the Hanumān Ghāt in Banaras, he gave a

of the school have tried to show that these different forms represent particular *līlās* of Kṛṣṇa. Although Rādhā is worshipped in the company of Kṛṣṇa in this school, she does not enjoy as much prominence here as she does in the Vaiṣṇavism of Śrī Caitanya.

[15] G. H. Bhatt, 'Viṣṇusvāmī and Vallabhācārya', *Proceedings of the Seventh All-India Oriental Conference,* pp. 449-465; *Proceedings of the Eighth All-India Oriental Conference,* pp. 322-328.

message to his sons and followers in words that should be written in letters of gold. He said, 'My dear followers, you should always serve the Lord to the best of your ability; you should not look upon Lord Kṛṣṇa as an ordinary worldly master; once you become His, He will always take care of you. But if, somehow or other, you forget the Lord and think of worldly matters, you will fall'.[16] The message of the Ācārya as embodied in his teachings is indeed sublime and inspiring, and will serve as an infallible guide to all lovers of truth in the realization of the ultimate end of human existence.

## CONTRIBUTIONS TO VEDĀNTIC THOUGHT

It is obvious from what has been said above that Vallabha has made a special contribution to the Vedāntic thought. The conception of Para-brahman as full of *rasa,* although found in the Upaniṣads, first received systematic attention from the Ācārya. Again, the idea of Akṣara Brahman, founded as it is on the basic works, received full treatment for the first time at the hands of the Ācārya. The doctrine of grace, the ideal of self-dedication, and the sublimation of human life are some of the peculiar features of the teaching of the Ācārya. And what is still more remarkable is the attitude of the Ācārya towards the Vedas and the allied literature. He has accepted the Vedas as the highest authority and followed them most faithfully, with the result that logic can never get the better of faith. It is because of this attitude that Vallabhācārya differs from Śaṅkarācārya.

[16] G. H. Bhatt, 'Last Message of Vallabhacārya', *Annals of the Bhandarkar Oriental Research Institute,* XXIII, pp. 67-70.

# 20

## BHEDĀBHEDA SCHOOL OF VEDĀNTA

### INTERMEDIARY BETWEEN ŚAṄKARA AND RĀMĀNUJA

VEDĀNTA as a philosophy of religion is a systematic exposition of the nature of Brahman as the cosmic ground and the supreme end of spiritual experience; by knowing Brahman everything else is known. It has its eternal foundation in the wisdom of the Upaniṣads, the *Gītā,* and the *Brahma-Sūtra,* which together form the *prasthāna-traya* or the triple sources of *Brahmajñāna.* The *Brahma-Sūtra* formulates the truths of Vedānta in a clear and distinct manner, but its language is too terse to be understood without the aid of Vedāntic teachers; among these are Śaṅkara, Rāmānuja, and Madhva who wrote commentaries on the *Brahma-Sūtra* in the light of ancient tradition as represented by *ācāryas* like Bādari, Kāśakṛtsna, Auḍulomi, Āśmarathya, and Ṭaṅka. In addition to the systems of Śaṅkara, Rāmānuja, and Madhva, there were other systems of Vedāntic thought, such as the schools of Bhedābheda expounded by Bhāskara and Yādava, of which very little is known in Indian philosophy today. They may be assigned to a period between the ages of Śaṅkara and Rāmānuja, and they are of profound interest to the student of comparative Vedānta, as they form a link in the chronological and logical transition from the Advaita of Śaṅkara to the Viśiṣṭādvaita of Rāmānuja. A brief summary of their teaching is attempted here.

First there is a logical inquiry into the validity of Vedāntic knowledge, the philosophic apprehension of the nature of Reality as Saguṇa Brahman, and the account of the origin of the universe from Brahman. The ethics of Bhedābheda describes the means by which Brahman is attained, and it includes both *jñāna* and *karma.* The religion of Bhedābheda refers to the attainment of *Brahmajñāna* and the nature of unitive consciousness. The philosophy of Nimbārka is a school of Bhedābheda; and its mono-dualism is more realistic than that of Yādava and seems to be midway between the teachings of Yādava and Rāmānuja.

### THEORY OF KNOWLEDGE

In his theory of knowledge, the Bhedābhedavādin posits the knowability of Brahman and regards the Śāstras or the Vedas as the ultimate source of knowledge. The validity of the Vedas is self-established, they contain their own criteria. They are a body of eternal, impersonal, and infallible truths which were intuited by the *ṛṣis* and clarified by the

Mīmāṁsaka rules of interpretation. There is unity of import in every Upaniṣadic topic, and its primary meaning can be gathered from the context. By applying these tests to the Upaniṣadic philosophy, Bhāskara and Yādava conclude that they support the system of Bhedābheda. This truth is confirmed by the knowledge given in sense perception and reasoning or *pratyakṣa* and *anumāna*. Every judgement connotes identity pervading difference, and the principle is clearly brought out in the relation between cause and effect and between genus and species. The *abheda* aspect is stressed in the causal state and the generic state, and the *bheda* aspect is stressed in the effect state and the specific state. In the propositions, 'This pot is made of clay', 'This cow is short-horned', the principle of unity in variety is clearly exemplified. The effect is a real manifestation of the cause, and it does not betray any inner contradiction. Likewise, the genus is realized in the species, and there is no inner discrepancy in the relation between genus and species or universality and individuality. Thus, according to the Bhedābheda, the one is realized in the many. The Absolute manifests itself in the finite and a supra-rational absolute is devoid of meaning and is unthinkable. There is no substance or subject without qualities or object, and every determination or predication affirms reality and does not deny it. The causal category is the keynote of the epistemology of the Bhedābheda. The effect is contained in the cause and is continuous with it (Satkāryavāda). Brahman is the unconditioned or the Absolute, and the unconditioned exists as and in the conditioned or *prapañca*. In this way, the Bhedābheda avoids the one-sidedness of monism and pluralism. Identity or non-difference is not alien to difference, but is its *prius* or presupposition. It is the whole immanent in the parts or particulars without losing its wholeness.

## ONTOLOGY

In the ontology of Bhāskara, the Absolute of philosophy is the God of religion or Saguṇa Brahman. According to him, Brahman is formless but not characterless. Predication affirms reality and does not pervert it; and when the Upaniṣads define Brahman as *satya, jñāna, ananta,* and *ānanda,* they refer to the Sat as the Sat without a second, as the all-Self that is unconditioned and infinite and blissful. It is immanent in all beings without being tainted by their imperfections and is therefore not the pantheistic all, which is nothing at all. The idea of *antaryāmin* brings out the Bhedābheda truth that Brahman is in the finite without being conditioned by the finite. The idea of the unconditioned as existing in, and yet not conditioned by, the forms of the world of nature and of Jīvas, satisfies all tests of revelation, reasoning, and sense perception; and it thus reconciles the extremes of the philosophy of identity of the monist who equates Ātman and Brahman, and the pluralism of the theists who assert eternal distinctions between Brahman and Jīva and *acit*. There is essential unity between Brahman and Jīva, and the difference is only *aupādhika* or adventitious, but the relation between Brahman and nature is *bheda* and *abheda* at the same time—identity persists in and through difference and gives it meaning. Like the one infinite space that is enclosed in pots and pitchers, the unconditioned Brahman, influenced by the *upādhis* or the psycho-physical complex of mind-body, exists as Jīva and thus there is a dualism between Brahman and the *upādhi*. But Yādava overcomes the dualism by his theory that Brahman is both identical with and different from *cit* and *acit*. While Bhāskara insists on the primacy of the *abheda* texts of the Vedānta and the real possibility of attaining *ekībhāva* or mystic union by removing the barriers of the *upādhis*, Yādava thinks that *bheda* and *abheda* express the eternal necessity of the Absolute. To Bhāskara, Jīva is essentially one with Brahman, though *acit* is both different and non-different from Brahman. Yādava regards both *cit* and *acit* as *bhinna* and *abhinna* or the one-many. Just as the sea contains foam, waves, and bubbles, Brahman the Absolute exists as Īśvara, *cit*, and *acit*, each having its own nature and function. The Absolute is God and the finite centres, and not God alone. They form a unity in trinity and are correlative and not contradictory. The finite is neither illusory nor self-contained, but is a real integral expression of the Absolute. According to Nimbārka, the Absolute or Brahman in Its *abheda* aspect is self-related; and in the Bhedābheda aspect It is the unity that pervades difference and also sustains it. Jīva has its source in Brahman and is also controlled by It.

## COSMOLOGY

Brahma-pariṇāmavāda strikes the keynote of the Bhedābheda theory of cosmology. According to Bhāskara, there is a twofold *śakti* (power) in Brahman known as *jīva-pariṇāma* (transformation as Jīva) and *acetana-pariṇāma* (transformation as matter) or *bhoktṛ-śakti* (power as enjoyer) and *bhogya-śakti* (power as the enjoyed). Brahman is the Sat without a second, devoid of differentiation in the *pralaya* state. In *sṛṣṭi*, Brahman wills to be the many and becomes the manifold by Its *pariṇāma-śakti* (power of transformation). The unconditioned one puts on a multiplicity of names and forms and becomes Jīvas or subjects of experience and *acetana* or the objects of experience. Absoluteness and relativity go together. Like the spider weaving its web, the Absolute by its energizing power becomes the pluralistic world and its explanation. It is the nature of the formless

Infinite to become the finite without losing its infinity and perfection, and to infinitize Jīva. Divine causality implies unity, immanence, and continuity. From the creative urge of Brahman emanates Brahmā, the totality of selves and the first born of the Absolute, who manifests Himself as the heterogeneous variety of living and non-living beings according to the moral needs of Jīva. *Sṛṣṭi* is followed by *pralaya,* and the cycle goes on endlessly. Every new creation is but a repetition of an earlier one, and soul-making is the cosmic purpose running through the ages. The universe is grounded in the divine nature ; the eternal works through the temporal ; and the whole is in and as the parts. According to Yādava, *Brahmatva* or pure being is the causal unity of the universe constituted by the trinity of Īśvara, *cit,* and *acit. Cit* and *acit* are real factors of reality and are its eternal self-revelation. Nimbārka rejects Bhāskara's theory of the *upādhis* and the Pariṇāmavāda of Yādava, and traces *sṛṣṭi* to the immanent *śakti* of Brahman. But all reject the pantheistic identification of Brahman with the world when they say that the one becomes the many without being infected by the imperfections of the many.

## PSYCHOLOGY

Bhāskara's psychology or the theory of the finite self is based on the two concepts of *upādhi* (limiting adjunct) and *aṁśa* (part). Jīva is not an appearance or mode of the Absolute, but is a fragment of Reality. Like the *ākāśa* enclosed in a jar and the coil of the coiled snake, the all-Self, influenced by the *upādhis* of mind-body or *deha-indriya-manas,* breaks itself, as it were, against these or limits itself and becomes the finite centres of experience. Finiteness is a defect inherent in Jīva. The formless Brahman as the Infinite limits Itself as Jīvas and acquires a spatial and temporal setting, is caught up in the perils of particularity and the hazards of the moral law of Karma, and suffers from the misery of *saṁsāra.* The *upādhi* is a complex of *avidyā, kāma,* and *karma,* and makes the limitless Brahman into the limited Jīva. Jīva has the qualities of cognition, conation, and feeling, and in all psychic states, normal and abnormal, the self persists in its self-identity in different degrees of limitation. Such limitation is only contingent and empirical in the state of *saṁsāra,* but in *mukti* (salvation) Jīva can become free from the limiting adjuncts and become one with Brahman. According to Yādava, *aṁśatva* implies identity in difference ; and Jīva is one with Brahman and different from It ; and both *abheda* and *bheda* are essential elements of Brahman. The finite self has infinite content and, owing to identification with mind-body, submits itself to the sorrows of finitude, isolation, and *saṁsāra.*

ETHICS AND SALVATION

The ethics of the Bhedābheda describes the moral and spiritual methods by which Jīva frees itself from the limitation of the *upādhis* and becomes the Infinite. The theory of *jñāna-karma-samuccaya* or the combination of *jñāna* and *karma* is the main Bhedābheda solution of the ethical problem of the *mumukṣu* (aspirant after salvation). Owing to the influence of *avidyā* and *karma,* Jīva is caught up in the cycles of births and deaths. Even the pleasures of *puṇya-karma* (good deed) are trivial and transient, and when the effect of good deeds is exhausted, Jīva is hurled down again into the world of *karma.* At long last he realizes the hardships of empirical life and desires emancipation. *Mukti* is not merely the apprehension of Brahman, but also the attainment of *Brahmaloka* ; and it therefore needs the combination of *jñāna* and *karma* or contemplation and activity. The Mīmāṁsakas insist on the performance of Vedic injunctions or duties as the goal of life ; but their theory of *apūrva* (unseen result) or *niyoga* (impulsion to duties by Vedic injunction) reduces morality to a mechanical process. The *Vedānta-Sūtra* restates the theory by substituting Brahman as the *niyantṛ* (ruler) of *niyoga.* The moral law is rooted in Brahman and not in *karma.* The Advaita brings out the self-contradiction between *karma,* which results from *ajñāna* and the sense of duality, and *jñāna,* which affirms the self-identity of the Absolute ; and it therefore extols the ultimate futility of *karma.* The Viśiṣṭādvaita recognizes the unity of the two Mīmāṁsās, Pūrva and Uttara, but it makes *karma* a means to *jñāna* and *bhakti.* The Bhedābheda rejects all these views by recognizing the equal value of *jñāna* and *karma,* and co-ordinating them in the synthetic view of *jñāna-karma-samuccaya.* The obstacles to *mukti* are both moral and intellectual, and wisdom consists in utilizing the values of both philosophic insight and moral endeavour, of *jñāna* and *karma* as the twin means to *mukti.* When work is done as duty or *niṣkāma-karma,* it is changed into worship ; *karma* is rationalized and spiritualized. Likewise, *jñāna* is changed into *vedanā* or *upāsanā* or inner meditation on Brahman. *Jñāna* is the aspect of apprehending the unity of the Absolute, and *karma* is the spiritual attempt to attain it. If *avidyā-kāma-karma* (ignorance-desire-action) causes the dualistic and the divisive consciousness of empirical life, *jñāna-karma* reverses the process ; and the finite grows into the infinite in the light of the Bhedābheda. *Mukti* thus implies an awakening as well as an activity.

The teaching of Bhāskara lays stress on the overcoming of the defects of the divided life due to the *upādhis* and the attaining of unitive consciousness or *ekībhāva.* The bonds of *bheda* are broken off and Jīva expands into infinity. *Mukti* is freedom from the embodied state (*videhamukti*) and not in the embodied state (*jīvanmukti*) and is the attainment of the world of Brahman. When *prārabdha,* together with the body of the *mukta,* is dissolved at death, he ascends to the Absolute by the straight and shining path of the gods and attains Brahman. If emanation from the One leads to the sorrows of the sundered life, the attainment of unity leads to ecstasy or eternal bliss. Unity or *avibhāga,* as the *Brahma-Sūtra* calls it, is not *aikya* or identity between Jīva and Īśvara by the removal of contradictions, nor inseparability due to coalescence of content, nor dependence, but becoming one with the all-Self or *ekībhāva.* Singleness of self, and not the self, is dissolved. In the vision of unity, every desire is at once fulfilled. It is the dissolution of the pluralistic consciousness and not of the pluralistic world. Consciousness without content is impossible. The highest values are conserved in the all-Self. Yādava's theory of *mukti* consists in retaining the finite self, but removing its sense of finitude and particularity. The self-feeling of the atomic self results in individualistic exclusiveness. When it sheds its distinctness and unites with the Absolute, it becomes Its moment or member and attains the sevenfold perfection referred to in the *'dahara vidyā'* (*Chā. U.,* VIII.1.1). According to Nimbārka, Jīva is a distinct entity that derives its being from Brahman and depends on It ; and his view seems to have more affinity with the Viśiṣṭādvaita than with the views of Bhāskara and Yādava.

## OTHER FEATURES

There are shades of difference among the Bhedābhedavādins which deserve the attention of the student of comparative Vedānta. While Yādava and Nimbārka insist on the equal validity and value of *bheda* and *abheda* in the relation between Brahman on the one hand and *cit* and *acit* on the other, Bhāskara regards non-difference between Brahman and Jīva as essential, and difference as adventitious, owing to the influence of *upādhis.* Nimbārka's view that Brahman is self-existent and Jīva and *acit* depend on Brahman differs from the Brahma-pariṇāmavāda of Bhāskara and Yādava. Both Śaṅkara and Rāmānuja reject the Bhedābheda on the ground that *bheda* and *abheda* are self-contradictory and cannot coexist. If Jīva is an emanation of Brahman, the imperfections of Jīva should belong to Brahman Itself. Good and evil will then follow necessarily from the divine nature. The Bhedābheda steers clear of the two extremes of theism and pantheism. If the *abheda* element is stressed, then Advaita is the logical conclusion ; if *bheda* is stressed, theism is the result. But the Bhedābheda has the supreme merit of being a corrective to the subjectivistic tendency of monistic idealism and the anthropomorphic tendency of naive theism.

# 21

## THE ACINTYA-BHEDĀBHEDA SCHOOL

IT is proposed to give here a short account of the views entertained by the Acintya-bhedābheda school of the Vedānta about Brahman, the Jīva, and the universe and the relation between Brahman and the rest. This school, also known as the Bengal school, was founded by Śrī Caitanya. His teachings were systematized and elaborated by his followers, Śrī Jīva Gosvāmin and others.

The views of this school differ widely from those of the Śaṅkara school on account of the difference in their modes of interpretation of the texts of the Upaniṣads. The Bengal school holds[1] that the Śrutis (Upaniṣads) are authorities by themselves and that interpretation in the *mukhyā vṛtti* (i.e. denotative and direct or primary meanings) only may reveal the true spirit of their texts and uphold their self-authoritativeness. The Śaṅkara school, however, bases its conclusions mainly on interpretations in the *lakṣaṇā* or *gauṇī vṛtti*[2] (i.e. indirect or secondary and derivative meanings) which is allowable only when the *mukhyā vṛtti* fails to give any admissible meaning. The meanings in *lakṣaṇā* or *gauṇī* are inferential and hence are not consistent with the self-authoritativeness of the Śrutis.

### BRAHMAN OR ŚRĪ KṚṢṆA

According to the Upaniṣads, Praṇava is Brahman;[3] and according to the *Gītā*, Śrī Kṛṣṇa is both Praṇava and Parama Brahman.[4] Etymologically, Brahman means 'One who is great' and 'One who can make great'.[5] The second part of the meaning implies existence of *śaktis* (powers or energies) in Brahman; and there are explicit texts in the Upaniṣads supporting His possession of an infinite number of active *śaktis*, super-

[1] *Caitanya Caritāmṛta* (*Cai. Ca.*), I. 7. 124, 125.

[2] *Lakṣaṇā* means a meaning connected with *mukhyārtha* (denotative or etymological meaning). It is to be resorted to only when the *mukhya* meaning is not admissible (*Alaṅkāra-kaustubha,* II. 12). An illustration: 'Devadatta lives in the Gaṅgā'. The denotative meaning of 'Gaṅgā' is a river of that name. It is not possible for a man to live in a river. Thus the *mukhya* meaning of 'Gaṅgā' is not admissible here. Hence it is inferred that Devadatta lives on the bank *connected with* the river Gaṅgā. *Gauṇī* is a variety of *lakṣaṇā* and is thus applicable only when *mukhya* meaning is inadmissible. In it, a *guṇa* (attribute) of the *mukhya* meaning is supposed to be the implication desired (*Sarvasaṁvādinī,* p. 19). An illustration: 'Devadatta is a lion'. The denotative meaning of 'lion' is a beast and is not therefore applicable to Devadatta, a man. Hence it is inferred that Devadatta is as valorous as a lion. Here 'lion' implies its valour, an *attribute* of a lion.

[3] *Pra. U.*, V. 2.

[4] *B. G.*, IX. 17; X. 12.

[5] *Viṣṇu Purāṇa,* I. 12. 57.

natural (*parā*) and inseparable (*svābhāvikī*) from Him.[6] He possesses both the aspects implied by the meaning of the word Brahman.[7] According to the *Viṣṇu Purāṇa,* He is Parama Brahman, only because He possesses both the aspects.[8] There is none equal or superior to Him.[9] Brahman is thus infinite in every respect—infinite in magnitude, infinite in *śaktis,* i.e. in the number of *śaktis* and also in the magnitude and activities of each *śakti.* He is the Infinite.

Brahman is Sat (absolute existence), Cit (absolute intelligence or consciousness, implying non-materiality), and Ānanda (absolute bliss).[10] Of His *śaktis* three are main, viz. *svarūpa-śakti, māyā-śakti,* and *jīva-śakti.*[11]

(1) His *svarūpa-śakti,* also known as *cit-śakti* on account of its being sentient, eternally exists in Him or His self and is very intimately connected with Him and His *līlās* (divine sports), and is thus called His *antaraṅga-śakti* (internal and intimate power). It has three aspects, viz. *sandhinī, saṁvit,* and *hlādinī,* corresponding respectively to His Sat, Cit, and Ānanda.[12] By *sandhinī,* He upholds His own existence and that of others ; by *saṁvit,* He knows and makes others know ; and by *hlādinī,* He enjoys and makes others enjoy bliss. These three cannot, however, be completely separated from one another ; but their proportion may differ in different cases. A combination of these three is technically called *śuddha-sattva* (pure existence) which is sometimes named after the *śakti* that preponderates in it. With the preponderance of *sandhinī,* it is called *ādhāra-śakti* (receptive power) ; with the preponderance of *saṁvit,* it is called *ātmavidyā* (knowledge about Brahman) ; and with the preponderance of *hladinī,* it is called *guhyavidyā* (*bhakti* or loving devotion).[13] *Śuddha-sattva* is so called on account of its being untouched by Mayā, implying that it is quite different from the *sattva* of Māyā.

(2) *Māyā-śakti* is that aspect of His power which is insentient and material (*jaḍa*) as opposed to *cit-śakti,*[14] and it cannot therefore move without His or His *svarūpa-śakti's* agency. It is also known as *bahiraṅga-śakti* (external power), as it cannot be in direct touch with Him. It has two aspects—*guṇa-māyā* and *jīva-māyā* ; the former consists of the three *guṇas*—*sattva, rajas,* and *tamas,* and, at the time of creation, is transformed into the constituents of the material universe ; and the latter helps the

[6] *Śvetāśvatara U.,* VI. 8.
[7] *Ibid.*
[8] *Viṣṇu Purāṇa,* I. 12. 57.
[9] *Śvetāśvatara U.,* VI. 8.
[10] *Cai. Ca.,* I. 4. 54 ; II. 20. 132 ; *Bhakti-sandarbha,* 51.
[11] *Cai. Ca.,* II. 8. 116.
[12] *Cai. Ca.,* II. 8. 118, 119.
[13] *Bhagavat-sandarbha,* 118.
[14] *Cai. Ca.,* I. 5. 51.

creation by making the Jīva forget its self and cling to the enjoyment of material pleasures.

(3) All beings, human or otherwise, are in essence His *jīva-śakti*, which is also known as *taṭastha-śakti* (marginal or intermediate power), as it is included in neither *māyā-śakti* nor *svarūpa-śakti*.[15]

Of the three main *śaktis* of Brahman, *svarūpa-śakti* is superior to the two others in every respect and is hence also called *parā-śakti*. *Jīva-śakti* also is superior to *māyā-śakti*, as the one is sentient and the other insentient.[16]

As the *śaktis* of Brahman are inseparably and eternally associated with Him, He cannot but be eternally qualified (*saviśeṣa* and *saguṇa*). He has endless, supernatural attributes (*guṇas*), all derived from His *svarūpa-śakti*, but none from His *māyā-śakti*. The texts that describe Him as *nirguṇa* (attributeless) imply that He possesses no *guṇa* from *Māyā*.[17] Thus He is both *saguṇa* and *nirguṇa*; and it is for this reason that in the different Upaniṣads and even in the same Upaniṣad, He is described as both.[18] He is omnipresent, omnipotent, and omniscient and is beyond the influence of time, space, and relativity.

He is Satya (the real), Śiva (the good), and Sundara (the beautiful). Brahman, being *ānanda* (bliss), which is essentially sweet and captivating, is the embodiment of sweetness and beauty and relishableness and is thus attractiveness itself. It is for this reason that He is called Kṛṣṇa, the supreme Attractor. Though both the words, 'Brahman' and 'Kṛṣṇa', have essentially the same implications and denote exactly the same ultimate Reality, yet the latter seems to carry with it much more vividly the idea of supreme attractiveness. Brahman appears at His best, so to say, in Śrī Kṛṣṇa, who is thus the most fascinating and hence the most appealing aspect of Brahman,[19] embodying in Him all the features of Brahman—His *śaktis*, attributes, etc.—in the most highly developed forms. It is for this reason that Śrī Kṛṣṇa is called the highest Brahman or Parama Brahman.[20]

Śrī Kṛṣṇa has a form, or strictly speaking, His self is a form,[21] resembling that of a human being,[22] or rather a human form is a poor resemblance of His. Though apparently limited like an ordinary human body, it is really infinite and all-pervading.[23] This form is bliss and

[15] *Paramātma-sandarbha*, 39; *Cai. Ca.*, I. 2. 86.
[16] *B. G.*, VII. 5.
[17] *Viṣṇu Purāṇa*, I. 12. 69.
[18] *Gopālatāpanī U.*, II. 97.
[19] *Cai. Ca.*, II. 8. 110.
[20] *Gopālatāpanī U.*, II. 44; *B. G.*, IX. 17.
[21] *B. S.*, III. 2. 14 (*Govinda-bhāṣya*).
[22] *Gopālatāpanī U.*, 11; *Viṣṇu Purāṇa*, IV. 11. 2; *Bhā.*, III. 2. 12.
[23] *Gopālatāpanī U.*, II. 97; *Cai. Ca.*, I. 5. 11; I. 5. 15.

consciousness solidified,[24] as it were, and is perfect, eternal, non-material, perpetually in the prime of youth, and enchantingly beautiful.[25]

Brahman or Śrī Kṛṣṇa performs His *līlās* (blissful sports or pastimes)[26] with His eternal *parikaras* (playmates or associates) in His own *dhāman* (abode) known as Goloka, Vṛndāvana, or Vraja, which is a particular expression of His *ādhāra-śakti.* He is self-complacent (*ātmārāma*) and self-sufficient (*svarāj*) ; but His self-complacency or self-sufficiency does not suffer on account of His pastimes with His associates, as they, being His own manifestations or manifestations of His *śaktis,* are not different from Him. They serve Him with intense love in His *līlās,* which therefore are rendered exceedingly charming both to Him and to His associates. They are ever eager to make Him happy with enjoyment of bliss, and He too in His turn is similarly eager for their happiness.

According to the Upaniṣads, Brahman or Śrī Kṛṣṇa is Rasa,[27] which denotes that He is astonishingly relishable and at the same time the best relisher (Rasika) too, the transcendental Rasika. Through the eternal activities of His *svarūpa-śakti,* He is the embodiment of infinite varieties of rasahood, which find their eternal expressions in His infinite manifestations, known as His different *svarūpas* (selves), such as Nārāyaṇa, Rāma, Nṛsiṁha, Sadāśiva, and others, who, apparently having separate existence, actually exist in, and owe their existence and status to, Him. It is He who in His one and the same *vigraha* (self) appears as so many.[28] He is one in many and many in one.[29] In Śrī Kṛṣṇa, who is also known as Parama Īśvara, Pūrṇa Bhagavat, or Svayam Bhagavat, His *svarūpa-śakti* and rasahood find the fullest, the highest, and the most perfect expression. The *svarūpa* (manifestation) in which *svarūpa-śakti* and rasahood find only the minimum expression, so as not to give it any noticeable qualifiedness, is known as Nirviśeṣa (unqualified) Brahman, generally, Brahman as referred to in the scriptures.[30] As *svarūpa-śakti* is inseparable from Brahman, it exists in His *nirviśeṣa* manifestation also ; but beyond giving this manifestation its own characteristic or feature such as all-pervading existence, it remains in a perpetual state of inaction. However, of the intermediate manifestations, the one nearest to Nirviśeṣa Brahman is known as Paramātman, the *antaryāmin* or immanent aspect of Śrī Kṛṣṇa, in whom *svarūpa-śakti* and rasahood find an expression higher than in

[24] *Brahma Saṁhitā,* V. 1 ; *Bhaktirasāmṛta-sindhu,* II. 1. 15.
[25] *Cai. Ca.,* II. 21. 83-122 ; *Bṛhadbhāgavatāmṛtam,* II. 5. 112.
[26] *B. S.,* II. 1. 33.
[27] *Tai. U.,* II. 7.
[28] *Cai. Ca.,* II. 9. 141.
[29] *Bhā.,* X. 40. 7 ; *Gopālatāpanī U.,* I. 21 ; *Ka. U.,* II. 3. 12.
[30] *B. G.,* XIV. 27 ; *Mu. U.,* III. 1. 3.

Nirviśeṣa Brahman so as to give this aspect a form.[31] It is from this aspect as locus (*āśraya*) and ground (*udgama-sthāna*) that the different *avatāras* or divine appearances and the phenomenal world of spirit and nature proceed. The other innumerable aspects lying between Paramātman and Śrī Kṛṣṇa possess higher expressions of *svarūpa-śakti* and rasa-hood in them in different degrees. They are all Īśvaras or Bhagavats, Śrī Kṛṣṇa being the Īśvara of Īśvaras. They all possess eternal forms of bliss and consciousness solidified, as it were, all-pervading though apparently limited.[32] All these *bhagavat-svarūpas* have their respective associates with whom they perform their *līlās* and thus relish their own sweetness in their respective *dhāmans* (abodes) which are only so many expressions of Vṛndāvana and hence of His *ādhāra-śakti*. The innumerable manifestations, being less perfect in respect of their *śaktis* and rasahood, are called *svāṁśas* (subjective portions) of Śrī Kṛṣṇa. It is now evident that Śrī Kṛṣṇa, the ultimate Reality, appears in three aspects, viz. Brahman, Paramātman, and Bhagavat, as referred to in the *Bhāgavata*.[33]

As already hinted at, the rasahood of Śrī Kṛṣṇa has two main aspects—relishable *rasa* (denoting astonishingly enjoyable bliss) and relishing *rasa* or Rasika. The relishing *rasa* is Śrī Kṛṣṇa Himself, the supreme Rasika. The bliss He enjoys has again two aspects— *svarūpānanda* (bliss of enjoying His own self) and *śaktyānanda* (bliss of enjoying His *śakti*), which constitute the two aspects of the relishable *rasa*. He being *ānanda* and nothing but *ānanda* is immensely delightful, and He enjoys Himself with the help of His *hlādinī-śakti* or rather *svarūpa-śakti* in which *hlādinī* preponderates. This *hlādinī*, being a *śakti* appertaining to His *ānanda*, is essentially delightful, but becomes much more richly relishable when thrown by Him into the heart of His devotees, *parikaras*, and others. There it is transformed into *bhakti* and *preman* or intense love for Him which finds expression in a flow, as it were, from the heart of His *parikaras* in course of their loving services in His *līlās*, and is enjoyed by Him with maddening relish. This is *śaktyānanda*; it is much more enthralling and covetable than His *svarūpānanda*. *Preman* is delightful to His devotees too,[34] who with the help of *preman* relish His all-round sweetness, which is so charming and attractive as to madden, with intense and anxious longing for relish, everybody including His different *svarūpas* and even Himself.[35] It seems indeed, Śrī Kṛṣṇa relishes *rasa* as His own self (*svayaṁ-rūpa*), as different *bhagavat-svarūpas*, and also as His *parikaras*, and it appears, He

[31] *Ka. U.*, VI. 17.
[32] *Laghubhāgavatāmṛtam*, I. 3. 86-90.
[33] *Bhā.*, I. 2. 11 ; *Cai. Ca.*, I. 2. 6, 7.
[34] *Prīti-sandarbha*, 64.
[35] *Cai. Ca.*, II. 21. 86-88 ; *Bhā.*, III. 2. 12.

manifested Himself eternally as all these, only to enjoy the *rasa* in all its varieties.

Of the *bhagavat-svarūpas,* other than Śrī Kṛṣṇa, Nārāyaṇa is the chief whose *dhāman* is known as *paravyoman* or *mahāvaikuṇṭha,* including in it the *dhāmans* of all the *svarūpas.* In *paravyoman,* where Śrī Kṛṣṇa appears as Nārāyaṇa, His *aiśvarya* (awe-inspiring grandeur and mightiness) preponderates over His *mādhurya* (sweetness) and stifles the *sevā-vāsanā* (desire for loving service) of the associates, who cannot therefore offer whole-hearted service. In Dvārakā and Mathurā, two *dhāmans* of Śrī Kṛṣṇa, both *mādhurya* and *aiśvarya* are equally evolved ; but the former is sometimes overtaken by the latter when the associates, being inspired with awe, have their *sevā-vāsanā* stifled. But in Vṛndāvana, although both *mādhurya* and *aiśvarya* find their fullest and most perfect expression, yet the former overwhelmingly predominates over the latter, so much so that even the consciousness of His Godhead, being immersed, as it were, in the bottomless ocean of sweetness, is lost to Him as well as to His associates. Here His *aiśvarya,* being steeped in sweetness, loses its awe-inspiring function, and disguised, as it were, in *mādhurya,* helps the enjoyment of bliss.

The love of the Vṛndāvana associates (*vraja-bhava*) is intense enough to inspire in them a sense of 'mine'-ness (a feeling of 'He is mine', *mamatva-buddhi*) as distinguished from a sense of 'thine'-ness (a feeling of 'I am Thine') in the *paravyoman* associates.

According to the degree of intensity, the love (*preman* or *bhāva*) of the Vṛndāvana associates has been classified as *dāsya, sakhya, vātsalya,* and *kāntā. Dāsya preman* is the love of the *dāsas* (servants) of Kṛṣṇa whom they regard as their loving and beloved master. But it suffers from a sense of inferiority on the part of the *dāsa,* whose *sevā-vāsanā* (desire for service) cannot therefore find an adequate expression. *Sakhya preman,* or the love of His *sakhis* (comrades), is immune from such a complex and is thus superior to *dāsya.* The *sakhis* regard Him as their equal in every respect and treat Him as such without the slightest hesitation, He too reciprocating their love exactly in a similar manner. *Vātsalya preman* is the love of parents for their beloved child. Though Śrī Kṛṣṇa, being the ultimate Reality, cannot have any parents, two of His associates, Nanda and Yaśodā, cherish a firm belief (*abhimāna*) that Kṛṣṇa is their own child, and Kṛṣṇa also entertains a corresponding belief. Thus with a loving sense of superiority, they regard Him as the object of their anxious parental care and kindness and sometimes even go so far as to chastise and punish Him[36]

[36] *Cai. Ca.,* I. 4. 21.

when they think it necessary for His welfare, but which the *sakhis* will not think of doing, as the love of the *sakhis,* though intense, is not so intense as to inspire in them a sense of 'mine'-ness regarding Kṛṣṇa, so crystallized as in the case of parents. In *kāntā preman,* the love is much more intensified and the sense of 'mine'-ness much more crystallized. It bears a resemblance to the mad love of a damsel for her amorous comrade or paramour, with the distinction that in *kāntā preman* there is not even a shadow of any desire for one's own pleasure. The cause of this distinction is that people under the bondage of Māyā are guided by Māyā and not by *svarūpa-śakti,* and this Māyā leads their mind to their own selves (i.e. away from Kṛṣṇa) and generates in them desires for their own pleasure; while the *līlā* associates of Kṛṣṇa are guided by *svarūpa-śakti* and not by Māyā which, being *bahiraṅga-śakti,* cannot even approach them; and this *svarūpa-śakti,* whose only function is to serve Kṛṣṇa for His happiness in all possible ways, leads their mind to Kṛṣṇa, but never away from Him, and generates in them desires for His happiness only. It is for this reason that the *Bhāgavata* says (X.22.26) that as fried or boiled paddy does not germinate, so does not the mind engrossed in Kṛṣṇa generate *kāma,* i.e. desire for one's own pleasure. However, the associates of Kṛṣṇa possessing *kāntā preman,* known as *gopīs,* are really the embodied expressions (*mūrta rūpa*) of His *svarūpa-śakti hlādinī* and are thus His own consorts (*svakīyā kāntās*); but in order that an extremely fascinating feature of the *kāntā rasa* (which, on account of its surpassing sweetness, is also known as *madhura*-[sweet] *rasa*) may be evolved, and also with a view to showing that *kāntā preman* is regardless of any hindrance that may confront the manifestation of their *sevā-vāsanā,* their relationship with Kṛṣṇa in His manifest *līlā* is, by the influence of *yoga-māyā,* conceived like that of a damsel with her paramour (*parakīyā*).[37] The distinction between the supersensible love of the *gopīs,* technically called *mahābhāva,* and that of the other associates of Vṛndāvana, is that the love of the *dāsas, sakhis,* or *vatsalas* (parents) is subject to their particular relationship with Kṛṣṇa and cannot therefore find an expression transgressing that relationship; while the relationship of the *gopīs* is subject to their love, which may therefore find an unrestricted expression in any direction and to any extent so as to make them forget everything concerning their own selves.[38] Such love of the *gopīs* again has various phases manifested in different *gopīs*; but all the phases, with infinitely superior manifestations unapproachable by any other, exist in their chief known as Śrī Rādhā, who is *pūrṇa-śakti* and is not therefore essentially different from Kṛṣṇa, the *pūrṇa-śaktimat* (the most perfect possessor of *śaktis*), though the

[37] *Cai. Ca.,* I. 4. 26; *Gopālatāpanī U.,* II. 23; *Śrīkṛṣṇa-sandarbha,* 177.
[38] *Bhaktirasāmṛta-sindhu,* I. 153-160.

two exist separately from eternity for enjoyment of the bliss of *līlās*.[39] Just as the other *bhagavat-svarūpas* are the manifestations of Kṛṣṇa, so are their *kāntās* (consorts) the corresponding manifestations of Śrī Rādhā,[40] who is thus the *mūlākāntā-śakti* (the main source of all the *kāntā śaktis* or the consorts of all the *bhagavat-svarūpas* as well as of the *gopīs*). However, all other *gopīs* minister to the enjoyment of His *līlās* with Śrī Rādhā by their most loving services.

The enjoyment of *rasa* may attain its fullest perfection only when it is relished not only as an object, but also as a subject of love. In Vṛndāvana, Śrī Kṛṣṇa, the transcendental Rasika, is the object of His associates' love and in certain cases, subject too ; but as regards *kāntā preman,* He is only the object of Śrī Rādhā's love and not at all a subject. And it is one's love that enables one not only to serve Him, but also to relish His overwhelming sweetness which is alluring even to Himself ; and the extent of enjoyment corresponds to the extent to which one's love is developed. It is Śrī Rādhā alone therefore who may relish His sweetness to the fullest extent possible, as it is in her alone that love finds its most perfect expression. In Vṛndāvana therefore Śrī Kṛṣṇa's fervent desire for relishing His own sweetness like Śrī Rādhā remains ever unfulfilled. It is, however, fulfilled in another expression as Śrī Caitanya or Śrī Gaurāṅga performing *līlās* in His eternal abode Navadvīpa, sometimes manifested in the phenomenal world like Vṛndāvana. According to the Bengal school, Śrī Caitanya is the embodiment of Śrī Rādhā and Śrī Kṛṣṇa,[41] of *pūrṇa-śakti* and *pūrṇa-śaktimat,* of Rasarāja (Kṛṣṇa, the highest expression of *rasa*) and *mahābhāva* (the highest expression of *kāntā preman*)—the object and the subject combined, in one and the same form, the subjective aspect preponderating. The associates of Śrī Caitanya in Navadvīpa are no other than His Vṛndāvana associates in appropriate forms and names. Thus the *līlās* of Śrī Kṛṣṇa and Śrī Caitanya are only two parts, as it were, of the same *līlā* current of the ultimate Reality, *rasa* of the Upaniṣads.

## JĪVA OR JĪVĀTMAN

According to the Bengal school, Jīvātman (individual soul) is a *śakti* (*jīva-śakti*) of Brahman, superior to *māyā-śakti* and is *cit* (consciousness) by nature.[42] It is called an *aṁśa* (part) of Brahman[43] on account of its being His *śakti,*[44] as a *śakti* forms a part of the *śaktimat* (possessor of *śaktis*). On

[39] *Cai. Ca.,* I. 4. 83-85.
[40] *Cai. Ca.,* I. 4. 63-68.
[41] *Cai. Ca.,* II. 8. 233, 238.
[42] *B. G.,* VII. 5 (and commentaries thereof by Śrīdhara Svāmin and Viśvanātha Cakravartin) ; *Viṣṇu Purāṇa,* VI. 7. 61.
[43] *B. G.,* XV. 7 ; *B. S.,* II. 3. 43-47.
[44] *Paramātma-sandarbha,* 31.

the authority of a verse in the *Bhāgavata*[45] in support of the transfusion of *tattvas* (elements) into one another, Jīva Gosvāmin holds that Jīvātman is an *aṁśa* of Kṛṣṇa, transfused with *jīva-śakti,* but not associated with *svarūpa-śakti.*[46] It is not separated from Him by Māyā, as Māyā being His *bahiraṅga-śakti* cannot touch Him, nor is it a part separated from Him, like a chip cut off from a block of stone, as He is not divisible.[47] Jīvātman does not possess *svarūpa-śakti*[48] and hence is called His *vibhinnāṁśa* (differentiated part)[49] as distinguished from His *svāṁśa* possessing *svarūpa-śakti.*

Jīvātman, being *cit* by nature, is a knower (*jñātṛ*)[50] and a doer (*kartṛ*),[51] though its power of doing is derived from Brahman.[52]

As to the magnitude of Jīvātman, it is the smallest thing imaginable.[53] Its magnitude is like that of an atom.[54] Residing in the heart of a living being[55] it spreads its consciousness throughout the whole body, just as a spot of sandal-paste placed somewhere on the body spreads its coolness beyond the spot,[56] or just as a flower spreads its fragrance beyond its own self.[57]

Jīvātman has a separate entity which is eternal.[58] The soul of a being in bondage does not therefore lose its existence and become one with Brahman when it attains liberation, as the Śaṅkara school holds. That the separate existence of the soul continues even after its liberation is evident from a text of the Upaniṣad[59] purporting that the Jīva realizing *rasa* becomes *ānandin* (blissful possessor of *ānanda* or bliss) and from a passage in Śaṅkara's *bhāṣya* on the *Nṛsiṁhatāpanī*[60] as well as from a *sūtra* of the *Brahma-Sūtra,*[61] implying that even the *muktas* (liberated souls) serve God or Brahman. Jīvātmans are infinite in number.[62]

Since Jīvātman is a *śakti* and an *aṁśa* of Brahman, the Bengal school holds that it is its intrinsic nature and duty to serve Him,[63] as a *śakti* is always found to serve its possessor, and a part the whole, like the roots and branches

[45] *Bhā.*, XI. 22. 7 ; *Paramātma-sandarbha,* 41.
[46] *Paramātma-sandarbha,* 31.
[47] *B. S.,* II. 3. 43 (*Govinda-bhāṣya*).
[48] *Viṣṇu Purāṇa,* I. 12. 69.
[49] *Paramātma-sandarbha,* 45.
[50] *B. S.,* II. 3. 18.
[51] *B. S.,* II. 3. 33.
[52] *B. S.,* II. 3. 41.
[53] *Bhā.,* XI. 16. 11 ; *Paramātma-sandarbha,* 17, 33 ; *Mu. U.,* III. 1. 9.
[54] *Mu. U.,* III. 1. 9 ; *Ka. U.,* II. 8, 13 ; *B. S.,* II. 3. 19-22.
[55] *Chā. U.,* VIII. 3. 3 ; *Pra. U.,* III. 6.
[56] *B. S.,* II. 3. 23.
[57] *B. S.,* II. 3. 26.
[58] *B. S.,* II. 2. 36 ; *B. G.,* XV. 7.
[59] *Tai. U.,* II. 7.
[60] *Nṛsiṁhatāpanī U.,* II. 15, 16, as quoted in *Cai. Ca.,* II. 24. 33.
[61] *B. S.,* IV. 1. 12 (*Govinda-bhāṣya*).
[62] *Paramātma-sandarbha,* 44 ; *Bhā.,* X. 87. 30.
[63] *Cai. Ca.,* II. 20. 101.

of a tree serving the tree. The Jīva is an eternal servant of Brahman, a loving servant, of course. Brahman or Śrī Kṛṣṇa, the object of the Jīva's loving service (being the most lovely and lovable, the most enchantingly beautiful and graceful, and the most loving one) is always eager to give bliss to His associates ; and the Jīvas, as His associates, are ever as eager to minister to His pleasures by loving services in His *līlās*. The Jīva's loving service is a constant source of ever-increasing joy (*sevānanda*) to both the subject and the object of love.

There are two classes of souls,[64] *nitya-mukta* (eternally liberated) and *baddha* (under the bondage of Māyā from eternity). The former serve Him as His eternal associates enjoying the bliss of loving services ; and the latter, because they forget Kṛṣṇa and their relationship with Him, have come under the bondage of Māyā, but may be liberated and become His associates by proper devotion.

The Jīva, being intrinsically His loving servant, cannot, unless prevailed upon by some extraneous circumstances such as a strong desire for merging into Brahman, be really satisfied with mere liberation from Māyā, as it is not in full consonance with his servanthood. Nor may Śrī Kṛṣṇa, the Rasika, if He be ever good and merciful which He certainly is, be fully satisfied with giving to the Jīva anything short of admittance to His blissful *līlās*.

However, there are mainly two classes of His associates—those who are the expression of His *svarūpa-śakti,* as already referred to, and those who are liberated Jīvas. The latter, being essentially His servants, may serve Him only under the guidance of the former.

But how to get rid of Māyā and realize one's essential servanthood and have one's *sevā-vāsanā* evolved?

As non remembrance of Brahman is the cause of the soul's bondage, the bondage may be removed only by removing non-remembrance, which may be done only by remembering Him, by knowing Him, and ultimately, by realizing Him, just as darkness may be removed only by bringing in light. Hence, remembrance of Brahman is the essence of all forms of *sādhanā* (means to be adopted for liberation).[65] But simple remembrance, unaided by His *svarūpa-śakti,* cannot lead one to realization, as He can be realized only in His *svarūpa-śakti,* or rather, in that aspect of His *svarūpa-śakti* which is known as His *ādhāra-śakti,* technically, Vāsudeva.[66] Hence the Bengal school holds that the only effective means of liberation and realization of Brahman is *bhakti,*[67] which at the stage of practice is graced

[64] *Cai. Ca.,* II. 22. 8-11.
[65] *Bhaktirasāmṛta-sindhu,* I. 2. 5.
[66] *Bhā.,* IV. 3. 23.
[67] *Bhā.,* XI. 14. 21 ; *B. G.,* XVIII. 55.

by *svarūpa-śakti* and is ultimately ripened into *preman,* a particular aspect of *svarūpa-śakti* in which *hlādinī* and *saṁvit* preponderate.[68] It is for this reason that this school holds that even *jñāna* and *yoga,* unaided by *bhakti,* cannot produce their desired effect,[69] while *bhakti* is efficacious independently of *jñāna* and *yoga. Māṭhara Śruti* says: 'It is only *bhakti* that leads the Jīva to Brahman, it is only *bhakti* that shows Brahman to the Jīva. Puruṣa or Brahman is subject to *bhakti.* Only *bhakti* is great'.[70] In the practice of *jñāna* associated with *bhakti, svarūpa-śakti* appears as *ātmavidyā* (knowledge of Self), and in the practice of pure *bhakti,* as *guhyavidyā* (mystic experience).

Broadly speaking, there are four ways (*mārgas*) that aspirants after salvation follow—*karma, yoga, jñāna,* and *bhakti.* These are all, more or less, technical terms. *Karma* signifies performance of *yajñas* and other Vedic rites, generally known as *varṇāśrama-dharma* (directions to be followed by persons placed in different *varṇas* or castes, at different *āśramas* or stages of life as enjoined by scriptures). *Karma* may lead one to prosperity and happiness in this world or to *svarga* (heaven in the perishable universe) after death, and even to *satyaloka,* but not to liberation from Māyā.[71] With the dedication to Kṛṣṇa of all fruits of *karma,* it may, however, pave one's path to liberation.[72] *Yoga* signifies meditation aimed at union with Paramātman. *Jñāna* (knowledge) signifies meditation with a view to *sāyujya-mukti* or merging into Nirviśeṣa Brahman. And *bhakti* signifies devotional practices, such as worship of God, chanting His names, attributes, etc., singing songs about His sweetness and beauty and *līlās,* and so on. This is known as *sādhana-bhakti* (*bhakti* at the stage of practice). When mixed with *karma, yoga,* or *jñāna,* it is called *miśrā* (mixed) *bhakti* and gives efficacy to the way associated with it. It is called *kevalā* or *śuddhā* (unalloyed) *bhakti* when it aims exclusively at the loving service of Kṛṣṇa, as the dearest and nearest one, for His happiness only, and not at anything else, not even at liberation from Māyā. This constitutes, as it were, the fifth *puruṣārtha,* going beyond *mokṣa* or liberation which is the fourth objective of the Jīva. But even with the practice of *śuddhā bhakti,* if one ultimately has a sense of His *aiśvarya* (awe-inspiring grandeur and mightiness) predominating in one's mind, one would attain in *mahāvaikuṇṭha,* the *dhāman* of Nārāyaṇa, any of the four kinds of *mukti* (liberation), viz. *sārūpya* (same appearance as that of Nārāyaṇa), *sāmīpya* (vicinity of Nārāyaṇa), *sālokya* (residence at

[68] *Bhaktirasāmṛta-sindhu.* I. 3. 1.

[69] *Cai. Ca.,* II. 22. 14 ; *Bhā.,* I. 5. 12 ; II. 4. 17 ; X. 14. 4.

[70] '*Bhaktireva enaṁ nayati, bhaktireva enaṁ darśayati, bhaktivaśaḥ puruṣaḥ, bhaktireva garīyasī*' (*Māṭhara Śruti*), quoted in *Prīti-sandarbha,* 64, 65 and many other places by Jīva Gosvāmin and also in *Govinda-bhāṣya.*

[71] *B. G.,* II. 37 ; IX. 20, 21 ; *Mu. U.,* I. 2. 7.

[72] *B. G.,* IX. 27, 28.

the same abode with Nārāyaṇa), and *sārṣṭi* (*aiśvarya* similar to that of Nārāyaṇa). A *śuddha bhakta* (devotee) wants neither *sāyujya* nor any of these four kinds of *mukti,* though the Bengal school recognizes them. He aims exclusively at the loving service of the transcendental Rasika, the attainment of which is known as *prāpti* (attainment of the ultimate Reality as the dearest and nearest one), and liberation from Māyā is only incidental to it.

A devotee of the Bengal school worships both Śrī Kṛṣṇa and Śrī Caitanya with their associates in the *līlā* he chooses to serve them in. He also meditates on their *līlās,* imagining that he himself, under the guidance of the *līlā* associates, is serving them there as an associate in each *līlā* with appropriate form (*rūpa*). Besides worship (*arcanā*) and meditation (*smaraṇa*), he may practise other items of *sādhana-bhakti,* the most important and the most efficacious item being the chanting of His names which are all *cit* and *ānanda,* and hence, not different from Him.

When by the practice of *sādhana-bhakti,* the heart of a devotee is purified, it is graced with the advent of a special aspect of *svarūpa-śakti* emanating from Śrī Kṛṣṇa,[73] which with the continuance of *sādhanā* develops into *sādhya-bhakti* (*bhakti* desired or aimed at) and *preman* (intense love for Kṛṣṇa) that leads him to his goal, which, according to the Bengal school, is the loving service of the transcendental Rasika in His *līlās* in Vṛndāvana as well as in Navadvīpa, under the guidance of any of the four classes of associates already mentioned, viz. associates with *dāsya, sakhya, vātsalya,* and *kāntā bhāvas.* On the success of *sādhanā,* when graced by *svarūpa-śakti,* he will be favoured with a form of *śuddha-sattva* befitting his desired service, in each of the two *dhāmans*—Vṛndāvana and Navadvīpa.

### THE UNIVERSE: CREATION

According to the Upaniṣads, Brahman is the universe and exists beyond it too.[74] It may mean that He is the cause of this universe or that He transforms Himself into the universe. The Bengal school holds that Brahman is the material and also the efficient cause of the universe and that He transforms Himself into the universe, Himself remaining unaffected by the transformation.[75]

Brahman creates the universe with the help of His *māyā-śakti. Māyā-śakti,* being inert, has no moving power of its own and remains in a state

[73] *Cai. Ca.,* II. 22. 57 ; *Bhaktirasāmṛta-sindhu,* I. 2. 2 ; *Prīti-sandarbha,* 64.
[74] *Mā. U.,* 1.
[75] *B. S.,* I. 4. 26. The example of a spider and its threads in the Upaniṣads supports the transformation theory. *Cai. Ca.,* I. 7. 117, 118.

of equilibrium before the creation begins. When He desires creation, He looks at Māyā and thereby transmits His sentient creative (moving) power to it, whereby the state of its equilibrium is disturbed and creation ensues.

It has already been noted that Māyā has two aspects—*guṇa-māyā* and *jīva-māyā*. The *guṇa-māyā,* with the help of the power transmitted by Brahman, transforms itself into the constituents of the infinite varieties of things in the universe and thus becomes the 'constituent' cause of the universe. And *jīva-māyā,* with the aid of the power transmitted, helps the creation by making the souls-in-bondage forget their selves and their relationship with Brahman and also by inspiring in them an attachment for things mundane; and thus it becomes the efficient cause of the universe. But it should be noted that Brahman is the principal cause and Māyā only the secondary cause of the universe, as neither *guṇa-māyā* nor *jīva-māyā* can help the creation unless and until Brahman's power is transmitted to them. However, it is now evident that according to the Bengal school, the *māyā-śakti* of Brahman, associated with the energy transmitted by Him, and not His self with *svarūpa-śakti,* is transformed into the universe, He in His self remaining unaffected.[76]

It has already been pointed out that this school admits the transfusion of *śakti* and *śaktimat* into each other,[77] and there are texts in the scriptures to show that Brahman spreads Himself in the universe like threads in a piece of cloth.[78] It therefore follows that the universe is the *pariṇāma* (transformation) of Brahman transfused with *māyā-śakti* (not with His *svarūpa-śakti*) but still remaining untouched by Māyā through His *īśvaratva* (inscrutable powers).[79] Here a question may arise, Since *svarūpa-śakti* exists eternally and inseparably in Brahman, how is it that the universe is the *pariṇāma* of Brahman transfused with *māyā-śakti* only, and similarly that the Jīva is an *aṁśa* of Brahman transfused with *jīva-śakti* only? How is it that *svarūpa-śakti* plays no part? The answer probably is that in the case of the Jīva and the universe, *svarūpa-śakti* no doubt exists in Brahman, but it exists in a state of perpetual inaction as in the case of Nirviśeṣa Brahman; and it is for this reason that the *Brahma Saṁhitā* asserts that the universe evolves out of Nirviśeṣa Brahman regarded as a halo (*prabhā*) of Śrī Kṛṣṇa.[80]

Besides Māyā, Jīva, *kāla* (time), and *karma* (destiny, the works done by Jīva in the previous births), all these being *śaktis* of Brahman, also play important parts in creation. It has already been pointed out how the Jīva,

[76] *Paramātma-sandarbha,* 73.
[77] *Ibid.,* 34.
[78] *Bhā.,* X. 15. 35; X. 46. 31; *B. G.,* X. 42.
[79] *Bhā.,* I. 11. 39.
[80] *Brahma Saṁhitā,* V. 40.

under the influence of *jīva-māyā,* finds its way into the universe and thus becomes an important factor of creation. *Kāla* helps the transformation of Māyā, just as it helps milk to be changed into curd. And *karma* or destiny determines the nature of the Jīva's material body and its organs and also the origin and nature of the things that the Jīva may, according to its destiny, enjoy or suffer.

However, as opposed to the Vivartavāda (theory of apparent transformation) of the Śaṅkara school, according to which the universe has only an illusory existence, the Bengal school holds that its existence is real though transitory. This theory of creation is known as Pariṇāmavāda (theory of real transformation).[81]

## ACINTYA-BHEDĀBHEDA EXPLAINED

There is a good deal of difference of opinion among the philosophers regarding the relation between the Jīva and Brahman. In one view, there is no difference (*bheda*) whatsoever; in another view, there is; and yet in a third view, there are both difference (*bheda*) and non-difference (*abheda*). In fact, the Upaniṣads contain texts in support of *bheda* and also of *abheda* between the Jīva and Brahman, and even in the same Upaniṣad may be found texts in support of both,[82] which fact is therefore suggestive of a reconciliation between the two sets of texts, based on equal importance attached to them, which they unquestionably deserve, as they equally convey the truths revealed in the Upaniṣads. Such a reconciliation has always been the aim of the Bengal school.

The Bengal school upholds a peculiar type of Bhedābhedavāda known as Acintya-bhedābhedavāda, which stands on a much wider basis than that of other schools, whose arguments are mainly as follows: (1) The Jīva and Brahman are *abhinna* (non-different) inasmuch as they are *cit* (consciousness), and they are *bhinna* (different) inasmuch as their attributes are quite different. Brahman is *vibhu cit* (all-pervading consciousness), while the Jīva is *aṇu cit* or '*cit*-atom' (the smallest imaginable portion of consciousness); the one is all-knowing, the other is too-little-knowing; the one is all-powerful, the other has very little power and that too emanating from Brahman; the one is the master of Māyā, and the other is susceptible to, and is under, the bondage of Māyā; the one is the Creator of the universe, the other, while under the bondage of Māyā, has his body created by Him; and so on. (2) As the Jīva is an *aṁśa* of Brahman, the relation between them must be one of simultaneous *bheda* and *abheda,* for such is the relation between *aṁśa* and *aṁśin*. The Bengal school accepts these views,

[81] *Cai. Ca.,* II. 6. 154, 157.
[82] *Chā. U.,* III. 14. 1; VI. 8. 7; *Bṛ. U.,* I. 4. 10; II. 1. 20.

but only as a corollary to its wider view regarding the relation between *śakti* and *śaktimat* in general.

It has already been said that the Jīva is an *aṁśa* of Brahman transfused with His *jīva-śakti* and that the universe also is Brahman transfused with His *māyā-śakti*. And the *dhāmans* of Brahman and His different *svarūpas* as well as their *parikaras* or associates also have been said to be essentially the different aspects of His *svarūpa-śakti* or, strictly speaking, Brahman transfused with the different aspects of *svarūpa-śakti,* as the latter cannot be separated from the former. Hence, since it is the different *śaktis* or their different aspects, and not Brahman, that give them their distinctive characteristics, it may be said that the Jīva, the universe, the *dhāmans,* and the *parikaras* are all essentially His *śaktis,* and their relation with Brahman will be the relation that exists between *śakti* and *śaktimat* in general.

But how is *śakti* related to *śaktimat*? Are they absolutely different from each other or are they absolutely non-different? Can they be separated?

The last question may be taken up first. According to the Upaniṣads, the *śaktis* of Brahman are *svābhāvikī,* inseparably connected with Brahman, as has already been pointed out. Such a relation between *śakti* and *śaktimat* is universal. It has been very aptly illustrated in the *Caitanya Caritāmṛta* with the help of the examples of musk and fire. As odour cannot be separated from musk, as heat cannot be separated from fire, so *śakti* cannot be separated from *śaktimat.* Indeed, inseparability seems to be the essence of *śaktitva* (state of being *śakti*). Red-hot iron emits heat, but it does so only so long as it is hot. Heat is not natural to iron, and hence heat is not said to be its property or *śakti,* as in the case of fire.

Then the other question about difference or non-difference. The answer is not an easy one. One cannot think of musk bereft of its odour; and, accordingly, one may be inclined to think that there is no difference between the two. But when one feels the odour of musk at a distance from the latter, one is again inclined to think that there is a difference between the two. Again, if the substance of musk and its odour be supposed to be different, both are to be regarded as constituents of musk; and consequently, the musk will lose in weight on emission of its odour, which, however, one's experience does not corroborate. Hence, the substance of musk cannot be said to be different from its odour.

The relation between Brahman and His *śaktis* also may be considered in the light of the above example. Brahman being *ānanda* is inseparably connected with His *śaktis. Ānanda* and *śaktis* of Brahman constitute one and the same thing.[83] If these two be supposed to be

[83] *B. S.,* II. 3. 43 (*Govinda-bhāṣya*).

different, like oxygen and hydrogen in water, *svagata-bheda* (internal difference) in Brahman becomes unavoidable, which, however, cannot be admitted. Nor can it be supposed that there is absolute non-difference between the two, as His attributes, such as grace, may be felt even when His self is not realized.

The relation is indeed a peculiar one ; and it is probably for this reason that the *Viṣṇu Purāṇa* regards the *śaktis* (properties or qualities) of things as *acintya-jñānagocara* (falling within the range of inexplicable knowledge).[84] *Acintya-jñāna* means the knowledge that cannot be accounted for. Sugar is sweet ; but why? Quinine is bitter and cures malaria ; but why? Poison kills a man, whereas milk does not ; but why? One cannot answer these whys. Still these are truths and have got to be admitted. Such knowledge of truths that cannot be accounted for and yet have to be admitted is known as *acintya-jñāna* or inexplicable knowledge.

However, it has been found that the recognition of mere difference between *śakti* and *śaktimat,* apart from non-difference, gives rise to insurmountable difficulties, and the recognition of mere non-difference too, apart from difference, gives rise to similar difficulties. Nor may the existence of either be ignored. Hence it cannot but be admitted that the relation is one of simultaneous difference and non-difference, and such a simultaneity is inexplicable (*acintya*). After elaborate discussion in his *Sandarbhas* and *Sarvasaṁvādinī,* Jīva Gosvāmin holds that the relation is one of *acintya-bhedābheda* (inexplicable difference and non-difference). By *acintya* he means 'incapable of being considered under either of the categories of absolute difference and absolute non-difference' (*Bhinnābhinnatvādi-vikalpaiścintayitum-aśakyaḥ*), as in the case of fire and its heat.[85] This is known as the Acintya-bhedābhedavāda (theory of inexplicable difference and non-difference) of the Bengal school.

## ADVAITA TATTVA

According to the Upaniṣads, Brahman is *advaya tattva, ekamevā-dvitīya* (one without a second), which, according to the philosophers of different schools, implies that He is without any of the three kinds of *bhedas* (difference), viz. *sajātīya-bheda* (*bheda* within the same species), *vijātīya-bheda* (*bheda* between alien species), and *svagata-bheda* (*bheda* within self or internal difference).

Both Śaṅkarācārya and Jīva Gosvāmin agree that Brahman is without these three kinds of *bhedas,* but the ways of their thinking are different.

In spite of there being explicit texts in the Upaniṣads regarding the

[84] *Viṣṇu Purāṇa,* I. 3. 2.
[85] *Krama-sandarbha* of *Bhāgavata,* XI. 3. 37.

eternal existence of inseparable *śaktis* of Brahman, Śaṅkarācārya does not recognize them, probably because he thinks that since *śaktis* give rise to differences or *bhedas,* Brahman, who is without any *bheda,* cannot possess them. In his opinion, the texts that speak of Brahman's *bhedas* or *śaktis* have no *pāramārthika* value (the value that may lead one to eternal truth) and possess only *vyāvahārika* value (the value that may help one in one's *sādhanā* and that, too, only during the period of *sādhanā* or *upāsanā*). In consequence of such a view he asserts that (1) the Jīva has no real existence as such and is nothing but Brahman under the influence of Māyā or nescience and will become one with Brahman on the removal of nescience ; (2) the universe has only an illusory existence and appears to be real only under the influence of Māyā ; (3) the *bhagavat-svarūpas* also are only Brahman under the influence of an aspect of Māyā ; and (4) only Brahman and nothing else has real existence. Thus Brahman is one without a second. In his attempts to establish his views, Śaṅkarācārya had generally to resort to *lakṣaṇā* or *gauṇa* meaning of the texts even where *mukhyā vṛtti* was admissible.

On the other hand, Jīva Gosvāmin recognizes the existence of Brahman's *śaktis,* as is quite evident from the previous discussions, and also the real existence of the Jīva as such, of the *bhagavat-svarūpas* and their *dhāmans* as such, and also of the universe, though as transitory. He holds that all the texts of the Upaniṣads have *pāramārthika* value, and none need be ignored as *vyāvahārika.* He resorts generally to the *mukhya* meaning of the texts. Herein lies the fundamental difference between Śaṅkara and Jīva Gosvāmin.

According to Jīva Gosvāmin, since the Upaniṣads speak of *bhedas,* they have got to be recognized ; but these *bhedas* are only apparent, not real ; otherwise, the Upaniṣads would not have spoken of Brahman as being one without a second in spite of these *bhedas.*

Then what is meant by *bheda*? According to Jīva Gosvāmin, *bheda* can be predicated of two things only when each of them is *svayaṁsiddha* (i.e. self-evolved, self-dependent, self-sufficient, and independent of everything else) ; and Brahman has no such *bhedas—sajātīya, vijātīya,* or *svagata*—as these are not *svayaṁsiddhas* unlike Himself.

As to *sajātīya-bheda,* both Brahman and the Jīva are *cit* in essence, and hence they belong to the same species, *cit,* and thus the Jīva appears to be a case of *sajātīya-bheda* in relation to Brahman ; but it is not really so, for the Jīva, owing its existence and status to Brahman, is not *svayaṁsiddha.*

As to *vijātīya-bheda,* the material universe, being in essence unconscious matter, belongs to a species alien to Brahman, the absolute consciousness, and thus may appear to be an instance of *vijātīya-bheda* ; but it is not really so, as it is not *svayaṁsiddha,* depending as it does on Brahman for its existence and status.

As to *svagata-bheda,* it is of two varieties, viz. of different ingredients and of different phases. In the material bodies of beings, there are five elements—*kṣiti* (earth), *ap* (water), *tejas* (light), *marut* (air), and *vyoman* (voidness)—all being different types of matter; and there is also the conscious soul. Hence there are *svagata-bhedas* in individual beings. But in Brahman there is nothing but *cit* or *ānanda,* nor is there any soul apart from His self. Hence there is no *svagata-bheda* in Him. Again, the different *bhagavat-svarūpas* existing in Him, being the different phases of His rasahood, do not constitute *svagata-bheda,* as they are not *svayaṁsiddha* or independent of Him. The attributes of Brahman also are not a case of *svagata-bheda,* as they too owe their existence to Him, or rather to His *svarūpa-śakti.*

In this connection, Jīva Gosvāmin considers in his *Sarvasaṁvādinī* a text of the Upaniṣad—*'Vijñānamānandaṁ Brahma'.* Here, if *vijñāna* (consciousness) and *ānanda* (bliss) denote the same thing, there will be redundance, which is inadmissible in the same text. If they denote different things, they will appear like *svagata-bhedas.* But they are not actually so for reasons stated above, just as a piece of ornament of pure gold, with nothing else intermixed with it, is not a *svagata-bheda* of pure gold, it being not independent of gold and there being nothing but gold in it. The *dhāmans* and *parikaras* of Brahman, owing their existence to Him or His *svarūpa-śakti,* are not also *bhedas.* Thus Brahman is *advaya* (one without a second) in spite of the *bhedas,* which are only apparent and not real.

The Bengal school bases its arguments and conclusions strictly on the *mukhyārtha* of the Śrutis, attaches equal importance to all the texts, and ignores none as *vyavaharika,* and tries to reconcile the different texts, the most striking feature being its Acintya-bhedābhedavāda and establishment of Brahman's *advayatva* in spite of His inseparable *śaktis.* The most outstanding feature of the Bengal school, apart from its philosophical aspects, is its Rasa-cult that brings into the limelight the most fascinating and the most attractive phase of the rasahood of Brahman, hitherto more or less undisclosed (being only hinted at in the scriptures), and points out ways and means for its realization, which surpasses even the charm of *Brahmānanda* (bliss of realizing Nirviśeṣa Brahman). This latter implies calm and quiet bliss as distinguished from the ever-effulgent, ever-overflowing, and ever-rising flood of *rasa* in all its phases as in the *līlās* of Śrī Kṛṣṇa.

PART III

# THE RELIGIOUS PHILOSOPHIES

## 22

# THE PHILOSOPHY OF ŚAIVISM

### SCHOOLS OF ŚAIVISM

THE Śaiva philosophy is, in a sense, typical of the entire range of Hindu thought. While, in all its forms, it subscribes to the belief in three *padārthas* (categories: God, soul, and the bonds) and thirty-six *tattvas* (principles), in the reality ascribed to the *tattvas,* and in the independence assigned to souls and matter, it varies from idealistic monism at one end of the scale to pluralistic realism at the other end. But all through there will be found the typically Hindu insistence on knowledge as essential to salvation and as the prime cause thereof, though in some forms of Śaivism, this requisite is diluted with (or as they would say, reinforced by) deeds. All such variations may be found even in the recognized orthodox forms of Śaivism, leaving out of account the Pāśupatas (who do not recognize that God is the material cause or that He has any regard for the *karma* of souls in creation), the Mahāvratas, the Kāpālas, etc. (who combine the beliefs of the Pāśupatas with obscure rituals of their own), and a host of other unorthodox types like the Bhairava, Vāma, and so on. These latter are near the gate of truth, but yet outside it; while even among those that have entered the gate there are numerous gradations. Which is placed higher will depend on the outlook of the system that makes the estimate. Thus, monistic Śaivism (Aikyavāda-Śaiva) is given a relatively low place in the estimate of the Siddhāntin, who is a realist. The basic teachings of Śaivism would thus seem to have undergone much the same vicissitudes as the Upaniṣads, being interpreted variously according to the metaphysical bent of the followers. We shall take up the fundamental conceptions and briefly note, where necessary, the varying interpretations made of them.

### THIRTY-SIX PRINCIPLES

The Śaiva system recognizes thirty-six principles as against the twenty-five of the Sāṁkhya and Yoga. No other system recognizes as many principles; even the Pāñcarātra, says the Śaiva, admits only twenty-four.[1] The recognition of more principles is treated as a discovery which other systems failed to make, and is thus considered a feature of merit in itself. To

[1] See *Pauṣkara Āgama,* pp. 559-562. The Advaita Vedānta reckons thirty-six principles, but the new principles in this scheme are not independent principles, being, for the most part, modifications of one principle, *vāyu* (cosmic force).

reckon more is to know more, and to know more is to know better.[2] The extra principles are not uncritically accepted, however, and we shall have something to say about the arguments for them in the proper place.

### TWENTY-FOUR IMPURE PRINCIPLES—BHOGYA-KĀṆḌA

To start with the last in the scheme of evolution, we have the five gross elements (*mahābhūtas*)—ether, air, fire, water, and earth ; the last possesses the five qualities of sound, touch, colour, taste, and odour ; water lacks odour ; fire lacks taste and odour ; air lacks colour, taste, and odour ; ether has sound alone. These qualities are called *tanmātras*. They are subtle as contrasted with the elements which are said to possess them ; and they cause the gross elements. The uncritical mind may not understand how a quality like sound can be the cause of a substance like ether ; but this is due to mere prejudice ; for there is no such thing as substance other than its qualities viewed collectively, just as there is no forest other than the trees viewed collectively.[3] Sound produces ether, while sound and touch produce air, and so on. Thus we have ten principles, viz. the gross elements and the *tanmātras* that cause them. The *tanmātras* are themselves evolutes of that variety of individuation (*ahaṅkāra*) wherein the quality of darkness and inertia (*tamas*) is predominant. This variety of *ahaṅkāra* is also called *bhūtādi*, since it is (indirectly) the cause of the elements. There are two other varieties of *ahaṅkāra*, distinguished by the predominance of *sattva* (quality of illumination, buoyancy, and goodness) or *rajas* (quality of activity and passion) ; they are called *taijasa* and *vaikṛta* respectively, marking a departure from the Sāṁkhya doctrine, where the *sāttvika* is called *vaikṛta* and the *rājasa* is called *taijasa*. Still another point of departure is that the Sāṁkhya derives all the organs of sense and action, including the *manas* (the mind in its deliberative aspect), from the *sāttvika ahaṅkāra*, making the *rājasa* merely an auxiliary to both the *sāttvika* and the *tāmasa* varieties, while Śaiva philosophy derives the organs of sense and *manas* from *sāttvika ahaṅkāra* and the organs of action from *rājasa ahaṅkāra*. In any case, the organs are derived not from the elements as in the Vedānta, but from varieties of *ahaṅkāra*. The enumeration of the organs of sense and action corresponds to that in any other system ; *manas* is, as in the Sāṁkhya, recognized to be an organ of both sense and action ; about its

[2] The estimation of the worth of knowledge by its extent seems to have been common to the earlier Upaniṣads, as, for instance, when different seers are criticized for knowing only one part or another of the cosmic Puruṣa, but not all the parts. See W. Ruben, 'Uber die Debatten in den alten Upaniṣads' (Z.D.M.G., 1929, pp. 238 ff). It is, however, possible that in the passages cited by Dr. Ruben, some emphasis at least is intended on the idea of a *whole* as contrasted with the idea of a *more*.

[3] See *Pauṣkara Āgama*, pp. 456-460; also *Śivajñāna-māpāḍiyam*, pp. 184-186. This is very much of an idealistic view of substance, with some affinities to Russell's theory in his *Lowell Lectures*; and it marks one of the affinities of the system to idealism.

function we shall have to say more presently in treating of the internal organs as such. *Ahaṅkāra* is itself derived from *buddhi* (the intellect). From the standpoint of the individual, *buddhi* is known as the determinative faculty. It is itself derivative, but about that which gives rise to it there is considerable difference of opinion in different Śaiva works. Some recognize a principle called *citta,* which is equivalent to the three *guṇas* (primal constituents of the universe), manifested but in equipoise ; above these they admit a principle called Prakṛti as the cause of the *guṇas,* for on the general principle that all that is manifold and non-intelligent is caused, the *guṇas* must have a cause, and this is Prakṛti ; it is other than the mere equipoise of the *guṇas.* Others, while recognizing Prakṛti, see no need for a separate principle called *guṇa,* and hence identify *citta* with Prakṛti. Yet others would say that *citta* is but a variety of the functioning of *manas,* that it is what may be called the faculty of attention and does not rank as a distinct principle at all. As the balance of opinion is in favour of reckoning only twenty-four principles from Prakṛti downwards, there is no room for *citta* as a separate principle. The matter is mentioned only to indicate the existence of diverse opinions even in the enumeration of the principles.

*Buddhi, ahaṅkāra, manas,* and *citta* (where it is recognized) constitute the internal organs. When the senses come into contact with objects, they give rise to indeterminate cognition. *Citta* (or *manas* in the first phase of its functioning) fastens itself on this or that element in this stream of indeterminate presentation. Then it analyses the datum into substrate and quality (*viśeṣya* and *viśeṣaṇa*), says that such and such qualities would belong to one substrate, while such other qualities would belong to another substrate, and doubts which of these substrates the object in front actually is. *Ahaṅkāra* resolves to decide the issue ; and *buddhi* supervenes and resolves that it is one or the other of the doubted substrates.

As in the Sāṁkhya, eight dispositions of *buddhi* are recognized, viz. *dharma* (virtue), *jñāna* (knowledge), *vairāgya* (dispassion), *aiśvarya* (lordship), and the opposite of these—*adharma, ajñāna, avairāgya,* and *anaiśvarya.* The subdivisions of these conform for the most part to Sāṁkhya teaching, though they vary in some details ; the total number of these products of the intellect (*pratyayas*) is 612.[4]

### SEVEN MIXED PRINCIPLES—BHOJAYITṚ-KĀṆḌA

*Mūla-prakṛti,* sometimes called *prakṛti-māyā,* is itself a product of *aśuddha* (impure)-*māyā,* through the evolute called *kalā* (lit. particle).

[4] They are 10 of *dharma* (5 *yama* and 5 *niyama*), 80 of *jñāna,* 100 of *vairāgya,* 64 of *aiśvarya,* 10 of *adharma,* 64 of *ajñāna,* 100 of *avairāgya,* 8 of *anaiśvarya,* and 176 of *aśakti* (impotence). See *Śivajñāna-māpāḍiyam,* p. 170.

*Aśuddha-māyā* evolves primarily into three principles—*kāla* (time), *niyati* (destiny or necessity), and *kalā*. Time should be admitted as an independent principle, since we find in experience that even when all necessary causes are present, the effect is not produced except with the passage of time. We find that different crops grow in different seasons; we find that time matures and time heals. If time be taken to be one, its distinction, and consequently its causal efficacy, would have to be explained by the adjuncts, e.g. the objects which differentiate it; and the empty husk of bare time would not be worth recognition. Time therefore is manifold; it is also non-intelligent; hence it is a product and, being a product, is non-eternal.

Destiny is that principle which sees that every soul has its due in the matter of the enjoyment of its appropriate fruit, that there is no improper filching of another's fruit or avoidance of one's own. Being non-intelligent, the soul has no doubt to be actuated by intelligence as the energy of the Lord (*Śiva-śakti*); but *Śiva-śakti* is the actuator in every case, and should therefore be endowed with different instruments for different purposes. Destiny is the instrument intended for the purpose of controlling the enjoyment of *karma*.

*Kalā* is the instrument whereby the darkness that envelops souls is removed in part. On one side it evolves into *mūla-prakṛti* and on another into *vidyā* (knowledge) and *rāga* (attachment). *Vidyā* and *rāga* have a tendency to be confused with *jñāna* and *avairāgya*, which are dispositions of the intellect. The latter are purely material; in order that they may attach to the soul, they should be actuated by *Śiva-śakti* which is pure intelligence. For their actuation intermediaries are needed which are neither wholly pure nor wholly impure; hence the recognition of *vidyā* and *rāga*. *Jñāna* as a disposition of the intellect would account for individual cognitions; but these would not be possible unless the cognitive faculty of man has been made manifest, and this is done through *vidyā*. If the cognitive energy of the Lord were directly active, bliss alone should be cognized, as pure bliss is of the nature of that energy; in order to account for our experiences of pleasure and pain, *vidyā* has to be admitted as an intermediary. Similarly, attachment appears in the intellect, only as controlled by the emotive faculty, which faculty needs to be manifested by *Śiva-śakti* through an appropriate instrument. This instrument is *rāga*.

These five—*kāla, niyati, kalā, vidyā,* and *rāga*—are called the five sheaths (*pañca-kañcuka*). It is as enveloped in these and endowed with five *kleśas* (hindrances), viz. *avidyā* (ignorance), *asmitā* (egoity), *rāga* (attachment), *dveṣa* (aversion), and *abhiniveśa* (clinging to life) that the soul is ready to have experience of *mūla-prakṛti*. The five *kleśas* are together called *puṁstva-mala* (human impurities); and the soul in this condition is admitted as a separate principle called *puruṣa-tattva*.[5]

From *aśuddha-māyā* up to and inclusive of Puruṣa, there are seven principles. While the twenty-four principles from Prakṛti are wholly impure, these others are mixed; hence they are said to belong to the *miśra adhvan* (the mixed way) as distinguished from the *aśuddha* (impure) *adhvan* and the *śuddha* (pure) *adhvan* (to which belong the *Śiva-tattvas* to be mentioned presently). The seven principles from *aśuddha-māyā* are also called *bhojayitṛ-kāṇḍa* (the part that brings about enjoyment), as distinguished from *preraka-kāṇḍa* (the directive part) and *bhogya-kāṇḍa* (the part consisting of objects of enjoyment). The functioning of the five principles—time, destiny, etc. in constituting finitude is well illustrated in the *Paramārthasāra* with reference to the judgement, 'Now this is something I know fully'. The infinitude of knowledge is contracted into finite knowledge (*vidyā*); it is limited to a part (*kalā*); the word 'now' indicates a present or future knowing of something unknown or a present or future doing of what is not yet done; this distinction constitutes time (*kāla*). The word 'something' indicates restriction (*kalā*) of the soul's powers; the word 'this' indicates a definite and necessary relation between the subject and object; necessity (*niyati*) restricts the object known. The word 'fully' indicates a sense of incompleteness, a desire for possession of everything and for continued existence; this is *rāga*. The words 'I know' express finite knowledge (*vidyā*); these five united with Māyā constitute what are known as the six cloaks (*ṣaṭ-kañcuka*) in that system.[6]

## FIVE PURE PRINCIPLES—PRERAKA-KĀṆḌA

The pure principles are five. *Śiva-tattva* is the first of these and the cause of the rest—*śakti, sadāśiva, īśvara,* and *śuddhavidyā*. *Śiva-tattva* is one, pervasive, and eternal; it is of the nature of both knowledge and action; it is the cause of the other pure principles. It helps to manifest the cognitive and conative energies of souls. It is not, however, to be identified with Śiva, for *in itself* it is not of the nature of knowledge or action which is non-intelligent. Neither Śiva Himself nor His inherent *śakti* (power) can be directly the cause of any principles, as they would then be

[5] See *Tattva-traya-nirṇaya,* v. 22, commentary, and *Śivajñāna-māpādiyam,* p. 158.

[6] Allied to the conception of the cloaks is that of the eightfold city (*puryaṣṭaka*), which is another name for the subtle body with which each soul is endowed. There are divergent accounts as to the eight constituents of this body. According to some accounts (e.g. the *Kālottara*), they are the five subtle elements together with *manas, buddhi,* and *ahaṅkāra;* according to others, they are *kāla, kalā, niyati, rāga, vidyā, manas, buddhi,* and *ahaṅkāra;* according to yet another account (Bhoja's *Tattvaprakāśikā,* v. 12), this body is made of thirty *tattvas* under eight heads: (1) the elements, (2) the organs, (3) *manas,* (4) *buddhi,* (5) *ahaṅkāra,* (6) *guṇa,* (7) Prakṛti, and (8) the five beginning with *kāla*.

liable to transformation and affected by inertness. *Śiva-tattva* is an evolution through *mahāmāyā* or pure Māyā, as distinguished from *aśuddha-māyā* mentioned earlier. But Māyā in either form cannot be an inherent power of the Lord; it is assumptive, taken on (*parigraha-śakti*).[7]

The first evolute of this is *śakti-tattva.* From *śakti* proceeds *sadāśiva-tattva,* wherein the cognitive and conative energies are held in equipoise; thence proceeds *īśvara-tattva,* in which the cognitive energy is subordinated to the conative; from that again comes *śuddhavidyā-tattva,* wherein conative energy is subordinated to the cognitive. Since time belongs to the class of inferior impure evolutes, it should follow that the pure principles are timeless and that there is no question of priority or posteriority among them. Such a conclusion is, however, not acceptable to some Śaiva Siddhāntins;[8] by these others therefore a pure time is recognized, pertaining to the pure principles. It is difficult to make intelligible this concept of a pure time. If it is free from the defects discovered by idealistic dialectic in the category of time, it is really timelessness; and if there is really a sequence among the pure principles, these cannot be as pure as they are claimed to be. The recognition of 'pure time' is significant of the Siddhāntin's constant desire to effect a compromise. It is questionable, however, whether this compromise is anything but a half-way house.

## WORLD OF SOUNDS

So far we have dealt with one aspect of the evolution of *śuddha-māyā* or *mahāmāyā,* the evolution into the world of things (*artha-prapañca*) as contrasted with the world of sounds (*śabda-prapañca*). Over and above the articulate sound cognized by all physically, the Siddhāntin recognizes three other forms—*parā,* which is absolutely supreme and subtle, *paśyantī,* which is relatively gross but is still undifferentiated as the colours of the peacock are undifferentiated in the contents of the peahen's egg, and *madhyamā,* which is grosser still and differentiated, though not articulate, being of the nature of words which we utter to ourselves without the use

[7] See Aghora Śiva's commentary on the *Tattvaprakāśikā,* v. 25. Even the realistic school has to admit Māyā to be a *parigraha-śakti.* While, however, the idealistic school draws what seems to be the natural inference and compares the product to the reflection in a mirror (see *Paramārthasāra,* verses 12 and 13: 'As in the orb of a mirror pictures such as those of a town or village shine, which are inseparable from it and yet are distinct from one another and from it, so from the perfectly pure vision of the supreme Bhairava this universe, though void of distinction, appears distinct, part from part, and distinct from that vision'; cf. also the opening verse of *Dakṣiṇāmūrti-stotra* ascribed to Śaṅkara), the realist school refuses to take the evolutes to be illusory, 'as such a manifestation would be false, though what is declared to be so is established as true by all the means of knowledge'. For the *Paramārthasāra,* Dr. Burnett's text and translation published in the J.R.A.S., 1910 have been used.

[8] Verse 32 of the *Tattvaprakāśikā* denies priority and posteriority among the pure principles. But the commentator, Aghora Śiva, condemns it as an interpolation; according to him, there is an order of evolution and involution even among the pure principles.

of the vocal organs. Articulate sound is called *vaikharī*. Of this there are two forms, subtle and gross; the latter abides in *śuddhavidyā-tattva*, and the former in *īśvara-tattva*; *madhyamā* abides in *sadāśiva-tattva*; *paśyantī* in *śakti-tattva*, also called *bindu-tattva*; and *parā* in *Śiva-tattva*, also called *nāda-tattva*. Just as *śakti* has to be distinguished from *śakti-tattva*, *bindu* has to be distinguished from *bindu-tattva*; the latter is an evolute of *śuddha-māyā*, while the former is *śuddha-māyā*.

## THEORY OF SPHOṬA

Meaning is made known not by letters nor by words, but by a capacity which is manifested through letters and words. This capacity (*śakti*) is what is called *sphoṭa* by the grammarians. It resides in the *nāda-tattva*, the first evolute of *śuddha-māyā*. The arguments whereby *sphoṭa* is established are well known. The individual letters cannot make known the meaning, for if each letter did so, the other letters would be unnecessary; and as the letter-cognitions are momentary, any aggregation of them is impossible. The contention that the residual impressions of letter-cognitions persist and that they may have this function is of no avail, since residual impressions are known to have the function of recalling their own causes (here the letter-cognitions); and there is no justification for imposing another function on them. Though *sphoṭa* or *śakti* or *nāda* is manifested by each letter, meaning as a whole is not fully manifest therewith; for it is manifested bit by bit by each succeeding letter as occurring in a particular sequence; the manifestation by the preceding letter or set of letters is a preparation for the manifestation of the succeeding letter, till the word is completed. Similar is the case in the expression of meaning by the words of a sentence. The Siddhāntin thus favours not a mere diversity, but a unity progressively manifested in the diversity.[9]

## SOULS AND THEIR BONDS

Souls are naturally infinite, pervasive, omniscient, etc. Yet they experience themselves as limited, finite, little-knowing. This is due to their bonds, of which there are three—*āṇava, karma,* and Māyā. *Āṇava* is a connate impurity; it is what may be called original sin, if by 'sin' we mean nothing more than imperfection. It is present without any beginning in souls, like the husk and bran in paddy or verdigris in copper. It

[9] The grammarians who defend *sphoṭa* are Advaitins, though not of the orthodox school. They are Śabda-brahma-vādins. Śaṅkara rejects the *sphoṭa* doctrine despite its monistic metaphysical implications. Vācaspati follows him in this, though the arguments of neither can be said to be very conclusive: see an article by the present writer on 'Vācaspati's criticism of the Sphoṭavāda', *Journal of Oriental Research,* Madras, December, 1932. The Siddhāntin's recognition of *sphoṭa* is one more link with monistic idealism.

is because of this impurity that the pervasive (*vibhu*) soul cognizes itself as finite, as if it were atomic (*aṇu*). Because of this limitation of cognitive and conative powers, souls act in certain ways which they take to be good or evil ; and these acts bear consequences which have to be worked out by being experienced. The consequences constitute the next bond called *karma*. But in order to experience the consequences and gain knowledge thereby, there should be objects of enjoyment, and instruments of cognition and enjoyment. These are provided by Māyā of the impure variety. The functions of *āṇava* and pure Māyā are thus opposed ; while *āṇava* obscures, Māyā illumines ; while *āṇava* binds, Māyā liberates ; but the illumination and liberation due to Māyā are very limited ; such knowledge as results therefrom is delusive.[10] All the same, there is sufficient contrast between *āṇava* and Māyā to warrant the non-identification of the two. Those who would avoid the recognition of *āṇava* have yet to admit ignorance as a positive entity obscuring the natural powers of knowledge and action. This ignorance itself is called *āṇava* by the Siddhāntins.[11]

Souls which have all the three kinds of bonds are called *sakalas*. Those for whom Māyā alone has been resolved by the involution of the worlds etc. in the periodical deluges, are called *pralayākalas*. *Karma* remains for these in addition to *āṇava* and has to be worked out in fresh worlds etc. in a fresh creation. Those for whom *karma* too is resolved, *āṇava* alone being left, are called *vijñānākalas*. These reside in the worlds constituted by *śuddha-māyā*.

## GOD AND HIS FUNCTIONS

God is pure, omnipotent, omniscient, gracious, eternally free from bonds.[12] He carries on the fivefold function of creation, preservation, destruction, concealment, and the bestowal of grace. The last is the culmination of all His other functions. Souls, in their essential nature, are the same as God ; but their potencies are concealed by beginningless

[10] See Aghora Śiva on v. 25 of the *Tattvaprakāśikā*: 'Though *aśuddha-māyā* too brings about knowledge and action through *kalā* etc. it yet serves only to delude, since that knowledge is of the particular and leads to the superimposition of the self on the not-self, whereas the knowledge brought about by the *mahāmāyā* is extensive knowledge of all things together; further, the latter is of pure entities like Śiva and comes through knowledge imparted by doctrinal works; hence *śuddha-māyā* produces real wisdom'.

[11] The arguments for the existence of *āṇava* constitute a striking parallel to the Advaitin's arguments for recognizing nescience of a positive nature (*bhāva-rūpa-ajñāna*). Yet another link with monistic idealism.

[12] He is both the material and the efficient cause of the world; through His *śaktis* He is the material cause and in His own nature the efficient cause. The distinction is relative and not indicative of a real difference, for there is identity between *śakti* and *śaktimat*, as between attribute and substance. While the monistic variety of Śaivism insists on both kinds of causality, the dualistic variety as presented in the *Śivajñāna-māpāḍiyam* considers the attribution of material causality to be figurative.

*āṇava.* To remove the obscuration and to reveal innate capacities is the purpose of God's functioning. The ignorance of souls can be removed partially through the bodies, instruments, etc. provided by *aśuddha-māyā,* i.e. by the physical world around us. The creation and sustentation of this world are therefore undertaken by God for this purpose. Aided by these bodies and instruments, the soul transmigrates, acquiring and spending *karma,* gathering experiences, and gradually weaning away the power of *āṇava* to obscure. The progress is not uniform nor invariable. Different souls require different lengths of time ; sometimes there is backsliding, because the identification with the material world and its enjoyments is too strong. The process of transmigration is in any case wearisome. It is necessary to give rest periodically to the evolving souls ; the flagging energies of *aśuddha-māyā* have also to be given time occasionally to get freshened up ; the function of destruction is thus an act of grace, not of cruelty. Souls left to themselves may not engage in activity leading to further experiences. And *āṇava,* being non-intelligent, is not active of itself. Since for their own good souls should be made to act, seeking the pleasures of this world as if they were ultimate happiness, and parviscience as if it were omniscience, God functions through His own energy called the energy of concealment (*tirodhāna-śakti*) and makes *mala* (original impurity) active ; hence this *śakti* too is figuratively spoken of as a *mala* ; and the function of concealment is the fourth function of God in the interest of the souls.

## SALVATION

When by long experience of transmigration the soul has learnt to equate empirical good and evil, realized that the one is as fleeting and intrinsically worthless as the other, and become indifferent to the acquisition of good *karma* as well as bad, the stage is set for release. The *mala* that so long obscured and hindered is now ripe and fit for the divine surgeon's knife. The soul no longer cognizes with the evolutes of *aśuddha-māyā* nor with its own feeble flickering intelligence, but seeks the omniscience that is at once its own nature and birthright. There is the onset of divine grace, quick or slow, relatively to the capacities of the soul and the activities of physical or mental worship or meditation that the soul betakes itself to. When grace has fully set in, the Lord reveals Himself and instructs the soul. To the *vijñānākalas* He reveals Himself as their own inner light ; to the *pralayākalas* in a divine supernatural form ; to the *sakalas* as a preceptor apparently like one of themselves. By seeing, touching, or instructing He performs the purification (*dīkṣā*). If the ignorance of souls were due to mere absence of knowledge, it could be removed by knowledge ; but *mala* is an entity ; it is of a positive nature and can be removed only by another positive entity ; hence the need for *dīkṣā*. The need for the help of the preceptor does not cease immediately with *dīkṣā*. He has to continue to help for a while, just as the surgeon is required not merely to operate the cataract, but also to bandage the eye for some days before proper vision is restored. With this restoration, the soul no longer looks on itself as of the nature of *pāśa* or *paśu,* matter or the finite little-knowing spiritual atom. It has been weaned away from association with them and educated to a realization of its own full stature. It realizes its own *Śivatva* ; and whatever is cognized is cognized as Śiva. There is no more misery or imperfection, since there is no cause thereof; when the cognizer and the cognized are both Śiva, who can cause misery to whom? This is the final stage of release. It is not dependent on or concomitant with release from the body ; for the change is not physical, but spiritual. Through mere momentum or through the residue of *prārabdha karma* (past work already bearing fruit), the physical body may persist for a while after spiritual illumination ; but it does not fetter the enlightened soul, since it is not cognized as such.

### ŚAIVA SIDDHĀNTA CONTRASTED WITH OTHER SYSTEMS

The attainment of *Śivatva* may be understood as complete mergence of being in Śiva or the realization of an identity of essence in spite of difference in existence. This is the difference between the idealist and realist schools of Śaivism, between what is ordinarily known as Kashmir Śaivism and the Śaiva Siddhānta of South India.[13] The latter contends that identity is not significant in the absence of difference and that when the scriptures teach non-duality (*advaita*), they mean to deny not the existence of two, but the duality of two ; they say, 'They are not two', not 'There are not two'. While both schools claim to maintain *advaita,* they differ thus in the interpretation of the term. Consistently with the starting point, the realist Śaiva cannot conceive of release as a mergence. The released souls continue to exist as souls ; if they ceased to be as such, who is there to enjoy release? Not God, for He is eternally released. The soul claims God's nature as its own too ; but it has not the effrontery to claim that it is itself God. On the contrary, it always professes to be a devoted servant of God. But it claims greater dignity for itself than in

[13] The contrast in localities is unsound; for many of the early writers of the realist school, e.g. Sadyojyotis, Rāmakaṇṭha, Nārāyaṇakaṇṭha, etc., seem to have belonged to Kashmir. Tradition has it that Tirumūlar, perhaps the earliest Tamil Śaiva, brought Śaivism to the South from the North, possibly Kashmir. The editors of the Kashmir Śaivism series recognize that dualist Śaivism too has a home in Kashmir; and one of the works published by them, the *Nareśvara-parīkṣā,* belongs to this school.

the Vaiṣṇava Viśiṣṭādvaita ; if the analogies of being secondary to God, being the body of God, and so on were pressed, it would follow that in release God experiences through the soul, as formerly the soul used to experience through its possessions, the body and the senses ; this is the proper consequence of the adjectival position of the soul. But the Śaiva Siddhāntin will have none of this ; he makes the soul the essential figure in the picture. In bondage the soul experienced through *pāśa* ; now it experiences through *pati* (the Lord) ; its knowledge is no longer *pāśa-jñāna* or *paśu-jñāna,* but *pati-jñāna* ; *pati-jñāna* means not the Lord's knowledge, but the soul's knowledge through the Lord. To the idealist critic, this will appear to be one more half-way house, a concession to the popular demand for individuality combined with an inability to avoid the fundamental position of non-duality. The other well-defined indications of idealism may be briefly resumed here: the recognition of *pramāṇa* (evidence of knowledge) as essentially one—*cit-śakti,* the varieties like perception, inference, etc. being but instruments which define that one ; the recognition of Māyā as not the inherent but an assumptive (*parigraha*) *śakti* of the Lord ; the admission of *sphoṭa* ; the acknowledgement of the essentially unstable and indeterminable nature of the Jīva (soul) as such, since he is said to be *sadasat* (real-unreal), i.e. both intelligent and non-intelligent, taking on the colour of his surroundings (this is not far removed from the Advaitin's doctrine of *jīvatva* as indeterminable) ; the notion that there is no substance as such in which qualities inhere ; and so on. But more than all these, the insistence on knowledge as the means of release is what places the system in the direct line of succession of Indian thought. The original defect is obscuration or ignorance of a positive character with the resultant non-intuition[14] of the Jīva's essential oneness with Śiva. The removal of this ignorance has to be worked up through discipline—*caryā* (observance), *kriyā* (rites), and *yoga*—and helped by the onset of grace ; but discipline and grace function only as culminating in *jñāna* ; it is knowledge that removes the sorrows of the soul. Throughout the course of transmigration, the soul has suffered in ignorance of its birthright, like the princeling brought up by the woodmen as one of themselves ; when the divine Preceptor removes the veil and reveals the true identity of the princely soul, there are no more false identifications, no more miseries. Discriminative wisdom is the supreme means of release ; all others are means only as subsidiary thereto. And this knowledge is not of the same texture as empirical knowledge. The external objects of cognition through *pāśa-jñāna* are *asat.*[15] Illustrations of things which are

[14] *Akhyāti,* as it is called in the Pratyabhijñā school.
[15] See *Śivajñāna-māpāḍiyam, sūtra* 6, topic 1.

*asat* are the writing on the water, the dream, and the mirage. For the Siddhāntin, who believes in Satkāryavāda (the view that effects are pre-existent in the cause), the *asat* cannot be the absolutely non-existent; what he means thereby is the mutable. It requires very little imagination to see the close resemblance of this conception of the world to the Advaitin's conception of it as *anirvacanīya* (indeterminable). It will not be forgotten in this connection that the Advaitin too is a Satkāryavādin. A further point of resemblance is the function assigned to scripture. Scripture too is a *pramāṇa* and its content can be but *asat*. The Siddhāntin says that scripture (like other *pramāṇas*) has a place in the knowledge of the pure *sat*, in that, though it does not have Śiva for its content, it helps to bring about the inward realization of the *sat*.[16] It is a case of the *pramāṇas* not revealing but fulfilling themselves in the *sat*.

## JĪVANMUKTI

Consistently with such a doctrine of release, one would expect not only the subordination of all forms of worship and meditation to knowledge, but also their elimination when knowledge is attained. The *jīvanmukta* (free while living) should have no duties to perform. If he does any virtuous acts, it may be by choice or purely by force of habit. Those who want to find him will see him in the company of the saintly or in places of worship; he will be found in the garbs of the saintly. But there can be no injunction of place or time or activity for such souls. The mention of what they do is to be treated as a description, not a prescription. In so far as any prescription is intended, that should be taken to apply to him who is yet in quest of wisdom, not to the enlightened man. Such a position is taken up not merely by the monistic Śaivism of Kashmir, but also by the Siddhānta. The twelfth *sūtra* of the *Śivajñāna-bodha* prescribes the consorting with godly men and the frequenting of temples *for the sake of* release, and not for the released.

The more extreme among the realists say that even though knowledge is attained, there is no unshakable realization. *Prārabdha karma* not yet having been exhausted, it will tend to uproot this new acquisition; and the performance of virtuous acts is enjoined for the sake of reinforcing the knowledge gained.[17] Such a position is not unintelligible in itself; but it is hardly consistent with the Siddhāntin's conception of the nature and supremacy of knowledge in the scheme of release.

[16] *Śivajñāna-māpāḍiyam, loc. cit.* Yet, strangely enough, the Siddhāntin is not tired of criticizing the Advaitin for his doctrine of a non-dual Brahman revealed by scripture, which is not real as Brahman is.

[17] See *Śivajñāna-māpāḍiyam, sūtra* 12. Compare this with Śivāgrayogin's *bhāṣya* on the Sanskrit version of the same *sūtra*.

Doctrinal variations like these do but lend point to our main contention that a whole gamut of variations has been played on a single fundamental theme, with a common stock of fundamental concepts based perhaps on common scriptural texts.[18] The Śivāgamas, no less than the Upaniṣads, have provided the basis for every shade of philosophic thought from monism to pluralism, idealism to realism, but throughout there is the insistence on knowledge as the saviour, the insistence characteristic of the best Hindu thought.[19]

[18] It is by no means certain that the remote basic texts of the idealistic school are different from those of the realist. Even the *Śivajñāna-bodha,* a cardinal text of the realist school, is susceptible of idealist explanation. Vidyāraṇya is credited with an idealist commentary on these twelve *sūtras;* in our own days, a very creditable attempt in this direction has been made by Kuppuswami Raju of Tanjore, the scholarly Tamil translator of many Sanskrit philosophical works.

[19] It is because of this cardinal feature that it was possible for Appaya Dīkṣita to construct (or, as some would have it, reconstruct) a bridge between Śaivism and Advaita Vedānta, through the system known as Śivadvaita; see further the *Śivādvaita-nirṇaya* and the *Śivādvaita of Śrīkaṇṭha* (both published by the University of Madras).

# 23

## THE PATH OF YOGA IN THE GĪTĀ

IT is significant that the *Bhagavad-Gītā* calls itself a Yoga-śāstra and not a Dharma-śāstra, though the scripture arises out of a moral problem. The question that is posed at the outset is whether, in the given circumstances, Arjuna's refusing to fight was an act of *dharma* or *adharma*. But the elaborate answer given by Śrī Kṛṣṇa, after a short preliminary reprimand, begins on a high metaphysical note: 'Never was there a time when I did not exist, nor thou, nor these kings of men. Never will there be a time when any of us shall cease to be' (II.12). This high note is continued through the next eighteen verses, rising at times to such a pitch as the following, before it comes down to the moral question: 'The unreal never is, the Real never is not; the conclusion about these two is well perceived by the seers of Truth' (II.16).

The procedure here adopted by the *Gītā* is quite in accordance with the Hindu spiritual tradition. For in Hinduism ethics is only a subordinate branch of metaphysics. Ethics is the science of human conduct and character. It is a study of what a man ought to do and to be. But what a man ought to do and to be depends upon the end and aim of human life; and this, again, depends upon the nature and purpose of the universe, of which he is an integral part. The universe is a vast arena where there is a perpetual conflict going on between the self and the not-self, giving rise to a hierarchical order of dual beings, till at last the dualism of spirit and matter is overcome, and the sundered spirit regains its original wholeness and becomes absolutely free from any kind of limitation—thus closing one cosmic cycle. This law of spiritual progression in the universe of time and space is one of the fundamental postulates of Hindu speculative thought. And on this law are based the Hindu views of human individuality, of human society, and of human history in general. Accordingly, progress on the part of individuals or communities or nations is always judged in terms of increasing spiritual values. And the consummation of all these values is called *mokṣa,* which means liberation. It is a liberation which takes place not *in* time but *from* time. It is a transformation into the eternal being of God.

### PLACE OF YOGA AND ETHICS IN THE GĪTĀ

*Mokṣa* is a negative expression, as it connotes freedom from the bonds of finitude. But *yoga,* as it is used in the *Gītā,* is a positive expression for the same experience. It connotes the positive aspect of *mokṣa,* as it means union with the Infinite. The Sanskrit word *yoga,* which is cognate with the English word 'yoke', is the key to the whole scripture. The *Gītā* is called a Yoga-śāstra, its message is termed *yoga,* the *avatāra* who delivers the message is designated Yogeśvara, and the ideal man whom the scripture describes is called a *yogin.* These four words—*yoga, yogin,* Yogeśvara, and Yoga-śāstra—have to be borne in mind by all who want to understand the import of the *Bhagavad-Gītā.* Also, it should not be forgotten that the word *yoga* is not used in the *Gītā* in any narrow or technical sense of thought-control, as in Patañjali's *Yoga-Sūtra.* It is used here in its primary sense of union or fellowship with God. The *Gītā* is called a Yoga-śāstra, because it teaches the way to that union or fellowship. And, as that union has to be achieved through right effort, right devotion, and right knowledge, we have the three well-known divisions of Karma-yoga, Bhakti-yoga, and Jñāna-yoga. It is idle to contend that there are only these three divisions of *yoga* or that there is any hard and fast line between one division and another. The *Bhagavad-Gītā* knows no such limitations, nor such rigid distinctions. For it speaks also of Buddhi-yoga, Dhyāna-yoga, and Sannyāsa-yoga, and very often in one and the same passage one aspect of *yoga* runs into another most naturally. The fact is that the various aspects of *yoga* cannot be really separated from one another, any more than the various functions of our minds can be separated from one another. It is only for purposes of analysis that we isolate the discipline of our will and call it Karma-yoga, the discipline of our emotions and call it Bhakti-yoga, and the discipline of our understanding and call it Jñāna-yoga. Spiritual life is a whole and it involves the direction of the whole mind—our will, our emotions, and our understanding. The path of light begins with right discrimination, goes through obedience to the law and moral action, and thence through self-forgetting love and service, and ends in spiritual freedom, where the individual realizes that he is part and parcel of the all-embracing Spirit. And all this lengthy way is a natural slope and not an artificial staircase in which one could count the steps. Therefore the *Gītā* treats *yoga,* which stands not only for the goal of spiritual life but also for the way leading to it, as one organic whole, though, for purposes of exposition, it often isolates and dwells upon one aspect of it to the exclusion of the others.

It is in the light of such a *yoga* that the *Gītā* wants us to consider all problems of *dharma* including the one posed by Arjuna on the field of battle. Any conception of *dharma* which consists only of some authoritative rules of conduct, without a living connection with *yoga,* which is the end and aim of human life, is *dharma* only for the ignorant. For rules of *dharma* are not ends in themselves. They are only means to an end and the end is *yoga*. Therefore their utility should be judged by the degree to which they promote the end. If at any time any rule is found to be retarding, instead of promoting, our progress towards the union, it has to be scrapped at once. True *dharma* is that which is ever in vital connection with *yoga*. It has to grow from within and adjust itself, as the personality of man progresses towards divine union. And all rules of *dharma* are dissolved at last in the fruition of *yoga*. That is the meaning of that famous verse in the *Gītā* which says, 'Surrendering all rules of *dharma*, come to me alone for shelter. Do not grieve. I will release thee from all sins' (XVIII.66).

We now see why the *Gītā* calls itself a Yoga-śāstra and not a Dharma-śāstra. *Yoga*, as understood in the *Gītā*, involves and transcends *dharma*, as religious life involves and transcends moral life. It stands both for the way and for the goal. The goal is God's being, and the way is man's becoming. The description of the goal and the description of the way are the two streams flowing throughout the *Gītā*. Sometimes one stream comes up and sometimes the other stream, and sometimes both of them intermingle their waters like the holy rivers, the Gaṅgā and the Yamunā.

### THE GĪTĀ AND THE UPANIṢADS

The *Gītā* is also termed an Upaniṣad. A well-known verse compares the Upaniṣads to cows and the *Gītā* to their milk. It is thereby admitted that the teachings of the *Gītā* are derived from the older scriptures. Only, in the later scripture we have an expansion of matter, a redistribution of emphasis, and a reinterpretation of the teaching for the benefit of men in all walks of life. For instance, the idea of Karma-yoga, which is so marvellously developed in the *Gītā*, is found in germ in the opening *mantras* of the *Īśa Upaniṣad*, which may be translated thus: 'Whatsoever moves in the world, is to be covered by the Lord. You should then enjoy by surrendering all. Do not covet the wealth of any man. Only by doing one's *karma* here, one should desire to live a hundred years. *Karma* will not cling to you if you live thus—and not otherwise'.

Mahatma Gandhi once said about this passage, 'If all the Upaniṣads and all other scriptures happened all of a sudden to be reduced to ashes, and if only the first verse in the *Īśa Upaniṣad* were left intact in the memory of Hindus, Hinduism would live for ever'. No wonder therefore that this passage and its expansion in the *Gītā* were the favourite texts of the Mahatma, who exemplified them in his own life as no other man did in recent history.

It should be observed that Karma-yoga, even in its first appearance in the *Īśa Upaniṣad,* was regarded as the solvent of *karma-bandha* or the so-called law of Karma. In the centuries that lay between the age of the Upaniṣads and the age of the *Mahābhārata* the law of Karma underwent an enormous development in Hindu religious thought, and *jñāna* (divine knowledge) coupled with *karma-sannyāsa* (renunciation of works) came to be looked upon as the only solvent of the inexorable law. The *Gītā* does not deny that *jñāna* is a solvent, but reaffirms that Karma-yoga is also an equally efficient solvent. Thus it supplied a much needed corrective to the over-emphasis on *jñāna* and renunciation, which had led to mere quietism. It may be said that the whole *Gītā* is a long and sustained protest against the dangers of quietism.

## BUDDHI-YOGA

In working out its doctrine of *yoga,* with its well-balanced emphasis on *karma, bhakti,* and *jñāna,* the *Gītā* begins with the preliminary discipline of the mind, which it calls Buddhi-yoga. Nothing shows the intellectual robustness of its teaching so well as the place which this scripture gives to *buddhi* (intellect) and the importance it attaches to its proper cultivation. In many theistic systems intellect is generally suspect, and an uncritical acceptance of things which cannot stand the test of reason is often encouraged. The result is that many people who are actually critical in all other things are notoriously uncritical in matters religious. There are, no doubt, some truths beyond the reach of reason. But there are a good many that lie within its province, and an over-emphasis on faith, at the expense of reason, generally results in an uncritical attitude to all religious teaching, culminating in gross superstition. The *Gītā* encourages no such attitude. Following the Upaniṣads, it gives to *buddhi* a very high place in its analysis of human personality. It says, 'The senses are said to be great, the mind is greater than the senses, and the understanding is greater than the mind, but greater than the understanding is He (the Ātman)' (III.42).

*Buddhi* or understanding is thus next only to the Ātman in man. The rational element in us is next only to the spiritual element. Therefore it is not by ignoring reason, but by exercising it fully, that we can rise to the level of the spirit. An enlightened understanding is preliminary to every kind of effective spiritual life. It is as necessary for Karma-yoga and Bhakti-yoga as for Jñāna-yoga. For the *karma* that is taught in the *Gītā* is not unenlightened action, nor is the *bhakti* that is taught there unbalanced emotion.

This will be seen clearly when we note the implications of what the *Gītā* calls Buddhi-yoga. The expression first occurs in II.49. This verse along with four others that follow may be taken as the exposition of the importance of *buddhi* in Karma-yoga. If we analyse these verses, we find that, according to the *Gītā,* Buddhi-yoga implies equanimity or evenness of mind, an attitude of detachment, freedom from error or delusion, and ability to rise above the mere letter of the law. In short, it is the preliminary discipline of the mind indispensable to every kind of spiritual life —whether it is Karma-yoga, Bhakti-yoga, Dhyāna-yoga, or Jñāna-yoga.

Further light on the importance of *buddhi* is thrown by the distinction which the *Gītā* seems to draw between *jñāna* and *vijñāna*—that is between intellectual enlightenment and spiritual realization. These two words occur in conjunction in five different places in the *Gītā* (III.41, VI.8, VII.2, IX.1, and XVIII.42), and if we examine the verses in which they occur together, we see what great importance the *Gītā* attaches to intellectual enlightenment. In fact, according to this scripture, realization is never complete without the enlightenment of the understanding. *Jñāna* is obviously connected with *buddhi.* The awakening of *buddhi* leads to *jñāna,* as the awakening of the Ātman leads to *vijñāna,* which is thus the fulfilment of *jñāna* and not its negation.

The *Gītā* is, however, not unaware of the dangers of the understanding. For it speaks of three types of *buddhi.* And the lowest type is described thus: 'The understanding which, being enveloped in darkness, regards wrong as right and which reverses all values—that, O Pārtha, is of a dark nature' (XVIII.32). The *Gītā* further illustrates this type of *buddhi* in its description, in the sixteenth chapter, of the wicked men who say, 'This world is false, without a moral basis and without a God. What is there that does not spring from mutual union? Lust is the cause of all' (XVI.8).

Thus the great scripture has no patience with those who are intelligent but devilish in character, any more than with those who are pious but foolish. It is aware that, without a disciplined mind, Karma-yoga would result only in rash action, Bhakti-yoga in superstitious worship, and Jñāna-yoga in vague abstractions. Though the *Gītā* is a theistic gospel, its object is not to bring to the feet of God a rash or a sentimental or an anaemic soul but a fully developed, well integrated, dynamic soul. Hence its insistence on the preliminary discipline of Buddhi-yoga.

### KARMA-YOGA

How a well integrated, dynamic soul should conduct itself in the world of men is the theme of those sections of the *Gītā* which deal with Karma-yoga. It has become almost a truism to say that Karma-yoga means performance of actions without caring for their fruits. But we have to distinguish here internal fruits from external fruits. We have to distinguish internal spiritual reactions of our works in ourselves from their external consequences in the world. If we draw a graph of our successes and failures in the world from day to day and another graph of our successes and failures in the internal kingdom of spirit, how different would these be! Very often the crest of the one would correspond to the trough of the other. For very often our worldly success is due to some compromise with evil, some sacrifice of principle ; and, contrariwise, some at least of our failures in life may be due to our reluctance to compromise with evil, to our dogged adherence to some principle of conduct. It may be that, when the world is congratulating us on some achievement of ours, our conscience is pricking us ; and, again, when the world is treating us with contempt and scorn, we are rejoicing inwardly that in the interests of our higher self the sacrifice was worth making. Happy, of course, is the man in whose life both the graphs of worldly success and spiritual progress approximate to each other. Ordinarily they do not, and give rise to the storm and stress of human life. On this conflict what the *avatāra* of the *Gītā* seems to say is this: 'Leave the outer curve to me and confine yourself to the inner. If you do so resolutely, you will find supreme happiness'. That is really the meaning of one of the most popular verses in the *Gītā*: 'Those who meditate on me and worship me exclusively and who are ever devoted to me—their welfare is my burden' (IX.22).

### KARMA-YOGA RESULTS IN A RICH MENTAL LIFE

If we shift our goal from the outside world to our own inward self and care only for the spiritual value of our actions and not for their material consequences, we gain a marvellously rich experience consisting of various elements.

First of all, a single aim takes the place of many conflicting aims and desires. The chaos of our mental life is reduced to order and harmony. As the *Gītā* says, 'In this, the resolute mind has a single aim ; but the thoughts of the irresolute are manifold and endless' (II.41). The single aim is what an English poet called soul-making—not money-making or pleasure-seeking or anything of the kind. All the given conditions of life will then be looked upon as only machinery for shaping the soul. They are not at all ends in themselves, but only means to an end. And the end is the expansion and enrichment of the soul, enabling it to realize its destiny in God.

Secondly, very soon there comes the realization that there is really no such thing as failure in life. When we fix our aim on some worldly object —wealth or power or pleasure—we may or may not succeed. But if we fix our aim on something inward like the improvement of the self, there can be no failure whatsoever. For every righteous act or noble feeling or kind thought automatically exalts the soul, whatever may be its consequence in the outer world. Here success is in our own hands and is not subject to chance, uncertainty, or fear. As the *Gītā* says, 'In this no effort is ever lost and no harm is ever done ; even a little of this law saves a man from great fear' (II.40).

Thirdly, with the realization that the kingdom of God is within us, to be traversed day by day with pure thoughts and noble deeds, we cease to expect too much from the world, we cease to look for things which our life on earth was never meant to give. For instance, we may ceaselessly work for improving the conditions of the society we live in, but we may not foolishly hope for the establishment of a social Utopia. We may as well expect our wooden horizontal or parallel bars to leap into life one day and bear blossom and fruit. Evil will remain in the world for all time to come. We can never eradicate it, however hard we may try. The paradise we work for is the paradise of the soul and not of the earth. It belongs to eternity, not to time.

Fourthly, when once we resolutely shift our aim inwards, we seem to touch the core of Reality amidst a thousand transient things. Everything falls into its place. The earth shrinks into a speck in the starry regions. A proper perspective is established, and with it comes a correct sense of values. We discover the golden thread that strings together the pearls of creation. We see order in disorder, unity in multiplicity, and design in chance and accident. The *Gītā* says, 'Deluded by the threefold disposition of Nature this world does not know me who am above them and eternal . . . But those who take refuge in me shall overcome the spell' (VII.13,14).

Fifthly, it is the beginning of a happiness which grows day by day and for which we have no words—happiness which, as the *Gītā* says, 'not even the heaviest of afflictions can take away'. The *yogin* begins to feel that experience, of which the scripture speaks so often, and which Mahatma Gandhi has exemplified throughout his life, viz. perfect rest and peace amidst ceaseless toil and incessant activity.

Thus Karma-yoga does not mean that the *yogin* reaps no fruits. On the contrary, he reaps a hundredfold. Only they are the invisible fruits of the spirit, far more lasting and valuable than the tangible fruits of the world.

## THE CONCEPTION OF SVADHARMA

But Karma-yoga is only the method of our work. It lays down only the manner in which we should discharge our duties. But what our duties are, what constitutes their content and substance, is indicated in the *Gītā* by the expression *svadharma.* In our religious tradition this expression is too often interpreted as meaning only caste duties. As there were—or it was supposed there were—four distinct castes in Hindu society, it was presumed that every caste had its own clear-cut profession or duty and that *svadharma* meant that, and nothing more. The *Gītā* itself seems to give room to this interpretation when it speaks of the *svadharma* of Arjuna. Arjuna is a Kṣatriya prince, and his *svadharma* is stated to be to fight in a righteous war. But we should not forget that in the *Gītā,* just as the battlefield of Kurukṣetra is only the starting point from which we are taken to far wider fields of man's endeavours, and just as the moral question raised by Arjuna is only the starting point from which we are led on to a hundred different questions of religion and metaphysics, so is the *svadharma* of the Kṣatriya prince only the starting point from which we are taken deep into philosophy which lies behind the concept of *svadharma.* If by *svadharma* the *Gītā* merely meant 'that the descendants of washermen should do nothing but wash clothes for all time and that the descendants of shoemakers should do nothing but make shoes for all time', it would not be a scripture with a universal message. So, by giving a narrow interpretation to the expression *svadharma,* we are doing great injustice to the *Gītā* and trying to hide its light under a bushel. In a remarkable verse in the eighteenth chapter the *Gītā* connects *svadharma* with *svabhāva,* one's duties with one's nature. It says, 'Better is one's own duty, though imperfectly done, than the duty of another done perfectly. He who does the duty imposed on him by his own nature incurs no sin' (XVIII.47).

It is one of the remarkable features of the *Bhagavad-Gītā* that it strikes an extraordinarily modern note in its clear and unmistakable recognition of the influence of natural dispositions on the individuality of man. It is only in a scientific age like ours that this emphasis on the part which Nature plays in the economy of spiritual life can be appreciated. No wonder that all our old commentaries on the *Gītā* have almost ignored this aspect of its teaching. The divine Teacher recognizes that man, like all other creatures on earth, is a dual being—child of both earth and heaven—and bases His teaching on this scientific fact. He says, 'From whatever womb living forms may arise, O Arjuna, great Nature is their womb and I am the generating father' (XIV.4).

If God is our father, Nature is our mother. And therefore in no scheme of spiritual discipline can the natural dispositions of the individual be ignored. The *Gītā* repeats this statement in a hundred different ways. It says, 'Fettered by thine own tendencies which are born of thy nature, that which through delusion thou seekest not to do thou shalt do, O Arjuna, even against thy will' (XVIII.60). 'One ought not to give up the work which is suited to one's own nature, O Arjuna, though it has its imperfections; for every enterprise is beset with its own imperfections, as fire with smoke' (XVIII.48). 'Even a man of divine knowledge acts in accordance with his own nature. All beings follow their nature. What can repression do?' (III.33). 'Everyone is driven to act, in spite of himself, by the impulses of Nature' (III.5). 'There is no creature here on earth, nor again among the gods in heaven, which is free from the three dispositions of Nature' (XVIII.40).

The almost overpowering influence of natural dispositions on the character and mind of man is further indicated in the *Gītā* (1) by its classification of men into two types—the godly and the ungodly—in the sixteenth chapter, and (2) by its elaborate analysis, in the seventeenth and eighteenth chapters, into three separate types of each of the following twelve concepts—faith, food, sacrifice, penance, charity, renunciation, knowledge, deed, doer, understanding, steadiness, and pleasure. The division is everywhere based on the three supposed fundamental qualities of Nature—*sattva, rajas,* and *tamas.*

Man thus belongs to two worlds—the natural world and the spiritual world. He has a body and a mind which belong to the former, and a soul which belongs to the latter. Now, the question arises, 'What should be the relation between the two? Are we to indulge the natural man, or suppress him altogether, or utilize him in the interests of the spirit?' No religion worth the name, of course, advocates the first view. It is only some secular systems of philosophy, called hedonistic systems, that make pleasure the end of life. The opposite extreme of hedonism is asceticism, which believes that Nature is ever the enemy of the spirit, and that therefore all natural desires and inclinations should be suppressed. All religions are, no doubt, based on the ascetic principle that the spirit should conquer the flesh. But in every religion there are puritan sects which carry this principle to an extreme, and glory in the torture of the flesh, and look with suspicion on all forms of art and beauty. The *Gītā* does not countenance this extreme attitude. On the other hand, it condemns in no uncertain terms all ascetic practices, as the following verses will show: 'Vain and conceited men, impelled by the force of their desires and passions, subject themselves to terrible mortifications not ordained by scriptures. And, being foolish, they torture their bodily organs and me also who dwell within the body. Know that such men are fiendish in their resolves' (XVII.5,6). '*Yoga* is not for him who eats too much, nor for him who eats too little. It is not for him, O Arjuna, who sleeps too much, nor for him who keeps vigil too long. But for the man who is temperate in his food and recreation, who is restrained in all his actions, and who has regulated his sleep and vigils, *yoga* puts an end to all sorrows' (VI.16,17).

No doubt, there is one passage where the *Gītā* seems to agree with the ascetics who want to eradicate all natural desires. In the third chapter, answering Arjuna's question, 'What is it that impels a man to commit sin, in spite of himself, driven, as it were, by force?' Śrī Kṛṣṇa says, 'It is desire, it is wrath, which springs from passion. Know that it is our enemy here, a monster of sin devouring all .... The senses, the mind, and the understanding are said to be its seat. Through them it veils true knowledge and deludes the soul. Therefore, O Arjuna, control thy senses from the beginning and slay this foul destroyer of knowledge and wisdom' (III.37-41). But this is not the real view of the *Gītā* taken as a whole. It is only when *kāma* or desire leads to sin that the scripture takes up this uncompromising attitude. For in an important verse, it identifies *kāma* which is not opposed to *dharma* with Īśvara Himself. The *avatāra* says, 'I am the desire in all creatures, O Arjuna, which is not in conflict with *dharma*' (VII.11).

According to the *Gītā* therefore, the natural man should neither be indulged nor suppressed but wisely directed. But how is this to be done? It is a problem which every established religion has to solve. Every religion dealing with large masses of men has to show a way through which they can sublimate their natural appetites, inclinations, and instincts. The *Gītā's* solution of the problem is contained in its doctrine of *svadharma*.

*Svadharma* in its ultimate analysis means the law of one's own being. Every man has, first of all, to be true to himself, to the law of his own being. He has to achieve the best he is capable of by perfecting his own natural endowments and by making the most of the circumstances in which he is placed. It is only then that he will become an efficient servant of God and an efficient member of society. The advantages of such a life of action are many. First of all, it is obviously the line of least resistance. *Svadharma* connotes ease and spontaneity. An action which is not done with perfect ease is not the best action. And an action which is really beyond one's capacity and which is undertaken only through ignorance and rashness is the worst. In the eighteenth chapter of the *Gītā* there is a division of all actions into three classes. Under the first class come those actions which are organically related to the nature of the man who performs them ; under the second, those which involve great strain ; and under the third, those which are undertaken by a man without regard to his own capacity and the consequences.. The *Gītā* view is that we should discharge our duties as a tree discharges its duty of putting forth flower and fruit—

with perfect ease and spontaneity. The gospel of *svadharma* demands that man should play his part in the world consciously and voluntarily as animals and trees play their part in Nature unconsciously and involuntarily.

When our duties are organically related to our natural endowments, they would be most efficiently discharged, whereas, when they are not, they go against the grain and are most inefficiently discharged. Therefore an ideal society is that in which all men are assigned the duties which they are most fitted to discharge, in which every man's *svadharma* is based on his *svabhāva*. *Cāturvarṇya,* or the system of four castes, conceived by the Indian sages, was one such ideal society. As far as historical records go, there have never been the four clear-cut divisions of Hindu society postulated in our sacred books, nor has there been at any time a rigid assignment of duties to each of these castes. The Indian sages meant by the four *varṇas* only an ideal society in which every man's position would be organically related to his aptitudes. At any rate, that seems to be the view of the divine author of the *Gītā*. For he says, 'The system of the four castes was created by me according to the division of aptitudes and works' (IV.13).

The pursuit of *svadharma* implies not only ease, spontaneity, and efficiency, but also beauty. For beauty is nothing but the inimitable grace which all creatures exhibit when they are true to the law of their own being. The most beautiful rose is that which most nearly approaches the ideal pattern of a rose. The most beautiful horse is that which most nearly exhibits all the parts and functions of an ideal horse. A horse is certainly not beautiful when its body or legs approximate to those of an elephant. The world is rich in individual forms of varied hues and shapes. And when any individual form acquires efficiency, strength, or beauty, it reveals and glorifies the work of God. The *avatāra* of the *Gītā* says, 'Behold my forms, O Arjuna, by hundreds and thousands—manifold and divine and of varied hues and shapes' (XI.5). 'Whatever being there is, endowed with grandeur, beauty, or strength—know that it has sprung only from a spark of my splendour' (X.41). And the way to acquire these qualities is to be true to one's self, to perfect one's own aptitudes, to improve one's own gifts, to progress along the lines laid down by Nature—in a word, to act according to one's *svadharma*.

The *Gītā* is thus in accordance with the educational theories of today in holding that every person's individuality is sacred and precious, and all that an educator has to do is to make every child who is entrusted to his care discover his *svadharma,* and allow him free play to develop along his own natural lines. Only, the *Gītā* does not stop there. It goes a step further and says that all our varied individualities find their fulfilment only in service to God. The scripture says, 'Whatsoever thou doest, whatsoever thou eatest, whatsoever thou offerest, whatsoever thou givest away, and whatsoever of austerities thou dost practise—do that, O son of Kuntī, as an offering unto me' (IX.27).

Nature, no doubt, is our starting point, but God is our goal. Hence all our actions should have only one ultimate aim, viz. to reach God. Our *svadharma* should, in short, be moulded and directed by our ideal of Karma-yoga.

The *Gītā* sometimes speaks of *svakarma* instead of *svadharma*. For it happens that many people feel that they have no special aptitude of any kind and that their profession was determined for them purely by external circumstances. Even then, the *Gītā* tells them, their professional duties may be made the basis of Karma-yoga. Suppose a man, having no special aptitude of any kind, becomes, say, a clerk. The *Gītā* says that even he can make his everyday duties in his office the basis of Karma-yoga as easily as a musical or a mathematical genius. Our spiritual progress depends not upon the kind of work we do, but upon the way in which we do it. One man may work in a small place with a large heart, another in a large place with a small heart. Selflessness illumines even a petty shop, while selfishness darkens even a palace.

### GOD HIMSELF A KARMA-YOGIN

The originality of the *Gītā* is seen not only in the formulation of the doctrine of Karma-yoga, but also in the telling illustration it gives of it from the way in which God works in Nature and in history. At every turn of its argument the scripture points to the example of Īśvara Himself as a great *karma-yogin*. For God is not a quietist sitting idle in a remote heaven. He is not a *sannyāsin* who has renounced all activity. His ideal is not a state of *naiṣkarmya* or actionlessness. He is ever creating, ever destroying. He makes Nature produce every day, every moment, innumerable forms of life. He makes the sun rise every morning and set every evening. He makes the winds blow, He sends down rain and dew, and makes the sap rise in trees. He is seated in the hearts of all creatures, making them breathe, live, think, forget, and remember. If He withdraws Himself even for a moment from His creation, the whole structure will collapse and fall. And what has He to gain by all this work? Is there anything at all for Him to gain which He does not already possess? The *Gītā* says, 'There is nothing in the three words, O Arjuna, for me to achieve, nor is there anything to gain which I have not gained. Yet I continue to work. For if I did not continue to work unwearied, O Pārtha, men all around would follow my path. If I should cease to work, these worlds would perish, and I should cause confusion and destroy these people' (III.22-24).

The Creator thus sets an example for all His creatures to follow. He is a perfect *karma-yogin,* for He works incessantly and selflessly. So man becomes most like God when he works as He works—silently, ceaselessly, and selflessly—not caring for the fruits of his action. When he thus follows the example of God, he soon ceases to feel that he is a separate agent. He feels that he is doing God's work, that he is only an instrument in God's hands, and that he is always at one with Him.

### CONSUMMATION OF KARMA-YOGA

The final step in the exposition of Karma-yoga is taken by the *Gītā* when it calmly states the paradox that God, who is the supreme *karma-yogin,* works incessantly, and yet He works not. Incessant work and absolute rest are mysteriously reconciled in Him. As Brahman, the Absolute, He is eternally quiescent ; and as Īśvara, the Creator, Protector, and Destroyer, He is always and everywhere active. The colourless beam of light breaks up into a spectrum of many colours when it passes through a prism, and yet it is the same light. Similarly, the Absolute emerges from the prism of time, space, and causality as Creator and a world of creatures. The practical lesson that the *Gītā* draws from the mystery of the divine Being is that man also should reconcile within himself activity and rest. He should find rest in work, and work in rest. The scripture says, 'He who sees no work in work, and work in no work,—he is wise among men. He is a *yogin,* and he has accomplished all work' (IV.18). In other words, a wise man should work ceaselessly and yet remain every moment unaffected by the results of his work. This is possible only when he eradicates the notion that he is a separate self with interests of his own, and allows the universal spirit to work through him.

### BHAKTI-YOGA

From this account of Karma-yoga, it will be seen that we have already passed unconsciously from *karma* to *bhakti.* In the statement that a man should give up not only the fruit of action, but also the agency of action, lies the germ of Bhakti-yoga. How can a man learn to give up the agency of action when he is a self-conscious individual with a will of his own and not a mere machine? It is only by gradually surrendering his will to God in self-forgetting love that he can do this. Hence the necessity of *bhakti* from the very starting point of his spiritual journey.

It is wonderful how the *Bhagavad-Gītā* traverses the whole range of *bhakti* from the crudest kind of worship practised by the ignorant to the highest kind of contemplation on the impersonal Absolute, of which only the most advanced souls are capable. In fact, its exposition of Bhakti-yoga, in its myriad phases of ritual, sacrifice, worship, surrender, meditation, contemplation, and realization, is as original a contribution to our religious tradition as its exposition of Karma-yoga. Just as the Karma-yoga of the *Gītā* is a marvellous expansion of a few *mantras* in the Upaniṣads, so its Bhakti-yoga is a marvellous expansion of the various kinds of *upāsanās* scattered throughout the Upaniṣads. But the most striking difference between the old *upāsanā* doctrine and the new *bhakti* doctrine lies in the appeal of the latter to the warm feelings of the heart. Had it not been for the teaching of the *Gītā* and similar scriptures in the post-Vedic age, our Vedānta would have been either a bleak metaphysics or a mystic ritual beyond the reach of ordinary man. It was the great *avatāra* of the *Gītā* that first brought into our Vedic traditions a warm current of love and beauty, which afterwards inundated the whole country and threw up innumerable literary forms, works of art, and ways of life—all of surpassing loveliness. The famous *Bhāgavata Purāṇa* is only one of such developments. In consequence, the *avatāra* of Kṛṣṇa has become the highest ideal of love and beauty—the Beloved of India. And the religion of love that he taught became so extensive, so refined, and so etherial that Swami Vivekananda, in one of his lectures, says that the Kṛṣṇa of the *Bhagavad-Gītā* belongs to a lower stratum than the Kṛṣṇa of the *Bhāgavata Purāṇa*. Speaking of the love of the *gopīs* of Vṛndāvana, as described in the *Bhāgavata,* the Swami says, 'That is the very essence of the Kṛṣṇa incarnation. Even the *Gītā,* the great philosophy itself, does not compare with that madness, for in the *Gītā* the disciple is taught slowly how to walk towards the goal, but here is the madness of enjoyment, the drunkenness of love, where disciples and teachers and teachings and books and all these things have become one, even the ideas of fear and God and heaven. Everything has been thrown away. What remains is the madness of love. It is forgetfulness of everything, and the lover sees nothing in the world except that Kṛṣṇa, and Kṛṣṇa alone, when the face of every being becomes Kṛṣṇa, when his own face looks like Kṛṣṇa's, when his own soul has become tinged with the Kṛṣṇa colour. That was the great Kṛṣṇa!'[1]

## CONCEPTIONS OF ULTIMATE REALITY

In all ages and countries, wherever the heart of man longed for God, his love expressed itself through some kind of symbolism. The ultimate divine Reality is conceived either as a place or a person or a spirit or a

[1] 'The Sages of India', *The Complete Works of Swami Vivekananda,* III. p. 259.

state of consciousness. When it is conceived as a place—a paradise or a heaven—the worshipper looks upon himself as a pilgrim on the way to it. When it is conceived as a person, various kinds of emotional relationship are established between the worshipper and the worshipped. The worshipper may conceive of God as a master and look upon himself as a servant ; or he may think of Him as a friend and look upon himself as a comrade ; or he may conceive of Him as a parent and look upon himself as a child. Or, again, he may conceive of Him as a lover and look upon himself as His beloved. When the ultimate Reality is conceived as a spirit, either immanent or transcendent, the worshipper becomes either a seer or a thinker, and this gives rise to what has been called Nature mysticism in one case and philosophical mysticism in the other. And lastly, when the ultimate Reality is conceived as a state of consciousness, the worshipper looks upon himself as a sleeper awakened—awakened from the sleep of *ajñāna* to the one universal consciousness of *jñāna*. It is well known that in the Hindu Bhakti-śāstras of later days these various conceptions of God as a person are termed *bhāvas—dāsya-bhāva, sakhya-bhāva, vātsalya-bhāva, kānta-* or *madhura-bhāva,* etc. But in the *Bhagavad-Gītā,* the divine Teacher, without using any such technical term, deals naturally with all concepts of the ultimate Reality mentioned above. When he speaks of it as a place, he uses the terms *loka, sthāna, pada, gati,* and *dhāman* ; when he speaks of it as a person, he uses, besides the ubiquitous first personal pronoun *aham* in all its seven cases, the terms Puruṣa, Īśvara, etc. When he speaks of it as an immanent spirit, he uses the words Ātman, Jīva, *kṣetrajña, vibhu,* etc. ; when he speaks of it as a transcendent spirit, he uses the terms *sat, tat, para, avyakta, akṣara,* Brahman, etc. And lastly, when he speaks of it as a state or condition, he uses the words *sthiti, siddhi, śānti, nirvāṇa, amṛta, śreyas, jñāna, yoga,* etc. But what is most remarkable is the way in which, in one and the same passage, several of these concepts are blended together without producing any incongruous effect. Take, for instance, the following: 'I am the father of this universe, the mother, the supporter, and the grandsire . . . . I am the goal and the support ; the lord and the witness ; the abode, the refuge, and the friend ; I am the origin and the dissolution, the ground, the resting place, and the imperishable seed' (IX.17,18). 'Then one should seek that place from which there is no return, saying "I seek refuge in that primal person from whom has come forth this eternal process" ' (XV.4).

### SYNTHESIS OF RELIGIONS

Thus we have in the *Gītā* a grand synthesis not only of various schools of religious thought and various ways and means of spiritual life—such as Karma-yoga, Bhakti-yoga, and Jñāna-yoga—but also of the various concepts of the ultimate Reality which we generally call God.

It may be observed that God, as He is in Himself, is an impersonal Absolute and is designated Brahman, and that God, as He is in relation to us and the world, is a personal deity and is designated Īśvara. The former is a scientific conception and the latter a poetic one. At the beginning of the twelfth chapter of the *Gītā* the question is raised whether we should meditate on the impersonal Absolute or the personal Īśvara. The answer of the Lord is that both methods lead to the same result, but that the former is naturally more difficult for the embodied beings than the latter. Elsewhere He goes further and says, 'Whatever may be the form which each devotee seeks to worship with faith—in that form verily do I make his faith steadfast. Possessed of faith, he worships that form, and his desires are fulfilled, granted, in fact, by me alone' (VII.21,22).

All forms of the Divine which men worship—from the crudest image to the highest Īśvara—are only symbols of the Formless. Therefore, while tolerating all forms, the *Gītā* says that the higher the form the better is the result, and that it is only the ignorant who think that the transcendent Spirit has any inherent form of its own: 'Not knowing my supreme nature, immutable and transcendental, foolish men think that I, the unmanifest, am endowed with a manifest form' (VII.24). This is a remarkable statement on the part of the *avatāra* clad in human form, who throughout the *Gītā* calls upon men to come to Him, worship Him, and seek refuge in Him. It is the best illustration of the Hindu doctrine of *adhikāra,* according to which the highest truth is not hidden, but only tempered for the time being according to the capacities of men who have to assimilate it. Accordingly, the *Gītā* tolerates all forms of worship, but, at the same time, gently leads the worshipper on to a pure and noble type of monotheism, whose distinguishing characteristic is its progressive spiritual freedom.

## SCRIPTURE AND INDIVIDUAL FREEDOM

At the beginning of the seventeenth chapter of the *Gītā* an important question is asked by Arjuna: 'Those who leave aside the ordinances of the scripture (Śāstra) but worship with faith (*śraddhā*)—what is their state, O Kṛṣṇa?' It is the question of authority vs. freedom, Church vs. individual, which every historical religion has to face. Therefore it is necessary for us to understand clearly what the *Gītā* has to say on this point, especially, as no direct answer is given in the text to Arjuna's question. That *śraddhā* or faith of the individual is an all-important thing in worship is, of course, recognized in a ringing verse at the end of the seventeenth chapter, which says, 'Whatever offering or gift is made, whatever austerity is practised, whatever rite is performed—if it is done without faith, it is called *asat,* O Arjuna. It is of no account here or hereafter'. This verse should be regarded as a counterpart of the verse which occurs at the end of the previous chapter, and which runs as follows: 'Therefore let the scripture be thy authority in determining what ought to be done and what ought not to be done. Knowing the scriptural law, thou shouldst do thy work in the world'.

These two verses are complementary to each other. Perfect worship is that in which there is implicit obedience to the Śāstra and a free exercise of *śraddhā*—that in which both the Church and the individual co-operate. And, conversely, the most imperfect worship is that in which there is neither obedience to the Śāstra nor exercise of *śraddhā*—that which is both untraditional and insincere, that which is the result of mere egoism. The former is termed *sāttvika* and the latter *tāmasika.* They are two extremes. And in between is the third type in which only one of the elements—either Śāstra or *śraddhā*—is present. This is the *rājasika* type. This type has naturally two subdivisions: (1) that kind of worship which is in accordance with the Śāstra but which has no *śraddhā* behind it, and (2) that kind of worship which is not in accordance with the Śāstra but which is the result of the individual's own *śraddhā.* Arjuna's question obviously refers to the second subdivision. Of these two types of worship which is the better? The *Gītā* says that the answer depends on the kind of *śraddhā* of the man, which again depends upon his own natural disposition. The *śraddhā* of one man may drive him to the worship of the gods; that of another, to the worship of demigods and demons; and that of a third, to the worship of ghosts and spirits. It is, again, the *śraddhā* of some men, unaided by Śāstra, that drives them to terrible mortifications and tortures of the flesh under the false notion that these constitute what is called *tapas.* Thus, while those types of worship which are in accordance with the Śāstra, but which are not sustained by *śraddhā,* may be simply futile, those which are not sanctioned by the Śāstra, but which are the result of a misguided *śraddhā,* may be positively harmful. There is no guarantee that an individual's unaided *śraddhā* will always lead him along the right path. It is therefore safe for the individual, especially in the early stages, to rely upon the guidance of law and tradition. At the same time, it should never be forgotten that law and tradition should fulfil themselves in the illumination and faith of the individual. *Śraddhā* should complete what the Śāstra has begun. Everywhere the *Gītā* holds the balance even between obedience to scriptural law and spiritual freedom. If tradition is over-emphasized, the growth of religion is retarded, and if individual freedom is over-emphasized, the continuity of religion is broken. The correct view that we should take of scriptures therefore is that they are our teachers, whose aim is to help us to think for ourselves and enable us to win our spiritual freedom and employ it wisely. It is significant that the *Gītā* includes the study of the Vedas in its list of virtues in several places, but says elsewhere that the vision of God cannot be gained through the study of the Vedas, nor through penances and gifts, but by the individual's exclusive devotion to Iśvara. And more significant still is the *Gītā's* own example in this matter. For the great scripture everywhere follows the Upaniṣadic tradition, but re-interprets and expands that tradition in such a way as to make it almost an original gospel.

The wisdom of the *Gītā* is further seen in that, while ending its message on the grand note of *prapatti* or the absolute self-surrender of the worshipper to God, followed by the divine promise of release from all sins, it never encourages the excessively emotional *bhakti* of later ages which is divorced from healthy action and thought. The *bhakti* that it teaches is well balanced by a life of disinterested action on one side and by a comprehensive vision on the other. It cannot be too often repeated that one of the most remarkable features of this great scripture is that, in its teaching, the various components of spiritual life, viz. *karma, bhakti,* and *jñāna,* are kept in perfect balance and harmony.

### DHYĀNA-YOGA

The intensive phase of Bhakti-yoga is called Dhyāna-yoga in the *Gītā*. It consists of moments of intense rapture when the soul is lifted to the heights of the eternal Being and rests satisfied but speechless. There is a remarkable description of it in the sixth chapter: 'As a lamp in a place sheltered from the wind does not flicker—that is the figure employed of a *yogin*, who, with a subdued mind, practises concentration of the spirit. That in which he knows the boundless joy beyond the reach of the senses and grasped only by the understanding, and that in which when he is established, he never departs from truth; that on gaining which he feels there is no greater gain, and that in which he abides and is not moved even by the heaviest of afflictions—let that be known as *yoga*. It is severance indeed of contact with pain and it is to be practised with determination and an untiring mind' (VI.19-23).

In the face of such verses it is absurd to say, as some do, that the *Gītā* is merely a gospel of duty for duty's sake, or that it is merely a gospel of humanitarian work or social service. The *Gītā* is a comprehensive gospel of *yoga,* and includes within itself all the ways and means by which man is brought into union with God.

### JÑĀNA-YOGA

The final stage in the path of light which leads to union with God is called Jñāna-yoga. The word *jñāna,* as it is used in our Vedāntic literature, has no word exactly corresponding to it in English ; for *jñāna* does not mean mere knowledge, though, coming from the same root, it is often translated as knowledge. It means, however, much more than ordinary knowledge. It comprises both knowing and being. We can never know God as we know any external object—a house or a tree. For God is not an object. He is the eternal subject. Accordingly, we cannot realize Him through intellectual knowledge, but only by inward spiritual growth. Here knowing and being are one. In other words, it is only to the extent of partaking of the nature of God that we may be said to know Him. Rightly does Arjuna say in the *Gītā,* addressing the Lord, 'Thou alone knowest Thyself through Thyself, O supreme Person'.

But it must be admitted that the word *jñāna* is also often used in a lower sense. It often means metaphysical knowledge, and not spiritual realization. And therefore those sections of the *Gītā* which are devoted to *jñāna* deal as much with metaphysics as with religious experience.

### RELATION WITH THE SĀṀKHYA SYSTEM

The metaphysics of the *Gītā* is influenced by two systems of philosophy —the Sāṁkhya and the Vedānta. Many verses in the *Gītā* cannot be understood without at least an elementary knowledge of the Sāṁkhya system. It should not be forgotten, of course, that at the time of the *Gītā,* the Sāṁkhya had not yet become a rounded system of thought. Its doctrines were still in a rather fluid state, and the words it used had not yet hardened into technical terms. And many ideas and expressions were common to the Sāṁkhya, Vedānta, and Buddhist schools. So it is rather uncritical to read into the language of the *Gītā* the clear-cut doctrines of the later Sāṁkhya. However, it cannot be denied that the Teacher of the *Gītā* was as much influenced by the speculations of Kapila, the reputed founder of the Sāṁkhya, as by the revelations of the Upaniṣads. He included Kapila among the *vibhūtis* or manifestations of Īśvara and tried, if possible, to work the speculation of that great thinker into the synthesis of His *Gītā*. The task was not an insuperable one. For at the time of the *Mahābhārata,* the Sāṁkhya thought was still theistic as in the Upaniṣads. It had not yet become a dualistic atheism.

Let us see how far the Sāṁkhya ideas are utilized in the *Gītā*. In the first place, it should be observed that the word *sāṁkhya* is used in five or six verses (II.39, III.3, V.4,5, XIII.24, XVIII.13) in the *Gītā*—not in the sense of the Sāṁkhya system, but in the sense of metaphysical knowledge. And in one of these verses (XVIII.13) the word *sāṁkhya* is interpreted by Śaṅkara actually to mean Vedānta. The Sāṁkhya as a system of philosophy founded by Kapila is, according to the commentator, referred to in the *Gītā* by the expression *guṇa-saṅkhyāna* in XVIII.19. Whatever that may be, the *Gītā* accepts the concept of Prakṛti, which is also found in the Upaniṣads. It whole-heartedly accepts the three *guṇas*—*sattva, rajas,* and *tamas*—as the fundamental dispositions of Prakṛti. It accepts on the whole the twenty-four *tattvas* (principles) in the evolution of Prakṛti (VII.4,5, XIII.5,6). It admits that our actions are to be attributed to the forces of Prakṛti in us, and not to the soul which is above these. It admits that the soul is deluded in thinking that it is the doer, while it is the senses, *manas* (mind), *ahaṅkāra* (principle of individuality), and *buddhi* (intellect) that are responsible for everything that is done. It also admits that the liberated soul is free from this delusion and knows its own nature and transcends the three *guṇas* of Prakṛti.

But the *Gītā* alters the trend of the whole Sāṁkhya system by its Upaniṣadic conception of the one Uttamapuruṣa, of whom the other Puruṣas are only individual manifestations. And this Puruṣottama is not merely a witness of the changes of Prakṛti. He is also the Governor. Prakṛti is His Prakṛti. Its changes are directed by His will. Prakṛti is His lower manifestation, while the souls are His higher manifestations. As Prakṛti is thus an aspect of God, contact with it is not evil. On the other hand, it is only by working in conjunction with it to carry out the purposes of God that the individual Puruṣa can get over his individuality. Furthermore, the liberated Puruṣa is not merely free from the thraldom of Prakṛti; he is in conscious union with God. Thus, at every step, the atheistic dualism of the later Sāṁkhya is avoided in the *Gītā*. The Teacher simply makes use of the Sāṁkhya analysis of Nature and the mind of man in His popularization of the Upaniṣadic teaching. It may be that the Sāṁkhya analysis is now superseded, and its account of the evolution of the world must give place to more scientific theories. But that does not in any way invalidate the teaching of the *Gītā* and the Upaniṣads based on religious experience.

### RELATION WITH THE YOGA SYSTEM

Similar to the *Gītā's* relation to the Sāṁkhya is its relation to Patañjali's Yoga system. Patañjali accepts the dualism of the Sāṁkhya and believes in the theory of the evolution of the world from the juxtaposition of Puruṣa and Prakṛti and prescribes a severely graded discipline of the mind for reaching *samādhi*. In fact, there is no essential difference between the Sāṁkhya and Yoga systems, except that the latter prescribes a detailed *sādhana* for liberation and makes a faint mention of Īśvara. Devotion to Īśvara is said to remove all obstacles in the path of *yoga*. Īśvara is defined by Patañjali as a *Puruṣa-viśeṣa* or particular Puruṣa, who is untouched by the actions and imperfections of the world. He stands outside the other Puruṣas and Prakṛti. He is not immanent in creation, nor is He the Creator. The evolution of the world does not depend upon Him. Nor is the liberation of souls directly brought about by Him, nor does salvation mean union with Him. He is only the model of a liberated Puruṣa and the first teacher of *yoga,* and by devotion to Him other Puruṣas can become like Him.

This short account of the system will show how different it is from the teaching of the *Gītā,* in both its theoretical and practical parts. First of all, the *Gītā* uses the word *yoga,* as we have seen, in a far wider and more varied sense. The *yoga* of Patañjali's system is a mere channel of mental discipline, while the *yoga* of the *Gītā* is an ocean of spiritual life. The eight accessaries of the former—*yama, niyama,* etc.—form a very small part of the latter. The *Gītā* does make mention of all of them, but not at all in the form of a cast-iron system. Particular care is taken to see that the regulations prescribed are not harsh or difficult. The *Gītā* advocates no difficult poses nor any prolonged breathing exercises. It advocates moderation in eating and sleeping, and not severe fasts and vigils. It roundly condemns all unnecessary mortifications of the flesh.

Again, there is no comparison between the conception of God which we have in the *Gītā* and that which we have in the Yoga system. According to the *Gītā,* God is both transcendent and immanent. He is present everywhere in creation and extends beyond it. He determines all the activities of Nature. He helps all souls with His kindly presence at their centre. He is a Redeemer within call. He has many different phases, as Brahman the Absolute, Hiraṇyagarbha the cosmic Soul, Īśvara the personal God, Śakti the creative Power, *avatāra* or God in human form, Jīva the individual soul, *vibhūti* or particular manifestation, and as Prakṛti of the eightfold Nature. Thus the Puruṣottama of the *Gītā* and the *Puruṣa-viśeṣa* of the Yoga system are poles asunder.

## NATURE AND OBJECT OF JÑĀNA

But Jñāna-yoga, as we have already seen, means not only knowledge of God and of His several manifestations, but also the realization of the soul's union with Him. It includes also the experience of the mystic unity of all things. The *Gītā* says, 'When he sees that the manifold nature of beings is centred in One and that all evolution is only from there—he becomes one with the Absolute' (XIII.30). 'When thou hast seen it, thou shalt no longer be deluded as now, O Arjuna ; for thou wilt see all things, without exception, in thyself and also in me' (IV.35).

The vision of *viśvarūpa,* the cosmic form of the Lord, which came to Arjuna in the middle of his thrilling discourse with Kṛṣṇa, is a symbol of this experience. We are told that a new sense—a third eye, as it were—was opened in him, and he saw to his great astonishment a transfiguration of the world. The *Gītā* says, 'There, in the person of the God of gods, Arjuna beheld the whole universe, with its manifold divisions, all gathered together in One' (XI.14).

## SUPREME BEING AS PERSONAL AND IMPERSONAL

There is a fundamental difference between the conception of God implied in *jñāna* and that implied in *bhakti.* In the exercise of *bhakti* we regard God as a being, outside ourselves, possessing in perfection all those spiritual values of which we have only glimpses in this world. But in the exercise of *jñāna* we view Him as a supra-personal spirit, of whom no predication can be made by man. Human conceptions of justice, mercy, love, goodness, etc. are such poor things that it is ignoble to clothe the supreme Being with them. That is why the great Upaniṣadic seers gave only a negative description of the Ātman, saying, 'not this, not this'. Though the *Bhagavad-Gītā* is a theistic scripture, the utterance of a personal God, we find scattered throughout its pages both conceptions of the ultimate Reality—what we in an earlier section called the scientific and the poetic conceptions. In chapter XIII, for instance, we find both of them in antithesis: 'I will now describe that which ought to be known, and by knowing which immortality is gained. It is the supreme Brahman, who is without beginning and who is said to be neither being nor non-being. His hands and feet are everywhere ; His eyes, heads, and mouths are facing in all directions ; His ears are turned to all sides ; and He exists enveloping all. He seems to possess the faculties of all the senses and yet He is devoid of the senses. He is unattached and yet He sustains all things. He is free from the qualities of Nature, and yet He enjoys them. He is without and within all beings. He has no movement, and yet He moves. He is too subtle to be known. He is far away, and yet He is near. He is undivided, and yet He is, as it were, divided among beings. He is to be known as the sustainer of all creatures. He devours and He generates. The light of all lights, He is said to be beyond darkness. As knowledge, the object of knowledge, and the aim of knowledge, He is set firm in the hearts of all' (XIII. 12-17).

Some scholars are of opinion that both the personal and the impersonal aspects of Divinity are included in the *Gītā* concept of Puruṣottama.

Whatever that may be, it must be admitted that the *Gītā* draws no hard and fast line between the highest *bhakti* and the highest *jñāna*. Take, for instance, the following passage: 'Four types of righteous men worship me, O Arjuna—the man in distress, the man who wishes to learn, the man who has something to attain, and the man who has attained supreme knowledge. Of these, the man of supreme knowledge (*jñānin*), having his devotion centred in One (*eka-bhakti*) and being ever attuned, is the best. For supremely dear am I to the man of knowledge, and he is dear to me' (VII. 16, 17).

Similarly, in the well-known description of *jñāna* in the thirteenth chapter (7-11) not only are the highest moral qualities mentioned, but also unswerving devotion to God. That is why the *Gītā* speaks only of the two paths of Karma-yoga and Jñāna-yoga and not of the three paths, as we do now, of *karma, bhakti,* and *jñāna*. The *avatāra* says, 'In this world, a twofold way of life was taught of yore by me, O Arjuna, that of knowledge for men of contemplation and that of works for men of action' (III. 3).

### SOCIAL MESSAGE OF THE GĪTĀ

In the preceding sections we have traced the path of *yoga* in the *Gītā* from its beginnings in the awakening of *buddhi* to its culmination in *jñāna*. But the unique feature of *jñāna,* as taught in the *Gītā,* is that it is never divorced from service to society. It is indeed remarkable how, even in its highest flights of description of the rapture of the saints, this great scripture never fails to mention love of all creatures as an inalienable element in it. Take, for instance, the following passage describing *Brahmanirvāṇa* or beatitude of the realization of God: 'The *yogin* who is happy within, who rejoices within, and who is illumined within becomes divine and attains to the beatitude of God. Those whose sins are destroyed and whose doubts have been removed, whose minds are disciplined and *who rejoice in the good of all beings*—such holy men attain to the beatitude of God' (V.24, 25). Or, again, the following verse which ends the section on Dhyāna-yoga in the sixth chapter: 'He who looks upon all as himself in pleasure and in pain—he is considered, O Arjuna, a perfect *yogin*' (VI. 32).

The teaching of the *Gītā,* in short, is that, starting with our natural endowments, we have to pass through the world, doing our duty to society in a spirit of detachment, and reach our home in God. *Svadharma, lokasaṅgraha,* and *yoga* are the three important terms which may be said to sum up the message of this scripture. A casual reader is apt to lose sight of the middle term, especially as it is a term not mentioned in the Upaniṣads. In fact, unsympathetic critics of Hinduism have often ignored it and said that social service forms no integral part of our religion. They forget that the service to society is fundamental to the very concept of Hindu *dharma*. *Dharma* etymologically means that which binds society together. The Hindu State had for its aim only the maintenance of *dharma*. Our ancient writers on political science seldom recognized either the divine right of kings or the divine right of States. *Dharma,* according to them, was above the secular power of the State. Again, the maintenance of society in *dharma* is the very purpose of an *avatāra,* as defined in the *Gītā*. And the whole object of the *Gītā* teaching is to make Arjuna do his duty by society and not run away from it, as he proposes to do at the beginning of the discourse. Lastly, the master stroke in the message is the representation of God Himself as a *karma-yogin* who is ever engaged in maintaining law and order in the universe of His creation.

# 24

# PHILOSOPHY OF THE YOGAVĀSIṢṬHA

THE *Yogavāsiṣṭha* is one of the finest works in Sanskrit. Its author, whoever he might have been, must have combined in himself a great mystic, a great philosopher, and a great poet. Quite a number of the later Upaniṣads, *Viveka-cūḍāmaṇi, Haṭhayoga-pradīpikā, Śiva Saṁhitā, Pañcadaśī, Jīvanmukti-viveka, Bhakti-sāgara, Rāma-Gītā,* and *Vedānta-muktāvalī* copiously quote from it. A Sanskrit writer on the Vedānta has stated very boldly, 'Another work like the *Yogavāsiṣṭha* has neither been produced nor is likely to be produced' (*Brahmāhnika,* 256). The author of the *Yogavāsiṣṭha* himself claims that his work is 'a veritable store of wisdom and contains all that is best anywhere' (III.8.12).

For various reasons it is difficult to ascertain the time when the *Yogavāsiṣṭha* was composed. Tradition, relying on the dramatic situation created in the work, attributes it to Vālmīki, the reputed author of the *Rāmāyaṇa.* Among modern scholars, there are two different opinions about the probable date of its composition. According to one, the work is post-Śaṅkara and must have been composed sometime 'between the eleventh and the middle of the thirteenth century'. The other regards it as a pre-Śaṅkara work which must have been composed before the advent of even Gauḍapāda, the grand-teacher of Śaṅkara.

### SOME OUTSTANDING AND DISTINCTIVE FEATURES

Whatever its date of composition may be, the work, however, is not meant for any particular period of history. It appeals to the modern reader as much as it might have done to those of the age when it was composed. The *Yogavāsiṣṭha* appeals in particular to the modern reader for its rationalistic outlook. All authority, ancient or modern, human or divine, is rejected as such. Truth is to be discovered by us by our own endeavour at rational interpretation of our own experience, which, of course, can be extended and deepened by our own aspirations and efforts. Thus says Vasiṣṭha, the philosopher, the sage, and the teacher, in the work: 'A devotee of reason should value the works even of ordinary persons, provided they are rational and advance knowledge, and should discard those even of the sages, if they are not such. A reasonable statement, even of a child, should be accepted, while the unreasonable ones should be discarded like a piece of straw, even though they are made by the Creator Himself' (II.18.2,3). 'No teacher or scripture can ever show us God. He is realized by one as one's own self, through one's own purified and perfected intuition' (VIa.118.4). 'There is only one ultimate source of knowledge, namely, one's own direct experience, which is the ground and source of all other *pramāṇas,* even as the ocean is the ultimate source of all waters' (II.19.16).

Another feature of the *Yogavāsiṣṭha* is its catholicity, generosity, and spirit of reverence for the views of others. Though unorthodox, the work is nowhere polemical. It respects every view and tries to understand it as sympathetically as possible. Thus we read: 'All the various views arising at different times and in different countries, however, lead to the same supreme Truth, like the many different paths leading travellers from different directions to the same city. It is ignorance of the absolute Truth and misunderstanding of the different views that cause their followers to quarrel with one another with bitter animosity. They consider their own particular dogmas to be the best, as every traveller may think, though wrongly, his own path to be the only or the best path' (III.96.51-53). 'The method by which a man makes progress is the best for him. He should not change it for another, which is neither proper for him, nor pleases him, nor is fruitful of good to him' (VIb.130.2).

Still another feature which distinguishes the *Yogavāsiṣṭha* from most of the other spiritual works of India is its belief in unqualified equality of rights in spiritual and worldly matters between man and woman. It does not regard woman as in any way inferior to man. Not only has she the capacity to rise high spiritually, but she often goes ahead of her male companion and leads and raises him up.

'A wife of noble descent can by her own effort lead her husband out of the deep and extensive darkness of ignorance. Even the scriptures, the preceptor, and the sacred incantations are not so effective in raising a man spiritually as an affectionate wife of a noble descent can be. She is to her husband a companion, a brother, a sympathizer, a servant, a teacher, a friend, a scripture, a refuge, a slave, wealth, and joy ; and all these at once' (VIa.109.26-28).

The *Yogavāsiṣṭha* teaches the brotherhood not only of all human beings but of all creatures. Thus tells Vasiṣṭha to his pupil Rāma: 'The idea that this one is my brother and that one is not is entertained only by petty-minded people. How can one be said to be a brother and another not, when the same Self equally pervades all? All classes of creatures, O Rāma, are your brothers. There is none here who is absolutely unrelated to you'.[1]

The author does not believe in dry and hair-splitting argumentation, which only a few people can understand. To make his teaching effective

[1] V.18.61; V.20.4; V.18.57.

he takes help of similies, illustrations, and stories. In his own words: 'All that is expressed in sweet and graceful words, and with easily comprehensible arguments, similies, and illustrations, goes direct to the heart of the listener, and expands there, just as a little drop of oil expands on the surface of water; whereas all that is said without suitable illustrations and arguments unintelligible to the hearer, in confused and obscure language, does not enter the heart of the hearer, and is a mere waste of words, like butter poured on the burnt ashes of oblation. It is only through appropriate similies and illustrations that subtle themes which are worthy of being known, can be made popular as it has been done in all great works' (III.84.45-47).

Finally, the *Yogavāsiṣṭha* is not a work expounding or supporting the teachings of any particular school of thought as distinguished from another. Its teachings are not those of any of the traditional schools of Indian philosophy. It synthesizes the best aspects of all systems of thought, particularly those of the Sāṁkhya, the Yoga, the Buddhist, and the Upaniṣadic. Its is a thoroughgoing, systematic, and comprehensive idealism, different from the view of all other idealistic schools of Indian thought.

### THE DRAMATIC SITUATION IN THE YOGAVĀSIṢṬHA

The *Yogavāsiṣṭha* pictures a situation in which the philosophy it expounds, in a literary and popular manner, originated. Rāmacandra, the young prince of Ayodhyā, whose life and activities are depicted in the *Rāmāyaṇa,* just on the eve of his departure with the sage Viśvāmitra to protect the latter's religious performances from the disturbing *rākṣasas,* fell a victim to serious intellectual doubts and consequent loss of interest in life, its pleasures, and activities. Finding no satisfactory solution of the riddle of existence, he cries in despair: 'Is there any view which is free from error? Is there any place where there is no suffering? Is there any creation which is not ephemeral? Is there any transaction which is free from deception?' (I.27.31). 'Is there any better state of existence which may be free from suffering, ignorance, and grief, and which may be full of undecaying joy?' (I.30.24). Vasiṣṭha, the family preceptor, is called in for formulating a proper philosophy of life. Rāma requests him to teach him 'the science and art of a perfectly happy life' (I.31.17). And thus we have the birth of a philosophy of Vasiṣṭha which is embodied in the *Yogavāsiṣṭha.* A brief outline of this philosophy is sketched in the following pages.

### THE ULTIMATE SOURCE OF KNOWLEDGE

As already mentioned, direct cognition or intuition is the only and ultimate source of all knowledge, be it of an external object, of the Self, or of God. There is no other *pramāṇa* (source of knowledge) admitted by Vasiṣṭha.[2] Lacking in direct personal experience, nobody can know anything completely from a mere description of it—none can know how sugar tastes except by tasting it himself (V.64.53). Others can only give us a hint or partial indication of things unknown to us by way of analogy and illustrations (*upamāna* and *dṛṣṭānta*) (II.18.51f).

## IDEALISTIC MONISM

Our experience and a little reflection thereon reveal that without a common substance immanent in both of them, two things cannot be related either as cause and effect or as subject and object. Knowledge can have for its object only that which is homogeneous with its nature. Being related and known to each other, all things, objects and subjects, must thus be modifications or forms of one and the same consciousness.[3]

Idealism: A modification or form of consciousness is called an idea, thought, or image (*kalpanā*). The entire world experience is thus a *kalpanā* or idea of the absolute Consciousness. Consciousness in its objective and manifested phase is called *manas* (mind) by Vasiṣṭha. The world of experience, with all its things, laws, time and space, and individualities, is a creation of *manas*, an idea. They are all made of the same stuff as dreams are. There is nothing absolute and purely objective about time and space. Both are relative and subjective, and they differ with different subjects. Both cease to be experienced by a *yogin* in *samādhi*. The laws of nature, those of identity, uniformity (*niyati*), etc. are also mental concepts and are relative and subjective. They are not applicable in the same form to the entire experience. The mind may undo them and introduce a different order. The order, stability, and persistence we find in our world are also *imaginary* like those of dreams.[4]

Waking and dream experiences: There is thus little or no difference between the waking and dream experiences. Both are alike in their nature as long as each lasts. From the standpoint of a higher realization, no difference is felt between the two. As hundreds of dreams are experienced in the sleeping hours of our life, so hundreds of 'waking dreams' are experienced by the self in its transmigratory journey. As we can remember the various dreams experienced throughout our life, so the enlightened ones (*siddhas*) can remember the numerous waking dreams experienced by them during their past career.[5]

[2] III.42.15; II.19.16; VIb.52.29.
[3] III.121.37; VIb.38.8.
[4] IV.11.23; VIa.42.16; IV.47.48,58,59; V.48.49; VIb.56.3; VIb.210.11; VIa.61.29; VIa.37.21,22; VIb.148.21; III.13.36; III.60.21-26; III.103.13; VIb.73.19,20.
[5] IV.19.11,12; VIb.34.29,30; IV.18.47.

Subjective idealism: According to the *Yogavāsiṣṭha,* every individual cognizes and perceives only that which is within his own experience; no mind perceives aught but its own ideas. The world experience of every individual has arisen individually to every one. Every mind has the power to manufacture its own world.[6]

Objective idealism: Vasiṣṭha also admits a cosmic world with countless objects and individuals within it, which in its original form is a system of ideas in the cosmic Mind called Brahmā. Brahmā imagines the world and all the individuals within it at the commencement of the creation, and they continue to exist as long as Brahmā lives (III.55.47).

Two idealisms reconciled: The ideas imagined by Brahmā (cosmic Mind) are the common objects of experience of us all, although in our own mind they are experienced as our own. It may also be said that they are the reals (*bimba*) which our minds imitate or copy (*pratibimba*). As every mind in itself is an idea of the same cosmic Mind, it is capable of representing within itself other individual minds also as its own ideas. One is an idea in the mind of others as much as others are ideas in that of that one. As it is possible that several men may see the same dream, it happens that we all experience the same objects. As the same person may be seen in imagination by many individually, so also the same world experience is imagined in every mind, in the same way as it has arisen in the cosmic Mind.[7]

### THE WORLDS WE EXPERIENCE

The terms cosmic Mind and individual mind are, according to Vasiṣṭha, relative. That which is an individual in relation to a wider and more comprehensive cosmic Mind and its contents, may, in its own turn, be considered to be cosmic in relation to the entities (ideas) within its own objective experience. For, according to him, every object has a subjective aspect, i.e. is a mind, in which is experienced a world peculiar to itself, as in a dream. Every idea, thus, is a monad in itself and has a world within its experience, every ideal content of which is, again, in its turn, in itself, an individual monad having another within itself. There is no end to this process of worlds within worlds. In this way, in each universe are contained millions of other universes, and this process goes on *ad infinitum.* All this is unknown and unreal to us, but is directly known to those who have attained perfection.[8]

All the worlds which thus arise successively or simultaneously are

[6] III.40.29; III.55.61,62; IVb.13.4.
[7] VIb.20.7; III.55.48; V.49.10; VIb.151.10; VIb.154.11; III.53.25.
[8] IV.18.16,27; IV.19.1; III.52.20; III.44.34; VIb.59.33,34.

not necessarily of the same kind. They are not governed by the same laws and evolved in the same way as our own world. Some of them may have more similarity than others and some none at all. The same is the case with individual persons. Mind is not bound by any law of creation to be followed always and everywhere. The theories of creation propounded in various systems of thought are idle fancies.[9]

The manifestation of an objective world within a mind proceeds by way of materialization and externalization of ideas in the form of things, body, and senses, consequent upon a wish, craving, or desire to enjoy particular objects. This process can be well understood by a study of the phenomenon of dream, for the law of evolution or rise of an objective world is the same as in the case of a dream, of an after-death experience, and of the present knowledge of a cosmos. The dynamic force behind the manifestation of all objects in one's experience is the desire to *be* something or to *have* something, which the creative imagination supplies forthwith.[10]

### THE MIND OR INDIVIDUALITY

Individuality, according to Vasiṣṭha, does not consist in being something like a simple, undecomposable, spiritual entity called soul. It consists, on the other hand, in being a mind (*manas*), which means a particular mode of the absolute Reality, determined by a particular movement, tendency, desire, or will to imagine. It is called by various names such as *buddhi* (intellect), *ahaṅkāra* (ego), *citta* (attention), *karma* (activity), *vāsanā* (desire), *indriya* (sense), *prakṛti* (root-matter), and others on account of its different functions.[11] Mind is not anything different and separate from the absolute Brahman. It is Brahman manifesting Itself as creative agent. It is the whole looked at from a particular point of view.[12] There are three grades of manifestation of the mind with reference to its grossness. It is called Jīva or monad when it originates in Brahman as a subtle and powerful individuality; it is ego when it becomes a little grosser and more objective; and it is a physical body when its grossness, limitedness, and objectiveness are complete.[13] There is no limit to the number and kinds of monads in the universe (IV.43.1-4).

### OMNIPOTENCE OF THOUGHT

As minds, we have limitless power at our command. Thought in the forms of desire, imagination, effort, and will is the most potent force in

[9] IV.47.14,17f; VIa.66.23,24.
[10] III.12.2; VIb.22.37; VIa.114.17; III.4.79.
[11] III.96.3,17-29; III.64.16; V.13.51,54; III.96.43.
[12] IV.42.18; V.13.53,54; VIa.96.19.
[13] III.64.12,14; III.13.18f.

the world. Mind is endowed with creative power. In its creative activity mind is absolutely free. We all attain to what we aspire after. All that we intensely desire and make efforts for comes to us sooner or later. In fact, our own efforts guided by our aspirations are the warp and woof of our destiny. Our lives are what we make them by our thoughts. The world around us changes in accordance with our own thought. Our perceptions are coloured by our own beliefs. The extent of space and the duration of time are relative to our thoughts and emotions. Faith is the secret of all success and achievements. Bondage and freedom are states of mind and are wrought by thought. The physical body is a creation of mind and can be shaped by it into a desired form. Most of the diseases of the body originate in the disturbances of the mind and can be cured by right thinking and re-educating the mind. If we did not allow our balance of mind to be lost or marred by ambitions, worries, anxieties, and cares, no disease could ever enter our body. Happiness is another name for the harmony of the mind. Right culture of the mind is then the secret of joyful living.[14]

The main secret of attaining supernormal powers, according to the *Yogavāsiṣṭha,* is affirmation of one's spiritual nature, which is above the limitations of the physical body. Through the process of constant denial of all false limitations, created by wrong thinking, and through thoughtful auto-suggestion and affirmation of the ideal perfection, extraordinary powers are manifested in us. We should not allow our mind to be governed by the idea of the limitations of the body and the senses.[15] Extraordinary powers can also be acquired through the awakening and control of the *kuṇḍalinī-śakti*[16] residing in our body and normally lying dormant.[17]

## THE NATURE OF THE JĪVA AND HIS DESTINY

The body, the senses, the mind, the intellect, the ego, and even the individuality, cannot as such be regarded as the Self, for each of them can be transcended on one or the other level of experience, each of them is an object of our consciousness, and each of them is moved to activity by something else from the deep within. The subject and the object must be unified in the Self, otherwise knowledge would not be possible. The

[14] III.11.16; VIb.139.1; III.4.79; III.45.12-14; III.56.28,30; III.60.16,17,20-22,28; VIb.148.33; VIb.100.3; IV.21.20-22,56-58; IV.17.4; VIa.51.3; III.98.3; IV.45.7; IV.11.19; IV.21.16; VIa.28.34; VIa.26.10-38; V.21.12,14.

[15] III.57.30-33; VIa.82.26.

[16] *Kuṇḍalinī-śakti* is the name of the great power which lies dormant in every individual and which when awakened and directed towards the brain makes him an enlightened and powerful individual capable of supernormal powers.

[17] VIa.24; VIa.80.36f; VIa.81.1f; VIa.82.

Self therefore is the Reality at the root of the universe, which manifests itself in all individual beings and things of the world.[18]

The physical body is only an external manifestation of the inner will to be, which, with countless desires and hopes, persists as an individual mind; and this, as a consequence of the unfulfilled desires, will have another body to experience another world after the death of the present body. Death brings about a change in the kind of the objective world of the Jīva. It shuts from him the world with which he is no longer in rapport after the death of the physical body. The mind does not go anywhere else in space but only experiences another objective world after a temporary insensibility consequent upon the shock of losing this body and this world. The after-death experience is what the dead morally deserve in accordance with their beliefs and imagination. Having enjoyed the joys of 'heaven' or suffered the torments of 'hell' according to their deserts, beliefs, and desires, they again experience the life of the world, dragged thereto by the residue of the unfulfilled desires. The desireless dead do not undergo any further experience of a world. After the dissolution of the physical body and individuality, when the contents of desires are fully emptied, they enter the state of *nirvāṇa,* in which they experience complete identity with the absolute Brahman. They may, however, unbound by any desire, choose to play the rôle of cosmic deities in any of the manifested worlds.[19]

## CREATION AND DISSOLUTION

The mind which creates the objects that the Jīvas take to be objectively real is called Brahmā in the *Yogavāsiṣṭha.* It is the cosmic Mind that has imagined the world idea. Brahmā creates the world through his imaginative activity with the freedom and skill of an artist. He is not conditioned by any previously existing plan, he being a fresh wave of creative activity in the ocean of the absolute Consciousness. He is the lord of our cosmos, which continues as long as his imagination is at work and will collapse when he desists from his play of imagination. The rise of Brahmā in Brahman, the Absolute, is the most mysterious occurrence. He is like a sprout come out of the eternal seed of the Absolute when Its creative power tends to evolve a cosmos out of Itself. The Absolute in Its creative aspect or power, in a merely playful overflow, by Its own free will, comes to self-consciousness at one point, which brings about the forgetfulness of the Whole, and on account of intensity of consciousness there, begins to vibrate, pulsate, or agitate in the form of thinking or imagining,

[18] VIa.78.18-27; VIa.6.15-16; V.73.4; IV.22.33; V.27.12; V.34.52f.
[19] V.71.64-65; III.20.31; III.40.45; IV.43.26; III.9.14-25.

and assumes a distinct existence for Itself, as if separated from the Whole, whose one aspect It is in reality.[20]

The creative impulse of Brahman (Śakti) which finds expression in Brahmā is an inherent energy, a motive power, a will to manifest in finite forms. It is ever present in the absolute Brahman either in actual operation or in potential rest. It is nothing different from, but ever identical with, the Absolute. When the power is active, it may temporarily assume a separate and distinct form for itself; but when it ceases to work, it turns back to its source, and merging therein, becomes undifferentiated, when there is no creation.[21]

## ABSOLUTE REALITY AND WORLD APPEARANCE

It is very difficult to describe the nature of the Absolute. The categories of our experience are, one and all, incapable of expressing the Reality which is in and beyond the world experience. No aspect of the whole can be equated with the whole. All our concepts—matter, mind, subject, object, one, many, self, not-self, knowledge, ignorance, light, darkness, etc.—comprehend one or the other aspect of the Reality, but not the absolute Reality (Brahman) as such. They prove unsatisfactory when applied to the Reality, which is inherent in all things denoted by these concepts and their opposites. Hence Reality, when described at all, should be done in all terms, positive and negative, and not exclusively in any of the opposite terms. We must either affirm or deny everything or better keep silent, realizing the utter futility of the attempt.[22]

One form of the same substance may be separate and distinct from another form as such, but it can never be separate and distinct from the substance itself. An ornament of gold is never different from gold with which it is ever one and identical. Bubbles, ripples, waves, etc. are never different from water, whose forms they are, and abstracted wherefrom they cease to be. In the same way, everything in the universe including ourselves is Brahman, the ultimate Substance—'Thou art That'.[23]

The test of reality is eternal persistence. All forms, however, persist temporarily. They come into existence and pass out of it. How can they be regarded therefore as real? Neither can they be said to be unreal, for they persist for some time at least. A new category is required to comprehend such facts as are neither absolutely real nor absolutely unreal. Vasiṣṭha uses the terms *mithyā* (not true), *avidyā* (that which does not exist

[20] III.55.47; III.3.33f; VIb.208.27-29; IV.44.14f; IV.42.4; VIa.114.15-16; VIa.33.21; III.114.10,20; VIa.11.37; IV.42.5.

[21] VIb.84.2-6,26,27; VIb.83.14,16; VIb.85.14-19.

[22] VIb.184.45,46; VIb.52.26,27; VIb.31.36,37; III.5.14; VIb.106.11; III.7.20-22; III.119.23.

[23] VIa.49.29-32; III.100.17; III.1.17-18; V.57.1f; VIb.60.28.

eternally), Māyā (that which is not), *bhrama* (delusion), etc., which are equivalents of the term 'appearance' used in modern philosophy to comprehend the objects of our experience. The world is an appearance, according to Vasiṣṭha, in another sense also. Being a thoroughgoing idealist, to him nothing of the objective world is real apart from its appearance in some mind. The reality and existence of every object and every world is only relative to the minds that experience them. Just like the vision of a ghost or things experienced by a hypnotized person they are nothing to other percipients.[24]

In Itself the absolute Reality is above all changes, divisions, differentiations, and relations. All these are relative and fall within the Absolute. But the Absolute in Itself is free from them. It is a distinctionless, homogeneous reality, which is blissful consciousness through and through. For the Absolute, as such, there is no creation or destruction ; no bondage or freedom ; no change, no evolution or involution. They are all relatively real, but quite unreal from the absolute point of view. Acosmism (Ajātavāda) is the ultimate and the highest truth which can be realized by everyone when he ceases to be interested in the relative, particular, and finite appearances and aspires to rise to the level of the Absolute.[25]

### THE PATH OF NIRVĀṆA

Nothing short of the realization of the absolute point of view in our consciousness will make us perfectly free and happy, which is our *summum bonum*. The absolute Whole is the abiding and real home of happiness which we are all seeking, and nothing short of it will satisfy us.[26] A glimpse of this joy can be had when the mind is at peace, when it is not functioning, not desiring or thinking this or that object, and is calm and quiet (VIa.44.26,27). How to attain to this deepest level of experience of identity with the Absolute is the problem of all problems, and all great sages have prescribed this or that method. Vasiṣṭha is very definite and clear in this connection and lays down a comprehensive scheme of self-realization which leads to *nirvāṇa* or annihilation of all limitations and sufferings and makes man absolutely free and happy here and now.

In the scheme of Vasiṣṭha there is no place for those beliefs and practices which are ordinarily prescribed by various religions of the world and are indulged in by the ignorant mass of humanity. He says, 'Liberation cannot be attained by merely living in a forest far away from human

[24] V.5.9; IV.45.46; III.4.62,63; III.65.6; III.44.27,41; VIa.114.20; III.54.21; IV.1.2,7,12; III.67.76; IV.41.15.

[25] III.4.67; IV.40.30; VIa.125.1; III.13.48,49.

[26] VIa.108.20; V.54.69,70,72.

society, by undergoing penances (VIb.199.30), by performance or renunciation of any particular action, by undergoing any prescribed rules of discipline of any sect (VIb.199.31), by pilgrimage to the sacred places, by making religious gifts, by bathing in sacred rivers, by learning, by the concentration of the mind, by some kind of yogic feats, by penances, by sacrifices (VIb.174.24), by reading scriptures, by obeying the orders of a preceptor, by worshipping a god (VIb.197.18), by good luck, by religious acts, by means of wealth, or by the help and kindness of friends and relations (V.13.8)'.

What then is the way suggested by the *Yogavāsiṣṭha* for the attainment or realization of *nirvāṇa* or the absolute point of view? Knowledge of Reality, acquired through one's own efforts at right thinking, together with living by the enlightenment one gets from that knowledge, is the only method of crossing over the ocean of misery and reaching the land of happiness.[27] Through one's own efforts at introspection, understanding, thinking, and intuition one must first reach the conviction that Brahman is the only Reality, that everything is Brahman, that nothing other than Brahman is real, and that Brahman is the very self of us all, and then one must live by this conviction.[28] To think correctly, the mind must be purified through a study of philosophical works, association with the wise, and cultivation of moral sense.[29] The chief problems on which one should think with all the light that one's thought and intuition can give are: 'What am I? How does the world experience arise in me? What are life and death?' (V.58.32).

Knowledge for Vasiṣṭha is not merely an intellectual conviction. One must live by it. Otherwise it will not stay. In order to know well, we have to *be* and to *feel* well. To know the Absolute truly, we have to expand into the Absolute (VIb.22.1-5). The process of this expansion into the Absolute by shaking off our limitations and breaking off the bonds of individuality is called *yoga* by Vasiṣṭha. And the *Yogavāsiṣṭha* abounds in this *yoga* or practical method of self-realization, which has imparted the name to this great work.

This *yoga* is a process along two lines, namely, *denial of individuality,* which is the same as limitation and imperfection, and *affirmation of the Self,* which is perfection, peace, and happiness. As our individuality does not consist only of *intellect* (cognition), but also of *feeling* and *activity,* and as the Self is not only absolute Consciousness, but also absolute Bliss and absolute Peace, the practice of self-realization may proceed along three

[27] III.7.17; II.11.36; V.83.18; V.13.85,89.
[28] V.79.2,3; VIb.190.5.
[29] V.5.5; V.21.11.

ways, or along any one of them, for they are only three aspects of the same process, namely, (1) an intellectual conviction of not being an individual, but of being the infinite Absolute (*Brahma-bhāvanā*) ; (2) an intimate feeling of a lack of individuality, of possessing nothing and desiring nothing —this negative process having a positive counterpart in the cultivation of equanimity, universal brotherhood, cosmic feeling of oneness with all beings, and an ecstatic love of the Self ; and (3) the practice of controlling and stopping the constant rising and setting of the vital currents (*prāṇas*), leading to the stoppage of the perpetual flux of our internal being, whose external expression the *prāṇas* are. This stopping of the activity of the *prāṇas* can be brought about by lengthening the usually unnoticed moments of rest which occur when one current of the vital breath has set and the other has not begun yet. This moment of rest in breathing activity corresponds to that experience of rest in consciousness, however fugitive it may be in our ordinary life, when one idea has ceased to occupy the focus of consciousness and the other has not appeared therein.[30]

## STAGES OF REALIZATION

Several stages may be marked on this progressive path of evolution of individual consciousness into the Absolute. Vasiṣṭha notices seven with slightly different nomenclature in different parts: the first, when a person having become conscious of the evils of individual and selfish living, aspires to transcend it (*śubhecchā*) ; the second, when he reflects over the nature of the Self and the world (*vicāraṇā*) ; the third, when, on account of the knowledge of its ultimate unreality revealed by philosophical thought, the individuality becomes less and less assertive and is little felt (*tanumānasa*) ; the fourth, when the aspirant begins to feel the being of the real Self within himself (*sattvāpatti*) ; the fifth, when clinging to the objects of the world is finally given up by rising above all desires (*asaṁsakti*) ; the sixth, when all things are realized to be unreal from the point of view of the Absolute (*padārthābhāvanā*), or (according to an alternative reading) when the individual affirms himself to be the ultimate Reality (*padārtha-bhāvanā*) ; and the seventh, when the mystic experience of being one with the Reality is realized in consciousness (*turyagā*). This is the last door which opens into the unspeakable *nirvāṇa*.[31]

Those who live in the seventh stage are called *jīvanmuktas,* the liberated ones living here in this world. The *Yogavāsiṣṭha* gives a description of how they live and work and feel.[32] A *jīvanmukta,* according to

[30] *Śrī-Vāsiṣṭha-darśanam,* pp. 204-237.
[31] III.118.2-16; VIa.120.1-8; VIa.126.12-73.
[32] See *Śrī-Vāsiṣṭha-darśanam* on *Jīvanmukti.*

the *Yogavāsiṣṭha,* is the happiest person on earth. He is neither delighted in prosperity nor dejected in distress. Outwardly discharging all the duties of life, he is free within. He is free from the bonds of caste and creed and is polite and friendly to all. He has nothing to attain, nothing to give up. Even in the midst of worldly activities, he is always in solitude and above life's turmoils. Having seen him, having heard about him, having met him, and having remembered him, all beings feel delighted. He has no longer any struggle for livelihood. The guardian angels of the world protect and support him, as they do the entire cosmos. The *jīvanmukta* grows more and more powerful, intelligent, and lustrous every day, in the same way as trees grow more and more beautiful in spring. He enjoys life, he is a great man of action, and he is capable of the greatest renunciation.[33]

[33] *Yogavāsiṣṭha and Its Philosophy,* pp. 96 ff.

# 25

## PHILOSOPHY OF THE TANTRAS

### THEIR SCOPE AND GOAL

LIKE the word Veda, Tantra is often used in the singular, which may suggest that there is a uniform formulation of doctrine and discipline covered by the term. But there exists no such formal uniformity as one may expect from the singular use. Tantras are profusely varied in their theme and in their expression, but they claim (and this is a point of uniformity) to have emanated from a divine source, and, as such, they call themselves by such names as Āgama, Nigama, etc. Leaving apart those that are avowedly of a Buddhistic character and also those that have a veiled affiliation to the tenets of Buddhism, the Tantras that have allied themselves to Vedic metaphysics and theology, if not to some extent also to Vedic practices, are of a varied nature and have divided themselves into diverse, and sometimes apparently divergent, cults, paths, and rituals. The Tantras, being pre-eminently ways of practical realization, have necessarily to bear reference to the diverse characters and competencies of different aspirants and seekers, and have, accordingly, designed the framework of their theory and practice suitably to actual conditions prevailing, and also evolving stages and states in the soul's journey towards its chosen ends and values.

But what are to be the ends and values of its choice? The highest and the best, of course. The seeker soul cannot give up its quest till it realizes *all* that it is potentially; in other words, till it realizes, in all the dimensions of its meaning and fulfilment, its own undiminished perfectness. This highest end has been called by a special name in the Tantra Śāstra—*pūrṇatākhyāti* (e.g. in *Paraśurāma Kalpa-Sūtra*). Commonly, however, the highest end is called *mokṣa* or liberation from bondage. If, for example, the highest Reality, as eternally realized perfectness, is Śiva, the Jīva or the individual is potentially Śiva; but he does not actually know and realize himself as That. How can you (or thou) equate yourself to That? Only by liquidating your 'bonds' or limitations.

This is realization. Then, 'Thou art That', 'Jīva is Śiva'. The limitations are mainly of two kinds: those that limit or detract from the pristine purity of the individual self (*mala*), and those that limit or restrict the sense as well as the degree of its freedom (*pāśa*). On a more comprehensive scale, the limitations are counted as five; and they are called the five *kañcukas* (contracting and restricting factors). These five, as we shall see, have their place and function in the descent of the universe from its ultimate perfect source, and have therefore got to be resolved and not simply 'by-passed' when ascent is sought from cosmic limitations to the purity, freedom, and perfection of the ultimate source. In other words, if realization is to mean the equating of thou to That, it cannot be effected except by reducing the factors that apparently make a 'little knower, little doer, little enjoyer, etc.' of the first term (thou) and thereby create all the world of difference between itself and the second term (That). So long as those limiting factors are permitted to operate and create a stupendous bar, what am I but a tiny drop of dew on a shaky blade of grass? The vast sublime choir of the starry heavens above and the 'still small voice' of moral consciousness within dealing in categorical imperatives, are the two things that set the great philosopher Kant furiously thinking, 'Have they or have they not a common source or origin?' The mighty master voice that leads that sublime heavenly chorus and the small masterful voice that speaks through moral injunctions; the mighty master ordaining the measure of cosmic harmonies and the little master regulating the inner springs of action in us—can 'That' and 'this' be equated to each other? This raises the eternal issue, The little mystery that dwells within and rules as the hidden *in*—can it be assimilated to the majesty and sublimity that rules as the displayed *out*? Kant's *Critique of Pure Reason,* as we all know, locked the front door, keeping only the back door ajar. One knocked but had no reassuring answer. But is there really to be no positive solution?

The issue primarily relates to the individual, but is not confined to him. The individual does not stand and function alone, abstractedly and cross-sectionally. His life is functionally integrated into a broader and ampler scheme of life, which enlarges itself into groups, classes, and societies, which, in their turn, are 'partials' of a grand cosmic scheme. His life cannot be the life in a 'frog hole' or even in the cloistered seclusion of the 'cave'. It must be a self-conscious and self-fulfilling component as well as exponent of the unmeasured immensity which is life divine. He cannot therefore pursue his ends and work out his values irrespective of the entire scheme into which he is integrated. In other words, his own realization—or as we have put it, the solving of his own basic equation of thou and That—cannot be effected by methods of simple negation, ignorance, and escape. The problem, the equation, must be solved upon the most complete and thorough appraisement of all the relevant factors and conditions, individual and extra-individual.

## SYNTHETIC APPROACH

Now, the great significance of the Tāntric approach, both as regards philosophy and discipline, lies in this that it sets the problem with the full burden of all the relevant terms involved; the conditions limiting the individual could not be assigned and assailed as though these pertained to him alone abstractedly and cross-sectionally; and therefore his own perfection could not be attained irrespective of whether the cosmic scheme and the cosmic process were his allies or were hostile to him or simply neutral.

But what should this mean and imply? Should it mean that the individual would not attain his perfection unless and until the whole cosmic scheme and process also attained perfection; that there is no place for individual perfection in a universe which, for example, may actually be 'running down' for aught we know? The physicists, at any rate some of them, are telling us that the universe is 'running down' physically; but are we on the other hand assured that the universe is 'looking up' spiritually? Supposing that it is spiritually advancing and even 'turning the corner', is the individual's own advance so scheduled as to move *pari passu* with the total advance? That there must be a continued vital exchange of personal effort and 'outside' assistance between the two cannot be denied. Redeeming forces of sufficient magnitude and adequate influence must descend as operative 'high level' aids. And forms of Tāntric discipline recognize and keep themselves alive to these supra-physical and supra-mental forces. The world can never be so bad, materially and spiritually, as to make those forces unavailable for the earnest seeker's reforming and transforming effort.

It is here that the philosophy and practice of the Tantras deliver their special meaning and message to a world sunk low in material and spiritual confusion. Independent, if not alien, objectivity of the universe is a theory and will perhaps ever remain a theory; but that each conscious centre, every appreciative individual, 'lives, moves, and has his being' in a universe of his own selection and acceptance is an indisputable fact. To him therefore the theoretical objectivity of an alien universe is of much less practical account than the fact that he has his own universe to live and function in. We may call this latter the universe of appreciation and acceptance. This implies that this universe grows in stature and brightens, or else, shrinks and darkens, in accordance with the individual centre's appreciative and reactive ratio, which, of course, varies in the same individual as also from case to case. The ratio means that not only is man what nature has made of him, but that nature is what man has made of her. The best or worst possible world is man's own world as determined by that ratio, so that by transforming his own appreciative angle and reactive momentum he can transform that world suitably to his highest ideals and noblest ends.

His own realization must therefore necessarily imply and require this transforming also in all dimensions. His realization, as we have said, requires the solution of a basic equation, thou = That. The equation would admit of no solution till that brute, blind factor entering into the constitution both of the individual and of nature could be reduced—reduced not by simple negation and elimination, for it could create only an untenable vacuum, but by transforming the *paśu* in us into Paśupati, Jīva into Śiva. Then what are bonds or limitations from the appreciative angle of the first must appear as forms of creative joy and fulfilment, when that appreciative angle is raised and that reactive index transformed into a vision and understanding and ecstatic enjoyment of the whole basic theme of creation. In other words, the whole creation must be realized as Śiva. The equation thou = That cannot be finally and perfectly solved unless it is realized that all is That, all is Śiva.

## SIX COROLLARIES FROM THE GENERAL POSITION

The corollaries that follow from this general position are: First, there is undoubtedly enough evil, physical and moral, in the universe of our appreciation and acceptance. We could not create, even if we would, a vacuum by simply negating it or equating it to some sort of transcendental nothing. Speculatively, it is just possible that in the balanced economy of the universe there may be an equal subtraction corresponding to any addition made anywhere, so that all the positive and negative terms added up yield a resultant zero. But how is this to be practically realized as the total reduction of evil in one's own life? Hence the compelling reason, the driving power (*śakti*) appearing as evil must be sublimated and transformed.

Secondly, Jīva has to work out his salvation, not simply by negating his limitations and his evil, but by so working them up that they become his allies, his helpers, and ultimately, his liberators. This is the principle: Man must rise with the aid of that *śakti* which made him fall. Or, as *Śāktānanda-taraṅgiṇī* puts it, 'The poison which kills becomes the elixir of life when suitably treated and tested by the wise physician'.

Thirdly, his own body and mind, and his whole environment, must be appreciated as and worked up into spiritual community and ultimate identity with his own inner imperishable Self (Ātman). The body, for example, must not be looked upon as 'flesh' only and therefore essentially alien and intransigent and sinful. Look upon it as an epiphany of the divine Consort (Śiva-Śakti), Her own vehicle for manifestation whether in play or in purpose; and therefore use that vehicle for the purpose of realizing your identity with Divinity. Make it Her temple, fill every fibre of it with Her divine presence. Then what was toiling purpose in the effort will be play in divine ecstasy (*ullāsa*) in the achievement. So treat and transform all the functions, including those that are commonly looked upon as 'carnal'. There is, essentially, nothing 'carnal' in what is, in reality, the 'incarnation' of Śiva-Śakti. The same sublimating attitude and enlarging 'ratio' must work up and exalt our psychical being and our environment.

Fourthly, neither the body and the mind nor the environment can be taken at their face value and worked as they are in ordinary usage. Their latent magazine of power (*kuṇḍalinī-śakti*) must be opened up and made available. If the body and the mind and everything be Śiva-Śakti incarnate, nothing in the universe can be a mere nothing or trifle. Microcosmically, as well as macrocosmically, all must be Śiva-Śakti. Science has found the magazine in the atom of matter. But has it not so far touched only the fringe, the 'outer rings'? Material mass is energy: this is now recognized. But the real and the whole thing is not what appears as material mass, so that the energy-equivalent of material mass is only 'crustal energy' or nature's stabilizing forces which maintain material things at their present creation level. When the foundational power (Śakti) has descended to the present material level, it applies the 'brake', so to say, and the creative momentum is in part arrested; and it is the brake or arresting part of the momentum which is represented by material mass and energy. But the part arrested and 'interned' is not represented by it. That is the inside power and pattern of what we appreciate as matter. A unit of matter therefore must possess an intrinsic economy of higher and higher, deeper and deeper energy levels, till the core is reached where resides *mahāmāyā* (Śiva-Śakti) as *mahākuṇḍalinī* (the great coiled power). The hooded serpent girdling Śiva's matted locks has now been roused; but every dynamic path must essay to lead the divine flow inside Śiva's matted locks deeper and deeper to the inmost core.

Fifthly, the ascent of the seeker (*sādhaka*) must be carried up to the 'mystery bridge' (*setu*) in order that it may first be co-ordinated and then integrated with the flow of divine descent. The 'bridge' is a necessary factor in the progress: it not merely connects *this* with *that*; it converts lower-level energy into higher and consummates it.

Sixthly, the ascent must be made in the order of creative descent, but with its sign reversed. The Tantras speak of the six paths or steps (*ṣaḍadhvā*). Physically as well as metaphysically, creative descent must start from a condition of immensely 'massed' probability-wave function which we may more simply express as unbounded potency to be and to become all. It is power regarded as unbounded *plenum* and *continuum*. What physics now appreciates as space-time-continuum is a 'descended' phase or specification of the basic continuum of power which is called *nāda*. The next state must be an infinite intentness or readiness of that power to evolve and create. This is power as continuum 'condensing' itself into dynamic point or centre or nucleus. This condensation, however, is not a process in space or in time, so that the power continuum is not contracted and reduced in magnitude and dimensions and does not suffer either in sense or in tense value when it is the dynamic point. It is a primordial causal transformation not renderable in terms in which causation is apt to be expressed in our planes. Hence, paradoxically, the dynamic point is the perfect potential universe. This is *bindu*. Words in common parlance can never express the basic idea or pattern (*hṛllekhā*). An aspect of the basic pattern is sought to be expressed in Tantra by the mystic syllable or formula *hrīṁ* (*māyābīja*).

## COSMIC DESCENT

Do not physics and biology and psychology illustrate the principle of polarity (*mithuna*) in ultimate as well as derivative forms? There is no need to wonder that they do, because the whole creative process starts as and from polarity. We have just referred to Śakti as *nāda* and Śakti as *bindu*. Each is partless, aspectless, though the entire process of cosmic 'partition' and 'aspectualization' must have its possibility grounded in the one and 'worked up and out' by the other. One is the 'soil', and the other the 'seed' for all cosmic generation and fruition. One is the extensive or expansive whole of power ; the other is the intensive or concentrated whole of power.

The relation of *nāda-bindu* is, undoubtedly, one of the hardest hurdles to negotiate in the way of understanding Tāntric principles. From *bindu* descends, next in order, the polarity of *kalā* and *varṇa*. The former term, as also many others, bears an elastic and flexible meaning in the Tantras and Vedas, as terms or symbols meant primarily for practical or 'experimental' use should. We are not here dealing with a speculative philosophy set in a rigid mould of logical terms. The term *kalā,* in the last analysis, must mean that aspect of Reality (Śiva) by which it manifests as power (Śakti) for evolving universes and involving them again. It is the *prakṛti* or 'nature' of Reality so to manifest itself. Hence Śiva in Śaiva-Śākta Āgama is both transcendent (*niṣkala*) and emergent and immanent (*sakala*). It is thus clear that *kalā,* in this ultimate sense, must logically precede all 'descending movements' of Reality. But here, coming after *nāda-bindu,* it means 'partial'. That is to say, when we come to this point, the whole, the entire, veils or covers up its wholeness, as it were, and manifests as partials, as predicables. It is the starting point of differentiation. It is here that time, space, thing, attribute, etc. are differentiated from an 'alogical' integrated whole (*nāda-bindu*). *Kalā,* in the basic sense of nature-aspect, is already implicit in *nāda-bindu,* but as partial it comes after. There is no derogation from dynamic wholeness and perfectness in *nāda* or in *bindu* ; but in *kalā,* as here derived, all gradation and gradualness (all ascending and descending series in the cosmic process) have their possibility of appearance. This possibility can be viewed in two ways—as object and as index or 'sense'. An object itself and the sense (sign or index of the object)—this is how the polarity principle appears when we come to partials.

But this does not mean that we have been already landed in the 'concrete' (*sthūla*) universe of our own acceptance. That is yet a far cry. In *kalā* and *varṇa* we are still in a 'prototypal' region (*para* it may be called). *Varṇa,* here, does not yet mean 'letter' or 'colour' or even 'class', but only the 'sense' or the 'function form' (natural *spanda* we may call it) of the primordial object projected from 'perfect activity' (*bindu*). *Varṇa* would mean therefore the characteristic measure-index (number, magnitude, etc. as rendered by us) of the function form associated with the object. Lower down, this may appear as 'chromosome number', 'probability function', 'atomic number', etc. In this primordial sense, *varṇa* sets and rules the order and harmony in creation.

Then, in the subtle (*sūkṣma*) or vital plane, this polarity manifests as *tattva* and *mantra.* The primordial object with its conceptual or mathematical function form is not yet a 'picturable' thing, not yet a localizable entity that can be 'rounded up' and seized upon as this, and not that, rendering a sufficiently categorical account of itself for the purpose of definition and usage.

The concept of *kalā* and *varṇa* as logically prior to and transcending the concept of *tattva* and *mantra* is, no doubt, a particularly hard nut to crack ; but it is noteworthy that new physics too in her newest theoretical ventures has found herself confronted with an analogous conceptual impasse. She has been able to 'crack' the hard atom, but her conception of 'wave packet' electron and of the wave itself as being a wave of probability, and many a vital postulate and conclusion incidental to her present theoretical position, have certainly rendered her 'physical' entity, mathematically quite reasonable and consistent though it be, very nearly a conceptual impossibility. But does it mean that it is in reality a non-entity, not a fact in nature but a mathematical fiction? No. It means only that there is reality transcending our conceptual limits, that there are facts beyond our perceptual frontiers. As we work up from our own level to the realm of reals, we are bound to cross frontiers one after another ; and as we do so, we come across postures and measures of the real which strike us not merely as novel, but as astounding and baffling.

Shall we, then, be surprised to know that what was to our understanding only 'cosmic dust' or 'cloud' in the higher stage, 'gathers' itself into things of definite shape and function when we descend to the stage next below? *Kalā,* as we have seen, is cosmic 'partial' that has not yet parted itself from the cosmic whole, and *varṇa* 'element' or 'elemental' (*varṇa*= *mātṛkā*=matrix) of cosmic function that has not yet differentiated itself from the cosmic 'integral'. They are therefore *terms* and *conditions* in a general cosmic equation which has not yet solved itself understandably. They are there, but we cannot as yet definitely assign distinctive sets of value, that is, we do not yet know the characteristic of each, its own appropriate formula. When we do, we come to the realm of *tattva* and *mantra.* The term *tattva,* like *kalā,* is used in an elastic sense ; but here it means a 'thing-in-itself' as this or that, and possesses therefore its own distinguishing characteristic. It is the thing or event regarded as inherent principle, the radix of relations, as distinguished from reactions due to varying incidents or accidents of cosmic exchange. Associated with it is there its own appropriate function form, its own basic formula, its 'natural name' (*mantra*). Now, the general cosmic equation has displayed to us the underlying principles—the characteristics of its terms and the shapes of its conditions. We are, however, still in the realm of dynamic (*śaktirūpa*) being and becoming. The universe of appearance, the universe of our acceptance and convention, the *chāyārūpa* (as *Śrī Caṇḍī* puts it), is not yet. With the emergence of this, we have the third and last polarity—*bhuvana* and *pada. Bhuvana* is the universe as it appears to apprehending and appreciating 'centres', such as we are, and, accordingly, it greatly varies. It is governed by reactive ratio. *Pada* (*padyate anena iti*) is the actual formulation (first by mind reaction and then by speech) of that universe in accordance with the ratio that subsists relevant to a given 'centre'.

## SPIRITUAL ASCENT

At this level the cosmic descent apparently stops. And as it stops it stabilizes its incalculably great, gathered momentum. So that incalculably great power is latent, 'coiled up', in the tiniest thing of creation, not to say of the self-conscious Jīva. What was in 'That' is really in 'this' also, that is, the whole undiminished glory of cosmic life and consciousness, joy and harmony. This is what is meant by *citī* or *cit-śakti* pervading (*vyāpya*) all creation. She has 'involved' Herself in this plane of *bhuvana* and *pada.* A 'centre' living and functioning in that plane must essay to 'evolve' to perfection what has been thus involved. By completing its evolution it can work out the realization of its inherent perfectness or divinity. For this, it must be able to reverse the gear of the whole working apparatus, individual as well as environmental. In other words, ascent must be made from the reactive plane of sense experience and expression (*bhuvana* and *pada*) to the dynamic realm of inherent principles (*tattva*) and natural 'function forms' (*mantras, yantras,* and *tantras*) ; and from these to the highest level of cosmic partials and *mātṛkās* (*kalā* and *varṇa*) which together weave a grand, seamless pattern of cosmic harmony. This is the positive or upward evolving sense of the *ṣaḍadhvā* as distinguished from the negative, downward involving sense. It has been said that one who knows *ṣaḍadhvā* knows all in Tantra.

From 'partials' and *mātṛkās* one must press forward into the unspeakable mystery beyond—the mystery of *bindu* and *nāda.* Here is the wonder of the partless and measureless in the travail of giving birth to the still united 'twin'—partial and measure. It is the *setu* or link connecting supreme experience in which magnitude (*pāda*) and measure (*mātrā*) are 'absorbed', with another posture of that experience in which they 'recognize' each other, though as yet held in each other's close embrace, so to say. Tantra, Upaniṣad, in fact all types of mystic experience, thus speak in symbols and parables: there is no help. Trace the curve of any vital concept (e.g. *guru* = spiritual guide) from below upwards till the apex is reached: (1) *guru* as embodied, physically and mentally, and his prayer and worship ; (2) *guru* as *tattva* or principle, and his *bīja mantra* ; (3) *guru* as the *kalā* (aspect) of Śiva as liberator, and as Śakti operative as *varṇa* (*mātṛkā*) ; (4) *guru* as combined *nāda-bindu* ; and (5) *guru* as *nāda-bindu-kalātīta* (transcending the three), and therefore the Absolute. The *sādhaka's* own self is to be ultimately equated to That.

## SUPREME EXPERIENCE

So we have somehow a dual aspect of the supreme experience—Parama Śiva—*niṣkala* and *sakala,* as they have been called. The former is experience or consciousness beyond *nāda-bindu-kalā* (the primary *trika* or triad) and all their derivatives as shewn in the 'six steps' (*ṣaḍadhvā*). The latter is Śiva as His own divine nature (Paramā Prakṛti or Parā Śakti) to be and become all. In Śrīvidyā (the type of Tāntrika doctrine on which we are especially working here for the sake of brevity), the supreme consciousness is often called Tripurā, which term literally means what is prior to (*purā*) or beyond the three. Even the word Caṇḍikā has been taken to mean (e.g. in *Bhuvaneśvarī Saṁhitā*) the Akṣara Brahman Itself of the Upaniṣads (the Reality that never recoils or relents), the fear of whom keeps Time itself flowing for ever, the Sun and Fire, Indra, the chief of the gods, and Death going their appointed rounds, and so on. Tripurā and Caṇḍikā, in this ultimate sense, must therefore be Śiva's own divine nature (*prakṛti*) to be and become all.

Śiva associated with His own nature, which is perfect, is Godhead (Parameśvara). As such there is fivefold expression of His perfectness—absoluteness (*svatantratā*), eternality of being (*nityatā*), eternal self-satisfaction (*nitya-tṛptatā*), supreme sovereignty and omnipotence (*sarva-kartṛtā*), and omniscience (*sarvajñatā*). As and when that divine nature is *involved* in creative descent, Her own perfectness is 'veiled' or limited, and this gives rise to the five 'contracting factors' (*kañcukas*) corresponding to the five 'perfections'. They are respectively called *niyati* (determining or binding factor), *kāla* (the 'tense' factor), *rāga* (desire or appetite factor), *kalā* (power delegated and 'parcelled out', so to speak, the devolving factor), and *avidyā* (the 'ignoring' or veiling factor).

## THIRTY-SIX PRINCIPLES OF ŚAIVA ĀGAMA

Śaiva Āgama traces the devolution of the ultimate Reality (which is Śiva = Śakti = Śiva's own nature) through thirty-six forms or principles (*tattvas*) as they have been called. We have dwelt at some length on the 'six step' scheme (*ṣaḍadhvā*), but this one is more elaborate and more common. Working from down upwards we meet the familiar twenty-four *tattvas* of the Sāṁkhya, reaching the 'peak' in Prakṛti (which is the equilibrium plane of the three cosmic factors of presentation, movement, and veiling); below this plane we meet, of course, three 'stages' in which the three factors, never in dissociation though they may be, respectively prevail—*sattva, rajas,* and *tamas,* yielding the three 'inner instruments' of *buddhi* (understanding), *ahaṅkāra* (apperception or self-reference), and *manas* (apprehending and desiring). Beyond Prakṛti is Puruṣa as individual soul (Jīvātman), also sometimes called *citta,* appreciating and reacting to the 'pulsations' of Prakṛti. The individual is subject to the five 'restricting factors' we have mentioned above. He is thus *apūrṇa* (imperfect). These five factors are therefore above him. And he must work up so as to outgrow them. Next in order comes Māyā which not only 'measures out' all that is held by and within her, but is primarily responsible for the non-realization of the fact that the creation (*jagat*) is in reality Śiva-Śakti. She makes the world appear as other than Brahman. All knowledge, all perception within the net of Māyā is therefore impure (*aśuddha*), and in that sense, unreal. Above and beyond Māyā is *śuddha-vidyā* (the realm of pure knowledge and principles). In this, and at the base of this, is Īśvara, the Lord of creation, who 'appreciates' and ordains all as 'this' (*idam*). Here we reach the root of any act or process of 'objectification' and of egression. The same *īśvara-tattva* regarding all as 'I' (not to be confounded with the 'inner instrument' of *ahaṅkāra* we met before) is the root and precondition of any act or process of 'subjectification' and of ingression. As such, He is *sadāśiva-tattva.* Next comes Śakti which combines the two roots of *idam* and *aham* and contains in Herself all that may 'shoot out' and evolve. She is Śiva's own desire (*kāma*) to be and become. *Śakti-tattva* is what projects, subjectively as well as objectively, everything as *nāda, bindu,* and *kalā,* and again absorbs all into Her. Śakti as identified with Śiva is the first and final Principle. It is Parama Śiva as Absolute.

## ŚAKTI AND TĀNTRIKA REALISM

The precise nature of the identity of Śiva-Śakti has been a matter of considerable metaphysical discussion. Bhāskararāya, Rāmeśvara, Lakṣmīdhara, and other writers and commentators have stoutly defended the non-duality of Śiva and Śakti vis-a-vis the Māyāvāda position as regards Brahman and Its Māyā. Śakti is distinguishable from Śiva only in theoretical and conventional analysis, but in realization She is identical with Śiva. Hence, if Śiva is *sat* (Being in itself), Śakti is *satī* (Being in itself as power to be such); if Śiva is *cit* (pure and perfect Consciousness), Śakti is *citī* (Consciousness as power); and if Śiva is *ānanda* (perfect Bliss), Śakti is *paramānanda-sandoha-rūpā* and *paramānanda-laharī* (the very soul of *ānanda* and its 'wave' of absolute play). If Śiva is Brahman, She is Brahmamayī. Should this relation be called *advaita* (non-duality) or not? We can only repeat what the *Mahānirvāṇa Tantra* says on this: 'Some say it is *advaita,* others *dvaita*; but in reality it is *dvaitādvaita-vivarjita*—neither the one nor the other'. It is beyond the reach of measure and nothing numerical can pertain to it.

As to the 'illusoriness' of the world appearance, the position is that the question does not arise on the principles as enunciated above. Even the 'appearance' (*chāyā*) is She and none other, and it is only by a dispensable convention, a certain form of definition and notation only, that one can maintain a dialectical hiatus or opposition between the world and reality. In reality the world is Śiva-Śakti, and it is wrong to think that the one is not the other. The object of realization in Śākta Tantra is to prove that the relation is first an equation and that the equation is ultimately an identity; the proving is not by 'purging' and 'emptying' one or the other relevant term, but by a method of perfecting, and realizing one into the integrated whole of the other. *Niṣkala* or pure Consciousness is the changeless background, and the changing world is Its own show by Itself as Śakti to Itself as Śakti.

This prepares the ground for the pre-eminently practical and essentially realistic and synthetic approach of Tantra. Action, devotion, and knowledge—all these must be harnessed into the service of the supreme object the *sādhaka* has in view. And the paths must be varied suitably to varying steps and stages of competence and temperament. Not only the paths, but even to some extent the principles are varied also, but always keeping within the basic framework necessary for working out complete realization. The path, Śaiva, Śākta, Vaiṣṇava, or whatever else it be, if followed with faith and courage, devotion and vision, will itself lead the way to the clarification of the principles and their harmonic integration. It will show how the divergent paths all meet at last, how the varying principles approach and blend into a final synthesis. And the appeal of the Tantras is not for the individual only: it is an all-dimensional comprehensive appeal for all seekers' societies toiling into the higher realms of power, light, and perfection.

# 26

## THE PHILOSOPHY OF MYSTICISM

### PHILOSOPHY AS A WAY OF LIVING

PHILOSOPHY in India is not mere speculation but a way of living. Nor is philosophical speculation only a systematization of concepts and theories. Indian philosophy is also the quest both of an immediate experience of reality and of an achievement of the good and just life. Again, the good man and the good society are nourished in India not by ethical and social, but by mystical and trans-social, doctrines and ideals. Metaphysics thus becomes the law of man's social living. Humaneness, benevolence, charity, tenderness, and even love can be best fostered on the basis of the realization of the supreme worth of the fellow-man, which essentially requires for stability also the sense of worth of the universe, totality or whole transcending nature, man, and society. This mystical notion alone can effectively sustain perennial, self-transcending human love, devotion, and enthusiasm. The fellow-man is too full of defects of character, and society too full of imperfections, injustices, and cruelties, to elicit man's unbounded love and service. It is the infinitely vast universe or whole, of which all beings, nature, and society are inseparable, organic parts, that can be the ultimate source of man's love and sharing, which must in the last resort be grounded on convictions regarding the nature of self, non-self, and the universe or whole. Thus do human allegiances and enthusiasms towards fellow-individuals and society imply and involve initiation into the deeper mystery of the beyond-human and beyond-social.

Indian ethical systems are thus built on the foundation of metaphysics, and Indian doctrines and symbols all invest morality with rich, trans-human meanings. The 'scientific' interpretation of the evolutionary march of organic life and mind cannot be soul-stirring and enthralling, nor elicit enthusiastic service, as it lacks identification of the cosmic goals with human values and purposes, without which the cosmic process cannot shed its bewildering immensity, insensibility, and alienness. It is the prerogative of man to criticize, evaluate, and direct both organic and human evolution ; he imports into evolution both control and direction by his own scale of values. Now, man derives values and norms not from the world stuff nor from the cosmic process, but from within his self and its relation to other selves and to the cosmos. Thus it is metaphysical notions and values that conserve and elevate his dignity in a fathomless universe, and inspire and energize him for his tasks of control of the evolutionary forces and of intellectual and moral adventure, in spite of his natural finitude and limited span of life. Metaphysics and religion both import beyond-human meanings to the evolutionary process and encourage mankind to evaluate, order, and direct it as frequently as it suffers defeat at the hands of nature. Such meanings and values make man indeed a creator and a participator in the immortal life, and evolution in the universe no longer holds any terrors for him.

## FOUNDATIONS OF MORALITY EXAMINED

Modern humanism replaces the deity not only by nature, but also by society, and seeks to elicit man's supreme self-surrender and sacrifice, although such devotion is too often restricted to the 'cause' of the country or nation—that 'mortal god' to which he owes his livelihood, peace, and defence—in times of crisis, and to blind conformity to established laws, customs, and institutions in times of peace. In each case society, taking the place of the 'immortal God', plays havoc with man's deeper non-collectivistic feelings, consciences, and values. Similarly, a mere 'social' or 'moral' meaning attached to the brotherhood of nations or commonalty of fellow-creatures remains an illicit fancy so long as it is unleavened by a real and profound affirmation and appreciation of the infinite worth of both self and non-self, which is the introduction of metaphysics into society. The notions of the organic perfectibility of man and the brotherhood of a free and unlimited society—the goals of scientific humanism—cannot stimulate flagging human enthusiasms without these latter being oriented and channelled in an infinite, superhuman, super-social frame of reference. This may best be illustrated by a reference to the Mahāyāna Buddhist metaphysical notion of the Buddha-essence (*dharmakāya*) filling the world, immanent in all sentient creatures, and inspiring the enlightened creature (Bodhisattva) to serve all. This idea has supplied the staying power of the most ardent emotions and altruism and compassion in the world's ethical systems. Here it is recognized that mere understanding or knowledge cannot give man unbounded feelings of love, sharing, and solidarity, but that he must take recourse to spiritual contemplation (*dhyāna, samādhi*), cultivate wisdom (*prajñā*), and practise the moral precepts (*śīla*) of non-violence and compassion, among others, as formulated by Buddha. The goal of Mahāyāna perfection is expressed in the following memorable words by Āryadeva: 'Those who feel only for themselves may enter *nirvāṇa,* but the aspirant to Buddhahood who feels for the sufferings of his fellow-creatures as though they were his own, how can he bear the thought of leaving his fellow-creatures behind, while he himself is making for salvation and reposing in the calm of *nirvāṇa*? *Nirvāṇa* in truth consists in rejoicing in others' being made happy, and *saṁsāra* means not feeling happy. Whosoever feels a universal love for his fellow-creatures will rejoice in conferring bliss on them and thus attaining *nirvāṇa*'. The above is but the amplification and enrichment of the ancient Hindu metaphysical tradition as expressed in the *Īśa Upaniṣad* and the *Bhagavad-Gītā*: 'He whose self is integrated and harmonized by *yoga* sees the self abiding in all creatures and all creatures in the self; everywhere he sees the same'. On the basis of his apprehension of non-duality, he overcomes ignorance and sorrow, attains peace, and never suffers degradation. On the moral plane, man, after the realization of oneness of understanding or equality in life with all sentient creatures, experiences a profound joy and absolute compassion, from which well forth infinite sharing with and service to the world. On the other hand, he achieves the supreme detachment and freedom of the *Homo universus* (Viśvātman) from whose nature the various passions and dispositions of unrighteousness and separatism have been completely eradicated. The culmination of *yoga* in Indian thought and practice is the adoption of the rule of identity in life that leads to instinctive happiness at the happiness of others and instinctive pain at the pain of others.

## MYSTICAL APPROACH TO UNITIVE LIFE

The stages of mystical progress may be indicated on the basis of the well-known *ślokas* in the *Bhagavad-Gītā* (chapter VI) as follows: the all-pervasiveness of knowledge or of self; the sense of equality of life rooted in the pervasiveness of self-knowledge; the life of detached and passionless altruistic devotion and service to all creatures; the realization of the absolute and the transcendental Divine that is immanent in the self and in all existence, sentient and non-sentient; and, finally, the consecration of life with all its activity as service to the Divine immanent in all sentient creatures; and at the same time the identification of a life of profound silence with the non-dual, undifferentiated, unconditional, and peaceful Absolute.

From the metaphysical establishment of oneness with the whole current of life and consciousness proceeds all creative spontaneous morality. The highest adept (*yogin*) described in the *Bhagavad-Gītā* is one who, on the basis of his identity with all sentient creatures and the identity of their happiness with his happiness and of their pain with his pain, serves everybody with compassion (*anukampā*). Kierkegaard has recently given a similar interpretation of Christian love as an interest in the true or eternal welfare of all other creatures. In loving 'the man one sees', regardless of merits and demerits, we not merely fulfil the divine command which is the law of our nature truly understood: in doing so we also love God in the truest and highest sense, through a sharing of His love for man. 'From the Christian standpoint to love men is to love God, and to love God is to love men; what you do to men you do to God.'[1] Mystical contemplation, Eastern or Western, demonstrates that the highest morality is reached, not through repression and asceticism, but through the way of unitive knowledge or communion, fused with love, compassion, and sympathy that imply positive self-transcendence, power, and service. With unitive consciousness and elimination of ego-centric impulses and desires all human activity becomes moral *per se,* spontaneously conducive to the good of all, the distinction between egoism and altruism, rightness and wrongness altogether disappearing. Man becomes totally unimpeded in his impluses, thought, and behaviour; he is beyond moral and social imperatives. Yet he can do no wrong, as all the while he is merged in the unitive consciousness, and, when engaged in action, is really inactive or has no separate action of his own. Such is the Indian conception of the liberated man of wisdom (*jīvanmukta*). Similarly, in the Mahāyāna Buddhist conception the Bodhisattva is the great Healer, who loves and serves for the sake of love and service on the basis of profound detachment and understanding that in *bodhi* nothing dual exists nor is any thought of self present. *Nirvāṇa* (enlightenment) and *saṁsāra* (the world of births and deaths) are in essence one (*yaḥ saṁsāras tat nirvāṇam*). It is contrary to reason to imagine that the one lies outside the pale of the other and therefore that we can attain enlightenment after we have annihilated or escaped the world of births and deaths. 'If we are not hampered by our confused subjectivity, this our worldly life is an activity of *nirvāṇa* itself.' 'All sins transformed into the constituents of enlightenment! The vicissitudes of *saṁsāra* transformed into the beatitude of *nirvāṇa*!'[2]

## MYSTICISM TRANSCENDS MORALITY

In *The Perennial Philosophy* Aldous Huxley speaks of three forms of modern higher idolatry as corrosive of human culture and progress, viz. technological idolatry, the most ingenious and primitive of the three, that attributes human redemption and liberation to material goods; political idolatry that substitutes the worship of redemptive social and economic organizations for that of gadgets as abolishing all human unhappiness and evils; and finally, moral idolatry that is the worship not of God but of human ethical ideals in which the acquisition of virtue is treated as an

[1] Kierkegaard, *Works of Love,* p. 309.
[2] The quotation is from Vasubandhu. See Y. Sogen, *Systems of Buddhist Thought,* p. 280.

end in itself and not as a means—the necessary and indispensable condition of the unitive knowledge of God. Aldous Huxley thus comments on the last form of idolatry: 'The idolatrous worship of ethical values in and for themselves defeats its own object—and defeats it not only because there is a lack of all-round development, but also and above all because even the highest forms of moral idolatry are God-eclipsing and therefore guarantee the idolater against the enlightening and liberating knowledge of Reality'.

His distinguished brother, Julian Huxley, while regarding technical and political idolatries as disastrous modern errors, considers, however, that communion with the Divine, which moral idolatry obscures owing to man's narrowness and projection of his limited joys and sorrows, frustrations and fulfilments upon the infinite universe, is scientifically 'unproven' and thus, presumably, cannot provide the basis of any scientific ethics.

Not only the mystical, but also the traditional ethical view in India on this point, is in agreement, however, with Aldous Huxley's position. Śaṅkara in his *Viveka-cūḍāmaṇi* (11) clearly states, 'Action is for the mind's purification, not for the understanding of Reality. The realization of truth is brought about by discrimination, and not in the least by ten millions of actions'. In the same key, the great Chinese teacher of the Chan school of Buddhism observes, 'Knowledge—this one word—is the fountain-head of all mysteries'.[3] The highest state of human consciousness, in which the self is completely absorbed in the vast numinous mystery of the non-self, maintains an ethical neutrality; for ethics belongs to the lesser reality of the human whole. It must be pointed out that the emphasis on moral obligations is absent from most ancient codes of morality, and has become prevalent in Europe only since the nineteenth century, the age of reason and ethics, which has also witnessed the lapse of the religious attitude. Kant has been the leading force in the establishment of the supremacy of the moral view-point dissociated from religious conceptions. Both metaphysics and religion, particularly in India and China, eschew all traces of sentimentality and the attachment of the code of morality to doctrinal principles. In post-Kantian thought in the West, the Hegelian, Marxian, and totalitarian ethics ultimately eclipsed the freedom and self-realization of the Kantian ethical individual and tended to subordinate spiritual values to a rigid moral, cultural, and economic determinism. Yet the Kantian delimitation of the autonomous spheres of religion and ethics still holds good in contemporary Western thought. Recently, however, Western ethicists have turned to the philosophy of intuition of Bergson and Croce and to the existence theory

[3] See Fung Yu-lan, *The Spirit of Chinese Philosophy,* XIII and XIV.

of Kierkegaard and Heideggar ; but, as Northorp shows, 'what they actually provide is neither a genuine religion of intuition of the Oriental type nor a genuine religion of doctrine of the theistic Western type but a muddled confusion of both'.[4] In Oriental religion *turīya,* Brahman, *nirvāṇa,* Tao, and Zen, which are all kindred conceptions, denote a phase of consciousness which rises above every sort of flux or motion, and which is characterized by a complete cessation of sensations, ideas, and concepts and the absence of the subject-object relation. The classical description of the 'transcendental' intuition (*turīya*) is given in the *Māṇḍūkya Upaniṣad*: 'The wise think that *turīya* is neither that which is conscious of the internal (subjective) world, nor that which is conscious of the external (objective) world ; neither that which is conscious of both, nor that which is a mass of all sentiency ; neither that which is simple consciousness, nor that which is insentient. It is unseen, unrelated, incomprehensible to the mind, uninferable, unthinkable, indescribable, essentially of the nature of consciousness constituting the Self alone with no trace of the conditioned world, the peaceful, all bliss, and the non-dual. This is the Self, which is to be realized (through meditation)'. With such realization, the sage not merely attains complete wisdom, freedom, and detachment, but also a profound identity of self with all creatures of the world. He practises non-violence to all creatures and becomes quiet, devoid of conflict between right and wrong, of ignorance and sorrow, and of discrimination between himself and the creatures of the universe.[5] Such is the silence of the universal man in mind, word, and deed.

## THEISTIC AND NON-THEISTIC SCHOOLS OF MYSTICISM

Indian schools of philosophy and mystical contemplation that stress the unitive consciousness are both theistic and non-theistic. But this makes no difference to ethics as long as their outlook is enlarged by communion with the vast and incomprehensible great Whole that is immensely larger and profounder than society and morality. The great Whole, the mystic's macrocosm, combines science and speculation, knowledge and apprehension, fact and ideal, physical happening and spiritual purpose. It not only safeguards him against all possible fears, anxieties, and darkness of the mind, giving him the most complete security of childhood experience, which Freud regards as the primary psycho-biological function of religion, but also unfolds the mind's limitless possibilities in relation to fellow-men. Out of both theistic and non-theistic unitive understanding emerges a human love and compassion of such numinous and mysterious strength and sweep as

[4] Northorp, *Logic of the Sciences and Humanities,* pp. 379-385.

[5] *Jīvanmukta-Gītā,* 2, 6, 8, 20.

embraces all sentient creatures in the vast universe and harnesses most effectively the human will and capacity for individual fulfilment and moral perfection and the achievement of human solidarity.

## MEANS TO MYSTIC CONSCIOUSNESS

The means to maintain unitive consciousness in life and action are fourfold: (1) the way of action with non-attachment grounded on the realization of the presence of the universal Self or God in every sentient creature (Karma-yoga); (2) the way of metaphysical knowledge or understanding of this unity (Jñāna-yoga); (3) the way of elevated contemplation for direct and intuitive apprehension of this unity (Rāja-yoga); and (4) the way of devotion to and feeling of the immanence of the universal Self or God through prayer and worship (Bhakti-yoga). Sometimes the above means are regarded as following one another in succession in spiritual progress and perfection; but at the same time, since man cannot always continue in the same state of consciousness, he takes to mystical contemplation, worship, metaphysical discrimination, or social action as he chooses according to his temperamental make-up or circumstances in life. Thus he becomes the perennial *yogin*—'like a lamp in a windless place that does not flicker' or 'that shines inwardly as when placed inside a jar'—whether he is in meditation or in action. 'Action is true worship when it serves the creatures of the world in whom the Divine is immanent; inaction is true worship when it is the profound silence or unitive contemplation', says Śaṅkara.[6] Similarly, in Mahāyāna thought the Bodhisattva, in spite of his unceasing activities of beneficence, succour, and relief of the sorrows of mankind, is completely detached and passionless. Asaṅga in his famous hymn to the Bodhisattva sings, 'Thou art free from every obstacle, thou hast mastery over the whole world, O *muni* (sage), thou occupiest all the knowable with thy knowledge. Thy thought is liberated. Thou hast impassivity, thou hast no attachments, thou art in mystical communion (*samādhi*). Night and day thou watchest over the world. Thou art given over to the great Compassion. Thou seekest only salvation'.

Since the publication of the well-known works of William James and Leuba, Western scholars have been apt to view man's intuitive transcendental experiences as somewhat abnormal and single-tracked. This view is due, to a great extent, to the exclusive attention paid in the West to the systems of discipline, control, and 'repression' (*nirodha*) of the impulses and desires as described in the Yoga system of Patañjali, to the neglect of the 'spiritual practices' in respect of the training and expansion of altruistic

[6] See the writer's *Theory and Art of Mysticism*.

emotions that are also largely practised in the Orient. In Buddhaghoṣa's *Visuddhi-magga* there is a detailed description of Buddhist methods of contemplation (*jñāna* and *yoga*) by which man, calming the passions and transmuting the false mind of life and death into the clear intuitive mind, makes this the starting point for its concentration upon, and inundation of, the universe with benevolence, compassion, sympathy, and happiness. His constant prayer is that all creatures of the world may be friendly, healthy, and unharmed, and may live in bliss and become free. We read in the *Metta-Sutta,* 'As a mother, even at the risk of her own life, protects her son, her only son, so let there be goodwill without measure between all beings. Let goodwill without measure prevail in the whole world, above, below, around, unstinted with any feeling of differing or opposing interests'. If a man remains steadfastly in this state of mind all the time he is awake, then is come to pass the saying, 'Even in this world holiness has been found'.

Thus the mind reaches successively the pure consciousness of infinite space (sky), of joy, and of void. Each successive level or sphere of cosmic consciousness, 'formless' and 'supra-mundane', brings to the adept its own depth, subtlety, and mystery of infinitude, 'just as cotton and silk textures vary in fineness and softness of wear although the size of the woman's cloth remains the same'. The metaphysical concept of beauty, infinite space, joy, and void seem to be correlates of the unbounded feelings of benevolence, compassion, sympathy, and serenity respectively.[7] Remaining constantly and steadfastly in an attitude in which he fills the world with benevolence, compassion, and sympathy that transcend the boundaries of space and time, the adept acquires a new sense of the worth of sentiency. Perfecting himself in the 'divine' emotional ecstasies (*Brahmavihāra*) or 'infinite' sentiments (*appamanna*) of benevolence, compassion, and sympathy, he prepares himself for the practice of serenity or equal-mindedness that is the threshold of *nirvāṇa.*[8] The Bodhisattva's life is humane and compassionate, but his mind is serene through his profound ecstasy and experience of the unreality of the phenomenal world and of the essence of the Buddha nature immanent in it. Such serenity (*upekṣā*) is also what is regarded as the final spiritual experience—even-mindedness (*samatā*), joy, and establishment in truth in the Upaniṣads and the *Bhagavad-Gītā*. The *Laṅkāvatāra-Sūtra* warns:

> Abide not with dualism,
> Carefully avoid pursuing it,
> As soon as you have right and wrong
> Confusion ensues and mind is lost.

[7] The English equivalents are the outcome of a discussion the writer had with a Buddhist monk from Ceylon. This interpretation is closest to the original, in his view.

[8] See *The Path of Purity* (*Visuddhi-magga*) translated by Maung Tin, and *Manual of a Mystic* by Woodward.

One in all
All in One
If only this is realized,
No more worry about your not being perfect.

In the *Aṅguttara-nikāya,* the disciple asks, 'We carry on life with different attitudes. Which mode of life is the best?' The teacher replies, 'Reverence is eternally dynamic. One who lives a life of constant activity acquires the supreme knowledge of Reality'.

### MYSTICISM AS A FORCE IN HUMAN PROGRESS

Man reaches his highest moral stature when his identity-feeling, joy, and reverence reflect themselves in his relations to the external world through a more sensitive, universalized conscience in terms of complete acceptance, peace, and transcending compassion or love. Such is the indispensable contribution of the mystical consciousness to the elevation of moral standards and the peace of the universe through the discipline and direction of human nature for human progress. The destiny of man, the microcosm, is linked, no doubt, with the law of the inter-stellar spaces and immensities of the macrocosm. But man must accept and appreciate it within the circumscribed fold of duties and obligations of his lesser, social macrocosm. His enlarged knowledge and intensified love lead to expanded sharing and service, strengthen his fight against misfortune, disease, ignorance, and poverty—both the handicaps of nature and the defects of his social organization—and, indeed, invest ethics with an indescribable purity and mystery, an overwhelming numinous significance. Widely practised, mysticism is the impulsion of any future evolutionary advance of man.

# 27

## PHILOSOPHY IN POPULAR LITERATURE

THERE is an idea in vogue that philosophy is the exclusive business of a learned few and that the common man has no access to it. Ouspensky was not unjustified in his fling that it is nothing but 'self-satisfied dialectic, surrounding itself with an impenetrable barrier of terminology unintelligible to the uninitiated'. The hyper-critical literature which goes under the name of philosophy sharpens reason and intellect like a razor blade that they may cut through all propositions. But it does not solve life's problems or give peace. On the soil of India, side by side with the feats of logic and the incisive polemics of learned controversialists, there is a stream of thought developed by and preached among the masses—thought which looks at the problems of life from a higher altitude than pure reason. There is a mystical popular philosophy side by side with the critical scholastic philosophy.

### FOLK MYSTICISM AND FOLK POESY

If philosophy is to solve the problems of life, it must occupy the life of the people ; and its elements must be drawn from all that is vigorous and creative in man. His emotion and will are faculties no less powerful than reason ; and all these must blend together if philosophy is to fulfil its mission.

Hence a people's philosophy does not express itself in dry prose, but seeks the medium of colourful poetry which is the natural and earliest vehicle of human expression. The utterances which rise from the heart must correspond with the rhythms of the heart. From the nursery the child is delighted in rhymes ; and in later life songs give vent to the deepest emotions. Since reason is only a tool to enunciate and explain the truth that flashes directly before a glowing imagination, it is in verse that fundamental experiences are proclaimed. This intuitive revelation of truth is known as mysticism ; and its instruments being feeling and emotion, it is aptly recorded in poetry. The philosophy of the Indian people is embedded in their folk poesy and folk mysticism which can be traced almost to the beginning of their civilization. These mystical lyrics are heard even today on the lips of masons beating the roof of a house, ploughmen following their furrows, carters driving along the highroad, or boatmen plying along the rivers. They have a philosophical strain spontaneously poured forth, remarkably uniform in ideas and woven into a complete and consistent texture in which all the parts are pervaded with the pattern of the whole.

### REALIZATION AND UNDERSTANDING

Popular philosophy starts with the assumption that truth which is beauty and joy is a thing for realization, not for understanding. Reality is never revealed to reason. It is revealed only when the subject achieves complete identity with the object; and this identity is achieved only by means of emotions that are elemental in man. Hence love succeeds where intellect fails. As the Sufi saint-poet would put it: it is not *aql* (intellect) but *ashq* (love) that shows the true *tariqā* (path) for identity. Or, as the Sahajiyā lyricist would say, it is the path of nature, the Sahaja way, lighted by simple emotions of the heart. This road is not for high-browed scholasticism or dialectical acumen which rests satisfied with the jugglery of words. As Kabīr, the great plebeian philosopher of the middle ages, sang:

> Reading and reading they have become stone,
> Writing and writing they are now bricks,
> Their heart has no place for a drop of love.

A half-literate peasant would babble out the truth while learned savants gloat over their dialectic. The language of the commoner is like 'a flowing stream'; the language of the savant is a 'stagnant well'. Like life-giving water, spiritual illumination 'never rests high, it goes down'.

There is a story that a Bāul, a plain unvarnished naturalist, was once given a scholastic exposition of some texts of the Vaiṣṇava philosophy. As the interpreter finished his discourse the listener blurted out:

> Alas, a jeweller has come into the flower garden!
> He appraises the lotus by rubbing it on his touchstone.

Truth, like a flower, is to be enjoyed with emotional insight, it cannot be appraised by logic.

### PRAGMATIC APPROACH

The philosophical songs of the people, e.g. the verses of the Sufis, of the mediaeval saints, and of the Sahajiyās are all marked by a naive spiritual fervour and by a frank admission of the pragmatic needs of life, and not by any abstract metaphysical speculation. There is a clear affirmation that truth is not outside life. The popular philosophers cut the chains of introspective analysis and soar high on the wings of lyrical ecstasy like birds whistling their notes in the wide expanse of the horizon.

On this philosophy the people were deeply fed and nurtured. It is not confined to a few chosen saints rising and preaching now and then, nor to some sects bound by rituals or theology. It is spread over the entire society of the villages ; the *yātrā* or rural opera, the *kavi* or the minstrelsy, the nursery rhymes, the festive chorus, all bear the same touch. Poets, not introduced to letters, appear in plenty, and compose and sing themes of spiritual love of abiding interest. They have no pretensions to any standard education or to any literary technique. Yet their songs penetrate into the soul and lift it above the inertia of daily routine.

### FROM BUDDHA TO THE SUFIS

The popular philosophy of India began from the time of Buddha whose gospel gave a new status to the commoner. The songs of the Pali canon are as rich in their emotional appeal as in their dialectical content. They are nearer to the feelings of the people than their Brāhmaṇical predecessors. Buddha preached the doctrine of salvation through love which lies in the hearts of all men, i.e. through nature's own way:

> As mother saves her only son with her own life,
> So among all beings grow your limitless love.
> Through space far-flung be your amity—
> High above, down below, all around—without rest or spite,
> Standing, walking, sitting, lying, till you are asleep
> To rest firm in amity ; this is *Brahmavihāra* (roaming in Infinity).
>
> —*Suttanipāta,* I. 8. 7.

The popular saints of the Jains, of the Bhāgavatas, and of the Śaivas carried this tradition forward. They decried all differences of caste, vocation, and race, and exhorted their followers not to imprison their religious life within the temple but to carry it into their lives. Then Islam knocked at the western gates of India ; and the Sufis, inspired by the Islamic idea of equality, came as the torch-bearers of a liberal folk philosophy. The faquir and the dervish emerged from the lowest orders of society ; and they spoke in a style understood by the masses. Their approach to the problems of life was similar to that of the Sahaja *sant* or the *sādhu*. Their spirit was free from those superstitions and rigidities which caused stagnation among the classical Indian and Islamic schools. Against the sterility of the orthodox systems, the new popular appeals awakened a fresh spiritual fervour and let loose great creative power which so long lay dormant. A new philosophy grew up based on the material of human values. It trusted in the latent divinity of the human soul, in the universality of love, and in the dynamic power of emotion. It released powerful spiritual energy hitherto pent up by social barriers among the dumb millions of the soil.

MEDIAEVAL SAINTS: A MASS REVOLUTION

Naturally, the call and the response came from the poor, illiterate commoners. The new masters, in spite of their humble birth or station, rose to the height of social esteem and popularity. The earliest examples were Nāmadeva, a tailor, and Sadnā, a butcher. Kabīr, who became the central figure of the spiritual revolution, belonged to a despised weaver family. Ravidās, who was a cobbler, claimed among his disciples, Jhālī, the queen of Chitore, and Mīrābāi, the famous princess-devotee. Senā, a barber, became the spiritual guide of the Rājā of Bandhogarh. Dhannā, a Jāt, and Pīpā, a Rājput, were among the principal disciples of Rāmānanda. Nābhā, the author of *Bhaktamāla,* was a pariah. Dādū and Rajjab came from cotton-ginning Muslim families. Many of them continued their low vocations side by side with their holy mission. They believed in the honest, useful, and devout life of a householder.

Kabīr and Dādū have several pungent thrusts against 'untouchability' and sectarianism. See how Kabīr, a weaver, strikes caustically at the touch-me-not attitude of the Brāhmaṇa:

> Oh Pāṇḍe! Why are you so sensitive to touch?
> Of touch the whole world is born.
> Is there blood in me and milk in you?
> How are you a Brāhmaṇa and I a Śūdra?
> So scrupulous about touch from birth,
> Why came you through the unclean womb?
> There is impurity at birth and impurity at death.
> Says Kabīr, only God's glory shines pure.

Dādū attacks the sectarians with biting sarcasm:

> You plead for the sects? The earth and sky,
> Water and air, day and night, moon and sun,
> Attend Him best. Of what sect are they?—
> Of none but the unseen and truthful, the Great Lord.

The Lord who dwells in all men has given them the stamp of equality with similar life and similar body, organs, and sensations, and has endowed them with the same hunger, the same thirst, the same pain and pleasure. The essence of the Lord is love. So, the widest extended love, love all-embracing and non-discriminating, is the foundation of all spirituality. The exercise of love requires no scriptures or rituals, no mosques or temples, no allurements of heaven or threats of hell, no rigorous austerities or self-persecution. The great quest is a quest of joy, not of sorrow. But neither is it a soft, easy journey. Love divine is of sterner stuff than tears and sobs. 'The path of love is hard and distant', says Kabīr. 'If you can cut and rest your head at His feet, you know the taste.' 'It is a perennial fight fought without sword.' 'The earth and the sky tremble, rumbling in the hollows above.' 'It is the path of heroes, not of cowards', says Dadū, 'the hero goes to war ; he knows no retreat.' The life of the seeker is a ceaseless war against the calls of family and secular life, against the obstacles put by his own individuality, against the opposition of orthodox sects, faith, and learning, against the hostility of vested interests, and sometimes against the persecution of ruling powers. It is because of this inherent militancy of the new movement, that Sikhism, founded as a religious fraternity by Nāṇak and nurtured in plebeian doctrines, grew into a fighting community under the hostile pressure of the times.

Sind and Bengal were the last nurseries of this syncretizing popular philosophy. In Sind, the gateway which introduced Islam and Sufism into India, a Hindu *murshed* or a Muslim *guru* was not at all extraordinary. The songs of the Sufi mystics—Bedil and Bekaś, Rohal and Qutb, and Śāh Abdul Latīf—were till lately sung by Sindhis of all communities. Till lately, before religious fanaticism worked its havoc upon India, Hindus and Muslims used to congregate at the tombs of these popular saints and sing in chorus, keeping all-night vigils. The practice of Sahaja had its last foothold in Bengal, thanks to numerous minstrel schools like Āul, Bāul, Dervish, Sāiñ, Kartābhajā, etc., who differed from one another in their forms of expression and religious exercises but not in their philosophical outlook. Sahaja is not a cult or creed. It is a path or *panth* which needs no formal conversion in faith. Literally, it is a return to what one is born with, i.e. to the divine in man. Love is the central theme of the Sahaja way. 'Man is above everything, none is higher' (Caṇḍīdāsa). 'God is never equal to living beings' (Kṛṣṇadāsa). Every act must be weighed in the scale of human values. The highest of all values is love ; and its fountain is in our body.

### THE BODY CULT

So, the Sahajiyā springs upon the learner the startling interdict, 'The worship must start with the body of man' (Mukundadāsa). In this mortal frame resides the immortal. The songsters assign a place within the body to all the gods of the diverse sects. The Lord Aesthete calls upon his devotee:

> Worship me with your own body.
> I am love in the shape of desire,
> I am the formless in forms.
>
> —*Ratnasāra*

Physical love is an instrument of training for promotion into higher spiritual love (*śuddhā parakiyā*). When that stage is reached all differences disappear. The seeker finds the state of beatitude and dissolves into an endless sea of beauty, joy, and love:

Once the puzzle of mind is broken
Contemplation of beauty turns it into molten gold,
Beauty flows like the singing wanderer
Blinding the earth.

—Akiñcanadāsa

The body pines for love. It is carnal passion, sensuous desire which seeks appeasement in the coils of flesh. This is nothing to be ashamed of. This is a manifestation on the plane of life of the cosmic attraction which gives mobility to all non-living phenomena from the electrons to the galaxies. The cosmic attraction emerges in animate flesh as desire for physical unity. Nature is beaming with love, so is man. Our sophisticated and repressive culture has sought to stifle this dynamic vital surge. Hence the Sahajiyā calls us back to nature, to the physical body, to the latent divinity in it. He recasts the amours of Rādhā-Kṛṣṇa with a frank and straightforward erotic appeal. The culture of erotics or physical love under right direction raises it to a higher plane, where the subject finds complete identity with the object, where beauty, joy, and love surpass all empirical limits, where evil, pain, and death lose their atrophic stings:

That love sports eternally in cosmos,
That love distracts primal nature,
Mad with love whirl the stars and planets,
Love in streams rolls into the sea,
Love within, love without, love in every home,
In riches, in abandon, in sickness showers love.

—Narottama

## MODERN FOLK PHILOSOPHY

Bengal still abounds with homeless wanderers without caste and creed who preach and live this philosophy of love. Their lays are wafted in melodious vibrations from mouth to mouth while the poets themselves sink into oblivion. They have no pretensions to literary excellence. The compositions well up spontaneously from the heart, full of passion and human appeal. A month's sojourn in a number of Bengal villages will give any casual observer a cross-section of this philosophy:

Virgin lay the field of man,
I made the furrows; but a thunder-storm burst,
And all was flooded by a sweeping tide.

Methinks the whole day's labour is lost.
I drove and drove the plough
Till the end of day,
Only the mark lies deep on my shoulder.

But the cry does not stop. It reverberates and is lost in the wilderness. Against soul-killing rancours, the voice of peace and love, stifled and smothered, rises up again and again. The torch must be kept alight and the call to return to the elemental goodness in man should never cease:

Primal man is an *ālef*[1] creeper,
Full of blooming flowers.
Their fragrance maddens the earth.
Alas! man is sealed within the chamber.
How can you find him outside?

Man flits about frantically after worldly pursuits in a blinding blaze of desires. He does not discover the true self within which alone gives satisfaction:

Oh mad mind! open your secret chamber,
See the lost wealth, if you have an artist's eye.
Your true self lies asleep there,
He will wake at your call,
The chamber will flash its beauty.

The process of discovery is given in the *yoga*. The lake of love is below the waist. There lies dormant the seed of spiritual growth. The creeper must be nursed and grown by concentration of will till the flower blooms at the chest. The body will be kept in a straight sitting posture, legs crossed, eyes fixed at nose tip, and breathing strictly regulated according to directions. This is the physical part of the exercise designed to make the body fit to receive and culture the tremendous onrush of spiritual awakening:

A flower has blossomed on the lake
—Allah, the Lord, knows its worth—
On the lake of the heart, from whence flows the river of breath,
The lotus has opened its beauteous hundred petals.
The flower shines with the lustre of lightning,
Do you know its name? It is Rasul (the Messiah).

Thus, quite unobtrusively the Sahajiyā absorbed the Islamic and

[1] *Ālef*—the first Urdu letter; in this case it means 'as simple and straight as the letter *ālef*'.

Tāntric cults in his practices. The corner-stone of all these systems is the *guru* or *murshed.* Spiritual practices require expert training by the guide. He knows the art of forging divine gold out of human clay:

> His training school is in the sky, which nobody knows.
> Strange workshop indeed is the master's.
> There was iron underground,
> The master traced and got it,
> Mixed a little alloy
> And transmuted it into gold.

### NIRVĀṆA AND MUKTI

The destination of the pilgrim is Rūpanagara, 'the city of beauty', where the journey ends. It is not a physical locality. It is the state of perfect beatitude when the mind has reached the highest aesthetic level and sees the world as a vast ocean of love. The Buddhists call this *nirvāṇa* and the Sufis call it *fanā.* The Sahajiyās of Buddhist inspiration have understood *nirvāṇa* not as a state of negation but as a state of bliss ; it is acquired not with reason but with the heart. *Nirvāṇa* is also the formless state which is reached through the appreciation of innumerable forms. When changing physical forms transcend their limits of materiality, the formless void (*nirañjana,* the stainless) is reached. The Sahajiyās of Vaiṣṇava inspiration do not differ substantially from this. Only they lay more emphasis on the forms and feelings which take the seeker towards illumination. The state of beatitude is not a formless void. It is a state of fullness rich in all forms.

The Jaina saint Rāmasiṁha of Gujarat, the author of *Pāhud Dohā* (A.D. 1000), writes about this equanimous state, 'To feel oneself spread in the All-pervading like salt in water is to be *samarasa* . . . . To find one's true self in one's self is *nirvāṇa*'. *Samarasa* is socializing of emotions. It aims at the voided mind, boundless as the sky (*khasama*). Thus the popular Sahajiyā philosophy resolves all differences, ritualistic and doctrinal, among the Buddhist, Jain, Vaiṣṇava, Sufi, and Tāntric, and gathers them all on a common ground—all, because its appeal is to the natural, to the simple urges of man for freedom from bondage.

Here, in the conception of *mukti,* is the starting point of all Indian philosophies. Philosophy begins with struggle against bondage. The sage of the *Ṛg-Veda* cried out, 'Oh Indra, pierce this darkness, fill our eyes with light, and free us from the bondage that ties us down' (X.73.11). The earliest sages sought release from the limitations of flesh—from hunger, pain, disease, senility, and death. They faced the challenge of death with *Brahmavidyā,* the mystic lore which converts mortality from a negation into a renewal. As philosophy descended down to the people, the flesh was no longer a brute to be tamed and death no longer an enemy to be conquered. The real slave-master is the ego that binds down the soul and converts the earth, essentially a paradise, into a prison-house. Under its spell man endlessly pursues the mirage of appearances, his thirst never appeased, his craze for material gains ever growing and encircling him like the coils of a spiral.

Thus multiply the fetters of life, and the soul yearns all the more passionately for liberation. The soul craves for identity with the Truth that is the unity underlying the phenomenal variety. *Mukti* is freedom from the isolation of self, from the urge of possession and grabbing, from the barriers of individuality that separate man from the reality of existence. This freedom is attained not by snapping the bonds here and there, not by discarding possessions, but by a positive realization of the truth that is unity and pure joy.

## EVIL AND PAIN

Then, why are there evils, why is there pain? Are they parts of truth? They are. It is because our intellect picks up single actions from the total truth that they appear evil or ugly. Truth, cut up into segments, is untruth. When man pulls down the walls of individuality and merges his activities in the universal flux, actions lose their moral colouring, and all distinctions between evil and good fade away. It is the same with the problem of pain. One who flows with the universal current has no grief or sorrow over passing events. Grief and sorrow are relative to our physical states. Children feel pain over trifles, which elders ignore. Elders forget pain after they have passed through it. And when the canvas of life is viewed as a whole, these pains appear as parts of joy. 'Our sweetest songs are those that tell of saddest thoughts.' Joy is not in pleasure, but in the discovery of life. This is why art is joy. Art (*rasa*) reveals the real, a fine blending of pleasure and pain which we enjoy. We feel the spirit of freedom in art because it gives a glimpse of reality. We enjoy a piece of art because in it we see truth where good and evil, happiness and grief, are in their proper place and setting.

And where is love without pain, love that is the source of the deepest delight? Pain takes us into the depths of feeling and stimulates the urge to seek the truth, bringing us nearer to our object. The pain that comes from the beloved is the sweetest of tastes. The Sufi martyr was not pained at the sword of Aurangzeb that was descending upon his head—'So this is the form thou hast taken now to meet me, my Beloved!'

If the goal is joy, and if suffering draws us nearer to the goal, then surely suffering is an inalienable part of joy. The picture which shows the dark background of the sky pierced with a bright flash of lightning blends the two into a finished piece of art. Evil and pain are like parts of a composite picture. They cannot be discarded; they can be overcome in our march towards a fuller realization.

### RENUNCIATION VS. ASSIMILATION

Hence the struggle for liberation is a slow course. Liberation is not attained by an outright rejection of possessions, by avoidance of pain or evil, by a hasty race along the path of renunciation. Bondage is self-created, not imposed from outside. Liberation is an inward process—a slow process at that—to be 'spread in the All-pervading like salt in water'. It cannot be hustled through by an external act. As Madan, the unknown village songster, would warn:

Oh cruel over-zealous, would you scorch the mind-bud with fire?
Can you make it blossom and spread perfume without patience?
Look at my master.
He takes ages to make a bud blossom without hustle or haste.
Your greed is great, so you rely on force.
Where is the remedy?
Prithee, hurt not the mind of the master.
One lost in the simple current can hear the voice,
Oh over-zealous!

When the secrets of matter were not understood, when knowledge of the sciences was poor, the material world seemed alien to man, and the philosopher was apt to seek relief in a flight of escape. It is now discovered that there is a harmony in the material order of the world with which our reasoning is in close accord. There is a profound chord of unity between us and nature. Once this unity is realized, man is free from the fetters that matter seemingly imposes on him. He is free to master it and transcend its limits. The function of life itself is to supersede matter. It first came into being by bursting the bonds of matter and of mechanical laws. A life mechanical and material is a life in bondage. Such a life heaps up wealth, but loses the soul. It sinks down into the inertia of matter, lost to the creativity that is life's function. In his creative activities man not only supersedes matter, he imbues his surroundings with his own life and love. Man's creative acts are those that liberate him from isolation; his struggle for freedom is the struggle to improve social relationships, to restore the disturbed harmony of the diverse forces and factors in society.

## THE FINITE IN TUNE WITH THE INFINITE

The harmony among the finites is a step to the infinite. The finites and the infinite are eternally linked together. The philosophy of life is that the reconciliation of apparent contradictions paves the way to the Absolute. Reconciliation is the art of living or *yoga*. *Yoga* is the synthesis of the finites with the infinite, of *avidyā* with *vidyā*. The *yogin* who has mastered this philosophy does not reject materiality. Like Wordsworth's skylark he soars 'true to the kindred points of heaven and home'. As Dādū said, 'When all the strings of the lyre are played on, the melody is entrancing. So when all the powers, faculties, and ideas of man are cultivated in the same degree, in tune with the wisdom of all cults, all ages, all climes, then does it become true *yoga*, the *Brahmayoga*. Such is the power of true striving that all deficiences are made complete, the bitter becomes sweet, the broken becomes whole. Such is the resulting wisdom that the very bonds become the means of freedom, the fettered are liberated, the enemy turns into a friend'.

Into this philosophy the people of India are initiated through their mystic folk poesy. It teaches that they are not mere automata of production under the wheels of mechanical laws. They are not slaves to the absorbing demands of material greed. They are creative beings, their souls pining to be liberated from the chains of the ego, to attain the freedom and joy of truth. The faculties for this attainment are inherent in man, in his emotional nature, which awaits to be exercised. Love leads man from the bondage of the finite ego to the infinity of existence. But the finites, the world of names and forms, survive after the realization. Only they acquire a new and sweeter meaning, for the two are inseparable:

> My heart-lotus is blossoming for ages,
> It is charged with sweet honey.
> Thou enamoured bee would not leave it ;
> So thou and I, both tied down, have no release.

This is the eternal sport or *līlā* between the finite and the infinite. The art of living is to taste the joy of this association. Life is not an evil to be escaped. It is to be discovered and enjoyed in its infinity, i.e. in its largest relations and identities.

PART IV

# THE PROBLEMS OF PHILOSOPHY

## 28

# RELIGION OF THE NYĀYA AND VAIŚEṢIKA

IN dealing with the 'religion' of a particular system, we have to consider it (1) in its theoretical aspect, i.e. its conception of God, and (2) in its practical aspect, i.e. its conception of the rules of life and conduct.

### NYĀYA CONCEPTION OF GOD

The world has the atoms for its constituent or material cause; its efficient cause is God, as influenced by men's acts. God is the Ātman endowed with two sets of qualities, negative and positive; the negative set consisting of the absence of demerit, wrong knowledge, and negligence, and the positive set consisting of the presence of merit, knowledge, and intuitiveness. He is also endowed with the eightfold *siddhi* (power), *aṇiman* and the rest. His merit follows the bent of His volition; He controls the residuum of the merit and demerit subsisting in each individual Jīvātman, as also the earth and other material substances. He is omnipotent in regard to His creation, not, however, failing to be influenced by the results of acts done in their past lives by the beings He creates. He has no ends of His own to serve by what He does. He continues to act for the sake of His own creatures, just as the father acts for the benefit of his children. From the scriptures we learn that God is the 'seer, cognizer, and omniscient'. He is discernible by the presence of *buddhi* and other such indicatives of the Ātman, and is beyond the reach of ordinary perception, inference, and words. If God were regarded as creating things irrespective of the acts done in the past by His creatures, then He would be open to the charge of being cruel and arbitrary, unjust and merciless. On the other hand, if His creation is influenced by the past record of His creatures, however 'merciless' He might be, He would be absolutely just and fair. The efforts of man and other creatures are aided by God in the sense that He stimulates the activity of man in due accordance with its true character and in due consideration of the time of its fruition in the course of the man's experience.

The existence of God is proved by the following reasoning: People have ascribed the origin of the world either (1) to primordial matter, or (2) to atoms, or (3) to *karma*, the collective residue of the acts of men. Any one of these can act only when, prior to the beginning of creation, it is controlled by an intelligent Being. As all these by themselves are lacking in intelligence, like an axe and other implements which can operate only when handled by the intelligent carpenter, so from the operation of primordial matter, or atoms, or *karma* in the making of the world, we infer the existence of the controlling agent, God.[1]

### NYĀYA CONCEPTION OF RULES OF LIFE AND CONDUCT

The four stages of life, *āśramas,* form the basis of our life and conduct according to all our systems except the system of Karma-Mīmāṁsā which deprecates *sannyāsa,* the fourth stage. This scheme of the *āśramas* embraces the entire code of life and conduct for all ; and there is no difference of opinion on this point. It is only in regard to the final culmination of human effort, *mokṣa* (liberation), that there are slight divergences.

That *mokṣa* is attained by means of true knowledge is practically the common ground among all *darśanas.* That which keeps man in bondage is what has been called 'the concatenation of aberrations', *kleśa,* viz. ignorance, egoism, affection, hatred, and yearning for life. These form the motive for all worldly activities. When therefore on the dawn of knowledge all these cease, there is either no activity at all, or there is just that amount of activity which is needed for the exhausting of the *prārabdha karma* ; and when there is no 'aberration', and hence no activity, the man attains *mokṣa.*

The knowledge that leads to *mokṣa* is the knowledge of that thing, the wrong notion whereof is the potent cause of birth and rebirth. This wrong notion consists in the conceiving as Ātman of what is not-Āman, i.e. the regarding of the body and other things as 'I'. This notion of 'I', *ahaṅkāra,* is at the root of the whole trouble. It appears as a rule in regard to the body, the sense-organs, the mind, feelings, and cognitions ; and it ceases with the dawn of true knowledge of 'the causes of defects', i.e. of all objects of cognition, viz. body, sense-organs, perceptible things, apprehension, mind, activity, defects, rebirth, fruition, and pain. These are called 'the causes of defects', because these are what form the subjects of wrong notion. Consequently, when the true knowledge of these appears, it sets aside the 'notion of I' with regard to them ; and there is a cessation of pain, which is followed by the cessation of birth, which in its turn is followed by the cessation of activity ; this again is followed by the cessation of defects, which leads to the cessation of wrong notion ; and this finally leads to *mokṣa.*

[1] Those interested in further discussions should read the *Nyāyavārttika,* translated in the *Indian Thought,* and the *Tātparyaṭīkā* thereon ; and also the *Nyāya-kusumāñjali.*

## VAIŚEṢIKA CONCEPTION OF GOD

God is the creator and controller of all things. He possesses innate intuition embracing all things. Being omniscient, He can have no illusions ; free from illusions, He can have no attachment or aversion ; free from these, He can have no activities, hence no *dharma* (righteousness) or *adharma* (unrighteousness). The process of creation by this God is as follows: For the sake of making the beings experience the fruits of the actions of their past lives, there arises in the mind of God a desire for creating the world over again, after the periodic dissolution that was brought about by God's desire to reabsorb the whole creation within Himself in order to provide rest for all living beings wearied by their wanderings. When this desire for creating things appears in God, it sets in motion all the potential tendencies and forces in all the Jīvas, which, operating upon the various atoms, lead to the formation of things suited to the experiences of the Jīvas going to function during the coming cycle. There is only one God, ever free from all limitations.

## VAIŚEṢIKA CONCEPTION OF RULES OF LIFE AND CONDUCT

*Dharma* is that quality in man which is conducive to happiness and ultimately to *mokṣa*. The qualities conducive to *dharma* are faith, harmlessness, benevolence, truthfulness, freedom from desire for undue possession, freedom from lust, purity of intentions, freedom from anger, cleanliness, purity, devotion to God, fasting, and alertness. These are common to all men. Then there are specific qualities prescribed for particular castes and life-stages. Here come in all the *varṇa-dharmas* and *āśrama-dharmas*. The contact of mind and soul, aided by all these qualities and kept on without a desire for visible results and with the purest of motives, brings about *dharma*.

So long as man has not attained the true knowledge of things, and hence is still under the influence of affection and aversion, if he does a righteous deed, he is born in the celestial regions in a body suited to the experiencing of pleasures resulting from his past righteous action. On the other hand, if he does an unrighteous deed, he is born in the lower regions, equipped with a body suited to the experiencing of pain resulting from his past unrighteous action. In due course, the man comes to be reborn on earth, where also his birth and life are determined by his past righteous and unrighteous deeds. Thus man passes through the various divine, human, and animal existences again and again. This is what constitutes the wheel of bondage.

When a man with due knowledge and intelligence performs righteous acts without any selfish motives, he comes to be born in a pure family and within holy surroundings. Thus circumstanced, he comes to be seized with a longing for learning the means of removing the triad of pain inseparable from birth and rebirth. With this end in view, he has recourse to a teacher and obtains from him that true knowledge of things which entirely removes his ignorance ; after this, through dispassion, he becomes free from all attachment and aversion and other feelings. Freedom from these leads to the cessation of all forces of *dharma* or *adharma,* the cause of birth and rebirth. All his acts henceforth tend towards peace and calm, contentment and disregard for the body. Finally, he attains the highest degree of bliss and peaceful contentment as the culmination of his *dharma,* whereupon this *dharma* also ceases ; and when his present body falls off, there is no further body for him. This cessation of equipment with bodies and organs constitutes what is called *mokṣa* (final deliverance).

29

# NATURE OF THE SOUL

OF all the subjects of philosophical discourse that have coloured the cultural life of India from the earliest stages of her history, that of the soul easily occupies the most prominent place. Political organizations, ethical codes, social institutions, and religious rites and observances have all been determined by the attitudes the Indian people have assumed to this supreme problem in the successive phases of their long history. Every change in the conception of the soul has been reflected in the cultural environment, which in its turn has called forth modification in older beliefs. Thus it would be scarcely an exaggeration to say that the cultural history of India is the history of the influence the problem of the soul has exercised upon the diverse aspects of her complex civilization through the centuries.

The richness of the Indian speculation on the soul has no doubt been due to the persistent belief that a correct knowledge of the Ātman provides the only remedy for the evils and sufferings incidental to human existence ; self-knowledge accordingly came to occupy the highest place in the hierarchy of man's duties and obligations. This has induced discussions which, though sometimes crude and superficial, gradually came to acquire a progressively rich and systematic character, till they reached a position that may still be considered to be a remarkable achievement in philosophy. What is more surprising is that this position should have been reached as early as the age of the Upaniṣads.

## DEVELOPMENT OF THE IDEA

It would therefore be wrong to suppose that the chronological history of Indian speculations on the Ātman has always corresponded to the stages in a progressively perfect analysis. On the contrary, the fact seems to be that some of the post-Upaniṣadic developments, when judged by the standard of logical correctitude, were symbolic of a retrograde process and a speculative decline. This was inevitable. Truth is as much a concern of him who discovers and transmits it, as of him who receives it ; and the most unfortunate thing is that men differ profoundly in their capacity to receive what has been discovered by a philosopher of genuine insight. The profounder an analysis, the deeper is the insight it needs for its correct appreciation. Thus it came about that a backward movement in the speculations on the Ātman set in even during what is generally known as the Upaniṣadic age, and this was due to the comparatively inferior intellectual equipment of the majority, who could not reach the dizzy height to which the minority's thoughts had moved.

The opinion that the Upaniṣads, as a whole, represented a period of infancy in the development of Indian philosophy, though widely prevalent, is, to say the least, an unwarranted assumption, prompted by the belief that whatever appears later in time must on that very account be profounder than the achievements of an earlier age. When we disabuse ourselves of this mischievous prejudice, the Upaniṣadic speculations appear as a heterogeneous mass of philosophical wisdom that bears evidence to the varying degrees of insight possessed by those who contributed to its growth. It is tolerably evident from the extant literature that the thinkers of that distant age had as acute differences among themselves as we have among the modern philosophers. Debates, dialogues, and discussions, conceit of the young, humility of the old, self-confidence born of maturity, impatience of the dogmatist, and the frustration of the sceptic—all these go to prove the identity of human nature from age to age. The doctrines of reality, evolved out of these discussions, were as numerous then as they are today. And it would not be an improbable hypothesis that the Upaniṣads heralded the advent of a critical period that had been preceded by a period of dogmatism. This critical attitude is discernible in the oldest of the Upaniṣads where thought moves cautiously and with the greatest circumspection.

With the advent of the critical period the search for reality started with a subjective note. It must have appeared to the philosophers of this new age that the only way out of the plethora of dogmatic assertions about reality was to replace the objective method by the method of subjective analysis. This was a momentous change. In pursuance of the innate objective tendency of human nature, the first impulse of man, when confronted by the riddles of the universe, is to seek reality in the world of objects ; and the problem of explanation is that of discovering unity underlying the multiplicity of entities. What is that out of which the world of multiplicity has come and into which it returns? Thought moves at this first stage in a cosmogonic setting, and the task of the philosopher is to find out the primeval stuff from which the world has originated. Thus, the authors of the Upaniṣads, like the speculators of ancient Greece, sought to unify knowledge by advancing various theories about the primeval element that was the source of the universe. According to some, what existed at first was water—*'Āpa evedamagra āsuḥ'* (*Bṛ. U.*, V.5.1) ; others believed space to be the fundamental principle. Similarly, being, not-being, air, life, and even Ātman were alternatively taken to be the first and fundamental principle. There was apparently no way out of these speculations, and philosophy came to be a cockpit of conflicting theories. A deeper analysis of experience found the old cosmogonic approach unsatisfactory. The next forward step was therefore taken when the method of subjective analysis was undertaken. Instead of seeking reality in the world of objects the philosophers now looked into themselves in search of a principle that would offer a sure foundation for philosophical knowledge.

As soon as the method of approach was changed, it brought with it the conviction that the only way of eliminating the chances of dogmatic assertions in philosophy must lie in self-knowledge; the self provides a principle which is so irrepressible that its reality is reasserted in the very act of doubting or denying. Metaphysics therefore should get its clue, not from the world of objects, but from the granite certainty of one's own existence. The most fundamental question thenceforth was not of the origin of the world, but that of a correct apprehension of the essential nature of the self whose reality defies all doubts and the exigencies of demonstration or refutation. Thus the problem of self forced itself to the foreground of metaphysics and became the philosophical problem *par excellence*.

### THREE STAGES OF UPANIṢADIC SPECULATION

A great obstacle before the modern student in the way of a correct appreciation of the earliest metaphysics of India, particularly of the changed perspective brought about by the replacement of the objective by the subjective attitude, lies in the vast interval that separates our age from that of the Upaniṣads. It has been remarked by T. H. Green that each generation requires the questions of philosophy to be put to it in its own language, and, unless they are so put, it will not be at the pains of understanding them. If the difficulty of understanding a philosophy is so great after the lapse of a generation only, it is likely to be immeasurably greater when the distance is of several centuries. The language along with the changed tradition not only renders the earlier analysis difficult, but, in the absence of a correct comprehension of its value, it encourages fruitless attempts at innovation, leading to the illusion of an infinite progress in philosophy. Some of the observations on the Upaniṣadic speculations have been due to this linguistic obstacle. To a sympathetic interpreter, refusing to yield to the difficulties, it would be evident that the Upaniṣadic teachings in respect of the Ātman represent three well-defined stages in the progressive movement of thought. They corresponded respectively to the doctrines that characterized the Ātman as a 'thing', those that looked upon it as the 'knower', and those that regarded it as the supra-relational conscious principle. For convenience of reference they may respectively be called the psychological, the epistemological, and the transcendental theories.

### THE PSYCHOLOGICAL LEVEL

Nothing seems more obvious to our ordinary thought than the psychological theory which regards the Ātman as a 'thing' alongside of other things, and knowledge as a relation of compresence. The self from this standpoint is on a level and co-ordinate with any other thing existing in the world, possessing a definite nature by which it may be recognized as distinct from other things. It may be then identified with any of the things suggested by the exigencies of the situation or the individual temperament of the philosopher. Thus in the *Bṛhadāraṇyaka Upaniṣad* the Ātman is defined as speech, breath, eye, ear, *manas,* or heart, each of which is rejected by Yājñavalkya as inadequate and false. Similarly, the Socratic method of instruction adopted by Sanatkumāra in the *Chāndogya Upaniṣad,* designed to lead Nārada through several stages of imperfect definitions, and of Bhṛgu's education in the *Taittirīya Upaniṣad* signifies the attitude of the Upaniṣadic thinkers to the all-too-common tendency of ordinary thought to grasp the Ātman, through the mechanism of the defining intellect, as a definite object in the democracy of the universe. Whether it is defined as *vāc, manas, āpas, ākāśa, citta, vijñāna,* or, as in modern psychology and realism, as the behaviour of the organism or the cross-section of the universe, the assumption remains identically the same, namely, that the Ātman is a definable entity by the side of other entities, or, to borrow Bosanquet's beautiful expression, it is a unitary being, a sort of angel inside the mind.

### THE EPISTEMOLOGICAL LEVEL: THE BHŪMAN

The criticism of the psychological theories of self marks the transition of the Upaniṣadic thought from the psychological to the epistemological level. As was to be expected, this epistemological level is clearly enunciated in the very dialogues that adopt the method of gradual instruction, sometimes compared to the mounting of a flight of stairs. Thus, for instance, Sanatkumāra, proceeding through a number of tentative positions, the defect of each being removed by the next higher stage of analysis, leads Nārada beyond the sphere of finite entities to the ultimate stage in which the analysis ends with the conception of the Bhūman or the infinite principle which, as a universal, cannot be defined in terms of finite categories. In a language that testifies equally to the poetic endowment as well as the depth of insight of Sanatkumāra, this ultimate analysis which reveals the Ātman as the infinite principle condemns all objectivistic definitions as falling short of the final ground in which is rooted the world of finite things. Every finite object implies duality and is consequently called *alpa,* while the Infinite in which it is grounded is beyond all dualistic categories. The Bhūman is that in which nothing different from itself is seen, heard, or known. Being the ground of all that exists, it is not itself grounded in a principle that might transcend it ; and in this sense it is grounded in its own richness (*sve mahimni*). To put it in the words of modern philosophy, the Infinite is the ultimate condition or presupposition of the finite entities or the universal ground of the finite individuals. This profound conception of the Infinite resting on its own glory or richness needs a few words of comment. Finite objects are determined by one another ; it is through this mutual determination that each is invested with meaning. The notion of cow, to take the example given in the dialogue, becomes significant only as contrasted with the notion of horse, each contributing to the meaning of the other. In this sense every definite content of thought needs something other than itself from which it is distinguished. In other words, a definite object of thought exists and maintains its individuality with the help of its 'other', which, consequently, may be characterized as its support. That is why it is said that *anyo hi anyasmin pratiṣṭhitaḥ* (one thing is grounded in another). But the Infinite which has nothing outside itself cannot seek its support in something other than itself ; it is therefore *causa sui* or a self-maintaining principle. While all finite things are rooted in the Infinite, the latter has nothing in which it itself may be rooted ; it is, in other words, the ultimate support (*āśraya*) or presupposition of all that exists. The famous principle of *determinatio est negatio,* which no doubt is universally true of the finite objects of thought, cannot therefore apply to the infinite principle.

### THE SELF AS THE BASIS OF KNOWLEDGE

The next step in the analysis of the Infinite, as envisaged in the same dialogue, is intended to remove the possibility of confusing the Infinite with anything different from the self. The knowing self, in the strictly epistemological sense, has nothing outside of itself ; I am the presupposition of all that exists for me, and except in relation to my knowledge the world would be as good as nothing for me. All distinctions that I might make between objects and objects must be within my knowledge, and it would therefore be impossible for me to distinguish something that I know and some other thing that I do not know. I am in this sense the universal or all-pervasive principle, and, as such, not limited by anything lying outside myself. In other words, everything that exists for me, however distinct from something else, can be so distinguished only because both fall within my knowledge. In this sense, I can have no 'support' in a thing lying beyond myself; I, as the subject of knowledge, am the ultimate presupposition of all objects. So far as my world is concerned I am therefore a self-supporting or self-maintaining principle. In the language of the Upaniṣad, that which is below and above, which is in front and on the back, which is to the south and to the north, may be represented either in terms of the individual self (*ahaṅkārādeśa eva*) or in terms of the universal Ātman (*ātmādeśa eva*). The implication is that no knowledge is possible except on the basis of an infinite, universal, conscious principle.

### IDEALISM IN THE UPANIṢADS AND WESTERN THOUGHT

It would be unnecessary to multiply examples to show that the Upaniṣadic thinkers have persistently adhered to this position in their analysis of knowledge, and that it is the linguistic barrier which is mainly responsible for promoting their misinterpretations and the tendency of the modern students to relegate their teachings to the care of the antiquarians. The entire world is supported by Brahman or the Ātman, and in this sense the world is *prajñānetram* (having *prajñā* or Ātman as its source), *prajñāne pratiṣṭhitam* (held or maintained by Ātman); the Ātman, on the other hand, is *pratibodhaviditam* (is known in every act of cognition, being its ground) as it is the *jyotiṣāṁ jyotiḥ* (the basic light or knowledge of all empirical knowledge) and *vijñānaghana* (it is all knowledge or consciousness), persisting through the waking, dream, and deep slumber states. Similar other conclusions of these ancient philosophers represent a remarkable type of idealism that may be favourably compared with the idealistic contentions of the modern age. There is, however, one interesting feature of the Indian prototype which, in view of the prevalent misunderstandings, requires elucidation. It is repeatedly said that the Ātman, though neither speakable, nor thinkable, nor provable, has yet to be known as an eternal principle—*'Ekadhaivānudraṣṭavyam etadaprameyaṁ dhruvam'*—though not amenable to being made an object of knowledge, it is the eternal unchanging ground of all (*Bṛ. U.*, IV.4.20). The problem is apparently insoluble inasmuch as it demands the reconciliation of two conflicting ideas, because there does not seem to be any philosophical justification for what cannot be thought or proved and yet is to be viewed as the foundation of the whole universe. The speculations directed to resolve this apparent paradox mark the transition of Indian idealistic thought from the epistemological to the transcendental level of analysis. A proper evaluation of this transition, particularly its value for philosophy, may be helped by a short outline of the development of the problem of self in modern idealism.

The real problem of the self in the history of Western thought was brought to the forefront of philosophy by Kant's analysis of knowledge. By a scathing criticism of rational psychology, Kant, in opposition to his predecessors, struck at the root of man's inherent tendency to misapply to the transcendental self the categories that are valid in the sphere of objects. The *viṣayin* (subject), being the universal pre-condition of the *viṣaya* (object), must repel the categories of object. Herein lies the mistake of rational psychology which applies the phenomenal categories to the 'I think', and thus, through a sort of illusion, makes the eternal *viṣayin* co-ordinate with the *viṣaya,* by superimposing the conditions of the latter upon the former. While, however, extricating himself from the disastrous error of misapplying the categories to the transcendental self, Kant drifted into the equally disastrous position of the Śūnyavāda. The eternal subject was reduced to a mere naught, empty of all content. Kant was thus caught on the horns of a dilemma. The 'I think', being the transcendental condition of experience, cannot be denied while the objects are affirmed; yet, on the other hand, it repels all the categories by means of which anything is capable of being a content of knowledge, and thus threatens to reduce itself to a contentless abstraction. Thus the problem bequeathed by Kant was that of avoiding *adhyāsa* (superimposition) without falling into Śūnyavāda.

The immediate task of the subsequent idealists therefore was to discover the way of saving the epistemological theory of Ātman from the predicament into which Kant's analysis had forced it. It was never doubted by them that Kant had once for all killed the psychological theory; but while escaping from the horn of the psychological analysis, he was thrown on the other horn of the dilemma, namely, agnosticism. This made peremptory the need for a further analysis of the Ātman and for reaching a higher synthesis that, while eliminating *adhyāsa,* will not degenerate into Śūnyavāda. The required synthesis, as effected by the post-Kantian idealists, put briefly, was reached by a criticism of the claim of the principle of abstract identity to represent the highest law of intelligence, a claim that remained unchallenged since the time of Aristotle. The only way out of the agnostic inconvenience was therefore supposed to lie in a fresh interpretation of the ultimate principle of thought by replacing the abstract law of identity by that of identity-in-difference. It is true that whatever has a meaning must have a nature of its own distinguishable from every other object of thought—it must maintain its identity in different and varied contexts. But, it was contended, this is only one aspect of the whole truth. What, however, it fails to emphasize is the complementary aspect of the truth that the identity of every significant concept is maintained in and through its difference from other concepts. Take any object of thought in its atomic self-seclusion, and it will be found that as the process of abstraction proceeds further and further, the concept will gradually approach to a mere *śūnya,* completely empty of content. It is therefore *in and through* its difference that every significant concept maintains its identity. Neither bare identity nor mere difference is capable of investing a concept with meaning. It was therefore no wonder that Kant was led to Śūnyavāda owing to his failure to see the mediated nature of self-consciousness.

The subject therefore must be conceived, on pain of being reduced to an empty abstraction, as maintaining its identity through its difference from the object. The object, accordingly, while different from the subject, helps the concept of subject to acquire significance. Except as mediated through the object, the subject would be a mere *śūnya.* Thus, the Ātman, according to the post-Kantian idealists, becomes self-conscious only by distinguishing itself from the *anātman* ; it is a self-distinguishing principle that distinguishes itself from the *anātman* (not-self) and, at the same time, overreaches the distinction.

Instead of pursuing further this remarkable theory of Ātman, it may be recalled that the critics have not been silenced. They find that in the idealistic elucidation and development of the position there is clearly discernible a see-saw that inclines it at one time to the pan-objectivist and at another to the agnostic consequence. As this has been shown in another context,[1] we may now return to the Upaniṣadic attempt to develop a theory of the Ātman that would free it completely from every type of *adhyāsa* and yet avoid its reduction to the *śūnya.*

### THE TRANSCENDENTAL LEVEL

The problem of Ātman in the Upaniṣads, as we have observed, is put in the form of a paradox. It is urged on the one hand that the Ātman is the ultimate transcendental principle which supports the world, and on the other hand, it is repeatedly said to lie beyond the region of thought and speech, and consequently, of all proof. We cannot deny Brahman while affirming the world, nor can we bring the Ātman under the conditions of thought and speech. The first and the most important step that is taken in resolving this paradox is represented by the statement that Brahman, which is the foundation of the world, is no other than the essence of the individual self, which is presupposed by all knowledge and experience. The 'I' of the 'I think' is essentially identical with the Ātman,

[1] A.C. Mukerji, *The Nature of Self.*

in which is rooted the entire world of plurality. If none can deny his own existence, a careful analysis of this irrepressibility of the self will show that none can deny the Ātman, which is at the foundation of the world.

The ontological status of the Ātman is accordingly to be discovered through an epistemological analysis, leading ultimately to the conclusion that there can be no knowledge without the presence in the knower of an infinite conscious principle that, though itself the presupposition of all distinctions, has no distinction within it. That there are apparently insoluble difficulties in this transition from the epistemological to the transcendental doctrine of the self has never been denied; and therefore there is no wonder that even among the Upaniṣadic thinkers, only a few succeeded in stepping beyond the frontiers of the epistemological doctrine. These difficulties are all resolvable into the apparent impossibility of establishing the reality of a supra-relational principle in view of the inextricably relational or discursive nature of thought. This being through and through relational, the supra-relational principle, when brought before the bar of thought, must inevitably shrink into a mere *śūnya.* Yet, the reality of an infinite conscious principle lying beyond thought and speech is brought home to us by an inexorable logic.

### THE SUBJECT-OBJECT RELATION IN KNOWLEDGE

That 'I know' is the ultimate presupposition of all knowledge has been a recognized tenet of idealism since Kant's analysis of the transcendental principles of knowledge. Pursuing the same line of analysis, it may be said that it is only in so far as I know 'a' and I know 'b', that I can ever know the difference between 'a' and 'b'. If 'a' had been within my knowledge and 'b' outside my knowledge, I could never know that one is different from the other. Similarly, my knowledge of any other relation implies that 'I know' is the pre-condition of the terms between which the relation obtains. Thus all relations, including the relation of difference, must presuppose the 'I know'. And it is a further consequence of this that the 'I' of the 'I know' cannot be strictly represented as different from, or related with, the entities that are themselves known as different from, or related with, one another. In other words, the knowledge of relation, and so of difference, would be impossible if the 'I' had been supposed to be itself a term of the relation. It is only against the background of the 'I know' that any relation has its meaning. The inevitable conclusion to which such considerations point is that the background or support of all relations, though something positive, falls beyond the relations, and, as such, cannot be conditioned or supported by anything different from itself. What is presupposed by all distinctions cannot itself be known through distinction. It is therefore the unconditioned support of all things that are related with one another and determined by mutual relations.

But, it may be asked, Can we not accept the idealist doctrine of the self as a self-distinguishing principle? The self as the subject, we have been repeatedly told, distinguishes itself from the object and through this process becomes conscious of itself as the subject ; the self is neither a mere subject nor a mere object, but a self-conscious principle in which the difference between subject and object is overreached without annulling their distinction. Cannot this theory be accepted as the last word in the philosophy of the self? It might be said in reply that even the idealists are themselves divided in their attitude to this account of self-consciousness. Bradley's criticism, for example, is well known. But instead of examining the theory in the context of Bradley's analysis, it may be questioned if the doctrine does not run counter to one of the valuable contributions of modern idealism, namely, that all relations presuppose the supreme subject-object relation. The very first point to be borne in mind is that difference itself is a relation, and, as such, it must, like other specific relations, fall under the generic relation of subject to object. This being so, it would be self-contradictory to insist that the subject-object relation itself implies the relation of difference. In other words, as all distinctions exist *for* the subject, it would be self-contradictory to urge at the same time that the subject distinguishes itself from the object. This is indirectly admitted in so far as the idealist accepts that the correlativity of subject and object exists *for* the subject. But in that case the subject for which the correlativity exists cannot itself be one of the correlated terms. To put it briefly, the pre-condition of all relations cannot itself be a term of the relation conditioned by it. Being the support of all relations, the self cannot be co-ordinated with the objects between which exists a relation, because this would be to dislodge the conscious principle from its foundational position and place it alongside of what it supports, and here the mistake would be identical with that of placing the universal alongside of the particulars, which has been emphatically rejected by modern idealists.

### SUPRA-RELATIONAL NATURE OF BRAHMAN

These considerations bring out an important truth about the nature of self-consciousness. It is only apparently that self-consciousness implies mediation. At first sight it seems to be true that as we can know a thing as *this* by contrasting it with *that,* the self, in order to be conscious of itself, must distinguish itself from the not-self. But this, as we have seen above, the self cannot do. Being the presupposition of all distinctions, it cannot distinguish itself from what it is not. This is but another way of saying that self-consciousness, when taken strictly, cannot be a mediated consciousness, or that the knowledge of the self is not a relational or conceptual knowledge. It is, on the contrary, an absolutely immediate consciousness which cannot be thrust into the mechanism of relational apprehension. It is something like the 'experienced experiencing' as put by some of the contemporary thinkers, or the 'non-objectifying experience' as it figures in the epistemological analysis of some philosophers of the recent past.

It may now be comparatively easy to appreciate the view of the Upaniṣadic idealists and their insistence on the much-misunderstood negative method of knowing the Ātman, as 'not this' and 'not that'. They were fully convinced of the fact that the only way of knowing 'this' is to limit it by 'that'. Every finite thing, in other words, must necessarily be known through its distinction from what transcends it. But this method of knowledge is inapplicable to the all-inclusive Ātman beyond which there is nothing. The Ātman, in other words, is the unconditioned ground of all finite entities. Being the *sarva-vikalpāspada* (ground of all distinctions), Brahman cannot be known in the ordinary way which implies identification through distinction. This is, again, another way of saying that the characters by which one finite thing is distinguished from another is inapplicable to the basic principle of all distinctions. The world of plurality is *ātmamaya* in the sense that nothing can ever be known except on the presupposed reality of the Ātman that defies the conditions under which the world is known. This technical meaning of *ātmamayatva* is explained by the later Vedāntins as *'Yatsvarūpavyatirekeṇa agrahaṇaṁ yasya tasya tadātmatvam'* (that peculiar character without which a thing cannot be grasped or known is its nature). Hence, again, Ātman is a non-object (*aviṣaya*) ; every object of knowledge has to be known as a definite *this,* but Brahman cannot be known in this way. That is why it is repeatedly urged that none can see the seer of sight or the knower of knowledge—*'Na dṛṣṭerdraṣṭāraṁ paśyeḥ'* etc. (*Bṛ. U.,* III.4.2). Such apparently paradoxical statements with which the Upaniṣads are replete are all intended to signify that discursive knowledge, which is universally applicable in the field of finite things, is absolutely inapplicable to the non-discursive foundational principle supporting the world of plurality.

This, briefly put, is the Upaniṣadic solution of the very difficult problem of soul which Kant bequeathed to those who came after him, namely, the problem of avoiding *adhyāsa* without falling into Śūnyavāda. The majority of the theories of Ātman that have made their appearance in the history of Indian or Western philosophy have either succumbed to man's inherent tendency to objectify what is essentially unobjectifiable, or have drifted towards some type of agnosticism. The former alternative has encouraged the democratic conception of the universe in which the Ātman, as aptly put by S. Alexander, has no privileged place. The latter alternative, on the other hand, has led to the self-refutation of denying the reality of what withstands all doubt. Modern idealism and the ancient idealism of the Upaniṣads, accordingly, represent two classical attempts at steering clear of the mistakes arising out of these two extreme attitudes. Both schools of idealism agree that the real problem of self will defy solution as long as the Ātman is regarded to be only one thing in the midst of other things, or even as a *primus inter pares.* While agreeing so far in the rejection of the purely objectivist doctrines, they differ from each other profoundly in their respective constructive suggestions. The modern idealists have persistently suspected the wisdom of transgressing the limits of epistemological analysis, because in their opinion this would inevitably lead to agnosticism. The self is a subject presupposed by all objects; and yet a self-conscious principle must reconcile the opposition of subject to object without reducing the one to the other. Such a reduction would altogether annihilate their difference, rendering the Ātman too indefinite to carry any meaning.

According to the Indian idealists, on the contrary, the epistemological analysis which remains at the relational level can never purge itself completely of the objectivist attitude leading to the confusion of the self with the not-self, of the subject with the object. The analysis therefore must be carried further into the transcendental level, and then the Ātman will be realized as the supra-relational immediate experience which, while itself free from all distinctions, is yet the support of all distinguishable entities. Even the distinction between existence and knowledge, implied by discursive thought, has no application to the self; here *sattā eva jñānaṁ, jñānam eva sattā* (existence is knowledge and knowledge is existence). To demand that it must be known through mediation is as absurd as to demand that one light must be revealed by another; the only appropriate description of it is therefore that the self is the ultimate principle of revelation. This explains why it is also described as something that is not amenable to proof, though itself the basis of all proof. Being an irrepressible principle it cannot be disproved, and as the basis of all proof it cannot itself be proved. The self, in other words, is *svayaṁsiddha* (self-existing) and *svaprakāśa* (self-revealing). Similarly, being the logical presupposition of the objects, it cannot itself be known as an object, or made co-ordinate with the objects. To put the whole position succinctly, the self is infinite (*ananta*), supra-relational (*asaṅga*), non-objective (*aviṣaya*), immediate (*aparokṣa*) knowledge or experience. This, according to the Upaniṣadic thinkers, is the only solution of the true problem of self, which was thrown into prominence by Kant's analysis of knowledge discussed above.

From this contrast of the modern with the ancient solution of the problem of self follow certain results of paramount importance for epistemology and metaphysics. If the contention of the Indian idealists be true, idealistic metaphysics must be reconstructed on the basis of the recognition of the indefinable, yet undeniable, conscious principle that does not owe its meaning to mediation. The process of mediation, no doubt, is the universal condition of all finite existence ; but the infinite consciousness provides a clear exception to the rule that mediation and meaning are inseparable. The principle of identity in and through difference represents, no doubt, a valuable improvement upon the law of abstract identity ; and the modern idealists, in emancipating thought from the agelong fallacy of bare identity, have done an invaluable service to the cause of sound philosophy. But it must not be forgotten that a principle that is universally applicable within a limited sphere loses its value and usefulness when accepted as a universal principle of unlimited application. Difference in some form or other must enter into the life of an intelligible identity which on that account implies limitation by what transcends it. Such an identity therefore is valid within the field of finite entities ; and this may be shown to be true even in the case of a self-determining principle. In other words, a self-determining principle, such as a concrete universal, must have internal differences through which it maintains its identity. It ought to be evident from this that the category of self-determination is inapplicable to what is the logical basis of all difference, the infinite conscious principle within which there is no difference.

## POST-UPANIṢADIC SPECULATIONS

The post-Upaniṣadic speculations on the self, though influenced either positively or negatively by the rich heritage left by the ancient thinkers, explored several avenues of approach to the problem, some of which marked new departures in the method as well as the general outlook of philosophical analysis. The tendency to rely on direct intuition or religious experience for reaching the deeper aspects of reality was gradually supplemented, and often replaced, by a growing emphasis upon an exclusively rational analysis and argumentative discussion. This was in a way inevitable, because every systematic growth of thought has to reckon with the intellectual *milieu* and fight its way to recognition as an independent philosophical position. Thus it happened that even the orthodox systems, in spite of their professed loyalty to the Vedic tradition and a consequent dislike of unaided reason, were compelled to define and clarify their respective positions against the rival systems that were growing along with them. This committed the philosophers to a rational defence of what was yet acknowledged to have its final support in the unquestionable authority of the Upaniṣads. The clear implication of this scholastic endeavour to reconcile reason with authority was that the latter was not only rationally defensible, but needed reason's assistance for making its voice distinctly audible even within the narrow circle of orthodoxy. Whenever a particular issue was at stake it was not so much the scriptural statements that acted as an arbiter as the preconceived idea of the system that dictated the particular interpretation of the scripture. And then the choicest dialectical weapons were brought into play in defence of the idea ; and consequently the repeated professions of allegiance to the Upaniṣads assumed the appearance of little more than lip-service to a tradition that was crumbling under the pressure of conflicting interpretations.

It would therefore be a mistake to think that the scripture-ridden systems left no room for independent and unbiased thinking and were ultimately based upon blind faith in authority. The fact is that reason, banned on the highway, discovered by-ways for self-assertion ; and that the orthodox systems, though ostensibly based upon the scriptures, could not help disclosing their respective rational foundations.

### CONSCIOUSNESS AS A QUALITY OF THE SELF

In every serious inquiry the different lines on which controversy develops are more or less determined by the different formulations of the problem ; the problem of the self is no exception to this. Bradley's formulation of the problem of the self may be easily taken to be one of the clearest with which modern thinkers are familiar. 'We are all sure that we exist,' he remarks, 'but in what sense and what character—as to that we are most of us in helpless uncertainty and in blind confusion.' In a surprisingly similar manner the mediaeval Indian philosophers formulated the same problem. Śaṅkara in his commentary on *Brahma-Sūtra* I.1.1 says, *'Sarvo hi ātmāstitvaṁ pratyeti,... tadviśeṣaṁ prati vipratipatteḥ'* (Nobody doubts the existence of Ātman, but there are differences as to its character). The problem of the self, according to this particular form of presentation, is not that of the *existence* of the self ; it is rather the problem of the *character* of what exists as the inexpugnable postulate of all knowledge and all experience. Thus, the very formulation of the problem has implicit in it the distinction between existence and character, the 'that' and the 'what'. In other words, the scope of the possible theories that may arise out of the attempts to solve the problem is predetermined and restricted by the postulate that whatever is real must conform to the conditions of discursive knowledge or discursive thought that understands everything by distinguishing it from other things by means of the character that the latter do not possess. It is therefore natural, while the postulate remains unchallenged, to regard the self as something possessing a peculiar character that distinguishes it from the not-self; and the self is then conceived as a substance with knowledge or consciousness as its peculiar quality. A large number of respectable theories of the self, in Indian and Western philosophical systems, have been developed in conformity with the requirements of discursive thought, and they are still popular.

Once we have taken this important step, a theory of the self may develop on one of two distinct lines according as knowledge is regarded as an inseparable or a separable attribute of the soul-substance. In the latter case, knowledge or consciousness reduces itself to a mere accidental or adventitious quality occasionally produced in the soul, which in between the intervals of consciousness is essentially unconscious. This position, again, contains, in a state of unstable equilibrium, the germs of materialism as well as what is generally known as spiritualism, as is to be found in Locke and the Nyāya-Vaiśeṣika. A substance that is essentially unconscious may easily be identified with matter; and when this identification is complete, consciousness becomes a by-product of matter or an epiphenomenon in the strict sense of the term. When, on the other hand, the identification of the soul with a bit of matter is rejected as paradoxical and outrageous, while still adhering to the theory of consciousness as a quality as in Descartes and Jainism, we get a theory according to which consciousness is an inseparable quality of the soul, so that the soul is taken to be conscious even in the intervals of apparent unconsciousness, such as sleep and swoon. The soul, according to this position, can never remain unconscious without forfeiting its claim to be a spiritual substance; thus while avoiding the apparent paradox of identifying the soul with matter, it is driven to the equally paradoxical admission that the soul thinks or is conscious even when there is apparently a total suspension of consciousness as in sound, dreamless slumber.

## THE SELF AS AN OBJECT OF PROOF

Now, as to the theory of the unconscious soul as developed by the Nyāya-Vaiśeṣika school. It is an ultimate postulate of the Nyāya thinkers that whatever is real must be capable of being proved, and so what cannot be proved is a mere nonentity. A second postulate that is equally vital to the Nyāya analysis lies in the assertion that whatever is real must possess certain attributes; mere existence without character is as inconceivable as character that does not characterize something. In conformity with these postulates they insist that the self, if it has to be taken as real at all, must be an object of proof for which it must be a 'that' and a 'what', i.e. it must have an existence and a character. Without going into further details we would be content in this short article to bring into prominence the perplexities and quibblings that are directly born of the assumption that the self can be proved in the ordinary sense of the term, so that it is only one of the objects that stand in need of proof.

Vātsyāyana, for example, inquires how the self as Ātman, that must be accepted as the logical presupposition of the process of proof, can itself be turned into an object of proof, how the *pramātṛ* may be taken to be a *prameya*. Apparently, the question is insoluble within the postulates of the Nyāya philosophy; and it must either be admitted that the process of proving implies the existence of the prover just as doubt implies the existence of the doubter, as Descartes said, or that every attempt to know the knower would inevitably lead to argument in a circle, as was seen by Kant. But Vātsyāyana, instead of following any of these courses, seeks to cut the Gordian knot by taking recourse to the case-endings of Sanskrit grammar, according to which the same thing may be regarded as being the subject of a sentence or its predicate depending upon the intention of the verb. A tree, for example, may be used in a sentence either as a nominative or as an accusative; this is supposed by Vātsyāyana to be a sufficient guarantee for the assertion that the self too may be the agent as well as the object of proof, the *kartṛ* as well as the *karma*. The appeal to the grammatical structure of a language for solving a philosophical issue has not perhaps assumed a more irrational form than what is illustrated here. The syntactical rules governing the construction of sentences cannot be brought in for the solution of an epistemological issue, and Vātsyāyana does not appear to see the ambiguity in the terms *kartṛ* and *karma* when they are used in sentence-construction on the one hand, and in the analysis of knowledge on the other.

Yet, however, he has himself characterized the self as the knower of all objects, the feeler of all feelings (*ātmā sarvasya draṣṭā, sarvasya bhoktā, sarvajñaḥ, sarvānubhāvī*). The clear meaning of this description, to put it briefly, is that it is the inexpugnable presupposition of experience in general. That the self, when regarded in this light, cannot be turned into an object of knowledge or of proof should be obvious to every dispassionate thinker, and the analogy of the tree makes the confusion worse confounded without offering a real solution of the problem. Similarly, Vātsyāyana's endeavour to prove the identity of the knower and the known by appealing to such experiences as 'I am happy' and 'I am unhappy' is mostly influenced by the dictates of unreflective ordinary thinking wedded to the grammatical structure of language; and if every form of linguistic expression is taken to correspond to the form of reality, the problem of knowing the self would not present itself as a problem at all. 'I am stout' or 'I am not stout' does not amount to the knowledge of myself; and, if so, there is no earthly reason why 'I am happy' should be taken to solve the problem of self-knowledge. The inherent paradox in such an uncritical acceptance of the identity of the linguistic form with the form of reality shows itself when, instead of saying 'I know myself as unhappy', a person says that he does *not* know himself to be happy. The former expression as little justifies the opinion that the self knows itself as existing in reality as the latter would warrant the conclusion that the self does not exist.

It is significant that Vācaspati, the distinguished exponent of the different systems, who possessed the wonderful capacity of entering into the spirit of each school of philosophy, remarked that the Nyāya analysis, when carefully examined, did not favour the doctrine that the self was literally an object of knowledge or *jñeya*. What Uddyotakara also implied was not the identity of the knower and the known; it was only through a sort of linguistic licence that the self, which is in reality the principle of revelation, was said to be the *object* of knowledge (*tatra vivakṣayā jñeyatvābhidhānam*). In reality, however, Vācaspati insists, happiness and misery that are the qualities of the self are the objects of knowledge and not the self itself. It is evident, then, that Vācaspati and Uddyotakara, as interpreted by him, were against the ordinary interpretation of the Nyāya analysis of such experiences as 'I am happy' and 'I am unhappy'; and this implied that the self, when taken strictly, could not be proved in the sense in which proof necessarily implies objectification of what is proved. To put it plainly, the self or Ātman being the pre-established reality of all doubt and refutation, proof and disproof, the attempt to prove it through perception or inference would be a paradoxical undertaking.

In the history of Western philosophy the false assumption that the self, like all other things, must be known through 'experience' led to perplexing quandaries in pre-Kantian empiricism; and it is Hume who drew the logical conclusion that what the philosophers called the self was nothing more than a bundle of 'perceptions' that were in constant flux. In a similar spirit the Buddhists insisted that the so-called self was but the common name for the flux of ideas or *vijñāna-santāna*. The denial of a permanent principle, in both these cases, was the inevitable consequence of the uncritical assumption that the self, if it is to be proved at all, must be proved in the same way in which every other thing is demonstrated; the assumption, to put it in another form, confuses proof with presupposition and implies that what is presupposed by proof must itself be subjected to proof, the *pramātṛ* must also be a *prameya*. It is as little realized by the modern empiricists as by the Indian empiricists of old that the presupposed principles of knowledge being the logical implicates of all proof, it is impossible as well as misleading to attempt their logical justification. The self, when taken in the strict sense of a knower, is therefore beyond the region of proof (*pramāṇa-nirapekṣa*) and the basis (*āśraya*) of all proof and disproof. In the language of the Advaita Vedānta, the self is *svayaṁsiddha* as distinct from *parataḥsiddha*. It is, however, important to note here that the assertion that the self is beyond proof and disproof is not to reduce it to a mere assumption, because an assumption, like a working hypothesis or postulate, does not exclude the possibility of its rejection at a future stage of investigation ; a *svayaṁsiddha* principle, on the contrary, is irrepressible in the sense that in doubting or refuting its reality one has to accept it at every stage of investigation.

### THE SELF AS TRANSCENDENTAL REALITY

Allied with the assumption that the self is a *prameya,* which the Nyāya philosophy along with some other systems accepts as an indubitable truth, there is another that is equally fundamental to its realistic and psychological outlook, namely, that all that exists must possess such characters as may distinguish them from one another so that each may be conceived as different from the rest. Under the influence, and considered in the light, of this assumption, the self is taken to be a thing or a substance having for its attribute knowledge or consciousness. Many a reputable doctrine of self in Indian and Western philosophy has found in it an unquestionable postulate that must be accepted by every intelligible doctrine of reality ; and if the self is not to be a mere nothing or myth it must also conform to that postulate. In Indian philosophy therefore all the different schools of thought have accepted it in more or less emphatic language, the only exception being the Sāṁkhya-Yoga and particularly the Advaita Vedānta associated with the name of Śaṅkarācārya. The highest level of analysis, as we have remarked above, was reflected in the transcendental doctrine of the self as discovered and propounded by the Upaniṣads ; the Ātman was then taken to be an integral experience above all relations, internal or external. It was consequently indefinable yet undeniable, and, as such, falling beyond speech and discursive thought. It was therefore quite natural for the majority of the later thinkers to re-interpret the Upaniṣadic teachings in conformity with the requirements of our ordinary knowledge. But Śaṅkara, impressed by the thoroughness and dialectical force of the arguments of the great thinkers of the Buddhistic tradition which assailed the belief in a permanent unchanging principle, must have realized the utter futility of defending the Upaniṣadic faith while leaving unchallenged the basic postulate that whatever is real must possess a character, as was evident from the way in which the different systems sought to criticize Buddhism. He therefore brought to prominence and developed the transcendental approach to the problem of reality as was suggested by the Upaniṣads, and believed that this alone held the key to a metaphysical position that would avoid the shortcomings of substantialism on the one hand, and those of the theory of universal becoming on the other. The Ātman therefore is neither a substance underlying the changing states of consciousness, nor is it a mere stream of consciousness. It is the indefinable yet *svayaṁsiddha* and *svaprakāśa* principle, or an eternal conscious principle in which existence is knowledge and knowledge is existence, and to which such objectivistic principles as space, time, and causality are inapplicable.

# 30

## NATURE OF THE PHYSICAL WORLD

THE physical universe was early recognized in India, as in other parts of the world, as a philosophical problem both of epistemology and of ontology. How we know the physical world, whether directly or indirectly, was a point of discussion, for instance, in the Buddhistic schools. Perception was universally acknowledged to be a source of knowledge, though there was difference of opinion regarding other sources, such as inference, analogy, verbal testimony, etc. and also regarding the objects that are perceived and the elements that enter into perceptual experience.

### VARIETY OF SPECULATIONS

Naturally therefore, a variety of speculations, in consonance with their respective ontological positions, arose in the different philosophical schools. There was, for example, the major question whether the physical universe was real. Two extreme views on this subject are represented by the Cārvāka and the Advaita Vedānta.

The Cārvākas are of opinion that matter alone is real, and that what we call mind or consciousness is nothing but a property of matter generated under certain conditions, just as grains of rice acquire by fermentation the power of intoxication. Not believing in any transcendental world, religion, or morality, the Cārvākas think that the body is the sole reality, and consciousness ceases with the dissolution of the body into its constituent elements. At the other extreme stands the Advaita Vedānta with its view that the physical world has only an illusory reality produced by the false projection of Māyā. The extreme Advaitin rejects all explanations except the *vivarta* or illusory projection guaranteeing no substantiality, and therefore no true being, to the physical world. A modified form of idealism is to be found in the Yogācāra system of Buddhism where the physical universe is regarded as a projection of consciousness, but not exactly illusory in character like the 'hare's horn' or the 'sky flower'. For all practical purposes, the world is real though changing every moment; but its origin is to be traced to the operation of the mind, which is the only reality; and though in an ultimate reference everything is void, yet, compared with the physical projection, the receptacle consciousness (*ālaya-vijñāna*) is relatively more real. An extreme form of subjective idealism is Dṛṣṭi-sṛṣṭi-vāda, the theory that holds that the *esse* of things is their *percipi,* not as modes of absolute consciousness but as mental creations of individual percipients. In between these extremes, we have any number of theories acknowledging in varying degrees and senses the reality of the physical world.

## THE SĀṀKHYA-YOGA VIEW

The Sāṁkhya-Yoga believes that Prakṛti or primordial nature is as real as Puruṣa ; but while the unmanifested (*avyakta*) Prakṛti is real as an ultimate principle, the same cannot be said of its manifestations (*vyakta*). They pass away for individual Puruṣas with the dawn of the discriminative knowledge that the soul and the embodied self are not identical. But even though phenomena are unreal, Prakṛti as such is real ; and when the process of manifestation, starting with *mahat* or *buddhi* and ending in the two parallel series with *mahābhūtas* and *indriyas,* terminates, there continues to be a process of multiplication of the constituent elements (*guṇas*) inside the primordial Prakṛti. The Sāṁkhya view therefore makes a distinction between two orders of reality in the physical universe, namely, in the manifest and in the unmanifest condition. The visible world is thought of as a product of five gross elements, viz. earth, water, fire, air, and ether (*ākāśa*), but in the unmanifest Prakṛti the gross and subtle elements cease to exist, and we have to think only of their strands, *sattva, rajas,* and *tamas,* as constituting its nature. It is obvious that the Sāṁkhya-Yoga was primarily interested in the different aspects in which nature appears to us, namely, illuminating, active, and stupefying, and that, obviously, this triple aspect was arrived at by a consideration of the ways in which the world of manifestations shows itself. For, according to this particular school, the effect is practically identical with the cause ; and unless these three aspects were really present in the original Prakṛti, they could not have found a place in the manifested universe. This Sāṁkhya view finds a modified expression in the *Caraka Saṁhitā* where a medley of categories combining the Nyāya-Vaiśeṣika and Sāṁkhya conceptions is to be found. In Kashmir Śaivism also the Sāṁkhya categories, mixed with theistic elements, make their appearance.

## THE VEDĀNTIC VIEW

In the Vedāntic schools, however, the major inquiry is about the relation between Brahman and the universe ; and consequently the nature of the physical world is seen from a theistic or pantheistic angle. While some are willing to accord a kind of ontological reality to the physical world in so far as it represents the transformation of Brahman Itself, others regard it as representing the body of Brahman, that is, the physical aspect or quality of the ultimate principle. Nature, according to the latter view, represents the unconscious extension aspect of Brahman, just as the Jīva represents the consciousness aspect. The Vedāntic dualists, not satisfied with this position, further postulate a fivefold distinction of God and matter, God and soul, soul and soul, matter and soul, and matter and matter (*bhedapañcaka*). In this system therefore, barring the dependence of the universe on God, the existence of the physical world could be regarded as real. Apart from their initial divergence on the problem of the origin of the universe out of Brahman, the Vedāntic schools, in dealing with the physical world in a practical manner, admit the combination of different elements as producing the protean forms in which nature makes its appearance. Thus even in the Advaita Vedānta we meet with the theory of *pañcīkaraṇa* (combining the five), according to which the five elements mix in different proportions to produce the *bhūtas* (gross elements). Other philosophical schools in their treatment of real things (*bhāva padārtha*) include four or five of these physical elements, though there is some discussion as to whether all the substances are perceptible or some are merely inferred. There is also a divergence of opinion regarding the necessity of admitting potency (*śakti*), resident in material things, which is responsible for manifesting their characteristic qualities.

### THE NYĀYA-VAIŚEṢIKA VIEW OF ELEMENTS

Our major field of discussion regarding the physical universe is, however, the Nyāya and Vaiśeṣika systems, which, starting as two different schools, latterly combined into a single unified mode of thinking. Taking up a realistic attitude towards the universe and not denying the necessity of admitting non-material principles, the Nyāya-Vaiśeṣika furnishes us with a systematic account of the different elements of the universe together with their differentiating qualities and their method of combination. Adopting the standpoint of the common man that the physical world, as it appears to our external senses, must be accepted as real, even though it might be necessary to assume or infer certain transcendental conditions (e.g. the deserts of the self) in order to explain the modes of combination of the atoms, the Nyāya-Vaiśeṣika broadly divides reality into self (*cetana*) and non-self (*acetana*). The latter may be divided into mental and extra-mental realities. Our everyday experience shows that every idea arising in the mind is not only very intimately associated with an external object, but has a corresponding reality in the objective world. These two realities stand to each other in a certain relation of causal sequence. The external reality concerned, however, is quite independent of the idea in so far as its existence is prior to the appearance, and is a condition of the possibility, of the phenomenon of our mental life,

This experience of our life has remained unchallenged throughout the ages and is at the root of all our dealings with the objective world. The discussion on the nature of the physical world therefore is mainly based on the experience of our mental life (*laukika-pratīti*) and the usage of the objective world for practical purposes (*laukika-vyavahāra*).

For the clear understanding of the nature of the physical world it is also very necessary to know something about the nature of its other aspect, the *cetana* (conscious) element. Neither of the two depends upon the other for its existence, but there does exist a peculiar relation between them in so far as the existence of the *cetana* element is manifested through the operation of the *acetana* aspect. Although these two are opposite entities, they co-operate in such a smooth manner that our life and our dealings with the world are harmonized. In between these two realities of opposite natures there exists an eternal and atomic inanimate element,[1] called *manas,* which brings about a close connection between the two and helps the working of the physical world.[2] Without *manas* it will not be possible to realize the aim of creation.[3]

The constituents of the physical world are the eight forms of matter—five atomic and three ubiquitous in nature—and their qualities. Matter, in its atomic or discrete form, consists of (1) the four productive elements, called *bhautika paramāṇus,* which enter into the composition of the insensate world, and (2) the non-*bhautika paramāṇu,* called *manas,* which, conceived as an eternal substance and associated with the individual self (Jīvātman), helps in the organization of the productive matter into structures or physical organisms capable of experiencing pleasure and pain under the stress of moral necessity and retributive justice.[4] The other form of matter, which is looked upon as a continuum, being substantive in character, is the eternal background of the creative process, namely, *kāla* or time, and *ākāśa* or space, and of the relative position involved therein, namely, *diś*. All these, together with their qualities, form what is called the physical world. Besides, as has been mentioned above, there is the conscious element which is essential for the clear understanding of the nature of the physical world.

## ORIGIN OF THINGS AND THE PHYSICAL WORLD

The physical world may be an object of immediate perception through the instrumentality of our external sense-organs where such cognition is

[1] *Nyāya-Sūtra,* III.2.59; *Vaiśeṣika-Sūtra,* VII.1.23.
[2] *Nyāya-Sūtra,* III.2.59.
[3] *Padārtha-dharma-saṅgraha* (Chowkhamba, 1923 Ed.), p. 36; *Vyomavatī,* p. 428; *Kiraṇāvalī,* p. 93.
[4] *Nyāya-Sūtra,* III.2.60.

possible, or else its notion may be arrived at through other means of right cognition. When closely observed, it is found that every product of this objective world undergoes some change or other. Production and destruction in some form are constantly taking place. Now, it is to be seen whether this change is in some regular order or not. This is a problem which everyone has to face from his own angle of vision ; and throughout the ages various views have been advanced on the problem. Some of these views are found summed up in the *Śvetāśvatara Upaniṣad* (I.2). It is mentioned there that time (*kāla*), nature (*svabhāva*), necessity or fate (*niyati*), chance or coincidence (*yadṛcchā*), elements (*bhūtas*), Puruṣa, and combination of these have been regarded by different thinkers at different times as the cause of the origin of the world. In the *Mahābhārata* (*Vanaparvan,* XXX.28), the *Mahābodhi Jātaka* (*Jātaka,* V), and the *Buddhacarita* (IX.53) there is a reference to Īśvara as the cause. Gautama in his *Nyāya-Sūtra* (IV.1.14,19) refers to void (*abhāva*) and God (Īśvara) as the causes. He also mentions one Nirnimittavāda with reference to a view-point according to which things are produced without any cause (IV.1.22). The authors of the *Suśruta,*[5] the *Buddhacarita,*[6] and the *Gomaṭasāra*[7] also refer to a similar view. Again, Gautama says that, according to some, everything of the universe is non-eternal, because it is produced and destroyed, and there exists nothing before the production and after the destruction (*Nyāya-Sūtra,* IV.1.25). As opposed to this view, he refers to another view according to which everything is eternal, for the five atomic elements which constitute this objective world are ultimately eternal. Hence, there is no need to establish any causality to explain the origin either of individual things or of the universe as a whole.

After a careful analysis of these views it is clear that some thinkers do believe in some sort of positive cause, while there are others who do not believe in any positive cause. As each school of thought faced this problem in its own way, it became very controversial. The following may be said to be some of the points on which the controversy is based: (1) Relation between cause and effect, (2) Identity or difference between the two, (3) Production of an effect out of something which is real, positive, and eternal, or out of mere void, (4) Is an effect only a modification of that which was present in the cause even before the causal operation, or is it entirely different from its cause, and as the effect has no existence prior to the causal operation, is it a new creation? and (5) The cause alone is real and eternal, while the effect is merely illusory. All these factors led to

[5] *Śārīrasthāna,* I.11.
[6] *Buddhacarita,* IX.52.
[7] *Gomaṭasāra,* V.883.

the standpoints of the four main schools, namely, the Nyāya-Vaiśeṣika, the Sāṁkhya, the Śaṅkara Vedānta, and the Mādhyamika school of Buddhism. These points of view are ordinarily called the Ārambhavāda, the Pariṇāmavāda, the Vivartavāda, and the Śūnyavāda respectively. Here in the present article we shall follow the theory of origination (Ārambhavāda) only, for it is this view-point alone which properly represents the nature of the physical world.

According to the theory of origination, there is an absolute difference between a cause and its effect, and the effect is entirely a new and fresh production. But, in spite of this, both are mutually bound together by a mysterious tie of relation, so that as long as the effect lasts it inheres in its cause, and even when it does not exist, as for instance, before its production and after its destruction, its non-existence, in both states, technically called *prāgabhāva* and *dhvaṁsābhāva,* is also attributed to the same cause. It is not possible to give any satisfactory reason for this. The upholders of this view attribute it to the very nature of cause and effect. They hold that the ultimate particles of the four productive elements are the ultimate cause of this world. These particles, through the operation of some conscious agency, combine together so as to form products, which are entirely new and which had no existence prior to their production. Nothing can come into existence without the operation of a cause ; and even in cases where no cause is obvious, it has to be assumed that the cause is hidden from sight (*adṛṣṭa*). In the case of animate beings, ordinarily called Jīvātmans, the differences found in them are neither inherent in them nor are they due to mere chance. These also are due to some cause. In other words, every birth of every animate being necessitates the assumption of a cause that can be traced to its past life alone, and that life in turn depends upon a cause in another previous life, and so on. This leads us to believe in the beginninglessness of this objective world.

### THE LAW OF KARMA AND DIVINE WILL

Tracing the causality of the birth of an animate being we come to the law of Karma. In fact, the birth of an animate being and the creation of the physical world are so closely connected that it is essential to attribute the ultimate causality of the world to the same law of Karma. It is for the sake of providing animate beings with facilities to experience pleasure and pain that the inanimate objects of this universe have been created.[8] In other words, all the inorganic constituents of this world have been created simply to meet the demands of the organic creation. What could have

[8] *Padārtha-dharma-saṅgraha,* pp. 135, 143.

been the aim of creation of the non-conscious objects except that the Jīvas might experience pleasure and pain through them? According to the law of Karma, all actions, mental and physical, bear some fruit that must be experienced by the doer himself. This experiencing of the results of deeds may be effected in one life or in many. But the doer cannot be freed from this until all the results of his actions are exhausted through experience. It is for providing facilities for the experiencing of these results that there exists the physical world with all its constituents.[9] Every time a being takes birth, it comes to this world with a fresh impetus provided by the results of its own deeds which accumulated in the past in the form of impressions (*saṁskāras*), also called *adṛṣṭa, dharma-adharma,* or *apūrva.* When that force with which the being started its fresh life becomes exhausted, the physical organism dies only to recoup itself with fresh energy and a new organism in order to exhaust those results of the past deeds which are still left to be experienced. It is not only that the Jīva reaps the fruits of its own past deeds in a fresh birth, but it also creates for its future experience fresh sets of impressions through the performance of fresh deeds according to the limited freedom which it has. In this way the cycle of births and deaths continues till eternity except in the case of those who realize the final emancipation (*mukti*). Similarly, all the organic productions individually undergo change, and a time comes when all these products, organic and inorganic, come to an end for some time in order to regain fresh energy out of the karmic forces of the past to enable them to function further. This period of universal dissolution is called 'cosmic rest' (*pralaya*). During this period, all the products are reduced to their ultimate particles, called *paramāṇus,* which are regarded as eternal. Besides, we find other eternal elements, such as *manas, ākāśa, kāla, diś,* and the Jīvas, together with their qualities, present during this period.

Accepting the view that nothing is created without the agency of a cause and that there are the karmic forces arising from the past deeds of the Jīvas to act as the cause, the question remains as to how these forces which are non-conscious in nature operate so as to bring about the cosmic world after the period of cosmic rest is over. A causal operation requires the agency of a conscious being who is present even during the period of cosmic rest. The Jīvas are, no doubt, present even then, but they are insensate at that time and so are not capable of imparting any productive motion to the elements to create fresh products. This leads us to believe in the causality of the divine will which is ever present to impart initial motion to the *paramāṇus* for creation. This divine will is influenced in

[9] *Ibid.,* p. 163.

a way by the cumulative *adṛṣṭa* of the Jīvas in imparting the productive motion to the *paramāṇus*. This is how causality leads to the production of motion at the beginning of a fresh creation.[10]

### CHARACTERISTICS OF FORMS OF MATTER

Before we proceed further, it will not be out of place to mention certain common characteristics of the forms of matter constituting the physical world and the special characteristics of the laws of causation and motion. Of the various properties of the forms of matter, the most important seem to be (i) inherent causality, that is, capacity for generating an effect with itself as its cause, (ii) an individual character in each of its ultimate forms which are eternal, and (iii) in its emergent aspect incapability of being destroyed, as an effect, by the cause concerned. Individually earth possesses motion which generates velocity (*vega*),[11] so that when any earthly object moves, it continues to move only because of the velocity inherent in it, which helps the existence of motion in that object for a certain length of time according to the strength of the impetus imparted to that object. The velocity once generated in an earthly object produces a series of motions in succession until the object stops due to gravity (*gurutva*).[12] By nature earth is solid, but under certain conditions when it comes in contact with heat and is reduced to *paramāṇus,* a certain attribute called liquidity is produced in it.[13] Water as a distinct entity possesses all the above-mentioned qualities of earth except that it is not solid by nature and that liquidity is not conditional but natural to it.[14] *Tejas* (heat, fire) also possesses the above-mentioned attributes except gravity. It is due to the lack of gravity that *tejas* always moves upwards. Liquidity is not intrinsic in it.[15] Air possesses oblique or transversal motion.[16] It does not possess gravity, and therefore it does not move downwards; and consequently there is nothing to check its movement, which ever continues to get a fresh impetus from the velocity possessed by it.[17] Of all the elements it is the swiftest.

Coming to the ubiquitous forms of matter constituting the physical world, we should know that these are the forms which are inseparably connected with the objective world as the necessary conditions of the creative process. We know that, according to the theory of origination, after the period of cosmic rest is over, a succession of fresh products comes

[10] *Padārtha-dharma-saṅgraha,* pp. 20 f.
[11] *Vaiśeṣika-Sūtra,* V.1.17; *Padārtha-dharma-saṅgraha,* p. 136.
[12] *Vaiśeṣika-Sūtra,* V.1.18; *Padārtha-dharma-saṅgraha,* p. 133; *Kiraṇāvalī,* p. 37.
[13] *Vaiśeṣika-Sūtra,* II.1.6,7; *Padārtha-dharma-saṅgraha,* p. 135.
[14] *Padārtha-dharma-saṅgraha,* p. 134.
[15] *Vaiśeṣika-Sūtra,* V.2.13.
[16] *Ibid.*
[17] *Padārtha-dharma-saṅgraha,* pp. 18, 19.

into being out of the causal material. The sequence of phenomena observed in creation implies the existence of a factor that is technically known as time or *kāla*. It is held to be a substance, supersensuous, pervasive, and eternal in nature. It is not subjective—a mental construction, as the Yoga believes, nor a specific power associated with the Supreme as the Āgamas affirm, but is objective and substantial in nature, in so far as it is the substrate of a number of qualities. That it is eternal is evident from the fact that it lies behind all worldly processes, creative as well as destructive, which involve succession.[18] This very fact presupposes its all-pervasive character as well. It is regarded as a necessary precondition of every kind of action in the physical world.[19]

With creation, the necessity of having a support for the created objects naturally arises. Objects of limited dimensions can be thought of only in relation to a substance of wider extension that may be said to hold them within it, and this latter substance, again, being similarly related to another of still greater extension, and so on, we come at last to an ultimate substance with infinite extension holding within itself all the limited and partially extended objects of the universe in common. This substance, technically known as *ākāśa* or space, is necessarily a continuum and is therefore eternal.[20] It is regarded as physical space with sound as its specific property.[21]

The last principle, which is inseparably connected with the cosmic order, refers to the relative position involved therein. In other words, it is a fact of common experience that two separate objects of limited dimensions cannot simultaneously occupy the same space. They must occupy separate spaces.[22] These created objects are related to one another, as is evident from the notions of proximity, distance, and so on, and this presupposes the existence of a separate substance technically called *diś*.

These three are the forms of non-conscious elements which form the very background of all creation in this physical world. No production of any object can be explained without these. Hence, though supersensuous in nature, they are dealt with here as being the necessary conditions of creation.

## LAWS OF CREATION AND MOTION

Regarding the characteristics of the law of causation, the only point which needs to be emphasized is that the cause must precede the effect and

[18] *Ibid.*, pp. 26, 27.
[19] *Upaskāra* on *Vaiśeṣika-Sūtra*, V.2.26.
[20] U. Mishra, *Conception of Matter*, p. 161.
[21] *Ibid.*
[22] *Nyāyalīlāvatī* (Nirnayasagara Ed.), p. 34; U. Mishra, *Conception of Matter*, p. 161.

that nothing can be produced without a cause. The effect, though inseparably connected with the cause, is yet entirely different from it and has no existence prior to its production.

It has been pointed out before that for the creation of the objective world motion is most essential. It is equally needed for the destruction of products. Motion, to come into existence, must have as its substrate some material object, though it is also a fact that no product can come into existence without motion. There can be only one motion at a time in one substance.[23] Motion never produces another motion,[24] nor does it produce any substance.[25] It produces an effect marking a particular direction.[26] It produces velocity as well as elasticity.[27] A single motion is produced through several causes, such as, weight, effort, and conjunction. Fluidity, velocity, impression, elasticity, and certain unseen forces also produce motion.[28] These are some of the more important characteristics of the law of motion.

With the help of motion, the ultimate particles representing the material cause begin to group together so as to form various products. The process of creation stops only when the last organic production (*antyāvayavin*) has come into existence. It has to be kept in mind that the motion with which creation begins does not continue for more than a few moments. It gives rise to some other causes which will help the creation further.

### LAWS OF CONSERVATION OF MATTER AND WEIGHT

In this process of change from cause to effect throughout the entire process of creation no material substance is ever lost. The *paramāṇus*, which are the ultimate cause of this world, are eternal. Throughout all the changes from cause to effect, these *paramāṇus* do not change either in number or in any other aspect. They give rise to various products which undergo changes, but they themselves remain unchanged. If any product is destroyed and is reduced to its ultimate particles, it will be found that the number of the *paramāṇus* out of which that object was produced remains as before. In other words, the ultimate matter remains the same throughout the entire process of change. This is what may be called the law of conservation of matter. It is also a fact that the weight of the totality of causes is equal to the weight of the particular effect produced

[23] *Vaiśeṣika-Sūtra,* I.1.17; *Padārtha-dharma-saṅgraha,* p. 147; *Upaskāra,* II.1.21.
[24] *Vaiśeṣika-Sūtra,* I.1.24.
[25] *Vaiśeṣika-Sūtra,* I.1.21; *Padārtha-dharma-saṅgraha,* p. 147.
[26] *Padārtha-dharma-saṅgraha,* p. 147.
[27] *Vaiśeṣika-Sūtra,* I.1.20; *Upaskāra* on the above.
[28] U. Mishra, *Conception of Matter,* pp. 202-205.

out of those causes, which means that in the creation of the physical world the law of conservation of weight also holds good. But this view is not shared by all. In certain cases the products gain in weight. The *Yājñavalkya Smṛti* says, 'Coarse wool and cotton yarn gain 10 per cent in weight in weaving; wool and cotton yarn of middling counts gain 5 per cent and those of the finer counts gain only 3 per cent. But in the case of pure silk (*kauśeya*) and tree-bark, the produced cloth does not gain anything, nor does it lose any weight. Again, in certain products, such as embroidery work, the product loses 30 per cent' (II.179,180). This view is also upheld by Uddyotakara in his *Nyāyavārttika* (II.1.33). From this it is concluded that the law of conservation of weight is believed only partially in Indian thought.

## THE THEORY OF CHEMICAL ACTION

This leads us to say a few words in connection with the theory of chemical action (*pāka-prakriyā*),[29] which is so intimately connected with the laws of change and motion. From our study of the nature of the qualities of the four productive elements of the world, it is clear that all possible changes can occur only in the qualities of earthly particles or products. These changes occur when objects come in contact with heat. This contact takes place only in earthly substances.[30] The earthly particles and products, after having come in contact with heat particles, change their qualities, such as colour, taste, smell, touch, and even sound. This law knows no exception. There is no other cause for producing such a change in their qualities.[31] Other substances, such as water, are not affected by chemical action.[32] It is only through contact with earthly particles that water, for instance, appears to have changed its qualities. But this is not a real change. For instance, water is naturally cool. It appears hot after it is boiled simply because earthly particles mixed with water have become hot due to its contact with heat. Similarly, if there appears any change in the taste, smell, and colour of water, after it has come in contact with heat particles, it is due to the presence of earthly particles in water. As a matter of fact, even after being boiled, water does not give up its natural qualities, such as, colour, taste, touch, and sound.[33] The same is the case with air. It appears hot not because the contact with heat has produced any change in its natural quality, which is neither hot nor

[29] *Padārtha-dharma-saṅgraha*, pp. 46, 47; *Nyāyabodhinī* on the *Tarkasaṅgraha* (Ed. Athalye and Bodas), pp. 16, 17.

[30] *Vyomavatī*, p. 446.

[31] *Ibid.*

[32] *Kiraṇāvalī*, p. 67; *Kiraṇāvalī-prakāśa* (Sarasvatibhavana Sanskrit Series Ed.), p. 267.

[33] *Kiraṇāvalī*, pp. 67, 68; U. Mishra, *Conception of Matter*, pp. 309-311; *Padārthaviveka*, MS. p. 7b; *Dravya-sāra-saṅgraha*, MS. Fol. 66.

cold, but because of the presence of earthly particles in it which have become hot due to the contact. Chemical action is responsible for all possible changes in this physical world where earthly particles and products alone predominate. All our food and drink produce various results according to this process. All growth and decay are attributed to it.

## OTHER CONDITIONS OF CREATION

This is how the products of the physical world proceed. The productive elements, the necessary conditions of creation, and the various laws of the physical world—all aim at one common goal, viz. to provide the Jīvas with the means of *bhoga* (experience), and ultimately, the attainment of final emancipation, which is the highest aim of all the systems. We have seen how the initial motion for creation comes from the divine will. Later, motion is produced from several causes through the agency of conscious beings who have come to exist by that time.

Amongst the more important conditions of creation, it is found that there can be no creation out of one single element.[34] There must be at least two. And these two should not be of the same class, as is quite obvious in the case of human creation.[35] A particular product is classed under one substance or the other on the grounds of the excess of the constituent elements of any one particular substance.

## CLASSIFICATION OF ORGANIC AND INORGANIC PRODUCTS

These products may be classed under two broad heads, namely, organic and inorganic. That class of products, which is the substrate of such activities as tend towards the attainment of what is favourable and liked and abstain from objects that are unwholesome and disliked, is called organic. This is the substratum of sense-organs and is the receptacle of the experiences of pleasure and pain derived through the contact of the sense-organs with the objects outside. It is through this kind of product that life and consciousness find their manifestations. It is in such organism that growth and the healing of wounds occur.

This organic production is generally divided into four heads: *jarāyuja* (viviparous), *aṇḍaja* (oviparous), *udbhijja* (germinating), and *śvedaja* (generated by heat and moisture). Of these, the first are born of the placenta, like man and beast; the second are born of eggs, like birds and reptiles; the third break through the earth, like trees; and the fourth are born of heat and moisture, like some small worms and insects. All these organisms come to possess life which manifests itself through them after the

[34] *Nyāya-Sūtra* with *bhāṣya,* III.2.65.
[35] U. Mishra, *Conception of Matter,* p. 268.

various productive elements have combined under the influence of the karmic force of the Jīva.

The inorganic product is that which does not possess any of the above-mentioned qualities. It is called *jaḍa*. In spite of the vital difference between these two types of products, as far as their production is concerned, the process is the same.

### MIND AND CONSCIOUSNESS

This completes the brief account of the nature of the physical world. *Manas* is not included directly in this, but as it helps the clear understanding of the nature of the world it has been introduced here. We have seen that the ultimate aim of this world is to provide *bhoga* for conscious beings. This *bhoga* is possible through the help of *manas* and not otherwise. *Manas* is atomic in size and is attached to every conscious organism separately. It is eternal and is the only factor which distinguishes one Jīva from another. It is the cause of all cognition. It is non-*bhautika,* and as such it has the quickest possible motion. As long as *manas* remains in an organism, so long that organism is alive, and as soon as it leaves the organism that organism is dead. Being eternal, it remains attached to every Jīva even during the state of cosmic rest. But it does not produce any cognition during that period for want of an organism.

Similarly, though the *cetana* element does not directly form part of the physical world, yet its presence cannot be overlooked. For, to supply the Jīvas with their objects of enjoyment, according to their deserts, is the ultimate purpose of the physical world.

# 31

## NATURE OF MIND AND ITS ACTIVITIES

MIND in the Indian philosophical systems is uniquely, though variously, conceived. The difficulty in appreciating the views they inculcate is due to the fact that their approach is entirely different from that of Western philosophy and psychology. In Indian philosophy, mind is different from soul (Jīva) and self (Ātman). But rarely do we come across such a view in the history of Western philosophy. Even during the ancient and mediaeval periods, when the conception of soul dominated over that of mind, never do we come across a system which regards mind as different from soul. The concept of mind as such belongs to the modern period of Western philosophy, in which the idea of soul as such has been relegated to the limbo, and in which mind is not an addition to, but a substitute for, soul, and is divested of all the mythological associations which the other had. Even then it does not exactly correspond to mind as conceived in Indian philosophy. Most schools of Indian philosophy propound three entities, namely, *buddhi* (intelligence or knowledge), *ahaṅkāra* (ego), and *manas* (mind), all of which in some way or other belong to Ātman (self). But mind in Western philosophy is an all-inclusive term connoting all the three entities besides Ātman. Although the Indian schools expound the relation between the four terms differently, none of them treats self (Ātman) as identical with mind (*manas*). The only philosophy that does not draw this distinction is Buddhism, which does not affirm the existence of Ātman. Further, Ātman is not the personality of Western psychology, for while this treats personality as an empirical product, Ātman is non-empirical. What corresponds in Indian philosophy to personality in Western psychology is *ahaṅkāra* (ego) or Jīva (soul), with its accumulated experience. We may therefore say that the 'mind' of Western psychology roughly corresponds in Indian philosophy to *buddhi, ahaṅkāra,* and *manas,* taken together and often called *antaḥkaraṇa* or inner sense.

### MIND IN THE UPANIṢADS

The Upaniṣads contain speculations about the nature of mind, which form the basis of the psychological doctrines of the systems that developed out of them. Even Buddhism and Jainism were not uninfluenced by the Upaniṣadic thought, though they rejected the authority of the Vedas.

The question, how mind (*manas*) is formed in Ātman, is not discussed in the Upaniṣads. We get some mythological stories of the formation of the individual (Jīvātman). In the *Kaṭha Upaniṣad,* we read that the knowledge of the world of sense is due to an externalizing process of Ātman, and is not the truth (IV.I). The same Upaniṣad says that objects are higher than the senses, *manas* higher than the objects, *buddhi* (intelligence) higher than *manas, mahat ātman* (cosmic person or cosmic intelligence) higher than *buddhi, avyakta* (unmanifest) higher than *mahat,* and Puruṣa higher than *avyakta.* Thus the externalizing process takes place from Puruṣa down to the senses, and Ātman can be realized only by a corresponding internalizing process (III.10,11). The *Kaṭha* account of *manas* was utilized in some Advaitic texts to deny the sense character of *manas* which is higher than the senses. But what we call mind includes both *manas* and *buddhi* of the *Kaṭha* psychology, and *buddhi* is a stage lower than *mahat ātman.*

The *Aitareya Upaniṣad* gives the following as the names (*nāma-dheyāni*) of *manas*: *saṁjñāna, ājñāna, vijñāna, prajñāna, medhas, dṛṣṭi, dhṛti, mati, manīṣā, jūti, smṛti, saṅkalpa, kratu, asu, kāma,* and *vaśa.* These are really the functions of *manas.* They may be translated as determinate knowledge, feeling of lordship, differential cognition, intelligence, wisdom, insight, fortitude, deliberation, thoughtfulness, impulse, memory, resolution, purpose, feeling of life, desire, and passion for the opposite sex (V.2). The *Bṛhadāraṇyaka Upaniṣad* gives the following functions of *manas*: *kāma* or desire for women etc., *saṅkalpa* or judgement, *vicikitsā* or doubt, *śraddhā* or faith, *aśraddhā* or disbelief, *dhṛti* or fortitude, *adhṛti* or unsteadiness, *hrī* or modesty, *dhī* or intelligence, and *bhī* or fear (I.5.3).[1] Some of these functions appear as independent categories in the *Chāndogya Upaniṣad* (VII.3.1f.).

Besides the word *manas,* the word *citta* also is used in this Upaniṣad. It is explained by some commentators as the *vṛtti* (function) that grasps the purposiveness of things by knowing the class to which they belong (*Chā. U.,* VII.5.1). *Citta* is what understands the pragmatic value of things. It has obviously little to do with the *citta* of the Buddhist Vijñānavādins.

## MIND IN ADVAITA VEDĀNTA

Mind, in the Advaita, the most important of the Vedāntic systems, is the internal organ (*antaḥkaraṇa*). The external organs are instruments of either action or perception. Hands, feet, etc. are organs of activity;

[1] For a more detailed treatment of Upaniṣadic psychology, see the author's articles, 'The Psychology of the *Bṛhadāraṇyaka Upaniṣad*', *The Journal of Oriental Researches,* June 1946, and 'Mind in Upaniṣadic Psychology', *The Vedanta Kesari,* May 1948.

eye, ear, etc. are organs of sense perception. The five sense-organs have as their objects sight, hearing, touch, taste, and smell. Mind is capable of establishing contact with all the external organs. The entire apparatus of the internal organ consists of four divisions: *manas, buddhi, ahaṅkāra,* and *citta.* The function of *manas* is doubting (whether the object is X or Y), of *buddhi* is determining (that it is X), of *citta* is recollecting, and of *ahaṅkāra* is the attribution of experience to the ego. Some clue to these functions may be given by saying that *buddhi* makes a cognition determinate by fixing it to be such and such, and *citta* brings it into an apperceptive mass by bringing it into an ordered whole. *Ahaṅkāra* is the 'I' or sense of mineness that accompanies this process. We are here reminded of Kant's theory of the ego as synthetic unity of apperception; but we should not equate one or all of these processes to it. The Advaitins often include *ahaṅkāra* in *manas* and *citta* in *buddhi,* and divide *antaḥkaraṇa* into *buddhi* and *manas* only.[2]

The operations of these functions are called *vṛttis.* In perceiving an object, *manas* takes on the form of the object, and cognition is the awareness of this *vṛtti.* We may say that *manas,* working through the senses, comes into contact with the object, takes on its form, and offers it to *buddhi,* which, in its turn, offers it to *citta*; and *ahaṅkāra* finally appropriates the form as its own perception.

This process naturally implies that *manas* is *vibhu* (all-pervading). The Advaita says that, otherwise, objects at a distance could not be grasped by *manas.* There is another reason why it should be all-pervading. *Manas,* as the *Kaṭha* says, is the *prius* or source of the senses and their objects, and consequently it should pervade all of them. But then why does it not know all the objects always? It could have done so; but it itself is a product of the unconscious Māyā, and so is overwhelmed by ignorance. It can know the objects only when Māyā permits it to know them. This unconscious energy (*śakti*) is of two kinds: *āvaraṇa śakti* or the energy that conceals and *vikṣepa śakti* or the energy that projects. *Āvaraṇa śakti* conceals the real nature of every thing from *manas*; but *vikṣepa śakti* projects the objects and the corresponding forms of *manas,* which then becomes aware of the objects. Māyā of the individual mind is a part of Māyā of the cosmic mind; and hence the objects seen by different minds can be common objects.

Though *manas* is all-pervasive, it is not static but dynamic. It is *cañcala* or unsteady and is always on the move. The peculiarity of the Advaita doctrine is that these divisions of *antaḥkaraṇa* are not qualities

[2] *Ātmānātmaviveka* of Śaṅkara in the *Minor Works of Śaṅkara,* IV, edited by Bhagavat.

but entities. For instance, *buddhi* or intelligence is not a quality or state of *manas,* but an entity *sui generis.* Perhaps, our acquaintance with the modern doctrine of the different levels of reality as emergent qualities may enable us to appreciate the Advaita view. What used to be a fundamental difference between substance and quality no longer holds now. For what was regarded by earlier philosophers as substance is now understood as a new form of process or a new emergent quality. So whether *buddhi* etc. are treated as substances or as qualities may not be a very important question to the modern student. Yet the Advaitin has a definite objection against treating *buddhi* etc. as qualities of *manas* (mind).

The nature of *vṛtti* is a sort of agitation (*saṁkṣobha*), out of which are produced projections of objects, perceptions, etc. Desire (*icchā*), memory (*smṛti*), etc. are attributed to *manas.*

## MIND IN VIŚIṢṬĀDVAITA

While the Advaita Vedānta regards *buddhi* as an entity, as a subject and not as a predicate, as a substance and not as an attribute, the Viśiṣṭādvaita of Rāmānuja treats it as a *dharma* or quality. Knowledge is called *dharmabhūtajñāna* (knowledge as quality). According to Rāmānuja, there is no knowledge which is *dharmin* or subject. Among its synonyms are *jñāna, saṁvit, buddhi, upalabdhi,* etc. Here the Viśiṣṭādvaita differs from the Advaita which treats *buddhi* as a *dharmin.* But curiously enough, the former system calls all the four entities, Jīva (soul), Īśvara (God), *dharmabhūtajñāna,* and *śuddhasattva* (pure *sattva*) by the name *jñāna.*[3] Further, this *dharmabhūtajñāna* is regarded as the chief *svarūpadharma* (natural attribute) of Īśvara, who is the *dharmin* possessing that property. What we have to note is that, even according to the Advaita, *cit* or *jñāna* is a *svarūpalakṣaṇa* (natural attribute) of Brahman as distinct from its *taṭasthalakṣaṇa* (accidental quality); yet this system would treat a *svarūpalakṣaṇa* as part of the substance of Brahman, but not as an attribute distinct from its substance. Thus, though both the systems treat *jñāna* as an essential attribute of Brahman, the Advaita treats it as forming the substantial essence also of Brahman.

Īśvara and Jīva become the knowers, agents of action, enjoyers, etc. by virtue of *dharmabhūtajñāna.* Pleasure, pain, desire, will, impressions and instincts, fear, shame, intelligence, merit, demerit, emotions, sentiments (*rasas*), in fact, everything that is internal except Ātman and *manas,* are states and forms of *dharmabhūtajñāna.* For instance, pleasure is agreeable *jñāna,* and pain is disagreeable *jñāna.*

[3] *Darśanodaya,* p. 210.

All cognitions arise through contact of *manas,* through the senses, with objects on the one side and through contact of *manas* with Ātman on the other. *Jñāna* is relational. The relation is of the form of contact in the case of substances; in the case of non-substantial entities, it is of the form of the basis contacted (*saṁyuktāśrayaṇa*). It may be asked how there can be contact in the case of objects belonging to the future and the past; for there can be no relation when one of the terms to be related does not exist. But the Viśiṣṭādvaitins say that all things are eternal, even past and future things exist; and so there can be the required relation. Even with regard to things belonging to far-off places and times, as mind can fly with infinite speed, contact is possible. With regard to objects of memory, the relation works through the impressions left on the mind.

*Manas* is posited as common to all the senses. Each sense perceives only one kind of objects—the eye, colours and forms; the ear, sounds; the nose, smells; and so on. But often these objects have to be co-ordinated and unified, and then they have to be presented to Ātman for final perception. In order to perform this process, there must be something other than the senses and Ātman; and that is *manas.*[4] Cognition arises when *manas* comes into contact with Ātman.

All perception, according to Rāmānuja, is determinate (*savikalpaka*). On this point, he differs from the Nyāya which accepts an indeterminate (*nirvikalpaka*) stage prior to the determinate and holds that when *manas* and the senses first come into contact with the object, a mere 'that' is cognized and the 'what' is known only later.

### MIND IN THE PŪRVA-MĪMĀṀSĀ

The theory of mind, according to the Pūrva-Mīmāṁsā, differs from that according to the Advaita. In general, it accepts the Naiyāyika position. The two leading exponents of the Mīmāṁsā are Prabhākara and Kumārila. According to Prabhākara, *manas* is a substance (*dravya*), atomic (*aṇu*), eternal, and extremely mobile. Kumārila, like Prabhākara, treats *manas* as an organ (*indriya, karaṇa*), but, according to him, it is never operative apart from the body.

Unlike the Advaita, which treats *antaḥkaraṇa* as being composed of four divisions, the Mīmāṁsā as a whole treats it as composed of only one entity, *manas.* Contact between *manas* and Ātman is external. Further, Ātman is the same as *ahaṅkāra* or ego.

The followers of Prabhākara give us an interesting analysis of volition. It consists of the following steps: 'The consciousness of something to be

[4] *Ibid.,* p. 208.

done (*kāryatājñāna*), which implies the consciousness that it can be done (*kṛtisādhyatājñāna*), volition (*pravṛtti*), motor reaction (*ceṣṭā*), and the act (*kriyā*)'.[5]

## MIND IN THE SĀṂKHYA AND ALLIED SCHOOLS

The Sāṁkhya account of mind is akin to that of the Advaita. Mind is called *antaḥkaraṇa* or inner organ, and consists of only three divisions, *buddhi, ahaṅkāra,* and *manas.* No place is given to *citta,* as in the Advaita, and *buddhi* is made to perform its duty also. Curiously enough, *manas* is called an *indriya* or organ, the number of *indriyas* thereby becoming eleven instead of ten. The reason for treating *manas* as an *indriya* is that, like the other *indriyas,* it has a special function to perform, namely, perceiving *sukha* (pleasure) and *duḥkha* (pain).

Ātman or Puruṣa is different from *antaḥkaraṇa,* and is pure *cit* or consciousness. *Antaḥkaraṇa* is due to the reflection of Ātman in Prakṛti, which is composed of three *guṇas* (constituents, elemental phases)—*sattva* (purity, quiescence), *rajas* (activity, agitation), and *tamas* (insensibility, stupefaction). These three *guṇas* can be appreciated if we compare them to *buddhi, vikṣepa śakti,* and *āvaraṇa śakti* of the Advaita. Now, owing to the reflection of Puruṣa in Prakṛti, the equilibrium of the three *guṇas* is disturbed, and the evolution of the world begins. The detailed process is: out of Prakṛti comes *mahat* or *buddhi,* out of *buddhi* comes *ahaṅkāra,* out of *ahaṅkāra* comes *manas* and the ten organs of sense and action, and the five *tanmātras* (subtle elements), and out of these subtle elements the world of five gross elements (*mahābhūtas*). *Ahaṅkāra* is of three kinds: the *sāttvika* called *vaikṛta,* out of which the eleven organs issue forth, the *tāmasika* called *bhūtādi,* out of which the subtle elements evolve, and the *rājasika* called *taijasa,* which participates in both the processes.

*Manas* is regarded as both an organ of sense and an organ of action, for the reason that it directs the activities of both kinds of organs.[6]

The function of *buddhi* is determining and willing (*adhyavasāya*). It has two aspects, the *sāttvika* and the *tāmasika.* To the former are due merit (*dharma*), intelligence (*jñāna*), dispassion (*vairāgya*), and lordship (*aiśvarya*); and to the latter their opposites. The function of *manas* is reflection and perceptual individuation. What is at first perceived as a mere 'that' is later perceived as a 'what', with the help of the peculiarities and the class concept. That is, *manas* renders indeterminate knowledge determinate. The senses give only indeterminate knowledge (*ālocana-mātra*). Though *buddhi, manas,* and *ahaṅkāra* have their own specific

[5] Dr. Ganganath Jha, *Pūrva-Mīmāṁsā in its Sources.*
[6] *Sāṁkhya-tattva-kaumudī,* 27.

functions to perform, they have a common function also, namely, the five *prāṇas* or life processes.

All the mental processes, *buddhi, ahaṅkāra, manas,* and the senses can operate either simultaneously or in succession, in the case of perceptible things. In the case of imperceptible things, as in inference, the first three occur only after the cognition of a perceptible object.

It should be noted that the derivation of *manas* from *ahaṅkāra* is the same in the Vaiṣṇava (Pāñcarātra) and Śaiva (Pāśupata) and Śākta Āgamas. The only difference is that the Sāṁkhya opposes Puruṣa to Prakṛti out of which mind issues, while the Āgamas trace both Puruṣa and Prakṛti to a higher source.

The account of mind as given by the Yoga system need not be presented separately, as it differs little from that given by the Sāṁkhya.

## MIND IN THE NYĀYA-VAIŚEṢIKA SCHOOL

The Nyāya and Vaiśeṣika systems, like the Sāṁkhya and the Yoga, are generally hyphenated and treated together. Unlike the Advaita, these four schools do not think that bliss, happiness, pleasure, etc. belong to the essential nature of Ātman. Ātman is, according to the Upaniṣads, *sat* (existence), *cit* (consciousness), and *ānanda* (bliss). So every form of happiness or pleasure, the Advaita maintains, should be derived from the *ānanda* of Ātman. But according to the Sāṁkhya, happiness is a *sāttvika* aspect of *buddhi* ; and as *buddhi* does not belong to the essence of Ātman, happiness should not be regarded as belonging to it. Ātman is essentially consciousness (*cit*), and the consciousness of *buddhi* is therefore due to the reflection of the consciousness of Ātman in it. The Nyāya and the Vaiśeṣika accept the Sāṁkhya view of happiness ; but they contend that consciousness also cannot belong to the essence of Ātman. *Buddhi* for them is not a distinct entity, but an adventitious quality, which Ātman obtains when it comes into contact with *manas.* Whatever objection there is to the attribution of *ānanda* to Ātman holds also against attributing consciousness to it. The Advaita, however, contends that just as *buddhi,* according to Sāṁkhya, becomes conscious by reflecting the consciousness of Ātman, so also it becomes bliss by reflecting its *ānanda* ; to be *sāttvika* means to be pure, and anything can be reflected only when the reflecting material is pure.

According to the Nyāya-Vaiśeṣika, Ātman has fourteen qualities: *buddhi* (knowledge), *sukha* (pleasure), *duḥkha* (pain), *icchā* (desire), *dveṣa* (hatred), *yatna* (striving), *saṅkhyā* (number), *parimiti* (size), *pṛthaktva* (distinctness), *saṁyoga* (contact), *vibhāga* (separation), *bhāvanā* (imagination, impression), *dharma* (merit), and *adharma* (demerit).

Ātman comes to have knowledge when it comes into contact with *manas,* which is atomic (*aṇu*). Both are substances (*dravyas*) or objects of valid knowledge (*prameya*). *Antaḥkaraṇa* consists of *manas* only.[7] The attributes of *manas* are: *paratva* (proximity), *aparatva* (distance), *saṁyoga* (contact), *viyoga* (separation), *pṛthaktva* (distinctness), *parimiti* (size), *saṅkhyā* (number), and *vega* (speed). Ātman presides over the activities of body and *manas.* The objects cognized by *manas* are *sukha* (pleasure), *duḥkha* (pain), *icchā* (desire), *dveṣa* (hatred), *mati* (knowledge), and *kṛti* (activity).

Though *manas* is atomic, it works with infinite speed, and hence are the apparent simultaneity of cognitions and the co-ordinating process of mind made possible. Otherwise, if *manas* be all-pervasive, all things would be known at all times simultaneously, and what is perceived as pain or pleasure at one part of the body would be cognized as such throughout the whole body.

*Buddhi* is of two kinds, experience and memory. Experience (*anubhava*) is again of four kinds, perception, inference, analogy, and word (verbal knowledge). Perception is of six kinds, perceptions of the five senses and of *manas* (*sukha* etc.). The senses as well as *manas* can perceive the respective substances, their qualities, the universals subsisting in them both, and other abstract entities like negation connected with both. All manifest (*udbhūta*) forms are perceived by the eye ; it perceives all substances possessing those forms, and also contact, separation, nearness, distance, oiliness (*sneha*), and liquidity, when they have size. It sees activity (*karma*), universals, and inherence (*samavāya*) also. But *āloka* (light) and *udbhūtarūpa* (manifest form) are the indispensable conditions for its perception. The skin (*tvac*) perceives manifest (*udbhūta*) touch, manifest form, and substances possessing them. Similarly, the other senses perceive their respective objects.

In all cases of perception, contact of *manas* with skin is a common indispensable factor. For in deep sleep, when *manas* loses this contact, no cognition arises.

Knowledge is of two kinds, *nirvikalpaka* (indeterminate) and *savikalpaka* (determinate). All knowledge originating through the senses is of the second sort. When, for instance, a pot (*ghaṭa*) is known, the pot shines in knowledge as a form (*prakāra*) of the latter. *Prakāra* is also called *viśeṣaṇa* (attribute). Of the pot in knowledge, again, potness (*ghaṭatva*) is the *prakāra* or *viśeṣaṇa.* Thus, there is a *prakāra* within *prakāra, viśeṣaṇa* of *viśeṣaṇa.* The second *viśeṣaṇa* is called *viśeṣaṇatāvacchedaka* (the

[7] *Nyāyamañjarī* (Vizianagram Sanskrit Series), p. 491.

peculiarity or specific mark of the *viśeṣaṇa*). Now, in indeterminate knowledge, this second *viśeṣaṇa* is absent. And the Nyāya-Vaiśeṣika school never accepts any cognition of a concrete thing as a cognition unless it possesses the second *viśeṣaṇa*. It is thought unnecessary only in the case of the cognition of universals and other abstract entities (*jātyakhaṇḍo-pādhyatirikta*).

Cognition is, again, of two kinds, false and true. Both involve the element of certainty (*niścayātmika*). It has been said that every cognition involves a *prakāra* (form, determination). Now, falsity is that cognition from which the *prakāra*, though perceived, is factually absent; and truth is that where it is factually present.[8] Falsity is due to some defect (*doṣa*) in the instruments and processes of cognition, and truth due to some specific good quality in the same. For instance, the presence of bile in the eyes makes one see all things yellow. The specific good quality in perception is the contact of the *viśeṣya* with the *viśeṣaṇatva*, for instance, the *ghaṭa* with its *prakāra* (*ghaṭatva*); in inference, *parāmarśa* or knowledge of reason (*hetu* or *liṅga*) as distinguished by invariable concomitance (*vyāpti*) with the major term (*sādhya*) and by being the property of a locus (*pakṣa*) of the minor term; in analogy, the perception of similarity in the right thing; and in verbal knowledge, correct cognition of *yogyatā* (compatibility of the meanings of words) and *tātparya* (intended meaning of the whole sentence).

Indeterminate knowledge is neither true nor false, because it has no *prakāratā* and is unrelated and unconnected.

The Naiyāyika theory that truth is due to some specific quality in the factors of cognition is often controverted. For though, in the case of false cognition, some wrong working of the senses and *manas* or the presence of an extraneous factor like bile can be accepted, true cognition is always due to the normal working of the senses and mind, and nothing extraneous is responsible for truth.

In doubt (*saṁśaya*), two *prakāras* along with *prakāras* of their negations are present. Thus doubt contains four *prakāras*.[9] Certainty (*niścaya*) is that cognition in which a *prakāra* is present, but in which the *prakāra* of its negation is absent. For instance, when we doubt whether the object at a distance is a man (*nara*) or a pillar (*sthāṇu*), in that cognition *naratva* (man-ness) and *sthāṇutva* (pillar-ness) along with not-man and not-pillar respectively are present. Not-man is present because of pillar-ness, and not-pillar because of man-ness. But when we are certain that the object is a man, even though it were a case of illusion, in that cognition man-ness only is present, but not not-man. The Naiyāyikas here give a very good

[8] *Tadabhāvavati tatprakārakaṁ jñānaṁ bhramaḥ,* and *tadbhāvavati pramā.*
[9] See commentary *Prabhā* on *Siddhānta-muktāvalī,* 129.

analysis, both psychological and logical, of doubt and its difference from certainty.

The Naiyāyikas treat recognition (*pratyabhijñā*) as a single act of cognition, but the Buddhists treat it as a combination of perception and memory. Again, for the former, *smṛti* or memory is not a valid means of cognition (*pramāṇa*), for a thing remembered may be non-existent. But the Mīmāṁsakas treat *smṛti* as valid, because Smṛtis are forms of verbal testimony. Smṛtis are remembered treatises and are authoritative, second only to the Vedas.

The Buddhists and some of the Vedāntins maintain that happiness (*sukha*), misery (*duḥkha*), etc. are different forms of knowledge (*jñāna*). But the Naiyāyikas do not accept this view.[10] Cognition takes in the form of the object; but the object is not the same as the cognition. We have cognition of happiness; and happiness here is an object of cognition, but is not the cognition itself. Our experience of the difference between the two cannot be explained away.

The Nyāya-Vaiśeṣika doctrine of striving (*yatna*) is of interest. It is of three kinds: *pravṛtti* or striving for a thing, *nivṛtti* or withdrawing from a thing, and *jīvanakāraṇa* or life-process, which is the cause of the functioning of the *prāṇas* and corresponds to the *conatus* of Spinoza.[11]

### MIND IN BUDDHISM

Like the Yoga philosophy and the Āgamas, Buddhist literature contains a large amount of psychological material. As already mentioned, it has no conception of *manas* apart from *buddhi, citta,* or *vijñāna.* Some of the Buddhists denied the reality of Ātman, and others remained indifferent to the question of its existence. Buddha himself kept silent over the question. However, the Buddhists subjected human personality, which they called *pudgala,* to a very minute analysis. They regarded it as composed of five *skandhas* (aggregates): *rūpaskandha* or the aggregate of matter, *vedanāskandha* or the aggregate of feeling, *saṁjñāskandha* or the aggregate of concepts, *saṁskāraskandha* or the aggregate of latent forces like instincts, and *vijñānaskandha* or the aggregate of consciousness. Everything except *rūpaskandha* is mental. Personality is just an aggregate of aggregates.

Mind arises out of *bhavaṅga* (being), which is mind in sound sleep (*vīthimuttacitta*). *Bhavaṅguppacceda,* the boundary between being and thought, is called the threshold of mind (*manodvāra*).

The *cetasikas* (mental properties) are of two kinds, good and bad. Each of the two, again, is of two kinds, universal and specific. There

[10] *Nyāyamañjarī,* pp. 74 f.
[11] For a detailed discussion, see commentaries on *Siddhānta-muktāvalī,* 150.

are seven universal good mental properties: contact (*phassa*), feeling (*vedanā*), perception (*saññā*), volition (*cetanā*), oneness of object (*ekāggatā*), psychic life (*jīvitindriya*), and attention (*manasikāra*). Contact is just awareness of an object such as colour or smell. It corresponds to *ālocana-mātra* of the Sāṁkhya. *Vedanā* is the feeling of being agreeably affected. Perception is the awareness of a physical object occupying space etc. *Cetanā* is willing, which, under favourable conditions, results in action. *Ekāggatā* is the process of individuating the object, i.e. perceiving it as one individual. *Jīvitindriya* is the whole psychic state, infusing life into one and all of these processes. *Manasikāra* is attention to the object.

The specific good mental properties are six: *vitakka* or the process of directing concomitant properties towards the object, *vicāra* or the process of continually exercising the mind on the object, *adhimokkha* or the process of freely choosing to attend to an object (that is, selecting the object for perception), *viriya* or the energy at the back of conation, *pīti* or interest in the object, and *chanda* or intention to act with regard to the object.

There are four universal and two specific properties (*cetasikas*) which are bad. The former are *moha* or delusion, *ahirika* or shamelessness, *ano-ttappa* or remorselessness, and *uddhacca* or distraction which is opposed to attention. The latter are *lobha* or greed, and *diṭṭhi* or error or erroneous view.

*Vīthi* is the order of thought (*cittaniyama*). There are three phases of thought: genesis (*uppāda*), development (*thiti*), and dissolution (*bhaṅga*), each phase occupying one instant. When an object enters the field of presentation, it produces a vibration in *bhavaṅga* (being). Then the faculty of reflection or mind proper (*manodvārāvajjana*) arises and the vibration is arrested. This reflection is then followed by apperception (*javana*), after which thought loses itself again in *bhavaṅga*. Then another sense object can enter into consciousness. Thus every object enters into consciousness at a nascent instant of being (*atītabhavaṅga*). Now, when the vibration by an object is checked, mind turns towards one of the five senses, and visual sensation (*cakkhuviññāna*), for example, comes into play. This sense operation is followed by a moment of reception called *sampaṭicchana*. Next, the investigating faculty comes into operation, and momentary examination of the object (*santīraṇa*) is made. Afterwards comes the determining or the fixing process (*voṭṭhapana*), which arranges the material into a definite object. After this comes the apperceptive (*javana*) process, and cognition becomes complete. Then follows the registering (*tadārammaṇa*) stage, in which the object apperceived remains identified for two moments.

All the above processes take place when the object is perceived vividly.

But when the vibration is weak and slow, cognition falls short of completion at one stage or another.

In the above process, not only the mind and senses but also physical objects are involved. So it is not *suddhamanodvāra* (purely mental). But there is a *suddhamanodvāra-vīthi* also. Mind can reflect on objects once seen, heard, etc., and also upon *a priori* entities developed by thinking (*viññāta* objects). Imagination, images (*uggaha*), fancy (*paṭilakkhaṇa-vīthi*), after-images (*paṭibhāga*), apperception, different forms of *jhāna* (concentration), dreams, etc. belong to this *vīthi*.[12]

### MIND IN JAINISM

The Jaina philosophy, like the orthodox schools, distinguishes between Ātman and *manas* ; and though it treats the latter as the *antaḥkaraṇa* of the former, it calls it *anindriya* (non-sense-organ), as, unlike the sense-organs which are limited to their own particular field of knowledge, this apprehends the objects given by all sense-organs. But it is more interested in studying the nature of Jīva or soul, which it equates with the Ātman of the Upaniṣads, than in discussing the nature of *manas*. So we get little information as to how *manas* is formed.

Somehow, Jīva comes into contact with body, speech, and *manas*. This contact is called *yoga* (union), which is the same as *āsrava* (flow). In other words, activity (*karma*) of body, speech, and *manas* is *yoga*, and cessation of this activity is liberation.

The conception of *manas* in Jainism is peculiar in that it is neither a single function nor a single entity. The name is given to two different things, *dravyamanas* or substantial *manas* and *bhāvamanas* or ideal *manas*. The former is matter or *pudgala*, and the latter is the same as *jñāna* or *buddhi* and so belongs to Ātman. Thus there is a material as well as a spiritual *manas*.

Knowledge is of five kinds: *mati* or knowledge of objects obtained through *manas* and the senses, *śruta* or that obtained through hearing (verbal knowledge), *avadhi* or fixed and determinate knowledge of things distant in space and time (the difference between the first and this seems to be that, though both are ordinary, senses and *manas* are involved in the former but not in the latter), *manaḥparyāya* or knowledge of other minds, and *kevala* or extra-normal perceptions.[13]

It is only in recent times that the question of extra-sensory perception

[12] For details, see Aung and Rhys Davids, *Compendium of Philosophy*. Stcherbatsky's *Central Conception of Buddhism* differs slightly in details. See also *Abhidharma-kośa*. Rhys Davids, *The Buddhist Manual of Psychological Ethics* may also be consulted.

[13] *Tattvārthādhigama-Sūtra* of Umāsvati, and Kundakunda's *Pravacanasāra*.

has cropped up in Western psychology, thanks to the activity of various psychical research societies. But the problem of extraordinary perception, extending to omniscience, is a very old one in Indian psychology. The Cārvākas naturally denied its existence, and the Mīmāṁsakas, who reserved this type of knowledge for Vedic injunctions only, severely criticized the Jaina theory that omniscience dawns after all *karma* matter has been destroyed. But all other systems, both orthodox and heterodox, believed in supernormal perception through the attainment of new dimensions by the mind. This is acquired by the practice of austerities, intense meditation, and, according to theistic systems, the grace of God. This includes not only hyperaesthesia of different kinds (clairvoyance, clairaudience, etc.), but also direct knowledge of the thoughts of other minds and of events in all parts of space and all dimensions of time. The supernormal knowledge is of the order of higher immediacy in which the mind is completely dominated, except of course in Buddhism, by the self that has attained equanimity through concentration and conquest of disturbing emotions and banishment of evil impulses. Whether as *yogi-pratyakṣa* (ecstatic vision) or as *ārṣajñāna* (intuition) or as *prātibhajñāna* (telepathy), direct knowledge other than sensory is available to man without the mediation of the sense-organs. The Jains denied that the mind had anything to do with such extension of knowledge and ascribed to the operation of the self the *avadhi, manaḥparyāya,* and *kevala* types of knowledge; but other systems, while recognizing that ordinary mentation was insufficient for extraordinary perception, did not deny the operation of *manas* in such knowledge and only emphasized the need of cultivating the moral and spiritual conditions for attaining it. If nescience and restricted knowledge are due to moral and spiritual limitations, these must be overcome to expand the operation of the mind to cover supersensuous things.

## 32

# EXTRA-SENSORY AND SUPERCONSCIOUS EXPERIENCES

### STUDY OF THE TOTAL MIND

STUDY of the total mind (conscious, unconscious, and superconscious) is the special interest of Indian psychology. Until the turn of the century, Western psychologists mainly studied the conscious states of mind; but for the last fifty years many of them have been interested in the unconscious states. Philosophers like Leibnitz, Schopenhauer, and E. von Hartmann had shared this interest earlier, and there had been traces of it in Plato. Indian psychologists have always laid great emphasis on the understanding of not merely the conscious, but also the various kinds of superconscious and extra-sensory perceptions. They have not been mere objective observers and speculative thinkers, so far as psychology is concerned, but they have also realized that the various states of mind cannot be properly understood without bringing in the subjective element, namely, training of the perceiving mind. They have never been inclined toward behaviourism of the Western type. In order to understand the objective validity of the superconscious and other forms of extra-sensory perceptions (and in order to know the unconscious) one must experience these states. Indian psychologists have also realized that verification of the different experiences is the best criterion of their validity. So, in their study and exploration, they have evolved methods of developing various extra-sensory experiences and superconscious realization.

It is an undeniable fact that the main emphasis of Indian psychology has been on religious experiences of various types (though some non-theistic systems were developed in the process of self-analysis). Both Hindu and Buddhist psychologists systematized their psychological concepts in the course of their religious experiences. As their investigation and development of mental powers progressed, they discovered that the unified mind could have some experiences which were not religious, even though they were extraordinary and extra-sensory. The mind, when concentrated and trained, develops tremendous power to understand and control the various gross and subtle laws of nature, though these may not be perceived with the naked eyes, just as the radiation of cosmic rays cannot be perceived. We can understand both the existence of cosmic rays and mental functioning by their effects. The mind can also control these laws through definite discipline and training.[1] Indian psychologists have not only recognized the existence of such powers, but they have also developed various methods of manifesting them. *Yoga-Sūtra* by Patañjali, *Haṭhayoga-pradīpikā,* and various Tantras like *Ṣaṭcakranirūpaṇa* and *Pādukāpañcaka* are thoroughgoing studies of various aspects of extra-sensory perception, in which different methods of developing these powers are described. Although these powers cannot be called spiritual, it cannot be denied that they are real functions of the human mind.

## EXTRA-SENSORY EXPERIENCES

Some individuals in India have been credited with the power of controlling many natural laws by psycho-physical means. There are also cases of *piśācasiddhi* and *vetālasiddhi* in which adepts are supposed to maintain a certain amount of control over departed souls and other subtle-bodied beings through different types of mental practices. In the West, such persons are called mediums. These powers can be placed in various groups—*siddhis, abhijñās, vibhūtis,* and *aiśvaryas.* The Buddhists call these powers the five *abhijñās*: (1) subtle, extra-sensory hearing, (2) subtle, extra-sensory sight, (3) knowledge of previous births, (4) thought-reading, and (5) magical powers. In *Saddharma-puṇḍarīka,* chapter XI, it is described how the Tathāgata (Buddha) levitated. In chapter XXVI, it is also shown that some of his followers had the power of moving through the air and controlling other elements. Again, *Vinaya* (*Mahāvagga*) contains passages on how one can become invisible and express other extraordinary powers. There are also references to these powers in Jaina literature and tradition. In the life of Śrī Kṛṣṇa many such incidents are recorded. It is described in the *Bhāgavata* that Śrī Kṛṣṇa assumed many forms simultaneously, and they were perceived simultaneously by many persons. The *Rāmāyaṇa* and other Brāhmaṇical works refer to the control of the burning quality of fire and of other elements in nature. It will not be out of place to mention here that there have been similar expressions of extraordinary power recorded in the life of Jesus and some of the Jewish prophets.

In chapter III of the *Yoga-Sūtra,* Patañjali discusses these supernatural powers elaborately. It is he who actually made a science of them by showing methods of not only developing the above-mentioned powers, but also of controlling the central and sympathetic nervous system and bringing about suspension of animation, breath control, etc. He also discusses the

[1] This is called parapsychology by Richard Müller-Freienfels. Dr. Gardner Murphy and Dr. Joseph Banks Rhine, following the leadership of Dr. William McDougall, have experimented with extra-sensory phenomena, known nowadays as extra-sensory perception (ESP).

acquiring of knowledge of past lives, future events, subtle elements of matter, and the power to become invisible, move through the air, appear in different places, walk on water, and so on.

In the *Bhāgavata*, Śrī Kṛṣṇa says, 'Eighteen are the powers (*siddhis*) declared by those who are thoroughly successful in the *yoga* of concentration, and of them eight are perfect in me'.[2] These eight are: *aṇiman, mahiman, laghiman, prāpti, prākāmya, īśitva, vaśitva,* and *kāmāvasāyitva.* Śrī Kṛṣṇa describes them thus: 'To be the minutest, biggest, and lightest things are the three powers relating to the bodily form ; to act with the senses of all beings in association with their presiding deities ; to be able to enjoy all the things spoken of in the Śāstras as well as those of the visible world ; the ruling power, i.e. to set aworking one's *śakti* (energy in the form of Māyā in the case of Īśvara, and lesser manifestations of it in the case of other beings) ; the power of self-control, i.e. to be free from the desire for sensuous enjoyments ; and finally to find any pleasure that is wished for. And these eight powers, O gentle one, are considered to be natural and essential. To be free from organic cravings like hunger and thirst in the body, to hear sounds and to see things at a distance, to take the body quickly where the mind goes, to assume any desired form, to enter another's body, to cast off the body at will, to have a vision of the gods sporting with *apsaras,* to have things accomplished as intended, to command unopposed, to know things of the three times (past, present, and future), to be not affected by heat or cold, to read others' minds, to neutralize the force of fire, sun, water, poison, and the like, and to suffer no defeat'.[3] In the same chapter, Śrī Kṛṣṇa also gives the methods for manifesting these powers.

The different Tantras no doubt stress real religious development, but they also give methods by which one can develop *śāntikarma* (cure of diseases and removal of outside influences on the body and mind), *vaśīkaraṇa* (control of and influence on the minds of others, thought-reading, clairvoyance, etc.), *vidveṣaṇa* (harmful acts toward others, black magic of various types), *uccāṭana* (removal of a person from a certain location), and *māraṇa* (destruction of beings).

*Haṭhayoga-pradīpikā, Gheraṇḍa Saṁhitā, Pavanavijaya-svarodaya,* and such other books describe not only these extra-sensory powers, but also some of the means of controlling the minds of other people. They also show other methods developed for the control of the elementary functions of man to keep the body strong and healthy ; *dhauti* (a process of cleansing which improves the respiratory system and other functions), *vasti* (cleansing of the lower channels of man), and so forth. There are six processes altogether for

[2] *Bhā.*, XI.15.3.
[3] *Ibid.*, XI.15.4-8 with Śrīdhara Svāmin's commentary.

purification of the physical nature which produce control over bodily functions.

The methods of these extraordinary perceptions are verifiable as prescribed by Patañjali in the *Yoga-Sūtra, Haṭhayoga-pradīpikā,* etc. There have been many cases of controlling the burning quality of fire, remaining buried for as many as six weeks, stopping the circulatory and elementary functions, and controlling other involuntary functions, such as the heart beat, which have been demonstrated in the presence of highly qualified scientific authorities.[4]

## MISUSE OF SUPERNATURAL POWERS

It is certainly true that some of the Buddhistic and Tāntrika practices and the more recent Haṭha-yoga and such other later practices are not conducive to spiritual growth. They are essentially the use of psycho-physical forces of man for obtaining certain powers of control and enjoyment. In earlier periods, the great thinkers discussed these practices with good intentions from the point of view of sublimation and transformation of human tendencies for higher spiritual realization. As scientists, Patañjali and others gave them elaborate treatment ; but unfortunately, in the course of time these practices deteriorated and degenerated and made many persons conscious of their physical nature more than their spiritual requirements. In fact, the *siddhis* or *aiśvaryas* are seriously condemned by Śrī Kṛṣṇa, Buddha, Patañjali, and Sri Ramakrishna. Patañjali says in the *Yoga-Sūtra,* 'By giving up even these powers comes the destruction of the very seed of evil, which leads to *kaivalya* (freedom). . . . The saving knowledge is that knowledge of discrimination which simultaneously covers all objects, in all their variations'.[5] Śrī Kṛṣṇa declares, 'But in the case of one who practises the best course of *yoga* of devotion to me and obtains my grace, these attainments are mere obstacles and waste of time'.[6] Again, it is stated in *Uttarādhyayana-Sūtra,* of Jaina tradition, that supernatural knowledge (*avadhijñāna*) and knowledge of the thoughts of other people (*manaḥparyāya*) are obstacles to liberation or supreme knowledge.[7] Sri Ramakrishna also says, 'Beware of these powers and desire them not. . . . *Siddhis* or psychic powers are to be avoided like filth. . . . He who sets his mind on *siddhis* remains stuck thereto, and he cannot rise higher. . . . For

[4] The demonstration of Khoda Bux of his ability to walk on fire and control the elementary functions of his body was witnessed by the London Medical Association and by authorities with scientific interest in Copenhagen ; and other such cases were witnessed in India and America. This incident has been reported in the *Proceedings of the London Medical Association* and by Prof. P. Plum, Rigshospitalet, Copenhagen, Denmark.

[5] *The Complete Works of Swami Vivekananda,* I. 285, 288 ; see also *Yoga-Sūtra,* III. 51-55.

[6] *Bhā.,* XI.15.33.

[7] *Uttarādhyayana-Sūtra,* discourse 33.

occult powers increase man's egotism and thus make him forgetful of God'.[8]

*Siddhis, aiśvaryas, abhijñās,* and certain other extra-sensory powers are indeed obstacles to spiritual realization. Yet many spiritual persons spontaneously develop these powers in the course of their spiritual realizations. On various occasions, Śrī Kṛṣṇa and Buddha showed some of these extraordinary powers. Jesus, the Christ, also manifested them. In the life of Sri Ramakrishna also we find that he manifested some of them, such as appearing in distant places.[9] Although a deeply spiritual man with superconscious realization can spontaneously develop these powers, they are regarded as obstacles in most cases, as they distract the mind from God, especially when they are consciously sought. There are many historical incidents to substantiate this point of view. A man by the name of Girija used to visit Sri Ramakrishna. He had the ability to emanate light from his back. Through the advice of Sri Ramakrishna he stopped using that power, and he consequently gained in spirituality. Another man, Chandra, who had similar powers, in spite of the warnings of Sri Ramakrishna, continued to express them. As a result, he gradually became demoralized and lost both his spiritual life and his extraordinary powers.[10] Buddha, as is well known, forbade his disciples to show magical feats either to win personal regard or to attract followers.

## SUPERCONSCIOUS EXPERIENCES CLASSIFIED AND EVALUATED

These extraordinary and extra-sensory powers are often confused with true religious expressions, even though a great spiritual man may also have them without any special practices for their development. Real superconscious experiences are of a different and higher order. Spiritual realization is based on the experience of the ultimate Reality, God. Valid religious experiences depend on mental purification and 'one-pointedness' (complete concentration) of consciousness. Unless a man is thoroughly unified, he cannot experience the ultimate Reality. It is said in the *Kaṭha Upaniṣad*: 'And he who is devoid of proper understanding, thoughtless, and always impure, never attains that goal, but gets into the round of births and deaths. But he who is intelligent, mindful, and ever pure, reaches that goal whence none is born again'.[11] It is also stated in the *Śvetāśvatara Upaniṣad*: 'First harnessing the mind and thought

[8] *Sayings of Sri Ramakrishna,* pp. 129, 130.

[9] While he was in Calcutta, he appeared to Vijaya Krishna Goswami in Dacca. A similar incident happened in the United States during the 1870's. Sri Ramakrishna appeared to a lady living in Lakehurst, New Jersey, at that period. His appearance to Vijaya Krishna Goswami is related in *The Gospel of Sri Ramakrishna,* p. 874.

[10] *Life of Sri Ramakrishna,* pp. 146 ff.

[11] *Ka. U.,* III. 7, 8.

with a view to realizing the Truth, and then having found out the light of the fire, the evolving Soul (Savitṛ) brought it out of the earth. With our minds controlled and inspired by the self-luminous immanent Soul, we endeavour for the attainment of vigour and supreme bliss. Controlling the heaven-aspiring senses with the help of the mind and the intellect, may the immanent Soul so regenerate them as to enable them to manifest the self-luminous infinite light!'[12] It is said in the *Dhammapada*: 'If a man's thoughts are unsteady, if he does not know the true law, if his peace of mind is troubled, his knowledge will never be perfect'.[13] Mystics all over the world who have direct awareness of God are one in their basic requirements for valid religious experiences.

Superconscious or religious experiences can be variously classified. Some are superconscious in the sense that a man is not aware of the objective world. He is conscious of God or Self alone. He is completely absorbed in Brahman in Its personal (Saguṇa) or impersonal (Absolute or Nirguṇa) aspect.[14] Patañjali classifies some of these experiences as *samprajñāta* and *asamprajñāta*.[15] According to him, in the former remains the seed of bondage while in the latter all the mental functions are emptied.[16] He also says that the deeper aspect of the latter form of superconsciousness, namely *asamprajñāta,* is *nirbīja* (seedless).[17] Other spiritual experiences are in the form of visions (*rūpa-darśana*). They are also satisfying and exalting from a spiritual point of view. Great religious personalities and mystics have had such realizations throughout the ages. They are not limited to people in any particular part of the world. In these states, a devotee directly sees or hears a personal aspect of God. *Samādhi* (superconsciousness) of a type higher than visions is generally classified in two stages. In the first (*savikalpa samādhi*), a devotee realizes the personal aspect of God and remains absorbed in the Beloved and becomes unconscious of the world. He is only conscious of a person, such as Śrī Kṛṣṇa, Buddha, Jesus, Sri Ramakrishna, divine Mother, and various other personal aspects of the divine Being. The human soul experiences and enjoys God, remaining separate. This is advocated by the devotional schools of Indian religion. In the second state (*nirvikalpa samādhi*), the seeker of truth is completely identified with Nirguṇa Brahman (absolute Existence-Knowledge-Bliss). Duality vanishes; awareness of the world ceases to exist; unity alone remains. Patañjali evidently describes something like

[12] *Śvetāśvatara U.*, II. 1-3.
[13] *Dhammapada* (Trans.), Max Müller, *Sacred Books of the East.*
[14] Here it is to be noted that the personal God in the Hindu thought means God with or without a body in various schools.
[15] *Yoga-Sūtra,* I. 17, 18.
[16] *Ibid.*, I. 50, 51.
[17] *Ibid.*

this, saying that at that time the perceiver remains in itself: *'Tadā draṣṭuḥ svarūpe avasthānam'*.[18]

In *Vedāntasāra* of Sadānanda these are classified as *savikalpa* and *nirvikalpa*. According to Sadānanda, 'Absorption attended with self-consciousness (*savikalpa samādhi*) is that in which the mental state, taking the form of Brahman, the One without a second, rests on It, but without the merging of the distinction of knower, knowledge, and the object of knowledge'.[19] He further states, 'Absorption without self-consciousness (*nirvikalpa samādhi*) is the total mergence in Brahman, the One without a second, of the mental state which has assumed Its form, the distinction of knower, knowledge, and the object of knowledge being in this case obliterated'.[20]

In *Viveka-cūḍāmaṇi* of Śaṅkarācārya, a similar distinction is made between *savikalpa* and *nirvikalpa samādhi*.[21] According to some authorities, superconsciousness is classified in three states. The first two are *savikalpa* and *nirvikalpa samādhi*, as described above. The third state of superconsciousness (*ānanda samādhi*) can neither be discussed nor described. It is beyond duality and unity (*dvaitādvaitavivarjita*), beyond one and many. Buddhists call the highest form of superconsciousness *lokuttara-citta*. They also classify *arūpa-jhāna* (knowledge of the formless) at various stages of experience. *Lokuttara-citta* transcends even the experiences of the generally known invisible. Jains call superconscious experience *pāramārthika pratyakṣa*. According to them, this knowledge originates in the self and not from external objects.

*Samādhi* is the primary objective of religious practices. Mystics or *yogins* are wholly interested in the attainment of superconsciousness, without which one cannot be directly aware of God or Brahman. They also become knowers of past, present, and future events (*trikālajña*), even though they may not always let it be known.

The real superconscious state is attained, as Patañjali says, by complete control of the mental states. A *yogin* or mystic gradually reaches one of these three main superconscious experiences step by step. There are certain states such as *bhāvas* and *mahābhāvas* (spiritual ecstasies) where physical and mental exaltations are experienced in the form of shedding tears, hair standing on end, hearing of divine sound, seeing cosmic light, and perceiving certain abiding divine forms. A *yogin* also attains a sense of cosmic unity in which he feels the meaning and purpose of events in

[18] *Ibid.*, I. 3.
[19] *Vedāntasāra* (Nirnayasagara Ed.), *khaṇḍā* 30, p. 45.
[20] *Ibid.*
[21] *Viveka-cūḍāmaṇi*, 362-365.

the world, as it is delineated in chapters X and XI of the *Bhagavad-Gītā* and in the *Bhāgavata, Saddharma-puṇḍarīka,* and *Yoga-Sūtra.* Then he reaches complete oneness, either through *savikalpa samādhi,* as it is described in *Viveka-cūḍāmaṇi,*[22] or directly in *nirvikalpa samādhi.* Finally, some reach *ānanda samādhi.* From any of these states he can return to the plane of multiplicity with the effect of his superconscious experience and feel the abiding Presence in all.

## MODERN CRITICISM OF SUPERCONSCIOUSNESS

The *nirvāṇa* of Buddha and *nirvikalpa samādhi* or superconscious realization have been construed by some mystical writers and thinkers of the West, such as Dr. Rufus M. Jones and Dr. Albert Schweitzer, as negative mysticism. They seem to be rather critical of these states as they think that these experiences sap the foundation of social consciousness by negating the world. They do not realize that a person who attains *nirvikalpa samādhi* finds *'Sarvaṁ khalvidaṁ Brahma'*, which means that he feels the presence of the Reality everywhere. Again, can we find a more socially conscious man than Buddha? In this modern age, Swami Vivekananda is an outstanding example of one who attained *nirvikalpa samādhi* and was at the same time one of the greatest of socially conscious persons. There have been others at different times in India who also reached *nirvikalpa samādhi* and yet remained lovers of humanity.

The question may arise as to the validity of these experiences. There have been many persons who have claimed that they experienced God or had higher superconscious realization; yet their personal lives definitely indicate that they are abnormal in their emotional reactions and interpersonal relationships. Some psychologists of religion, like Leuba and others, conclude that religious or superconscious experiences are abnormal states of mind, akin to experiences caused by drugs. They also say that persons with a strong sex urge have such experiences. In other words, they feel that these experiences are pathological, perhaps epileptic, certainly abnormal. However, they do state that such persons direct their sex energy to God or Self instead of giving it lower expression. Freud and such other thinkers condemn religion as the real cause of repression and consequent mental and nervous disorder. Behaviourist psychologists, like Watson and others, completely deny the reality of mind, not to speak of the validity of superconscious experiences and extra-sensory perceptions. Some thinkers seem to feel that these superconscious experiences are attained by certain kinds of hypnosis. But auto-suggestion or hetero-

[22] *Ibid.*, 362.

suggestion in the form of hypnosis cannot bring in new knowledge, which has not been experienced by the hypnotizer or the hypnotized. According to some groups, a man is established in the Self during these superconscious experiences. According to others, the seekers of truth are established in Reality, Truth, God, or Absolute—Saguṇa or Nirguṇa Brahman. This is a unique state which cannot be attained by self-hypnosis or by any other kind of suggestion, the reason being that the hypnotized or the hypnotizer has not reached this state of mind. It brings a new knowledge which is not experienced until one reaches superconscious realization. Moreover, in cases of hypnotism of any type, the individual is not the gainer; he is rather a loser in the field of knowledge. It is observed that a hypnotized person, instead of being integrated, becomes more and more dependent and weak in emotion and volition. On the other hand, a man of superconscious realization is unified, integrated, and strengthened in his emotional reactions and volitions.

These psychologists and scholars who adopt an extremely narrow scientific point of view ignore the actual facts of experience. It is admitted that there have been epileptic and other persons who have claimed to be religious, and that there have also been other persons who have claimed to have spiritual experiences. However, the best test of their validity is in the development of personality. A man of higher experiences is a pure person. His emotions are unified; his behaviour pattern is uniform; he is rational in his understanding and in his inter-personal relationships; and his activities are based on higher ethical principles of love, purity, and truth. A man of superconscious realization is definitely supernormal. In fact, he is not only integrated himself, but he can help others to become integrated. The lives of great saints all over the world show how even questionable personalities can be transformed by mentally unified men and women. Two of Sri Ramakrishna's disciples, Girish Chandra Ghosh and Kalipada Ghosh, were thoroughly transformed because of the effect of Sri Ramakrishna's spiritual power and love. Jagāi and Mādhāi were similarly transformed by Caitanya, and Mary Magdalene by Jesus. In previous periods of history, Buddha and others changed a number of such personalities. If the pathological psychologists and psychologists of religion, like Leuba, were to study religious experiences with no preconceived notions, they would perceive the validity of these statements. On the other hand, Professor William James in his *Varieties of Religious Experience* and James B. Pratt in *The Religious Consciousness* give many interesting descriptions of exalted religious experiences.

Carl Jung of Zurich identifies *samādhi* with the unconscious state of mind. He says, 'There are dreams and visions of such an informative kind that the people who have them refuse to believe that they are derived from an unconscious psyche. They prefer to suppose that they issue from a sort of superconscious. Such people usually distinguish between a quasi-physiological or instinctive unconscious and a psychic sphere or logos, "above" consciousness, which they style the superconsciousness. As a matter of fact, the psyche, called the superior or the universal in Hindu philosophy, corresponds to what the West calls the unconscious'.[23] He further says, 'The *yogīs* wind up with *samādhi* an ecstatic condition that seems to be equivalent to an unconscious state. . . . A universal consciousness is logically identical with the unconscious'.[24]

## MENTAL PREPARATION FOR REALIZATION

It is a fact that superconscious states cannot be really understood unless one experiences them. As chemical laws cannot be verified without laboratory experiments, so superconscious realization or *samādhi* of various types cannot be properly understood by unprepared or untrained minds, however intellectual and well-intentioned they may be. Dr. Jung misunderstands the nature of *samādhi*. It is not equivalent to an unconscious state, as he declares, even though a man remains oblivious of the objective world. He is then fully aware of the Reality or God, not conceptually but actually and really; and he attains full coherency and rationality. He is directly and immediately aware of Him or is established in the Self or Ātman. *Samādhi* is vivid and definite; as we have already mentioned, in its higher state it is integral unity. Nay, it is consciousness itself on the highest plane.

Some writers seem to think that religious experiences satisfy the emotions, but they make no contribution to the cognitive element in man. This conjecture is not based on fact. A man of *samadhi* enters that state as a comparatively ignorant person, but he comes out of it fully illumined. He is fully aware of the true nature of Saguṇa or Nirguṇa Brahman (personal or impersonal aspects of God) or the Self. There remains no darkness in his consciousness regarding the validity of the existence of the real Self or Godhead, even though he cannot always communicate it conceptually to others, as unitary and unique emotional experience cannot be intellectually expressed. However, superconscious states can be gained directly and immediately, as has been demonstrated in the lives of great personalities.

The natural sciences study objective phenomena; so they do not require unusual mental preparation for observation itself. But the study

[23] Carl G. Jung, *Integration of the Personality* (Translation), Stanley Dell, p. 15.
[24] *Ibid.*, p. 26.

of superconscious realization requires rigorous mental training in the form of ethical living, purity, and the practice of concentration and meditation. It is also difficult because the subject and object of study are the same. Nevertheless, the lives of saints, mystics, *yogins, arhats, tīrthaṅkaras,* and dervishes (Mohammedan saints) reveal that they have verified these superconscious experiences and directed their followers to do likewise. Such realizations are illustrated in the lives of Śrī Kṛṣṇa, Buddha, Jesus, Sri Ramakrishna, and their great disciples.

Bhakti-yoga, Karma-yoga, Jñāna-yoga, and Rāja-yoga of the Hindus, Buddhists, and Jains in India are various methods for realizing the superconscious state. According to Patañjali, *yoga* means cessation of mental waves through active effort and consequent establishment of the self in its own essence. According to others, it means union with God or realization of the Self or Brahman (Absolute) and also methods for attaining that goal. In Bhakti-yoga, a person is to direct his emotions and love towards God. Bhakti-yogins establish an individual relationship with God according to the predominance of their natural emotional tendencies. The different types of relationships that one can establish with God are those of (1) a placid devotee (*śānta*), (2) a servant (*dāsya*), (3) a friend (*sakhya*), (4) parents (*vātsalya*), (5) a lover (*madhura-bhāva*), and (6) a son (*āpatya*). By cultivating a particular relationship, and through it directing human love to God, one attains to *savikalpa samādhi* and in some cases to the realization of unity with Him. It is said in the *Bhāgavata* that the *gopīs* attained complete unity with their beloved at a certain stage. Generally speaking, however, devotees prefer the dual relationship with God, so that they can enjoy Him. Karma-yoga teaches a person how to perform unselfish work in the spirit of consecration and devotion without caring for the results. This path also leads one to the highest realization. In Jñāna-yoga, a person learns to discriminate the real from the unreal, the permanent from the temporary, and to reject the unreal and the transitory. By this process he becomes established in Nirguṇa Brahman, in *nirvikalpa samādhi.* The steps in Rāja-yoga teach one to unify the mind by controlling it. This leads the aspirant to the superconscious state. There are many subdivisions in these various *yogas,* such as Kuṇḍalinī-yoga and Mantra-yoga of the Tāntrika schools, which can be classified under the four major *yoga*-systems of Indian thought. The Buddhist and Jaina schools also more or less follow some of these *yogas* in a broad sense.

The Tāntrika schools and Vaiṣṇavas also made special studies of the *mantra* or symbolic name of God. Some of the Tantras definitely emphasize that by repeating a special *mantra* which is suitable to the individual temperament, one can realize God (*japāt siddhiḥ*). According to them, one can realize the superconscious state by repeating the *mantra* in accordance with the instructions of the *guru*.

Through the practice of the methods of superconscious experiences, Indian psychologists have definitely discovered various unconscious states. They are of the opinion that mere knowledge of the unconscious tendencies (*saṁskāras*) cannot help a man in removing his complexes or other mental disturbances. It is their opinion that *saṁskāras* or unconscious tendencies can be controlled and transformed only in the very process of total psychological development.

Indian psychologists are convinced that superconscious realization cannot be imparted unless a teacher is himself established in those experiences. A teacher of the psychology of the unconscious must himself also be an integrated person of higher spiritual realization in order to straighten out effectively the mental crookedness and conflicts of his students or clients. Superconscious realization can generally be attained only with the help and guidance of a dynamic, spiritual personality (*guru*), even though there have been a few cases in which persons have stumbled unaided into such experiences.

PART V

# THE PHILOSOPHICAL SCIENCES

# 33

## INDIAN THEISM

### NATURE OF GOD: EARLY SPECULATIONS

INDIAN thought-record begins with the Vedas. In them there are definite statements regarding God and His nature. At first the ideas were polytheistic. But this polytheism soon developed into henotheism[1] (i.e. each god being elevated in turn to the position of the supreme Deity). Henotheism, in due course, evolved into monotheism,[2] which culminated in monism.[3] So, the idea of the Absolute of later thought had germinated already in the mind of the Vedic seers.

In the Upaniṣads we find more definite statements regarding the being and nature of God. The main current of Upaniṣadic thought flows towards a monistic conception: 'There is One without a second'.[4] 'All this is Brahman'.[5] This conception of God has been called the *nirguṇa* aspect. He is devoid of all attributes.[6] Nothing can be positively postulated about Him. He can be indicated only by 'not this, not this'.[7] But side by side with this there is another current of thought. This is the conception of God as the ruler of the universe. He is the source of everything. He is the creator and destroyer.[8] He is endowed with all virtues (*guṇin*) and with omniscience. He is the cause of bondage and liberation.[9]

From the Upaniṣads to the systems is not a far cry. What was in an embryonic state in the Upaniṣads appeared in fully developed forms in the philosophical systems. The Indian systems of philosophy can be classified into two groups: heterodox and orthodox, those that do not believe in the Vedas and those that do. Under the former come the Cārvāka, the Jain, and the Buddhist, and under the latter the Sāṁkhya, the Pātañjala, the Nyāya, the Vaiśeṣika, the Pūrva-Mīmāṁsā, and the Uttara-Mīmāṁsā.

The Cārvākas, who accept perception as the only valid means of knowledge, consistently reject God, who does not come within the purview

[1] Max Müller, *Six Systems of Indian Philosophy*, p. 40; *Three Lectures on Vedānta Philosophy*, pp. 27,28.

[2] *R.V.*, X.82.3; IV.40.5; X.121.1.

[3] *R.V.*, X.129.2.

[4] *Mu. U.*, II.2.11; *Chā. U.*, VI.2.1.

[5] *Chā. U.*, III.14.1.

[6] *Ka.U.*, I.3.15; *Mu.U.*, I.1.6; *Mā.U.*, 7,12.

[7] *Br. U.*, II.3.6; III.9.26; etc.

[8] *Mā. U.*, 6.

[9] *Śvetāśvatara U.*, VI.16,17.

of perception. If any God is at all to be postulated, then the visible king who is known to everybody should get that appellation.[10]

Buddhism in its original form does not concern itself with the problem of God. The main problem that confronts mankind is, according to it, the way out of the miseries of the world, for which no extraneous help is necessary. In later Buddhism, however, arguments are adduced for proving the non-existence of God as creator and organizer of the world.[11] But later still, Buddhism had to concede to the inborn weakness of the common man for an object of worship and support. Thus it ended by adopting and adapting various Hindu gods and incorporating Buddha as the supreme and central figure of a divine hierarchy. The historic Buddha was considered in the Mahāyāna school to be a manifestation of the ultimate Reality called *dharmakāya,* which is something possessing attributes of personality, viz. intelligence (*prajñā*) and love (*karuṇā*).

Jainism is atheistic in its outlook in so far as it denies the existence of a supreme Deity, the creator and ruler of the universe. But the Jains believe in the existence of various minor deities, above whom are the *jinas,* the liberated ones, the *paramadevatās,* who, however, do not vouchsafe any boon, mercy, or pardon to the worshipper, but who, when prayed to, help one to follow the path of discipline leading to salvation.

## GOD IN THE SIX PHILOSOPHICAL SYSTEMS

The Sāṁkhya system also is atheistic in its outlook. Though Max Müller thinks that the 'denial of an Īśvara or personal Lord did not probably form part of the original Sāṁkhya, as presented to us in the *Tattvasamāsa*',[12] according to traditional as well as modern consensus of opinion, earlier Sāṁkhya is positively atheistic.[13] The eternal existence of souls or Puruṣas, who are permanent and supreme, is inconsistent with the infinity and creatorship of God. But the Sāṁkhya does not say directly that there is no God whatsoever. It simply affirms that the existence of an eternal God cannot be established by proof.[14] The Sāṁkhya admits the godhood of certain souls. These are individual souls who are merged in Prakṛti, each emerging as a god in the beginning of a new cycle of creation and lording it over all during that cycle.[15] Such a god can be established by logic.[16] The Sāṁkhya further accepts the popular gods, who are only

[10] *Sarva-darśana-saṅgraha* (Abhyankara's Ed.), *Cārvākadarśana,* pp. 6,7.
[11] *Bodhicaryāvatāra,* IX.119 f.
[12] Max Müller, *Six Systems of Indian Philosophy,* p. 230.
[13] Radhakrishnan, *Indian Philosophy,* II. p. 316. Cowell and Gough's translation of *Sarva-darśana-saṅgraha,* XIV. p. 230.
[14] *Sāṁkhyapravacana-Sūtra,* I.92; V.10.
[15] *Ibid.,* III.56.
[16] *Ibid.,* III.57.

more highly organized and happier beings than men, but who are equally subject to the laws of *saṁsāra*. Whenever the word 'Lord' (Īśvara) is used in the scriptures, it is in reference to the liberated souls or these beings.[17]

Later Sāṁkhya, however, had to concede a place to God in the system. Vijñāna Bhikṣu, for example, holds the view that it was for the sake of argument and to prove that God was no integral part of the system, and not to assert its antagonism to theism as such, that the Sāṁkhya had not included God in its philosophy.[18]

Apart from this later innovation, however, the Sāṁkhya system does not believe in God. That is why it has been called 'Nirīśvara (atheistic) Sāṁkhya' in contrast with the system of Patañjali, which is called 'Seśvara (theistic) Sāṁkhya'.

Patañjali opens the topic of God with the *sūtra 'Īśvara-praṇidhānād vā'* (And also by devotion to God).[19] He means thereby that *samādhi* can be attained, among other means, by devotion to God also. Garbe[20] and Geden[21] hold that the concept of God is an extraneous graft on the system, loosely fitted and superficial and due to pragmatic considerations, a view with which it is difficult to concur, inasmuch as God is a metaphysical necessity in the system. Vācaspati Miśra says, 'And in the case of Īśvara we must understand that His activity is limited to the removal of obstructions with a view to securing a basis for merit'.[22] Vijñāna Bhikṣu says, 'The disturbance leading to the disequilibrium of Prakṛti is due to Īśvara's will'.[23] Bhoja says, 'The association and dissociation of Prakṛti and Puruṣas cannot be established without postulating the will of God'.[24]

God in Pātañjala philosophy is a particular Puruṣa who is ever untainted by troubles, actions, and their effects and deserts.[25] There are some Puruṣas who have become liberated and are free from all taints. There are others who are merged in Prakṛti (*prakṛtilīna*) and who are free from such blemishes at present, but may again be affected by them. God is, however, one who never was and never will be tarnished by any blemish whatever. Moreover, God's attributes are the highest. He in whom pre-eminence reaches the zenith is God. He is not a different category but is a singular type of Puruṣa. He is the first Teacher, because, unlike other teachers, He is not limited by time. Though He has

[17] *Ibid.*, I.95.
[18] *Sāṁkhyapravacana-bhāṣya*, Introduction, *'Tasmād abhyupagamavādapraudhivādādinaiva sāṁkhyasya vyāvahārikeśvarapratiṣedhaparatayā Brahmamīmāṁsāyogābhyāṁ saha na virodhaḥ'*.
[19] *Yoga-Sūtra*, I.23.
[20] Garbe, *Philosophy of Ancient India*, p. 15.
[21] *Encyclopaedia of Religion and Ethics*, VI. p. 285.
[22] Vacaspati's *ṭīkā* on IV.3.
[23] *Yoga-vārttika*, I.24.
[24] *Yoga-vṛtti*, I.24.
[25] *Yoga-Sūtra*, I.24.

no desire, yet out of His grace towards all beings He saves people immersed in *saṁsāra* by imparting knowledge and virtue (*dharma*) to them. He is made up of the purest *sattva*; He is ever free and ever the pre-eminent. And He is omniscient.[26]

In the *Nyāya-Sūtra* of Gautama, God has not been mentioned as one of the twelve *prameyas*. From this it has been concluded by some modern scholars[27] that the *Nyāya-Sūtra* originally was not theistic. But to this, Vṛttikāra Viśvanātha and others say that Ātman as postulated among the *prameyas* includes both Jīvātman and Paramātman. That is why no separate mention of Īśvara has been made.

There are three aphorisms in the *Nyāya-Sūtra* which discuss God.[28] Leaving aside the difference in the niceties of interpretation between Vācaspati on the one hand, and Vātsyāyana, Uddyotakara, and Viśvanātha on the other, the arguments boil down to the following points: (i) that God is the efficient cause of the world, (ii) that for dispensing man's fruits of action He is dependent on man's action, and (iii) that this dependence of His does not in any way interfere with His sovereignty, inasmuch as man can neither work nor reap the fruits of his work but by and through the divine will.

This God of the Naiyāyikas is omnipotent. He is a particular kind of Ātman possessing benign attributes, devoid of vice, wrong knowledge, and mistakes, and is eternally endowed with what are known as the eightfold superhuman powers (minuteness, lightness, etc.).

In the *Vaiśeṣika-Sūtra* of Kaṇāda, God is not openly referred to. The *sūtra 'Tadvacanād āmnāyasya prāmāṇyam'* (Being His words, the validity of the Vedas)[29] has been held by some scholars to mean that the Vedas are the works of the seers,[30] and that the *sūtra* has no reference to God. Without entering into this useless controversy, it can be safely said that whatever might have been the position of the early Vaiśeṣika, the system in its later form is unequivocally theistic, subscribing to the Nyāya view of God, one might say, *in toto*.

The Pūrva-Mīmāṁsā, according to the traditional view, is atheistic in its outlook. The universe having neither beginning nor end does not require any creator. God also cannot act as a supervisor of *dharma* and *adharma*, as the Naiyāyikas hold, since *dharma* and *adharma* belong to the performer, and God cannot have any knowledge of them. God can have neither conjunction with nor inherence of *dharma* and *adharma* in Him,

[26] *Yoga-Sūtra*, Vyāsa's *bhāṣya* on I.23-26.
[27] Garbe, *Philosophy of Ancient India*, p. 23, and Muir, *Original Sanskrit Texts*, III. p. 133.
[28] *Nyāya-Sūtra*, IV.1.19-21.
[29] *Kaṇāda-Sūtra*, I.1.3.
[30] Radhakrishnan, *Indian Philosophy*, II. p. 226.

because conjunction is possible with substances and not qualities which *dharma* and *adharma* are, and because they inhere in individual souls and cannot inhere in an extraneous God.[31] Perception, inference, and scriptures do not prove God. But scholars like Max Müller and P. Shastri[32] infer that the Pūrva-Mīmāṁsā rejects God only as creator of differences in the lots of men, but not God as such. But this view does not seem to be tenable, because the early Mīmāṁsakas are silent about the question of God and the later ones reject the proofs of God. This system cannot even be called polytheistic, because even the deities invoked by it are not said to have existence anywhere except in hymns that describe them. But the Mīmāṁsakas of a later period introduced God into the system. Veṅkateśa, the author of *Seśvara-mīmāṁsā,* grafted Vedānta doctrine on Mīmāṁsā. Āpadeva and Laugākṣi Bhāskara hold that if sacrifices performed are dedicated to God, they will lead to the highest good (*niḥśreyasa*).[33] This inclusion of *apavarga* ideal in the system is a later innovation.

The *Vedānta-Sūtra* of Bādarāyaṇa is a systematic presentation of the Upaniṣadic teaching. Different interpretations, offered by different commentators, have given rise to different schools of thought. The main schools are Advaitism of Śaṅkara, Viśiṣṭādvaitism of Rāmānuja, and Dvaitism of Madhva.

### VIEWS OF ŚAṄKARA, RĀMĀNUJA, AND MADHVA

God, according to Śaṅkara, can be viewed from two standpoints: empirical (*vyāvahārika*) and transcendental (*pāramārthika*). From the first standpoint, the world is considered to be real and God is the creator, preserver, and destroyer of it. 'That omniscient omnipotent cause from which proceed the origin, subsistence, and dissolution of this world—which world is differentiated by names and forms, contains many agents and enjoyers, is the abode of the fruits of actions, these fruits having their definite places, times, and causes, and the nature of whose arrangement cannot even be conceived by the mind—that cause, we say, is Brahman.'[34] So 'a Lord possessing the stated qualities' can be the creator of the world. He is free from all sins. He is the Being within the self of all beings, to Him belong all works, all desires. He can assume a bodily shape formed of Māyā in order to gratify thereby His devout worshippers.[35] He creates

[31] Keith, *The Karma-Mīmāṁsā,* p. 62.

[32] Max Müller, *Six Systems of Indian Philosophy,* pp. 210 ff, and P. Shastri, *Introduction to the Pūrva-Mīmāṁsā,* III.

[33] *'Śrī Govindārpaṇabuddhyā kriyamāṇastu niḥśreyasahetuḥ'*—Āpadeva's *Mīmāṁsā-nyāya-prakāśa.* *'Īśvarārpaṇabuddhyā kriyamāṇastu niḥśreyasahetuḥ'*—Laugākṣi Bhāskara's *Artha-saṅgraha.*

[34] *Brahma-Sūtra, Śaṅkara-bhāṣya,* I.1.2; I.1.11.

[35] *Ibid.,* I.1.20.

the world in a spirit of sport.[36] In creating the world, He is guided by the merits and demerits of the living creatures. Hence no blame can attach to Him for inequality etc. existing in the world. In this aspect, God is called *saguṇa*. In this condition, He is said to be an object of nescience (*avidyā*).[37]

But, considered from the second standpoint, the world is unreal ; and nothing but God, as the ground of everything, is ultimately true. He is referred to as Brahman. Brahman is thoroughly devoid of all attributes. This is called the *nirguṇa* aspect. It can be referred to only as 'not this, not this'.[38] This view is absolutely monistic.

But from the above discussion are we to assume that Brahman has a double nature? No, because the *saguṇa* aspect has no transcendental validity. 'Hence Īśvara's being Īśvara, His omniscience, His omnipotence, etc. all depend on the limitation due to the adjuncts whose self is nescience ; while in reality none of these qualities belong to the Self whose true nature is cleared, by right knowledge, from all adjuncts whatever.'[39]

According to Rāmānuja, God is the only reality, but within Him exist as parts (*aṁśa*) the conscious (*cit*) individual souls (Jīvas) and the unconscious (*acit*) world. There is nothing outside of Him whether different in kind (*vijātīya*) or of the same kind (*sajātīya*). But in Brahman, there is internal (*svagata*) distinction (*bheda*) constituted by Jīva and *jagat*. 'The whole aggregate of intelligent and non-intelligent beings constitutes Brahman's body.' 'All imperfection and suffering are limited to the sentient beings constituting part of Paramātman's body, and all change is restricted to the non-sentient things which constitute another part.'[40] But this body is controlled by Him and He is its Self. God creates, preserves, and destroys the world. He is both the efficient as well as the material cause.[41] God modifies Himself into the world. But He is not intrinsically touched by this modification and no imperfection attaches to Him by the change. During *pralaya* (dissolution) the world resolves into an ultra-subtle form and is absorbed into Brahman, to be modified again into the world at the beginning of another cycle of creation. He creates in a spirit of sport. He is the ruler of all, endowed with infinite auspicious qualities like knowledge, blessedness, etc., is omniscient, omnipotent, and supremely merciful.[42] He possesses a divine form, peculiar to Himself, not made of

[36] *Ibid.*, II.1.33.
[37] *Ibid.*, I.1.11.
[38] *Ibid.*, III.2.17.
[39] *Ibid.*, II.1.14.
[40] *Brahma-Sūtra, Rāmānuja-bhāṣya*, I.4.27.
[41] *Ibid.*, I.4.28.
[42] *Ibid.*, I.1.2.

the stuff of Prakṛti nor due to *karma*.[43] 'In Him are combined energy, strength, might, wisdom, valour, and all other noble qualities.'[44] When it is said that He is devoid of qualities, it is simply meant that He is free from all touch of evil.[45] He is endowed with a personality and is identified with Viṣṇu.[46] Prajāpati, Śiva, etc., all refer to the supreme Reality who is Nārāyaṇa.[47]

According to Madhva, God, Jīva, and the world are eternally distinct. The last two, though eternal, are subordinate to God. God is the independent principle (*svatantra tattva*), and the other two are the dependent principles (*asvatantra* or *paratantra tattva*). There are five real and eternal distinctions (*bhedapañcaka*), viz. (1) between God and Jīva, (2) between God and matter, (3) between matter and Jīva, (4) between Jīva and Jīva, and (5) between one particle of matter and another. God is free from all blemishes and endowed with all auspicious qualities. He is not limited by His qualities. He is identified with Viṣṇu. Brahmā, Śiva, Indra, etc. are non-eternal and are designated as *kṣara*. Lakṣmī is His creative energy, is coeternal with Him, has no material body, and is all-pervading. Lakṣmī is eternally free (*nityamukta*) and is called *akṣara*. Still She is dependent on Viṣṇu. Viṣṇu is superior to both the *kṣara* and *akṣara* deities. He is endowed with independence, strength, knowledge, bliss, etc. He is the efficient, but not the material cause of the world. He is the absolute ruler —punishing some and rewarding others. He is both transcendent as well as immanent, because He is *antaryāmin* (inner ruler) of all souls. He is guided by the individuals' *karma,* but cannot be said to be dependent on *karma,* because, for their existence, *karmas* have to depend on Him.[48] The conception of the identity of God and individuals is a heinous offence for which a person will be punished. He explains the identity texts of the Upaniṣads in a dualistic sense.

## PROOFS OF GOD'S EXISTENCE

In the systems, both orthodox and heterodox, attempts have been made either to prove or to disprove the existence of God. The Cārvākas, as we have already noted, believe only in perception as the valid means of knowledge. Merit, life after death, heaven, hell, soul, and God are not objects of perception. So they do not exist. According to the Buddhists, a thing that has nowhere been perceived cannot exist. As God has not

[43] *Ibid.,* Introduction to I.2.1.
[44] *Ibid.,* III.2.11.
[45] *Ibid.,* I.1.1.
[46] *Ibid.,* I.1.1; III.2.11.
[47] *Ibid.,* II.2.36.
[48] *Brahma-Sūtra, Madhva-bhāṣya,* II.1.37.

been perceived by anybody anywhere, He does not exist. According to the Jains, God's omniscience is not valid knowledge, because right knowledge is that which is produced only in the case of an object not known before. But as God knows everything, His knowledge is necessarily of known objects and hence untrue. So even if God exists, none can direct any faith to Him. According to the Sāṁkhya, there is no logical proof of the existence of God. The inherent teleology in Prakṛti is sufficient to explain creation, and the intervention of God is superfluous and unnecessary. The Mīmāṁsakas believe in the eternality of the Vedas. So the argument of the Naiyāyikas that God exists because He is the creator of the Vedas is not tenable. By the performance of religious rites one gets to heaven, the *summum bonum* of human aspiration. So, more than this, it is not necessary to conceive, nor can it be proved.

The great Naiyāyika, Udayanācārya, who has written an elaborate thesis on the proofs of the existence of God in his famous treatise *Kusumāñjali,* has examined the foregoing arguments and found them wanting. At the beginning of his book, he says, 'What doubt can there be in God, experience of whom is admitted throughout the world?'[49] So, any argument in support of His existence is unnecessary and redundant from the standpoint of the Naiyāyikas. But even then proofs of His existence have been adduced. Because, as Udayanācārya writes, 'This logical consideration of God is tantamount to thinking (*manana*) about Him. It follows hearing (*śravaṇa*) about Him, and is undertaken as a form of worship (*upāsanā*)'.[50]

In putting forward the various inferential proofs, the author writes, 'From effects, conjunction, support etc., from the use of things, from the authoritativeness of the Vedas, from the composition of the Vedas, from sentences, and from particular numbers, an immutable all-knowing God can be deduced'.[51] The first of these is the causal argument—from consideration of effects (*kārya*) God can be deduced. The earth etc. must have a maker since they are effects like the pot. Everything that is composite must possess an intelligent cause. Without such a cause, the material causes cannot produce definite effects. To be this cause entails possessing direct knowledge of the material causes, a desire to realize some aim, and the power of will to accomplish this aim. God must be such a cause. The second proof is from conjunction (*āyojana*). At the beginning of creation two atoms must join to form a molecule. All works require an intelligent agent. At the beginning of creation, when two atoms join together to form

[49] *Kusumāñjali,* I.
[50] *Ibid.,* I.3.
[51] *Ibid.,* V.1.

a dyad, even that, being a work, must also require an intelligent agent, who must be God. The third proof arises from the consideration of inhibition of celestial bodies from fall. Just as a piece of wood is supported in space by a bird, so also the universe is withheld from falling down by someone's support. And that someone is God. The word 'etc.' (*ādi*) signifies dissolution. God is the author of the destruction of the world. 'From the use of things' (*padāt*) denotes that there must be a teacher for imparting the knowledge of the use of things. We find that instructions are needed for teaching the modern arts. So for the traditional arts, which are current from endless time, there must be an instructor. And that instructor must be God. The next proof is had from the authoritativeness of the Vedas (*pratyayataḥ*). The knowledge from the Vedas is authoritative like all true knowledge. So that authoritativeness must have a cause which is God. Another proof is from the inference of composition of the Vedas. The Vedas are composed by some person as Āyurveda is. Now, as the authorship of the Vedas cannot be ascribed to any human being, its author must be God. The argument 'from sentences' (*vākyāt*) denotes that since the Vedas contain sentences, so they must have been composed by some person, just as our sentences have ourselves as the authors. That author is God. Then comes the argument from number (*saṅkhyā-viśeṣāt*). According to this argument, the magnitude of the dyad is not caused by individual atoms; it depends on number, because atomic magnitude is eternal and insignificantly minute. But number requires the distinguishing perception (*apekṣā-buddhi*) which must be somebody's. As the number two of the atoms that go to form the dyad at the beginning of creation could not have been the object of our distinguishing perception, so that distinguishing perception must have been God's. That scriptures independently prove the existence of God has been accepted by Udayana.[52] By these various arguments the Naiyāyikas try to establish God. The Vaiśeṣika system believes inference and scriptures to be the valid means of the knowledge of God. God is proved by the inference of an active principle as the creator of the world, independent of *adṛṣṭa*. As the author of the Vedas also He can be inferred.[53]

Patañjali describes God as 'a particular spirit (Puruṣa) untouched by troubles, works, fruits or deserts'.[54] The next *sūtra* of Patañjali is, 'In Him does the germ of omniscience become infinite'.[55] Everything that admits of comparison or degree must have an acme. The ultra-sensorial knowledge of the past, present, and future existing to a greater or less degree

[52] *Ibid.*, V.15.
[53] *Kaṇāda-Sūtra*, I.1.3; II.1.18,19; X.2.9 with Śaṅkara Miśra's commentary.
[54] *Yoga-Sūtra*, I.24.
[55] *Ibid.*, I.25.

in every human being constitutes the germ of omniscience ; and this germ of omniscience reaches the apogee in someone ; and that someone is God. Thus we infer God generally ; but since inference does not conduce to particularity, His specific nature, e.g. omniscience etc. is to be learnt from the scriptures. So, for establishing God, inference and authority are both necessary according to this system.

According to Śaṅkara, the Vedas are the only valid means of the knowledge of God. Reason in itself is futile. 'On account of the diversity of men's opinions, it is impossible to accept mere reasoning as having a sure foundation.' He, however, concludes, 'Our final position therefore is that on the ground of scripture and of reasoning subordinate to scripture, the intelligent Brahman is to be considered the cause and substance of the world'.[56]

Rāmānuja, more or less, agrees with Śaṅkara's view that the scriptures are the only means of the knowledge of God. He says, 'Because Brahman, being raised above all contact with the senses, is not an object of perception and the other means of proof, but to be known through scripture only'.[57] But reasoning plays a secondary part. 'With regard to supersensuous matters, scripture alone is authoritative, and reasoning is to be applied only to the support of scripture.'[58]

According to Madhva also, God transcends all perception.[59] But His nature is not indefinable, because we can know His nature through a study of the Vedas.[60]

This is the general attitude of the Vedāntins of all shades. But that does not prove that they have not produced cogent proofs in support of the existence of Brahman.[61]

### GOD'S RELATION TO NATURE AND MAN

In the Saṁhitās, God has been spoken of as the efficient cause and in some places as the material cause of the world.[62] God is regulated by *ṛta* (order) in His dispensation. Through His grace man prospers both in this world and the next.[63]

In the Upaniṣads we find that Brahman has been thought to be both the efficient and the material cause of the world.[64] But this creation is

[56] *Brahma-Sūtra, Śaṅkara-bhāṣya,* II.1.11.
[57] *Brahma-Sūtra, Rāmānuja-bhāṣya,* I.1.3.
[58] *Ibid.,* II.1.12.
[59] *Brahma-Sūtra, Madhva-bhāṣya,* III.2.23.
[60] *Ibid.,* III.3.1.
[61] *Brahma-Sūtra,* scattered through I.1.1; I.1.4; II.3.7; and *Bṛhadāraṇyaka-bhāṣya-vārttika,* 189; *Pañcadaśī,* I.1-10; and later polemical writers.
[62] *R.V.,* X.90.
[63] *Ibid.,* I.1.8; I.23.5.
[64] *Mu. U.,* I.1.7.

unreal, because there is no diversity in the world.[65] The individual beings, though appearing as many, are really one and the same as Brahman.[66] The individuation is really the result of ignorance. When this ignorance is dispelled, then the finitude of individuality is transcended, the supreme realization of unity dawns, and the end of spiritual life is reached.[67]

The Cārvākas hold that the world is a fortuitous and spontaneous growth promoted by the chance combination of material elements, and no intervention of God is needed in creation. They admit the existence of consciousness, but only as an epiphenomenon or a by-product of matter. Hedonistic calculus is the only principle that should guide human beings, since there is neither God nor heaven or hell. The Jains hold that the world is created by the permutation and combination of the four primary ingredients, time, space, soul, and matter (*pudgala*) in their subtle form. In their various arrangements they are guided by (1) time, (2) environment, (3) necessity or destiny, (4) action, and (5) effort. According to the Jains, a Jīva or soul is a conscious substance. But consciousness exists in different Jīvas in varying degrees. At one end of the scale are the perfected souls possessing omniscience, and at the other end plants and minerals showing no apparent sign of consciousness, and yet possessing consciousness. Individual souls who have limited knowledge and power are subject to miseries. But they have the potentiality of infinite consciousness, power, and happiness. They are debarred from attaining these because of *karmas*. By transcending *karmas* the souls can realize their potentiality, which is liberation. Buddha himself was averse to any metaphysical speculation. Yet he could not avoid it altogether. Since Buddha's time some philosophical ideas came to underlie his ethical teachings. These are (1) the doctrine of dependent origination, (2) the doctrine of universal change and impermanence, (3) the theory of the non-existence of soul, and (4) the doctrine of Karma.

According to the Sāṁkhya system, there are two types of eternal ultimate realities. The first is Prakṛti which is unconscious, and the second is self (Puruṣa) which is conscious. The self is many and the subject of knowledge. Prakṛti evolves into the world by coming into relationship with Puruṣa. But the Sāṁkhya does not explain how this relationship is brought about. The followers of the Pātañjala school say that this is brought about by the agency of *avidyā* and God. *Avidyā* rests on *buddhi* and involves Puruṣa in the world when he is reflected in *buddhi*. But this *avidyā* is something insentient. So it is difficult to see how it can bring

[65] *Bṛ. U.*, IV.4.19.
[66] *Ibid.*, I.4.10.
[67] *Ka. U.*, II.1.15; *Ī. U.*, 7.

about the contact of Puruṣa and Prakṛti. So, according to the Yoga school, without the intervention of God this association is not possible.[68] According to the Nyāya-Vaiśeṣika school, the world is created by God out of the eternal, unalterable, causeless atoms, taking into consideration the moral deserts of the individual souls who are eternal. The individual souls are something distinct from body, mind, etc. They are many and not necessarily conscious, and they possess contingent attributes like desire, aversion, intellection, action, pleasure, and pain. Souls are not conscious, but consciousness is 'a quality of the soul produced in the waking state by the conjunction of the soul with *manas*. It is an intermittent quality of the self'.[69] God is thus the moral governor of the world and dispenses fruits of Jīva's actions. The Mīmāṁsā system avers that atoms, which are the ultimate constituents working under the autonomous law of Karma, form the world. No postulation of God is necessary for explaining this. But the system has to postulate individual souls. The Vedic injunctions hold out promises of reward to be enjoyed in another world. But this would be impossible if some real self did not exist. The selves are many. They are eternal infinite substances. Consciousness is not their essence, but is an adventitious quality which arises under suitable conditions.

We have seen above that in Śaṅkara's system God has been conceived as both the efficient as well as the material cause of the world. At the same time He has been spoken of as devoid of all attributes and as the only reality. In this context any theory of creation seems to be logically unsound. But Śaṅkara escapes this logical insufficiency by enunciating the concept of Māyā or illusion. Brahman no doubt transforms Itself into the world and is therefore both the efficient as well as the material cause. But this is only apparently. Really there is neither transformation nor the world. This is the famous Vivartavāda, according to which the change is not real but due to imaginary attribution (*adhyāsa*) only, just as a rope is taken to be a snake due to imaginary attribution.[70] The Jīva also in such a background is illusory. His real nature is the same as the ground of everything. It is through ignorance that he considers himself limited and sees the diversity in the world. As soon as ignorance is dispelled, he realizes his true self and goes beyond the sufferings of the world. But all this is from the transcendental and ultimate standpoint.

From the empirical standpoint the world is the creation of God through His power of Māyā. Brahman is the efficient cause of the world and also the material cause in so far as He is associated with Māyā.

[68] *Bhojavṛtti,* I.24.

[69] Radhakrishnan, *Indian Philosophy,* II. p. 149.

[70] *Brahma-Sūtra, Śaṅkara-bhāṣya,* II.1.33. 'Finally, we must remember that the scriptural doctrine of creation does not refer to the highest reality.'

Brahman associated with Māyā is Īśvara, God. Māyā directed by God changes into the world. The Jīvas are the products of the particular adjuncts into which Māyā specializes herself. In their real nature they are Brahman Itself. Their body, mind, etc. are the creation of Māyā. At each creation the Jīvas are endowed with natures which are the results of their past merits and demerits.[71] God has no purpose for creation, because all His desires are ever fulfilled. He creates out of play.[72]

Rāmānuja holds that at the beginning of a cycle of creation God alone remains, and matter and souls remain in Him in a dormant and subtle condition. By an act of volition the Lord sets the process of creation going. Subtle matter evolves into gross state. The individual souls also assume bodies corresponding to their past *dharma* and *adharma*. But, after all, matter and souls are not different from God, and in the subtle state less so. So it is God who can be said to modify (*pariṇāma*) Himself into the world and soul. The soul, who, assisted by the grace of the Lord, contemplates Him and cognizes Him as He has been described in the Vedānta, attains liberation. In the liberated condition he becomes similar to and not the same as God. He never possesses the powers of creation, preservation, and destruction of the world.

Madhva holds that God creates the world out of Prakṛti, in which heterogeneous principles are located in a subtle form. God in creation takes into account the moral deserts of individual souls. The individual souls are infinite in number and are distinct from God and from one another. The Jīvas are atomic in size. The souls are eternal and dependent entirely on the Lord. Liberation can result only from the grace of God, which can be obtained by the worship of the Lord.

[71] *Brahma-Sūtra, Śaṅkara-bhāṣya,* II.1.34; see also II.1.35,36.
[72] *Ibid.,* II.1.33.

# 34

# INDIAN EPISTEMOLOGY

## PLACE OF EPISTEMOLOGY IN PHILOSOPHY

EPISTEMOLOGY or the theory of knowledge has acquired special importance in European philosophy in the modern period, particularly in the philosophies of Locke, Hume, and Kant. Kant thought that without a prior critical examination of the elements, sources, and limits of knowledge we should not engage in metaphysical discussion. So he regarded all previous philosophy as dogmatic as contrasted with his own critical philosophy. In more recent times, however, the American neo-realists have tried to oppose the general modern European trend, initiated by Kant, that the theory of knowledge should precede the theory of reality. They have chosen to be consciously dogmatic. They are led to this position by a kind of reaction against the use of epistemology made by most modern idealists for establishing idealistic theories of reality.

But in India the position has been otherwise. From the very beginning of the different systems of philosophy until recent times, discussions on the problems of knowledge (including those of doubt and error) have formed an essential part of philosophy. The reason for this striking and continued unanimity can be found in the fact that all schools of Indian philosophy, without exception, regarded ignorance as the root cause of human suffering, so that they were all bent upon discovering the means and processes of true knowledge by means of which reality could be known and life could be so lived as to overcome misery or minimize suffering. Vātsyāyana voices the feelings of all Indian thinkers on this matter when, in commenting upon the first *sūtra* of Gautama, he says that the study of the sources of knowledge (*pramāṇa*) is necessary, because through it alone can we properly know reality and thereby guide our actions so as to be able to attain desirable ends and avoid suffering.

Epistemology thus becomes closely linked up with ontology and both of them again with ethics. Knowledge and moral perfection are regarded as necessary to each other in almost all systems of Indian thought. Sometimes knowledge is regarded as the means to the good life, sometimes again moral purity is regarded as indispensable for perfect knowledge, so that morality and knowledge are regarded as the two inseparable aspects of perfection.

In the course of the development of the Indian systems interest in epistemology increased and it began to claim a large share in the philosophical discussions of almost every school. The motives were sometimes theoretical, sometimes practical, sometimes simply polemical. But all led to the enrichment of epistemological thought and literature.

### ANALYSIS AND SOURCES OF KNOWLEDGE

The factors constituting and connected with knowledge (*jñāna* or *pramā*) are usually analysed into the subject (*jñātṛ* or *pramātṛ*), the object (*jñeya* or *prameya*), and the means of knowledge (*pramāṇa*). But consciousness is not always regarded as the product of any relation between the subject and the object. The Sāṁkhya, the Vedānta, and the Jaina schools conceive the self as possessed of intrinsic consciousness, so that knowledge is nothing more than the relation of the object to an already existing consciousness of the self. The Sāṁkhya, the Yoga, and the Vedānta assert the possibility of the existence of consciousness even when there is no object. But the Nyāya-Vaiśeṣika and the Mīmāṁsaka hold, as do some Western thinkers, that consciousness—and so knowledge—is a product of the relation of the self, previously unconscious, to some object in some appropriate way. The Buddhists also regard consciousness, like every other phenomenon, as a momentary product of several conditions.

A distinction is maintained, however, by the Sāṁkhya-Yoga and the Vedānta between consciousness as it is in itself (*svarūpa-caitanya*) and empirical consciousness or consciousness of objects (*vṛtti-caitanya*). With the help of this distinction these schools can also maintain the common-sense notion of knowledge (as beginning in time and depending on the relation of the self to some object), because such knowledge only means empirical consciousness of some object. But they point out, like Green, that consciousness in itself is original and eternal ; and it transcends time and space. In fact, such intrinsic consciousness is regarded as identical with the self (Ātman) itself. According to the Sāṁkhya and the Yoga, the self as the knower is real, and it is distinguished from objects as known. The relation of the self to objects is not possible, according to these schools, unless the object produces through the senses and *manas* some image of itself in the intellect (*buddhi*). This modification of *buddhi* (technically called *vṛtti*) is illuminated by the self or consciousness, resulting in the knowledge of the object. But as the Advaita regards the distinction between the knower and the known as a practical make-shift, untenable in the ultimate analysis, it does not hold, like the Sāṁkhya, the reality of even the rôle of the self as the knower. The knower and the known are but the two apparent aspects of one basic reality, the real Self or Brahman. Knowledge should not be considered therefore to be really an external relation. It is only the self-shining consciousness that is the very nature of existence, including the apparent subjects and objects. But to explain knowledge in terms of the dualistic beliefs of the ordinary man, the Advaitin adopts to a certain extent the Sāṁkhya theory of knowledge, with the important difference that he does not regard knowledge as an external relation. The object in contact with the external sense or directly present to the internal sense (*antaḥkaraṇa*) causes a modification (*vṛtti*) of the latter. This *vṛtti* only serves to remove, though to that extent and in that respect only, the illusory distinction between the knower and the known. For the Buddhist idealist, the Vijñānavādin, every objective knowledge is an illusory externalization or external projection of a subjective idea.

Knowledge, in the strict sense of correct cognition, is called *pramā,* and a source of knowledge is called a *pramāṇa.* Unlike Western logic that generally admits two chief sources of knowledge, perception and inference, Indian epistemology admits, in the different schools, one to six sources of knowledge. We shall briefly discuss them one by one.

### PERCEPTION OR PRATYAKṢA

Perception, generally called *pratyakṣa,* is admitted by all the schools to be the basic source of knowledge. The Cārvākas regard it as the only source. According to them, inference is not reliable, since every inference, to be true, must be based upon *some* universal proposition containing the knowledge of an invariable relation between two phenomena ; and such a universal proposition cannot be established by observations. We cannot observe, for example, whether all cases of smoke—those in the unobserved past, or in the future, or in regions beyond perception—were, will be, or are even now invariably accompanied by fire. Inference cannot therefore be relied on with certainty. About authority as a source of knowledge the Cārvākas point to the innumerable examples in daily life where we find ourselves deceived and misled by the testimony of other persons. Even the scriptures are not beyond doubt. The Vedas contain many meaningless words and enjoin rituals which may merely go to swell the fees of the officiating priests. They may therefore be the work of cunning priests.

Regarding the exact origin of *pratyakṣa* or perceptual knowledge, there is, however, a good deal of controversy among the different schools. The ordinary view is that *pratyakṣa* is that kind of knowledge which is generated by the relation of sense (*indriya*) to some object (*indriyārtha-sannikarṣa-janya-jñāna*). In accordance with the Nyāya-Vaiśeṣika view, there are six senses or *indriyas*—the five external ones of sound, sight, touch, taste, and smell, and the internal one, mind (*manas*). If the object is an external one, like a tree, the knower (the soul) directs the mind through the external sense, say the eyes, to the tree, and gathers thus the visual knowledge of the tree. If the object to be perceived is internal, say a pleasure (which according to this school is a quality of the soul itself), the soul has simply to attend to it through the *manas,* which does therefore, in this case, the double duty of an organ of attention as well as that of an internal sense.

According to the Sāṁkhya-Yoga school also, the contact of the object with some one of the senses is necessary for ordinary external perception. But such a contact must generate some modification in the internal sense, as was mentioned in the previous section. The internal organ is sometimes considered to be a whole and called *antaḥkaraṇa* or *citta,* but sometimes distinguished by its different functions (of explication, self-reference, and determination) into the three aspects called respectively *manas, ahaṅkāra,* and *buddhi.* The account of the origination of perception is therefore differently given by different writers of this school. But on the whole it is admitted that if the internal organ in some aspect does not assume the form of the object and present it to the self or the self-shining consciousness, there cannot be any knowledge of the object. This clue is utilized by the Yoga when it teaches that the modification of the *citta* into the form of the object should be stopped, so that no object may appear before consciousness and tempt it into attachment and bondage. *Yoga* is thus defined as the arrest of the modification of the internal organ (*Yogaścitta-vṛtti-nirodhaḥ*).

A question often discussed in connection with the possibilities of perceptual knowledge is whether there can be any perception of entities not related to any sense. Some Vedantins, who do not regard *manas* as a sense (unlike the Naiyayikas and Sāṁkhyas), point out that internal perceptions (of pleasure, pain, etc.) prove that no sense need mediate in such cases. Moreover, they ask, 'If perception be not possible without some sense, how can the Naiyāyikas and others think of God as perceiving the world?' The Yoga system admits that there can be knowledge of external objects which are not accessible to any sense, if the mind can be sufficiently concentrated on them. The later Naiyāyikas agree that there are exceptional cases of extraordinary perception in which immediate knowledge of external objects, not related to an external sense, is possible ; and they admit in that connection the possibility of yogic perception. Gaṅgeśa, the founder of the later Nyāya, states in his famous work *Tattva-cintāmaṇi* that it is not necessary to conceive and define perception in terms of sense-object relation ; immediacy is the essential character of perception. This point is further emphasized and elaborated by the Jaina and the Advaita thinkers.

The Jains very aptly observe that ordinary perception in which the self knows the object through the medium of some sense cannot rightly be called immediate. It is only less mediate than inference, testimony, etc. But real immediate knowledge, worth the name, is that knowledge which the self can acquire by its direct relation to the object without the intermediation of any organ whatsoever. Such absolutely immediate knowledge can be gained only when the self can free itself of the obstructing influence of its many *karmas*. Everyone can attain such omniscience through the necessary moral perfection.

The Advaitins, the followers of the monistic Vedānta school of Śaṅkarācārya, also hold, in another way, the potential omniscience of every man. According to this school, the self being really identical with the absolute Brahman, what limits its knowledge is its ignorance of its real nature. When ignorance is overcome, what remains is the self-shining consciousness, the pure Self or Brahman. Immediacy is primarily the nature of this basic consciousness; only secondarily it belongs to a sense perception. Every such perception takes place by a sort of removal of the ignorance that divides the knower from the known. Perception is therefore a momentary restoration of the lost identity between the two and the flashing forth of the basic consciousness which underlies all—the knower, the known, and the entire mechanism of knowledge. The ideal of immediate knowledge is not, however, attained in sense perception or any other knowledge in the objective attitude. It is attained when the objective attitude is altogether overcome and the underlying unlimited consciousness, Brahman, is allowed to reveal Itself.

The question is often discussed in the Indian schools as to what exactly is revealed by sense perception. The subjective idealists among Buddhist thinkers—the Vijñānavādins or Yogācāras, as they are variously called—hold that external perception is really an external projection of mind's own ideas, which emerge into consciousness by the maturation of some of the innumerable unconscious ideas that form the total mental substratum (*ālayavijñāna*) underlying the individual. The Sautrāntika school of Buddhism believes, however, that sense perception produces in the mind the ideas or copies of external objects, which can therefore be inferred as the originals of these copies. But the Vaibhāṣika school of Buddhism holds that external objects themselves, and not merely the ideas of them, are directly given in perception. The Nyāya-Vaiśeṣika, Sāṁkhya, Mīmāṁsaka, and Vedāntin, including even Śaṅkarācārya, hold this last view about perception.

Consistently with its thoroughgoing realism, the Nyāya-Vaiśeṣika school holds that all the elements that we can find by analysing the different perceptual judgements—in fact, all the basic categories of reality—are given in perception from the beginning, though the relation among them is established by the judging mind subsequently. The Buddhists, in general, hold that perception reveals only unique particulars—their class-characters, names, etc. are later superimposed by the judging mind. Some later followers of Śaṅkara maintain, on the contrary, that perception reveals only pure Being (*sanmātra*); all particular characters are the superimpositions of the interpreting mind.

Can the self be perceived? This question is variously answered. The older Nyāya tries to prove the existence of the self by inferences of different kinds. But the later Nyāya-Vaiśeṣika writers hold that though the self as such cannot be perceived, yet it is possible to perceive it in such introspective knowledge as 'I am happy'. The self as possessed of some perceptible quality (like happiness or sorrow) is the object of such internal perception. The Bhāṭṭa Mīmāṁsakas also think that the self is knowable as the object of occasional self-consciousness. The Prābhākaras strongly feel that the self, which is the subject, cannot possibly be an object of knowledge without losing its own nature. According to them, every act of knowledge reveals itself, as well as the self as the knower and the object as the known. The Sāṁkhyas and the Advaitins believe that as the self is identical with consciousness, it is self-revealing. Only it is not known in its purity, so long as it is not isolated from the empirical objects with which it is confused and mixed up in the form of objective consciousness. The self is not known objectively—not even as the object of introspection—but as the consciousness which immediately manifests itself.

### INFERENCE OR ANUMĀNA

Except the Cārvākas, all other schools consider inference to be a valid and important source of knowledge. In reply to the Cārvāka objections against inference, it is pointed out (1) that even the theory that inference is invalid can be established only by an inference, so the Cārvāka theory is suicidal, and (2) that it is not impossible to establish universal propositions (as premises necessary for deductive inference) with the help of various inductive methods (discussed below).

Gautama and his later followers of the Nyāya school devoted special attention to inference, which occupied these thinkers almost exclusively for centuries, particularly in Mithilā and Bengal. The views of other schools were greatly influenced by them. In the course of their intensive cultivation of this narrow field of inference, they discovered many subtleties, and developed above all a unique algebraic language for the precise formulation of ideas. This became the standard language of philosophical discussion in all schools and made all later philosophical treatises unintelligible to the general reader.

The common conception of inference—rather *anumāna*—is that it is the kind of knowledge which is derived from the previous knowledge of an invariable relation between a sign (*liṅga*) and something bearing that sign (*liṅgin*). For example, when we know the existence of fire on the distant mountain from the smoke perceptible on it, we have an *anumāna* based on the invariable relation between smoke and fire. Such a relation is technically called *vyāpti* or pervasion (the cases of the existence of smoke being pervaded by those of the existence of fire).

This invariable relation is established by different inductive methods. The Buddhist logicians adopt the five-step method of observation (called *pañcakāraṇī*), namely, (1) cause is not perceived, effect is also not perceived, (2) cause is perceived, (3) effect is also perceived, (4) cause disappears, (5) effect also disappears. In his *Positive Sciences of the Ancient Hindus* Sir Brajendra Nath Seal characterizes this Buddhist method of establishing induction through causal connection as the double method of difference and notes its superiority to the ordinary single method of difference adopted by Western logicians.

The Naiyāyikas, commencing with Gautama, recognize that it is possible to have *vyāpti* or invariable connection of the causal as well as of the non-causal type, e.g. all animals with horns have tails. In most cases, according to them, such a relation can be established by the observation of agreement in presence (*anvaya*), e.g. by observing in many cases that wherever there is smoke, there is fire, and by the observation of agreement in absence (*vyatireka*), e.g. by observing in many cases that where there is no fire, there is no smoke. This would constitute the joint method of agreement. But in some exceptional cases we may have to depend on the single method of agreement in presence only (*kevala-anvaya*), e.g. when we have to establish a relation like 'All nameable things are knowable things' (where, from the nature of the case, we cannot possibly observe any negative instance like 'This thing is not knowable, and it is also not nameable'). In other exceptional cases, of an opposite type, we may have to depend only on agreement in absence (*kevala-vyatireka*), e.g. when we have to establish a proposition like '(Of the five elements) whichever is not different from the other (four) elements (e.g. ether, air, fire, and water) has no smell' (where we cannot observe any positive instance except earth since earth is the only element having smell).

To make induction more certain the Naiyāyikas also insist on the elimination of doubts arising from the existence of any unnoticed condition (*upādhi*) that might be responsible for the invariable coexistence of two phenomena in the cases observed. For example, someone may observe in many cases the existence of fire accompanied by smoke ; and, failing to notice that in all such cases wetness of the fuel was a condition responsible for smoke, he might erroneously lay down the universal proposition, 'Wherever there is fire, there is smoke'. Only by repeated and careful observation can such errors be eliminated.

Gautama speaks of three kinds of inference, *pūrvavat, śeṣavat,* and *sāmānyatodṛṣṭa.* According to the common interpretation, they stand respectively for inference from cause to effect (e.g. from the gathering clouds to rain), from effect to cause (e.g. from flood in the river to rainfall up-stream), and lastly from a generally observed non-causal type of relation (e.g. from the changing position of the sun to the movement of the sun).

Later Naiyāyikas classify inference on another principle, namely, in accordance with the inductive method on which the major premise of the inference is based. So they have the three kinds of inference called respectively *anvaya-vyatirekī, kevalānvayī,* and *kevala-vyatirekī.*

Gautama lays down five steps as necessary for an inference when it is required to demonstrate a conclusion without straying from the point to be proved and without committing any formal or material fallacy. For such a purpose one should proceed as follows:

(1) State the proposition to be proved (*pratijñā,* e.g. 'That hill has fire', i.e. there is fire on the hill).

(2) State the reason in support (*hetu,* e.g. 'Because it has smoke').

(3) State the invariable relation between the sign (the reason or middle term) and the signified (the major term) supported by some concrete instance guaranteeing material validity (*udāharaṇa,* e.g. 'Whatever has smoke has fire, as the fire-place', i.e. wherever there is smoke there is fire).

(4) Show how the above relation applies to the case in hand (*upanaya,* e.g. 'This hill has smoke which is invariably accompanied by fire').

(5) Draw the conclusion (*nigamana,* e.g. 'Therefore, the hill has fire').

It will be observed that *anumāna,* as conceived here, is not only the formally valid deductive inference of Western logic, it is also, as Seal calls it, a formal-material, deductive-inductive process.

The fallacies of inference mentioned by Gautama and discussed by other thinkers after him are chiefly the different kinds of material invalidity arising from the middle term not being invariably, or at all, related to the major, or not actually existing in the minor, or leading to a conclusion contradicted by observation or by a more reliable inference. Gautama is never tired of insisting in various ways on the necessity of keeping truth as the goal of all argument and debate and the consequent necessity of desisting from all unfair use of the intellect, such as quibbling, using false analogy, arguing merely for victory, and so on.

Though the other schools do not accept *in toto* the Nyāya view of inference, their deviations are not so important as to deserve special mention in this brief essay.

### TESTIMONY OR ŚABDA

Except the Cārvāka school and Kaṇāda, the founder of the Vaiśeṣika (who admits only perception and inference), the Indian logicians accept testimony or authority as a third source of valid knowledge. Kaṇāda thinks, like Western logicians, that knowledge from authority is really a kind of inference, based on the reliability of the authority. But the Naiyāyikas and others point out that the process by which such knowledge is derived is so different from that of inference that it deserves a separate status. For, in order that *śabda* or verbal statement may yield knowledge, the following conditions have to be fulfilled:

(1) Each word of a sentence must carry some meaning which is by itself incomplete and raises some expectation (*ākāṅkṣā*).

(2) The meanings of the different words should possess mutual compatibility (*yogyatā*) and thereby fulfil the expectation raised by one another.

(3) The words to be construed must have mutual proximity (*sannidhi*), that is, they should not be written or uttered at long intervals.

To these three conditions some thinkers add a fourth, namely, understanding of the context (*prakaraṇa*) or the intention of the speaker of the sentence (*tātparya*).

Now, it will be seen that these conditions of verbal cognition do not involve the knowledge of *vyāpti* which is essential for inference. So knowledge derived from the words of an authority cannot be the same as inference.

Of course, it is true that only the words of a reliable person (*āpta*) can yield valid knowledge. But similarly only undisturbed perception and unvitiated inference can yield valid knowledge. In other words, the possibility of doubt and error is common to all sources of knowledge; and this should not prevent us from admitting authority as a source of knowledge. If we disbelieve authority, we have to go without so much of valuable knowledge obtainable from the statements of specialists, experts, and the scriptures. The Mīmāṁsā school tries to show in this connection that if we do not accept the authority of the Vedas, we have no other means of knowledge by which we can ascertain which ritual has to be performed for which purpose and with what result. The Vedas are the only source of knowledge of the various injunctions (*dharmas*).

### KNOWLEDGE FROM SIMILARITY OR UPAMĀNA

A fourth source of knowledge admitted by Gautama and his followers, as well as by the Mīmāṁsā and Vedānta schools, is what is called *upamāna* (literally, comparison). It is, however, variously conceived. According to Gautama, it is that kind of knowledge which we have about an unfamiliar thing on the basis of its similarity with a familiar thing. The later Nyāya conceives it as the knowledge of the denotation of an unfamiliar word on the basis of a knowledge of similarity. We do not, for example, know the denotation of the word *gavaya*. An expert tells us that it denotes an animal like a cow, but without a dewlap. We go to the forest and, observing such a creature there, we know it to be a *gavaya*. This resulting knowledge is obtained through *upamāna*.

But the Mīmāṁsā and Advaita schools think that this knowledge can be said to be obtained in part by testimony and in part by inference, and does not require to be classed apart. According to them, *upamāna* is the knowledge of similarity about an absent object obtained from the perceived similarity of a present object. For example, when a man sees the animal *gavaya* in the forest, he feels, 'This *gavaya* looks like my cow at home'; and then he may think, 'The cow at home is like the *gavaya*'. The first judgement is derived from perception since the subject is being perceived; but the second is obtained through the knowledge of similarity contained in the first, and it is therefore called knowledge from similarity, or *upamāna*. It cannot be said to be *deduced* from the first, since deduction involves the knowledge of an invariable relation between some sign and something signified, a *vyapti*, which we are not conscious of using here.

### IMPLICATION OR ARTHĀPATTI

A fifth kind of knowledge, different from the four already mentioned, is recognized by the Mīmāṁsā and the Advaita schools. It is called *arthāpatti* and means the supposition of what is necessary for explaining any fact either observed (*dṛṣṭa*) or heard about (*śruta*). The stock example is: A person, Devadatta, is observed to be fasting the whole day, but growing stouter and stouter. To explain this, we are forced to suppose that he must be eating (unperceived) during the night. This last knowledge is arrived at through *arthāpatti*. Similarly, by this very method we suppose a word in a sentence where it remains understood, or we suppose the secondary, figurative meaning of a sentence where the primary meaning does not suit.

This process of knowledge is different from inference, because here we do not draw a conclusion from given premises—rather we have to discover here the explanation of what is given. It resembles the method of hypothesis recognized by Western logicians; but the difference is that here the supposition is not provisional but necessary.

### NON-COGNITION OR ANUPALABDHI

In addition to these five sources of knowledge, the Bhāṭṭa school of Mīmāṁsā and the Advaita school of Vedānta admit appropriate (*yogya*) non-cognition as a unique source of knowledge. The necessity of admitting this arises thus: Looking round the room we say, there is not a single jug of water here. How do we know the non-existence of the jug here? The common-sense reply would be, 'We *see* that it does not exist here'. But the difficulty is that we can see a thing or sense it only when it is something positive, so that it can stimulate the sense concerned. But how can non-existence stimulate the sense? The Nyāya school, which is the philosophical advocate of common sense, tries to get over this difficulty by holding that though non-existence itself cannot be directly related to any sense, it is indirectly related to it through its locus, say the room, which is related to the sense. Non-existence is like an adjective, a qualifying character, to its locus; and as the locus (e.g. the room) is perceived, so also is the non-existence (e.g. absence of the jug) along with it.

But this Nyāya view is not accepted by the Bhāṭṭas and the Advaitins who point out that *any* character that qualifies a thing is not necessarily perceived just because the thing itself is perceived; for instance, when we see a jar we do not perceive its weight, though it is there in the jar. So, only qualities which can be related to and stimulate the sense concerned can be perceived, and non-existence is not of this kind.

The Prābhākaras and Sāṁkhyas try to obviate the difficulty in another way. They say that non-existence is not at all an entity additional to its locus. In fact, it is a turn of expression signifying the bare locus, or the mere locus. To say that there is no jug in the room is to say that only the room is there. And when we perceive such a bare room, we say, we perceive the non-existence of the jug in it.

But even this explanation is not accepted by the Bhāṭṭas and the Advaitins. They point out that we cannot understand a bare or empty room without thinking of the non-existence of things in it. So non-existence is found to be an additional entity.

It has to be admitted therefore that non-existence cannot be said to be perceived through the senses. Nor can we infer it from anything else unless we have previous knowledge of an invariable relation of non-existence with that thing, which would presuppose some knowledge of non-existence and thus beg the very question.

Non-existence can be said to be known, however, by non-cognition. Just as positive cognition is the source of the information about positive entities, absence of the knowledge of a thing (under circumstances in which it should have been known had it existed) yields us the information about its non-existence. That is how we primarily know non-existence, according to the Bhāṭṭas and the Advaitins.

In addition to these six sources of knowledge there are a few more like tradition (*aitihya*), presentiment (*pratibhā*), possible entailment (*sambhava*), etc. admitted by other minor schools.

## TRUTH AND ERROR

The conceptions of truth and error and their metaphysical outlook vary from school to school. Buddhist sceptics, who disbelieve the validity of even normal perception, hold that all such knowledge is *prima facie* unreliable. But still they adopt, for practical purposes, the distinction between true cognition and false cognition with the pragmatic criterion of practical utility (*artha-kriyā-kāritva*).

The Nyāya-Vaiśeṣika realist thinks that the distinction between truth and falsity is not simply a practical one, but is based on objective conditions. If a knowledge reveals something as it really is or some character as belonging to a place or substratum where it really is, it is true ; and if, on the contrary, it shows the thing to be what it really is not or shows it to belong to a place or substratum where it does not really exist, it is false. Truth and falsity can be ascertained only inferentially from the soundness or defectiveness, respectively, of the condition generating the knowledge ; or from the harmony (*saṁvāda*) or disharmony (*visaṁvāda*), respectively, of the knowledge with other knowledge or with the practical consequences following therefrom. Immediate knowledge under normal conditions is free from error. But illusions sometimes occur under extraordinary conditions ; when, for example, a rope seen in twilight revives in our mind, by reason of its great similarity, the vivid idea of a snake perceived in the past at some other place, we have the illusion of a snake. A thing which has never been perceived in the past, however, can never appear in illusion. Illusion is only the dislocation of really perceived objects from their own locus to another. It is not the creation of something new. So this theory of illusion is called Anyathākhyātivāda, that is, the theory of something (previously perceived) appearing in some other place or time.

According to the Mīmāṁsā school and Rāmānuja, all knowledge worth the name is self-evidently valid, since whenever knowledge arises it claims belief, and we act on it without suspicion. This is known as the theory of the self-validity of knowledge (Svataḥprāmāṇyavāda). The Mīmāṁsakas point out that if the validity of any knowledge were to depend on another knowledge, e.g. inference, then the validity of this second knowledge would require to be certified by a third knowledge, and so on. There would thus be an infinite regress (*anavasthā*).

As to illusion, the Prābhākara Mīmāṁsakas say that there is no positive mental state like error. When a rope is said to appear as a snake, what really happens is that we have the true perception of something long and tortuous and this revives in our mind very vividly the idea of a snake perceived in the past ; and owing to a lapse of memory there is lack of discrimination (*bhedāgraha*) between the perceived and the remembered. This view is known as the theory of the denial of illusory appearance (Akhyātivāda). The Bhāṭṭas hold, however, the theory of reversed appearance (Viparītakhyātivāda) which maintains, like that of the Nyāya-Vaiśeṣika, that in illusion the elements truly perceived are presented in a distorted, dislocated, or reverse relation and cause wrong behaviour.

Rāmānuja defends his theory of non-illusion (Satkhyātivāda) by showing that as all objects are made of the mixture of the same basic elements of matter (*bhūtas*) in different proportions, there is really something common to the rope and the snake ; and it is this common element which appears in so-called illusory perception, which is therefore not illusory.

The Advaita Vedānta agrees with Mīmāṁsā that all knowledge is self-evident. But it adds that if knowledge is contradicted by any experience, it ceases to be knowledge and turns into error. Truth, according to the Advaita, consists therefore in the uncontradicted (*abādhita*) and self-evident (*svaprakāśa*) character of knowledge. Practical efficiency is not, by itself, a safe criterion of truth, since even an illusory snake can produce fear and death. It is useful, however, as revealing non-contradiction to a certain extent, but mere non-contradiction would not suffice for truth, had not knowledge possessed also the positive characteristic of self-evidence.

But the objection may be raised that if non-contradiction be the character of truth, the most that we can say about any knowledge is that it is not yet contradicted and is provisionally true ; how then can we ascertain any knowledge to be finally or absolutely true? The reply to this is that such truth can belong to knowledge, the possibility of whose contradiction is not conceivable. Knowledge like 'This tree is green' may be liable to contradiction in future. But if the tree is considered *sub specie aeternitatis*, or from the *pāramārthika* point of view regarded as pure existence (without any specification), there is no logical possibility of contradiction. For, even if the tree turns out to be illusory, even as an appearance it possesses an undeniable 'beinghood' (though not of the specific objective character). Here we have absolute or uncontradictable truth.

Regarding illusion, the Advaitins hold that in every such case there is an undeniable positive appearance directly present to the mind; and it is a misrepresentation of experience to explain it either as the vividly revived memory-idea of something perceived in the past or to explain it negatively as a lack of discrimination between the perceived and the reproduced. The illusory snake is as objectively present to consciousness as a real snake. Only it is momentary and contradicted by subsequent experience. It cannot be described as absolutely real, because it is contradicted; nor as absolutely unreal, because unlike such an unreality as the son of a barren woman, it can appear to consciousness. So the illusory object should be recognized as indescribable. The Advaita theory of error is known therefore as the theory of thc appearance of the indescribable (Anirvacanīyakhyātivāda). Moreover, it is admitted that the illusory object is the temporary creation (*sṛṣṭi*) of ignorance (*avidyā*) which is responsible for all errors.

# 35

# THE ART OF PHILOSOPHICAL DISPUTATION

## SIXTEEN CATEGORIES OF NYĀYA

THE Indian art of philosophical disputation has been exhaustively dealt with in the aphorisms of Akṣapāda, and is embodied in the Nyāya philosophy, which is therefore sometimes called Tarkavidyā or Vādavidyā (the science of debate or discussion). It is the method initiated by Akṣapāda that has been adopted by Indian philosophy in general, though Buddhists, Jains, and some others have registered their partial disagreement with it.

The Nyāya school of philosophy has examined sixteen categories, viz. *pramāṇa* (means of right knowledge), *prameya* (object of right knowledge), *saṁśaya* (doubt), *prayojana* (purpose), *dṛṣṭānta* (familiar instance), *siddhānta* (tenet, conclusion), *avayava* (members of a syllogism), *tarka* (indirect reasoning), *nirṇaya* (ascertainment), *vāda* (discussion), *jalpa* (wrangling), *vitaṇḍā* (cavil), *hetvābhāsa* (fallacy), *chala* (quibble), *jāti* (futile objection), and *nigrahasthāna* (a point of defeat). Among these sixteen categories, all, except *pramāṇa* and *prameya,* are accessaries to the art of disputation. Some categories like *saṁśaya* describe the preliminary conditions of philosophic discussion; some constitute its main body; others, again, make up its final stage. *Nirṇaya,* for example, is the final product of *vicāra* or discussion. Vātsyāyana in his commentary on the *Nyāya-Sūtra* has pertinently posed the question why the fourteen categories beginning with *saṁśaya* have been separately mentioned after describing *pramāṇa* and *prameya,* which evidently include them.[1] In his elaboration of this part of the commentary, Uddyotakara, the author of the *Nyāya-vārttika,* has stated that as all the categories are no other than *prameyas,* naturally categories like *saṁśaya* etc. are all included under that of *prameya.* Why, then, has Akṣapāda made separate mention of *saṁśaya* etc.? Vātsyāyana anticipated this objection in his statement that unlike the subject-matters of the three recognized *vidyās,* viz. the *trayī* (three Vedas), *vārttā* (commerce and agriculture), and *daṇḍanīti* (polity), the fourth one, viz. the *ānvīkṣikī* or the science of Nyāya or argumentation, has for its specific subject these fourteen categories like *saṁśaya* etc. A system of thought becomes altogether pointless if its specific subject-matter is not separately indicated. If the *Nyāya-Sūtra* had done nothing beside

[1] *Nyāya-Sūtra,* I.1.1.

elaborating the twelve *prameyas* like Ātman (soul), *śarīra* (body), *indriyas* (senses), etc., it would have lost its distinctive character and would have been indistinguishable from such purely philosophical texts as the Upaniṣads. So *saṁśaya* etc. which are implied in *vicāra* (discussion) are specifically mentioned and treated in the study of Nyāya.[2]

### CLASSES OF DISPUTATION

*Vicāra,* according to the Indian style, is called *kathā* (controversy). These are synonymous terms. Vātsyāyana says, 'There are three kinds of *kathās*: *vāda, jalpa,* and *vitaṇḍā*'.[3] *Vicāra* has been called *tadvidyasambhāṣā* (discussion with people versed in the relevant science) in *Caraka Saṁhitā.*[4] This *sambhāṣā* (discussion) is of two kinds: *sandhāyasambhāṣā* (friendly discussion) and *vigṛhyasambhāṣā* (aggressive debate). The former, also called *anulomasambhāṣā,* is known as *vādakathā.*[5] The latter refers to *jalpa* and *vitaṇḍā.*[6] Hence the ratiocinative procedure adopted in the Nyāya philosophy and *Caraka Saṁhitā* is fundamentally the same. It is only a seeker after truth (*tattvajijñāsu*) that is entitled to hold *vādakathā.* Uddyotakara says that *vāda* should be entered into with persons like preceptors and others of like status. This *vāda,* according to Vācaspati Miśra, the author of *Tātparyaṭīkā* on the *Nyāya-Sūtra,* yields three results—knowledge of unknown truths, removal of doubts, and confirmation of previous knowledge.[7] It has been stated in the *Vimānasthāna* of *Caraka Saṁhitā* that *tadvidyasambhāṣā* increases the ardour and critical acumen of the inquirer, strengthens his argumentative power, and invests him with fame. Moreover, doubts regarding his previously acquired knowledge are dispelled, firmness of conviction gained, and new knowledge added. One should not enter into *vigṛhyasambhāṣā* with one's preceptor or men of similar position; *sandhāyasambhāṣā* with them is recommended for augmenting one's knowledge. Some have recommended *vigṛhyasambhāṣā* with eminent persons. But Caraka is definitely against this.

The Nyāya philosophy and *Caraka Saṁhitā* have given elaborate accounts of the threefold *kathā—vāda, jalpa,* and *vitaṇḍā.* Caraka has given in addition a detailed description of the types of assemblies (*pariṣad*), namely, whether of the learned or of the ignorant, the components thereof (whether friendly, neutral, or hostile), and the kinds of opponents taking part in them (whether superior, inferior, or equal), and laid down the

[2] *Nyāya-bhāṣya* (Metropolitan Ed.), pp. 34,35.
[3] *Nyāya-bhāṣya,* I.2.1.
[4] *Caraka Saṁhitā, Vimānasthāna,* VIII.
[5] *Nyāya-Sūtra,* I.2.1 enumerates the characteristics of *vādakathā.*
[6] *Ibid.,* I.2.2,3 enumerate the characteristics of *jalpakathā* and *vitaṇḍākathā.*
[7] *Nyāyavārttika-tātparyaṭīkā,* I.2.1.

procedure for tackling each opposing type. The *kathā* meant for the philosophic inquirer is *vāda.* This *vādakathā,* which is the best of *kathās,* will continue until truth is arrived at. Almost all the philosophical treatises we know of have adopted *vādakathā. Vijigīṣukathā* (discussion for scoring a victory), which includes *jalpa* and *vitaṇḍā,* is different from it. It is not resorted to for ascertainment of truth, though *jalpakathā* has sometimes been introduced, under special circumstances, in certain contexts in treatises generally employing *vādakathā.* There are three classes of people —*apratipanna* (ignorant), *vipratipanna* (having a contrary view), and *sandigdha* (in doubt). Preceptors or persons of their status, desirous of doing good to *apratipanna* persons, should generate doubt in the latter in regard to matters that await ascertainment. When doubt is generated in them, they should be initiated in *vādakathā* that would dispel doubt by ascertaining the truth. A *vipratipanna* person, on the other hand, takes up a contrary position. Unless his counter convictions are repudiated, he would not entertain any healthy doubts, his vanity blocking the way; *jalpakathā* is necessary to destroy this vanity. When the contrary position of a *vipratipanna* person is countered by *jalpa* and *vitaṇḍā,* he becomes a *sandigdha* person, i.e. he begins to doubt the validity of his original standpoint. Then by initiating him in *vādakathā* and by consequent ascertainment of truth, his doubt can be removed. This is why the end of *vādakathā* is ascertainment of truth by removal of doubt. The person in doubt (*sandigdhapuruṣa*) is considered fit for *vādakathā.* Owing to this, *saṁśaya* has been called the forepart of disputation. Of the fourteen accessaries of *vicāra* the first is *saṁśaya.* Although *saṁśaya* forms a part of *vicāra, bhrānti* (wrong apprehension) does not. Akṣapāda has listed *saṁśaya,* and not *bhrānti,* as forming an integral part of *vicāra.* In *vijigīṣukathā* the mere defeat of the disputant is aimed at. *Vijigīṣukathā* is employed to expose the ignorance or to demolish the contrary conviction of the disputant, and it ceases with his discomfiture. *Vādakathā,* on the other hand, does not come to an end till the definite ascertainment of truth is reached. Śrī Kṛṣṇa has also said in the *Gītā,* 'I am *vāda* in relation to disputants'.[8] When Indian philosophers write treatises or expound certain truths in the seclusion of their seminaries, even then they present the *prima facie* objections of their opponents (*pūrvapakṣa*) and meet them. While doing so, they assume the presence of these opponents and invest them with the freedom of advancing contrary arguments. They also assume the presence of neutral persons, give expression to the latter's doubts, and suggest solutions. When an author writes a treatise, he thus imagines himself to be present in an assembly of the enlightened.

[8] *B.G.,* X.32.

Śaṅkara Miśra in his *Vādivinoda* has stated that the knowledge of a hitherto unknown truth, the conservation of this knowledge, the 'practice' of the conserved knowledge, and its transmission to others—these constitute the ends of the threefold *kathā*. Those entitled to resort to this threefold *kathā,* whether bent on the ascertainment of truth or on winning a debate, should satisfy these conditions: they must not go against universal experience, they must have unimpaired powers of perception, and they must not be quarrelsome. They should, besides, be able to maintain their own position and expose the weakness of the opponents' view-points. They should be cautious and be conscious of the defects on both sides. Those entitled to *vādakathā* should, again, have some additional qualifications. They should not be given to deception, should have presence of mind, and should be averse to unnecessary refutation of the opponent. They must put forward only those arguments that go to prove the point under discussion, and should also be capable of appreciating the reasonable points of the opponent. They must, above all, be keen about the ascertainment of truth. Two persons having the same qualities are entitled to *vāda*. Two persons entitled to *jalpa* and *vitaṇḍā* should also have similar qualities. In this way are the fruits of the threefold *kathā* fully obtained. Those who are endowed with contrary qualities have no right to engage themselves in any *kathā*. Persons, not entitled to *kathā,* are called *kathābāhya* (outside the pale of discussion).

## TECHNIQUE OF DEBATE

The *kathā* of the philosophic inquirer is *vādakathā*. In *vādakathā* and *jalpakathā* there is the adoption of a *pakṣa* (thesis) and a *pratipakṣa* (counter-thesis). Two contradictory qualities attributed to an object are called *pakṣa* and *pratipakṣa*. When to an object the disputant attributes a quality and his opponent attributes a contradictory quality, the quality attributed by the former is called *pakṣa* and that attributed by the latter is called *pratipakṣa*. That the contradictory qualities relate to the selfsame object should be admitted by both. So, *vāda* consists in attributing contradictory qualities to an object by both the disputant and his opponent. The attribution of contradictory qualities to an object will, however, lead to *saṁśaya*. Two contradictory qualities cannot coexist in the same object. If they coexist at all, they cannot be said to be contradictory. An object cannot be established by *pramāṇas* as possessing mutually contradictory qualities. Such a contingency will make for never-ending doubt. To illustrate: If the disputant says that sound is non-eternal, and his opponent argues that sound is eternal, the contradictory qualities of eternality and non-eternality will be attributed to the same object 'sound'. This will lead to the doubt as to whether sound is eternal or not. This doubt cannot be removed as long as there are not forthcoming proofs establishing one *pakṣa* and disproving the other *pakṣa.*

The procedure of disputation is decided upon before the disputant and his opponent begin their disputation. The appointment of a *madhyastha* (umpire) and an *anuvidheya* (president) is an item in the settlement of procedure. Before the discussion starts, the umpire decides what procedure the disputant and his opponent should adopt. The umpire should know the truth and should be free from bias or attachment. Such an umpire should set a limit to the discussion and should give a *résumé* of the arguments of both the disputant and his opponent. He should also assess the merits and demerits of both sides. If either of the parties violates the accepted procedure, it is the duty of the umpire to explain the fact of violation immediately to the offending party. The umpire will also have to declare the result of the discussion.[9] These duties of the umpire and the *anuvidheya* have no relevance to *vādakathā* ; they are essential in *jalpa* and *vitaṇḍā.* Sincere philosophic inquirers can themselves carry on *vādakathā* and may not stand in need of any umpire. The choice of an *anuvidheya* means the installation of a king or a person wielding similar influence in the council of disputation. When the results of the discussion have been declared by the umpire, this *anuvidheya* will eulogize the disputant and his opponent according to their merits. This choice of an *anuvidheya* is also not necessary in *vādakathā.* The persons who are competent to hold *vādakathā* are not eager for fame or honour. They seek the truth. *Saṁśaya,* which is occasioned by the adoption of *pakṣa* and *pratipakṣa,* has already been referred to. The statement that presents this *saṁśaya* is called *vipratipattivākya.* The person who is chosen an umpire in the discussion will present this *vipratipattivākya.* The presentation of *vipratipattivākya* is counted among the various duties that have been assigned to the umpire beforehand.

There cannot be any ascertainment of truth without the removal of doubt, and the result of discussion is the removal of doubt. The *vipratipattivākya* engenders doubt in the disputant and his opponent. This will be followed by the awareness of doubt, and this awareness will finally be followed by the knowledge of the absence of doubt. This knowledge of the absence of doubt constitutes the knowledge of the fruit of discussion. When this knowledge of the fruit is obtained, one will feel inclined to it. This will lead to discussion of the means of attaining the fruit. The necessity for such *vipratipattivākya* has been shown by the

[9] *Vādivinoda,* p. 112.

authors of various works. The neo-logicians and the teachers of Madhva school, however, have not accepted doubt as the forepart of disputation. According to them, the *vipratipattivākya* is of no use. But the adherents of the Nyāya school down to the time of Udayanācārya, and different Advaitic teachers as well, have regarded doubt as the forepart of disputation and *vipratipattivākya* as the introducer to that doubt.[10] 'This presentation of *vipratipatti* is made only in conformity with the convention of the logicians; it has not any real standing in actual discussions.'[11]

## PROCESS OF ARGUMENTATION

Anyway, after the presentation of the point at issue, the disputant will take up one of the *pakṣas* and his opponent will take up the other. That is to say, the two contradictory positions appearing in the *vipratipattivākya* will be taken up by them. The disputant, after having taken up his position, should state the *hetu* (reason or middle term) that is capable of establishing his own position. This is called *sthāpanā*. To do this, the disputant will have to adduce a fact which is to be 'a case of', and which has to be in the 'locus' of, what is sought to be proved. As for instance, if doubt is generated by the *vipratipattivākya*—'Is sound non-eternal or not?', the disputant seeking to prove 'non-eternality' will employ the *hetu* 'having an origin'. That which has an origin is called *kṛtaka*. This *hetu* 'having an origin' is 'a case of' 'non-eternality' and exists in sound which has been accepted as the 'locus' of 'non-eternality'. These two facts represent what is called *vyāpti* (invariable concomitance) and *pakṣadharmatā* (condition of being an attribute of the subject), which constitute the strength of a *hetu*. With the help of these two, the *hetu* establishes what is sought to be proved (the *sādhya*). That the *hetu* is 'a case of' the *sādhya* has also to be demonstrated and this is to be done by citing instances from experience, as for example, 'Whatever has an origin is non-eternal, e.g. a pot'. This example shows that there is an invariable relation of the *sādhya* to the *hetu*. Now, a *sadhya* comes to be established in a *pakṣa* (subject of a syllogism), if a *hetu* with the *vyāpti* of that *sādhya* is found in that *pakṣa*. The disputant will therefore have to employ the *upanaya* (application). This will be done by saying that the *hetu* (here, 'having an origin') with the *vyāpti* of the *sādhya* (here, 'non-eternality') is actually found in the *pakṣa* (here, 'sound'). The disputant will next end with the *nigamana* (conclusion), 'Therefore sound is non-eternal'. The original thesis regarding the non-eternal character of sound is thus established on the ground of *kṛtakatva*, i.e. 'having an origin', for the mark *kṛtakatva* establishes *anityatva*,

[10] *Advaitasiddhi* (Nirnayasagara Ed.), pp. 16,17.
[11] Cf. *Nyāyāmṛta* (Madhvavilasa Press Ed.), I.1. p. 8.

i.e. non-eternality. These statements constitute the five parts (*avayava*) of the comprehensive statement called *nyāya*.

There is a wide divergence of views among logicians in regard to the five constituent parts of the *nyāyavākya* shown above. Logicians of the very remote past regarded *upanaya* to be the only constituent of the *nyāyavākya*. The Buddhist dialecticians accepted only *upanaya* and *udāharaṇa* (example). The Mīmāṁsakas admitted *pratijñā* (proposition), *hetu,* and *udāharaṇa.* It has already been stated that the logicians of the Nyāya school have admitted five constituents of the *nyāyavākya.* Some logicians of the old Nyāya school accepted *jijñāsā* (desire to know), *saṁśaya, śakyaprāpti* (belief in the possibility of a solution), *prayojana,* and *saṁśaya-vyudāsa* (removal of doubt) in addition to the five mentioned above, and they were accordingly known as Daśāvayavavādins. It is to be noted here that the five constituents like *jijñāsā* (inquiry), *saṁśaya,* etc. precede *pratijñā.* After settling the constituents—*jijñāsā* etc.—*pratijñā* has to be applied. This is the view of some logicians of the old Nyāya school. The commentator Vātsyāyana has referred to this view in his commentary on the *Nyāya-Sūtra.*[12] These constituents have also been referred to in the introduction of Jagadīśa's commentary on *Tattva-cintāmaṇi.* In his interpretation of a couplet of *Sāṁkhya-kārikā,*[13] the author of *Yuktidīpikā* has given an elaborate account of the pentad—*jijñāsā, saṁśaya,* etc. The employment of a new *avayava* called *kaṇṭakoddhāra* after that of the five-standard constituents of the *nyāyavākya* is mentioned in some treatises, e.g. in Śaṅkara Miśra's *Vādivinoda.*

## ADAPTATION OF NYĀYA TECHNIQUE BY OTHERS

We have set forth in brief the character of philosophic disputation. The *Caraka Saṁhitā,* in the section called *Vimānasthāna,* throws much new light on the subject. Buddhist philosophers like Vasubandhu, Diṅnāga, Dharmakīrti, and others have made a detailed examination of the art of disputation as set forth by Akṣapāda. The Jaina philosophers have also done something in this direction. An elaborate reply to their objections has also been given by Uddyotakara, Vācaspati Miśra, Udayana, and others. It is by adapting the art of disputation as settled by them that the teachers of Vedānta, Sāṁkhya, etc. have elaborated their respective doctrines. In later times, Vedāntadeśika, a teacher of the Rāmānuja school, in his *Nyāyapariśuddhi* and Vyāsa Tīrtha, a celebrated teacher of the Madhva school, in his *Tarka-tāṇḍava,* have attempted an examination of the art of philosophic disputation initiated by Akṣapāda. They have

[12] *Nyāya-Sūtra,* I.1.32.
[13] *Sāṁkhya-kārikā,* 6.

also said a good deal against the methodology advocated by the Nyāya school.

The utility of these constituents of Nyāya has been demonstrated by their application to disputations in other systems of philosophy. It may be added here that the Mīmāṁsakas and the Vedāntins have designated each unit of discussion as an *adhikaraṇa.* Each *adhikaraṇa* of the Mīmāṁsakas has five parts, viz. *viṣaya* (topic), *saṁśaya, pūrvapakṣa, siddhānta,* and *saṅgati* (relevance). In *Bhaṭṭadīpikā* and other treatises, Khaṇḍadeva has stated that an *adhikaraṇa,* like the Vedas, has six subsidiary parts. The sixth that he has added is called *prayojana,* which states the necessity of both *pūrvapakṣa* (*prima facie* view) and *uttarapakṣa* (conclusion) separately. The *pūrva* and *uttara* or *siddhānta* standpoints have been different in view of the divergence of *prayojana.* Śabara Svāmin, the commentator of the *Mīmāṁsā-Sūtra,* has also referred to the difference between the *pūrvapakṣa* and *siddhāntapakṣa* consequent on their estimation of necessity (*prayojana*).

Many are under the impression that it is customary with the Mīmāṁsakas only, and not with the Naiyāyikas, to reserve one *adhikaraṇa* for one discussion. This is erroneous. Vātsyāyana has stated, 'Akṣapāda, the author of the *Nyāya-Sūtra,* has demonstrated the *pūrvapakṣa* and stopped short of the *siddhāntapakṣa* under the belief that a general knowledge of the tenets of the Śāstra will enable people to guess the *siddhānta* in that section. Take the case of Ātman or *ākāśa.* According to the Nyāya school, it is without any parts, yet the author of the *Nyāya-Sūtra* has nowhere stated that this is the case. He imagined that people would know this from the tenets of the Śāstra. Akṣapāda has not composed *sūtras* bearing upon objects that are known by implication or from the Śāstras'. It can be gathered from the statement of the commentary that the aphorisms were composed with a view to defending the Nyāya doctrines that were already in vogue. The Nyāya commentator has himself designated a unit of discussion (*vicāra*) as an *adhikaraṇa.* A closer thinking will reveal that the five-limbed *adhikaraṇa* and the *nyāyavākya* are not very different from each other. The *dharmin* (bearer of predicates) is indicated by the constituent '*viṣaya*' ; two contradictory predicates are attributed to the *dharmin* by the constituent '*saṁśaya*' ; to establish the undesirable thesis with the help of argument is '*pūrvapakṣa*' ; to establish the desirable thesis by the refutation of the argument favouring *pūrvapakṣa* is '*siddhānta*' ; to show the relation between the prior and the posterior discussion is '*saṅgati*' ; the *phala* or the result is '*prayojana*'. It should be remembered in this connection that the argument favouring *pūrvapakṣa* is only a semblance of reason (*yuktyābhāsa*), and that favouring *siddhāntapakṣa* is valid reason (*sadyukti*). The aim of philosophical discussion is to establish the *siddhānta* (conclusion) by the refutation of the semblance of reason with the help of reason proper.

### DISCUSSION BY VĀDA

The three kinds of *vicāra,* i.e. *vāda, jalpa,* and *vitaṇḍā,* have already been discussed. We shall now show the method of discussion by *vāda.* 'Sound is non-eternal' (*pratijñā*) ; 'because it has an origin' (*hetu*) ; 'whatever has an origin is non-eternal, e.g. the pot' (*udāharaṇa*) ; 'sound has thus a feature, "having an origin", which is a case of "being non-eternal" ' (*upanaya*) ; 'therefore sound is non-eternal' (*nigamana*). After having applied this five-limbed *nyāyavākya,* the disputant will demonstrate the process of 'extrication of thorns' (*kaṇṭakoddhāra*) either in brief or in detail. The brief procedure would be to say that the ground 'having an origin', which has been adduced for establishing 'the non-eternality of sound', is not merely an apparent ground ; or that it is not faulty ; or, to put it in a different way, that there is no fallacy (*hetvābhāsa*) about this ground. The detailed process of 'extrication of thorns' is done in the following manner: 'The *hetu* "having an origin" is not *"vyabhicārin"* with reference to "non-eternality". Here, "non-eternality" has to be established and "having an origin" is the *hetu.* If the *hetu* "having an origin" were sometimes coexistent with the absence of the *sādhya* "non-eternality", it would have been *"vyabhicārin"* (discrepant) or *anaikāntika* (indeterminate) with reference to that *sādhya.* It is not, however, *"vyabhicārin",* for it is not sometimes coexistent with the absence of the *sādhya* ; nor *"viruddha"* (contrary), for it is never coexistent with the absence of *sādhya.* It is neither *"asiddha"* (unfounded), for it is subsumed under the *sādhya* and is also present in the *pakṣa* ; nor *"satpratipakṣita"* (counterbalanced), for the counter-*hetu* establishing the absence of *sādhya* is not forthcoming ; nor *"bādhita"* (contradicted), for the *hetu* "having an origin" does not exist in that in which there is demonstrably the absence of the *sādhya*'. The process of 'extrication of thorns' consists in showing that the fivefold *hetvābhāsa* (fallacy) is not present in the demonstrated *hetu.* In his commentary on *Avayava,*[14] Mathurānātha Tarkavāgīśa has exhibited the 'extrication of thorns' in a different way. According to him, 'extrication of thorns' consists in a kind of interrogative sentence. As for example, the premise, 'The mountain has fire', got in reply to the question, 'What is on fire?', constitutes the *pratijñā.* Next comes the question, 'What is the ground for that assertion?' The reply, 'Because there is smoke', is the application of *hetu.* Then comes the question, 'What of that?' The reply, 'Whatever is with

[14] *Avayava* is a section of *Tattva-cintāmaṇi* on which Mathurānātha wrote his celebrated commentary.

smoke is also with fire', is the statement of *udāharaṇa*. It appears to us, however, that the process of the 'extrication of thorns' as elaborated in *Vādivinoda* is the proper one.

Having extricated the thorns in this way, the disputant will stop ; and then his opponent will point out the faults in the *hetu* put forward by the former. He will, for instance, say that since 'having an origin', which has been stated by the disputant to be the *hetu,* is *asiddha* (unfounded), it cannot really prove the *sādhya.* In this exposure of the fault, the application of the five-limbed statement would not be required. That the unfounded *hetu* cannot accomplish the *sādhya* is admitted both by the disputant and by his opponent. This is why it would not be necessary to make any statement like the following: 'Having an origin does not prove the *sādhya,* for it is unfounded ; nothing that is unfounded is competent to prove anything'. Why the posed *hetu* does not establish the *sādhya* has only to be shown. This done, the opponent will seek to establish his counter thesis in the following way: 'Sound is not non-eternal ; rather, it is eternal, because it is a property solely of *ākāśa* ; and whatever is a property solely of *ākāśa* is eternal, e.g. the property of "unity" inhering in ether'. In this connection it should be remembered that the Naiyāyika postulates non-eternality and the Mīmāṁsaka eternality or ever-existence of sound. Here the Naiyāyika is the disputant and the Mīmāṁsaka the opponent. We have shown here three *avayavas,* because the Mīmāṁsaka admits only three *avayavas* of the *nyayavakya.* The parts in question are *pratijñā, hetu,* and *udāharaṇa.*

When the opponent will stop after having established his own position by extricating the thorns of his *hetu,* the disputant will endeavour to meet the charges of the opponent.[15] He will, first of all, seek to free his position from the objections alleged by the opponent. The opponent contends that the *hetu* 'having an origin' in regard to sound is unfounded ; the disputant, on the other hand, will urge that it is not so. That sound has an origin is perceived by all. Everybody perceives that the letters *ka* etc. are produced. These letters constitute sound. Whatever is produced has an origin. The letters *ka* etc. are produced ; so they must have an origin. This being the case, why should the *hetu* 'having an origin' in regard to sound be unfounded? Sound is *pakṣa* ; if the *hetu* 'having an origin' does not inhere in it, this will lead to the fallacy of *svarūpāsiddhi* (essential unreality) of the *hetu. Asiddhi* is one of the fallacies. There are five fallacies—*vyabhicāra* (inconstancy), *virodha* (contradiction), *asiddhi* (unfoundedness), *satpratipakṣa* (counterposition), and *bādha* (incongruity). If

[15] *Vādivinoda,* p. 14.

any of these five fallacies is detected in the *hetu*, the *hetu* cannot prove the *sādhya*. The fallacy (*hetvābhāsa*) indicates the incompetence of the *hetu* in proving the *sādhya*. It is not only the syllabic, but also the non-syllabic *śabda* (*dhvani*), that has an origin. In the perception of the sound produced by a drum, the fact of having an origin is perceived in regard to sound which is non-syllabic (*dhvani*). In this way the disputant will first meet the opponent's objections and then find fault with the latter's *hetu*. The disputant will argue in this way: 'In order to prove the eternality of sound the *hetu* that has been posited by the opponent is "being a property solely of *ākāśa*". But this *hetu* cannot prove "eternality" which is the *sādhya*. This *hetu* has a limiting adjunct (*upādhi*), and a *hetu* with a limiting adjunct cannot prove a *sādhya*'. In this way, when the disputant will stop after having met the opponent by freeing his own position from objections and finding fault with the latter's argument, the opponent will, in his turn, free his own position from the objections urged by the disputant and will seek to reinforce his own contention regarding the fallacious character of the disputant's *hetu*.

The general procedure adopted by the teachers of old is that one has to point out the defects in the other's arguments after having freed one's own argument from the stigma of illogicality. The study of the Indian dialectical literature clearly reveals that philosophic disputation is a battle of words. The combatants on both sides first provide for self-defence and then plan the demolition of the argument of the adversary. An offensive without adequate defensive measures brings on one's ruin. Hence the general procedure is to refute the opponent's position after having defended one's own. Śaṅkara Miśra, however, is of opinion that this order is not absolutely binding.[16] One may start with finding fault with the opponent's argument, and then may seek to free one's own from the fault attributed by the opponent. But whatever may be the order, the dual procedure is imperative both on the disputant and on his opponent. We cannot say that one is fundamental and the other non-fundamental. Both are equally important. This is why Śaṅkara Miśra has stated that of these two, viz. finding fault with the opponent's argument and freeing one's own from the fault attributed by the opponent, whichever presents itself first to the mind ought to be resorted to.

## THEORY OF UPĀDHI

It is to be noted by the way that the analysis of the concept of *upādhi* or the 'limiting adjunct', forms an important topic in logic. The *hetu*

[16] *Ibid.*

that is subject to an *upādhi* cannot prove the *sādhya.* The entity that is 'wider' (*vyāpaka*) than the *sādhya* but not 'wider' than the *hetu* is called an *upādhi.* The theory of *upādhi* is a highly complicated topic. From the time of Uddyotakara down to the present day, Naiyāyikas have discussed quite a lot about this *upādhi.* The theory of *upādhi* forms an important topic in the chapter on *vyāpti* in the section on *anumāna* in *Tattva-cintāmaṇi.*

Now, the opponent suggests the *hetu* 'being a property solely of *ākāśa*' in order to prove the eternality of sound. But the disputant suggests that the *hetu* is vitiated by an *upādhi.* The opponent, however, asserts that this suggestion is unfounded for the following reasons. What is the disputant's view about the suspected *upādhi*? Is it knowable (*yogya*) or not? Now, it is a fact that there is no knowable *upādhi* in the *hetu* put forward by the opponent. The absence of any knowable *upādhi* in the *hetu* is proved by non-perception. It is everywhere the rule that non-cognition of the appropriate kind establishes the absence of a knowable entity. If the *hetu* were vitiated by a knowable *upādhi,* the *upādhi* would have been known ; but as there is no such knowledge, it follows that there is no knowable *upādhi.* Let us now consider the other alternative, viz. that the suggested *upādhi* is unknowable. Now, it is doubtless true that the possibility of an unknown *upādhi* is not ruled out by non-cognition, but this possibility can be imagined in the *hetu* put forward by the disputant as well. To explain: If the disputant argues that the opponent's *hetu* to prove the eternality of sound is inconclusive because it is vitiated by an unknowable *upādhi,* then the *hetu* employed in this argument, viz. 'being vitiated by an *upādhi*', may with equal cogency be regarded as vitiated by an unknowable *upādhi,* and thus the disputant's contention will fall to the ground. The point is that the suggestion of an unprovable *upādhi* is self-stultifying. It cuts both ways and leads only to a stalemate in the discussion. The upshot of all this is that the opponent's *hetu* under reference is free from both kinds of *upādhi* and is thus not open to the charge of inconclusiveness brought forward by the disputant. To prove that the *hetu* 'having an origin' is present in the *pakṣa* 'sound', the disputant has asserted that the feature 'having an origin' is established in regard to 'sound' by such perceptions as 'the sound *ga* is produced now', 'sound is produced by the drum', etc. But this is improper. Such perceptions might have for their object merely the manifestation of sound, that is to say, they may not so much show that sound has an origin as that sound has manifested itself. The drum does not produce but manifests the sound. The sound *ga* is not produced ; it is manifested.

The disputant might next argue—and this would be the fifth stage in the discussion—that the contention of the opponent, viz. 'The non-existence of the knowable *upādhi* is established by its non-perception', is not valid. For the character 'not being produced' is the *upādhi* here in the *hetu* (being a property solely of *ākāśa*). This *upādhi* has not been negatived by non-perception of the appropriate kind. The feature that is found in the *dṛṣṭānta,* but not in the *pakṣa,* is the *upādhi.* This is the broad principle whereby *upādhi* is determined. As it is found in the *dṛṣṭānta,* the *upādhi* is 'wider' (*vyāpaka*) than the *sādhya* ; and as it is not found in the *pakṣa,* it is not 'wider' than the *hetu.* The property that is 'wider' than the *sādhya* and not 'wider' than the *hetu* is an *upādhi.* The Mīmāṁsaka, who is here the opponent, has 'being a property solely of *ākāśa*' as the *hetu* in order to establish the eternality of sound. The properties which are solely found in *ākāśa,* like its infinite magnitude and numerical unity, are eternal. Sound is also the quality of ether (*ākāśa*). So sound is eternal. This is the contention of the Mīmāṁsaka. But the disputant Naiyāyika would here argue as follows: Is the infinite magnitude of *ākāśa* eternal, or its numerical unity? Is it eternal because it is not a 'product' or because it is the quality of *ākāśa*? Evidently the magnitude of ether is eternal, because it has no origin ; it is not eternal, simply because it happens to be the quality of *ākāśa.* So, the property of 'not being produced' is found in the *dṛṣṭānta,* viz. the magnitude of *ākāśa,* and not in the *pakṣa,* that is to say, sound. Now, whatever is eternal is incapable of being produced. This is why the property of 'not being produced' has been 'wider' than the *sādhya* (i.e. 'eternality') and the *hetu* (i.e. 'being the property solely of *ākāśa*') is found in the *pakṣa* (i.e. sound), but the property of 'not being produced' does not exist in sound. Owing to this, the *upādhi* has been exclusive of the *hetu.* That sound is produced is evident from the production of the sound *ga* etc. The statement of the Mīmāṁsaka that the perception of the origination of sound is to be interpreted differently is unreasonable. To take the perception of origination as that of manifestation is not proper. The verdict of perception can be set aside only if there be superior evidence to the contrary. Otherwise, all perceptions would have to be invalidated, leading to a complete suspension of our practical activities.

## OTHER FACTORS IN VĀDAKATHĀ

In this way, the flow of disputation may run through several stages in which the argumentative skill of both the disputant and his opponent may find its best expression. This is why the argumentation may continue for a long time. But the flow of reasoning will abruptly stop if there be flagging of enthusiasm on the part of either of the parties. In this connection it should be remembered that the disputant and the opponent, even though wise and enthusiastic, should be particular about economy of words. The parties should use just as many words as are necessary for meeting the argument of the adversary and must not use more. Although they might have many things to say, none of them must utter even a letter that might be considered irrelevant or redundant.

In trying to exhibit the nature of philosophic discussion, we have shown the form it takes when a Naiyāyika is the disputant and a Mīmāṁsaka the opponent. When the disputation is with a Naiyāyika, all the five constituents will have to be applied in *vādakathā* ; but when it is with a Mīmāṁsaka or a Buddhist, the employment of the 'pentad' need not be adhered to. The employment of *avayava* should be in accordance with the conclusions of the parties concerned. Madhusūdana has said exactly this in his *Advaitasiddhi*.[17] There cannot be any fixed rule about *avayavas* in a disputation, because all the disputants may not admit the five *avayavas*. Akṣapāda has said that the disputant should establish his position and refute that of his opponent with *pramāṇas* helped by *tarka*. The opponent will also take to the same procedure. When Akṣapāda speaks of the employment of '*pramāṇas* helped by *tarka*' in *vādakathā*, he means that *chala, jāti,* and *nigrahasthāna* cannot be employed therein. With these one cannot establish one's position, but can only find fault with the argument of the opponent. Akṣapāda does not recommend this in *vādakathā*, which is meant for the seekers of truth.

### CHALA, JATI, AND NIGRAHASTHANA

The knowledge of *chala, jāti,* and *nigrahasthāna* is indispensable for a proper understanding of the art of disputation. There are three kinds of *chala*, twenty-four kinds of *jāti*, and twenty-two kinds of *nigrahasthāna*. These require special understanding, but the treatment of these is beyond the scope of this article. *Chala* consists in repudiating the statement of the disputant by wilfully twisting its meaning.[18] As for instance, 'This man has come from Nepal, for he has a *navakambala* (new blanket) with him'. Here the disputant has evidently used *navakambala* in the sense of 'new blanket'. But the opponent, with a view to showing the falsity of the disputant's statement, construes the word *nava* in the sense of '*nine*' and queries, 'Where are his nine blankets?' The implication is that the *hetu*, i.e. the possession of a new blanket, does not inhere in the *pakṣa*. So it is unfounded. *Jāti*, on the other hand, consists in finding fault with the disputant's *hetu* on the strength of mere similarity or difference apart from

[17] *Advaitasiddhi*, p. 31 (with Balabhadra's commentary *Siddhi*).
[18] *Nyāya-Sūtra*, I.2.10.

*vyāpti* or invariable concomitance. Akṣapāda says, '*Jāti* consists in meeting the disputant on the strength of similarity and difference'.[19] The disputant's thesis was, 'Sound is non-eternal because it has an origin, for instance, a pot'. To find fault with this proposition the Mīmāṁsaka might employ *jāti* in this way, 'If sound, which has origin, be non-eternal like a pot, it would have colour like a pot and be visible like it'. The *hetu* 'having an origin' has invariable concomitance with non-eternality, but it has no such invariable concomitance with 'possession of colour or visibility'. Only there is coexistence of the *hetu* 'having an origin' with 'possession of colour and visibility' in the pot. This is a reply of the kind called *jāti,* because here fault has been found with the disputant's position on the strength of mere similarity apart from *vyāpti* or invariable concomitance.

Sustaining a defeat is called *nigrahasthāna.*[20] Akṣapāda says, '*Nigrahasthāna* consists in contrary comprehension or non-comprehension'. These two lead to the defeat of the disputant. Vātsyāyana says, 'The person comprehending the contrary has to own defeat. Non-comprehension consists in not doing what was to be done'. If the opponent does not know how to contradict the *hetu* advanced by the disputant, he is open to defeat. Similarly, if the disputant is not in a position to remove the fault suggested by the opponent, he suffers the same fate. Out of twenty-two *nigrahasthānas* some are included under 'contrary comprehension' and some under 'non-comprehension'.

Generally, *nigrahasthāna* should not be employed in *vādakathā. Vādakathā* is the disputation among the seekers of truth. In it one should not employ *nigrahasthāna* to defeat another person. Although *nigrahasthāna* has generally been interdicted in *vādakathā,* yet those *nigrahasthānas* which help in the ascertainment of truth may be employed in it. It is to indicate this that Akṣapāda says that a *vāda* must not contradict accepted tenets.[21] If it were to do this, it would not lead to ascertainment of truth. This is why the *nigrahasthāna* called *apasiddhānta* may be employed in *vādakathā.* The author of *Nyāyavārttika* says that three *nigrahasthānas* called *nyūna* (incomplete), *adhika* (redundant), and *apasiddhānta* (deviation from the accepted theory) may be employed in *vādakathā.*[22] These three are so employed because they are favourable to the ascertainment of truth. The remaining nineteen *nigrahasthānas* are not to be employed in *vādakathā.*

If we closely discuss these *nigrahasthānas,* we shall be in a position to comprehend the strength and profundity of the technique of philosophic disputation. Out of these twenty-two *nigrahasthānas* one is called *niranuyo-*

[19] *Ibid.,* I.2.18.
[20] *Nyāya-bhāṣya,* I.2.19.
[21] *Nyāya-Sūtra,* I.2.1.
[22] *Ibid.,* I.1.1.

*jyānuyoga*. Suppose both the disputant and the opponent have advanced faultless *hetus*. In spite of that if any one of them imputes fault to the *hetu* advanced by the other, the imputer of the unreal fault would be guilty of employing this *nigrahasthāna*. Suppose either the disputant or the opponent has advanced a faulty *hetu*, but if that is not pointed out, the omission will involve the *nigrahasthāna* called *paryanuyojyopekṣaṇa*. Making uncalled for statements leads to the *nigrahasthāna* called *adhika* (redundant). Employment of more *avayavas* than are necessary also leads to this *nigrahasthāna*. The statement of a feature of the *hetu* that is not relevant to the discussion also leads to this *nigrahasthāna*. The failure, again, to state what is necessary leads to the *nigrahasthāna* called *nyūna*. The five *hetvābhāsas* (fallacies) that have been referred to above are also *nigrahasthānas*. Although *hetvābhāsa* is a *nigrahasthāna*, the separate mention of *hetvābhāsa* is due to the fact that all the five *hetvābhāsas* might be employed in *vādakathā* but not any *nigrahasthāna* other than *nyūna*, *adhika*, and *apasiddhānta*. Ascertainment of truth is impossible if *hetvābhāsas* are not considered and refuted in *vādakathā*. The employment of *hetvābhāsa* is thus necessary in *vādakathā*.

### JALPAKATHĀ

We shall now discuss *jalpakathā*. The characteristics of *vādakathā* will be found in *jalpakathā* also.[23] The additional characteristic of *jalpakathā* is that in finding fault with the opposite party one is here permitted to employ *chala*, *jāti*, and *nigrahasthāna*. The principal aim of the *jalpa* form of disputation is the defeat of the disputant. The parties engage in the debate just to test the polemical skill of the opponent. The ascertainment of truth is only incidental. If *jalpa* disputation leads to the discovery of truth, it would not for that reason cease to be a *jalpa*. When a wrongly comprehending person out of incorrigible vanity engages in disputation, the *jalpakathā* might be employed to crush his egotism. Even without ascertaining the truth, one can initiate *jalpakathā* for sealing the mouth of the disputant. In *Nyāya-kusumāñjali* this silencing of the disputant has been resorted to.[24] Although *Nyāya-kusumāñjali* is a *vāda* text, it has introduced *jalpa* also in certain contexts.

There are certain stipulations, especially agreed to, between the parties in *jalpakathā* or a trial of polemical strength, one of them being that the disputant and the opponent do not leave the subject under discussion and digress into irrelevant topics. The employment of a dispassionate umpire and *anuvidheya* is also imperative. Besides, it has to be determined how

[23] *Ibid.*, I.2.2.
[24] *Nyāya-kusumāñjali*, III.7.

*nigrahasthāna* etc. are to be used. The fault that will justify the closure of disputation also requires to be ascertained. If the proceedings are to be put down in writing, there must be a scribe to do that job. The scribe must be acceptable to both the parties. Both the disputant and the opponent must be of equal erudition. Otherwise the argumentative skill of the parties cannot be properly tested, and the disputation becomes futile. The board of judges of such disputation should be acceptable to both the parties. They should be well posted in the respective philosophical positions of the parties and should maintain strict impartiality. They should, besides, be in a position to fully comprehend and explain the view-points of the disputant and his opponent. The number of the judges should be odd, i.e. 3, 5, 7, etc. In that case the majority verdict can decide victory or defeat in favour of either side. The person presiding over these deliberations should be impartial and acceptable to the disputant, the opponent, and the judges.

The procedure of *jalpa* disputation is as follows. When a neutral person states the doubt as to whether air is perceptible or not, the stipulations will be agreed to, and the Mīmāṁsaka will employ an inference in favour of the positive side (*sthāpanā*). According to the Naiyāyika, air is imperceptible ; by touch etc. its existence is inferred. Now, the Mīmāṁsaka will present his case thus: 'Air is perceptible, because it is the substratum of perceptible touch. Whatever is the substratum of perceptible touch is perceptible, e.g. the pot'. He will also employ the 'extrication of thorn' in this way: 'This is not a wrong *hetu,* as it has no characteristics of *hetvābhāsa*'. The Naiyāyika is here the opponent. He will initiate the second stage thus: 'When air is the substratum of perceptible touch, it need not be itself perceptible. To be the substratum of perceptible touch and to be itself perceptible need not always go together'. According to the Mīmāṁsaka, to be the substratum of perceptible touch is the *hetu,* and perceptibility is the *sādhya.* The *hetu* which is inseparable from the *sādhya* proves the *sādhya.* But this *hetu* not being so does not establish the *sādhya.* This is how the Naiyāyika will continue: 'Air is imperceptible, because it is a colourless external substance ; whatever is a colourless external substance is imperceptible, e.g. *ākāśa.* This has the character of being such—a fact which entails imperceptibility. Therefore this is imperceptible'. The Naiyāyika is committed to the use of five constituents or *avayavas* in an argument. So he has exhibited these five. The Mīmāṁsaka, being committed to the use of three *avayavas,* has employed three constituents only. Then the Naiyāyika will 'extricate the thorn' and say, 'This *hetu* is not spurious, because it has no characteristics of *hetvābhāsa* in it'. In the third stage of the argument the Mīmāṁsaka will say, 'We advance "to be the substratum of perceptible touch" as the *hetu.* To prove that this *hetu* does not accomplish the *sādhya,* the Naiyāyika has argued that this *hetu,* being variable (*vyabhicārin*) cannot establish the *sādhya.* But the *hetu* advanced by us not being *vyabhicārin,* the one advanced by the Naiyāyika has become unfounded (*asiddha*). So, it has not proved the incompetence of our *hetu.* The Naiyāyika further argues that the imperceptibility of air can be proved by the *hetu* "being a colourless external substance". This is also not right. This *hetu* of the Naiyāyika does not prove the imperceptibility of air, because "being without a touch quality" is the limiting adjunct (*upādhi*) in this *hetu,* and a *hetu* subject to an *upādhi* cannot prove the *sādhya.* In the inference of the Naiyāyika air is the *pakṣa* and *ākāśa* is the *dṛṣṭānta.* The feature "being without a touch quality" is found in the *dṛṣṭānta* but not in the *pakṣa* and is thus an *upādhi* with reference to the *hetu*'. Such *jalpa* disputation will proceed by stages as long as *nigrahasthāna* does not snap the thread of discussion.

## VITAṆḌĀKATHĀ

This very *jalpa,* when employed without the presentation of any counter thesis or *pratipakṣa,* is called *vitaṇḍā.*[25] Vātsyāyana, while commenting on the aphorism defining *vitaṇḍā,* says, 'Two contradictory predicates with reference to the same subject are called *pakṣa* and *pratipakṣa*'. The employer of *vitaṇḍā* does not advance any of these two. His only business is to contradict the other party. The disputant will present a proposition, and the employer of *vitaṇḍā* will refute that. This *vitaṇḍā* is also the disputation of persons wishing victory in debate. In the statement of the point at issue (*vipratipattivākya*) two alternatives are presented. The presentation of an argument establishing any of these two alternatives is called *sthāpanā.* The employer of *vitaṇḍā* does not exhibit a *sthāpanā,* he only exposes the adversary's fault. So, in *vitaṇḍā* disputation, an argument is adduced only to establish a single thesis. *Jalpakathā* and *vitaṇḍākathā* are meant for the trial of argumentative strength. It must be noted here that the strength of one's position is not determined either by exclusively proving or disproving something. If one party simply defends its own position and the other party finds fault with that, how can there be a real trial of strength? It may be asked, 'If relative strength could be ascertained in this way, what is the necessity of *jalpakathā*?' In reply to this it may be said, 'In *jalpakathā* both the disputant and the opponent defend their respective positions and find fault with their

[25] *Nyāya-Sūtra,* I.2.3.

opposite party. So the polemical strength of each is ascertained by his defence as well as offence. In *vitaṇḍākathā*, however, the disputant only defends his position, and the opponent simply finds fault with his defence. So, here the strength of the disputant lies in his defence, and that of the opponent in his offence'.

The celebrated *Khaṇḍana-khaṇḍa-khādya* of Śrīharṣa is a pre-eminent example of this *vitaṇḍā* disputation. The nihilist Mādhyamika and the Advaitin have both employed *vitaṇḍā*. The nature of *vitaṇḍākathā* will be properly understood from a perusal of *Khaṇḍana-khaṇḍa-khādya*. In the treatise *Advaita-ratna-rakṣaṇa* the definitions of *pramātva* (validity) as set forth by the Naiyāyikas have been refuted.[26] Madhusūdana Sarasvatī has first stated the ten definitions of *pramātva* as enumerated by the Naiyāyikas and then refuted them. He finally concludes, 'As it is not thus possible to give a definition of validity the claim that difference is the object of valid knowledge is hard to establish'. Dualists in reply say that the concept of valid knowledge or *pramā* is universally accepted. Everybody makes use of it. How can the Advaitins themselves account for the universal use of this concept? If *pramātva* or validity is incapable of being defined, how, again, would the Advaitin himself use it at all? If the Advaitin cannot justify the use of the concept of *pramā* or valid knowledge, he cannot possibly be looked upon as versed in the Śāstras. So by repudiating the concept of *pramātva*, the Advaitin would simply be stultifying himself. Madhusūdana in reply has argued that as the employer of *vitaṇḍā* the Advaitin cannot be asked how he will justify the use of the concept of *pramā*. The *kathā* called *vitaṇḍā* proceeds on the understanding that one will establish one's standpoint and the other will refute it. So how the Advaitin will give an account of *pramā* is quite an irrelevant question. Madhusūdana has wound up the discussion by quoting a couplet from *Khaṇḍana-khaṇḍa-khādya*, which purports to state, 'Whoever sets about clarifying the nature of the knowledge of reality and of practical life must ultimately fail in his object. So all disputants will eventually have to accept the doctrine of *anirvacanīyatā*, i.e. inexpressibility'. This concludes the analysis of *vāda*, *jalpa*, and *vitaṇḍā*, which are the three types of discussion generally recognized.

[26] *Advaita-ratna-rakṣaṇa*, p. 32.

# 36

## INDIAN PSYCHOLOGY

BEFORE discussing the main problems, it is necessary to ask what psychology is and has been in the West, so that we can next raise the same question about Indian psychology. The root of the word 'mind' was originally used in the sense of thinking; that of 'soul' in the sense of a substantial principle different from the physical body and having its own identity and individuality, of which 'the individual mental life and development are manifestations'; that of *nous* in the sense of reason, which is not merely subjective, but has objectivity like logos; and that of *anima* in the sense of breath, the life principle, which is a sort of double of the body.[1] The ideas of soul and logos are now discarded by Western psychologists, who now confine themselves only to the empirical and experimental study of mind and its activities like sensing, imagining, thinking, feeling, and willing. Even in Western philosophy, the ideas of soul and logos are now in disuse, and the idea of mind is preferred as a more tangible and less mythical and supernatural conception. The former two are now used only in Western theology.

What we call personality or empirical self is the same as mind, and the idea of the identity of the two belongs also to modern philosophy and psychology. Mind is not one of the aspects or functions of the self, but is the self. Most of the modern psychologists do not use the word self because of its metaphysical associations. Some of them are not very clear about the reality of mind, that is, about what mind in itself is. Mind is what mind does, they say. They are satisfied with the study of its behaviour, and the behaviourists are the extremists in this line of thinking, reducing mental to bodily activity.

For a long time what was unconscious was refused the adjective mental. But as a result of the researches of Freud, Jung, and Adler, the reality of unconscious mental activities has been recognized, and mind is thought of as having unconscious and subconscious depths, which affect its conscious level.

### ĀTMAN AND MIND

The difference between mind and Ātman in Indian philosophy perplexes the Western student who is not accustomed to this differentiation.

[1] See the relevant articles in *The Encyclopaedia of Religion and Ethics.*

It is *manas* or *antaḥkaraṇa* that performs what are regarded as mental functions; and Ātman is the basic residue one experiences when one gets behind all mental functions that can be objectified. Hume, Kant, and Bradley rejected the knowledge of the self for different reasons. But Indian philosophy and psychology claim that we can experience self or Ātman, that self-realization in the literal sense of the word is possible. Practically the whole of Indian philosophy and psychology is meant to prove the possibility and desirability of that experience for man. Mind with its functions belongs to a lower order of reality and is the connecting link between Ātman and the world of nature. If this distinction is not kept in view, the psychology of the Indian philosophical systems cannot be understood.

It would, however, be wrong to say that the distinction between Ātman and mind existed from the beginning of Indian speculations. The word Ātman, even in classical Sanskrit, has many meanings. What strikes us as important is that the word variously means the physical body, mind, the individual self, and the absolute Self also. Not only in classical Sanskrit, but also in the Upaniṣads, is the word Ātman used in all the four senses, though sometimes the word *para* is prefixed to it in order to denote the absolute Self. The *Kaṭha* (VI.7) uses the word in the sense of the human intellect (*manuṣyabuddhi*). The *Taittirīya* (I.5.1), the *Aitareya* (II.1), the *Chāndogya* (II.22.2), and the *Bṛhadāraṇyaka* (I.2.4,7 ; I.6.1) use the word in the sense of the physical body. In the senses of the individual self and the Absolute, the word is used too many times to need reference. What is important to note is that the word is used in the sense of *prāṇa* (life principle) also (*Pra. U.*, III.6), often associated with *vāyu* (air),[2] which, as conceived in the Upaniṣads, is not merely physical air and even its subtle counterpart, but is the principle producing movement (*karma* or action) in the original fullness of Ātman, and which in its cosmic form is the support and sustainer of the world and is its unifying principle (*sūtrātman*).

In spite of the different meanings of the word Ātman, the Upaniṣads usually draw a clear distinction between Ātman and *manas* (mind), and declare that the latter cannot grasp the former.

## INDIAN AND WESTERN APPROACHES TO PSYCHOLOGY

In Western thought, the disparity between mind and matter began to be felt from the time of Descartes, whence the problem of the relation between the two became acute. But the early Greeks did not feel this

[2] Cf. '*Tvameva pratyakṣaṁ Brahmāsi*' (*Tai. U.*, I.1).

disparity, and so how mind acts on body and body on mind was not a problem for them. The soul, *nous,* or logos was to them as much a substantial principle as matter, and, according to Aristotle, the relation between soul and body is the same as that between form and matter. Even to the mediaeval philosophers, it was not the unreality of matter but its transience that troubled them.

In Indian philosophy, particularly in the Upaniṣadic tradition, mind is understood more from within than from without.[3] It is formed in Ātman and out of it. Only the Cārvākas treated consciousness as a by-product of matter. But they have no followers, and it is even said that the school is a hypothetical one like pure subjectivism in Western philosophy. For all the other schools, mind is a distinct reality and not a mere product of matter.[4]

## THE ĀTMAN PSYCHOLOGY AND ITS METHOD

What is the method used to study mental phenomena? It is direct perception, which we may call introspection.

The distinctive feature of Indian psychology is that it declares that the method of looking within can be perfected so as to make the subject of experience itself completely conscious of itself without residue.[5] It would be wrong to say that it did not use reason to establish its principles. But generally speaking, only after having discovered an inner principle, did it begin rationally to establish its reality. Only in a few cases were the principles rationally established first and then experientially confirmed. In any case, no principle is the result of mere speculation and postulated as only regulative of some of our experiences, as only a hypothesis to explain some facts. Even the concept of *śūnya* has a psychological reality corresponding. It is that state in which the knot of the subject (*hṛdayagranthi*) disappears and experience is of the form of pure space (*gaganasama*). Even the orthodox schools have a place for this psychological or trans-psychological state, though the Mādhyamika Buddhists treat it as the highest state. This is also the psychological state corresponding to the category (*tattva*) Lakṣmī of the Vaiṣṇavas.[6] *Śūnya* is the name of Viṣṇu in the night of the great dissolution when everything determinate disappears.[7] Even for the Śaiva

[3] The Nyāya and Vaiśeṣika are exceptions. Though they owe allegiance to the Upaniṣads, they do not, in many details, belong to the Upaniṣadic tradition.

[4] It should be remembered that though *antaḥkaraṇa* is a product of Prakṛti in the Sāṁkhya, this school is not regarded as materialistic. Max Müller even poses the question, 'Is Sāṁkhya Idealism?' in his *Six Systems of Indian Philosophy,* pp. 293 f.

[5] There are differences of view about the nature of the Ātman at this stage among Indian schools. The Nyāya and Vaiśeṣika differ from the Upaniṣads on this point and say that the Ātman becomes completely divested of consciousness at this stage.

[6] *Ahirbudhnya Saṁhitā,* V. 3.

[7] Schrader, *Introduction to the Pañcarātra,* p. 86.

Āgamas, it is *mahāvyoman*,[8] the great space (or ether), a stage lower than the highest. Again, the principle of *mahat* in the Upaniṣads is super-individual and cosmic, and yet is to be realized within ourselves. It has the significance of the objective reason or logos of Western philosophers.

The real difficulty in selecting an appropriate name for Indian psychology from among the psychological schools of the West is that psychology and metaphysics become identified in Indian thinking. So far as such mental functions as emotions go, psychology may be treated as different from metaphysics. But when the question is asked, where ultimate Reality is to be found, the answer given by Indian philosophy is, right within our self. Speculative reason may construct any number of stages (*bhūmikās*) within, but that construction would be merely metaphysical. The actual realization of the stages is a psychological process akin to introspection ; and these inner stages of reality are as much psychological as metaphysical. There seems to be no word more suitable for us than Ātman psychology.

### MANAS, PRĀṆA, AND VĀC

But does Ātman correspond to psyche or mind? Indeed not. The Buddhists alone have no place for Ātman ; their *citta* corresponds to mind. The main motive of the Upaniṣads is the discovery of the self or Ātman. The story of Virocana and Indra, each trying to learn from Prajāpati what self is (*Chā. U.*, VIII.7) ; the story of Ajātaśatru and Bālāki, in which the former finally points out that Brahman is the same as Puruṣa residing in the innermost heart (*Bṛ. U.*, II. 1) ; the dialogues between Janaka and Yājñavalkya (*Bṛ. U.*, IV) ; the teaching of Sanatkumāra to Nārada (*Chā. U.*, VII) ; the story of Śvetaketu and Uddālaka (*Chā. U.*, VI) ; and a large number of other statements are unequivocal declarations of the motive. But how is Ātman to be known? If it is to be discovered in our innermost heart (*antarhṛdaya*), then it has to be discovered within our mind. Hence the discussion of the nature of mind. The essential conception of the Upaniṣads is that Brahman is the same as Ātman and has to be discovered in our innermost heart.

The method prescribed for the realization of Brahman is that speech should be merged in *manas, manas* in *buddhi, buddhi* in *mahat, mahat* in *avyakta*, and *avyakta* in Ātman (*Ka. U.*, III.13). Further, it is said that objects are higher than senses, *manas* higher than objects, *buddhi* higher than *manas, mahat* higher than *buddhi, avyakta* higher than *mahat*, and Ātman higher than *avyakta* (*Ka. U.*, III.10,11). At another place, *manas*

[8] Vasugupta, *Spandakārikā*, 13,25.

is given as higher than senses, and reference to objects is omitted (*Ka. U.*, VI. 7, 8). The Upaniṣads thus give the method of converting the world of objects and senses into Ātman. The reverse process of evolving the world out of Ātman is therein implied and is elaborated by the Sāṁkhya and the Āgamas in slightly different ways. The *Muṇḍaka* gives three examples to illustrate this process: the spider producing the web out of itself, plants sprouting from the earth, and hair coming out of our body (I.1.7). The *Kaṭha* says that the senses are created as outgoing (*parāñci*), and exhorts man to turn them inward (IV. 1). The senses and objects are the results of the externalizing process of Ātman. The *Aitareya* describes how the world issued progressively out of Ātman. Stripped of all personification, the statement means that in Brahman exist the cosmic propensities for the division into senses and their corresponding objects, and that the human individual partakes of these propensities; and this gives rise to the division of the enjoyer (*bhoktṛ*) and the enjoyed (*bhogya*).

The Upaniṣads treat *prāṇa* (air and life principle), *manas* (mind), and *vāc* (speech) as made for the Ātman and their presiding deities Vāyu, Indra, and Agni as the highest, next only to Ātman.[9] To the three again correspond *kriyā* (activity), *rūpa* (form), and *nāma* (name) (*Bṛ. U.*, I. 5. 3; I. 6. 1). Of the three again, *prāṇa* is often regarded as the highest (*Pra. U.*, IV. 8; *Chā. U.*, IV. 3. 3; VI. 8. 2); but in the *Kena*, Indra, as the deity of *manas*, is assigned that place for having known the great *yakṣa* as the nearest form of Brahman and for having been told so by the goddess who appeared to him (IV. 3).

The origin of speech (*vāc*) received considerable attention presumably because all revelation is received as verbal inspiration and transmitted through verbal instruction (*śruti*). The Word was actually made flesh in the different religious speculations, for out of it all creation was supposed to proceed. The Vaiṣṇava Saṁhitās, the Śaiva Āgamas, and the Śākta Tantras had all their respective theories of the origin of *nāda* (sound) from which the world was supposed to have arisen, following in this the tradition of the Brāhmaṇas that the Lord of Creation (Prajāpati) used his breath or speech to bring the world into being and recuperated his strength by speech. The Āgamas refer to the *prāṇas, manas,* and *vāc* as the different *śaktis* of God (*icchā, jñāna,* and *kriyā,* including *nāda*). The *Ahirbudhnya Saṁhitā,* a Pāñcarātra work, says (III.29,30,38; XVI.36-40) that when the divine creative activity, which is identical with desire (*saṅkalpa*), vibration (*spanda*), and vital airs (*prāṇa*), is bringing the world into existence, the *nāda*

[9] *Bṛ. U.*, I.4.1; I.5.3; V.8. *Chā. U.*, VI.5; VI.6; VI.8.4,6. Sometimes the sun and the moon also are associated with *manas* (*Ai. U.*, II.5). In ordinary enumeration, Agni or the Vasus, Indra or Vāyu or the Rudras or the Maruts, and Sūrya or the Ādityas really represent the terrestrial, atmospheric, and celestial gods respectively (*Bṛ. U.*, I.2.3).

rises in the form of a bubble called *bindu* (drop), which divides into name (*nāma*) called Śabda Brahman (the logos), and that which is named called *rūpa* (form) or *bhūti* (being). A typical Tāntrika account runs thus: The supreme Bindu (point, drop), Śiva, splits into *bindu* with the Śiva-aspect prevailing and *bīja* (seed) with the Śakti-aspect dominant; these two again unite and *nāda* (sound), with the Śiva- and Śakti-aspects equalized in strength, is formed. The great sound, generated during the splitting of the Bindu, is called Śabda Brahman, which, as uniting the three principles of *bindu, bīja,* and *nāda,* is represented as a triangle and is also known as *kula-kuṇḍalinī*. This *nāda* is to be distinguished from the *nāda* produced by the interaction of *bindu* and *bīja*.[10] Now, whatever be the account so far, Śabda Brahman is *avyakta* (unmanifest), corresponding to the *avyakta* of the *Kaṭha,* and *mṛtyu* (I. 2. 1) and *avyākṛta* (I. 4. 7) of the *Bṛhadāraṇyaka*. Through the operation of the *kriyāśakti* (energy as activity) of Śiva, the original supreme Bindu is split into *bindu* and *bīja,* and this process of splitting appears as the *avyakta nāda* (unmanifest sound).[11] In what is called *avyakta* or *avyākṛta,* the split between Śiva and Śakti is latent, and the resulting *nāda* also is latent. This is called the *parā* or supreme state of sound. Sound has four states and four names: *parā* (supreme), *paśyantī* (cognitive), *madhyamā* (middle), and *vaikharī* (gross).

Avalon quotes from *Nitya Tantra* the connection between these four forms and the plexuses (*cakras*): 'The *parā* form rises in the *mūlādhāra* produced by "air" (*prāṇa*); the same "air" rising upwards, manifested in the *svādhiṣṭhāna,* attains the *paśyantī* state. The same slowly rising upwards and manifested in the *anāhata,* united with understanding (*buddhi*), is *madhyamā*. Again rising upwards, and appearing in the *viśuddha,* it issues from the throat as *vaikharī*'.[12]

The *parā vāc* (supreme Word) corresponds to the logos or Word of the Bible. It is Śabda Brahman itself, unmanifest (*avyakta*), the spread of pure *nāda,* and can be experienced in deep sleep. Here the *kriyāśakti* of Śiva is dominant. The *paśyantī* form of speech is connected with *manas* (mind); in its cosmic form it is associated with Īśvara; it is a movement towards ideation, goaded by *icchāśakti* (energy as desire) to display the universe in its seed (*bīja*) form. The *madhyamā* form is connected with *buddhi* and is experienced in dream. It is the sound we hear in dreams, also called '*āgneyī vāc*'. In it *jñānaśakti* is dominant. From the *madhyamā* begins the distinction between the individual and the cosmos. In its

[10] *Serpent Power,* p. 178. See the other accounts in the preceding and following pages.
[11] *Ibid.,* p. 100.
[12] *Ibid.,* p. 174.

cosmic form, *madhyamā* is associated with Hiraṇyagarbha. The *vaikharī* is gross speech, associated in its cosmic form with Virāj.

To appreciate the distinctions between the individual and the cosmic forms, reference should be made to the Upaniṣadic doctrine of the relation between the Jīva and the cosmos. The Jīva passes through three states, *jāgrat* or waking, *svapna* or dream, and *suṣupti* or deep sleep. Beyond the three falls the *turīya* or fourth state, namely, Ātman. In the waking state, the Jīva is called *vaiśvānara,* in dream *taijasa,* and in deep sleep *prājña.* In the fourth, he becomes absolutely identical with Brahman (*Mā. U.,* 3-7). In it there is no difference between the finite and the infinite, the individual and the cosmos. Now, corresponding to the first three states, the cosmic states are Virāj, Hiraṇyagarbha, and Īśvara. These three are associated with the three lower forms of speech. Above Īśvara comes *avyakta* or *avyākṛta* in which the highest form of speech is found. There is this difference, however, between the *Māṇḍūkya* and the Āgamas that, according to the former, Brahman is above *avyakta.*

The doctrine of *prāṇa* is important in the Upaniṣads. It is of five kinds: *prāṇa, apāna, samāna, udāna,* and *vyāna.* These five are responsible for the voluntary and involuntary activities of the body and the cosmos. In the body, *prāṇa* resides in the heart and is responsible for respiration ; *apāna* resides in the anus and governs the excretory functions ; *samāna* has its abode in the navel and is responsible for the heat of the body and for the digestive processes and assimilation ; *udāna* is in the throat, and to it are due speech and other activities belonging to the upper part of the body ; and *vyana* pervades the whole body and co-ordinates the various parts of the body and their functions. Besides these five *prāṇas,* five more are mentioned: *nāga, kūrma, kṛkara, devadatta,* and *dhanañjaya,* which are manifest in hiccup, closing and opening of eyes, hunger, yawning, and in what is present in the corpse after death.[13]

The *Praśna* (III) tells us that *prāṇa* is both cosmic and individual. *Prāṇa* is born of Ātman and is related to it as the shadow to man. Presided over by *manas,* it enters the human body and divides its functions among the latter's parts. It itself resides in the eye and the ear, in the mouth and the nose ; *apāna* in the penis and anus ; *samāna* in the middle, carrying food to all the parts of the body ; *vyāna* in the hundred and one *nāḍīs* (nerves) spreading from the heart ; and *udāna* in one *nāḍī* going from the heart to the head, leading the soul either to hell or to heaven or to the earth according to its deeds. These are the forms of *prāṇa* in the individual. In the external world, the sun is the *prāṇa* ; the presiding

[13] *Triśikhi-brāhmaṇopaniṣad,* 77-87 ; *Darśanopaniṣad,* IV.23-34.

deity of the earth is *apāna* ; *ākāśa* is *samāna* ; air is *vyāna* ; and fire (*tejas*) is *udāna*.

According to the Sāṁkhya,[14] the five *prāṇas* of the individual are the common functions of the three divisions of *antaḥkaraṇa* (inner sense). That is, though *buddhi, ahaṅkāra,* and *manas* have their own specific functions to perform, together they do all that the five *prāṇas* are said to do in the Upaniṣads. Thus according to the Sāṁkhya, *prāṇa* is not an entity distinct from *manas*.

The Nyāya and the Vaiśeṣika schools say that the functioning of the *prāṇas* is due to an imperceptible striving called *jīvanayoniyatna,* corresponding to the *conatus* in Spinoza's philosophy. It is imperceptible, because it works even during deep sleep, when *manas* is not active. The Neo-Naiyāyikas do not accept this view.[15] In Buddhist psychology, the corresponding conception is that of *jīvitindriya*.

## THE CAKRAS OR NERVOUS PLEXUSES

The idea of nerves is not unknown to the Upaniṣads. They are called *nāḍīs, śirās, dhamanīs*.[16] The *Praśna* says that from the heart spread one hundred and one *nāḍīs,* each splitting into one hundred, and each of the latter again into seventy-two thousand ; and *vyāna* starts the process of all of them (III.6). The *Bṛhadāraṇyaka* speaks of these *hitā nāḍīs* proceeding from the heart. They are as fine as the thousandth part of a hair and are of various colours (II.1.19 ; IV.2.3 ; IV.3.20).

The Tantras give a very interesting account of the nervous system and the plexuses (*cakras*).[17] *Prāṇa* moves along these *cakras,* and the true co-ordination between the cosmos and the individual can be known only when *prāṇa* is mastered in these *cakras*. The absolute Truth can be mastered by mastering *prāṇa*. The senses and *manas* may err ; but *prāṇa* never (*Chā. U.,* I.2), because the split into microcosm and macrocosm is a split in it and the two divisions are held together by it. That is the reason for calling *prāṇa* by the name *satya* (truth) (*Bṛ. U.,* II. 3. 6), though Ātman is called the Truth of truth (*satyasya satyam*).

*Prāṇa,* as the creative power of Ātman, Śiva, or Viṣṇu, lies, according to the Āgamas, as the latent power of *kuṇḍalinī,* coiled up like a serpent round the *mūlādhāracakra* between the anus and the genital organ at the lowest end of the *suṣumṇā nāḍī,* which runs through the spinal chord (*merudaṇḍa*

[14] *Sāṁkhya-kārikā,* 29. According to Gauḍapāda, the circulation of the vital airs is a function of all the thirteen organs, internal and external, taken together.

[15] See *Dinakarī* on *Siddhānta-muktāvalī,* 152.

[16] For details, see Seal, *The Positive Sciences of the Ancient Hindus* ; Dasgupta, *A History of Indian Philosophy,* II. pp. 344 ff.; and the works of Woodroffe (Avalon).

[17] Rele, *Mysterious Kuṇḍalinī*.

or *Brahmadaṇḍa*). *Kuṇḍalinī* is the cosmic *śakti* (power), stored up but asleep. In order to realize the highest or the deepest reality within us, which is both individual and cosmic, we have to rouse *kuṇḍalinī* and make it go up through the higher and higher *cakras* till it reaches the highest in the brain called *sahasrāra* (the thousand-petalled).

The most important *nāḍī* running through the spinal chord is the *suṣumṇā*. Two other *nāḍīs, iḍā* and *piṅgalā,* run along with it on its right and left sides respectively. At the lower end of *suṣumṇā* is the *mūlādhāra-cakra* (sacro-coccygeal plexus). The next higher is the *svādhiṣṭhānacakra* (sacral plexus) situated near the root of the genital organ. The third is the *maṇipūracakra* (lumbar plexus) in the region of the navel. The fourth is the *anāhatacakra* (cardiac plexus) situated near the heart. The fifth is the *viśuddhacakra* (laryngeal plexus) found near the throat. The sixth is the *ājñācakra* found between the eyebrows. The six centres control the five elements—earth, water, fire, air, and ether together with their corresponding senses, and *manas.* Above all these and situated in the cerebrum is the *sahasrāra.* When *prāṇa* is carried up to it, we become conscious of the ultimate Truth.

## THE KOŚAS AND ŚARĪRAS

An important doctrine of psychological interest in the Upaniṣads is that of the five *kośas* or sheaths (*Tai. U.*, II). They are *annamayakośa* or the sheath of matter, *prāṇamayakośa* or the sheath of life, *manomayakośa* or the sheath of conscious activity, *vijñānamayakośa* or the sheath of intelligence (*buddhi*), and *ānandamayakośa* or the sheath of bliss. The *Taittirīya* says that each succeeding one is the soul (Ātman) of the preceding one, which forms its body, there being nothing beyond bliss which Brahman is. The theory of *kośas* is applicable to both the individual and the cosmic person. So far as the individual is concerned, *annamayakośa* is his physical body ; *prāṇamayakośa* consists of the five organs of action and the five *prāṇas* ; *manomayakośa* consists of *manas* and the five organs of sense ; *vijñānamayakośa* consists of *buddhi* and the five organs of sense again ; and *ānandamayakośa* consists of individual nescience dissociated from bodily and mental functions, as, for example, in deep sleep, when it assumes the form of bliss, because in that state objectivity and subjectivity become one and there can be no object of unattained desire for the subject. These are, according to a different account, the five levels of reality that have to be transcended in order to realize Ātman. The *kośas* are so called because Ātman is supposed to envelop itself by them after projecting them out of itself.[18]

[18] Śaṅkara's commentary on the *Brahma-Sūtra,* I.1.12-19 and on *Tai. U.,* II.2 and III.6.

The Advaita, closely following the Upaniṣads, gives four states of Ātman in its individual aspect—waking (*vaiśvānara*), dream (*taijasa*), deep sleep (*prājña*), and the state of pure Ātman (*turīya*), corresponding to the four cosmic states of Virāj, Hiraṇyagarbha (also called Sūtrātman), Īśvara, and Brahman. They are outwardly cognitive, inwardly cognitive, an undifferentiated cognition mass, and a mere witness respectively. According to this school, the individual has three kinds of bodies—the *sthūlaśarīra* or the gross body, the *sūkṣmaśarīra* (*liṅgaśarīra*) or the subtle body, and the *kāraṇaśarīra* or the causal body. The first, determinant of individual waking consciousness, is composed of the gross elements (*annamayakośa*); the second, determinant of individual dream consciousness, consists of the subtle elements (*tanmātras*) and the subtle body (*prāṇamaya-*, *manomaya-*, and *vijñānamaya-kośas*). If *antaḥkaraṇa* (inner sense) is divided into four parts—*manas, buddhi, citta,* and *ahaṅkāra*—the subtle body would consist also of the last two parts. The *kāraṇaśarīra* (corresponding to *ānandamaya-kośa*) is all one without distinct parts and is the determinant of individual deep sleep consciousness. Another name for it is *antaryāmin* (*Mā. U.*). Sleep in Indian philosophy is not regarded as a mere negation of consciousness, as a mere privation, but as the latency of the forces, instincts, impressions, etc. which are inherited from the earlier births also and which are responsible for manifesting the world of dream and waking consciousness.

Besides the *kāraṇaśarīra*, the Advaita speaks of *sākṣin* or the witness self (also called *kūṭastha* or *kūṭasthasākṣin*). The Jīva or soul, as identified with the subtle body, is the agent and enjoyer of actions. But the *sākṣin* is a mere witness thereof. It is therefore purer than the Jīva.

But the Āgamas give five states or supernals above the individual *sākṣin*. According to the Vaiṣṇava Āgamas, *kūṭastha* is like a bee-hive in which a plurality of Ātmans is to be found, the whole being controlled by the lowest super-individual reality. By the Vaiṣṇavas, the five higher levels are called Viṣṇu, Lakṣmī, Saṅkarṣaṇa, Pradyumna, and Aniruddha. According to the Vaiṣṇava Āgamas, Viṣṇu has six *guṇas* or attributes: *jñāna* or knowledge, *aiśvarya* or lordship, *śakti* or ability, *bala* or strength, *vīrya* or virility, and *tejas* or splendour. Lakṣmī as the Śakti of Viṣṇu is regarded as inseparable from him. Out of their unity emanate the three *vyūhas*—Saṅkarṣaṇa, Pradyumna, and Aniruddha—when two of the six attributes dominate in turn. When *jñāna* and *bala* dominate, Viṣṇu becomes Saṅkarṣaṇa; when *aiśvarya* and *vīrya* dominate, he becomes Pradyumna; and when *śakti* and *tejas* dominate, he becomes Aniruddha. From Aniruddha downwards, the duality of Prakṛti and Puruṣa becomes manifest.

The Śaivas, however, do not stick to this conception. According to the Pāśupata and Śaiva Āgamas, the Śakti as the *ānanda* (bliss) aspect of Śiva, the *cit* (intelligence) principle, has three forms—*jñānaśakti* or energy as knowledge, *icchāśakti* or energy as desire (will), and *kriyāśakti* or energy as activity. Now, Śakti as such is the state of equilibrium of the three forms. But when the equilibrium is disturbed and *icchāśakti* predominates, Sadāśiva or Sādākhya *tattva* issues out of Śiva; when *jñānaśakti* dominates, Śiva becomes Īśvara; and when *kriyāśakti* dominates, he becomes Śuddhavidyā or Sadvidyā. Through these three emanations the split between subject and object becomes manifest. Śiva and Śakti are absolutely identical at first. But at the level of Sadāśiva, consciousness takes the form, '*I* am *this*'; but the *this* is not as clear and emphasized as the *I*. At the next level, that is, of Īśvara, consciousness takes the form of '*This* is *I*' and the *this* is more emphasized than the *I*. And at the level of Sadvidyā, both the *this* and the *I* are equally well emphasized. However, at the levels of these supernals, the *this* is not impenetrable to the *I*, but thoroughly transparent to it—the *this* does not overwhelm the *I*.

Creation so far is absolutely pure. But there is semi-pure (*śuddhāśuddha*) creation according to both the Śaiva and the Vaiṣṇava schools, though their accounts of the categories of this creation vary. This intermediate creation, according to the Pāñcarātra, consists of *kūṭastha* and *māyāśakti*, both of which are the next higher forms of Puruṣa and Prakṛti as we find in the Sāṁkhya. *Māyāśakti* has two bodies: *guṇamayavapu* or the body of *guṇas* (attributes) and *kālamayavapu* or the body of time, which latter consists of *niyati* (rule, law, limit) and *kāla* (time). This time is not our gross time but subtle and spiritual or psychological. The same creation, according to the Śaiva Āgamas, has six categories: *māyā, kalā, vidyā, rāga, niyati,* and *kāla* (illusion, skill or ability, knowledge, attachment, law, and time). The categories of this intermediate stage are responsible for binding down the individual Ātman to limitations and conditions; and from them is born the impure creation of Puruṣa and Prakṛti, out of the union of which, again, issue forth what we generally understand as mind and the world.

Mind is not completely opposed to matter, nor is it purely spiritual. According to the Vedānta, Sāṁkhya, and Yoga, mind itself is an evolute out of an original subtle matter, whatever the ultimate nature of that matter may be. The distinction between the subjective and objective poles of our experience is a distinction within mind. What we generally call matter would be a division within the objective pole of our experience. According to the Nyāya and Vaiśeṣika, *manas* is a substance like earth and water. According to Buddhism, the higher four *skandhas* together constitute mind and the mental. In Jainism, which has two kinds of *manas, dravyamanas* and *bhāvamanas,* the former is a substance. Hence in none of the schools does the difficulty of contact between the substantial and the non-substantial crop up. Parallelism, if it is found at all, can be found not between mind and matter, but between senses and their corresponding objects.

*Prāṇa* and its parts control the functions of the body ; and *manas* and the senses are intimately associated with *prāṇa.* That is why yogic teachers prescribe control of *prāṇa* in order to control *manas.* During dream and deep sleep, *manas* leaves the physical body in charge of *prāṇa* and enters the *hitā nāḍīs* that branch out from the heart. During dream, the *sūkṣma* (subtle) body is active ; it is not mind without a body but with a subtle body that exists in dream, and the objects it works with are made of subtle elements. The body of deep sleep is the causal (*kāraṇa*) body, in which *antaḥkaraṇa* disappears, though the subtle body is retained in a potential form. During the process of transmigration, the physical body is given up and the subtle body moves from one physical body to another.

Personality is what corresponds to the ego (*ahaṅkāra*) with its accumulated experiences of present and past births. The Upaniṣads give a somewhat mythological account of the original formation of the individual. Out of *avyakta* or *avyākṛta* (called death in the *Bṛhadāraṇyaka*) are born the presiding deities (*devatās*) of mind and the senses and their corresponding objects. But these deities want an abode (*āyatana*) ; and this abode is the human individual, who is the medium for the activity of these deities. Stripped of the mythological element, this explanation amounts to saying that the forces of *manas,* senses, and their objects work through the individual and become manifest. The other such factors are the typal and individual impressions of past experiences and *karmas* that become forces in the shape of instincts and dispositions. The individual or Jīva is a knot (*granthi*) of all these forces, formed in *hṛdaya* (*buddhi*) ; and liberation consists in dissolving this knot.

Though the Buddhists do not accept that Ātman would be the residue after this dissolution, their view of personality is very similar to the Vedāntic *nāma-rūpa* conception. Personality (*pudgala*) is analysed into *skandhas* (aggregates)—*rūpaskandha* or the aggregate of matter, *vedanāskandha* or the aggregate of feeling, *saṁjñāskandha* or the aggregate of perceptions, *saṁskāraskandha* or the aggregate of instincts, impressions, and dispositions, and *vijñānaskandha* or the aggregate of consciousness. When the constituents of the *pudgala* are separated, nothing is left, which is the state of liberation.

## THE BHŪMIKĀS OR THE STAGES OF REALIZATION

Buddhist psychology discusses several psychological states which are supernormal and which appear while personality is being dissolved. Many of these are found in the Yoga philosophy also. These higher stages are reached by a gradual and systematic process of disciplining our mind (*citta*). The difference between these supernal stages and those given by the Āgamas is that the former are not personified and are divested of mythology.

The Yoga says that, when the process of *citta* is obstructed, Ātman, which is a pure perceiver (*draṣṭṛ*), regains its original nature. Otherwise, it identifies itself with its *citta*. The processes (*vṛttis*) of *citta* are five: knowledge (*pramā*), false knowledge or illusion (*viparyaya*), abstraction, imagination, or ambiguity engendered by word (*vikalpa*),[19] sleep (*nidrā*), and memory (*smṛti*). True cognition (*pramā*) is of three kinds: perception, inference, and verbal knowledge (scriptural testimony). False knowledge relates to the five *kleśas* (afflictions) mentioned below. Sleep is that mental function in which the mind is overpowered by the *tamas* (torpor) element and there is absence of all external sensory functions. It is still a function, because after sleep our memory that we slept well or ill would not have been possible without some experience or *vṛtti*. Memory is the rising into consciousness of a past experienced object. These functions are obstructed by yogic practice and non-attachment to worldly objects. When mind is made steady and *vṛttis* are obstructed, *samādhi* is attained. *Samādhi* is basically of two kinds: *samprajñāta* and *asamprajñāta*. *Samprajñāta* is that fixed state in which the object focussed upon by mind is most clearly cognized. It is of eight kinds: *savitarka, savicāra, sānanda,* and *sāsmita,* and their opposites, *nirvitarka, nirvicāra, nirānanda,* and *nirasmita*. They are due to concentration on more and more subtle forms of our being. *Savitarka* is that fixed state of mind in which the distinction between the object concentrated upon and its name subsists. The objects of this state are gross while those of *savicāra* are subtle but determinate and are limited by space and time. The object of the next state is the *antaḥkaraṇa* only; yet in it a little of *rajas* and *tamas* persists. It is full of bliss because of the dominance of *sattva,* the nature of which is bliss. In the fourth state, the object is still the *antaḥkaraṇa*; but in it even *sattva* is suppressed and the mere being of consciousness dominates. The *asmitā* of this state is not the same as *ahaṅkāra*; for the latter is the active ego appropriating every experience as its own, but the former is the *antaḥkaraṇa* turned inward and aware only of its own being. In the first

[19] For instance, the phrase 'consciousness of the Ātman' gives the meaning of a possessive; but in truth, consciousness and Ātman are identical for the Yoga.

two, the objects fixed upon are the objects of cognition ; in the third, it is the instrument of cognition ; but in the fourth, the object is the cognizer himself. These three divisions are called *grāhya-samāpatti, grahaṇa-samāpatti,* and *grahītṛ-samāpatti* or *grāhaka-samāpatti.*

Just as there is *savitarka-samādhi,* there is its opposite *nirvitarka-samādhi,* in which the distinction between knowledge and object is suppressed, and the object alone shines. Similarly, there is *nirvicāra-samādhi. Nirānanda* and *nirasmita* are the opposites of *sānanda* and *sāsmita.* These two are admitted by Vācaspati but not by Vijñāna Bhikṣu. When this lower *samādhi* is perfected, a peculiar power of knowing (*prajñā*) called *ṛtambharā* (full of truth) is attained, which is different from the usual ways of knowing like perception, inference, and verbal testimony.

*Asamprajñāta-samādhi* consists in rejecting every function as not the final truth. The arrested functions remain in it only as latent forces. And as there is nothing cognized or present before mind in this *samādhi,* it is called *nirbīja* or seedless. *Asamprajñāta* is of two kinds: *bhavapratyaya* and *upāyapratyaya.* Those who attain the first become higher supernatural beings after death and live with subtle bodies for a time, after which they are born again ; for they do not realize the difference between Puruṣa and Prakṛti. But those who attain the second through faith (*śraddhā*), enthusiasm (*vīrya*), unforgetfulness (*smṛti*), concentration (*samādhi*), and discrimination (*prajñā*) attain the highest *samprajñāta,* and through it the highest *asamprajñāta.*

The five *kleśas* (hindrances, difficulties) which are the causes of misery are *avidyā* (ignorance), *asmitā* (the feeling that one is so-and-so), *rāga* (attachment), *dveṣa* (hate), and *abhiniveśa* (the desire to continue to be what one is). When these *kleśas* or impurities are removed and our mind is able to enter various forms of *samādhi,* it attains many supernatural powers. The different forms of *samādhi* described above may be called *bhūmis* or stations or stages of mind in its higher attainment. They are also called *samāpattis* or attainments. The states of *citta,* corresponding to the power of attention or fixation it develops, are *kṣipta* (agitated), *mūḍha* (stupefied), *vikṣipta* (fitfully steady), *ekāgra* (attentive), and *niruddha* (obstructed, controlled). They represent a progressive advance towards the ultimate suppression of all mental modifications. The line of progression lies through *ekāgratā,* in which the rise of new experiences (*pratyaya*) is checked, and *samādhi,* in which even the latent impressions (*saṁskāras*) show signs of decay, until it terminates in *nirodha* when a complete cessation of all mental functions, including latent tendencies, takes place ; thereafter a direct knowledge of the pure self is obtained.

The Buddhists have a different account of the *bhūmis* or *bhūmikās* in the progress of the spiritual pilgrim. The majority of them accept ten. As given by the *Daśabhūmika-śāstra,* they are *pramuditā* (joyful), *vimalā* (pure), *prabhākarī* (brilliant), *arciṣmatī* (blazing), *sudurjayā* (difficult to attain), *abhimukhī* (face to face), *dūraṅgamā* (far-reaching), *acalā* (immovable), *sādhumatī* (good intelligence), and *dharmameghā* (cloud of *dharma*).[20]

The apparent difference between the *bhūmis* of the Yoga philosophy and those of Buddhism is that while the former are attained by *dhyāna* (meditation) upon the categories of existence, the latter are attained by *dhyāna* upon the ethical properties of things. But even for the former, moral qualities are indispensable preliminaries for *yoga* practice ; and the latter presumes right knowledge and realization of the categories of existence.

### WRONG PERCEPTION: HALLUCINATION AND ILLUSION

As in Western psychology, perceptual errors were classified under the three major heads of hallucination, illusion, and dream. Of these illusion received the most careful treatment not only psychologically, but also epistemologically and even ontologically. In addition to these, disorders of the sense-organs which produce defective perception were noticed. Excessive use, disuse, inadequate use, and injudicious use of the sense-organs tend to produce disorders of sensation and affect perception. The stimulus, the external medium of transmission, the sense-organ, the bodily constitution, the mental factor, and the moral equipment might operate jointly and severally to produce erroneous perception. Indefiniteness of the stimulus is sometimes responsible for producing doubt (*saṁśaya*), as when a man is unable to make out whether a distant object is a tree or a man, or indeterminate perception (*anadhyavasāya*) lacking in the apprehension of the exact nature of the object perceived and ending with the bare acquaintance with a *that* without its *what.* Failure to comprehend the nature of a perceived object may also come from inattentiveness and psychic blindness. Hyperaesthesia and anaesthesia may also affect the nature of perception.

Positive misapprehension may take the form of hallucination or illusion. For the latter the co-operation of the sense-organs is needed, but the former owes its origin to the mind alone. Past experiences and latent impressions, aided sometimes by the disturbance of the humoral balance

[20] For differences between the Mahāyāna and the Hīnayāna, and also between the various sub-schools, see Har Dayal, *The Bodhisattva Doctrine.* See also D. T. Suzuki, *Outlines of Mahāyāna Buddhism,* XII; R. Kimura, *A Historical Study of the Terms Hīnayāna and Mahāyāna and the Origin of Mahāyāna Buddhism,* pp. 133 f. Similarly, the Jains have their fourteen stages of excellence (*guṇasthānakas*).

in the body, attain sensory vividness under the stress of a strong emotion or due to mental preoccupation with an idea or on account of the operation of the moral factor (*adṛṣṭa*).

Illusion, in which both presentative and representative factors operate, may be due to (i) the ambiguous or indistinct nature of the stimulus itself, as when one sees silver in an oyster-shell, or water in desert sand, or a snake in a rope, or a city (*gandharva-nagara*) in the sky due to clouds, (ii) defect in the medium, as when in the dark one thing is mistaken for another, (iii) physiological disturbance in the sense-organ or the bodily system, as when excess of bile makes sugar taste bitter, jaundice makes a white thing yellow, and pressure on one eye-ball dislocates binocular vision and gives a double image of the moon, (iv) mental disturbance, as when habit, expectation, emotion, etc. prompt us to interpret a stimulus wrongly, and drowsiness and inattention lead to erroneous perception. To these may be added illusions due to movement which include physical and physiological factors and also magic (*indrajāla*) and other types of suggestion. The nature of the illusion sometimes depends upon the moral factor, the same situation causing different illusions to different persons according to their merit.

The most controversial issues were raised round the problem of illusion, specially the rôle played by recollection in its origination. The relation between the presentative and the representative factor was differently viewed by the different systems, giving rise to the various theories of illusion. These are *akhyāti* (either non-apprehension of an object, i.e. mistaking a hallucination for an illusion, or *smṛtipramoṣa,* failure to distinguish the presentative and the representative element), *asat-khyāti* (mistaking a non-existent thing as existent), *ātma-khyāti* (projecting a mental state into the external world), *anirvacanīya-khyāti* (mistaking an undefinable entity for a real thing), *alaukika-khyāti* (mistaking an extraordinary presentation as a real percept), *sat-khyāti* (objective error in which for the time being something real corresponding to the illusion is presented to the mind), *sadasat-khyāti* (apprehension which is partly real and partly unreal, the *that* being real and the *what* unreal), and *anyathā-khyāti* or *viparīta-khyāti* (mistaking the represented element for the presented due to common traits between the two). Some of these are closely related, but others are radically different ; and each theory has its own philosophical background.

## DREAMS

Dreams are due to impressions left by experiences of our waking life. But one is not conscious of the impressions as impressions ; hence dreams are different from memory. In a dream, one is in one's *liṅgaśarīra* (subtle body) and one's world is made up of subtle elements.

In the transition from wakefulness to dream, the physical body is left in charge of *prāṇa* or vital force ; and *manas* and other mental functions are withdrawn and used in dreams. Higher than *manas* is *vijñāna,* which works in both the waking and dream states. During deep sleep also, the physical body is left in charge of *prāṇa* ; but *manas* and the senses are withdrawn into *vijñāna* ; and *vijñāna* itself, in a germinal state, enters *avidyā* (ignorance), which is, for the Upaniṣads, a positive entity, psychical and metaphysical. This is the *kāraṇaśarīra* or causal body. In dreams the *vāsanās* or *saṁskāras* work as dynamic universals or forces producing experiences split up into subject and objects. The world of dreams is different from that of the waking consciousness, and the two are utterly unconnected. The dream time cannot be measured in terms of the time of the waking consciousness ; during dream, in what we call an hour according to the latter time, we might have telescoped events that take years of waking consciousness. The standards of measurement in dream must therefore be different.

One important point in this theory of dreams is the doctrine of the causal body (*kāraṇaśarīra*). It is the unconscious and unmanifest state of the individual and his world. It is the microcosmic *avyakta.* It is *prajñā* (intelligence)—*prājña* is the name of Ātman in deep sleep—but with all the forces that make up the individual's world lying latent. Praśastapāda (IX.2.7-9) refers to somatogenic and psychogenic dreams as depending respectively upon obscure organic stimulation and past impressions reviving veridically the image of an object even in the absence of the operation of the sense-organs. The character of the dream images depends upon the predominating humoral constituent—wind (*vāyu*), bile (*pitta*), or phlegm (*kapha*) ; upon the dominant thought, emotion, and attitude just before sleep ; and upon merit (*dharma*) and demerit (*adharma*). He also refers to dream within dream.

The Vedāntins say that the senses are collected in *manas* which alone functions in a dream and creates out of the impressions of past percepts as-if-external objects. Ātman then resides in the subtle body (*liṅgaśarīra*). The objects perceived therefore are made of subtle elements. Also the place, time, cause, and manner of refutation of dreams are totally different from those of waking consciousness.

Discussion about dreams is recent in Buddhistic literature. But the Buddhists have not made use of the difference between the gross and the subtle forms of our body. So, though they recognize that we see all the sense objects, they say all take the form of vision only and hence only the mind but not the senses can be operative in dreams.

There are four classes of dreams: (1) dreams due to organic and muscular disturbances, (2) recurrence of earlier dreams and dreams due to previous experiences, (3) dreams due to suggestions from spiritualistic agents, and (4) prophetic dreams. The first two do not correspond to facts. Prophetic dreams, the Buddhists say, are always true. The third class may be true or false according as the spiritualistic agent sends a true or false message. According to the Buddhists, all dream except the *arhants* who belong to the highest class and whose minds do not suffer from *viparyaya* (hallucination). Nāgasena says that a dream is neither sleep nor waking, but occurs in the transitional state. Is a dream thought or dream act moral (*kuśala*), immoral (*akuśala*), or unmoral (*avyakta*)? Do dreams produce effects? These two questions are answered together. Now, in a dream volitional control is suspended, and the monk is absolved from sins committed in dreams. Further, it is said that the power of will in dreams is not strong enough to produce rebirth; but if strengthened by earlier experiences, it may have after-effects in this very life. Praśastapāda also believes that dream experiences, though not original, may leave impressions (*saṁskāras*) behind.

## PSYCHOLOGICAL ASPECTS OF PRAMĀṆAS

*Pramāṇas* or valid forms of knowledge, accepted by the schools, though of much more logical interest, have their psychological aspects as well. Generally, more attention is given to the psychological aspect of perception than to that of the other forms. The Naiyāyikas admit inference (*anumāna*), analogy (*upamāna*), and verbal cognition or authority (*śabda*) in addition to perception (*pratyakṣa*) as sources of knowledge.

Aristotle divided inference into three steps. Some of the Indian schools like the Advaita and the Mīmāṁsā do the same. But the Naiyāyikas contend that it has five steps. Their classical example is:

The mountain has fire;
Because of smoke;
Wherever there is smoke there is fire, as in the kitchen;
The mountain has smoke implying fire;
Therefore the mountain has fire.

Logically, the first three steps are enough and the other two are redundant. But the Naiyāyikas say that, unless it is known that the smoke in the mountain implies fire, it would not be possible to make the judgement, 'The mountain has fire'. That is, besides asserting the major and minor premises separately, they should be asserted conjointly also.

The Naiyāyikas solve the problem of induction psychologically and avoid the insoluble problems of the unity of nature, its universality, and its uniformity. They admit that the major premise is not obtained by exhausting all the instances. But, unlike the Buddhists who hold that each thing has its own unique character (*svalakṣaṇa*), they believe in concepts or general ideas and classes (*jāti*) based on resemblance or essential similarity. According to them, there are two kinds of contact with the objects of perception, ordinary and extraordinary; the latter is again of three kinds, *sāmānyalakṣaṇa* or contact with the universal, *jñānalakṣaṇa* or contact with a cognition, and *yogaja* or supernatural (yogic or extra-sensory). When the eye first comes into contact with smoke and fire in a particular place, then simultaneously *dhūmatva* (smokeness) and *vahnitva* (fireness) are also contacted. Through the contact with these two universals all instances of smoke and all instances of fire become objects of knowledge, and the major premise, asserting their connection, is cognized. Through *jñānalakṣaṇa* contact, an attribute associated with another attribute directly cognized is known. When I see a red rose with the eye, the cognition of its sweet smell also arises, because that particular smell is associated with that colour. Thus though the object directly perceived is a 'red rose', the percept can be of the form of a 'sweet red rose'. *Yogaja pratyakṣa* is of two kinds, *yukta* and *yuñjāna* (eternal and temporary). Through this contact, the *yogin* can perceive objects, far, hidden, and subtle, and also objects of the past and the future. The first gives a constant knowledge of all things at all times, but the second can give the same knowledge only with some effort.

Some schools like the Sāṁkhya treat analogy as a process of inference, but the Naiyāyikas contend that it is a distinct form of obtaining knowledge (*pramāṇa*). Similarity itself, without leading to definite formulation of a syllogism, gives rise to a new judgement. The controversy on this point is similar to the one whether recognition is judgement or inference.

The problem of verbal knowledge has more of psychological interest than inference or analogy. Naturally, in order to understand a sentence uttered by another, one must have knowledge of the word, of the object denoted by the word, and of the fact that the word means the object. The Naiyāyikas say that each dying sound leaves an impression, which is connected by mind with the sound of the last part of the word, and the word as a whole is thereby grasped. But Mīmāṁsakas generally maintain that no part of a word or sentence by itself or along with the rest, can produce the whole meaning of a word or sentence, which is a unity. So this school says that over and above these sounds, there is what it calls *sphoṭa,* the essence of the sound of the word (or sentence) as a whole, which, brought up into consciousness by the different sounds of the word (or words of the sentence), produces the cognition of what is meant by the word (or sentence) as a whole.

The Naiyāyikas say that ordinary (*laukika*) contact is of six kinds: in the cognition of substance, it is simple contact with substance (*saṁyoga*); in the cognition of entities like qualities, it is of the form of contact-cum-inherence (*saṁyukta-samavāya*); in the cognition of entities that subsist in such entities, it is contact-cum-inherence-cum-inherence (*saṁyukta-samaveta-samavāya*); sound is contacted only through inherence (*samavāya*), for *ākāśa* (ether) in which sound inheres cannot be contacted by the ear and is contacted through inherence-cum-inherence (*samaveta-samavāya*); the relation of inherence itself is contacted as only an attribute (*viśeṣaṇatā*); and absence is likewise contacted through *viśeṣaṇatā* (the relation of being an attribute), when the idea, 'Had it been there it would have been perceived', is applicable.

These forms of *sannikarṣa* (contact) of senses with objects are rejected by some schools, like the Advaita, as fanciful. First, how can there be contact with absence? For instance, there can be contact between the eye and the table; but there can be no contact between the eye and the absence of the pen on the table, for contact is possible only between positive entities. *Samavāya,* again, is the relation that obtains between a substance and its quality, the individual and its universal, and so forth. But to say that colour, for instance, is contacted in one way and the relation between colour and substance in another is to introduce differences for which there is no justification.

Do all the senses go out to contact the objects?—is an interesting question. The Nyāya, Vaiśeṣika, Sāṁkhya, and Mīmāṁsā think that all the sense-organs go out to the object, contact it, and then produce cognition.[21] Accordingly, the physical eye, with which we see and which cannot leave the body in order to touch its objects, is not the visual sense proper, which is invisible to the naked eye. But the Jaina school makes an exception in the case of the eye and also in the case of *manas,* which is not, of course, a sense-organ for them. The Buddhists treat the eye and the ear also as not going out to contact objects. They are *aprāpyakārins.*

There are some among the Buddhists who treat the whole body as one sense-organ; some, again, among them treat only *manas* as such, and some others only touch (*sparśa*) as the sense-organ and say that eye, ear, etc. are differentiations of the same.

The Jaina philosophers distinguish between beings with five senses

[21] They are called *prāpyakārins* (those who work after reaching the object). See Sinha, *Indian Psychology,* Perception, pp. 20 ff.

(eye, ear, nose, taste, and touch), with four senses (ear, nose, taste, and touch), with three senses (nose, taste, and touch), with two senses (taste and touch), and with one sense (touch).[22] They divide senses, as they do *manas,* into two kinds, *dravyendriyas* (physical senses) and *bhāvendriyas* (mental or spiritual senses). The latter are obviously subtle.[23] The Naiyāyikas, of course, would say that the former are the real *indriyas.*

The correlativity of sense-organs and the corresponding objects has also been referred to ; eye and fire (sun, light), ear and *ākāśa* (ether), touch and air (*vāyu*), taste and water, smell and earth, are, in each case, two poles, as it were, of the same entity, which is personified as a *devatā* (deity) in the Upaniṣads. The Mīmāṁsakas maintain that it is not *ākāśa* (ether) but *diś* (space) that is correlated to the ear. It should, however, be said that the Upaniṣads contain both the views.

We have referred to the Naiyāyika view that sense-organs cannot produce cognitions simultaneously. For senses can do nothing without the co-operation of *manas* ; and *manas,* being an *aṇu* (atomic), cannot be at the service of all the senses at once. The Jains therefore contend that the omniscience of the sages cannot be a property of the atomic *manas,* but must be a quality of the self.

Reference need only be made to the stages of indeterminate and determinate perception recognized by most schools and the stages of *avagraha* (outlinear grasp), *īhā* (discrimination), *avāya* (judgement), and *dhāraṇā* (retention) of the Jains.

### RASA OR AESTHETIC PLEASURE

A psychological theory that is a peculiarly Indian contribution is that of *rasa,* which is very often, though wrongly, translated as sentiment. *Rasa* is aesthetic pleasure, which is said to be akin to the sublime bliss of God-realization (*Brahmāsvāda-sahodara*). The Upaniṣads say that the nature of Brahman is *ānanda* (bliss). But according to the Sāṁkhya, Yoga, Nyāya, and Vaiśeṣika, the nature of Ātman by itself is not *ānanda.* For the latter two, it is not even consciousness. The first two schools attribute *rasa* or *ānanda* to *buddhi,* and say that it is a *sāttvika* form of *buddhi.* And as *buddhi* is the principle of illumination, *rasa* or *ānanda* becomes a form of consciousness or knowledge (*jñāna*). But for the other two schools, *buddhi* is not a substantive entity but an adventitious attribute of Ātman, appearing when *manas* comes into contact with it. Like *buddhi,* pleasure (*sukha*) also is an adventitious attribute.

[22] *Tattvārthādhigama-Sūtra,* II. 10-14.
[23] *Ibid.,* II. 16.

The writers on *alaṅkāra* (rhetoric, poetics) follow the Upaniṣadic view generally, and say that *rasa* is one and is Brahman. But it can take different forms, which are usually accepted as nine, corresponding to nine *bhāvas* (emotions or sentiments). *Bhāvas* are of two kinds, *sthāyibhāvas* or stable *bhāvas* and *sañcāribhāvas* or unstable *bhāvas*. It is the former that can become *rasas*. They are *śṛṅgāra* (love), *vīra* (heroism), *karuṇa* (pity), *adbhuta* (wonder), *hāsya* (laughter), *bhayānaka* (dread), *bībhatsa* (disgust), *raudra* (fury), and *śānta* (quiet or peace). At their base lie the corresponding dominant feelings of *rati* (sexual craving), *utsāha* (energy), *śoka* (sorrow), *vismaya* (astonishment), *hāsa* (mirth), *bhaya* (fear), *jugupsā* (aversion), *krodha* (anger), and *nirveda* (self-disparagement), which must be assisted by favourable excitants (*vibhāva*), both essential (*ālambana*) and enhancing (*uddīpana*), by reinforcing ensuants (*anubhāva*), namely, voluntary and involuntary (*sāttvikabhāva*) expressions and also by certain accessaries or subordinate feelings (*vyabhicāribhāva* or *sañcāribhāva*) which follow in the wake of the dominant sentiments and diversify the same.

*Sthāyibhāva* as such is not *rasa*. It should be made sweet or pleasant (*ānīvamānaṁ svādutvam*) by a number of accessaries, some of which are *sañcāribhāvas*. *Bhāvas* may be based upon instincts, and some of them are sentiments and combinations of instincts. But an instinct is not reflective, whereas a *bhāva* is reflective (*hṛdayāvasthāvedaka*), and *rasa* is much more so. It is even said that all cannot have these *rasas*; they are experienced only by men of taste. However, both the *sthāyi-* and the *sañcāri-bhāvas* are common to all humanity.

Besides a description of the various *rasas*, there are elaborate discussions about their mutual congruence and conflict, which must be taken note of when presenting them in a drama. They have been given different colours in consonance with their respective natures. Thus the furious, the terrible, the comic, the erotic, the pathetic, the horrible, the marvellous, and the heroic are supposed to be red, black, white, dark, grey, dark blue, orange, and yellow respectively, and they are even credited with presiding deities, who are Rudra, Kāla, Pramatha, Viṣṇu, Yama, Mahākāla, Brahmā, and Indra respectively, and when the quietistic is added to the list, it is invested with jasmine as the colour and Nārāyaṇa as the presiding deity.

The relation of *rasa* to Ātman is differently understood by different systems. The chief writers on *rasa* themselves accept the Advaita theory. The *bhāvas* are different forms (*prapañca*) of *buddhi*; and the *rasas* therefore are also forms of *buddhi*. When a particular *bhāva* of *buddhi* is made *sāttvika*, the original *rasa* of Brahman is reflected into it, and the *bhāva* becomes a *rasa*. Thus all *rasas* are forms of the original *rasa*.

## PLEASURE AND PAIN

But aesthetic delight is only one species of pleasurable feeling. More fundamental is the general problem of pleasure (*sukha*) and pain (*duḥkha*) which are responsible for swaying our will positively (*icchā*) and negatively (*dveṣa*) respectively. Acute analysis of the feelings of pleasure and pain, together with the conditions, both phenomenal and non-phenomenal (e.g. moral), responsible for the same, is to be found in many systems. Pleasure (*sukha*), happiness (*prīti*), and bliss (*ānanda*) may be supposed to form an ascending series. Naturally the question of a neutral feeling which characterizes the state of dispassion or indifference (*vairāgya*), so necessary for attaining the highest condition of the mind or soul, crops up in most of the systems, as the essential condition of release is supposed to be transcendence of all duality (*dvandva*) and the attainment of an impassivity or serenity that goes beyond all sense of pleasure and pain and their effects, desire or attraction, and aversion or repulsion. The question whether pleasure or pain is the positive feeling is also discussed in connection with the nature of salvation, and except in Advaita Vedānta and some theistic systems, where bliss (*ānanda*) is regarded as characterizing the released soul, cessation of pain (*duḥkha-nivṛtti*) is laid down as the ultimate objective of spiritual endeavour. The basic impulses that lead to actions have also been classified, though the primary intention is in most cases to relate them to merit and demerit. Being mainly intellectualistic in outlook, practically every system traces the feeling life to some kind of obscuration of the intellect—*moha* (thoughtlessness or delusion), *avidyā* (false knowledge), *ajñāna* (ignorance), *aviveka* (non-discrimination)—and the trinity of *rāga* (attraction), *dveṣa* (aversion), and *moha* (delusion) figure in both heterodox and orthodox systems as the cause of the empirical life with its divergent sympathies and antipathies. Variants of these basic feelings in accordance with the objects towards which they are directed have been carefully laid down, as for instance, different types of positive desires like *kāma* (in the narrow sense, sex craving and in the wider sense, any longing for pleasure here or hereafter), *abhilāṣa* (desire for food and drink), *rāga* (recurrent passion or attachment of any kind), *bhāva* (concealed desire), and *cikīrṣā* or desire for specific types of action (knowing, hearing, seeing, taking, etc.). They may relate to the benefit of the self or to that of others. Similar classifications of aversions and delusions with their various modified forms are also to be found. Lower feelings which tend to disturb mental peace or social relation, like anger, rashness, meanness, unbecoming fear, impatience, intolerance, pride, arrogance, jealousy, envy, malice, revengefulness, cruelty, greed, deceitfulness, etc., are carefully listed and distinguished. Higher feelings are those connected with spiritual elevation, e.g. contentment, peace, magnanimity, loving-kindness, humility, honesty, etc., and those proceeding from an enlightened interest in the well-being of fellow-creatures, which are classified under the four forms—*maitrī* (friendliness towards all), *karuṇā* (compassion at the misfortune of others), *muditā* (joy at the prosperity of others), and *upekṣā* (indifference to, or non-emphasis on, the lapses of others). Devotion (*bhakti*) as representing the highest type of sentiment receives careful analysis specially on its expressive side (*lakṣaṇa*). It goes without saying that the helps and hindrances to various types of emotion are brought out with meticulous care and the control of the emotional life is systematically taught in the various philosophies as a necessary training for attaining higher reaches of spirituality. Here, as in the psychology of cognition, the ultimate motive of spiritual exaltation is never lost sight of, and therefore feelings are assessed on the grounds of their moral and spiritual value. The nearest secular classification is to be found only in *alaṅkāra* (aesthetic) literature, where not only are the sentiments classified but even a genetic explanation is sometimes attempted, namely, whether any particular feeling like *eros* (*śṛṅgāra*) or pathos (*karuṇa*) is at the root of the others.

### SPRINGS OF ACTION

'Springs of action' is one of the topics in which Indian psychology was deeply interested. These springs are treated not only as the cause of *action* in this life, but also as the cause of *life* itself.

Besides the urges from behind our personality, there are four ideals of life which prompt man to act. They are *dharma* (duty), *artha* (wealth), *kāma* (desire), and *mokṣa* (liberation). These ideals are accepted by all schools.

*Nirvāṇa* or *śūnya* of the Buddhists and Ātman of the other schools are pure by nature and do not contain activity or its roots in themselves. So *avidyā* (ignorance) is the first root cause of our actions. For the Buddhists, it is the first of the twelve-linked chain of causation. *Kleśas* or impurities or pain-givers are five in number: *avidyā* (ignorance), *asmitā* (self-feeling), *rāga* (attachment), *dveṣa* (hate), and *abhiniveśa* (desire to continue to be what one is). These five *kleśas,* according to Patañjali, are the root causes of all good and bad actions, and together form *karmāśaya* or the repository of *karma.*[24]

*Karmāśaya* corresponds to *ālaya* or *ālayavijñāna* of the Buddhists. *Ālaya* means a storehouse; it is the storehouse of all the latent forces (*vāsanās, saṁskāras*) some of which become kinetic. The group of

[24] *Yoga-Sūtra,* II. 15.

kinetic forces is called *pravṛttivijñāna*. The concept of *apūrva* or *adṛṣṭa* (unseen), developed by the Mīmāṁsakas and accepted by other orthodox schools, performs a function similar to that of *ālaya* and *karmāśaya*. Actions performed now duly produce their effects afterwards. But no causal relation can be established without temporal contiguity between cause and effect. So the Mīmāṁsakas maintain that actions performed remain in a latent unseen state till they produce their effects. In some form or other, the rest of the Indian schools accept this view. Thus what are called *saṁskāras* would be of two kinds, *vāsanārūpa* (of the nature of dispositions) and *dharmādharmarūpa* (of the nature of merit and demerit). Thus the *ālaya* of the Buddhists, the *kāraṇaśarīra* of the Vedāntins, the *karmāśaya* of the Yoga and the Sāṁkhya, the *apūrva* and *adṛṣṭa* of the Mīmāṁsakas and the Naiyāyikas play a common rôle, namely, of being the reservoir of the latent forces (*vāsanās* etc.) that burst out into activity when the occasion comes.

The Śaiva Āgamas give six super-individual forces which are to account for our activity in this world. They are called *kañcukas* (sheaths) that introduce limitation into the infinitude of Ātman. They are *māyā* (illusion), *kalā* (skill), *vidyā* (knowledge), *rāga* (attachment), *niyati* (law), and *kāla* (time). Buddhist psychology mentions four *āsavas* (intoxicants, impurities) which make a man go wrong as if he is drunk. They are sensuality (*kāmāsava*), becoming (*bhāvāsava*, rebirth), wrong views (*dṛṣṭyāsava*), and ignorance (*avidyā*).[25] In Jaina philosophy we come across the concept of *āsrava* which comes very near to that of *vṛtti* in the Yoga. *Asravas* are the channels through which *karma* flows into the Jīva (Ātman) and binds him.

Though a big part of voluntary action is connected with the obeying of scriptural injunctions, performance of appointed duties, and the cultivation of spiritual disciplines, subtle analysis of conation occurs in many systems of philosophy. Jainism gives the longest list of actions that men perform to their moral elevation or undoing, but it is in the Nyāya-Vaiśeṣika and Yoga systems that we get the most elaborate analysis of the springs of action. As is expected, the distinction between voluntary and involuntary action is drawn in order to indicate the limits of moral responsibility. Volitional acts have reference to the memory of past experiences of pleasure and pain as also to the idea of attaining a future state which brings about pleasure or avoids pain or gets rid of both. The origin and effect of habit (*abhyāsa*) and latent impression (*vāsanā*) are

[25] For further explanation of the terms, see Rhys Davids, *Buddhist Manual of Psychological Ethics,* pp. 268, 269, and Aung and Rhys Davids, *Compendium of Philosophy,* pp. 170, 171.

discussed, the latter in great detail, and the procedure for annulling or counteracting undesirable unconscious tendencies is laid down. The method of using the body as an aid to attention and concentration was carefully worked out, and in later *yoga* practices even the control of the autonomic system was achieved. The psychology of habit was extended to include not only the creation of latent traces (*saṁskāras*) responsible for the revival of past acts and thoughts later in life, but also the specific instincts of each species as determined by the present bodily structure. The re-embodied soul, in its previous births, must have assumed many animal forms and acquired different characteristic habits, but it must revive only those habits of past lives which are useful in the present bodily form, e.g. the instinct of eating grass when embodied as a cow and of flesh when a tiger.

It was accepted as a cardinal tenet that, in spite of the limitations imposed according to the law of Karma by the residual impressions of past lives, the will was free to choose between alternative modes of action by proper deliberation and decision (*saṅkalpa*) and a consciousness of freedom accompanied every deliberate act. A voluntary action involves not only a desire to attain a foreseen objective, positive or negative, but also a belief that it is achievable under existing conditions through personal effort, thus converting a mere wish into a motive ; the adoption of necessary bodily movements to bring about the desired change and the discharge of energy to produce the desired effect successively follow the impulse generated by the two mental factors mentioned above. The object aimed at may be either some objective good, whether rightly or wrongly conceived to be such, or some better condition of the self, whether that be pleasure or happiness or absence of pain or complete apathy. Moral and scripturally ordained actions involve in addition a sense of obligatoriness or imperative that they must be performed by the agent himself in the interest of personal righteousness (*dharma*), but a sense of duty does not compel the will and so violation of ordained actions always remains a possibility. There is no belief in predestination nor, except as a devotional exaggeration, any idea that God uses the human will as a mere tool for the realization of His own purposes and absolves finite beings from the moral responsibilities of their actions. This remark applies to both prescriptions (*vidhi*) and prohibitions (*niṣedha*) so that both propulsion (*pravṛtti*) and repulsion (*nivṛtti*) are under the agent's control.

The nature of the deterrents that check volitional acts and the mode of overcoming them were also discussed in some detail. A similar analysis of the different types of promptings or suggestions that lead to action was also made. It was acknowledged that no moral responsibility attached to acts dreamt to have been done by the person dreaming. The wise advice is also given that *dharma* is not to be preached to a person whose will power is temporarily at a low ebb, namely, one who is drunk, agitated, mad, tired, angry, hungry, in haste, in fear, or under the influence of an overpowering passion like greed or lust or some such inordinate desire. As usual, both empirical and transcendental elements entered into the motives of moral action, and the problem of disinterested action and dedicated life cropped up in connection with religious conduct in the theistic literature, e.g. the *Bhagavad-Gītā*. Different types of solemn vows (*śapatha, pratijñā, divya, vrata, praṇidhāna,* etc.) indicated the deliberate adoption of certain abiding will attitudes regulating the conational life in both secular and sacred matters, the abandonment of which entailed spiritual degradation.

It will thus be evident that Indian psychology tried to tackle most of the problems of mental life with which we are familiar in modern psychological literature of the West. The psychology of thinking received the greatest attention and some of the subtle distinctions drawn in Buddhism, Jainism, and Brāhmaṇism will still repay careful attention. The psychology of feeling was comparatively less developed in philosophical literature, though the defect was partially made good in the aesthetic literature. The psychology of willing, however, was fairly well developed in the interest of morality and religion which dominated every philosophical system of India. In the Āyurvedic (medical) literature is to be found a description of the physiological system as then known, the tradition having come down from the times of the *Atharva-Veda,* and this is repeated in the Tantra and later Yoga literature. Naturally, it is in the medical literature that we come across a description of the aetiology, symptoms, and treatment of the various types of mental diseases, generally classified under the two major heads of insanity (*unmāda*) and epilepsy (*apasmāra*).

# 37

## TYPES OF HUMAN NATURE

### IMMENSITY OF THE PROBLEM

HUMAN nature, in its richness and variety, in its heights and in its depths, in its psycho-physical expansion or what may be called its horizontal plane, and in its spiritual transcendence along its vertical plane, is at once an attractive and a baffling study. In the language of Aldous Huxley it is too vast a territory to be exhaustibly explored. Within this human continent we encounter on the psychical plane all those infinite varieties from the idiot to the genius, from the sneak to the braggart, from the cruel to the kind, from the communicative to the reserved, from the lustful to the continent, from the abnormal to the supernormal. On the physical plane, too, we are baffled by all manner of bodily constitution, from the big-boned, fat, and rounded to the small-boned, lean, and delicate. And when these physical varieties and psychical diversities are permuted and combined the enormity of the problem increases beyond comprehension. Further, if we include, as we should, the element of spirituality in man's total constitution, the spiritual coefficient of his body-mind constitution, then the problem acquires a still greater complexity.

In the West in earlier times medical men undertook to study human nature in terms of two main habits—the phthisic and the apoplectic ; or in terms of the four humours—blood, phlegm, black bile, and yellow bile, answering to the Indian medical classification of men according to the preponderance of *vāyu* (wind), *pitta* (bile), and *kapha* (phlegm), or in terms of the four qualities of hot, cold, moist, and dry. We have also the nineteenth and twentieth century classifications, e.g. of Paolo Mantegazza and his predecessors, based on the physiognomy of the human face, yielding variable data for anthropology ; the psychological dichotomy of human nature into the introvert and the extrovert introduced by Dr. C. G. Jung ; and the psycho-physical classification proposed by Dr. Kretschmer in his work *Physique and Character* and the very comprehensive scheme worked out by Dr. W. Sheldon in his two volumes, *The Varieties of Human Physique* and *The Varieties of Temperament*.

Psychology that confines itself to the study of man's mental constitution and considers him in the exclusive terms of his sensibility and intellect in abstraction from his aesthetic, moral, and religious ideals and aspirations, has proved itself inadequate. Further, a closer study of human nature reveals that structural and humoral influences, considered in their purely biological context and out of relation to mental influences, present many lacunae.

It seems further that there are two distinguishable aspects of human nature. One is the aspect of uniqueness that makes every man to be himself and nobody else ; and the other is the aspect of commonness and sharability which supplies the basis of classification for the sciences. But human nature in itself is an integral whole in which these two aspects act and react upon each other. The aspect of uniqueness seems to be as yet beyond analysis ; and this is why scientists are ultimately baffled in their attempts at classification. But science, committed to classifications, must make them on pain of failure or inadequacy. We know only too well, however, how ill fares the psychology of education in the matter of mental tests and education of children ; how inadequate is the Freudian scheme of the unconscious and the preconscious and the conscious to cope with all the phenomena of the normal, the abnormal, and the supernormal mind.

Human personality lies deeper than what the empirical sciences have penetrated. This unfathomed deep of human personality should therefore be sought in the metaphysical background, without which all our accounts will furnish only a truncated cone of the whole integrated phenomenon that is human nature. All empirical or scientific study, the study of man not excluded, proceeds on the assumption of pragmatic necessity, which inevitably makes the results of their investigation fall into water-tight compartments. The symbolic representations they lead to always stand in need of a reference to a world of reality, and this only can complete the circuit of human knowledge that longs to transcend the limitations of the pragmatic level. Ancient Indian thinkers are characteristically synthetic in their views and always alive to the futility of purely empirical investigation, excluding all reference to the larger whole of reality without which knowledge yields only half-truths. They do not deny altogether the pragmatic importance of the scientific level of experience, but they do not make a fetish of scientific knowledge. The phenomenal and the real, they believe, imply each other, because they involve each other.

## ORIGIN AND DEVELOPMENT OF PERSONALITY

According to the Indian conception, human personality is not the accidental offshoot of an unconscious evolving nature, appearing at the end of a process as a historical episode, but has its root, like every other thing, in the being of an absolute, self-existent Consciousness. The supreme Reality, free from all activity, manifestation, and mutation, is a principle of absolute identity without dynamism and differentiation. But the universe, in its aspect of many, is a field of manifestation, activity, and differentiation for the One. The universe is not out of relation to the Absolute. Hence dynamic differentiation, necessary for the manifold universe, must break through the absolute concentration of this primordial self-existent principle. This dynamic differentiation is due to Māyā or nature. But Māyā or nature is not always conceived as blind and unconscious. It is regarded as a conscious force of this absolute self-existence itself. It is the *ātmaśakti* or the conscious creative force of the Ātman, the Absolute.[1] This conscious force of nature or Prakṛti creates modes and relates them to the Ātman, which now becomes immanent as against its primordial absolute self-existence. All these modifications of the *ātmaśakti* are the real matrices of all plurality and individuality; but they do not mean any subjection of the Ātman to the *ātmaśakti,* which is none other than the Ātman. If this subjection means anything, it is only apparent and not real. From the point of view of pragmatic truth, the self of man appears as a distinct entity, among such other distinct entities, with original freedom and consciousness of its own. But when this pragmatic truth is made into an absolute truth, the result of this tendency of human thought is the development of a realistic and scientific attitude with pluralism as its corollary.

In the Sāṁkhya system of philosophy an over-emphasis on this pragmatic view of the relation between the Ātman and Māyā is clearly noticeable. In it the Māyā of the Upaniṣadic tradition, where it was a conscious universal force of Ātman, is metamorphosed into an unconscious universal reality, and its creative agency is not only retained but made absolute. The unconscious Prakṛti now performs all the activities necessary for the creation of all things, physical, biological, and conscious, with their varieties of qualities and function. The universal, self-conscious principle of Ātman is finitized, and becomes plural or many; and each unit is an independent centre of personality, a Puruṣa. From this pragmatic or empirical angle the Puruṣa is the finitized complex of body and mind; it is the doer and the enjoyer and the cognizer. The spiritual transcendence, freedom, and unity of the original absolute Ātman is necessarily thrown into the background and Puruṣas become the *de facto* empirical creations of the despiritualized Prakṛti, which is conceived as constituted of *sattva, rajas,* and *tamas* that, in their mutual relation and in varying preponderance of the one over the other two, determine the structures, qualities, and functions of all existents—physical, biotic, and psychical. The human individual is no exception to this general law of the creative operation of Prakṛti. His bodily make-up, his pleasure and pain, his action and cognition, desire and temperament, with all their variations of love, hate, and love-hate are what they are owing to these essences of Prakṛti in their

[1] *Śvetāśvatara U.,* IV.10.

varying but universal operations. Thus the self of man has its root in the being of the absolute self-conscious Reality, but grows into an empirical finitized conscious centre with its physical, biotic, and mental components, with its varieties of form, relation, and reaction, under the differentiating dynamic force of the supposedly unconscious Prakṛti.

Another metaphysical force that is conceived, in Indian systems of thought in general, to contribute to the empirical make-up of the personal self is the law of Karma or the inescapable law of moral action. Every being, living and conscious, is determined in its origin, career, and destiny by this inevitable law. As the *Śvetāśvatara Upaniṣad* has it, the self of man is an infinitesimal manifestation of the infinite self-conscious Reality ; it is originally undifferentiated into sex and varieties of bodily dimensions, *sthūla* and *sūkṣma* (stout and slender), or into bodily and mental qualities and tendencies ; it develops sexual, morphological, and psychical differences under the force of *karma*.[2] Even birth, parentage, longevity, and course of life are not accidental, but are determined according to this universal law of Karma. The biological units or *genes* as the determinants of the individuality of man thus become only a link in the whole chain of causes and effects started into operation by *karma*. Thus *karma*, coupled with the triplicate constituents of Prakṛti, is responsible for the phenomenon of individuality and its empirical relations with its environment.

The *Yogavāsiṣṭha*, in conformity with the Sāṁkhya metaphysics, lays down that the core of human personality is *citta*[3] whose real pivot is desire.[4] The importance of desire (*vāsanā*) as the *svarūpa* (real nature) of *citta* has its Vedic corroboration, as we are told there that *kāma* (desire) existed from the first as the very seed of *manas*.[5] The same pivotal character of activity is emphasized in the Sāṁkhya scheme of evolution where the intellect (*buddhi*) evolves into ego (*ahaṅkāra*) in which *rajas* predominates, and this leads later to subject-object differentiation.[6] The desire of the individual then directs the intellect to know its object and translate that knowledge into action. In modern psychological expression desire is the will-to-live in its two forms, namely, will-to-multiply and will-to-power. The will-to-live is thus the wider energy and gives rise to its narrower manifestation, the will-to-multiply. We may call this will-to-live *libido* in the wider sense in which Dr. Jung takes it,[7] and not in the narrower sense of will-to-multiply in which it has been taken by Dr. Freud. To desire or will-to-live

[2] *Ibid.*, V.9-12.
[3] *Yogavāsiṣṭha* (*Pūrvārdha*), III.23.
[4] *Ibid.*, VI.94.
[5] *R.V.*, X.29.4.
[6] See Dasgupta, *The Study of Patañjali*, p. 53.
[7] Dr. Jung, *Collected Papers on Analytical Psychology*, pp. 347-348.

have been traced the very origin, growth, forms, shapes, and even magnitude and bulk of the body that encloses the Jīva or the individual. For desire is a want, and it must therefore create that which removes the want. That which it will first create must be of the nature of an atom, a primitive seed energized under the force of desire, its creator, and moving in a regular way, just as the electron of the modern scientist is supposed to be whirling round a nucleus. This lays the foundation of the human trunk, the neuraxis, the seat and pathway of the *kuṇḍalinī* (the coiled-up power). The *kuṇḍalinī* consists of the central *suṣumṇā* and the *iḍā* and *piṅgalā* nerves, the latter two behaving like semi-material positive and negative to start into action the free spiritual current of the *suṣumṇā*.[8] Now, as desire or the will-to-live is everlasting and never to be completely fulfilled, it will always move in a dual manner in the alternate extremes of attraction and repulsion, love and hate. So desire, having an endless creative impulse, will come under the law of Karma, the producer of all varieties of sheaths or bodies.[9]

## TYPES OF PERSONALITY

Most writers are not so particular about explaining the varieties of physical structure in human beings as about distinguishing their temperamental diversities, though in the erotic literature a physiological classification of men and women with the limited objective of sexually matching them has been made. They have, however, drawn up a pretty comprehensive scheme of the varieties of temperament on the basic principle of desire. The two fundamental tendencies of hate and love, into which desire naturally moves, account for the development, in human persons, of the derived tendencies of inhibition and exhibition, introversion and extroversion, with their ambivalence of love-hate, inhibited-exhibited, introverted-extroverted. While thus distinguishing the varieties of temperament as emphasized by ancient scholars, one should not overlook their emphasis on the determining conditions of the three *guṇas* of *sattva, rajas,* and *tamas* in their different preponderances. The *sattva* is held to be the fountain-head of all knowledge and enlightenment that modify our very being; and our modified being does not fail to react upon our power of knowing. The combined effect of all this is that the three governing forces of love, hate, and love-hate will themselves be modified by the cognitive consciousness of superiority, equality, and inferiority between Jīva and Jīva. The modification of temperament, following from the factors and forces mentioned above, may be generalized under two heads:

I. Jīvas belonging to one or other of these two extreme categories of

[8] H. P. Blavatsky, *Secret Doctrines,* V. p. 520.
[9] *Mbh.,* XIV.16.29-37.

love and hate will exhibit in their relation to Jīvas of the same category the following traits according as they are superior, equal, or inferior to them.

II. Jīvas belonging to the mean between these two extremes of love and hate, and to neither of them strongly or exclusively, will exhibit in relation to Jīvas of the same category mental traits that are counterparts of their own. Hence we may draw up the following schemes.

I. (1) A Jīva belonging to the love-group with the element of *sattva* predominating and characterized by selflessness and *nivṛtti* will exhibit to a Jīva of the same group:

(i) A. Benevolence, if superior to other Jīvas showing fear with humility.
B. Friendliness, if equal to other Jīvas showing fear with humility.
C. Humility, if inferior to other Jīvas showing fear with humility.

(ii) A. Love, if superior to other Jīvas showing anger, sullenness, and moroseness.
B. Affection, if equal to other Jīvas showing anger, sullenness, and moroseness.
C. Sympathy, if inferior to other Jīvas showing anger, sullenness, and moroseness.

(iii) A. Humility, if superior to other Jīvas showing pride.
B. Friendliness, if equal to other Jīvas showing pride.
C. Pity, if inferior to other Jīvas showing pride.

(2) A Jīva belonging to the hate-group with the element of *tamas* preponderating and characterized by selfishness and *pravṛtti* will exhibit to a Jīva of the same group:

A. Disdain, if superior to a Jīva showing love or fear.
B. Anger, if equal to a Jīva showing love or fear.
C. Fear (suspicion), if inferior to a Jīva showing love or fear.

II. A Jīva belonging to the mixed group of love-hate and characterized by *pravrtti-nivrtti* will exhibit to a Jīva of the same group:

A. Pride and scorn, if superior to a Jīva showing fear and distrust.
B. Love and anger, if equal to a Jīva showing love and anger.
C. Fear, scorn, and vindictiveness, if inferior to a Jīva showing pride, scorn, and oppressiveness.

The above scheme is adapted from *Viṣṇu Bhāgavata*[10] and is a brief indication of the possibility of a far vaster scheme that can be constructed on data to be acquired from more patient and extensive observation of human nature.

The understanding of human nature with its classification has such a wide interest that, on the basis of the fundamental principle discussed above, others also have attempted, with their own respective predilections, various other classifications. The *Dharma Śāstra* has given a psycho-sociological

[10] *Viṣṇu Bhāgavata,* II, IV.

scheme of classification in order to establish the fourfold social structure (*caturvarṇa*) on the basis of mental qualities and abilities of men exhibited under the general influence of *sattva, rajas,* and *tamas,* and under the distinctive influence of the *svadharma* of each class. Division of labour, based on the principle of *svadharma* (duties peculiar to each class) thus developed, rendered the classification apparently stereotyped and artificial ; yet it had a value of its own in that it was based on the view that the laws of Karma and heredity were very great determining factors in the development of human nature. Astrological writers have also distinguished human types in the light of various traits of character as exhibited under stellar and planetary influences and the signs and lines on human palms, feet, and foreheads, which, they claim, play a significant part in determining the character of men.[11] Individual human beings, like all other entities of the world, are never isolated phenomena, but are always related to the cosmic whole whose different forces are pooled together to make them what they are.

## CARAKA ON HUMAN NATURE AND ITS TYPES

Caraka, the expounder of the Āyurveda system of medicine, has analysed the human constitution as a mind-body complex with a view to discovering the aetiology of bodily and mental diseases and their remedies. He has noted, in his analysis, psycho-biological materials which help in the scientific understanding and classification of human nature. He has shown that scientific study does not mean a purely empirical endeavour completely cut off from its metempirical moorings. He has taken experience in its radical sense to include the experience of all orders of existence and has not narrowed it down to external experience through the sense-organs. Inner experience of a finer being, rendered transparent by yogic concentration, is to him the real instrument in understanding the true nature of anything ; and it is far more so in the case of complex human nature. In tracing diseases to their causes he accepts the traditional assumption that the human constitution is what it is due to the proportionate or preponderant operation of the three *guṇas* of *sattva, rajas,* and *tamas,* and claims that the complete aetiology of diseases, both physical and mental, can be established by the consideration of the influence of the three *guṇas,* coupled with the humoral influences resulting from the undue preponderance of one or other of the three humours of *vāyu* (wind), *pitta* (bile), and *kapha* or *śleṣman* (phlegm). The ancient doctors, including Caraka, have given us the key in therapeutics in the conception of *sātmya,* which means restored natural condition of identity, deviation from which is equivalent to disease. Disease is called *vikāra* or *anātmyatā* or a state in which a man is other than his own being.

[11] Varāhamihira, *Bṛhat Saṁhitā,* LXVIII.

To cure a being is to restore its true normal self. This applies equally to cases of physical and psychical pathology. If disease, whether of the body or of the mind, is disorder or maladjustment, cure or healing is the restoration of the natural factors and conditions of the body or the mind needing readjustment or *sātmya*. Further, we come across passages repeatedly stressing the bodily and mental balance of the physician; it is only a physically and mentally balanced physician, having a perfect *sātmya* in himself, who can restore *sātmya* or the native balance to the diseased in body or mind. This is in line with the Freudian technique of treatment and corroborates the efficacy of the simple and friendly exploration of the neurotic's mental state by a mentally balanced physician.[12]

Now, preponderance of *sattva, rajas,* or *tamas* will divide mind into three types. When *sattva* predominates, the mind of man will be *śuddha* (pure), and its activities will be productive of what is good both to the individual and to society and will be called *kalyāṇāṁśa-viśiṣṭa* (with a preponderance of the beneficial elements). With the preponderance of *rajas,* mental activities will take all forms of anger or hate and will be called *roṣāṁśa-viśiṣṭa* (with anger predominating). And, again, when the mind is dominated by *tamas,* the activities will manifest themselves in all forms of fatuity and will be called *mohāṁśa-viśiṣṭa* (with predominating mental inertia or darkness). Caraka, be it noted, while determining differences in mental types, takes cognizance of the differences in parentage; thus heredity to him has much to do with such differences. And these mental differences will be accompanied by differences in bodily structure and activities due to the reciprocal influence of the element of *sattva* on body and of body on *sattva,* so that differences in human nature will be innumerable. Similar remarks hold good of *rajas* and *tamas* and their influences.

### CARAKA'S CLASSIFICATION

A. The following, named after some of the principal gods and demigods, are the classes in which the element of *sattva* predominates:

1. *Brāhma-sattva* type: Highly intellectual and moral, capable of scientific, philosophical, and religious discourses, not over-powered by emotions and lower impulses, truthful, having restraint over the senses, and impartial to all beings.
2. *Ārya-sattva* type: Endowed with keen perception, with power of persuasion and of understanding scientific truth, given to performance of religious rites enjoined by the Śāstras, hospitable to guests, restrained in senses, and not over-powered by emotions and impulses.

[12] McDougall, *An Outline of Abnorml Psychology,* p. 417.

3. *Aindra-sattva* type: Energetic, powerful, unfatigued by activities, endowed with foresight and with powerful speech, and given to religious, economic, and pleasure-giving activities.
4. *Yāmya-sattva* type: Having regard for secular duties, endowed with presence of mind, indomitable in pursuits, endowed with strong memory, and unaffected by lower impulses and emotions.
5. *Vāruṇa-sattva* type: Calm but courageous, abhorrent of the unclean, fond of aquatic pastimes, unfatigued in strains, discriminate in the show of anger and resentment, and giving patronage to the deserving.
6. *Kaubera-sattva* type: Fond of family life, given to the performance of religious and secular duties, indiscriminate in the show of pride and pleasure, and favouring and chastising fellow-beings according to their merits and demerits.
7. *Gāndharva-sattva* type: Fond of music and dancing, interested in stories, histories, and Purāṇas, having liking for scents, flowers, and cosmetics, and fond of the company of women.

B. The following, named after demoniac and aggressive animal species, are the classes in which the element of *rajas* predominates:

1. *Āsura-sattva* type: Characterized by physical prowess, furiousness, gluttony, self-conceit, and love of money.
2. *Rākṣasa-sattva* type: Marked by enduring wrath, aggressiveness, cruelty, fond of eating (specially flesh), malicious, hardy, and sleep-loving.
3. *Paiśāca-sattva* type: Indolent, unclean, cowardly, intimidating, and sensual.
4. *Sārpa-sattva* type: Heroic in anger but cowardly in other moods, expert in counsels, strong in habits, and given to the pleasures of the senses.
5. *Praitya-sattva* type: Loving food, unpleasant by nature and in conduct and dealing with others, pained at others' prosperity, intolerant, unconscientious, greedy, and lethargic.
6. *Śākuna-sattva* type: Given to sensuous desires, gluttonous, fickle, ruthless, and extravagant.

C. The following, named after lower animals and vegetation, are the classes wherein the element of *tamas* predominates:

1. *Pāśava-sattva* type: Dirty in dress, ignoble in dealings, given to eating, drinking, and sensuality, sleepy, and prone to rejection of everything.

2. *Mātsya-sattva* type: Cowardly, stupid, gluttonous, fickle, given to anger and sensuality, and fond of travel and of water.
3. *Vānaspatya-sattva* type: Living a purely vegetative life, inactive, food-seeking, and totally devoid of intellectual activities.

## CLASSIFICATION IN RELIGIOUS LITERATURE

The religious literature of India, of which the *Bhagavad-Gītā* is the quintessence, attempts a classification of human nature, always pointing to the goal of transcendence of its psycho-biological components by its spiritual element, and to the attainment of the highest spiritual values by way of recovery of its own unity with the divine. Answering to the main faculties of human mind—thinking, feeling, and willing; knowledge, devotion, and action—and to the emphasis with which they are pursued, there have been conceived three *mārgas* or ways of life. All the three *mārgas* are not open to all, though they are not antagonistic to one another. And human nature, as it pursues with emphasis one or other of these three, falls into three classes. The individual in whom will prevails takes to the Karma-mārga and is called the *karma-yogin*. The *bhakti-yogin* pursues the Bhakti-mārga, the path of devotion. Jñāna-mārga or the path of contemplation is adopted by the *jñāna-yogin* or the contemplative. But in each case, what is essentially required is the purging or purification of one's being by the proper acquisition and retention of the influence of the element of *sattva* followed by the gradual elimination of the influences of the elements of *rajas* and *tamas*. There are stages, necessary stages, in the process of spiritual elevation; there are degrees of worthiness of the aspirants. Corresponding to the aspirants' worthiness and spiritual eminence, there are varieties of human nature. Those who have attained to the highest spiritual values by positive appropriation of mental and spiritual qualities resulting from the *sāttvika* purification and from the avoidance of untruth, anger, aggression, greed, and similar other disvalues are classed by the *Gītā* as the possessors of the *daivī sampad* (divine treasure). Those who are given to pride and anger, egoism and ignorance, and similar other spiritual depravities are known as the holders of the *āsurī sampad* (demoniac treasure). The *Gītā* attempts another classification of man's nature according to his *śraddhā* (preponderant desire)—*sāttvikī, rājasikī,* or *tāmasikī*—resulting from the dominating influence of the fundamental constitutional components of *sattva, rajas,* or *tamas* on his life of desire. A man is what he is according to his *śraddhā*.[13] The threefold *śraddhā* brings about differences in the vegetative, active and rational, and spiritual com-

[13] *B.G.,* XVII.3. See also *Mbh.,* XIV.36-39.

ponents of man ; but the inherent energy of his spiritual component always endeavours to raise him in the scale of being, knowledge, and value as his *śraddhā* succeeds in lifting itself from the *tāmasikī* to the *rājasikī* and from the *rājasikī* to the *sāttvikī,* until his life of action transforms itself into the life of contemplation and dedication, and this is finally transformed into the life of divine love.

In the Buddhist ethical literature, too, attempts at classification of men and women have been made from the ethical and religious points of view. The *Puggala-paññatti,* the *Dhātu-kathā,* and the *Dhamma-saṅgaṇi,* which form parts of the *Abhidhamma Piṭaka* of the Buddhists, contain valuable contributions to the classifications of human nature.[14]

The Jains, who have developed an independent system of ethical personalism, also formulated, in their own way, a scheme of classification of human nature. The Jīvas, according to them, are subject to the influence of karmic matter, which affects their originally pure nature in various degrees. The souls of the Jīvas, though originally pure, become contaminated by what the Jains call *yoga* and *kaṣāya,* i.e. vibration of matter and passions that tinge the souls. The immediate consequence of these two forces is to generate what the Jains style *leśyās* (emotions), bad or good. They have been realistically associated with six colours—black, blue or indigo, grey, yellow or fiery, red, and white. These six kinds of *leśyās* supply us with a classification of human nature on an ascending scale of ethical perfection. (1) The soul affected by the first is ruthlessly destructive and relentlessly misanthropic. Such a soul is compared to a man who wants to eat mangoes, but who, coming to the mango tree, will forthwith uproot the whole tree. (2) The second kind of *leśyā* would affect the soul in a less harmful manner ; and though it would make a man greedy and indolent, yet some amount of patient consideration would be found in him. He is like a man who spares the roots but cuts the trunk of the mango tree to get at the mangoes. (3) The third kind of *leśyā* would make a man envious and wanting in discrimination but soften his instinct of destruction. The Jains have described the nature of this type of man by pointing out that he is like one who spares the root and trunk of the mango tree but chops down its big boughs unnecessarily.

The last three kinds of *leśyās* indicate the emotions that give a rising scale of merit and purification. (4) The fourth kind of *leśyā* makes a man prone to goodness but careless. He is like a man who breaks the twigs of the mango tree to secure the mangoes. (5) The fifth kind of *leśyā* will prompt a man to be forbearing and to inflict the least injury to the mango

[14] T. W. Rhys Davids, *American Lectures,* First Series, *Buddhism,* pp. 62,63.

tree, as when mangoes are only plucked without affecting the branches in any way. (6) When we come to the white *leśyā* that presents the soul with purity, compassion, and perfect equanimity, causing injury is avoided altogether. A man of this tint is like one who does not touch the mango tree at all but merely picks up the ripe fruits that have fallen to the ground. Such a person is freed from all contamination with matter and is on the way to *mokṣa*.[15] The soul, when it throws off the karmic matter entirely and attains siddhahood, becomes altogether rid of *leśyās* and regains its innate purity.

[15] *Uttarādhyayana-Sūtra,* XXXIV; *Gomaṭasāra, Jīvakāṇḍa,* pp. 488, 489, 492-507. For comparison with Buddhistic, Ājīvaka, and Yoga speculations on the same subject, see A. N. Upadhye, 'The Leśyā Doctrine', *Proceedings of the Seventh All-India Oriental Conference,* pp. 391-398.

# 38

## INDIAN ETHICS

### HINDRANCES TO INDEPENDENT GROWTH

LIKE some other philosophical disciplines, ethics is not to be had as a separate study in Indian philosophical and religious literature. In fact, logic is the only philosophical science that attained independence at a later time, the other studies like psychology and ethics remaining embedded within the general organization of philosophy and religion. In order to study ethics therefore, it is necessary that the ethical elements should be extricated from their general religious and philosophical settings. Again, the attitude of the different philosophies has affected the nature of the moral problem and its solution. But, irrespective of the philosophies, it is possible to trace in broad outlines certain fundamental questions and postulates of morality with which all the philosophies of India deal.

It has been generally admitted that ethics proper begins when the freedom of the individual will is conceded. The Kantian dictum, 'Thou canst ; therefore thou oughtest', holds true of all ethical speculations, though philosophical theories that imply a denial of the reality of the finite in an ultimate reference have tended to raise the question whether freedom of the will has any meaning beyond the realm of the empirical. It has been sought to be proved, for instance, by the critics of Indian speculations on morals, that, logically speaking, there cannot be any science of ethics in India, specially in Brāhmaṇical literature, because of certain philosophical presuppositions. Thus it has been argued that if the absolutistic position of the Advaita Vedānta be accepted as true, then the reality of the finite disappears altogether and there is no sense in talking of the freedom of a being that does not exist in reality. If the agent is himself unreal, obviously his actions cannot be treated as possessing any reality. The distinction drawn by Advaitism between the world of reality and the world of practicality is supposed to be a very lame excuse to get out of a difficult situation. For it is with the individual as real that we have to deal in any problem of ethical conduct ; and there must also be a field in which that conduct is manifested, that is, there must be other selves towards whom ethical action is directed. Thus without acknowledging the reality of a world of finite selves we cannot broach the moral problem at all.

There is this other objection that the admission of the law of Karma as governing human actions seriously imperils the freedom of the will. If the law is to be strictly interpreted, it is urged, then the past lives of any individual have a determining voice in controlling his actions of the present life. In other words, the actions that a man is capable of doing depend not only upon what he wishes to do in this life, but also upon what capacity was left to him to perform them freely by the moral results of the actions of his previous lives. Thus if a man has so acted in the past that his mind naturally turns towards evil, he cannot be expected to follow the dictates of a righteous will. Either his intelligence is so clouded that he cannot determine the moral aim or, even when he knows what is right, he is obliged to do the wrong because of the strong passions to which he is subjected in this life as a result of evil actions of his previous lives.

Then, again, theorists that are theistically inclined may go to the extreme of supposing that the only true agent whose will is being carried out in the world process is God. The finite cannot go against the ordinances and determinations of the Infinite. For the converse supposition would make the universe a field of two contending forces, viz. God and man. As this is inadmissible, we must accept the position that it is only the divine will that is carried out through the world process and that man is a mere tool in the hands of the divinity and has no independence of his own in the matter of shaping either his own destiny or the future of the world process. Man is not a co-worker with God, for he is after all a conduit through which divine energy is flowing to its ideal end or predetermined destination. We may be conscious of *how* we are working but not of *why* and *whither* ; and certainly we do not guide the course of our life.

## ETHICS PRESUPPOSED BY ALL RELIGIOUS SYSTEMS

Thus from both pantheistic and theistic sides the possibility of ethics may be assailed. It is significant, however, that in none of these lines of thought is the ethical problem absent, nor is it admitted by any one of them that morality is not a human responsibility. As a matter of fact, it has been claimed that the moral problem has been most persistently pursued and successfully tackled in India, and even those who did not connect morality with religion had not the least hesitation in denouncing those who believed that the world was ruled by chance or by inaction in the moral field. Witness, for instance, the severe criticisms to which the heretical teachers were subjected in the Buddhistic systems, because some believed in materialism, others in fortuitous origination, still others in automatic attainment of final destiny, and a few in the unimportance of drawing any distinction between good and evil. The wonder, in fact, is that without any kind of theistic presupposition some of the Indian systems should be so highly moralistic, and should have set a pattern for all those in the East and the West who believe that morality needed no theological support and could be based upon an innate propensity towards goodness or a social consideration with which all individuals are by nature endowed.

It has been pointed out also that the Indian philosophical systems are more intellectualistic than moralistic in their outlook, and that what they really aim at is not a purification of the will but a clarification of the understanding. This charge, though partly justified in the sense that in India the Socratic identification of virtue with knowledge was more widely practised than anywhere else in the world, is not wholly just, because the intellect was never viewed as totally uninfluenced by moral activities. Manu, in fact, forbids the imparting of instruction to persons swayed by passions, and the *Gītā* promises knowledge to the man of faith (*śraddhā*). It will be a strange misreading of Indian philosophy to suggest that morality was not a necessary element in man's ascent to higher realms of truth. Again and again do we meet with the declaration that man does not attain clarity of understanding without performing the duties of his station, and that whosoever eschews the obligations of life is destined to lose vision of absolute truth. Morality, in fact, was regarded as a necessary ground of philosophical competence (*adhikāra*). It is indeed true that in India moral action did not always have the same connotation in the different systems; but then the same is true of other parts of the world where also the different systems do not advocate an identical definition of morality. We cannot define the nature of concrete moral duties without reference to the social organization of the locality. What conduct was ethically correct in the city-states of Greece was not necessarily so in Imperial Rome. India with its belief in castes (*jāti*) and classes (*varṇa*) and stages of life (*āśrama*) had necessarily to orient its moral philosophy to the actualities of a social situation which is to be found nowhere else in the world. Its classification of duties and virtues was naturally influenced by its social organization; and no one who is not familiar with its social life is likely to have an intimate knowledge and appreciation of its ethical code. Thus the rights and duties of the different castes and classes were not identical because of the different functions that they were expected to perform in the social body. Those that advocated a uniform code of morals had to impugn, first of all, the Brāhmaṇical system of social stratification. Again, where life was divided into different stages, it was natural that duties appertaining to them would also vary. Then there are transcendental considerations that have a bearing upon man's conduct. Belief in God, departed ancestors, and future life would naturally dictate certain types of conduct, and ethics would have some reference to the unseen universe with which man has to hold commerce. It is obvious therefore that the moral problem is an intricate one in Indian thought, specially when we take into account the types of speculations that men in India had regarding the ultimate destiny of the human soul and the factors that were supposed to influence the attainment of that destiny.

### ETHICAL BELIEFS IN THE VEDIC PERIOD

In the formulation of its ethical doctrine Brāhmaṇism was fortunate in having a scriptural basis of great antiquity. The Vedas were regarded as the ultimate source of all *dharma*—an elusive word that might stand for law, virtue, duty, and religion, either jointly or severally. All other sources of *dharma,* such as the Smṛti (legal literature), *sadācāra* (the pattern of good conduct set by men deeply versed in the Vedic lore), and *svasya ātmanaḥ priyam* (actions pleasing to individual conscience), were ultimately based upon the mental and moral equipment of the Vedic scholars. In fact, when latterly the question arose whether the good points in the heterodox systems should not be accepted as patterns of belief and conduct, it was immediately pointed out that those who committed the one supreme mistake of not recognizing the validity of the Vedas could not be relied upon to give a correct lead in matters of thought and conduct.

Now, the Vedas, specially the *Ṛc, Yajus,* and *Sāman,* enunciated one great principle, viz. that the universe was governed by order (*ṛta*) and truth (*satya*)—a conception which probably goes back to the Indo-Iranian times, because in the Avesta also Asha appears as one of the guardian angels (Spenta Mainyu), and Ahura-Mazda himself is supposed to have fire (Atash) as his body and truth (Arta = *ṛta*) as his soul. In fact, the Vedic speculation went to the length of supposing that the first products of the divine fervour (*tapas*) were these two (*ṛta* and *satya*), which means that before there could be a cosmos there must first be regularity in the behaviour of things, and that before there could be a social organization there must first be mutual trustfulness based upon truthful speech and conduct. In the light of this thought we come across the belief that the gods obey order (*ṛtavat*) and are protectors of law (*ṛtasya gopā*) and fixed ordinances (*dhṛtavrata*). From this belief follows the logical sequel that the gods do not transgress the limits of their authority, nor do they quarrel among themselves. In fact, in many a hymn the gods are invoked together, and men are directed to follow the example of the gods in their social dealings in order that they might have, like them, identical objective, common counsel, and concerted action. The path of austerity and abnegation, which we meet with in later literature as the proper way of life, is to be met with in the Vedas themselves. *Tapas,* for instance, as a mystic practice is to be found associated even with the gods in the Vedic literature, and anchorites with long hair (*keśin*) are also referred to there. It will not therefore be correct to say that austerities were a later importation, and that the joyful attitude towards life in Vedic times did not have occasional exceptions. It is necessary to keep in mind, however, the supreme importance attached to law in the Vedas, for we find that the law of Karma in its various forms, as adopted by Brāhmaṇism, Buddhism, and Jainism and, in fact, all schools of philosophy, can be easily affiliated to this law of cosmic order adumbrated in the Vedic literature. It is quite possible that the Vedic Aryans, who had to regulate their life, whether nomadic or settled, by the observation of certain cosmic phenomena, came to a very early understanding of the laws governing the different departments and phenomena of nature, and could therefore record some astronomical happenings in their religious literature and regulate their religious practices in conformity with their discovery of cosmic laws.

One other notable fact that was responsible for the continuity of the moral tradition was the recognition that the bond between man and the higher powers was broken by the invasion of sin. We come across a large number of words in the Vedas signifying sinfulness, which shows that the religious-minded were keenly aware of lapses in their moral conduct and were solicitous about re-establishing their moral relation with the gods through appropriate means. It is not very much a matter of surprise that sin should sometimes be conceived almost as a kind of physical stain removable by some physical means, such as ablution or the sprinkling of water. Even much later religious beliefs of other lands have prescribed water as a means of purification not only of the body but of the soul. But genuine repentance, unconnected with physical lustration, is frequently met with in the Vedas, and it was widely believed that human conduct was subject to the constant scrutiny of overseeing powers and that sins could not be hidden from their gaze. The god with whom morality was specially associated was Varuṇa, and to a lesser extent Bṛhaspati, Aditi, and the Ādityas also were supposed to protect the pious. The Sun is the eye of Mitra-Varuṇa to whom he reports the conduct of men and whose spies could never be hoodwinked or fail to report correctly. No wonder that it should be stated that Varuṇa is the invisible third when two men are plotting together, for nothing can be hidden from the gaze of this moral god. But Varuṇa and also other gods, e.g. Agni, Savitṛ, Uṣas, Dyaus, Pṛthivī, etc., were conceived of as forgiving sins. Conversely, the righteous were assured of a good reward for their rectitude and promised the fruit of their charity, benevolence, and sacrificial acts (*iṣṭāpūrta*). The Vedic seers could justifiably claim that the religious could be regarded as relations of the gods and address the latter as such. The broken link between god and man could be repaired by recourse to confession and penitence, and continuance in sin entailed not only failure in life, but also physical ailment which could be removed only by proper prayer to the gods and the abandonment of the immoral life.

### DEVELOPMENT DURING THE PERIOD OF THE BRĀHMAṆAS

The period of the Brāhmaṇas is regarded by Western scholars as a period of stagnation in religious thought and of a gradual preponderance of the magical factor as contrasted with the properly spiritual. It is indeed true that faith in the efficacy of the *mantras* began to grow apace ; but it would be a misreading of the spiritual history of India to suggest that human arrogance dispensed altogether with the need of divine help and proper devotion in this period. *Śraddhā* or faith continued to be the prime necessity of a religious life ; and purity, which sometimes went to fastidious lengths, was still demanded as an indispensable necessity of spiritual perfection. What really gained in strength is the belief that there was a subtle relation between acts and their fruits, and that certain sacrifices properly done inevitably brought forth certain results. This change of attitude towards the function of the gods in joining merit to fruition was responsible at a later time for the enunciation of the doctrine that there were certain mystic forces in words and acts which every agent must take note of while performing his religious and moral duties. We have, in fact, interesting discussions about the relative superiority of mind and speech symbolized by the quarrel between Indra and Sarasvatī, and a fairly uniform conclusion, with rare deviations, that a mere act without an intention is not enough to produce moral result. This, it is obvious, cuts at the root of the belief that formality is sufficient for fulfilling the conditions of a moral and spiritual life. When we consider that by the end of this period the pendulum swung almost to the opposite pole and extolled contemplation as the principal means of attaining the spiritual objective of human existence, we can well believe that the ground was being imperceptibly prepared in the preceding age for placing increased emphasis on the mental side of all ethical and religious operation.

### MORALITY IN BUDDHISM AND JAINISM

The Upaniṣads constitute a landmark in the development of Indian spirituality, because by now the belief in the doctrine of Karma, which includes as a subsidiary feature the belief in transmigration, has taken a firm hold of the Aryan mind. When we remember that the religion of the Upaniṣads, Buddhism, and Jainism, which were almost contemporaneous movements, based themselves on this doctrine, we can well realize that something must have happened in the meantime to necessitate an emphasis on the ethical need of spiritual living. In Buddhism and Jainism the gods of the Vedas either disappear altogether or continue in colourless subsidiary existence ; the loss of belief in gods did not, however, entail the encouragement of antinomian living. On the other hand, we find that in these austerities harden, renunciations are more insistently demanded, and attachments of all kinds are denounced in gradually stronger language. This is a marvel in the religious history of the world, because too often has it been believed that without a theistic support morality tends to collapse. It is obvious that in India a substitute for faith in divine pleasure was found in the belief in the efficacy of moral life, and those who did not subscribe to the dogma that pious souls go to the eternal heavens of merciful and pacified gods could still believe that spiritual advancement was possible by ethical actions alone. It is possible that the declining faith in the eternity of heavenly abodes and their denizens was responsible for suggesting a surer mode of eternal existence, though the nature of this was not uniformly conceived, and each system had its own way of formulating the condition of the emancipated soul finally freed from the travails of empirical existence. The tone now becomes definitely more sombre as the incentive to moral life is not the attainment of a blissful celestial life, but escape from the sorrows and tribulations of earthly existence. In consonance with this changed conception of the nature of human life we find that the apparent joys which men hanker after are stigmatized as sorrows in disguise, and the philosophical disciplines that systematized this vein of thought practically took it for granted that enjoyments did not really advance the cause of the soul so much as abstention and abnegation did. The charge that Indian ethics is mainly negative and escapist in its conception is based upon this Indian idea that in the search for salvation all ties that bind man to the universe and to society are to be sundered and a kind of isolation is to be attained by intense meditation and spiritual culture.

But this aspect may be over-emphasized. While the ascetic preachers possibly inclined to the view that perfection (*śreyas*) was to be preferred to pleasure (*preyas*) and preached that the highest spirituality was synonymous with renunciation of the world and that men of the world would find it extremely difficult to tread the narrow path of spiritual progress, they did not condemn the householders' life as useless, but prescribed for it a milder discipline which would not be regarded as an unbearable burden by men who had obligations of different kinds to fulfil and could not devote their entire time and energy to contemplation and spiritual practice. Thus in the Buddhist and Jaina systems the ethical obligations of religious persons, both monks and nuns, were heavier, and it was expected that if they were to set a pattern of conduct for the people at large, they must lead a life of severer discipline. In fact, in Brāhmaṇical literature also a higher caste connoted at the same time a more austere form of life. A Brāhmaṇa was expected to practise certain virtues which it was not obligatory on the other castes to follow. He was expected to pass his time in study and devotion, to be self-restrained and forgiving, to be satisfied with little, and not attached inordinately to any worldly possession. But Vaiśyas were not expected to practise all these virtues, because as the producers of the means of sustenance they had other obligations to fulfil. Generally speaking, the higher the caste the greater the restraint. If therefore a Brāhmaṇa had certain privileges in the eye of the law and commanded greater respect in society, these were hard-won honours based upon sterner self-discipline and higher spirituality. Any occupation that was degrading or brought inordinate wealth was forbidden to the Brāhmaṇas, nor could they ordinarily take to the profession of a soldier in view of the fact that it involved cruelty and lust of conquest. Even in the heretical systems a true Brāhmaṇa has therefore been extolled in no uncertain terms. What they objected to was the system of hereditary caste which believed that virtue came by birth and not through personal nature and effort. Buddhism and Jainism proclaimed a charter of individual worth as against the Brāhmaṇical institution of settling the question of merit on the basis of birth. Thus, as against the *varṇāśrama* scheme of Brāhmaṇical life, was enunciated the principle of individual worth attainable by all persons by pursuing the path of purity.

## BRĀHMAṆICAL IDEA OF MORAL ACTION

Let us turn now to the Brāhmaṇical idea of moral action. It is obvious that in India, as elsewhere, the conception of what constitutes morality would materially depend upon the moral standard ultimately adopted. So long as men think that human actions are controlled by the need of pleasing the gods, the scriptures, as embodying the divine will, naturally determine the nature of moral obligation. Religion then becomes the source of morality, and the divine will the ultimate determinant of duty. Similarly, scriptural authority is stressed in the Mīmāṁsā school of thought where the nature of the various duties is delineated. We are told, for instance, that *dharma* is what is prescribed (*codanā-lakṣaṇo'rtho dharmaḥ*). The scripture may direct that certain actions should be performed; and yet they would be obligatory simply because the scripture has said so, though no reward has been promised and no reason assigned. The non-performance of such actions would entail sin. These are called *nitya karmas* or duties of perfect obligation. But the scriptures may sometimes be more kind and specify what benefit would accrue to the performer of actions of certain other types. These would be *kāmya karmas* or duties of imperfect or contingent obligation: one is not obliged to perform them if one has no desire to have the fruits thereof. For instance, only those who aspired to go to heaven or to attain mundane objectives like the birth of a son or the attainment of wealth were under an obligation to perform relevant sacrifices. Besides these, there were other duties that were contingent in the sense that their performance depended upon certain specific things happening, but they were obligatory in the sense that if those things happened, the relevant actions had to be performed (*naimittika karmas*). Thus various sacraments associated with certain happenings like birth, death, etc. had to be performed when those events occurred. Similarly, certain rites were periodic like the new moon and full moon sacrifices, or were performed on certain special occasions such as an eclipse. These sacrifices were moral actions in the sense that they were performed in fulfilment of certain scriptural injunctions. Detailed instructions are to be found in the various rules of interpretation about the way in which certain Vedic injunctions, prescriptions, laudations, etc. were to be understood as having a binding force of different types. It was believed that as religion dealt with many transcendental matters, unaided human reason could not possibly fix religious duties without reference to some infallible authority. The intrusion of argument into such matters amounted not only to a daring presumption, but also to a gross blasphemy.

Now, if, judged by the human standard of value, a particular action like killing in a sacrifice appeared to be cruel, the justification for indulging in such an apparently immoral action could be found only in a scriptural prescription. The informed reader would remember in this connection a similar discussion the European scholastics had about certain items of religious belief being either according to reason or beyond reason or contrary to reason. In the wake of a discussion of this nature it was inevitable that the question should be raised whether the prescription (*niyoga*) was divinely ordained or independent of all personal command. Those theistically inclined saw in prescribed duties the divine will manifested through seers and prophets, that is, persons specially privileged by divine grace to know divine intentions and proclaim the same for human guidance. Those who upheld, however, the autonomy of the moral law went further and saw in the scheme of human duties the operation of certain eternally valid ethical laws which even the Almighty could not alter but had simply to acknowledge. The mediaeval controversy in Europe between the Scotists and the Thomists over the primacy of the divine intellect or that of the divine will readily comes to the mind in this connection. Ultimately, however, the majority verdict in India went in favour of those who upheld the eternity of the moral law and divine creation being controlled by the law of Order and Truth. Seeing that the heterodox systems also formulated their moral law without a theistic basis, the majority view had influential support from an unexpected quarter. Thus, the Mīmāṁsā, Buddhism, and Jainism conspired together to establish firmly the self-sufficiency of the moral law and to lay the basis of the classical doctrine of Karma according to which moral actions produced their own fruit without reference to any kind of divine dispensation. The Nyāya theory and the theistic schools had great difficulty in introducing modifications into this theory and finding scope for divine intervention in the operation of the moral law. In the words of William James, the thinkers of India were 'tough-minded' and not 'tender-minded', as they expected each man to bear the cross of his own iniquities and not to look up to a merciful Providence to come to his rescue. This obviously could not have been to the taste of those like the Rāmānujists who endowed God with all auspicious qualities, including the capacity of cancelling evil and human imperfection. God not only possesses knowledge and power but is also forgiving, compassionate, and indulgent towards the weak. These attributes will have no meaning if God cannot come to the help and rescue of sinners and out of His superabundant grace take back to His heart the penitent sinner. But this consideration had no appeal to the resolute ethicists, who resisted the importation of divine intervention in man's moral affairs for fear that laxity would grow when there was a hope that an indulgent God would be swayed by prayers and thus the moral law would be indirectly negated.

In addition to the positive prescriptions, the Mīmāṁsakas admitted the existence of *niṣedhas* or negative injunctions. Taking it for granted that the occasions for temptation are many and that human understanding and will are weak, the moralists thought that the first necessity of a moral life was resistance to evil solicitations. Social justice and social harmony would demand forbearance from certain types of acts which were anti-social or subversive of social discipline. Hence it was felt that prescriptions must be supplemented by prohibitions, incentives by restraints. It is much more difficult to persuade people to do positive good than to stop them from doing evil. Frailty is such an abiding feature of human nature that constant reminder about the possibility of transgressing moral limits was necessary to keep people in the straight path of virtue. It is only rarely, however, that man was supposed to be evil by nature and morality to be a constant restraint to suppress the evil that is in man. More frequently it was held, on the other hand, that man had an innate goodness which turned into evil on account of the obscuration of his intellect.

Hence, virtue is knowledge; the proper means of making men virtuous is to give proper enlightenment to their soul. Men perform evil actions under the impression that they are achieving thereby some kind of good. Once they see that their conduct is not conducive to the realization of their highest potentiality as rational beings, they would automatically desist from unwholesome ways of life. Here again, an insignificant minority were of opinion that men might know the good and yet do the evil deliberately. A comparison of the Indian decalogue with the Jewish will show that positive and negative prescriptions are to be found in both.

### BRĀHMAṆICAL MORALITY—UNIVERSAL DUTIES

We have observed already that the principle of moral obligation in Brāhmaṇism rested upon a recognition of specific duties attached to each caste and each stage of life. It will be incorrect to think, however, that beyond performing the duties of their particular class there were no universal duties which every man was expected to perform. Both the legalists and the philosophers drew a distinction between general and special duties. Society is composed of all sorts of people in mutual interaction and is not a homogeneous fraternity of persons belonging to the same caste or profession. Hence there must be certain duties which cut across all sectional divisions and are necessary for maintaining the strength and progress of the social organism. Then again, there are transcendental matters towards which all people must bear the same type of attitude. Thus even if a Brāhmaṇa has a prerogative of direct approach to a divine image, religious faith can never be a monopoly with his class, and all men are expected to possess devotion and perform their religious duties. Similarly, doing good to others, entertaining guests, feeding the animal creation that frequents human homes, and offering oblations to ancestors are enjoined on all irrespective of their castes and professions. Similarly, abjuring injury to living beings, as also forcible and unjust possession of others' properties, is one of the fundamental conditions of social existence and is therefore a universal duty. Sexual purity and continence of all kinds are as much personal perfections as necessities of social concord. Then again, keeping the senses under control and practising truthfulness in word, thought, and deed are essentials of moral purity. The abjuration of the six deadly sins—lust, anger, greed, infatuation, pride, and jealousy—is a human obligation which all must fulfil. The distinctive Indian contribution to this list is the renunciation of excessive attachment and hatred of all kinds, which are both disturbances of the soul in a positive and a negative manner respectively. A sage is expected to rise above both, to go, in fact, beyond all duality in order to practise that indifference without which he cannot escape being troubled by his environment and losing the composure of his mind. Not only in the *Bhagavad-Gītā,* but elsewhere also, this direction to avoid being unduly attracted or repelled by the world is given to all. In addition to these, and as following more or less as a corollary from them, men are advised to practise forgiveness and patience, and, in fact, returning good for evil, love for hatred, charity for miserliness, and honesty for deceit.

The ultimate ideal being the securing of justice in society, it may sometimes happen that patient suffering fails of its purpose. The problem of counteracting evil in such a contingency found advocates of different remedies. Those who held that violence of every kind was a taboo trusted to an ultimate change of heart in the oppressor consequent on the non-opposition of the oppressed. But the advocates of the rival theory thought that that might prove an encouragement to the continuance of iniquity and oppression. They therefore advocated a resistance to evil in the interest of the greater good to the world at large. The Brāhmaṇical theory of God descending on earth not only to succour the righteous, but also to put down the unrighteous, took note of the fact that divine government sometimes necessitated the infliction of evil to restore the social balance disturbed by iniquitous persons. As such, it is the duty of those entrusted with the task of maintaining order to co-operate with God in preventing social disturbance and political upheaval not conducive to the realization of moral perfection. Not to do so would be a shirking of moral responsibility and would entail sin. It is true that in India, as elsewhere, the worldly-wise and the spiritually advanced did not have the same conception regarding the applicability of private ethics to international relation. Broadly speaking, human objectives were divided into four categories—moral action (*dharma*), economic activity and statecraft (*artha*), propagation of the race (*kāma*), and emancipation (*mokṣa*). It was taken for granted that the rules of morality and the rules of the state would not always tally, and therefore it was conceded that certain actions that would not be permissible in furtherance of private interests were allowable for the safety of the state. Murder, for instance, would be a heinous private offence, but a just war might be a moral duty of the state, although every war would involve the killing of enemies. Similarly, punishing the guilty was a kingly obligation. We are not concerned here with certain other types of state activities such as spying, wanton aggression, etc. the moral quality of which might be questioned. But on the whole the art of government (*daṇḍanīti*) was generally conceived in humane terms, and the lords spiritual had a large share in determining the state policy, seeing that the chief minister was almost invariably a Brāhmaṇa and the priest had a seat in the state executive council.

### PLACE OF PHYSICAL HEALTH AND PURITY IN ETHICS

An elaborate scheme of discipline is to be found in the Yoga system where under the title of the accessaries of *yoga* (*yogāṅga*) are to be found the various actions and abstentions that a spiritual aspirant was expected to practise in the interest of self-discipline, social concord, and spiritual advancement. Similar attempts at classifying duties are to be found in the legal and philosophical literature, e.g. in Manu and Praśastapāda's commentary on the *Vaiśeṣika-Sūtra.* It is acknowledged here that the condition of the body has some hand in determining the state of the mind, and hence prescriptions cover not only the discipline of the mind, but also the control of the body. Cleanliness, steadiness, concentration of the sense-organs, withdrawal of the same from unholy and unseemly objects, regulation of the breath, and assumption of characteristic bodily attitudes were also pressed into the service of controlling the mind, dissipating wayward thoughts, and bringing about a meditative pose. The objective always was to make the body an ally instead of an enemy. It is indeed true that meditation on the impurity of the body constituted the negative fifth meditation (*aśubhabhāvanā*) in addition to the four positive ones of friendliness (*maitrī*), compassion (*karuṇā*), sympathetic joy (*muditā*), and ignoring of human frailties (*upekṣā*). But it was acknowledged at the same time that the body could be brought under spiritual control and transformed into a seat of holiness. In the Tāntrika system, for instance, various deities or forms of the same deity are supposed to reside in different parts of the body, so that the human organism is looked upon as a veritable holy temple. The identification with the deity might go to the length of supposing that the devotee was justified in worshipping his own body as God incarnate; and in later times philosophies extolling this aspect of human body became widespread and popular. We are not thinking only of the worship of preceptors and saints and veneration to the earthly monarch as if they are gods; we are referring to the fact that both in one's own body and in those of others divinity was supposed to be resident, and a guest was supposed to be a representative of all the gods. It is doubtful whether the doctrine of the incarnation of God or the representation of the Godhead by images could have made any headway, if the human body were considered to be absolutely impure. Possibly, the pantheistic view that the whole universe is Brahman reinforced the belief in the sanctity of all forms of existence including the material.

The general attitude of the philosophers and moralists was, however, hostile towards the body because of the fact that the usual philosophical position was either dualistic or spiritualistic, in neither of which the body could claim an equality in pure existence with the soul. Those who thought of morality in terms of the regulation of mind naturally looked down upon the needs of the body and considered them in the light of troublesome impediments to spiritual advancement. They did not always agree as to why spiritual endeavour should be made, but they were fairly unanimous that the interest of the body should not figure in ethical calculation except in so far as it helped in the performance of one's moral duties. Thus the rules of health must be obeyed if the spiritual aspirant is to keep under sufficient control his flighty thoughts and impulsive propensities. Ablution and other types of cleansing were ordained because they helped to bring in a helpful mental attitude. If, however, it were to be believed, as was actually done by some, that even this small attention paid to the body was a distraction for the soul, then the proper moral attitude would be to keep the body dirty and to grow matted locks. The practice of austerity, again, might bring in a propensity towards spiritual outlook, and *tapas,* e.g. mortification of the flesh, could be defended on the ground that it enabled the soul to gain control over the body.

## ETHICAL SANCTIONS

The materialists like the Cārvākas did not recognize the reality or priority of the spirit ; still they prescribed a code of duties, taking care to point out that this was not a prescription of God or the scripture but the order of the only visible authority, namely, the king. In other words, positive laws as enacted by the earthly king constitute the entire body of moral truths. And if people do agree to put up with some inconveniences and pains, it is because thereby they would be assured of enjoyment of pleasures. Thus there was a mixture of the standard as law and the standard as pleasure.

In between those who upheld the authority of the king and those who made ethical imperatives impersonal in character, there were others who upheld the theory that social prescription was the final determinant of moral conduct. The conduct of the good is imitated by the people at large ; and as customs vary from place to place and from time to time, in certain matters at least ethical relativity was inevitable. In any matter of doubt or where alternative prescriptions are to be found, one would not commit any wrong if one were to follow the customs of one's own locality (*deśācara*), community (*lokācāra*), or family (*kulācāra*). If the ultimate object of moral conduct is to maintain the social equilibrium and ensure social peace, then obviously nothing that disturbs them should be practised.

The implicit assumption in this view-point is that the collective wisdom of the community or the race cannot go wrong, and an individual judgement is not always the safest criterion of moral quality.

To this view-point it was possible to demur, for in that case social laws would become as rigid as the laws of the Medes and the Persians, and there would be no scope for the operation of an enlightened conscience or reforming zeal. Hence some upheld the position that it is not social convention or custom that should determine the moral conduct, but it is the law of moral life as laid down by seers, prophets, and saints that should govern human behaviour. A Buddha or a Mahāvīra has laid down the law of moral life for his followers, and it is this that constitutes the ethical code. By their strenuous moral life and their perfected intelligence these prophets have peered into the realm of truth, and because they have the good of the people at heart and are moved by compassion at the sight of their misery they have spread the truths of moral life as perceived by them and thereby enabled them to ford the stream of *saṁsāra*. Something like prophetic infallibility is the basis of the acceptance of the moral laws.

The theists obviously could not accept this position. To them omniscience belonged only to God, and freedom from all disturbing elements was only a divine prerogative. The eternal, omniscient Being who has never been infected by any kind of ignorance, sin, or incapacity can alone lay down the laws of moral life. Hence morality is a divine prescription, and human endeavour should be directed to discovering and following the moral prescriptions of God. The extreme section went to the length of supposing that as God was the source of morality and He was not constrained by any external factor, the nature of a moral action depended entirely upon the divine will. The moderate section, however, did not support the idea of a possibility at any time of God prescribing a new set of moral rules according to His caprice, and supported the view that the divine nature has an eternal vision of unalterable verities, within which laws of morality are included. Moral laws are therefore not arbitrary prescriptions of God but communications through God of unchanging moral rules. We are coming back, in fact, to the theory of moral law as impersonal, which is the view of the Mīmāṁsakas, by a different route.

## ETHICAL RELATIVITY

One other point that needs recording is a new conception of ethical relativity to be found in Indian thought. The word 'relativity' has been generally understood as implying the possibility of truths as alternatives or even as transitory. Thus what action is regarded as moral in one place may not be so in another. A comparison of the moral prescriptions of different races and religions would reveal the startling fact that while there is fundamental similarity in respect of certain moral duties there is wide divergence in respect of others, so much so that a moral prescription of one religion would be considered as grossly immoral in another. Similarly, our conceptions of morality alter from age to age and the index of civilization is the acknowledgement of the superiority of more humane virtues over those more gross. Many of the moral prescriptions of an earlier time are no longer countenanced, and it is likely that in the course of time many of our modern prescriptions would share the same fate.

India knew of similar changes in moral conception and worked off many of the cruelties of past times in formulating new ethical creeds. In such matters theological presuppositions had obviously a large hand in determining change in moral attitude. But what is peculiar in the Indian conception of ethical relativity is the fact that duties had reference to degrees of illumination obtained. Not being a 'scripturary' religion, Brāhmaṇism at any rate had not to accept an authoritatively laid down code of morals binding on all. Its institution of castes and stages of life (*varṇāśrama*) made it possible to recognize relativity in moral duties of the different sections of the people in their different stages of spiritual life. Each caste had its own specific duties in addition to others which were common to more than one caste or to all men alike. Similarly, each stage of life had its own special duties, though here again certain universal duties were also present. The philosophers of India improved upon this conception by linking moral obligation with the stage of spiritual attainment. A man who has succeeded in seeing through the illusory character of the mundane existence feels himself under no further obligation to follow certain moral prescriptions, just as he considers himself free not to observe certain modes of social custom or religious worship.

Thus, according to the Vedānta, a seer who has been able to realize his oneness with Brahman can no longer observe the ordinary duty of religion, thinking of God as the worshipped and himself as the worshipper. For the practical world of experience God is a necessity, and duties towards a Creator are obligatory. But in an ultimate reference neither the worshipper nor the worshipped has any being, and a person who could rise above all distinctions was not required to follow a code of religious ethics based upon the recognition of an eternal Creator. In fact, a spiritual insight into the nature of truth was the only activity in which man at his highest was expected to indulge. Thus ethics, religion, and philosophy all culminated in a realization of the ultimate unity of absolute existence (*ekamevādvitīyam*). Knowledge and virtue entirely coincide, and good and evil cease to have any meaning to one who has gone beyond all duality (*dvandvātīta*). Many have seen in this position the danger of an antinomian culmination of moral life and have pointed to certain passages in the Upaniṣads and elsewhere where it has been said that such a person commits no sin even though he indulges in some of the lowest vices. An exaggerated and esoteric language has always its danger, as we know too well, from a misinterpretation of such prescriptions and also of certain Tāntrika practices. A more correct way of understanding such passages would be that a sage in such a stage would not only lose all sense of distinction, but would also be so absorbed in his own vision that he would practise no moral activity and perform no social action, good or bad, at all. A man who has passed through a life of the severest discipline is not likely to land himself in the paradox of suddenly turning vicious after attaining the highest vision of reality. The Buddhists taught, in fact, that after a certain stage of perfection (*bhūmi*) has been attained, there is no possibility of backsliding for the spiritual aspirant. Similarly, emphasis upon charity from the Vedic times downwards has been construed by some as aiming at satisfying the greed of priests. When it is remembered that in the classic symbolism of religion (*dharma*) as a bull, truth, cleanliness, compassion, and charity are regarded as its four feet and that in innumerable passages charity has nothing to do with gifts to the Brāhmaṇas, we at once see the weakness of such criticisms. The prevailing attitude of the Upaniṣads is to advise men to desist from all actions right or wrong and to take to the path of meditation and realization, forgetting altogether the distinction of good and bad. We have repeated assertions, however, that a man who has wisdom does not sin, and that a sinner is not purified by scriptural study or by any penance or sacrifice.

## MORAL ACTIONS AND THEIR GOALS

Naturally, the question arose about the types of actions in which men indulge and the results of such actions. Broadly speaking, actions (*karma*) are divided into good (*śukla*), bad (*kṛṣṇa*), mixed (*śuklakṛṣṇa*), and neither good nor bad (*aśuklākṛṣṇa*). In the famous Yājñavalkya-Ārtabhāga dialogue in the *Bṛhadāraṇyaka Upaniṣad* we have the cryptic saying that good begets good, bad bad. What those good and bad destinies were became the subject of active speculation at a later time, and the procedure of assessing the moral value of an action was laid down. The different theories of heaven and hell, as are to be found in Brāhmaṇism, Jainism, and Buddhism, took effective note of the different destinies of the good and the evil. Regarding mixed actions, there was trouble, and alternative theories were suggested about the way in which good and evil bore their respective fruits in subsequent embodiments. It was admitted that the preponderance of either determined the nature of the next embodiment, which in its turn had a hand in determining the spiritual possibilities of the new being. A distinction was drawn between modes of existence which were merely meant as punishments or rewards of actions done here below (*bhogabhūmi*) and modes of existence in which fresh accumulation of merit and demerit might take place (*karmabhūmi*). The heterodox systems practically limited the field of moral activity to this mundane world of ours and extolled human life to the extent of supposing that salvation could come to man and man alone and other types of beings, higher or lower, had to be reborn as men before they could obtain the saving knowledge. The Brāhmaṇical view that salvation was possible through ethical behaviour in other realms also is to be found in the Vedāntic theory of progressive salvation (*kramamukti*) that spiritual progress could be attained even by gods who were supposed to be already half-way towards salvation through their earlier ethical activities. But heaven and salvation were not identical, and even desire for heaven was a kind of desire from which the enlightened were expected to extricate themselves. The Sāṁkhya describes the gift to the sacrificing priest (*dakṣiṇā*) as a kind of bondage (*bandha*), for sacrifices which lead to heavenly existence (*svarga*) simply postpone the attainment of salvation (*mokṣa*). It was difficult to decide what actions were ethically indifferent on the human level, but it was agreed that spiritual enlightenment (*Brahmajñāna, bodhi, samyakjñāna*) was certainly included within this category, for at this stage the spiritual aspirant was regarded as having transcended all distinctions of good and evil and established an attitude of apathy towards all earthly happenings and as having conquered completely all attachment (*rāga*), aversion (*dveṣa*), and ignorance (*moha*). To some the attainment of such a condition came as a gift of nature because of the merits acquired in a previous life. But in almost all cases, it had to be effected by effort along a very slippery path of which the spiritual novice was asked to beware. In fact, minute prescriptions were laid down in Buddhism, Jainism, and Brāhmaṇism about attaining the different stages of this ascent of the soul (*bhūmi, guṇasthānaka*), and warnings were sounded about the lurking dangers of each stage, and also the powers (*ṛddhi, vibhūti*) and insights (*abhijñā*) that higher stages bring were described. Moreover, the *yogin* is cautioned not to cling to any intermediate stage but to pass on to the final state of liberation, variously described as *mokṣa, nirvāṇa, niḥśreyasa,* etc. In the pluralistic systems this coincided with a kind of spiritual isolation (*kaivalya*), though through omniscience the emancipated souls were regarded as becoming mutually pervasive. In the monistic and monotheistic systems some kind of association with the ultimate Reality, whether God (Īśvara) or Brahman, was established.

### GITĀ SCHEME OF MORAL ACTION

The *Gītā* made a notable departure from the beaten track by denying that *karma* could be avoided at any time, though it admitted that dualities could be successfully transcended by a *yogin*. In a series of discourses which have become classical, the *Gītā* discusses the various types of actions and points out that as no being, even God not excepted, could be entirely free from action, spirituality had to be defined in terms other than those of inaction. The spiritual act is not exclusive of the performance of the ordinary duties of life, but is a transformation of the same viewed from a higher standpoint. So long as we claim personal agency for all actions and desire their fruits, we get entangled in successive embodiments. To get rid of the contingency we must abjure all desire for the fruits of our meritorious actions and dedicate the same to God. This is not intended to be a vicarious enjoyment as when people pass on their merit for the benefit of a fellow-soul in spiritual distress ; for God is a being who is not affected by the results of actions, whether performed by Himself or dedicated to Him by devout souls. In so far as man is able to efface self-reference, he escapes the inevitable results of moral action ; and the easiest mode of such self-effacement is to dedicate them to God, to whom really belongs the initiation of all worldly happenings. This theory of *karma-sannyāsa* presupposes a belief that ultimately the finite beings are to consider themselves as tools for the working out of divine plans. Now, in the scheme of the divine government of the world there is need of all types of action. If the good have to be helped and rewarded, the evil are to be put down and punished ; whosoever tries to avoid unpleasant duties that might involve cruelty is neglecting a portion of the divine purpose under the mistaken notion that chastisement is only of the Lord. It is primarily in and through finite spirits that God works out His plans, and therefore both injury and non-injury may become parts of human duties. What one is to avoid is the spirit of attachment towards good and that of aversion towards evil. Injury (*hiṁsā*) is bad as a subjective feeling, but may be good as an objective fact needed to redress iniquity and outrage done by the evil. Kṛṣṇa's exhortation to Arjuna to fight the unrighteous Kauravas cannot be justified on any other ground: it is not an incitement to violence but an exhortation to fulfil the obvious duty of a Kṣatriya to keep all evil in the state in proper check.

The *Gītā* with its Sāṁkhya-Yoga leanings could also exploit the theory of the *guṇas* in the interest of ethics. There are some natures which are essentially good and spiritual (*sāttvika*), others which are active and somewhat spiritually indifferent (*rājasika*), while there are still others which are lethargic and prone towards evil (*tāmasikā*). Obviously, the incentives and restraints would not be identical in the cases of these three, nor would their actions be of the same type. Obviously, the paths of discipline have got to be adjusted to the constitution of each type. The *Bṛhadāraṇyaka Upaniṣad* has referred to the cardinal virtues that gods, men, and demons should practise, viz. self-control, bounteousness, and mercy or compassion. The *Gītā* also refers to the distinction between the divine (*daivī*) and the demoniacal (*āsurī*) tendencies, as it does to the distinctive character-traits and tendencies of the *sāttvika, rājasika,* and *tāmasika* types. In an acute analysis the *Gītā* discusses the moral value of the different types of actions as prompted by the different elements (*guṇa*) and leaves no one in doubt about its partiality for those who are prompted by the purest motives in the performance of their actions. It takes note also of the fact that all natures are not fitted for the performance of spiritual activities of all kinds. The temperamentally meditative, the naturally active, and the essentially devout may all yearn towards a spiritual life and get their suitable paths, which may not be identical. Duties prescribed in the line of least resistance are most easily performed; and once this truth is recognized, as was done by Patañjali, we shall cease to insist upon a uniform pattern of moral conduct from all. Then again, man's conception of God varies, and so the method of approach will naturally correspond to their idea of divinity. God as working in this world as its creator, God as co-extensive with this universe as an indwelling impersonal spirit, and God as both transcendent and immanent cannot exact the same type of response from the spiritually minded. Moral action, devotion, and meditation are each a spiritual way of approaching God according to the constitution of the believer and his conception of God. Thus the *Gītā* scheme of moral action has a universal appeal, because it provides for that latitude in moral choice which differential constitution, innate or acquired, and speculation demand.

## FREEDOM OF WILL

Adverting to this problem of choice, it may be argued that man has really no freedom to choose either because he is after all a wheel in the divine machinery or because actions of his previous lives fatally fix his constitution and determine him to a particular line of action. Reference has often been made to one or two celebrated passages which say that it is not man's personal knowledge of good and evil but divine dispensation that decides how a man will act. Seeing, however, that Indian spiritual thought has systematically fought against all tendencies towards predestination, it would be unwise to lay excessive emphasis on such exceptional utterances. If God were ultimately responsible for man's acts of commission and omission, then the doctrine of transmigration would lose all meaning; and yet it is this belief in repeated embodiments due to moral action that has governed the lives of spiritual India through untold generations. That man is his own friend or his own foe has been so often repeated, that one's own actions find one out even after millions of births as a calf finds out its mother has been enunciated so often in different languages, and that it is only by personal endeavour that man deserves a state of beatitude has been so often laid down as a basic creed, that it is not necessary to adduce further proof that human freedom being responsible for the choice of the way of life was never questioned seriously at any time. There would have been no confession of sin nor the practice of any austerity or expiation to wash it away had not man felt that the responsibility for spiritual well-being was his own. In popular tales we do indeed come across stories of God coming to the rescue of a hopeless sinner in His superabounding grace, but they are mostly designed either to bring home to us the compassion of a merciful Providence or to show that only through such divine approach the evil-doer comes at last to realize the iniquity of his previous conduct.

If any evidence is needed to show the recognition of the freedom of will in Indian thought, one need only turn to the philosophical systems for elaborate discussions about the elements of a voluntary action. Thus the primary distinction between moral and non-moral action was recognized, and to the latter were assigned all automatic acts that did not have their origin in consciousness. In the volitional act proper were included the objective or end, the desire, the impulse towards realization of the end, the movements necessary for the purpose, and the realization. Minute distinctions occur about the possible and the impossible in connection with the origin of desire, the consideration of the objective or end as likely to yield satisfaction of some kind or at least to remove some existing want or imperfection, the affective elements like desire and aversion that are prompted by the memory of pleasure and pain associated with previous activities of the same kind, the means that are to be adopted to bring about the desired result, the deterrents that keep one back from willing and the ways in which they can be overcome or circumvented, and the sense of duty that supervenes, in certain specific situations and acts, as an added incentive to, or prohibition against, an intended action. In all cases it is in the interest of the self, however conceived, that the agent moves; and in his progress towards the attainment of his objective he does not feel at any time that he is being driven by any extraneous force, whether another spiritual agent of a higher type or the impulsion of the accumulated tendencies generated by the acts of a past life. Even a scriptural injunction is not a compelling force, but only a moral directive leaving it to the discretion of the agent either to follow it for some specified or unspecified good or to incur the risk of committing some sin. If that were not so, the sense of sin in case of failure to perform one's duty would never have arisen, and there would have been no scope for regret, repentance, or remorse or for any expiation, all of which figure so prominently from the Vedic time downwards.

It is obvious therefore that man is a maker of his destiny, so much so that it was freely admitted that by taking proper steps a man could even annul the moral effect of voluntary acts done in this life and thus prevent the fructification of the seeds of *karma* in a life to come. We need not discuss whether it is the favour of God or the attainment of saving knowledge or the performance of some counteractive moral or religious act that could offset the results of actions previously done. The fact remains that man himself was expected to take the initiative to counteract the forces of evil actions done by himself. The doctrine of vicarious enjoyment of merit, though not totally absent, plays a very minor part in the doctrine of Karma. This doctrine finds expression in the Buddhistic belief that gifts made to monasteries could redeem *pretas* (ghosts) in distress. The system of offering funeral oblations or *piṇḍas* at Gaya, so closely associated with Buddhism, that is supposed to be the most efficacious method of improving the condition of the dead, perhaps served as the prototype of this Buddhistic practice. We should recognize in this connection that birth in a particular caste in this life has no relation to the type of embodiment that will take place in a future life. The possibility of ascent and descent belongs to all, and social gradations of this life may be entirely reversed in a future life. Irrespective of the caste in which a man may be born, he enjoys the privilege of possessing the capacity to improve his lot in a life to come or to get release from the wheel of *saṁsāra* altogether. As performance of sacrificial rites is not the only passport to a pleasurable re-embodiment in a future life, those not possessing the right of doing so do not fare worse than those who have it in the matter of improving their lot. Within the limits of one's own opportunities, as fixed by the *karma* of a previous life, each individual has an ample scope for exercising freedom and determining his future fate. In fact, the yoke was deliberately made lighter for those who were not socially or spiritually privileged in this life.

## SOCIAL AND PUBLIC DUTY

It has been charged against Indian ethics that it lacks the crusaders' zeal for improving the world. It prescribes methods of self-improvement without reference to social duties and advises men, in fact, to look after their own spiritual well-being and become a lamp only unto themselves. This charge is difficult to maintain in view of the fact that again and again has it been repeated that without performing the duties of one's own station, one cannot remedy the spiritual myopia that blurs one's vision for truth, without which spiritual illumination and final deliverance are impossible. The five great sacrifices (*mahāyajñas*) were ordained to fulfil one's duties not only to the self, but to the entire creation and even to gods and manes. The universe was regarded as a unitary whole, composed of different types of beings, all of whom shared in the gifts of man. Hospitality, tending the sick, and providing food and medicament for the dumb creation were regular features of a householder's life. Duties to relations did not mean only showing respect, friendship, or affection, as the case may be, but also succouring them in distress and maintaining cordiality of social relationship by a system of give and take. *Dāna* is therefore to be understood in a comprehensive sense as including not merely gifts to Brāhmaṇas and priests, but also scattering bounty all around in the form of planting trees, building highways, excavating wells and tanks, and providing places of shelter and treatment of which all persons and even animals might avail themselves. One of the earliest dogmas is that man is joined not only with the fruits of his sacrifices, but also with those of his gifts.

We may go even further and say that not only was there charity to those who sought it, but there was also active beneficence by wandering ministers of religion who roamed all over the country and even crossed mountains, deserts, and seas to bring the message of salvation to all. The missionary activities of Hinduism and Buddhism in Insul-India and the Far East fill a glorious chapter in the annals of India. Those who were ordained by their castes to defend the weak and to protect the realm never failed to respond to the call for help when holy sacrifices were disturbed or the weak were oppressed by the strong. It was considered dishonourable not to do one's utmost to save the life of one who had taken refuge, even though it might mean the loss of one's life and property. When we turn to Mahāyāna Buddhism, we notice at once how the conception of charity has altered to such an extent that a saint is now prepared to forgo or postpone his entry into *nirvāṇa,* if thereby he can be of use to any sinning or suffering soul. In both Brāhmaṇical and Buddhist literature are to be found passages in which lofty sentiments are expressed, prayers offered, and resolutions made that instead of getting any temporal power or personal pleasure or even final liberation one might be given opportunities of serving humanity at large. The matter was put, as usual, in the paradoxical form that the saint was prepared even to sin, if thereby good to any part of creation could be achieved. Sages were advised to direct their benevolent or friendly gaze in all directions so that all might be happy. Whether Brāhmaṇical or Buddhistic, the code of ethics proceeded on the assumption that in spite of their differences all souls were at bottom swayed by the same feelings and tendencies and yearned after pleasure. The identity of the human race was further accentuated by the Vedāntic theory of the identity of all souls in and through Brahman. Men were therefore advised to practise the golden rule and not to treat others as they did not like to be treated themselves. All seek pleasure and are interested in self-preservation: if this is kept in view, much tendency to oppress and injure others would disappear. We are to keep always in mind the fact that others feel pain and sorrow as keenly as we do, and that all have equal right to enjoyment.

Hindu ethics would not have had such an abiding hold on such a vast country, if Brāhmaṇical literature had not immortalized certain ideal types of character in its heroes and heroines. The kingly acts of Rāma, the brotherly affection of Lakṣmaṇa and Bharata, the chastity of Sītā, Sāvitrī, and Damayantī, the generosity of Karṇa, the compassion of Śibi and Jīmūtavāhana, the truthfulness of Yudhiṣṭhira, the steadfast vow of Bhīṣma, the devotion of Dhruva and Prahlāda, and the sacrifice of Dadhīci, have served as beacon lights through the ages and illumined the path of conduct of waverers and wanderers. Through countless tales of courage, forbearance, nobility, and character the three great religions of India have tried to impress upon the minds of people the necessity of following moral ideals through all hazards in order to achieve that spiritual perfection without which final liberation is impossible. That India still holds the world's record in religious toleration is due to the fact that forcible conversion and oppression of the heretics were not counted among the moral virtues. No wonder therefore that the benediction of peace (*śānti, svasti*) should be uttered at the end of all religious ceremonies!

If one were minded to seek in one place a summary of the moral precepts by which spiritual life in India is guided, one may turn with profit to the *Taittirīya Upaniṣad*, eleventh *anuvāka*. Here a teacher is delivering his valedictory advice to a pupil about to depart for home in order to assume the next rôle, i.e. a householder's life. The latter is directed not to neglect truth, virtue, and scriptural study, but to practise them all through his life without neglecting personal welfare and prosperity. He is further advised to look upon his parents, the teacher, and the guest almost as visible gods and to support and help them in a proper manner. He is reminded of his relationship with a wider world in which gods and departed ancestors figure as dependent upon his attention and reverence, and hence these gods and fathers must not be neglected, but they must be approached with faith and proper respect. The guests are to be entertained with alacrity and without niggardliness, while help to the needy must be offered not in an offensive manner but only in a spirit of modesty and sympathy and with fear lest offence should be taken at the mode of giving. In any case of doubt about the proper way of dealing with a social situation, the prospective householder is advised to turn always to such persons as are rational, sincere, upright, devoted to virtuous acts, and free from (personal) desires.

India recognized like other countries that international relations could not be fully governed by the laws of private morality, if the state was to survive. It evolved a science of statecraft (*arthaśāstra*) in addition to a scheme of salvation (*mokṣaśāstra*) and kept apart these four objectives of human life (*catur-varga*)—morality or sacrificial duty (*dharma*), earthly prosperity including economy and statecraft (*artha*), conjugal necessity (*kāma*), and emancipation (*mokṣa*)—though it advised the pursuit of all these objectives. The king and those in power had many unpleasant duties to perform to maintain order and discipline in the state ; and while the objective of a righteous war (*dharmayuddha*) was steadily kept in view and humane treatment of enemies and criminals was recommended, this paramount necessity of maintaining the integrity of the state was not allowed to be overridden by personal considerations. Injustice and wanton oppression were not allowed to go scot-free, and a king not punishing a criminal incurred moral guilt as not performing an appointed duty. Succouring the virtuous and weeding out the vicious were laid down as equal moral obligations. But unpleasant duties were not to be performed in a spirit of anger or vengeance, and the reformation of the character of evil-doers was a primary duty to be attempted with kindness and patience in the first instance in all cases, and was to be handled with sterner measures only when absolute necessity forced their adoption. On the whole, it is the gentler virtues that came in for greater approbation and were more frequently emphasized. In close association therewith was preached the necessity of keeping in constant remembrance the solidarity of the human race, the primary task of self-discipline, and the spiritual basis of all moral activity.

# 39

## PHILOSOPHY OF VALUES

INDIAN thinkers commonly speak of two functions of knowledge—one which is theoretical, viz. revealing the existence of some object (*artha-paricchitti*), and the other which is practical, viz. affording help in the attainment of some purpose in life (*phala-prāpti*).[1] The results of these two functions of knowledge are respectively what we mean by 'fact' and 'value'. A thirsty traveller, who happens to come upon a sheet of fresh water, discovers a fact; and, when later he quenches his thirst by drinking the water, he realizes a value. These functions are regarded as closely connected with each other, since the knowledge of a fact usually leads to the pursuit of some value. The number of facts that may be known, it is clear, are innumerable; and the values that may be realized through their knowledge are equally so. It is with the latter that we are concerned here. The Sanskrit word used for 'value' means 'the object of desire' (*iṣṭa*), and the term may therefore be generally defined as 'that which is desired'. The opposite of value or 'disvalue' may be taken as 'that which is shunned or avoided' (*dviṣṭa*). For the sake of brevity, we shall speak only of values; but what is said of them will, with appropriate changes, apply to disvalues also.

### FOUR CLASSES OF VALUES

One of the distinguishing features of Indian philosophy is that, as a consequence of the pragmatic view it takes of knowledge, it has, throughout its history, given the foremost place to values. Indeed, they form its central theme; and questions like those of 'being' and of 'knowing' come in only as a matter of course. It may, on this account, be described as essentially a philosophy of values. There are various problems connected with value. For instance, it may be asked whether we desire things because they are of value, or whether they are of value because we desire them. For want of space, we cannot consider such general questions here, however important and interesting they may be. We shall confine our attention to the values included in the well-known group of four, viz. *dharma* (virtue), *artha* (wealth), *kāma* (pleasure), and *mokṣa* (self-realization). We shall only observe, in passing, that values may be either instrumental or intrinsic. Thus in the example given above, water is an instrumental

[1] See Vātsyāyana's commentary on *Nyāya-Sūtra*, I.1.1,3.

value ; and the quenching of thirst by means of it is an intrinsic value. That is, though the term 'value' is primarily used for the ends that are sought, often the means to their attainment are also, by courtesy, called so.[2]

Though all the above four are ordinarily reckoned as values of life, a distinction is sometimes made within them, according to which only the first three are regarded so, excluding the last one of *mokṣa.* Early works like the *Rāmāyaṇa* and the *Mahābhārata,* for example, often refer to them alone. But it would be wrong to conclude therefrom that the fourth value of *mokṣa* was not known at the time,[3] for these epics and other early works themselves refer to it also. In fact, the ideal of *mokṣa* is at least as old as the Upaniṣads. The restriction of the name of 'value' to 'the aggregate of three' or the *tri-varga,* as this group is designated, probably only means that the writers of the works in question address themselves chiefly to the common people, for whom the final ideal of *mokṣa* is of little immediate interest. Whatever the reason for this inner distinction may be, it is a convenient one ; and we shall adopt it in our treatment of the subject here.

### INSTRUMENTAL AND PSYCHOLOGICAL VALUES—ARTHA AND KĀMA

To take up the *tri-varga* for consideration first: In this group of three, *artha* may be said to stand for economic value ; *kāma,* for psychological value ; and *dharma,* for moral value. To speak in the main, *artha* is an instrumental value, for it is helpful in satisfying one or other of the diverse needs of life. Their satisfaction is *kāma,* which is an intrinsic value, since it does not admit of the question 'why?' We may, for example, ask why we seek food ; but we cannot similarly ask for what we seek the satisfaction arising from the partaking of it. We describe it as a 'psychological value', not in its usual sense of subjective value in general, but in that of an end which satisfies the natural impulses of an individual as such. These two values of *artha* and *kāma* are sought not only by man, but by all sentient creatures.[4] The only difference is that, while man can seek them knowingly, the other creatures do so instinctively. In this distinction, we find the characteristic feature of *puruṣārthas* or 'human values', viz. that they represent ends that are *consciously* pursued by man. When they are sought otherwise by him, as they sometimes are, they may remain values but cease to be *puruṣārtha.* The possibility of his seeking them unconsciously is due to the fact that man combines in himself the character of an animal and that of a self-conscious agent—that he is not merely a

[2] See *Vedānta-paribhāṣā,* VIII.

[3] Possibly it was not once acknowledged by some like the early Mīmāṁsakas or Yājñikas.

[4] Robert Burns, in one of his well-known poems, speaks of finding ears of corn hoarded in the 'nest' of a mouse when it was turned by a plough.

spiritual but also a natural being. The wants which are common to man and the lower animals and whose urge is natural, rather than spiritual, are self-preservation and the propagation of offspring, or, as it may otherwise be stated, race-preservation.

### MORAL VALUE—DHARMA

The case is quite different as regards *dharma,* for its appeal is restricted to man. While it is virtually unknown to the lower animals, man may be said to be innately aware of it.[5] In this consists its uniqueness as compared with the other two values of *artha* and *kāma,* and we shall presently see in what respect it is superior to them. We have rendered it as 'moral value' ; and some forms of Indian thought, like early Buddhism, will bear us out completely. But in others, especially the so-called orthodox systems, the connotation of the term is much wider, for they include under it not only moral but also religious values, such as are detailed in the ritualistic portions of the Vedas. But, in accordance with a principle recognized from very early times, viz. that ceremonial is of little avail to those who are morally impure,[6] the practice of virtue becomes a necessary condition of ritualistic life. We also find it stated in some ancient works of this tradition that, as between ritual and virtue, the latter is certainly to be preferred. The *Mahābhārata,* in a familiar verse, declares that 'speaking the truth is far better than celebrating many horse-sacrifices'.[7] Gautama, one of the oldest among the law-givers, places what he terms the 'virtues of the soul' (*ātma-guṇa*), like kindness and purity, above mere ceremonial.[8] These are the reasons why we have rendered the term as 'moral value', and we shall confine our attention in what follows solely to that aspect of *dharma.*

The notion of *dharma,* thus restricted, is so familiar that it is hardly necessary to refer to examples of virtues whose cultivation it signifies. Yet to give a general idea of them, we shall refer to one of the several lists of them found in old works. Yājñavalkya, in the Smṛti which goes by his name, reckons them as nine[9]—non-injury, sincerity, honesty, cleanliness, control of the senses, charity, self-restraint, love, and forbearance. It will be seen that some of these, like non-injury and charity, have a reference to the good of others or are altruistic, while others, like sincerity and self-restraint, serve to develop one's own character and will. It should not,

[5] *Bṛ. U.,* I.4.14.

[6] *'Ācārahīnaṁ na punanti vedāḥ'*—Vasiṣṭha's *Dharma-Sūtra,* VI.3.

[7] *'Aśvamedhasahasrāt tu satyam ekaṁ viśiṣyate.'*

[8] *Gautama Dharma-Sūtra* (Anandashrama Ed.), I.8.24,25.

[9] *'Ahiṁsā satyam asteyaṁ śaucam indriyanigrahaḥ, dānaṁ damo dayā kṣāntiḥ sarveṣāṁ dharmasādhanam'* (I.122).

however, be thought that this division into self-regarding and other-regarding virtues is a hard and fast one; for, as an individual has no life of his own independently of society, the former has a bearing on the latter, as surely as the latter has on the former.

### RELATION OF DHARMA TO KĀMA

What is the relation of *dharma* to *artha* and *kāma*? Or, as *artha* is ordinarily but a means to *kāma*, we may narrow the scope of our question and ask, 'What is the relation of *dharma* to *kāma*?' If *kāma* stands for pleasure, as stated above, we may say that it is desired by all, for pleasure is always welcome to everyone. Indeed, we cannot help desiring our own felicity. But not everything desired is necessarily *desirable*. A sick person may long for a certain kind of food, but it may not at all be advisable for him to partake of it from the standpoint of his physical well-being. That is, *kāma*, while it may be an object of desire, may not always be desirable; and, though appearing to be a true value of life, it may not really be so or may even prove to be a disvalue. How then can we distinguish these two kinds of *kāma*? To speak with reference only to the *tri-varga* which we are now considering, *dharma* furnishes the necessary criterion. That variety of *kāma* is a true value, which is in accord with the requirements of *dharma*, but not any other. In thus helping us to discriminate between good and bad *kāma* or in rationalizing life, as we might put it, consists the superiority of *dharma*, which is thus reckoned as the highest of the three values. This conception of *dharma* as a regulative principle is so important in the philosophy of conduct that all the Śāstras and all the higher literature of India (the latter, though only impliedly) emphasize it. That is, for example, what Śrī Kṛṣṇa means when he says in the *Gītā*, '*Dharmāviruddhaḥ . . . kāmo'smi*' (I am *kāma*, not at strife with *dharma*).[10]

### DHARMA AS A MEANS AND AN END

Having considered the general nature of *dharma* and its relation to *kāma*, and therefore also to *artha*, which commonly is but a means to it, we may ask whether its function is limited to regulating the pursuit of these two values or whether it has any purpose of its own. There are two answers to be given to this question.

(1) The popular view, and probably also the older of the two, is that it has a purpose of its own. In this view, then, *dharma* is conceived as an instrumental value. A steadfast pursuit of it, in its double aspect of self-regarding and other-regarding virtues, results in one's good here as well

[10] *B.G.*, VII.11.

as elsewhere ; and this good—whether it stands for worldly happiness or heavenly bliss—is, as a whole, designated *abhyudaya* or 'prosperity'. Further, it is believed that *dharma* not only leads to the good, but that it does so invariably. Here is another reason for its superiority over the other two values, whose pursuit may or may not be successful. But it should be added that, for the attainment of the fruit of *dharma,* one may have to wait for long. The important point, however, is that it is sure to yield its fruit at some time, even though it be after many vicissitudes. It is the possible postponement of the result to an indefinite future that explains the common indifference of men towards *dharma,* notwithstanding their awareness of its excellence. It is this human shortsightedness that Vyāsa, for example, has in his mind when, in concluding the *Mahābhārata,* he says, 'Here I am, crying out with uplifted arms that *dharma* brings with it both *artha* and *kāma* ; but no one listens to me'.[11] The same feeling of sad astonishment at human folly is echoed in a common saying that 'people want the fruits of *dharma,* but not *dharma* itself'.[12]

(2) The other view is that *dharma* is an intrinsic value, and therefore an end in and for itself. It is maintained by some Mīmāṁsakas, viz. those of the Prābhākara school. They ridicule the idea that virtue should appeal to man's interest for being practised. That would be to look upon man as a creature of inclination and forget that he is a moral agent, who has the power to do what he ought and to abstain from doing what he ought not.[13] Further, they allege that such a view makes *dharma* not only a means, but also a means to the admittedly inferior value of *kāma,* by making it minister to the doer's felicity. However unexceptionable the *kāma* pursued may be in its nature, and whatever altruistic activity it may incidentally involve, it finally stands for a subjective end or, in plainer terms, for self-love. If there is a moral principle, it must be absolute in the sense that it has nothing to do with our likes and dislikes and that it should be followed solely out of respect for it. It is the nature of *dharma,* they say, to be thus ultimate. Here we have the well-known principle of practising virtue *for its own sake* ; and the student of Western philosophy will see in it a general kinship with Kant's teaching of the 'categorical imperative', that is, a command about which there is nothing contingent or conditional.

This will, no doubt, appear at first as a very exalted view of *dharma* or 'duty', if we may use that term instead, worthy to evoke our admiration.

[11] *Mbh.,* XVIII.5.62.

[12] *'Puṇyasya phalam icchanti puṇyaṁ necchanti mānavāḥ.'*

[13] The Prābhākaras might admit the distinction, made above, between good and bad *kāma.* But they would not attach any moral value to the former, for, while it may connote prudence, it is not altogether free from bondage to inclination.

But it is really untenable, because it is based upon unsound psychology. It assumes that voluntary activity is possible without any end in view or, to put the same in another way, that it forms its own end (*svayaṁ-prayojanabhūta*).[14] But how can anything be its own consequence? To accept such a view, as Śaṅkara observes, changes what is put forward as a gospel of duty into a 'gospel of drudgery'.[15] For, in that case, devotion to duty would mean present toil ; and dereliction of it, future evil, so that whether a person does his duty or leaves it undone, he has only trouble as his lot in life. Hence this view of *dharma* has not come to prevail. It was once for all given up in India when Maṇḍana, a contemporary of Śaṅkara, enunciated the principle that 'nothing prompts a man to acts of will, but what is a means to some desired end'.[16]

## DHARMA SUBSERVES MOKṢA

So much about the *tri-varga*. When we shift our standpoint from the system of the three values to that of the four (*catur-varga*) including *mokṣa*, we find the conception of *dharma* undergoing a profound change, which makes it superior to that in either of the above views. It continues here to be regarded as an instrumental value, as in the first of them, but the end which it is taken to serve is not the agent's 'prosperity'. It is rather the purification of one's character or, as the term used for it in Sanskrit means, 'the cleansing of one's mind' (*sattva-śuddhi*) by purging it of all lower or selfish impulses. This cleansing is effected through the performance of the duties for which *dharma* stands in the manner taught in the *Gītā*, that is, without any thought whatsoever of their fruit. Thus, if the former view commends partial abnegation of *kāma* and thereby rationalizes life's activities, as we have said, the present one commends its total abnegation and thus spiritualizes them. Its true character of a higher value is restored to *dharma* here, for, in contrast with the other view, it wholly ceases to be subservient to *kāma*. The weakness of that view, then, is not in its conception of *dharma* as a means to an end, but only in its insistence that the end is some form of happiness for the doer. In this rejection of 'prosperity' or personal benefit as the aim, the present view resembles that of the Prābhākara school ; but, at the same time, it differs vitally from that view in holding that *dharma* has an end, and thus denying that there can be any voluntary activity without an appropriate motive. It is this changed conception of *dharma* that has come to prevail in Indian philosophy, and not either of the above.

[14] *Tantra-rahasya* (Gaekwad Oriental Series), p. 70.
[15] See commentary on *B.G.*, III.1; IV.18.
[16] *'Puṁsāṁ neṣṭābhyupāyatvāt kriyāsu anyaḥ pravartakaḥ'—Vidhiviveka,* p. 243.

AIDS TO MOKṢA—MORALITY AND KNOWLEDGE

But it may be said that moral purification or the conquest of the lower self is too negative in its nature to prompt voluntary activity. So it is necessary to add that actually, in this view, self-conquest is only the immediate end of *dharma,* while its final aim is *mokṣa* or self-realization.[17] This is the ultimate value ; and its conception is quite positive, since it consists not merely in subjugating the lower self, but also in growing into the higher one ; it implies also the transcending of the narrow, grooved life and the gaining of a larger, ampler life. This change in the older view of *dharma* or its transvaluation, viz. that it is a means to *mokṣa,* is already made in the Upaniṣads.[18] But it is not the only means and requires, as indicated by our characterization of the final goal, to be supported by a knowledge of what the higher or true self is. And it cannot be known fully and well, unless it is known in its relation to the rest of reality. This knowledge of the self in relation to its environment, social and physical, represents philosophic truth. Like the good, then, the true also is here conceived as an instrumental value, both alike being means to *mokṣa.*[19] The several systems differ in the place they assign to these two means in the scheme of life's discipline. But it will suffice for our purpose to say, following Śaṅkara, that a successful pursuit of the good is required as a condition indispensable for the pursuit of the true.

We have seen that seeking the good is essentially for the purification of character. The search after the true is for removing our ignorance (*avidyā*) about the ultimate reality, which is the necessary implication of all our efforts to philosophize. But for such ignorance, man's desire to know the nature of reality, which is so natural to him, would be wholly unintelligible. This desire, so far as it is theoretical, is satisfied when we learn the final truth and are intellectually convinced of it. But intellectual conviction is not all that is needed for reaching the goal, since the actual effects of the ignorance are directly experienced by us in daily life and require, if they are to be removed, an equally direct experience of the truth about reality. For example, most of us feel the empirical self to be the true Self, while the fact, according to many of the systems, is that it is not so. But a mere intellectual conviction, which is what is commonly meant by philosophic truth, is scarcely of use in dismissing such beliefs. A perceptual illusion, for instance, is dispelled only by a perceptual

[17] The ultimate goal is God-realization in theistic doctrines ; but it, too, is to be achieved, generally speaking, through self-realization.

[18] *Br. U.,* IV.4.22.

[19] This does not mean that the good and the true should not be pursued for their own sake. What is meant is only that they find their fulfilment in self-realization.

experience of the fact underlying the illusion and not, say, by a hearsay knowledge of it. Seeing, as they say, is believing. Hence all the Indian schools prescribe a proper course of practical discipline to bring about this consummation, viz. transforming a mere intellectual conviction into direct experience. The chief element in it is *dhyāna* or *yoga* which means learning to steady the mind and, thereafter, constantly dwelling upon the truth, of which one has been intellectually convinced, until it culminates in direct experience. It is then that the aspirant realizes himself and becomes spiritually free.

## NATURE OF MOKṢA

What is the exact nature of this ultimate ideal called *mokṣa*? It is held by some to be a state of absolute bliss ; and by others, as one merely of absence of all pain and suffering. The distinction depends upon a difference in the conception of the self in the various systems. Bliss or joy is intrinsic to it, according to some, and it therefore naturally reveals itself when the self is released from bondage. According to others, neither bliss nor its opposite belongs to the self, and it is therefore without either in the condition of *mokṣa* when its true nature is restored to it. Before describing this condition further, it is necessary to refer briefly to an objection that is sure to occur to the reader at the above characterization of *mokṣa* in terms of pleasure and absence of pain, viz. that the ideal is hedonistic—a view which is now regarded as psychologically quite faulty. This is an objection which, on a superficial view, applies to the whole of the Indian theory of value ; but whatever the answer to that general objection may be, the charge of hedonism does not, in the least, affect the conception of the ultimate value with which we are now concerned. For the pleasure for which it stands should be unmixed, and there should be no lapse from it when it is once attained—conditions which the kind of pleasure the hedonist has in view does not, and is not meant to, satisfy. In fact, *mokṣa* means absolute or unconditioned bliss (or, alternatively, absence of suffering), which is vastly different from the pleasure that hedonism holds to be the supreme end of life.

Now to revert to the consideration of the nature of *mokṣa*. Śaṅkara has remarked that attaining the goal of life signifies nothing more than perfecting the means to it.[20] That is to say, the end here is not external to the means, but is only the means stabilized. This gives us a clue as regards the kind of life which a knower leads, and enables us thereby to

[20] See commentary on *B.G.*, II.55—'*Sarvatraiva hi adhyātmaśāstre . . . yāni yatnasādhyāni sādhanāni lakṣaṇāni ca bhavanti tāni*'. Cf. commentary on XIV.25.

grasp the exact meaning of *mokṣa*. We have mentioned two aids to the attainment of the goal, pursuing the good and acquiring a knowledge of the true self. Corresponding to these, the life of the knower, broadly speaking, will be characterized by two features. In the first place, it will be entirely free from the tyranny of the egoistic self, and therefore also free from the feverish activity for gratifying personal desires, which can never be completely gratified. In the second place, it will be marked by an unshakable conviction in the unity of all, and consequently by love for others—love for them, not as equals but as essentially one with oneself. Such love will necessarily prompt the freed man to work for their good, for while there is nothing that he wants for himself, he sees them immersed in so much ignorance and suffering. No doubt, he was doing unselfish work even before he became free ; but that was, more or less, the result of conscious strife. Now it becomes quite spontaneous. This is in monistic schools. In pluralistic systems also, the same will be the case, the only difference being that the enlightened person will help others, prompted by pity or compassion rather than love in the above sense. Thus, whether it be in monistic or pluralistic schools, the knower, after gaining enlightenment and freedom for himself, will strive to spread that enlightenment among others and secure for them the same freedom, so far as it lies in his power. There is in this regard the magnanimous example of Buddha who, we may remark by the way, is only one instance among several that have appeared in the spiritual history of India. Hence, though the final aim of life or the ultimate value is here stated to be self-realization, it is really very much more, for it also signifies doing one's utmost to secure universal good.

We have described the state of *mokṣa* from the standpoint of what is called *jīvanmukti* or 'liberation while one is still alive', for it is sure to make a better appeal to the modern mind. This ideal, however, is not accepted in all the systems, but only in some like the Advaita, Sāṁkhya-Yoga, and Buddhism. The others insist that spiritual freedom will not actually be attained until after physical death. It is known as *videha-mukti*. But even these systems may be said to admit *jīvanmukti* in fact, though not in name, for they postulate final release in the case of an enlightened person as soon as he leaves his physical body, implying thereby that there is nothing more to be done by him for attaining *mokṣa*. The distinction between the two views reduces itself finally to whether or not the discipline prescribed for the spiritual aspirant should as such (that is, under a sense of constraint) continue in the interval between the dawn of true knowledge and the moment of physical death. According to those who do not accept the ideal of *jīvanmukti*, it should continue, while according to the rest, it need not.

## INDIAN OPTIMISM

The question that now remains to ask is whether such an ideal can be achieved at all. In one sense, the question is not legitimate, because *mokṣa,* standing as it does for a progressive attainment, is being realized at every stage. But it may be taken to mean whether the process of self-realization is an endless one or has a culminating stage ; and if it has such a stage, whether it is attainable. All the Indian systems, including the non-Vedic ones, are of opinion that this process is directed to a definite goal, and that that goal can assuredly be achieved. According to them, the evil of *saṁsāra* or bondage carries with it the seeds of its own destruction, and it is sooner or later bound to be superseded by the good. In other words, none of the Indian schools is finally pessimistic, and the present-day criticism that they are 'gospels of woe' is entirely wrong. We have more than one interesting indication in the Sanskrit language of this faith of the Indian in the ultimate goodness and rationality of the world. The Sanskrit word *sat,* as noticed by Max Müller long ago, means not only 'the real' but also 'the good'. Similarly, the word *bhavya,* we may add, means not only 'what will happen in the future' but also 'what is auspicious', implying that the best is yet to be.

Besides the ultimate value of self-realization, we have referred to truth and goodness. But the latter are only two of the three, including beauty, which are now grouped together and are termed the 'trinity of values'. Aesthetic value, however, is not being treated in the present paper.

# BIBLIOGRAPHY AND INDEX

# BIBLIOGRAPHY

## GENERAL

AIYANGAR, T. R. SRINIVASA, AND MURTI, G. SRINIVASA, *Śaiva and Śākta Upaniṣads.* Translation. The Adyar Library, Madras

———, *Ten Major Upaniṣads.* Translation. The Adyar Library, Madras

———, *Vaiṣṇava Upaniṣads.* Translation. The Adyar Library, Madras

———, *Yoga Upaniṣads.* Translation. The Adyar Library, Madras

AIYANGAR, T. R. SRINIVASA, AND SASTRI, S. SUBRAHMANYA, *Sāmānya Vedānta Upaniṣads.* Translation. The Adyar Library, Madras

BARUA, B. M., *A History of Pre-Buddhistic Indian Philosophy.* Calcutta University

BELVALKAR, S. K., *Four Unpublished Upanishads.* Text and translation. Poona

BHANDARKAR, R. G., *Vaiṣṇavism, Śaivism, and Minor Religious Systems.* Strassburg, Germany

BHATTACHARYA, ASUTOSH, SASTRI, *Studies in Post-Śaṅkara Dialectics.* Calcutta University

BHATTACHARYA, SATISH CHANDRA, *Hindu Philosophy.* Calcutta

BRAHMA, NALINI KANTA, *The Philosophy of Hindu Sādhanā.* Kegan Paul, London

CARPENTER, J. E., *Theism in Mediaeval India.* Constable & Co. Ltd., London

CHATTERJEE, S. C., AND DATTA, D. M., *An Introduction to Indian Philosophy.* Calcutta University

COWELL, E. B., AND GOUGH, A. E., *Sarva-darśana-saṅgraha* of Mādhavācārya. Translation. Kegan Paul, London

DASGUPTA, SURENDRANATH, *A History of Indian Philosophy* (4 Vols.). Cambridge University Press

DATTA, D. M., *The Six Ways of Knowing.* London

FARQUHAR, J. N., *An Outline of the Religious Literature of India.* Oxford

GUÉNON, RÉNÉ, *Introduction to the Study of Hindu Doctrines.* Translated by Marco Pallis. London

HASTINGS, JAMES, *Encyclopaedia of Religion and Ethics* (13 Vols.). New York

HIRIYANNA, M., *Outlines of Indian Philosophy.* George Allen & Unwin, London

HOPKINS, E. W., *The Ethics of India.* Yale University Press

HUME, R. E., *The Thirteen Principal Upanishads.* Oxford University Press

KEITH, A. B., *The Religion and Philosophy of the Veda and Upanishads* (2 Vols.). *Harvard Oriental Series,* Cambridge (Mass.)

MACNICOL, NICOL, *Indian Theism.* Oxford University Press

MAITRA, SUSHIL KUMAR, *The Ethics of the Hindus.* Calcutta University

MAX MÜLLER, F., *The Six Systems of Indian Philosophy.* London

RADHAKRISHNAN, S., *Indian Philosophy* (2 Vols.). George Allen & Unwin, London

RADHAKRISHNAN, S. (Ed.), *History of Philosophy: Eastern and Western* (Vol. I). Sponsored by the Ministry of Education, Government of India

RAU, C. V. SANKARA, *Glossary of Philosophical Terms* (Sanskrit-English). Tirupati

SEAL, BRAJENDRANATH, *The Positive Sciences of the Ancient Hindus.* Longmans, London

SINHA, J. N., *Indian Psychology: Perception.* Kegan Paul, London

VIVEKANANDA, SWAMI, *The Complete Works of Swami Vivekananda* (8 Vols.). Advaita Ashrama, Calcutta

ZIMMER, HEINRICH, *Philosophies of India.* Edited by Joseph Campbell. Routledge & Kegan Paul Ltd., London

## SĀṀKHYA

BALLANTYNE, J. R., *Sāṁkhya-Sūtras* of Kapila. Translated with extracts from Vijñāna Bhikṣu's commentary. Asiatic Society, Calcutta

———, *Lectures on Sāṁkhya Philosophy.* With text and translation of *Tattvasamāsa* and *Tattvasamāsa-sūtravṛtti* (*Sāṁkhyakramadīpikā*). Calcutta

BANERJI, SATISH CHANDRA, *Sāṁkhya Philosophy* (*Sāṁkhya-kārikā* with Gauḍapāda's scholia and Nārāyaṇa's gloss). Text and translation. Calcutta

COLEBROOKE, H. T., AND WILSON, H. H., *Sāṁkhya-kārikā* (with the *bhāṣya* of Gauḍapāda). Text and translation. Bombay

GARBE, R., *Die Sāṁkhya Philosophie.* Translated by R. D. Vadekar. Poona

———, *Sāṁkhya-Sūtras* of Kapila (with Aniruddha's commentary). Text and translation. Calcutta

———, *Sāṁkhya and Yoga.* Strassburg, Germany

GHOSH, J., *Sāṁkhya and Modern Thought.* Calcutta

JHA, GANGANATH, *The Sāṁkhya-kārikā* of Īśvarakṛṣṇa (with *Tattvakaumudī* of Vācaspati Miśra). Text and translation. Bombay

KEITH, A. B., *The Sāṁkhya System.* New York

MAZUMDAR, A. K., *The Sāṁkhya Conception of Personality.* Calcutta University

SASTRI, GOVINDA DEVA, *Sāṁkhya-tattva-pradīpa.* Translated in *The Pandit.* Banaras

SASTRI, SURYANARAYANA, S. S., *The Sāṁkhya-kārikā* of Īśvarakṛṣṇa. Text and translation. Madras University

———, *The Sāṁkhya-kārikā* (with *Māṭharavṛtti*). Studied in the light of its Chinese version and translated into English from the French translation. Madras

SINHA, NANDALAL, *Sāṁkhya-pravacana-sūtram.* Text and translation. *Sacred Books of the Hindus,* Allahabad

## YOGA

AUROBINDO, SRI, *Bases of Yoga.* Arya Publishing House, Calcutta

———, *The Synthesis of Yoga.* Arya Publishing House, Calcutta

COSTER, G., *Yoga and Western Psychology.* Oxford University Press

DAS, BHAGAVAN, *The Concordance Dictionary to the Yoga-Sūtra and Bhāṣya.* Indian Bookshop, Banaras

DASGUPTA, SURENDRANATH, *The Study of Patañjali.* Calcutta University

———, *Yoga as Philosophy and Religion.* Kegan Paul, London

———, *Yoga Philosophy in Relation to Other Systems of Indian Thought.* Calcutta University

JHA, GANGANATH, *Yogadarśana* (with the *sūtras* of Patañjali and the *bhāṣya* of Vyāsa with notes from Vācaspati's *Tattva-vaiśāradī*, Vijñāna Bhikṣu's *Yoga-vārttika,* and Bhoja's *Rājamārtāṇḍa*). Text and translation. Bombay

———, *Yogasāra-saṅgraha* of Vijñāna Bhikṣu. Text and translation. Bombay

MITRA, RAJENDRALALA, *The Yoga Aphorisms of Patañjali* (with the commentary of Bhoja). Text and translation. Calcutta

RAMA PRASADA, *Yoga-Sūtras* of Patañjali (with *Vyāsa-bhāṣya*). Text and translation. *Sacred Books of the Hindus,* Allahabad.

VASU, SRISCHANDRA, *Haṭhayoga-pradīpikā.* Text and translation. Panini Office, Allahabad

———, *Gheraṇḍa Saṁhitā.* Text and translation. Panini Office, Allahabad

———, *Śiva Saṁhitā.* Text and translation. Panini Office, Allahabad

VIVEKANANDA, SWAMI, *Rāja-yoga* (with the *sūtras* of Patañjali). Text with translation and explanation. Advaita Ashrama, Calcutta

WOODS, JAMES HAUGHTON, *The Yoga-system of Patañjali* (with the commentary of Vyāsa and the explanation of Vācaspati Miśra). Translation. *Harvard Oriental Series,* Cambridge (Mass.)

———, *Yoga-Sūtra* of Patañjali (with *Maṇiprabhā*). Translated in *Journal of the American Oriental Society*

## NYĀYA-VAIŚEṢIKA

ATHALYE, Y. V., AND BODAS, M. R., *Tarkasaṅgraha* (with *Dīpikā* and *Nyāya-bodhinī*). Text and translation with notes. *Bombay Sanskrit Series*

BALLANTYNE, J. R., *Nyāya System of Philosophy* (with the Ontology of Vedānta). London

———, *Bhāṣā-pariccheda* (with *Siddhānta-muktāvalī*). Text and translation. Calcutta

CHATTERJEE, SATISH CHANDRA, *The Nyāya Theory of Knowledge.* Calcutta University

CHATTERJI, J. C., *The Hindu Realism.* Indian Press, Allahabad

COWELL, E. B., *Nyāya-kusumāñjali* of Udayana (with the commentary of Haridāsa). Text and translation. Calcutta

FADDEGON, BAREND, *The Vaiśeṣika System.* Described with the help of the oldest texts. Amsterdam

GOUGH, A. E., *Vaiśeṣika-Sūtras* of Kaṇāda (with comments from Śaṅkara Miśra's *Upaskāra* and Jayanārāyaṇa's *Vivṛti*). Text and translation. Banaras

GURUMURTI, D., *Saptapadārthi* of Śivāditya. Translation. The Adyar Library, Madras

INGALLS, D. H. H., *Materials for the Study of Navya-Nyāya Logic. Harvard Oriental Series,* Cambridge (Mass.)

JHA, GANGANATH, *Nyāya-Sūtras* (with *Bhāṣya* and *Vārttika*). Translated in *Indian Thought.* Allahabad

———, *The Nyāya Philosophy of Gautama* (Sadholal Lectures). Allahabad

———, *Tarka-bhāṣā* of Keśava Miśra. Translation. Poona

———, *Padārtha-dharma-saṅgraha* (with the *Nyāya-kandalī* of Śrīdhara). Translated in *The Pandit.* Banaras

KEITH, A. B., *Indian Logic and Atomism.* Oxford

MADHAVANANDA, SWAMI, *Bhāṣā-pariccheda* (with *Siddhānta-muktāvalī*). Text and translation. Advaita Ashrama, Calcutta

MISHRA, UMESH, *Conception of Matter* (according to Nyāya-Vaiśeṣika). Allahabad

RAVI TIRTHA, SWAMI, *Nyāya-kusumāñjali* of Udayanācārya. Translation. The Adyar Library, Madras

SASTRI, S. KUPPUSWAMY, *A Primer of Indian Logic.* Text and translation of *Tarkasaṅgraha.* Madras

SINHA, NANDALAL, *Vaiśeṣika-Sūtras* of Kaṇāda (with *Vivṛti* and notes from Candrakānta's commentary). Text and translation. Panini Office, Allahabad

UI, H., *The Vaiśeṣika Philosophy* (according to *Daśapadārtha-śāstra*). Chinese text with translation. London

VIDYABHUSHANA, S. C., *The Nyāya-Sūtras of Gotama.* Text and translation. Panini Office, Allahabad

———, *A History of Indian Logic.* Calcutta University

## PŪRVA-MĪMĀṀSĀ

EDGERTON, F., *Mīmāṁsā-nyāya-prakāśa* or *Āpadevī.* Text and translation. Oxford University Press

GOKHALE, D. V., *Arthasaṅgraha* of Laugākṣi Bhāskara. Text and translation. Poona

JHA, GANGANATH, *The Pūrva-Mīmāṁsā-Sūtras* of Jaimini. Text and translation. Panini Office, Allahabad

———, *Pūrva-Mīmāṁsā in its Sources.* Banaras

———, *Prābhākara School of Pūrva-Mīmāṁsā.* Allahabad

———, *Śabara-bhāṣya.* Translation. Oriental Institute, Baroda

———, *Śloka-vārttika* (with extracts from *Kāśikā* and *Nyāyaratnākara*). Translation. Allahabad

KEITH, A. B., *The Karma Mīmāṁsā.* Oxford University Press

MADHAVANANDA, SWAMI, *Mīmāṁsā-paribhāṣā.* Translated and annotated. Ramakrishna Mission Sarada Pitha, Belur Math

RAJA, C. KUNHAN, AND SASTRI, S. S. SURYANARAYANA, *Mānameyodaya.* Text and translation. The Adyar Library, Madras

SASTRI, PASHUPATINATH, *Introduction to the Pūrva-Mīmāṁsā.* Calcutta

MATERIALISTS, SCEPTICS, AND AGNOSTICS

SASTRI, DAKSHINARANJAN, *A Short History of Indian Materialism*. Calcutta

———, *Cārvāka-ṣaṣṭi*. The Book Company, Calcutta

ADVAITA

BALLANTYNE, J. R., *Vedāntasāra* of Sadānanda. Text and translation. Allahabad

BELVALKAR, S. K., AND RANADE, R. D., *The Creative Period*. Poona

CHATTERJI, MOHINI MOHAN, *Ātmānātmaviveka* and *Ātmabodha* of Śaṅkarācārya. Translation. Bombay

COWELL, E. B., *Tattvamuktāvalī* of (Gauḍa) Pūrṇānanda. Translated in *Journal of the Royal Asiatic Society*

———, *Hastāmalaka* of Śaṅkarācārya. Translated in *The Indian Antiquary*. Bombay

DAS, R. V., *The Essentials of Advaita* (*Naiṣkarmyasiddhi*). Translation. Calcutta

DAS, S. K., *A Study of the Vedānta*. Calcutta University

DEUSSEN, PAUL, *Outlines of the Vedānta System of Philosophy according to Śaṅkara*. Translated by J. H. Woods and C. B. Runkle. New York

———, *The Philosophy of the Upaniṣads*. Translated by Rev. A. S. Geden. Edinburgh

———, *The System of the Vedānta*. Translated by C. Johnston. Chicago

DHOLE, N., *Pañcadaśī* of Vidyāraṇya. Translation. Calcutta

DIVANJI, P. C., *Siddhāntabindu*. Translated with the commentary of Puruṣottama. Baroda

DUTT, N. K., *Vedānta: Its Place as a System of Metaphysics*. Calcutta University

DVIVEDI, M. N., *Vākyasudhā*. Translation. Bombay

GHATE, V. S., *The Vedānta*. Poona

GOUGH, A. E., *Advaitamakaranda* of Lakṣmīdhara Kavi. Translated in *The Pandit*. Banaras

JAGADANANDA, SWAMI, *Upadeśasāhasrī* of Śaṅkarācārya. Text and translation. Ramakrishna Math, Madras

JHA, GANGANATH, *Advaitasiddhi* of Madhusūdana Sarasvatī. Translated in *Indian Thought*. Allahabad

———, *Khaṇḍana-khaṇḍa-khādya*. Translated in *Indian Thought*. Allahabad

MADHAVANANDA, SWAMI, *Bṛhadāraṇyaka Upaniṣad*. Text with translation of Śaṅkara's commentary. Advaita Ashrama, Calcutta

———, *Vedāntaparibhāṣā*. Text and translation. Advaita Ashrama, Calcutta

———, *Vivekacūḍāmaṇi*. Text and translation. Advaita Ashrama, Calcutta

MAHADEVAN, T. M. P., *Gauḍapāda: A Study in Early Advaita*. Madras University

———, *The Philosophy of Advaita* (according to Bhāratī Tīrtha Vidyāraṇya). Madras

MAX MÜLLER, F., *Three Lectures on Vedānta Philosophy*. London

MODI, P. M., *Siddhāntabindu* of Madhusūdana Sarasvatī. Translation. Bhavnagar

MUKHARJI, NALINIMOHAN, SASTRI, *A Study of Śaṅkara.* Calcutta University

NIKHILANANDA, SWAMI, *Ātmabodha.* Text and translation. Ramakrishna Math, Madras

———, *Dṛg-dṛśya-viveka.* Text and translation. Ramakrishna Ashrama, Mysore

———, *Māṇḍūkyopaniṣad* (with Gauḍapāda's *Kārikā*). Text with translation of Śaṅkara's commentary. Ramakrishna Ashrama, Mysore

———, *Vedāntasāra* of Sadānanda. Text and translation. Advaita Ashrama, Calcutta

NITYASWARUPANANDA, SWAMI, *Aṣṭāvakra Saṁhitā.* Text and translation. Advaita Ashrama, Calcutta

RANADE, R. D., *A Constructive Survey of the Upanishadic Philosophy.* Poona

ROY CHAUDHURY, ANIL KUMAR, *The Doctrine of Māyā.* Calcutta

SARKAR, M. N., *The System of Vedāntic Thought and Culture.* Calcutta

SASTRI, PRABHU DUTT, *The Doctrine of Māyā.* Luzac & Co., London

SASTRI, KOKILESWAR, *An Introduction to Advaita Philosophy.* Calcutta University

———, *A Realistic Interpretation of Śaṅkara-Vedānta.* Calcutta University

SASTRI, S. SUBRAHMANYA, AND AIYANGAR, T. R. SRINIVASA, *Jīvanmuktiviveka.* Translation. The Adyar Library, Madras

SASTRI, S. S. SURYANARAYANA, *Siddhānta-leśa-saṅgraha.* Translation. Madras University

———, *Vedāntaparibhāṣā.* Text and translation. The Adyar Library, Madras

———, *Vivaraṇa-prameya-saṅgraha.* Text and translation. Madras University

SASTRI, S. S. SURYANARAYANA, AND RAJA, C. KUNHAN, *Bhāmatī* (*Catuḥsūtrī*). Text and translation. The Adyar Library, Madras

SASTRI, S. S. SURYANARAYANA, AND MAHADEVAN, T. M. P., *Bhedadhikkāra.* A free translation under the title *A Critique of Difference.* Madras University

SASTRI, VIDHUSEKHARA, *The Āgama-Śāstra of Gauḍapāda.* Translated and annotated. Calcutta

SHARMA, H. D., *Brahma-Sūtra* (*Catuḥsūtrī*). With text and translation of Śaṅkara's commentary. Poona

SHARVANANDA, SWAMI, *Īśa, Kena, Kaṭha, Praśna, Muṇḍaka, Māṇḍūkya, Aitareya,* and *Taittirīya Upaniṣads.* Text and translation with notes. Ramakrishna Math, Madras

SREERAM, LALA, *Vicārasāgara: Metaphysics of the Upaniṣads.* Calcutta

TAYLOR, J., *Prabodhacandrodaya* and *Ātmabodha.* Translation. Bombay

THIBAUT, G., *The Vedānta-Sūtra* (2 Vols.). Translation of Śaṅkara's commentary. *Sacred Books of the East,* Oxford

TYAGISANANDA, SWAMI, *Śvetāśvatara Upaniṣad.* Text and translation with notes. Ramakrishna Math, Madras

VENIS, A., *Pañcapādikā* of Padmapāda. Translated in *The Pandit.* Banaras

———, *Vedānta-siddhānta-muktāvalī* of Prakāśānanda. Translated in *The Pandit.* Banaras

VENKATARAMAN, S., *Select Works of Śrī Śaṅkara.* Text and translation. Madras

VIMUKTANANDA, SWAMI, *Aparokṣānubhūti.* Text and translation. Advaita Ashrama, Calcutta

VIRESWARANANDA, SWAMI, *Brahmasūtras.* Text and translation with notes. Advaita Ashrama, Calcutta

## VIŚIṢṬĀDVAITA

ADIDEVANANDA, SWAMI, *Yatīndra-mata-dīpikā.* Text and translation. Ramakrishna Math, Madras

JOHNSON, J. J., *Vedānta-tattvasāra* of Rāmānuja. Translated in *The Pandit.* Banaras

KRISHNAMACHARYA, V., *Vedānta-kārikāvalī* of Veṅkaṭācārya. Text and translation. The Adyar Library, Madras

KUMARAPPA, B., *The Hindu Conception of the Deity as culminating in Rāmānuja.* London

PAUL, MANOMATHA NATH, *The Vedānta Tattvatraya* of Piḷḷai Lokācārya. Translation. Panini Office, Allahabad

RAMANUJACHARI, R., AND SRINIVASACHARYA, K., *Nītimālā.* Text with introduction and notes. Annamalai University

RAMANUJACHARI, V. K., *The Three Tattvas of Śrī Rāmānuja.* Translation. Kumbakonam

———, *The Vedānta-Sūtra.* Translation of Rāmānuja's commentary. Kumbakonam

RANGACHARYA, M., AND AIYANGAR, M. B. VARADARAJA, *The Vedānta-Sūtra.* Translation of Rāmānuja's commentary. Madras

SRINIVASACHARI, P. N., *The Philosophy of Viśiṣṭādvaita.* The Adyar Library, Madras

THIBAUT, G., *The Vedānta-Sūtra.* Translation of Rāmānuja's commentary. *Sacred Books of the East,* Oxford

VARADACHARI, K. C., *Rāmānuja's Theory of Knowledge.* Tirupati

## DVAITA

MAITRA, SUSHIL KUMAR, *Madhva Logic.* Calcutta University

RAGHAVENDRACHAR, H. N., *Conception of Svatantra.* Mysore University

———, *Dvaita Philosophy and Its Place in the Vedānta.* Mysore University

RAO, P. NAGARAJA, *Vādāvalī* of Jaya Tīrtha. Text and translation. The Adyar Library, Madras

RAU, S. SUBBA, *Pūrṇaprajña-darśana* (*Vedānta-Sūtra* with the commentary of Śrī Madhvācārya). Translation. Madras

## BHEDĀBHEDA AND ŚUDDHĀDVAITA

CHAUDHURI, MRS. ROMA, *Doctrine of Nimbārka and His Followers.* Asiatic Society, Calcutta

CHAUDHURI, MRS. ROMA, *Vedānta-pārijāta-saurabha* of Nimbārka and *Vedānta-kaustubha* of Śrīnivāsa. Text and translation. Asiatic Society, Calcutta

MAJUMDAR, SRIDHAR, *The Vedānta Philosophy on the Basis of the Commentary by Nimbārkācārya.* Bankipur

PAREKH, MANILAL C., *Śrī Vallabhācārya: Life, Teachings, and Movement.* Rajkot

SRINIVASACHARI, P. N., *The Philosophy of Bhedābheda.* The Adyar Library, Madras

## ACINTYA-BHEDĀBHEDA

DE, S. K., *Early History of the Vaiṣṇava Faith and Movement in Bengal.* Calcutta

GOSWAMI, BHAKTI-SIDDHANTA SARASWATI, *Relative Worlds.* Gaudiya Math, Calcutta

———, *Vedānta: Its Morphology and Ontology.* Gaudiya Math, Calcutta

MUKERJEE, PRABHAT, *Mediaeval Vaiṣṇavism in Orissa.* Calcutta

SEN, DINESH CHANDRA, *Chaitanya and His Age.* Calcutta University

VASU, SRISCHANDRA, *The Vedānta-Sūtra of Bādarāyaṇa with the Commentary of Baladeva* (including Baladeva's *Prameya-ratnāvalī*). Translation. Panini Office, Allahabad

## BHĀGAVATA AND PAÑCARĀTRA

DUTT, M. N., *Bhāgavata Purāṇa.* Translation. Calcutta

RAU, S. SUBBA, *Bhāgavata Purāṇa.* Translation. Tirupati

SCHRADER, F. O., *Introduction to Pañcarātra and the Ahirbudhnya Saṁhitā.* The Adyar Library, Madras

## BHAGAVAD-GĪTĀ

ARNOLD, EDWIN, *The Song Celestial.* Allahabad

AUROBINDO, SRI, *Essays on the Gītā* (2 Vols.). Arya Publishing House, Calcutta

NIKHILANANDA, SWAMI, *The Bhagavad-Gītā.* Translation. New York

PRABHAVANANDA, SWAMI, AND ISHERWOOD, CHRISTOPHER, *Gītā.* Translation. Hollywood

RADHAKRISHNAN, S., *Bhagavad-Gītā.* Translation. George Allen & Unwin, London

SARMA, D. S., *The Bhagavad-Gītā.* Text and translation with notes. Madras

SASTRI, A. MAHADEVA, *The Bhagavad-Gītā.* Translation of Śaṅkara's commentary. Madras

SUBEDAR, MANU, *Gītā Explained by Dnyaneshwar Maharaj.* Translation. Bombay

SWARUPANANDA, SWAMI, *Śrīmad-Bhagavad-Gītā.* Text and translation. Advaita Ashrama, Calcutta

TELANG, K. T., *Bhagavad-Gītā* (with *Sanatsujātīya* and *Anugītā*). Translation. *Sacred Books of the East,* Oxford

VIRESWARANANDA, SWAMI, *Bhagavad-Gītā*. Text with gloss of Śrīdhara. Translation. Ramakrishna Math, Madras

## ŚAIVISM

BARNETT, L. D., *Paramārthasāra* of Abhinavagupta (with Yogarāja's commentary). Translated in *Journal of the Royal Asiatic Society*

CHATTERJI, J. C., *Kashmir Śaivism*. Srinagar

IYENGAR, P. T. SRINIVASA, *Śivasūtravimarśinī*. Translated in *Indian Thought*. Allahabad

LIEDECKER, K. F., *Pratyabhijñāhṛdaya*. Translation with notes. The Adyar Library, Madras

PANDEY, KANTICHANDRA, *Abhinavagupta*. Banaras

PILLAI, NALLASWAMI, *Studies in Śaiva Siddhānta*. Madras

RAO, C. HAYAVADANA, *The Śrīkara Bhāṣya* (a Vīraśaiva commentary on the *Vedānta-Sūtra* in 2 Vols.). Text and translation. Bangalore

SASTRI, S. S., SURYANARAYANA, *Śivādvaita-nirṇaya* of Appaya Dīkṣita. With introduction, translation, and notes. Madras

## YOGAVĀSIṢṬHA

AIYAR, K. NARAYANASWAMI, *Laghu-Yogavāsiṣṭha*. Translation. Madras

ATREYA, B. L., *The Philosophy of the Yogavāsiṣṭha*. The Adyar Library, Madras

———, *Yogavāsiṣṭha and Its Philosophy*. Indian Bookshop, Banaras

DAS, BHAGAVAN, *Mystic Experiences or Tales of Yoga and Vedānta from Yogavāsiṣṭha*. Indian Bookshop, Banaras

MITRA, VIHARILALA, *The Yogavāsiṣṭha-Mahārāmāyaṇa of Vālmīki* (4 Vols.). Translation. Calcutta

## TANTRA

AVALON, ARTHUR (Sir John Woodroffe), *The Great Liberation* (*Mahānirvāṇa Tantra*). Text and Translation. Ganesh & Co. Ltd., Madras

———, *The Principles of Tantra* (2 Vols.). London

———, *The Serpent Power* (*Ṣaṭ-cakra-nirūpaṇa* and *Pādukāpañcaka*). Ganesh & Co. Ltd., Madras

———, *Shakti and Shakta*. Ganesh & Co. Ltd., Madras

———, *Varṇamālā* (*Garland of Letters*). Studies in the *Mantraśāstra*. Ganesh & Co. Ltd., Madras

———, *The World as Power* (6 Vols.). Ganesh & Co. Ltd., Madras

BAGCHI, P. C., *Studies in Tantras* (Part I). Calcutta University

CHAKRAVARTI, P. C., *Sakti in Indian Literature*. Calcutta

DAS, SUDHENDUKUMAR, *Sakti or Divine Power*. Calcutta University

JHAVERY, M. B., *Comparative and Critical Study of Mantraśāstra*. Sarabhai Manilal Nawal, Ahmedabad

PAYNE, E. A., *The Saktas of Bengal*. Oxford University Press

## POPULAR PHILOSOPHY

BASU, MANINDRAMOHAN, *Post-Caitanya Sahajiyā Cult of Bengal.* Calcutta University

BOSE, ATINDRANATH, *Crossroads of Science and Philosophy.* Calcutta

BRIGGS, G. W., *Gorakhnāth and the Kānphaṭa Yogīs.* Calcutta

DASGUPTA, SASIBHUSAN, *Obscure Religious Cults.* Calcutta University

HOOPER, J. S. M., *Hymns of the Alvars.* London

KEAY, F. E., *Kabīr and His Followers.* Calcutta

KINGSBURY, F., AND PHILIPS, G. E., *Hymns of the Tamil Saivite Saints.* London

MACNICOL, N., *Psalms of Maratha Saints.* London

RANADE, R. D., *Mysticism in Maharashtra.* Poona

SEN, KSHITIMOHAN, *Mediaeval Mysticism of India.* Calcutta

SINGH, MOHAN, *Gorakhnath and Mediaeval Hindu Mysticism.* Lahore

TAGORE, RABINDRANATH, *One Hundred Poems of Kabir.* Macmillan & Co., London

———, *The Philosophy of Our People.* Visvabharati, Santiniketan

# INDEX

Implication (see *arthāpatti*)
Incarnation (see *avatāras*)
Inconclusive probans (see *hetvābhāsa*)
Indefinable (see *anirvacanīya*)
*Indian Logic and Atomism* (see Keith, A. B.)
Individuality, 217, 234, 245-47, 276
Indra, 166-67, 172-73, 541, 584-85, 625; doubters of existence of, 169
*Indriyas,* 324, 429, 495, 511, 550
Inductive method, 142, 553-54, 598
Inference (see *anumāna*), 17, 106, 152, 158, 237; barred by previous knowledge, 98-100; Buddhists on, 554; Cārvākas on, 550; conditional (see *upādhi*); conditions of, 104; deduction and induction in, 142, 553-54; essential elements in, 142; fallacies of (see *hetvābhāsa*); Lokāyata school on, 174; Madhva on, 318-19, 321-23; Nyāya on, 96-102, 141-43, 553-56; in relation to perception, 100-2; reply to Cārvāka's objections against, 553; subject of, 97, 100; two types recognized by Madhva, 324; two types recognized by Nyāya, 142
Infinite regress (see *anavasthā*)
Inherence (see *samavāya*)
Injunction (see *vidhi*)
Inner Ruler (see *antaryāmin*)
Intellect (see *buddhi*)
Introspection (see *anuvyavasāya*)
Intuition, 218, 220, 231, 519
Invalidity (*aprāmāṇya*), 276
Invariable concomitance (see *vyāpti*)
Iron age (see *Kaliyuga*)
*Īśa Upaniṣad,* 315, 402, 451
Islam, 460, 462
*Iṣṭāpūrta,* 624
*Iṣṭasiddhi* (see Vimuktātman)
Īśvara (see God and Lord), 53n., 64, 81, 162, 192, 202, 209, 245, 249, 260-61, 266, 270, 275, 296, 302, 305-11, 498, 510, 522; according to Sureśvara, 264; in Advaita Vedānta, 248; and Brahman, 202, 248-49; in connection with *niyama,* 50; controller (*niyāmaka*) of effect, 192; distinguished from *devāḥ,* 89n.; his dual form, 249; material cause of dreams, 200; His relation to individual selves and the world, 248, 330; resembling a *guru,* 51; Yoga and Vedānta conception of, contrasted, 50-51; *-bhāva,* 202
*Īśvarapraṇidhāna,* 49, 85n., 87n.
*Īśvara-Gītā,* 14
Īśvarakṛṣṇa, 13-14; his *Sāṁkhya-kārikā,* 13, 53n., 59n.-60n., 63n.-64n., 67n., 265, 568, 588
Iyer, K. A. Krishnaswami, his *Vedānta or the Science of Reality,* 235n.

Jābāli, 178
Jacobi, 4; on age of *Sūtras,* 34
*Jaḍa* (see matter), 242-43, 268, 270, 330, 506; *-tva,* 278
Jagadīśa, 8, 568; on disjunctive judgement, 135; on memory, 136; his *Pakṣatā-ṭīkā,* 135n.
Jagāi, 528
Jaimini, 5, 33, 151-52, 159, 162-63, 171, 187; on infallibility of Vedas, 181; question of his identity, 151; silent on existence of God, 167
Jaina Āgamas, 10
Jaini, J., his *Outlines of Jainism,* 58n.
Jainism, 9-13, 63-64, 74, 82, 86, 183, 489, 507, 518, 523, 549, 551; its belief in minor deities, 536; its conception of mind, 518; contrasted with Yoga system, 89; on delivered souls, 56; Digambara school of, 10; its epistemology, 28; on perception, 551-52
*Jalpa,* 562-63; *-kathā,* 564, 577-79; procedure of, 578-79
James, William, 131, 455; on formation of habit, 63; his *Principles of Psychology,* 57n., 63n., 81n.; on thinkers of India, 629; his *Varieties of Religious Experience,* 528
Janaka, 218, 584
*Jātaka,* 498
*Jāti,* as caste, 622; as futile objection, 562, 575-76; as a universal, 262, 274, 599
Jayanta (Bhaṭṭa), 38, 94, 182-83; denies memory as valid knowledge, 135; his *Nyāyamañjarī,* 182
Jaya Tīrtha, 8; his *Tattvaprakāśikā,* 313
Jesus, the Christ, 521, 524-25, 528, 530
Jewish prophets, 521
Jha, Ganganath, demarcates Prācīna-Nyāya from Navya-Nyāya, 125; on modern logic, 125; his *Pūrva-Mīmāṁsā in its Sources,* 512n.
Jhālī, queen of Chitore, 461
*Jhāna,* 70, 518; *arūpa-,* 73, 526; fourfold, 71
*Jijñāsā,* 188, 206, 265, 317, 319-20, 322-23, 327, 330-31; its nature and object, 317-18
Jīmūtavāhana, 643
Jinas, 13, 64
Jīva (see *cit,* self, and soul), 40, 80, 146, 181, 191-97, 200-4, 242, 249, 255-61, 263, 266-67, 270, 273, 275-76, 278-79, 284, 287, 296, 330, 437, 440, 471, 473, 496-97, 499, 500-1, 505-7, 510; *anādikarma* of, 208; ascent and descent of, 191; *-bhāva* (see individuality); characterized by *pravṛtti-nivṛtti,* 613; its condition in *mukti,* 201-6, 208, 210, 244, 249, 295-96, 302, 309-12, 331, 339-41, 352, 364, 375-77, 619; -consciousness, 205; -hood, 242; its ignorance as cause of creation, 266; *-māyā,* 378; its nature, 162, 194-97, 207, 209, 237-39, 264, 308, 316, 327-28, 336-38, 352, 363, 373-74, 518, 618; *-pariṇāma,* 362; its relation with Brahman, 197, 205, 209, 240-42, 244, 248, 281, 304, 308, 339-40, 363, 379, 382; *-śakti,* 367-68; with *sattva* predominating, 613; substratum of knowledge, 197; with *tamas* predominating, 613; theory of one (see Ekajīvavāda); three states of, 587
Jīva Gosvāmin, 9, 366, 374, 381-83; his *Sandarbhas,* 367n., 370n., 372n.-74n., 377n.-78n., 381; his *Sarvasaṁvādinī,* 366n., 381
*Jīvanmukta(i),* 45-46, 50, 73n., 244, 257, 261-62, 269, 274, 277, 296, 330-31, 365, 435-36